ENGLAND
IN THE REIGN OF
CHARLES II

ENGLAND
IN THE REIGN OF
CHARLES II

DAVID OGG

SECOND EDITION

Oxford   New York
OXFORD UNIVERSITY PRESS

Oxford University Press, Walton Street, Oxford OX2 6DP

London Glasgow New York Toronto
Delhi Bombay Calcutta Madras Karachi
Kuala Lumpur Singapore Hong Kong Tokyo
Nairobi Dar es Salaam Cape Town
Melbourne Auckland

and associated companies in
Beirut Berlin Ibadan Mexico City Nicosia

Oxford is a trade mark of Oxford University Press

First published 1934 in two volumes
Second edition 1956
First issued as two Oxford University Press paperbacks 1963
Reprinted 1963
Reissued in one volume 1984

British Library Cataloguing in Publication Data

Ogg, David
England in the reign of Charles II.
1. Great Britain—History—Charles II,
1660 – 1685
I. Title
942.06'6   DA445

ISBN 0-19-285142-X

Printed in Great Britain by
The Guernsey Press Co. Ltd.
Guernsey, Channel Islands

PREFACE

THIS book is not a biography of Charles II, but an attempt to depict, as it were in cross-section, one of the most formative stages in the growth of English civilization.

As will be seen from the list of chapter contents, a number of chapters are descriptive or analytical, and the others (distinguished by the addition of dates to their titles) are intended to provide a consecutive narrative of the events of the reign. The distribution of these different types of chapter has been conducted on this principle—in volume i, which brings the narrative down to 1674, there are chapters devoted to social and economic conditions, commercial rivalry, and naval organization, the volume concluding with an account of the last two Anglo-Dutch wars, and the subordination of English policy to France. In volume ii, three chapters in succession (XII, XIII, and XIV) describe the financial, the parliamentarian, and the legal institutions of the period, as an essential preliminary to the two episodes in which these institutions were strained and tested, namely the Popish Plot and the Stuart Reaction. The chapters on Scotland and Ireland and on the Plantations are necessarily of somewhat limited range.

The facilities and assistance placed at the author's disposal have made the preparation of this book a singularly pleasant task, and he wishes to thank heartily all who have helped in either of these ways. To the Most Hon. the Marquess of Bath he is indebted for the privilege of access to several volumes of the Coventry Papers at Longleat. For liberty to use manuscripts in their custody the author owes a debt of thanks to the authorities of New College and Worcester College, Oxford; Magdalene College, Cambridge; Winchester College, and the Royal Society. To Mr. J. P. R. Lyell he owes many references in rare tracts and books. Dr. G. R. Y. Radcliffe helped with the technicalities of law, Dr. Joscelyn Arkell with geology, and Mr. R. V. Lennard with agriculture. Mademoiselle Aliette Charlot of Paris rendered valuable help in the Archives des Affaires Étrangères. Mr. E. S. De Beer kindly read through the typescript and enabled the author to effect many important changes; numerous corrections and suggestions were made by Mr. C. R. M. F. Cruttwell, Principal of Hertford College, Oxford, and by Professor Andrew Browning of the University of Glasgow. Professor Browning allowed me to consult the typescript of his forthcoming *Life and Letters of Thomas Osborne, earl of Danby*, a book which will take its place as one of the standard biographies of English History. For the arrangement of the two volumes here prefaced, or for the opinions expressed, none of these coadjutors is responsible.

Finally, to Sir Charles Firth the author owes both encouragement to undertake the work and guidance in the problems of its completion.

D. O.

July, 1934.

NOTE TO THE THIRD IMPRESSION

A number of minor corrections have been made and important items have been added to the Bibliographical Note at the end of Volume II.

April, 1961.

D. O.

PUBLISHER'S NOTE 1984

In this reissued edition the original two volumes have been published together, with the original continuous pagination. The references to Volume I and Volume II in the footnotes and index have been allowed to stand. Volume II began with Chapter XI (p. 389).

CONTENTS

CONTENTS

ABBREVIATIONS

Acts and Ordinances of the Interregnum, ed. C. H. Firth and R. S. Rait. 3 vols. — *Acts and Ord.*

Additional Manuscripts, British Museum. — *Add. MSS.*

Affaires Étrangères, Archives des, Paris. — *Aff. Étr.*

American Historical Review. — *A.H.R.*

Aubrey, J. Brief Lives, chiefly of contemporaries, ed. A. Clark. 2 vols. — *Aubrey.*

Baschet, A. Transcripts of reports by French ambassadors in England from originals in the Affaires Étrangères, Paris (Record Office). — *Baschet.*

Bodleian Library, Oxford. — *Bodley.*

British Museum, London. — *B.M.*

Burnet, Gilbert. History of My Own Time, ed. O. Airy. 2 vols. with supplement by Miss Foxcroft. — *Burnet.*

Calendar of Clarendon State Papers, ed. J. Routledge. — *Cal. Clar. S.P.*

Calendar of State Papers, Domestic. — *Cal. S.P. Dom.*

Calendar of State Papers, America and West Indies. — *Cal. S.P. Amer.*

Calendar of State Papers, Ireland. — *Cal. S.P. Ire.*

Calendar of State Papers, Venetian. — *Cal. S.P. Ven.*

Calendar of Treasury Books, ed. W. A. Shaw. — *Cal. Tr. Bks.*

Camden Society. — *Camd. Soc.*

Clarendon, Edward, earl of. Life . . . in which is contained a continuation of the Great Rebellion. 3 vols. 1827. — *Clar. Cont.*

Clarendon, Life and Administration of, by T. H. Lister. 3 vols. — *Lister.*

Clarendon Manuscripts, Bodleian Library. — *Clar. MSS.*

Clarendon State Papers, ed. R. Scroope and T. Monkhouse. 3 vols. 1767–86. — *Clar. S.P.*

Colenbrander, H. T. Bescheiden uit vreemde archieven omtrent de groote Nederlandsche zeeoorlogen. 2 vols. The Hague, 1919. — *Colenbrander.*

Commons, Journals of the House of. — *C.J.*

Dictionary of National Biography. — *D.N.B.*

Dumont, J. Corps universel diplomatique . . . (8 vols. 1726–31). — *Dumont.*

English Historical Review. — *E.H.R.*

Grey, Anchitel. Debates of the House of Commons, 1667–94. 10 vols. 1769. — *Grey.*

Halifax, George Savile, marquis of. Life and Letters by Miss H. C. Foxcroft. 2 vols. — *Halifax.*

Historical Manuscripts Commission Reports.	*H.M.C. Rep.*
Instructions données aux ambassadeurs de France depuis la traité de Westphalie, Recueil des. Angleterre, éd. J. J. Jusserand, 1929.	*Instructions Données.*
Lords, Journals of the House of.	*L.J.*
Ludlow, Edmund, Memoirs, ed. C. H. Firth. 2 vols.	*Ludlow.*
Mignet, F. A. M. Négociations relatives à la succession d'Espagne. 4 vols. 1835–42.	*Mignet.*
Navy Records Society.	*N.R.S.*
Ormonde, James, duke of. Life . . . with a collection of letters, by T. Carte. 6 vols. 1851.	*Ormonde.*
Prinsterer, G. Groen van. Archives de la maison d'Orange-Nassau. 2nd series.	*Prinsterer.*
Parliamentary History of England, ed. W. Cobbett. 36 vols. 1806–20.	*Parl. Hist.*
Pepys, Samuel. Diary.	*Pepys.*
Rawlinson Manuscripts, Bodleian Library.	*Rawl. MSS.*
Record Office, London.	*P.R.O.*
Register of the Privy Council (Record Office).	*Reg. P.C.*
Register of the Privy Council of Scotland, ed. T. Hume Brown.	*Reg. P.C. Scot.*
Royal Historical Society, Transactions of the.	*Trans. R.H. Soc.*
Scottish Historical Review.	*S.H.R.*
Shaftesbury Papers (Record Office).	*Shaftesbury.*
State Papers, Domestic (Record Office).	*S.P. Dom.*
State Papers, Foreign (Record Office).	*S.P. For.*
Tudor and Stuart Proclamations, ed. R. Steele. 2 vols.	*Steele.*
Venetian Transcripts (Record Office).	*Ven. Trans.*
Victoria County History.	*V.C.H.*
Wood, Anthony. Life and Times of, ed. A. Clark. 5 vols.	*Wood.*

I

THE END OF PURITAN EXPERIMENT

THE obsequies of Oliver Cromwell were prolonged and impressive. For nearly two months (Sept.–Oct. 1658) his effigy, draped in black velvet, lay in a darkened room at Somerset House, through which defiled a curious but not irreverent multitude, gazing on this dolorous memorial of him who had lived 'serviceable, even to the last'. Then the scene was completely transformed. The wax image, having been adorned with sceptre and crown and clothed in crimson velvet, was placed erect on the bed, which was draped in fabric of like colour, while the light of five hundred candles, reflected on figure and pedestal, revealed Oliver in a deep-red glow of glory after his allotted period of purgatorial seclusion.[1] Thus was accorded to him in death that regal state with which he had toyed in life; and it was in the trappings of monarchy, challenging and effulgent, that he was at last withdrawn from the view of men who had grown docile under his rule.

Behind the symbolism of this posthumous coronation was the fear that a precarious alliance of personality and chance was on the point of dissolution, and that the rule of single person must either die or be reincarnated in more traditional guise. This fear attested the cleavage of opinion between those who deplored and those who welcomed the change whereby the Protectorate had come to face more and more in the direction of the traditional constitution; and already the Humble Petition and Advice, with its tentative return to older forms, served as a watershed from which these two streams of opinion took their course. With the first moved all the political purists, military and civilian, ready to do and undo at the behest of conscience; with the second went men who, weary of change and experiment, were willing to sacrifice the austere glories of Zion for the known amenities of Babylon. The one party, claiming religion and piety as the sole qualifications for office, looked backward to the pioneer exploits of the Long Parliament and to pre-Protectorate

[1] Burton, *Diary*, ii, app. vii; *Ludlow*, ii. 47–8.

republicanism; the other, convinced that an estate was a qualification more easily gauged than virtue, was prepared to compromise high principle for settled government. Though the latter
party proved to be in a majority it was still impeded by the
inertia of ostracism; nor, until it had gathered momentum, was
the restoration of monarchy possible.

Succeeding events accentuated this division of thought. For
Richard's parliament (Jan.–Apr. 1659) a return was made to
the old, unreformed franchise, on which a large proportion of
Presbyterians, lawyers, and country gentlemen were returned.
This assembly recognized both the Protectorate and the 'Other
House', and some of its members even expressed willingness to
restore the hereditary peerage to its place in the constitution.[1]
Hence the chance that a majority of the elected representatives
of the nation might go far in the direction of reinstatement, if
not of restoration; but their debates suggested a more imminent
possibility—that parliament might hold an inquiry into the past
conduct of army officers.[2] Accordingly when, on April 18, 1659,
the Commons passed a resolution that, during the sittings of
parliament, there should be no general councils or meetings of
the officers without the consent of the Protector and both
Houses, the hint was accepted by the Army as a challenge.
Three days later Richard, yielding to pressure from Desborough,
dissolved parliament. There then ensued a revolution within the
Army itself, precipitated by intense searchings of hearts and
scriptures. The superior officers assembled under Fleetwood
at Wallingford House wished to retain two things—an upper
chamber as a check on the Commons, and a Protector as 'a
round O or cypher' to serve their turn;[3] while the subordinate
officers in session at St. James's, convinced that the Millennium
had at last arrived, demanded the restoration of the Long Parliament, ever memorable for 'its great shaking of kingship', and
still revered as the sacred ark of the Good Old Cause.[4] Forced
by the necessity of raising supplies, Fleetwood and Desborough

---

[1] Burton, *Diary*, iii. 525, 531, and iv. 89.   [2] *Cal. S.P. Ven., 1659–61*, 13.

[3] *Ludlow*, ii. 61, 99; also, *A seasonable word or certain reasons against a single
person* (1659).

[4] For a full account of the Army's politics see C. H. Firth, *Cromwell's Army*,
ch. xiv.

yielded to their subordinates; and so on May 7, 1659, there reappeared in the Commons' House Speaker Lenthall, accompanied by about eighty survivors (mainly Sectarians and Anabaptists) of those members who had sat between 1649 and 1653. This return of the purged Long Parliament necessarily meant the end of the Protectorate, because the former connoted government with neither Protector nor upper chamber. Richard accepted the change in this sense, and remained at Whitehall only to avoid his creditors. On their side, the army officers hoped with the help of the restored legislators to end the backsliding which Richard's representative parliament had inaugurated, and thereby preserve the Elect from the steep declivities of hereditary peerage and single person.

Under the watchful eyes of their custodians, the parliamentary veterans did their best to maintain the civil government. They ordered the raising of an assessment of £50,000 per month; but even thus, sufficient money could not be found to pay the arrears of the fighting services; and, as if to protect themselves from their guards, they summoned three regiments from Dunkirk, and proceeded to raise a force of militia. Fleetwood, it is true, was appointed by them to the coveted post of commander-in-chief, but only for the duration of parliament; and there was much dissatisfaction when, after revising the list of commissions, the Commons resolved that in future they should all be signed by the Speaker. Such was the partnership resulting from the army revolution of April–May 1659.

There were several potential leaders. Now that he was the official head of the Army, Fleetwood might have taken the initiative. But, both by sentiment and personal relationship, he was a representative of Cromwellian tradition, and was handicapped by personal loyalties. To the soldiers, he was merely 'a godly man'; to others he seemed irresolute, and his tendency to weep in public was, even then, considered unbecoming in a cavalry officer. Like Richard he was destined soon to fade into obscurity. Both men were now displaced by the three apostles of the Good Old Cause, each anxious to undo the evil wrought by Oliver— sir Arthur Hesilrige, sir Henry Vane, and general Edmund Ludlow, all of whom, as leading members of the new Council of State, had reached that difficult point when an opposition suddenly finds itself in power. Hesilrige had become estranged from Cromwell after the latter's expulsion of the Long Parliament in 1653; and as parliamentary leader after May 1659 he was both the enemy of army rule and the costive exponent of constitutionalism as it was supposed to have been interpreted between 1648 and 1653. He had helped to pull down, he gloomily boasted, but always by prayer and humiliation. Because of his belief in the omnipotence of the Commons he was able for a time to command a respectable following; but on the other hand the extent of his landed acquisitions in Durham raised him many enemies, and his retrospective politics won few converts.

Principles similar to his found a more graceful exponent in sir Henry Vane, who preached 'freedom and self-government' and the inviolability of fundamentals, doctrines so conveniently elastic that he may be regarded as a party in himself. Looking on the nation as unacquainted with its own good and unfit to be trusted with power, 'he would have some few refined spirits (and those of his own nomination) sit at the helm of state . . . till the people be made familiar with a Republique and in love with it'.[1] But this educative process might have proved lengthy, and meanwhile the nation was impatient. Vane was convinced that, provided the foundations were sound, Providence would make good the deficiencies; on this basis he was able for a time to mediate between army and parliament. Equally opposed to compromise was Edmund Ludlow, who had rendered important service as commander-in-chief in Ireland. He had never recognized the Protectorate, nor did his scruples permit him to support any government that was not clearly the expression of popular consent. In vain Oliver had tried to elicit from him where that consent was to be found. Important as the strongest link between the army politicians and the civilian republicans,[2] Ludlow was staunch but limited, too querulous and pedantic to realize the place of expediency in practical politics.

The inevitable breach between Army and the restored Long Parliament commenced in August with the suppression of the presbyterian-royalist rising of sir George Booth. Credit for this triumph of the Commonwealth was due mainly to John Lambert, 'the army's darling', the reputed agent of Providence in

---

[1] *Nicholas Papers* (Royal Historical Society), iv. 161.   [2] *Clar. S.P.* iii. 484.

the miraculous victory of Dunbar, the Rupert and the Wallenstein of Cromwellian generals. His prestige with the Army and a section of the nation was steadily increasing. He had refrained from taking part in the unhorsing of Richard; he had turned a deaf ear to royalist offers; as one of the Council of State he eclipsed both Fleetwood and Desborough. For his services the apprehensive Commons offered him a jewel, but declined to raise him to the rank of general, or to make permanent Fleetwood's commission of commander-in-chief. Their distrust was patent when on October 11 they passed an ordinance[1] prohibiting the raising of money without parliamentary consent. This Act contained provisos confirming purchases of lands in England and Ireland, but definitely excluding everything else done in the period between the Long Parliament's eviction and recall (Apr. 1653–May 1659); moreover, violation of the ordinance was declared to be high treason; in effect, therefore, the conduct of the Army during these six non-legal years might be called in question by the civil power. Having gone so far, the Commons decided to emancipate themselves altogether from army tutelage; so they annulled Fleetwood's commission, cashiered Lambert and eight of his fellow officers, and vested the government of the Army in seven commissioners. The reply of the Army was prompt. Having seized the Mint, Lambert and his soldiers took up station in Palace Yard on October 13; and when the Commons came to take their seats they were presented with a display of massed and silent force. The legislators walked off in dismay; no blow was struck; there was not even a speech.

In its capacity of self-governing corporation the Army would now do its own constitution-making. Having confirmed Fleetwood in his office of commander-in-chief and restored Lambert and his colleagues, the Army next purged the Council of State of dissentients, and set up a military-civilian Committee of Safety, in which were included Desborough, Ludlow, Ireton, Hewson, and Whitelocke. This Committee annulled the orders passed by the late parliament in the last days of its session, and proceeded to discuss the fundamentals of government in order to draw up a written constitution. Fleetwood, mediating in disputes between soldiers and apprentices, displayed

[1] *Acts and Ord.* ii. 1351.

leanings towards Hesilrige, the vociferous champion of liberty, parliament, and a republic, at the same time giving sympathetic hearing to Harrington's apotheosis of Rotation as the sovereign means of preserving political equilibrium. His doubts and misgivings helped to confirm the eminence to which Lambert had raised himself by his spectacular termination of the Long Parliament's activities. Lambert might have declared for Restoration, knowing as he did that he was regarded with some favour by the exiled Court;[1] or he might have set up a dictatorship on the strength of his popularity with the Army. But he was the victim of his own virtues. Able and impressionable, daring and out-spoken, Lambert the tulip-fancier was incongruous in a society which set an excessive premium on piety or the reputation for it; nor did he consort well with a world habituated to the imagery of the Old Testament, and suspicious of aesthetic diversions. As an avowed cynic he was out of place in the Rule of the Saints; still worse, in his handling of the Commons he had shown himself woefully lacking in Oliverian technique; for Cromwell would not have evicted an assembly by merely locking the doors and parading outside. He would have unburdened himself in an impassioned speech; or at least quoted a seasonable text, or performed some gesture to make the occasion memorable and corroborative:

> For had old Noll been alive, he had pulled them out by the ears
> Or else had fired their hive and kicked them down the stairs,
> Because they were so bold to vex his righteous soul,
> When he so deeply had swore that they should never sit more.[2]

In taking upon himself the mantle of the Prophet, Lambert had shown how ill it fitted him; thereafter he and his army colleagues proved dumb, or at best mumbling exponents of the sacred mysteries entrusted to their charge. This prompted men to seek for another revelation, soon to be announced in language which they could understand.

Interference with an institution more cherished than church or monarchy was not the only irregularity of which the commonwealth leaders might have been accused. After his fourth dissolution of parliament in February 1658 even Cromwell had found it

[1] *Clar. S.P.* iii. 599.
[2] *A proper new ballad on the old parliament*, in Bodley, *Pamph. Wood*, 416, xvi.

difficult to balance the military and civilian elements in the constitution; indeed, the problems of appeasing army leaders and obtaining the return of the right members from the constituencies had so engaged the Protector that his health had suffered.[1] Still more, the policy of muffled security at home and military prestige abroad had cost money; and, with the accumulation of debt, pensions and army pay were in continual arrears; moreover, the war with Spain, coming so soon after the war with Holland, was held accountable for an alleged decline in the cloth and shipping trades.[2] In these circumstances the heavy taxes were a serious, and in some cases an impossible, economic burden. Ship-money had been opposed on principle; but against the far heavier monthly assessments there had arisen no Hampden; and against the hated Excise there had appeared only Prynne, who brought out his folios to convince a collector that the Excise on hops was illegal.[3] Nor were commonwealth financiers dependent only on national revenue; for, in consequence of confiscation, estates were sold at uneconomic prices, or their owners were forced to realize in a falling market in order to pay the fines imposed on them. These burdens, accentuated by the unhealthy summer of 1659 when men and horses were carried off by an obscure disease, proved realities in face of which the constitution-making of soldiers and orators seemed worse than futile.

But while these exactions and deficits were a source of disquiet, they can hardly be quoted as a direct cause of the Restoration. At what period are there no complaints of heavy taxes? or of accumulating debt? or of decaying trade? English commerce was certainly suffering from the war with Spain, but was benefiting from an enterprising foreign policy; wages were relatively high; the national debt seemed large, because the device of saddling it on posterity had not yet been thought of. The economic difficulties of the Commonwealth were those of a government which had to maintain large armies at home and a vigorous policy abroad. Had that government been legitimate, these heavy commitments would have been considered inevitable, or

[1] *Cal. S.P. Ven.*, 1657–9, xvii. 168, 169.

[2] For this question see M. James, *Social problems and policy during the Puritan Revolution.*

[3] Prynne, *A declaration ... against ... Excise*, 1654.

even commendable; but the difficulties consequent on these commitments have traditionally been selected for special emphasis because they appear to provide in a simple economic formula the reasons for the change from Commonwealth to Monarchy.

The consistent, economic motive which may regulate the actions of men to-day did not necessarily have the same force in the seventeenth century, when men were still influenced by religion, and there was more scope for personality; moreover, public opinion, as it is now understood, was non-existent in the older England of segregated provincialism; and so history might be 'made' by one man or by a group. By his personality and his control of the Army Cromwell had forced these groups into cohesion or impotence; as soon as he was gone, they began to fall apart or assert themselves; nor was the semblance of unity restored until Monck intervened. The groups were numerous, but they may be roughly divided according as they favoured experiment or tradition. In the first category were included, among others, the Army, the Levellers, and the Sects, notably the Independents; in the second were Royalists, Lawyers, and Presbyterians.

'All laws in favour of liberty spring first from the disagreement of the people with their governors.'[1] This was the keynote of Puritan reform; it sought to achieve constructive results by discussion and debate. That the people do not know what is good for themselves and must be guided or compelled—such was its second assumption; but public insistence on this truth showed that the reformers were not always good political strategists. As they rejected all secular precedent and authority, they propounded a rich variety of schemes. Thus, in the Army were some who favoured a written constitution, with a Senate to control the Commons; others were for single-chamber government; as a body, the officers were opposed to the effective rule of a single person, but were divided on the subject of the relations between the military and the civil power. They sought for guidance by prayer, and revelation was liable to be succeeded by revolution. More single-minded were the Levellers, the most zealous advocates of liberty of the subject, who held that Cromwell's rule was

---

[1] *Vox plebis, or the people's outcry* . . . (1646).

at least as tyrannical as the monarchy which it had displaced. They believed also that to all human laws should be applied the touchstone of the 'law eternal' which is implanted in every man's breast. So violently were they opposed to the Protectorate that many of them were willing to see Charles restored, provided he would accept their scheme of government, according to which authority is originally in the people; the chief magistrate should be elective and devoid of both military power and legislative veto; parliaments should be regularly summoned, and all penal laws for religious differences should be abolished. The royalist agents negotiating with the Levellers did not attempt to dispel the optimism inspiring these proposals.[1]

The Leveller belief in the need for reform of law and legal procedure was shared by most of the Sects; indeed it was in this respect that the Puritan Revolution was to achieve some of its most constructive results. Demand for legal reform was sometimes based on a historical theory, according to which the Civil Wars were regarded as contests between the Norman and the Saxon elements in the nation.[2] On this assumption, the true history of England had not begun at the Norman Conquest but had ended there; for the invading foreigners had swept aside the 'laws' of Edward the Confessor, and had enforced on ingenuous Englishmen such iniquities as law-French, tithes, prelates, extortion, and tyranny. Now that the 'Norman yoke' was gone, reform must start from national origins, and must begin with the lawyers, who are the agents of prerogative, bigotry, and wealth. To Hugh Peters, 'vicar general and metropolitan of the Independents in Old and New England,' we owe the most comprehensive code of social reform based on these principles.[3] He proposed that, if lawyers were necessary, they should be state servants; that civil litigation should be settled by local committees; that entails should be cut off for ever; that all judges should have their salaries from 'some public stock'; that small debtors should not be imprisoned; that freedom of bequest should be instituted. Having reformed the law, Peters would introduce many social

---

[1] *Clar. S.P.* iii. 430–1.

[2] e.g. Hare, *The Norman Yoke* (1647); also *St. Edward's Ghost* (1647), and *The Lawyer's Bane* (1647).

[3] Hugh Peters, *Good work for a good magistrate* (1651).

and economic improvements: a national bank; more humane prisons; speedy trial of persons under indictment; registers for recording sales of land; alms-houses for the impotent poor, work for the able-bodied; improved internal communication by making rivers navigable; complete freedom of trade in towns; development of London docks; and maintenance of the sovereignty of the seas by a strong navy. Finally, he would have non-intervention in continental politics. As he would sweep away all the accumulated abuses of the past, Peters proposed that all the old records in the Tower should be destroyed. Unfortunately, this was the one suggestion singled out from his code and levelled against him.

Contrasted with all this was the traditionalism of Royalists, Lawyers, and Presbyterians. Throughout the Commonwealth the Royalists were ostracized, and many of them were ruined by fines; as a class therefore they were not able to exercise influence on the course of events; nor did the plotters among them achieve any definite success. The most influential of them were abroad in exile; but those who remained in England preserved at least the sentiment for the old order of things. Another class which was subjected to specially heavy taxation was the Lawyers. They had troubled James I and Charles I with their wrangling, and they had helped to precipitate the Civil Wars by their questioning of the prerogative. But the respectable and learned opposition of such as Coke and Selden was very different from that of the men who came to dominate the Long Parliament and the Army after 1643; for, while the lawyers would at times dictate to the crown, they did not therefore wish to destroy it. To them the king was the fountain of justice; they sought only to regulate the streams which flowed therefrom. Furthermore, the English common-lawyer had an instinctive respect for legitimacy, as well as a dislike of the amateur, however well intentioned; in kingship he found the tangible embodiment of that authority of which he was the interpreter; for in contrast with the idealist, who would have reason and morality first and law afterwards, the lawyer insisted that the validity of a code must precede its equity. He therefore maintained something of the instinct for monarchy. Of the practitioners who bridged the gulf some of the most noteworthy were sir Matthew Hale, sir Edward Atkyns the senior,

Oliver St. John, and sir John Maynard, the last of whom lived to congratulate William III in 1688. Also, the lawyers proved more dexterous than any other profession in emerging from the avalanche of 1660.

This instinct for tradition was absent from the numerous sects into which the Puritan cause had degenerated; it is to be found, however, in the Presbyterians, whose alliance with a Stuart king had already caused the Second Civil War, an alliance which had its logical outcome in the reinstatement of his son. As then befitted an established church, the Presbyterians were uncompromising and intolerant; they had a standardized system of church government; in Scotland, they had a very definite theology, and in both England and Scotland they believed in limited monarchy and hereditary peerage. Their preachers were affirmed to be superior alike to the 'dumb dogs, the bishops', and to the testifying troopers and cobblers favoured by the Independents; even more, they had no association with the nebulous benevolence of the Independents, and nothing but horror for the vagaries of Quakers and Fifth Monarchy Men. Nor at that time did they have the characteristics associated with Dissent; for their system was a branch of continental Calvinism, and in the period 1648–60 it was in Scotland actually, and in England nominally, the established system of worship; moreover, it was still a religion fit for 'gentlemen', though there was soon to be a falling-off in the number of titled communicants. A limited monarchy and a powerful aristocracy—for profession of faith in these twin institutions the Presbyterians were then censured as the Whigs were afterwards eulogized. Among the most notable of the moderate Presbyterians before the Restoration were the earls of Manchester, Northumberland, and Warwick; Arthur Annesley, sergeant Maynard, and general Monck.

The knowledge that there existed in England a strong body of opinion in favour of kingship may have encouraged the exiled Stuart to persevere in his efforts to win the crown by negotiation or force. In receipt of a small pension from France and Spain (irregularly paid) Charles and his makeshift Court were ever on the alert for a change on the horizon. Would Mazarin continue the English alliance now that the Protectorate had gone and the Commonwealth was in difficulties? Would he not, in the interests of France, help to terminate English anarchy by restoring the lawful sovereign? Failing Mazarin, might not Condé[1] or Turenne[2] be induced to use his troops and prestige for the reinstatement of Charles? So too with the Dutch. They had never been enthusiastic allies of Cromwell, and might now be expected to wipe off old scores against their commercial enemy.[3] There was still a chance that Spain would help, if only to recover Jamaica; but the fall of Dunkirk (June 1658) and the comparative peace which followed the death of Cromwell served to make Spanish diplomacy still more cautious and dilatory. Moreover the wandering king was badly served, and his advisers included too many effeminate hot-heads and bellicose priests. Accordingly when, after the failure of Booth's rising (Aug. 1659), Charles decided to go to Fuenterrabia in the desperate hope of inducing Mazarin to make some provision for him in the Franco-Spanish settlement (the treaty of the Pyrenees), he was refused even an interview, because the French minister considered him a bad investment.[4] Nor were these the only disappointments. The threat of hostilities between English and Dutch remained only a threat; and nothing came of projected offers of help from Saxony[5] and Brandenburg.[6] These rebuffs served to teach Charles the rudiments of diplomacy.

Thus by the autumn of 1659 it seemed that the contest between experiment and traditionalism had reached stalemate. On both sides there was much talk but little action; Lambert's foolish act was followed by discussion and negotiation, while the failure of Charles's agents to effect a successful demonstration in England was succeeded by discouragement and recrimination. Events proved, however, that it was better for England to work out her own salvation than to have a dissolute Court imposed upon her by force.

From the moment when (in October 1659) the officers in London shook off the incubus of the revived Long Parliament, a note of trepidation may be detected in their pronouncements.

[1] *Cal. Clar. S.P.* 49, 327.
[2] *Carte MS.* 213 ff., 360–6.   [3] *Cal. Clar. S.P.* 128, 163.
[4] *Lettres du cardinal Mazarin* (ed. G. d'Avenel), ix. 356.
[5] *Cal. Clar. S.P.* 354.   [6] Ibid. 359.

'This is a great work,' they wrote to Monck[1] (then commanding
in Scotland), 'and we acknowledge we are weak and insufficient
to maintain it, but our eyes are towards the Lord.' Monck,
steadily gazing in the same direction, agreed that his correspondents were insufficient to carry through the enterprise on which
they had embarked; he had regarded the recall of the Long
Parliament in May as a dispensation, but its eviction clearly was
not. His conduct on receiving the news of Lambert's doings was
ominous. He ordered a fast; he directed his officers to seek the
presence and direction of God, and he put all the Anabaptists in
his army under restraint. Ever since his service under the Dutch
he had held inviolate the principle of soldierly obedience to
civilian authority;[2] now was the opportunity for vindicating that
principle by one whose hands were unstained in post-Oliverian
politics. Having announced to the Scottish Estates that he had
a call from God to march into England 'for the liberty and being
of parliaments . . . and a godly ministry'[3] (Nov. 15), he received
a generous supply, and took up his quarters at Coldstream. These
evidences of displeasure caused misgivings among the officers at
Whitehall, who well knew that without Monck's co-operation
they were only a faction; indeed, some of the more astute observers such as Whitelocke perceived that Charles Stuart, who could
not come in by foreign force might well come in by English disunion.[4] For these reasons Fleetwood was advised to risk a free
parliament and take upon himself the enterprise of restoring the
king, but he could not be prevailed upon to adopt such a decisive
course, and his indecision spread like a paralysis over the army
and republican idealists in London. Already they had acquiesced
in the second folly of Lambert—his departure (Nov. 3, 1659) at
the head of an army on a mission of negotiation to Monck. It was
a disastrous enterprise. Monck's three commissioners met Lambert at York and convinced him of the peaceable intentions of
their principal, but by then most of Lambert's horses had died
from disease, and his men had begun to desert from lack of pay.
The futility of Lambert's mission intensified the menace from the

---

[1] *Clarke Papers*, iv. 67, Oct. 20, 1659.

[2] Firth, *Cromwell's Army*, 383.   [3] *Clarke Papers*, iv. 113–14.

[4] e.g. *Clarke Papers*, iv. 77, Lambert to Monck, Oct. 25. Cf. also B. Whitelocke, *Memorials of the English Affairs*, 373, 382.

north; and so by the end of November there were pitted against each other two armies—that of Monck in Scotland and that of Fleetwood in London.

These two forces were not divided on the simple question of monarchy, because both were committed against the heresy of government by single person; but they were sharply opposed regarding the recent eviction of the Long Parliament, and they disagreed on the question whether Fleetwood and his associates provided an adequate substitute for the civil government. Their first skirmish was with the pen[1] and resulted in a crushing defeat for the southern brethren. Protesting against the imprisonment of their Anabaptist sympathizers, the Whitehall junto wrote to their associates in Monck's army inviting them to cross the Jordan in order to enjoy in peace and brotherly union the blessings provided for them by the most recent dispensation of Providence. Monck's officers were in exile, but an exile where the theological standards were high; they replied[2] as follows:

Dear brethren and fellow soldiers in the Lord.

Great are the thoughts of our hearts for the divisions in Reuben; and we are (as you express it) deeply affected and afflicted in our own spirits when we consider what cause we have to be dissatisfied with you, our dear brethren; you, with whom we have lived and conversed together; with whom we have prayed, and fought together; with whom we have taken sweet counsel together in the house of God as friends. . . . We shall deal with you with that plainness and freedom and sincerity that becometh brethren.

We could not be satisfied that there was any such need of general officers as that the parliament should be pressed to it so unseasonably. . . . We are less satisfied that you should endeavour by a new way to wrest the power of their [parliament's] hands; thus making the Army a corporation in a manner independent from the civil power. That you should so soon return to former sins, and for the apparent interest of nine or ten persons . . . that is that lieth so sore upon our spirits; that is it that must of necessity make the three nations slaves to the Army. We cannot but in the name of the Lord tell you that these actings make us stink in the nostrils of the Good People, and cause the name of God to be evil spoken of, and his enemies to rejoice. How

[1] The correspondence was printed in *A letter from the officers at Whitehall . . . with the answer of General Monck and his officers*, 1659. The originals are in the *Clarke MSS.*, Worcester College, Oxford. See the *Clarke Papers*, iv. 105, n. 1.

[2] Nov. 7, 1659.

can you be for good things when you do that which is evil? How can you be for a free state and commonwealth when, for the sake of nine or ten persons you dissolve parliament? To what purpose is it to be against a single person if you be for nine or ten? Or for reformation, if you return so soon to former sins? Our daily prayer to God is that we may not be necessitated to make war on you.

And now, brethren, as yet dear and precious in our sight, we beseech you to lay these things to heart and repent... with a repentance not to be repented of. Lay not up your treasure in this world, but seek first the kingdom of God: do not evil because you think good may come of it. Finally, brethren, be not entangled with the yoke of bondage. The grace of Our Lord Jesus Christ be with you, Amen.

[Postscript] We entreat you not to put so harsh a name on the necessary and short restraint of our brethren as Bonds; we shall own them and use them as brethren ... their pay is still continued.

The crisis was reached in December. On the thirteenth of that month the General Council of Officers in London announced the principles on which they were agreed;[1] these included (a) no kingship, (b) no single person, (c) no house of peers, (d) separation of the legislative and executive, and (e) a senate and lower chamber to be elected by duly qualified persons. In addition there were to be twenty-one Conservators of Liberty whose duty it was to preserve inviolate the fundamentals of the constitution—an innovation, the initiative for which was claimed by Ludlow, who may have derived it from Harrington.[2] In this scheme was embodied some of the most advanced political thinking of the Commonwealth, such as specially commended itself to those who wished to steer a middle course between the Scylla and Charybdis of single person and single house; and the proposals as thus formulated might have had at least a chance of trial if they had been the substitute for Richard's Protectorate. But the conditions of December 1659 were totally unlike those of the preceding May. Then the Army had had a free hand, as well as the good-will of many civilians; now it had forfeited that good opinion by disunion and violence, and had to contend with the increasingly insistent demand that (since fundamentals were in question) some semblance of civil authority should first be restored. In his attempt to emulate Cromwellian traditions Lambert had

---

[1] *Mercurius Politicus*, no. 598; also *Steele*, i. 3141.
[2] *Ludlow*, ii. 99, 172–4; Firth, *House of Lords in the Civil War*, 266–7.

suddenly awakened Englishmen to the fact that the partnership and direction of Providence are not necessarily the monopoly of one man or one clique, and before the end of the year both he and Fleetwood had forfeited their claim to be the channels through which alone God's mercy flowed to the long-suffering nations. Lambert was already discredited by his frankness; Fleetwood, who prayed hard until two in the afternoon, was obliged at last to confess that 'God had spit in his face'.[1] By the time they had announced the terms of their panacea, men were looking elsewhere for guidance.

As in so many national crises the lead was taken by the city of London. In her civic organization, backed by the great city companies, London possessed an influential community having a prestige second only to that of parliament itself. This factor was now to influence events at a time when there were no leaders and scarcely a government. There was a strong Presbyterian element in the city; also a party of youth—the apprentices; and there were many not actively concerned with politics who held that the trade of the metropolis suffered by the absence of parliament. These different interests expressed themselves so vociferously by way of petition that the Committee of Safety was obliged to issue a proclamation prohibiting this method of seeking redress;[2] but (on the pretended score of illness) the lord mayor refused to publish this edict, so it was read outside the Exchange by a sergeant, supported by a troop of horse, to the accompaniment of a shower of ice and tiles.[3] For several days the trade of the city was at a stand; many citizens armed; conflicts between soldiers and civilians were matters of everyday occurrence; hand grenades were stored in St. Paul's[4] for emergencies, and the young gentlemen of the Inns of Court, anxious for a scrap, undertook to lead the townsmen; but prompt arrests served to avert serious bloodshed. Disaffection within the Army itself both prevented civil war and completed the discomfiture of the military leaders. Soldiers were heard to say that rather than wage war they would make a ring for their officers to fight in;[5] they soon went farther, for the Irish troops in London arrested their officers, and when

---

[1] *Cal. Clar. S.P.* 492.   [2] Dec. 1, 1659; *Steele*, i. 3137.
[3] *Clarke Papers*, iv. 165, News-letter of Dec. 6.   [4] Ibid. 186, Dec. 13.
[5] Firth, *Cromwell's Army*, 384.

Portsmouth suddenly declared for parliament, the regiment sent to overawe it seized its leaders and carried them as a spectacle through the cheering town.[1] The next defection was even more serious—Lawson, in command of twenty-two ships at Gravesend, having declared for parliament, proceeded to sail up the Thames in order to enforce his demand. The revolution was completed when the soldiers, after parading in Lincoln's Inn Fields, marched by companies to the Rolls House, where they acknowledged old Speaker Lenthall as their commander, from whom they professed willingness to receive orders until the return from Portsmouth of Hesilrige and the other army commissioners.[2] Torn by divided counsels and deserted by all but Desborough and Vane, Fleetwood had to yield to the clamour; writs were hurriedly issued, and on December 26 there reassembled at Westminster the sorry remnant (about forty members) of the Long Parliament. They would serve at least to maintain the apostolic succession at Westminster; it was a Rump, but a civilian Rump, and from it, as from a rib, the whole political anatomy might one day be reassembled.

The parliament of December 1659 was certainly not a monarchist assembly, for it was still the embodiment of the Good Old Cause; but if it could be enlarged and reconditioned by the inclusion of those Presbyterians who had been expelled by Pride's Purge in December 1648, then the link with the past would be strengthened, and such an assembly might restore Charles on definite conditions. If, moreover, this extended Rump could be induced to 'go to the country' there was a possibility that a complete body would be returned, on the head of which the crown might safely be placed. A gamble on such a series of possibilities might ultimately justify itself, but it would be a gamble nevertheless; for almost anything might have happened—the Rumpers might have established a republic with Hesilrige as its president; or Lambert might have retrieved his mistakes and established a Protectorate; or he might have secured a son-in-law and restored a king at the same stroke; or Charles Stuart might have been brought back by a foreign power, or by a royalist rising in England—there was an endless series of possibilities, and speculation in these feverish markets would depend for success on

[1] *Clarke Papers*, iv. 216. [2] Ibid. iv. 219.

silence, caution, and detachment from the bonds of personal allegiance.

The one man gifted with these qualities was George Monck. Prudence and brevity were the mottoes of his varied career, and even his wooing was said to have been conducted on these principles; for (according to Aubrey) when Clarges, his prospective brother-in-law, went to tell him that Anne Clarges was brought to bed:

'Of what?' asked Monck.

'Of a son,' replied Clarges.

'Why then,' said Monck, 'she is my wife.'[1]

The unobtrusive circumspection which preceded his nuptials had served him at every stage of his career. After his detachment from the royalist cause in 1646 he had become a faithful servant of the Commonwealth, and was believed to have signed the Covenant, a relinquishment of his old allegiance which was rendered less obtrusive by the fact that his career was then mainly in Ireland. As commander-in-chief in Scotland he was again able to render distinguished service while remaining personally at some distance; indeed it had been jestingly said that Cromwell could not have got Monck out of Scotland even if he had tried. Faithful to Richard, he had advised him to reduce the Army, strengthen the Navy, and increase the power of the Presbyterian element, measures which, had they been capable of adoption, might have saved the Protectorate. 'Old Monck', though scarcely turned fifty, had the advantage of being thought older than he really was by men who distrusted youth. By twice declining a seat in the 'Other House' he had continued to maintain his equilibrium in the more spacious orbit through which he revolved.

As he followed Lambert's career through the summer and autumn of 1659 Monck saw his opportunity. To his own soldiers he imparted something of his own neutrality and ostensible obedience to the civil power; he professed joy at the news of Booth's defeat, and expressed the hope that the mere mention of Charles's return would be rewarded with hanging. He was for parliament only, but what lay beyond that, no one knew. What seemed certain was his fidelity to anti-monarchist principles;

[1] *Aubrey*, ii. 73. But see under 'Clarges' in *D.N.B. Corrigenda*.

otherwise he preserved his own counsels. His taciturnity was aided by the habit of chewing tobacco, and when, amid rumination, he interjected his contributions to a debate whether a man could be godly who said the same prayer twice, it was clear that he was still faithful to the old ritual.[1] Having taken up his station at Coldstream with about seven thousand foot and horse (Dec. 8) he was far enough off to make ineffective Lambert's attempts at compromise, but near enough to the border for a speedy march into England. There he remained until his military rivals in London had sufficiently discredited themselves; nor did he set out until, by the second recall of the Long Parliament in December, there was a civil institution in need of his support, in a city which expected much from his coming. Ostensibly 'the better countenancing' of the forty Rumpers was a good reason for intervention; nearer hand was Fairfax, who had roused Yorkshire in the cause of a free parliament,[2] and was willing to co-operate against Lambert, the common enemy; in the remoter distance were the possibilities of what a 'free' parliament might do after these years of purges and evictions. In the knowledge that he could depend on Fairfax against Lambert and on his own secretiveness against both republican and royalist, Monck crossed the Tweed on January 2, 1660.

South of the border Monck had no official status other than his commissionership of the Army; for it was doubtful whether the office of commander-in-chief to which he had been appointed by a few members of the old Council of State on November 24 still held good.[3] At Wooler he received letters from parliament which confirmed him in his resolution. At Newcastle he came upon Lambert's army, now but a shadow of its former self; part of this he disbanded, part he enlisted. His next stop was at Nunappleton, where he discussed events with general Fairfax, now openly advocating the return of the king; but Monck would not be drawn beyond his usual formula, that he would support parliament. Throughout his journey he was presented with addresses

[1] J. Price, *Mystery and method of His Majesty's happy restoration* (1680), 15.

[2] For the negotiations between Monck and Fairfax see *H.M.C. Rep.* vi, app. 466.

[3] *Clarke Papers*, iv. 137-9; and G. Davies, *The early history of the Coldstream Guards*, 97-100.

from the gentry and freeholders pressing him to recall those Presbyterian members who had been 'secluded' from the House of Commons by Pride's Purge; he was also urged to dispense with oaths and engagements. The petition from Suffolk[1] contained these words: 'it is tedious to see government reeling from one hand to another; it is in your power to fix it'; while that from Devonshire,[2] Monck's native county, was more explicit in its statement that the majority desired a monarchy, and that the most strenuous opponents of restoration were the holders of confiscated estates. Elements of similarity in these documents suggest a common origin;[3] indeed their simultaneous appearance throughout the greater part of the country at this time may have been one of the few successes in royalist propaganda on behalf of Charles.

But to all these requests the stereotyped reply was returned. At Newark he was still a 'black Monck', since no one could see through him, though his granting of commissions to men of profligate lives and anti-parliamentarian principles caused misgiving in the Rump, so that colonel Martin compared him to one 'that being sent for to make a sute of cloathes brought with him a budget full of carpenter's tools'.[4] Two spies, Scott and Robinson, sent by parliament to meet him, could extract nothing incriminating. London was reached on February 3, and three days later the general was thanked in the Commons by Speaker Lenthall, who compared[5] the deliverer to 'the little cloud no bigger than a man's hand which is in an instant become the refreshment of the whole nation'. This greeting was met with a characteristic reply. On his march south, he reported, the people had demanded a free and full parliament, the admission of the ex-members, and the determination of the proceedings of the existing assembly.[6] As for advice, he counselled them to bind themselves with as few oaths as possible—words of ominous import to a now apprehensive audience.

Since the memorable twenty-sixth of December 1659 England

---

[1] *Cal. S.P. Dom., 1659–60*, 332.   [2] Ibid. 330.

[3] Possibly Prynne. For the development of propaganda in relation to public opinion see C. S. Emden, *The People and the Constitution* (1933).

[4] *Ludlow*, ii. 207.   [5] *Continuation of Baker's Chronicle*, 683.

[6] *Ludlow*, ii. 216.

had been progressing through an intensive course of political evolution. Then the choice had been simple and fundamental—the Army or Parliament; now it was more complicated—the perpetuation of the Good Old Cause by the Rump, or the termination of that cause by the admission of the Presbyterians and a completely fresh start from a free or representative parliament. That the forty legislators had a divine call was evident from the fact that this was their second summons from oblivion; and now that they had freed themselves from the weighty loins of Fleetwood and Lambert, they professed to have no fears of the little finger of their deliverer. It is true that, apart from a congratulatory address sent by the London watermen,[1] they could not instance any demonstration of popular support; but, as venerable and select Levites claiming to have no inheritance in Israel, they asserted the prerogative of guiding the nation, and in this enterprise it was thought that they might carry Monck with them; for he was busily 'countenancing' their persons, while his wife plied their ladies with sweetmeats and wine, talking of her husband's self-denial and irreproachable republicanism.[2] Some members, with an eye on Monck's veterans, feared that he was bringing a pick-axe and spade for a job requiring only needle and thread; but he brushed aside these remonstrances with the assurance: 'it matters not; I will do your work well enough, I warrant you.' Soon the forty Rumpers were as forty interrogation marks personifying the great national conundrum: whither did these things tend?

The studied neutrality of Monck and the eager calculations of the Good Old Cause were upset by the city of London. In January there had been elected a new Common Council of a type likely to be impatient of the Rump; for it was 'such a one as has not been seen since the beginning of these troubles, of the best and wealthiest of the city, amongst whom there is not one Anabaptist, or one who hath purchased crown lands, church lands or delinquents' lands'.[3] An immediate consequence of this was that two London aldermen were able to raise a considerable sum on behalf of the exiled king.[4] But the position of Monck was now one of

---

[1] Jan. 31, 1659/60. *Steele*, i. 3149. It was ordered to be printed with an expression of the Speaker's thanks.   [2] *Ludlow*, ii. 217.

[3] *Clar. S.P.* iii. 641.   [4] Ibid. 649–52, and *Cal. Clar. S.P.* 532.

some difficulty, for he was placed between two rival representatives of the civil power. He was ostensibly the protector and presumably the servant of parliament ('Now, George, we have thee body and soul', Hesilrige had exclaimed in the House), but he had no intention of being a tool; on the other hand, he knew that the enmity of the city was not lightly to be invoked. When the city refused to pay taxes on the ground that it was not represented at Westminster, Monck was suddenly forced to choose between London and the Rump. For hours he was locked up with Hesilrige and the Council at Whitehall; so prolonged into the night was their session that Mrs. Monck knocked at the door, demanding to see her husband on important business; and when at half-past two in the morning he at last emerged, it was clear from his pallor that he had passed through a severe ordeal. His news explained his dishevelled looks. All was naught, he said; for he had been ordered to arrest ten prominent citizens, pull down the gates of the city, and reduce London to the level of a village.[1] He had no choice but to obey. In the process of executing these orders he begged his taskmasters to mitigate their severity, but their reply was to send even more insistent orders;[2] and soon the city was reduced to 'as very a dorp as Islington'.[3] His apology for this catastrophe was sympathetically received at the Guildhall, where he explained that he had undertaken a disagreeable duty in order that it might not be done more thoroughly by his enemies; he had broken down their gates as the servant of parliament and the friend of London. In this way was cemented the union between the general and the corporation, and while he was banqueting with the City Fathers, the Rump was burnt in effigy in the streets.

There were two consequences of the failure of this plot to discredit Monck, namely, the Rump lost what prestige it had possessed, and the generalissimo was securely entrenched in the position from which parliament had tried to drive him. Hence the forty legislators were obliged to acquiesce in the popular demand for a free parliament; and, as a preliminary thereto, they had to submit to the return of their old Presbyterian colleagues.

[1] Ashley Cooper's account (*Shaftesbury*, vi b, 442 sqq.) and Christie, *Shaftesbury*, i. 207.

[2] *Continuation of Baker's Chronicle*, 684, and *Steele*, i. 3151, Feb. 9, 1659–60.

[3] *Cal. Clar. S.P.* 568.

Gathering together what remained of the secluded members, Monck addressed them thus:[1]

> When I consider that wisdom and self-denial which I have reason to be confident lodgeth in you, and how great a share of the nation's sufferings will fall on you in case the Lord deny us now a settlement, I am in very good hopes there will be found in you all such melting bowels towards these poor nations that you will become healers and makers-up of all its woeful breaches. . . . I have nothing before my eyes but God's glory and the setting of these nations upon Commonwealth foundations.

Having then adjured them to provide for the Army, appoint a new Council of State, and agree to issue writs for a new parliament to meet in April, he secured their admission under the protection of his guards (Feb. 21)—the only exhibition of force in the events leading directly to the Restoration. As the secluded members took their seats Hesilrige and others cried out that Monck was a traitor, and several 'sitting' members left the House; but a tense situation was saved by a touch of humour when there appeared a ghastly apparition from the past in the form of 'crop-eared' Prynne, trailing a long sword between the legs of his fellow seclusionists, and settling himself firmly in a seat from which he had already been twice ejected by force. The Rump, now the inspiration of a facile and uniformly obscene muse, was only a bare bone; but movement was at last possible, because parliament was again in gear:

> The parliament now will
> Come into their Geers,
> For secluded Pryn
> That once lost his eares,
> March't in with his rapier
> For Commons and Peers.
> To fill up the parliament full, full, full,
> To fill up the parliament full.[2]

This event was speedily followed by changes serving still further to discredit the Good Old Cause and to forge the links with the historic past. Of the old leaders, Hesilrige was obliged to secure

[1] *Bodley, Godwin Pamph.* 1272.
[2] *England's triumph or the Rump routed,* in *Bodley, Pamph. Wood,* 416, xlviii.

his safety by a secret compromise with Monck;[1] Lambert, bereft
of his army, was in London, hiding from arrest; Fleetwood, in the
language of a contemporary,[2] was left in the briars of Wallingford
House garden, having been deceived and deserted by the woman
whom Oliver had given him; all the fallen grandees were commemorated in mock petitions and lampoons scribbled by the
scurrilous. Meanwhile the work of reinstatement had begun.
Booth and other political prisoners were released; the Common
Council of the city was confirmed in office; the gates and portcul-
lises of the city were restored at public expense, and a grateful
London devoted a day of prayer and thanks for the return of the
secluded members. The old Council of State was displaced by a
new one, in which appeared Fairfax, Ashley Cooper, sir Harbottle Grimstone, Denzil Holles, and sergeant Maynard—all of
them known to have Presbyterian leanings. Monck himself
acquired official status by his appointment to the office of commander-in-chief of all the land forces, in which capacity he dealt
severely with what remained of army politics and army politicians. Lambert was captured and sent to the Tower; Fleetwood's
army was disbanded; all unemployed officers were ordered to
stations assigned them by Monck and required to stay there.
Throughout these critical days of February and March 1660
Monck never lost his head, not even at the frequent Guildhall
banquets which he attended;[3] for neither wine nor success could
thaw his constitutional moroseness and taciturnity. He was still,
according to his speeches, against monarchy, as that would bring
back prelacy; he was anxious to secure a moderate as distinct
from a rigid Presbyterianism; he was for a gospel ministry, and
universities devoted to sincere piety and sound learning. No
one could quarrel with such professions, even in this, the most
'accusative' age of English history. He declined the specious
offer of Hampton Court, knowing as he did that real estate,
particularly crown land, was then a very dubious investment.
'Such a merit as his could be rewarded only with death,' it was
said.[4] He was content, however, with a parliamentary gift of
£20,000.

---

[1] *Clarke Papers*, iv. 302, app. D.   [2] *Bodley, Pamph. Wood*, 276 a, cci.
[3] See *Ludlow*, ii. 244, for Ludlow's strictures on these entertainments.
[4] *Continuation of Baker's Chronicle*, 693.

Thus by the month of March 1660 the position was this—a decayed remnant of parliament had been reinvigorated by a transfusion of Presbyterian blood in order to provide the energy required for committing suicide; a Council of State had been appointed composed chiefly of Presbyterians harbouring royalist sympathies; Monck, still elusive, was nominally the enemy of the Stuarts, but his army, perceiving 'that the abandoned interest of Charles Stuart doth seem to shine in the face of public transactions',[1] was unwilling to be fooled any further. Having just emerged from the contest between parliament and city, how would the general fare in the threatened conflict between his army and parliament? He had successfully disposed of the Rump and retained the goodwill of London; but would the men who had marched and prayed and fought with him allow this dallying with the Scarlet Woman who held both Presbyterian and Royalist in her thrall? So long as Monck hedged he was safe: a feather might disturb the balance and precipitate a decision.

The feather was vigorously thrust into the scale by the prize heavyweight of his age—William Prynne. A Presbyterian in religion and politics, and a rigid Puritan in the forbidding austerity of his morals, 'marginal' Prynne had hitherto so timed the pulsations of his vituperation as to guarantee, in an age of quick change, a remarkable continuity of punishment and imprisonment for himself. He had begun, in the happier days of Charles I, by attacking 'love-locks', face painting, drinking of healths, and the appearance of women on the stage, thereby losing his ears; when Laud was omnipotent, he assailed Arminianism, Prelacy, Free Will, Jesuits, and Ship-Money, suffering in consequence further fine and imprisonment as well as losing what little remained of his ears; in the Second Civil War he was again in trouble for advocating the unpopular causes of Monarchy and the Lords, and was among the most loud-voiced of the secluded Presbyterians; the advent of the Commonwealth he greeted with unmeasured attacks on Cromwell, the Army, and Free State tyranny, for which he again went to prison; and when released declaimed with greater ardour than ever against Jews, Quakers, Levellers, Independents, and lay preachers. By that time, however, the hope of silencing him had been abandoned. Of a

[1] Ibid. 691.

saturnine and witch-like countenance, a grimy burrower into hidden works of darkness, he had been so constructed that the ordinary human instincts of self-interest and calculation were completely displaced in him by chronic vertigo and an incurable itch for scribbling. In the early days of 1660 he found to his surprise that he was on the winning side. As one of the secluded members readmitted in February he procured the removal from the *Journals* of the oath of fidelity to the Commonwealth, and he had already supplied royalist agents with material for the petitions presented to Monck on his march,[1] services which earned for him a personal letter of thanks from Charles Stuart.[2] By a characteristic gesture this 'rhinoceros in blinkers'[3] now stampeded into a breach which Monck feared even to approach. On March 12 the Commons passed an Act placing the Militia in the hands of men known to be enemies of the Commonwealth; whereupon Monck, urged by his officers, was obliged to beg the Commons to forbear putting the Act into force, since he might thereby forfeit the support of his troops. A risk had to be taken and at this time Monck was not the man to take it; whereupon Prynne himself took the Act to the printers and had it published.[4]

Thus did Prynne make explicit what every one now believed to be implicit in Monck's designs. If from nothing else, these designs might have been deduced from the general's choice of personnel; for he appointed sir Horace Townshend governor of Lynn, Charles Howard of Carlisle, sir P. Killigrew of Pendennis Castle, and his kinsman William Morrice he made governor of Plymouth. It was Morrice who had most strongly urged Monck to readmit the secluded members;[5] it was he who, acting as intermediary with sir John Grenville, provided a link in the chain connecting the general with Charles's Court. On March 19 Monck interviewed Grenville in the presence of Morrice and accepted a letter from Charles, delivery of which he had refused in the previous year.[6] Still unwilling to put anything on paper,[7] the generalissimo sent a message by Grenville to the effect that while he much desired

---

[1] *Cal. Clar. S.P.* 532. *Supra,* 20.   [2] His reply is in *Carte MS.* 30, f. 592.
[3] The phrase is David Masson's (*Life of Milton,* v. 449).
[4] *Ludlow,* ii. 248.   [5] *Nicholas Papers,* iv. 195.   [6] *Clar. S.P.* iii. 622.
[7] As late as Apr. 6 the Council of State was ignorant of Monck's communications with Charles (ibid. 722).

his Majesty's restoration, it must be cautiously attempted.[1] He advised Charles to declare a free and general pardon to his subjects, except such as should be excepted; and that none should be punished for differences in matters of religion. He added also that he had intelligence of a Spanish design to detain the king in Flanders, and therefore advised him to leave Spanish territory and go to Breda or some Dutch town. On his arrival at Ostend Grenville put this advice into writing; the Declaration of Breda, drawn up with the concurrence of Hyde, Ormonde, and Nicholas was the result (Apr. 4/14). Its promise of toleration was valid only in so far as a 'free' parliament ratified it.

The reinforced Rump was now engaged in winding up its affairs, many of its members acting on the conviction that they would be returned by their constituencies to the parliament which was to follow;[2] and meanwhile the Army was pacified by a circular letter wherein Monck promised to intercede with the new legislature for an Act confirming them in their lands. On March 15 the Council of State (presided over by Arthur Annesley, an old secluded member) was empowered to act in the interval between the two parliaments, and on the following day the Long Parliament was formally dissolved by a bill containing this important proviso[3]—'that the single actings of this House, enforced by the pressing necessities of the present times, are not intended in the least to infringe, much less take away the ancient, native right which the House of Peers, consisting of those lords that did engage in the cause of the parliament . . . had and have to be a part of the parliament of England'. A resolution[4] that April 6 should be kept as a day of national fasting and humiliation was the last and characteristic act of a parliament which, once famous for pulling down, was now busily putting back.

It was generally assumed that the king's return would be a conditional one; indeed the Council of State, after a week spent in examining the treaties of Oxford, Uxbridge, and Newport,[5]

---

[1] *Continuation of Baker's Chronicle*, 695–6.

[2] 'They say the Rumpers bid great sums of money in many borough towns to be elected in the next parliament.' Massey to Hyde, Mar. 16, 1660. *Thurloe State Papers* (1742), vii. 855. The term Rumper here includes Presbyterian.   [3] *C.J.* vii. 880, Mar. 16.   [4] *Steele*, i. 3165, Mar. 16, 1660.

[5] *Cal. Clar. S.P.* 634. For the scheme in which Manchester was to be lord treasurer see ibid. 614.

negotiated with Manchester and the Presbyterian peers for the imposition of terms such as Charles I had been willing to accept in 1648, terms which wrested control of the Militia from the crown and provided some guarantee of parliamentary government. Moreover, the Presbyterians were not alone in desiring such conditions; for in this they had the support of Monck and his Army, the Council, the City, and the Navy;[1] nor was the desire for limitations of merely academic import, since among the men now co-operating to restore monarchy there were many who desired immunity for their own past conduct, and still more who were anxious to secure some degree of toleration for the beliefs which they professed. Why did Charles eventually return without conditions?

The answer may be that the Presbyterians were completely submerged by the ridicule and odium showered on them by a country fast becoming more royalist than the king himself. It was Charles's opinion that by negotiating secretly with Monck he was avoiding a conditional return; and it seems to have been held by the Court that, with the failure of Booth's rising, there was no reason why terms should be imposed. Monck might have secured conditions on behalf of his fellow Presbyterians before the king's return; but by his fear of taking a false step he left the way open for more adventurous managers, and so unwittingly betrayed the party which he represented. Also, the Presbyterian nobles assumed too lightly that it was for them to formulate conditions, forgetting that, even if they managed to veto the cavalier peers, there was growing up a younger generation of nobility which could not reasonably be excluded;[2] so too, the rank and file of the party over-estimated their chances at the general election of April 1660; indeed, few of the older men appear to have realized that a younger generation was growing up to whom the Civil Wars were only recollections of childhood, and Solemn League and Good Old Cause but outworn tags of an

---

[1] *Carte MS.* 30, ff. 590–1.

[2] 'These fourteen [Peers] that sat in '48 would very fain make themselves a noble Rump, if they could find out any counsellable way to effect it.' Barwick to Hyde, *Clar. S.P.* iii. 729, Apr. 16, 1660. For the contest between these lords and the younger peers, represented by Oxford, Peters, and Rivers, see Coventry to Ormonde, Apr. 27, in Carte, *Collection of original letters and papers* (1739), ii. 328.

evil past. Nor had allowance been made for the great wave of loyalism which, gathering force like a torrent, swept the country of everything but devotion to the crown, thrusting even the most moderate Presbyterianism into the wreckage, and defeating the hopes of those who had done most to effect Restoration by peaceable means. 'It must be a king surrounded with majestick beams,' wrote one of Manchester's public correspondents, 'consecrated with holy oil, invested with inviolable authority and power . . . such a prince and nothing else will answer our expectations. A duke of Venice is now a byword: chief magistrate is grown a nick-name.'[1] This change was observed by the French ambassador Bordeaux,[2] who reported that there was a general desire to recall the king without conditions; he noted also that the Presbyterians had been abandoned by Monck. Not compromise, but revenge was the danger to be anticipated, and it is significant that throughout the month of April 1660 there were numerous declarations from the royalist gentry expressing the hope that animosity might not be shown to their former enemies.[3]

The interval between the dissolution of the Long Parliament and the meeting of the Convention (Mar. 17–Apr. 25) was a critical period. As 'Keepers of the Liberties of England' the Council of State decreed the removal of disbanded troops from London[4] and forbade meetings until the assembly of parliament; army agitators were ordered to be arrested;[5] suspicious persons passing to and from the seas were taken into custody. The writs issued to sheriffs for the new parliament contained an express veto[6] on the election of those persons or their sons who had fought on the royalist side, a veto afterwards found to be ineffective. The chief danger was from Lambert, who, having escaped from the Tower, was suspected of plotting an insurrection with Hewson, Okey, and colonel Richard Lilburne; but his capture near Daventry by colonel Ingoldsby (Apr. 21) removed the last impediment to a settlement. Monck still retained something of his detachment; he would take no decisive step until the results of the general election were known and the complexion of the

---

[1] *Vox et Votum populi Anglicani*, by T.C., 1660 (*Bodley, Pamph. Wood*, 608).

[2] *Baschet*, 107. Bordeaux to Mazarin, Apr. 30/May 10, 1660.

[3] *Bodley, Pamph. Wood*, 276 a, cvii sqq.   [4] *Steele*, i. 3166, Mar. 17.

[5] Ibid. 3174, Mar. 24.   [6] Ibid. 3171 and 3176, Mar. 18 and 28.

new parliament revealed. He had saved Israel from the Midian-
ites, but it was not for him to rule; so like Gideon he conducted
himself with meekness, and the chiding Ephraimites he sent away
with smooth words.

The elections proved a disappointment to the Presbyterians.[1]
In several boroughs there had already begun a reinstatement of
persons excluded during the Commonwealth,[2] a change seldom
in favour of the Presbyterians, who, moreover, were chosen for
few counties, and in those instances only where the royalist element concurred. In spite of the prohibition excluding them,
about 100 members were returned who had taken up arms
against parliament;[3] these were royalist almost to a man, as were
also the large proportion of young men whom the French ambassador noticed in the House.[4] By superior management the
Presbyterians succeeded in obtaining the Speakership for an old
secluded member—sir Harbottle Grimstone; but they never had
a clear majority, and the by-elections may have further diminished
their strength. For the moment, however, the two parties were
united, and the personnel of the Convention is of special interest
because it combined representatives of families that had played
a notable part in Civil War struggles with members who, on the
basis of their territorial connexion, were destined to exercise a
profound influence on the politics of the succeeding century;
indeed, it was in the Convention that these latter families were
present for the first time in great force. In the former category
were a Hampden for a Buckinghamshire borough, an Eliot for
a Cornish borough, a Fiennes for Oxfordshire, and a Cromwell
for Huntingdonshire; in the latter class an Onslow for Guildford,
a Howard for Cumberland, a Stanley for Liverpool, a Godolphin
for Helston, a Walpole for King's Lynn, a Townshend for Norfolk,
a Temple for Buckingham, a Cavendish for Derbyshire, a Harley
for Herefordshire, a Russell for Tavistock, a Somerset for Monmouth, and a Pelham for Sussex. Thus the Convention which
effected a bloodless revolution was representative not of the town
but of the landed estate, and was dominated not by the tradesmen

[1] For this see *Clar. S.P.* iii. 731; *Clar. Cont.* i. 329; *Autobiography of Sir John Bramstone* (Camd. Soc.), 115; and Miss L. F. Brown, in *E.H.R.* xxii. 51 sqq.
[2] J. H. Sacret, 'Restoration government and municipal corporations' in *E.H.R.* xlv.   [3] *Cal. S.P. Dom., 1659–60*, 395.   [4] *Baschet*, 107, May 24/June 3.

and craftsmen of Commonwealth constituencies, but by the ancestors of most of the statesmen and prime ministers of the eighteenth century. Its temper was not that of a continental convention, but of a British House of Lords. Hence its conservatism.

Just as from the nucleus of the Rump there had developed the 'free' convention of April 1660, so the small body of Presbyterian peers expanded gradually into the House of Lords, though the time for the return of the bishops was not yet. On April 27 Monck consented to the admission of the 'young lords', thereby enveloping the presbyterian or parliamentary peers with about thirty sons of Royalists.[1] The question of admitting those peers who had fought for the king was more difficult; but Charles himself intervened at this point with a request that they would forbear pressing their claims, since otherwise they might raise the difficulty of 'unqualified' members of the Commons. On May 14, however, several of these lords were invited by their House to resume their seats, and this provided a precedent for the return of the others without summons; by June 1, indeed, about eighty peers were in session, whereas on April 25 only ten had made an appearance. Thus, by postponing vexed questions of principle, many of the elements of the constitution as it had existed before 1645 were quietly reinstated. Abroad, there was soon to be a renaissance of personal absolutism, strengthened by a preceding period of experiment or anarchy; in England, however, it was not the king that was restored, but the king in parliament.

This passage from Commonwealth to Monarchy was effected with extreme deliberation. Acting in co-operation with the few lords who at first took their seats, the Commons maintained contact with the Council of State, through its president (Annesley), and with the city of London, through the lord mayor and aldermen. Conjunction with the City was necessary not only for assistance in raising money, but because the presence of the magistrates at functions of national importance, such as the proclamation of Charles in Westminster Hall on May 8, served to give a more general sanction to the proceedings of the two Houses. No Convention ever acted with less precipitance than did this. On Wednesday, April 25, they began with a sermon

[1] Firth, *House of Lords in the Civil War*, 283 sqq.

from Dr. Reynolds at St. Margaret's, and set apart the following Monday as a day of fasting and humiliation; on Thursday, after appointing a committee for privileges and elections, they voted their thanks to Monck, 'our physician, who hath cured us with his lenitives'; Friday was occupied with the double returns; Monday was the fast day.[1] Meanwhile the western burgesses were arriving in London,[2] and on Tuesday, May 1, the 'great business touching the settlement of the nations' was at last taken in hand. Three documents, hitherto kept back by Monck, were communicated by the Council of State, which, after being read, were entered in the *Journals*. These were the Declaration of Breda, a letter to Monck, and a letter to the House of Commons. 'We shall always look upon your counsels as the best we can receive' was Charles's assuring message for his faithful Commons; the letter to Monck deprecated the evils of power 'assumed by passion and appetite and not supported by justice'; the Declaration of Breda invited all Englishmen, save such as should be excepted, to rely on the word of a king, and gave hints that, subject to parliamentary approval, there would be a measure of toleration for all who desired to live in peace.

Warmed by these assurances, the Commons resolved to grant a gift of £50,000 to the absent king, directing that a committee should consult with the lord mayor and aldermen on the best means of raising this sum; an assessment of £70,000 per month was also ordered to be levied. The Lords then took the lead. Having placed on record the principle that 'according to the ancient and fundamental laws of the kingdom the government is and ought to be by king, lords and commons', they voted that means should be devised to secure the king's return to his people.[3] With both these resolutions the Commons expressed their concurrence.[4] To maintain public order, the commissioners of the Navy, Customs and Excise and all sheriffs, justices, mayors, and constables in office on April 25 were ordered by proclamation to continue in the exercise of their duties.[5] On May 7 the two Houses agreed that Charles should be proclaimed on the following day, and the form of proclamation[6] used on May 8 declared

---

[1] *C.J.* viii. 2 sqq.   [2] Carte, *Collection of original letters*, ii. 328.
[3] Annesley's report from conference with the Lords, May 1, in *C.J.* viii. 7.
[4] Ibid. viii. 8.   [5] *Steele*, i. 3186, May 7, and 3201, May 11.   [6] Ibid. 3188.

that the imperial crown of England 'by inherent birth-right and lawful and undoubted succession' had descended on Charles immediately on the death of his father; in effect therefore the year of his restoration was reckoned as the twelfth of his reign.

It needed only the presence of the king in order that the Restoration might be complete. The duty of escorting him was entrusted to Edward Montagu, afterwards first earl of Sandwich, one of the Montagus who had thrown in their lot with the parliament while dissociating themselves from the king's trial and execution. Like Monck, Montagu had performed brilliant naval service for Cromwell in spite of complete lack of experience at sea. The fall of Richard Cromwell dissolved his bonds of obligation, and in the summer of 1659 he had been won over to the royalist cause by his cousin, an active agent for Charles.[1] In command of the fleet ordered to the Sound in order to mediate peace between Sweden and Denmark, Montagu, on his own initiative, had brought his ships home in the hope of assisting the operations of sir George Booth—a glaring breach of discipline; but he was too late, and he was fortunate[2] in that he was allowed to resign his command. The events of January 1660 restored his prestige. His intense dislike of Monck did not prevent his accepting joint control of the fleet with him (Feb. 23, 1660), and thereupon, with the help of Pepys, he 'purged' the Navy, dismissing Anabaptists and Sectaries, or sending them to distant stations,[3] and so securing from the eminence of the quarter-deck that uniformity of opinion unattainable in the camp. Shouts of 'God bless King Charles' greeted the admiral's announcement (May 3) that a naval council of war had decided for monarchy, and the last act in the drama of the royal home-coming could now be staged.

With eighteen commissioners Montagu proceeded to the Dutch coast in order to bring the king home to England,[4] and on the 25th day of May 1660 the restored exile stepped briskly ashore

[1] *Cal. Clar. S.P.* 244–6.

[2] The Commons were then preoccupied with Lambert—Sandwich, *Journal* (ed. Anderson, *N.R.S.*), 47. For the proceedings of the Council of State in regard to Montagu's return see the Council's Minutes in *Rawl. MS.*, A 134, Sept. 17, 1659.

[3] F. R. Harris, *Life of Edward Montagu, first earl of Sandwich*, i. 175.

[4] Sandwich, *Journal* (*N.R.S.*), 76–7.

at Dover, where he received the homage of Monck (whom he greeted as Father), while a large concourse of nobility and gentry offered their welcome from a marquee erected on the shore. From the mayor, Charles received a bible; and tears were shed as the king assured the donor that it would be the most treasured possession of his life. Therein he might at least have found a clue to some recent happenings in his kingdoms; for search would have revealed these words: *This kind goeth not out but by prayer and fasting*. But it was no time for such explanations. The royal equipage then proceeded by easy stages to London, through highways resounding with the cheers of a populace which rejoiced that its king had returned.

II

THE LAND: ITS PRODUCTS AND INDUSTRIES

1. PROVINCIAL ENGLAND: A BRIEF SURVEY

THE England to which Charles had returned was rich in two beautiful things, her poetry and her parish churches. These things, now numbered among the most graceful elements in the English heritage, were the products of a distinctive and rapidly maturing civilization; it is with the material conditions which made possible this civilization that the present chapter is concerned.

No survey, however brief, can ignore the geological conformation which predetermines so much of human activity. Within the compass of England are to be found many differences of rock-structure of vital importance to the agriculturist, and of interest to the student of history, differences which are most clearly evidenced in variations of soil and rainfall. Thus, in the south-east the annual rainfall seldom exceeds 24 inches, and on the Thames estuary it averages 18–19 inches; whereas in the north and west it often exceeds 30 inches, and in parts of the Lake District it exceeds 100 inches. One result of this diversity is the great variation of pastures, and hence the variety of wool—a factor of supreme economic importance in English history. It is more difficult to generalize about soils, because, in addition to difference of geological structure, there are glacial drifts and other deposits due to various forces, such as wind and the flow of rivers; with the result that in the same county many kinds of soil may be found. An example is Yorkshire, where there are (1) the Pennine moors in the west, composed of Carboniferous Limestone, Millstone Grit, and Coal Measures; (2) the Vale of York, from the Humber to the mouth of the Tees, composed of soft Trias, and Lias covered with Boulder Clay; (3) the North York Moors (including the Cleveland Hills and Tabular Hills) composed of hard Jurassic Sandstones; (4) the Vale of Pickering, a glacial-period lake-bed, composed of Kimmeridge Clay covered with alluvium; (5) the Chalk Wolds, forming a broad strip from the Humber to the mouth of the Tees; and (6) the levels of Holderness and Humber Mouth, composed of Boulder Clay and alluvium. Such is the diversity to be found within the limits of a single English county. In other counties a somewhat greater degree of uniformity may be traced. Thus in Cheshire there are substrata of Keuper Marl and Bunter Sandstone, overlaid with 'drift' or Boulder Clay, the result being a stiff soil best suited to pasture and cheese-making. Conditions are somewhat similar in Leicestershire and parts of Warwickshire, where there are glacial drifts over the Trias Sandstone and Lias Clay, providing pasture on the heavier lands and good arable on the Limestones and Ironstones;[1] farther south the Kimmeridge Clay favours dairy farming in the Vales of Aylesbury and White Horse.[2] Contrasted with these districts are Herefordshire and parts of Worcestershire, where the Old Red Sandstone has (exceptionally) worn down to a very rich soil, accounting for some of the best pasture and fruit farms in the country. Geology may well determine the uses to which the soil is put, and may therefore indirectly influence the character and habits of many generations of men.[3]

It is possible to distinguish two areas of England contrasted in the geological age of their respective rock formations. The southern of these includes three zones of very different size: (1) a strip bounded on the north by the Tees and on the west by the Pennines and the Yorkshire coal-fields; (2) a strip bounded on the east by the Pennines and on the north by the Lancashire coal-fields, roughly conterminous with Cheshire; and (3) the zone defined on the north by the southern extremity of the Pennines, on the west by the Welsh Marches, the Shropshire Hills, and the Malvern Hills, on the south-west by the Mendips, Exmoor, and Dartmoor, and by the sea on the south and east. Within this, the third of the above triple set of limits, lies that part of England to which the name the English Plain has been given, in contrast with the uplands of the north, the north-west, Wales, and the Cornwall-Devon peninsula. This name does not denote a district

---

[1] R. H. Rastall, *Agricultural Geology* (1916), 256.   [2] Ibid. 268.

[3] Reference should be made to *Great Britain, Essays in Regional Geography* (ed. A. G. Ogilvie, 2nd ed. 1930), and H. J. Mackinder, *Britain and the British Seas* (2nd ed. 1907). Good geological maps of England have been published by the Ordnance Survey.

of geological uniformity, but implies a preponderance of the softer and more recent formations, such as clay, chalk, marl, and sand, watered by old rivers which have worn down their beds to gentle and sinuous courses, with wide lateral deposits of fertile silt. Geologically, the two smaller zones as already described are similar in structure to the English Plain, and are its northern continuations; the secondary and tertiary deposits of all three are sharply contrasted with the hardened slates, quartzites, and igneous rocks which preponderate outside the above-mentioned limits. The general difference between the two parts of England as thus indicated can be seen not only in contour, but in climate. Along the north-western coast-line the high average rainfall accounts for the prevalence of oats over barley; while in the eastern and south-eastern midlands there are sharper frosts, and periods of drought are more frequent; but these extremes can be tolerated by wheat, because it is more deeply rooted. In consequence these lowlands are, on the whole, better adapted for cereals; while the best grass is to be found in the cultivable portions of the north and west.[1] There are many qualifications which prevent such distinctions from being absolute. Thus Devon is composed of the same types of materials as the north-west of Scotland; but the high average temperature combined with the rainfall helps to promote agriculture in many parts of that county.

Much of English history was inexorably dictated by the broad geological contrast between the north and west on the one hand, and the south and east on the other. Thus it is possible that in the English Plain history has moved more rapidly than elsewhere. In the order of creation its surface was younger than that of its northern and western neighbours; its long and navigable rivers, open to the Continent, were standing invitations to invasion; and it was here that first Teuton and then Dane most quickly established their civilizations. It was in the midlands and eastern midlands that, from ancient kingdoms there emerged the new grouping of the county, having its centre in a fortified town situated on a river; here also, on the drift and alluvium imposed on the clays of Warwickshire, Leicestershire, Oxfordshire, Northampton, Rutland, and Bedfordshire, conditions specially favoured

[1] For this see H. J. Mackinder, *Britain and the British Seas*, 61–5, and 172–3. This book, now a classic, should be read by all students of English history.

the common-field cultivator who, as he worked on a subsistence level, needed land cleared and cultivable, whereon he might grow corn and wool with the minimum of agricultural equipment and the maximum of agricultural waste. Here also the two-field system was succeeded, as early as the fourteenth century, by the three-field, as later by the four-field system;[1] here were brought into sharper contrast the archaic 'champion' farming and the more scientific economy destined to take its place. Within this area change continued to be rapid. In the central and eastern midlands was that part of England where the earliest pioneer work had been done by both Providence and Man; for there were no mountains, no great stretches of forest, no precipitate rivers, few mine workings, no large centres of population to invite intensive cultivation for a busy market; but a comparatively flat or undulating country of clay, or sand, or chalk, best adapted first for the squatter, because just fertile enough to provide him with a livelihood; then for the capitalist improver, because sufficiently unproductive to invite the application of pains and ingenuity; and lastly for the fox-hunter, because its scattered copses provided some cover for the fox, and its great stretches of turf and ploughed land long runs for the horse. The fields now pounded by the horses of the fashionable are those where the hand-to-mouth existence of the open-fielder survived longest, and where the experiments and evictions of the improver commenced first.

Nor is it only our agriculture that has been predetermined by geology; for it may not be altogether fanciful to trace, through this intermediate stage, some influence on our political history. Thus, it is noteworthy that most of the movements now considered comparatively progressive succeeded best in the English Plain; while the advocates of obsolescent tradition or awakened sentiment came mainly from outside its borders. The Yorkists had found most of their best supporters in the families of the midlands and south-east, whereas the Lancastrians and the upholders of the older régime had their strength mostly in the north and south-west; in the Civil Wars there was a similar distribution of the areas associated with the new cause and the old; indeed in 1644 the part of England held by the parliamentary forces was (except for the district round Tamworth) conterminous with the

[1] H. L. Gray, *English Field Systems*, 109, 154.

greater part of the English Plain, and included all of its eastern portion. The Second Civil War was decided on its north-western fringe—at Preston and Wigan. So too, the great risings of English history have sometimes met their fate on the borders of the Plain; for Perkin Warbeck, after finding supporters in Cornwall, had to submit at Taunton, and Monmouth met his fate at the same south-western corner—at Sedgemoor. The '15 penetrated no farther south than Preston; the '45 was held up at Derby, just within the Plain. Between these invaders and the capital there were soldiers; but there was a more effective barrier—an almost level country, every part of which was being put to some use by a settled population of squires and small men; here, in the continental angle of England, there was conservatism, but also progress, and these are the two qualities which have moulded the destinies of the race. Against this barrier the sentiment for the Stuarts was finally shattered, and one is tempted to conclude that while reaction or novelty might stir into agitation the extremities of the old provincial England, the heart still beat with measured pulse.

Better than description, the map[1] will serve to indicate those natural features which have helped to direct the course of English industry. For one thing England was indebted to the Roman occupation—for a road system; and the convergence of the highways on London facilitated the later development of the capital. Even more obvious is the importance of the rivers. Like France, England has been favoured in this respect by nature, and the waterways have been avenues not only for the transit of goods, but for the spread of civilization; hence few of the earlier towns were distant from a river, or more than a few hundred feet above sea-level. Three main river systems may be noted. In the northern midlands the Trent, utilized by the counties of Stafford, Derby, Nottingham, and a part of Lincolnshire, served for the conveyance of lead, timber, wool, corn, pottery, and cheese, and provided also an outlet for the products of Cheshire and Warwickshire. A second great river valley is that of the Severn, by which merchandise could be shipped between Bristol, Gloucester, Worcester, Bridgnorth, and Shrewsbury, while its tributary the

[1] See the map of seventeenth-century England published by the Ordnance Survey, with preface by G. M. Trevelyan.

Wye facilitated the transport of corn and fruit from Hereford-shire. The third important river valley is that of the Thames, the reservoir of numerous small tributaries, including the Colne, Lee, Wandle, and Roding, which served districts in Essex, Hertford-shire, Bedfordshire, and Surrey; farther down is the Medway, on which timber was conveyed to the naval base at Chatham. Thus the rivers of England, with their predominantly eastward flow, helped to predetermine three industrial areas—first, that across the country from Lancashire and Cheshire on the west to south Yorkshire and north Lincolnshire on the east, a band watered by the Trent, Humber, Ouse, Don, Aire, Calder, Mer-sey, and Irwell. This area was comparatively undeveloped. The second zone was the south-western, including most of Gloucester-shire and Worcestershire, with parts of Shropshire, Herefordshire, Wiltshire, Berkshire, and Somerset, supplied by the Severn, the Wye, the upper Thames, the three Avons, and the Frome. In this district were centres of the weaving, fruit, coal, and iron industries. Most fully developed was the south-eastern area, where the Thames and a network of small streams provided quick transport for a district of intensive cultivation and active industries, such as ship-building, tanning, brewing, dyeing, bleaching, calico printing, brick and glass making. Here was concentrated most of the industrial wealth of England.[1]

There were numerous schemes for the better utilization of water transport. A patent for making navigable 'all or any rivers' was granted for six years to one Arnold Spencer, but nothing appears to have come of it.[2] In 1670 it was proposed to link up the rivers so as to make communication possible between London and Bristol[3] and between Lynn and Yarmouth. More successful were the schemes of Andrew Yarranton, whose concern in the Worcestershire iron works prompted him to devise means for improving rivers and making canals. He began with the stretch of the Stour between Kidderminster and Stourbridge, and in his capacity of consulting engineer he surveyed the Wilt-shire Avon, the Thames, Humber, and Severn, suggesting and

---

[1] For a good study of this subject see W. T. Jackman, *Development of trans-portation in modern England*, i, ch. 3.   [2] *Rawl. MS*. A. 477, f. 1.

[3] F. Mathew, *A mediterranean passage by water from London to Bristol*. Mathew proposed that the water-mills should be replaced by wind-mills.

effecting several improvements. Lack of money, opposition by mill-owners, and the absence of concerted action prevented progress in these designs; but at least attention was directed to the possibilities of river transport, and in practice the rivers were then of much greater economic importance than they are to-day.

If, in place of the river, we adopt the more artificial boundary-line of the county, it is possible to indicate several types of agricultural and industrial area. This division into agricultural and industrial is, however, by no means rigid; nor were the workers comprised in these categories so clearly differentiated as they are now; for in the seventeenth century the husbandman might help to make his own cloth; the miner often had a small holding; the families of both classes usually engaged in part-time occupations such as spinning; and moreover, in the period prior to the Industrial Revolution, the word 'industrial' can be used only in a special sense, since the cottage, not the factory, was the unit. But nevertheless it is possible to enumerate some of the districts where one or the other form of activity had the greatest economic importance.

In the first class (that of the agricultural, including the pastoral, districts) was Wales, a country where an older economy was fast yielding to the penetration of English legislation and administration. Thus, the old heritable tenures were being displaced by year-to-year tenancies; primogeniture was taking the place of gavelkind; and by 1660 the Principality had become an area of small, detached farms, mainly of the peasant and family type, interspersed with the mansions of an unpretentious squirearchy.[1] Few of the landlords were said to be worth £1,000 a year; consequently, they could not hope to emulate the political and social influence exercised by their English compeers; but within the bounds of their estates they were supreme, and, together with the conforming clergy, they dominated a loyalist and Anglican Wales; for the great days of Welsh nonconformity were not yet. Wales was best known to English neighbours for wool and butter; there was increasing export of coal from South Wales, and there were local slate industries. Otherwise the Principality remained almost unknown to the Saxon, until its beauties were revealed in the landscapes of David Cox and the prose of George Borrow.

[1] J. Rhys and D. Brynmor-Jones, *The Welsh People*, 429–33.

Of distinctively agricultural counties, Bedfordshire, Leicestershire, Northamptonshire, and Herefordshire may be cited as examples. The first county was for the most part given over to arable, and was noted for the good quality of its wheat and barley; Leicestershire, abounding in clay and loam, produced some of the best wool, and most of the county was enclosed by the end of the century, when Celia Fiennes described its appearance thus: 'you see a great way upon their hills and bottoms full of enclosures, woods and different sorts of manureing and herbage, among which are placed many little towns which give great pleasure to the traveller to view.'[1] Northamptonshire, as befitted a county where good soil predominated, was a district of tillage and grazing; it was said to contain less waste ground than any other county in England;[2] and here, as in Warwickshire and Oxfordshire, it was thought that flax might be grown in order to provide an industry.[3] Herefordshire ranked as one of the most fertile and best-cultivated of English counties, producing abundant fruit, corn, and hops, and rearing great herds of cattle. It might be compared with Kent, where the wages and standards of husbandry were at their highest: a county already abounding in well-kept parks and estates.

Of counties not so completely dependent on agriculture, Gloucestershire and Essex are examples. Gloucestershire was richly endowed, because in addition to the coal and iron of the Forest of Dean, and the textiles and bleaching of the Stroud Valley, there were arable lands and orchards, and some of the best grazing in the country was to be had on the Cotswolds. There was also a tobacco-growing industry (in so far as the legislation could be evaded) at Winchcombe, and mustard was grown locally. More obviously, the county of Essex illustrated the conditions which then favoured prosperity. It was highly enclosed; its roads were comparatively good, and its water-ways numerous; it had benefited by early settlements of Dutch and Huguenots, and its strong Lollard and Independent traditions were blended with industry and thrift. Cheese and corn were shipped from Maldon; and at Saffron Walden was obtained the saffron still

---

[1] C. Fiennes, *Through England on a side-saddle*, 133.

[2] Blome, *Britannia* (1673), Northants.

[3] Yarranton, *England's Improvement by Sea and Land* (1677).

in demand as a perfume, a dye, and a drug. At Harwich there was ship-building; Colchester was the head-quarters of the New Draperies;[1] the villages were enterprising communities, engrossed in the activities of the field and the loom. The county was noted also for calves, oysters, agues, and sedition, these last attributed to its marshes and its proximity to Holland.[2]

In a similar class were those counties where husbandry was supplemented by local industries, some prosperous, some in decay. Thus, in the Wealden district of Surrey glass and iron were moulded, and at Croydon a community of charcoal burners made 'coal' for London. Wandsworth on the Wandle was then engaged in bleaching and calico printing. Of Surrey's natural products one of the most valued was fuller's earth, found at Nutfield, an absorbent clay used for removing oil and grease from woollen cloth. At Guildford there was a cloth industry.[3] Where the heavy clay preponderated Sussex was thickly wooded, and the county preserved an iron industry, about twenty furnaces being at work in 1660; but imports of Swedish ore led to a falling-off in the demand for the native iron-stone, and increasing shortage of timber made it difficult to provide for the working of the native ore.[4] Nevertheless, Sussex was industrially of greater relative importance than now. Cloth was made at Chichester; there was ship-building at Shoreham and Arundel; elsewhere were tanneries, brick works, rope lofts, pottery kilns and (at Battle) gunpowder mills. Another county which combined agriculture with extensive industry was Buckinghamshire, noted for its beech woods, which supplied the material not only of chairs and furniture, but of wooden implements such as mallets and the pins or nails used in the building of ships and houses. These last were gradually being displaced by the nails and hammers made from the softer type of iron known as 'blend metal', such as was worked in the district round Walsall (Staffordshire), where the hardening process was effected in fires made from wood and old shoes.[5] In

---

[1] Infra, 45.   [2] Bagford Ballads (ed. J. B. Ebsworth), ii. 752.
[3] V.C.H., Surrey, ii passim.
[4] Ibid., Sussex, ii. 199 sqq., and J. L. Parsons, The Sussex Ironworks in Sussex Archaeological Collections, xxxii.
[5] J. Houghton, Collection for the improvement of husbandry and trade (1727 ed.), ii. 319–29. This important source was commenced in 1681–3 as a series of

Staffordshire there was also a pottery industry; otherwise the county consisted of little but heath and moor, on which sheep grazed in company with rabbits. There was a more even distribution of activity between town and country in Nottinghamshire, which was known for the diversity of its products, as it supplied leather, flax, and coal; and its industries included weaving, hosiery, tanning, shoe-making, silk-weaving, and the making of candle-wicks.[1]

Examples of counties well endowed in neither agriculture nor industry are Berkshire, Shropshire, Oxfordshire, and Cambridgeshire. Berkshire was well cultivated in parts, notably on strips bordering the Thames and Kennet; elsewhere, however, downland and heath predominated; but the county's two towns were of some importance, Reading for brewing and tanning, Newbury for hosiery and hat-making. Shropshire yielded barley, wool, and grass, with a limited quantity of coal; comparatively it was a poor county, because many parts were uncultivable. In Oxfordshire there were many open fields where the cultivation was seldom above subsistence level; but the local deposits of iron-ore gave some employment, and there were several small industries, such as glove-making at Woodstock and brewing at Henley, where the household fire of wood served as a kiln for drying hops. Cambridgeshire was then poor and undeveloped, and in parts was still unreclaimed fen; here is a glimpse of the Cambridge-Suffolk border as described by a contemporary:

The level from Mildenhall to Ely being nothing but turf or peat, and by its insufferable heat and dryth having exhausted all the moisture out of the ditches, it was so suffocating hot by means of the brimstone or sulphury vapours that we could hardly breathe or endure it, so that I verily think it was possible to set the country on fire, the earth was so dry. As we rode along we saw here and there some poor cottages and wretched farms where some poor souls at a wretched rate do weather out a winter to look after the cattle that feed there. But doubtless there is incomparable fowling to make those amends that will undertake that pleasant toil, for the Red Shanks and other birds were very tame. In this passage between the ale-house and Ely

---

letters on trade and agriculture. See G. Davies, *Bibliography of British History, Stuart Period*, no. 1870.

[1] *V.C.H., Nottingham*, ii. 296.

we saw many Jacks sunning in the ditches between the highway and the enclosures.[1]

The counties of East Anglia had enough in common to justify inclusion in one group. Lincolnshire at this time was passing through a period of depression consequent on the decline of the wool trade from its pre-eminence of the sixteenth century, when the city of Lincoln had ranked fourth in the kingdom.[2] But as the reclaiming of fen-land[3] proceeded, the agriculture of the county improved, so that the rent of arable increased from 3s. per acre to 6s. 6d.[4] Boston was one of the busiest ports on the east coast, and then as now its graceful tower was a landmark for seaman and landsman alike. Norfolk was the home of the worsted industry, and its coast still retained some of its maritime importance; Yarmouth was the metropolis of herring-fishing and curing; moreover the city of Norwich was one of the great weaving towns of England. In East Anglia, however, the old cloth industry was being displaced by what were termed the New Draperies,[5] fabrics supposed to be more flimsy than the broadcloth and kerseys woven from short, carded wool. These more modern textiles were woven in Essex, and also in the small towns and villages of Suffolk, which still ranked as a rich county; for, in addition to grazing and weaving, its industries included ship-building (at Ipswich) and the working of flints at Brandon. On the coast there was fishing, and in 1670 the county of Suffolk had a fleet of thirty-three fishing vessels.[6] Thus the counties of East Anglia still ranked as industrial areas; but the same degree of prosperity was not to be found throughout, and variation was influenced by the demand for wool, and by changes in sartorial taste.

Like the south-east of England, the south-west was an area of industrial activity. Somerset was one of the greatest of the cloth-making districts,[7] and few cottages in Frome, Ilminster, Taunton, or Bridgwater were without their looms. The county, some portions of it still undrained, was one of manufacturing towns and

---

[1] Baskerville, *Journey* (1681) in *H.M.C. Rep., Portland MSS.* ii. 263–314.

[2] *V.C.H., Lincoln,* ii. 322–8.   [3] *Infra,* 55–6.

[4] *V.C.H., Lincoln,* ii. 334.

[5] Bayes were woven like serge; there is a specimen in the Colchester Museum. Sayes were used for bed-hangings and tapestry. *V.C.H., Essex,* ii. 386. See also G. Unwin, *Studies in Economic History,* 277–91.

[6] *V.C.H., Suffolk,* ii. 296.   [7] *V.C.H., Somerset,* ii. 313 sqq.

villages where the long and coarse wool of Somerset and Devon was made into serge and carried in bales by pack-horses, proceeding in single file by the 'pack and pen' ways. Wool cards were made at Frome, and woad for dyeing was grown locally. Minehead was a busy port, with Irish and Welsh sailings; Bath was developing as a health resort. At Taunton, which was full of conventicles in the later years of Charles, the anniversary of the town's relief from the royalist siege (May 11, 1645) was said to be more generally observed than Christmas Day.[1] In Devon, tin and lead mines were being worked, but the chief industry was the making of kerseys and serges in villages and towns. Bone lace was made in the vicinity of Honiton; in the valleys, and especially within a strip bordered by the sea and Dartmoor, there was arable farming on the red Devonshire soil. Tin mining[2] was the chief occupation in Cornwall; there was pilchard fishing on the coast, and garlic, the 'countryman's treacle', was grown and eaten. Though Cornishmen still thought of the Tamar as the boundary with England, they all talked English; and in 1661 it was said that only one man in the county could write Cornish.[3]

Thirdly and finally, there is the group of counties in the north of England comprising Cumberland, Westmorland, Northumberland, Durham, Yorkshire, and Lancashire. The first two were dependent mainly on sheep and salmon, but there was some coal-mining at Whitehaven; Carlisle still ranked as a port, and Kendal was the active centre of a cloth industry. Hadrian's Wall, covered with rowans and heath, provided medicinal herbs, and in some places served as a causeway, and also as a quarry for the builder.[4] Northumberland had a population of fishermen, shepherds, and small farmers; Berwick was noted for its salmon-curing, and in Newcastle the north of England had a community renowned for its shipping, salt, and grindstones. Durham was a hive of industry. From the sea could be seen the long line of coal fires at South Shields for the evaporation of brine in salt pans; iron was being worked in the blast furnaces leased from the bishop; at Ravens-

---

[1] *Cal. S.P. Dom.*, *1682*, 208.   [2] For this see *infra*, 78–9.

[3] John Ray, *Itinerary* (1661) in his *Memorials*, ed. E. Lankester (ed. 1846), 190. For a valuable study of social and economic conditions in Cornwall see Miss M. Coate, *Cornwall in the Great Civil War and Interregnum* (1933).

[4] *Rare observations of Cumberland and Westmorland* in *Newcastle Tracts*, vii. 13.

worth and Seaton Delaval were primitive railways of wood whereon coal was conveyed in wagons drawn by horses.[1] In its variety
of product and activity Yorkshire was more like a small state than
a county. Of the towns, Leeds was considered rich and populous,
full of clothiers, proud of the church lately built for them by one
of the Harrisons; Sheffield and Hallamshire were brightly illuminated by the forges of the cutlery makers; Wakefield, Halifax, and
Bradford were clothing towns, suffering to some extent from the
decay of their staple manufacture, a decay attributed by many to
the Civil Wars which had fallen heavily on Yorkshire. Rural
Yorkshire abounded in pastures and moorland; and there was
the vale of Cleveland, noted for its horses, its fruitfulness, and its
sticky soil:

> Cleveland in the clay,
> Bring in two soles, carry one away.[2]

In spite of its decline from former prosperity, Yorkshire would
have seemed a rich county in comparison with Lancashire, which
was, on the whole, poor and unfertile, producing a moderate
amount of corn, grass, and flax. But its mineral wealth was not
unknown, because the coal seams were found to be at least three
yards deep,[3] and Wigan was renowned for its coal, pewter, and
brazier work. Manchester, a small town with an ancient collegiate church, was making friezes and fustians with the help of an
inferior cotton wool imported from Smyrna and Cyprus; Bolton,
Rochdale, and Leigh were engaged in similar manufactures.
Liverpool, important for its Irish trade, was steadily overtaking
Chester, and in the later seventeenth century harboured shipping
amounting to a total of 3,000 tons.[4]

Such were the leading economic characteristics of the most important English counties. Economically, the unit of the county is
far from satisfactory, and has here been used only for convenience
of classification; but in spite of its semi-artificial dividing lines, the
county or 'country' as it was called was coming to be accepted as
a distinctive unit. This is shown by the holding of county dinners
in London.[5] But of life in the provinces there is a singular lack of

[1] V.C.H., Durham, ii. 238–426; The Lives of the Norths (Bohn ed.), i. 177 sqq.
[2] Ray, Itinerary (1661) in op. cit., and V.C.H., Yorkshire, ii passim.
[3] Grey, i. 232.   [4] V.C.H., Lancaster, ii. 300 sqq.
[5] e.g. a dinner for Oxfordshire men was held at Grocers' Hall on Nov. 20,

information; for country correspondents, while they are generally full of gossip about strange events, almost always avoid those normal, everyday matters on which posterity seeks information. The memoirs of the period relate mainly to the Court; the travellers were continually resorting to sepulchral monuments and 'gentlemen's seats'; and the evangelists were too much engrossed in sin and humanity to concern themselves much with material surroundings. Pepys saw the country with the eye of a townsman; as guide-book, Evelyn's *Diary* is not always distinguished for illumination; and so the modern reader is obliged to depend mainly on North[1] and Reresby.[2] There is therefore an absence of original material on which generalizations might be based. It may be affirmed, however, that throughout the country there were clear-cut differences of dialect and custom, and that local communities of workers, especially fishermen, weavers, and miners, were bound by a certain solidarity of sentiment and language. A Derbyshire lead-miner would have found it difficult to make himself understood outside the Peak district; still more, a northern dalesman would have been incomprehensible in Cornwall. It is in such provincial dialects that obsolete Old English words may still be traced; in the seventeenth century the number of such words in current use must have been large, a fact which may have restricted personal communication between Londoner and countryman.

This paucity of information about provincial England makes it impossible to determine with certainty even the relative size of the towns. None of these was even a good second to London; for the largest, Bristol, with about 30,000 inhabitants, had less than a tenth part of the population of the capital. Nevertheless, Bristol was prosperous and progressive,[3] partly owing to increased imports of sugar and tobacco; its merchants, many of them Noncon-

---

1662, 'for the continuance of our mutual society and acquaintance'. It was preceded by a sermon (at 9 a.m.) at St. Michael's, Cornhill. A ticket of admission (price 2s. 6d.) will be found in *Bodley, Wood*, 276 b, no. 119.

[1] *The Lives of the Norths* (Bohn ed., 3 vols.). The first volume, containing the life of lord Guilford, is of great value for the study of provincial England.

[2] In the complete text of the *Memoirs* of sir John Reresby, which has been edited by Professor A. Browning, much information will be found about Yorkshire and social conditions there.

[3] For a good account see J. Latimer, *Annals of Bristol in the seventeenth century*.

formists after 1664, maintained an estate which aroused the envy of neighbouring squires, and so keen was appreciation of the public prestige of wealth that it was not uncommon for the third part of a Bristol merchant's estate to be spent on his funeral. Early in the eighteenth century the third largest town in the kingdom was said to be Liverpool;[1] but meanwhile this honour may have been due to the city of York. In the northern capital the minster had been preserved unharmed during the Civil Wars; grouped closely round the cathedral were narrow streets, the tall houses so close at the top that sociability and even intimacy were forced on the inhabitants, who rejoiced that their famous city, with its lord mayor, twelve aldermen, and twenty-four assistants was, histori-cally at least, the second in the kingdom. In its social activities York was excelled only by London, and in 1665 it was visited by the duke of York. Almost equally populous was Newcastle, the houses of which were reported to be comparable in height and show with those of London.[2] Its long quay, a bridge of nine arches, and the newly-built Exchange were the wonder of travellers, who found its inhabitants a specially vigorous race of town-dwellers; for they were said to settle their disputes not by going to law, but by 'bang-ing it out bravely' among themselves. They were many of them speculators in coal and retailers of jokes against the Scots, boasters that their products were ubiquitous—'a Scot, a rat, and a New-castle grindstone you will find all the world over.'[3] Norwich was another industrial city, but of a very different type, because it had thirty-seven old churches; its streets still retained some of their medieval squalor, and its weavers were said to be as proficient in the pulpit as at the loom. There was a vigorous and distinctive life in these towns, but it did not assume a literary form.

The towns may have been distinguished not so much according to their size, but according as they were close or open. In the former category were most of the incorporated boroughs, where trade and industry might be controlled by gilds or a mercantile oligarchy, to the exclusion of all but freemen; the open town, on

---

[1] This is said to have been brought about by the development of the planta-tion trade and the influx of London merchants after the Plague and Fire. *Kenyon MS.* 430, quoted in A. P. Wadsworth and J. de L. Mann, *The cotton trade and industrial Lancashire, 1600–1780* (1931), 71.

[2] Ray, *Itinerary* (1661), in op. cit. 150.   [3] *Harleian Miscellany*, xi. 463.

the other hand, was generally the product of more recent economic development, unimpeded by the hampering restrictions which had survived from the medieval past. This contrast was specially noticeable in Lancashire; for while such corporate towns as Liverpool, Wigan, Lancaster, and Preston jealously insisted on their exclusive privileges and kept out all 'foreigners', the towns of Manchester, Bury, and Blackburn imposed little more than market regulations, and so were attracting fresh population and industry.[1] The same difference may be seen by comparing Coventry with Birmingham. The first, though much decayed from its medieval greatness, was still a centre of civic activity; the second, on the contrary, was a mean place, given over to nail-makers, endowed with no past and only one church. It was reached by turning off the main road at Coleshill, and was so 'open' that a claim to its citizenship had been advanced by Charles Stuart, who, at one stage in the flight from Worcester, tried to pass himself off as 'the son of a Bremicham naylor'.[2] But the new-comer had already begun its vigorous career; and before the end of the century it was reported[3] to be 'full of inhabitants, resounding always with hammers and anvils', by which time its solitary church was no longer sufficient for the population.[4]

As the towns changed in relative importance, so did the ports. From various causes, including the application of the Navigation Acts, a process began whereby the ports on the west gradually developed at the expense of those on the east, thereby relieving the congestion in the Thames, and diminishing the pre-eminence of Boston and King's Lynn. Newcastle and Hull were able to survive this change, the former because of its coal; the latter because it was a great garrison town, its harbour was not silted up, and it had a staple industry—the curing of Iceland stock-fish, a food-stuff greatly prized on account of its durability. Some conclusions regarding the status of English ports may be deduced from the details of the salaries and establishment charges incurred for their Customs administration. Thus, in 1680 the total cost for the port of London was £20,000 per annum; next came

[1] For this see A. P. Wadsworth and J. de L. Mann, op. cit. 55–60.
[2] J. Dauncey, *History of his sacred majesty Charles II* (1660), 121.
[3] S. Dunstar, *Anglia Rediviva* (1699), 77.
[4] *H.M.C. Rep., Portland MSS.* iii. 135.

Bristol, with an expenditure of £2,000; then Newcastle, Plymouth, and Hull, each approximately £900; Southampton, £500; Ipswich, £450; Liverpool and Dover, £320, and Chester, £280. At the other end of the scale were Padstow, £30; Truro, £44; Rochester, Faversham, and Fowey, each £120. Intermediate between these extremes were Sunderland, Lyme Regis, Swansea, Falmouth, Rye, Bideford, and Carlisle. If the cost of such establishment charges bears any relationship to the amount of tonnage handled, then these figures[1] may be taken to indicate approximately the comparative position of the ports in this period; with the reservation however that the figure for London includes salaries of commissioners and expenses of management not incurred by the other ports.

A survey of Restoration England, however imperfect, suggests two general conclusions: the disparity between north and south, and the contrast between town and country. The first of these can be illustrated in various ways. Thus, if a line be drawn from Gloucester to Boston dividing England (without Wales) into two very nearly equal areas, it will be found that in the assessments on which the property taxes were based[2] the wealth of the northern section (as here defined) compared with the southern was reckoned in the proportion of 5 to 14; and in the amounts for which the Excise[3] was farmed the disparity was sometimes greater, being estimated in 1665 at about 1 to 4. These figures suggest that in the seventeenth century the population south of this line may have been about thrice as great as that north of it; whereas to-day the majority of Englishmen live to the north of this imaginary boundary, though there are signs that the difference is being lessened by recent industrial developments in the south and midlands. The north was undeveloped and under-populated in comparison with the south.

Even more, this artificial line represented a social barrier. South of it were the metropolis, the Court, the more important industrial areas, the majority of the large ports, the homes of the more noteworthy among the peerage, the most frequented

---

[1] Customs Establishment Papers, *P.R.O.*, bundle xviii.

[2] Those for 1661 and 1679 have been taken for this purpose. The figures are in *Statutes of the Realm*, v. 326–7 and 897–9.

[3] From the figures in *H.M.C. Rep.*, x, app. vi. 178.

race-courses, and the two universities. In politics, the gentry of
the north were not so influential as those of the south, possibly
because they included a larger number of Roman Catholics;
important exceptions, however, were Danby, whose career was
helped by the influence of the duke of Buckingham in Yorkshire,
and Halifax, another Yorkshireman, whose eminence may be
attributed to remarkable gifts of mind and character. This
barrier of north and south had been broken down by the Civil
Wars, as earlier by the Wars of the Roses; but with the Restoration, the north retired into a social obscurity from which it did
not emerge for more than a century, when it contributed to
politics an entirely different type of personnel—the iron-master
and the cotton magnate. Few Englishmen of the south ever paid
a voluntary visit to the north; Pepys went no farther afield than
Edinburgh, but Evelyn's northern limit was York. Francis
North (lord Guilford), when on circuit, found in the border
country a more primitive and speedy justice than that of the
south; for when he thought inconclusive the evidence against a
Scot accused of cattle stealing, he was advised by a border commissioner to speed on the business: 'Send him to Huzz, my laird,
and ye'll see him nae mair.'[1] Northern England was for long
denied even a sight of her kings. Charles Stuart did not travel
again; his brother as king went to Shrewsbury and Chester only
for electioneering and Irish affairs; William III and a succession
of Irish lords-lieutenant crossed the line in order to reach Holyhead
or Milford Haven on the way to Ireland; the Georges ignored
that part of their dominions, though George IV visited Scotland
(by sea), as well as Ireland and Hanover. Not till 1851, the year
of the great Exhibition, was the north of England officially recognized by royalty; for in that year queen Victoria (on her way to
Balmoral) visited Liverpool, Salford, and Manchester. A statue
in Peel Park, Salford, commemorates this discovery of the north.

Another contrast was that between town and country. Our
towns which can boast a Roman origin had to be made twice, for
they completely lost what ancient civilization they had possessed;
and when they came to the surface again in the early Middle
Ages they were intruders into an agricultural world. The provincial towns have never quite made up for this handicap.

[1] *The Lives of the Norths* (Bohn ed.), i. 179.

Because of temperate climate and the attractiveness of the English country-side the nobility and even the bishops were not usually town-dwellers, and many of them still retain their head-quarters in remote places. London was exceptional because of its social life and the increasing importance of the financial interests in the city; but nevertheless the increasing size of the city and its suburbs was a source of disquiet to the government, and the earlier Stuarts had striven by means of proclamation to prevent the nobility from spending more than a modest part of the year in the capital.[1] The new buildings about London were the objects of animadversion and special taxation;[2] for it was held that they were drawing population and money from the country; moreover, as churches could not be built quickly enough for the new-comers, these men remained churchless, as they were already lordless; they were therefore dangerous. Nor did the inhabitants of the towns fit into the categories recognized in the country, these categories being: (1) the freeholder, having land as security for his conduct, (2) the copyholder, amenable to manorial jurisdiction, (3) the labourer, controlled by the employer with the help of the justices, (4) the itinerant beggar, licensed by a justice, and (5) the vagabond, driven from parish to parish by relays of village constables. So too the London pillory was no substitute for the village stocks, because while the former provided exemplary punishment for the notorious, the latter, within sight of one's door-step, was both a deterrent to wrong-doers and a salutary reminder to the well-behaved.

This antithesis came to be specially emphasized in the later seventeenth century. The distinction was partly religious, because nonconformity had its strongholds in the towns,[3] partly political, for the small tradesmen and craftsmen of London and the East-Anglian weaving towns had been the backbone of the Puritan revolution. It was economic, because towns, it was thought, attracted money, leaving a scarcity elsewhere; 'all tradesmen', said a member of the House of Commons, 'seem to

---

[1] e.g. that of 1615 (*Steele*, i. 1177) required that noblemen should live in their chief mansions for nine months in the year in order to exercise hospitality.

[2] *Infra*, ii. 437–8.

[3] Though nonconformity was rural as well as urban in Essex.

be turning bankers,'[1] and these were 'the commonwealth's men
who destroy the nobility and gentry'. 'As interest goes up, land
goes down like a pair of scales';[2] 'the farmer starves when things
are cheap, the poor when things are dear';[3] such were some of the
parliamentary utterances which voiced a widely held economic
theory based on these two axioms: namely, rents are always
falling; secondly, this fall is due to anything which threatens to
disturb the balance between town and country, whether it be the
importation of Irish cattle, or the erection of new buildings about
London, or the Dutch Wars, or the development of manufactures
in towns, or the increase in the number of stage coaches: or,
more generally, the increase of debauchery. These axioms were
scarcely even debated; moreover land had a national and uncontested sanctity so long as most of the property taxes were
levied thereon. The contrast was also social; for the county gentry
did not live in towns, and frequented London only for a season.
Townsmen, it is true, had their civic titles and regalia; but these,
it was held, were merely plebeian imitations of the privileges of
their betters; and before the end of the reign burgesses were
drastically reminded how precarious were their franchises.[4]

But, it may well be asked, how does this comport with the
increasing power of the House of Commons wherein the boroughs
were so strongly represented? Surely trade and money were
determining factors in society and politics? Even here, however,
the townsman was the inferior; for in the Commons, not only was
there the territorial core of the knights of the shire; but, by the
later part of the seventeenth century, an increasing number of
boroughs were conferring their seats not on burgesses (in the
strict sense of the term), but on sons of peers, or neighbouring
gentry, or outsiders who had acquired an estate and were anxious
to enjoy the public status and influence now conferred by membership of the House. This fact is reflected in the parliamentary
debates, which show that the Commons were more concerned
with popery and dissent than with maritime development, more
interested in game laws than in manufactures, in rents than in
trade; only thus indeed could they have achieved their unique

---

[1] Nov. 3, 1670, *Grey*, i. 274.

[2] Col. Birch in the Commons, Nov. 1670 in *Grey*, i. 273.

[3] Remark by the same speaker; *Grey*, i. 95–6.   [4] *Infra*, ii. 517–19; 634–6.

part in the constitution; for a House composed of true burgesses could not have held its own with a landed House of Lords. It is true also that the temporary importance assumed by the cobblers and weavers during the Usurpation served later to confirm this hegemony of the landlord, just as the influence afterwards acquired by merchant and capitalist have helped to obscure it.

Finally, while the provincial townsman had neither the social nor the political power of the landlord, the ranks of the latter were constantly being filled up from the former, because the eligibility of the country-side attracted generations of wealthy townsmen who, endowed with landed property and a title, quickly forsook the habitudes of desk and counter for the responsibilities of agriculture and the amenities of sport. In this respect a contrast is provided by France, where the richer nobility thronged Versailles, while their poorer brethren of the country shared their penury with the peasants. In England the power of money was exercised at first not directly, but through the medium of land.

2. DEVELOPMENT OF THE COUNTRY-SIDE

There are many indications supporting this view that in the reign of Charles II the English country-side was offering increased opportunities for both pleasure and profit. For example, there was the reclaiming of marsh land. This was conducted mainly in the levels of the Fen country—an area of about 300,000 acres, in shape not unlike a horseshoe, penetrating from the Wash to parts of the counties of Norfolk, Suffolk, Cambridge, Huntingdon, Northampton, and Lincoln. Many attempts had been made to reclaim these wastes, which were liable to inundation not only from the sea, but from the rivers Ouse, Nene, and Welland; for which reclamation, commissions of sewers had frequently been granted to neighbouring corporations and landlords. But these detached enterprises were mostly foredoomed to failure, since only by concerted action in such a vast undertaking could success be achieved. Already, however, a start had been made. Charles I had granted to the earl of Bedford and other adventurers a patent for the draining of 95,000 acres, and the services of the Dutch engineer Vermuyden had been enlisted; but the Civil Wars delayed progress; until, at the Restoration, the work was resumed, and in 1663 its furtherance was entrusted[1] to a corporation consisting of governor, conservators, and bailiffs, authorized to act as commissioners of sewers, and to make local levies for the furtherance of their enterprise. The rate of progress was steadily increased; in Lincolnshire alone about 25,000 acres were added to the available arable, thus enabling the county to make up in agriculture for some of the prosperity which had departed with the wool trade. The rivers were deepened and straightened, and their banks assumed the artificiality which they still retain.

Opposition to the fen draining in East Anglia came from several sources, including the port of King's Lynn, which claimed that its navigation was impeded because of the alleged silting up of the channel from Denver Dam to the sea. More strenuous hostility was shown by an indigenous race of fen-dwellers, the Slodgers, who in spite of chronic agues contrived in their huts of wattle to maintain a semi-aquatic existence by snaring, fishing, and reed-cutting. These men were lawless in their attempts to preserve a separate dominion of weed and mud, destroying the works of the drainers, flooding the land, and thereby drowning people in their beds. But the draining proceeded nevertheless, and one more distinctive community was removed from English life. In 1670 Evelyn visited the district, to see the engines and mills (worked by wind and water) draining away the mud in rivers or graffs cut by hand; and there he noted the fertility of the reclaimed land; for weeds grew as high as a man on horseback.[2] Not potatoes, but hemp and cole seed were the crops grown on this fertile soil; and like the water-ways the drained marshes had their poet.[3]

---

[1] 15 Car. II, cap. xvii.   [2] Evelyn, *Diary*, July 22, 1670.

[3]
    I sing Floods muzzled and the Ocean tam'd,
    Luxurious rivers governed and reclaimed,
    Water with banks confined as in a gaol
    Till kinder sluices let them go on bail.
    Streames curb'd with bridles, taught t'obey
    And run as straight as if they saw their way.
    When, with a change of elements suddenly
    There shall a change of men and manners be;
    Hearts thick and tough as hides shall feel remorse,
    And souls of sedge shall understand discourse,
    New hands shall learn to work, forget to steal,
    New leggs shall go to church, new knees to kneel.

Draining was one of the 'improvements'; so too was enclosing. There was no acute enclosure problem as in the sixteenth century, when many landlords had suddenly found it more profitable to grow wool than corn; by 1660 the lower price of wool, owing to over-production and deterioration, had helped to restore the balance between pasture and arable, and so the enclosures of the later seventeenth century were dictated mainly by the demand for a more adequate utilization of natural resources than that provided by the old open-field system with its cumbersome distribution of small strips. The counties wholly or partially enclosed by 1660 included Essex, Kent, Hereford, Middlesex, Somerset, and Durham; in some midland counties, notably Leicester, enclosures were proceeding and causing complaint, while in Northamptonshire, Oxfordshire, Cambridgeshire, Lincolnshire, and Bedfordshire there was still a predominance of the open-field system.[1] Proximity to London or to centres of such industries as weaving, coal mining, and dairy farming account in part for this distribution of the more intensive system of cultivation: in part also, enclosing was adopted by a number of improving landlords equipped with capital. Reclaimed land was almost invariably enclosed.

Against the enclosing of arable for pasture opinion was

Footnote [3], p. 56 (*continued*):

> Poor curate, whom thine envious stars prefer
> To be some hide-bound parson's pensioner,
> On such hard terms, that if the flock were fed
> As ill as thou, their souls might starve for bread;
> When these fair fields are ploughed, then cast with me
> How large, how fat the livings here must be.
> Ye busie gentlemen that plant the hop,
> And dream vast gains from that deceitful crop,
> Or by manureing what you ought to let
> Thrive backwards and too dearly purchase wit,
> Leave off these lotteries, and here take your lot,
> The profit's certain, and with ease 'tis got.
>
> J. Moore, *History of the great level of the Fens* (1685), 72.

[1] See E. C. K. Gonner, *Common Land and Enclosure* (1912). Prof. Gonner's estimates are to some extent derived from a study of the maps in Ogilby's *Britannia* (1675), where open fields by the road-side are indicated. These estimates are valuable, but are to a large extent necessarily conjectural. See also W. H. R. Curtler, *The enclosure and redistribution of our land.*

practically unanimous—it was held to cause unemployment and
depopulation. But on the general question of champion, that
is, open cultivation versus enclosed farming, whether for arable
or for arable and pasture, opinion was almost equally unanimous,
and was more emphatically expressed as enclosing proceeded,
for the latter system was simply a more economic, if less traditional method; moreover, as it generally led ultimately to the
employment of more labour than it had displaced, it was an
'improvement'. Like so many improvements it caused dislocation when first applied; and evicted commoners, as in Leicestershire, went round the country vainly inquiring for 'land to be set'.[1]
Where the open fields remained there was the old independence
and the semi-democratic regulation of agriculture by a community of sharers in the open strips; but there were the old abuses; for
though the cultivator was his own master, yet he had to 'toil and
moil' for a bare livelihood. There was often inequality also, since
the man with abundant stock might take more than his share of
pasture, and enterprising neighbours ploughed farther than they
ought to have done, or removed landmarks. Cattle wandered
over the crops, consuming more with their hooves than with their
mouths, or they might easily be lost, or harried by dogs, and in
hot summers the skinny survivors wilted on the shadeless flats.
At best, it was a hard and merely self-sufficing existence; at worst,
it was the avenue, through the ale-house, to vagabondage and
beggary. Nevertheless, the open fields and their inhabitants still
retained a certain sanctity for many Englishmen, and enclosures
were condemned by agitators such as the Levellers, who classed
them with the 'Norman' iniquities of tithes and French law.
Such a place-name as Hinton-in-the-Hedges[2] still serves to
commemorate this intrusion of hedged ownership into the
patchwork pattern of the old system.

'It ascertains every man's just proportion of land';[3] such was
the most obvious justification of enclosure. The hedges delimit-
ing that proportion were in themselves an advantage; for they
provided shade to cattle in summer, and some protection against

[1] John Moore (minister of Knaptoft, Leicestershire), *The Crying Sin of
England . . . wherein Inclosure is arraigned, convicted and condemned* (1653).
[2] Northants.
[3] R. Blome, *The gentleman's recreation* (1686), 208.

cold winds in winter; they might even be a source of timber, or fuel, or fruit. Ownership once established, private experiment would be a possible consequence, and it is only by experiment that agricultural progress can be made. Hence it was chiefly, though not solely, on the enclosed land that men tried their hand with the new French grasses, such as sainfoin, clover, and lucerne, as later they were to try the turnip; and so, by providing a winter food for cattle the agriculturists brought into existence the stock-breeder. For these enterprises both capital and initiative were needed, the two things lacking in the old self-contained village community. There were numerous facilities for enclosing; indeed in many manors the freeholders having lands lying in the common fields might enclose against those having rights of common there;[1] and Chancery sanctioned[2] several of these enclosures, generally insisting on the consent of all the freeholders concerned, and in some cases stipulating for the allocation of sufficient common to the commoners. Moreover, a Bill was introduced into the Lords enabling all who desired to enclose to apply to the chancellor for the appointment of a commission of substantial neighbours to effect an equitable distribution between the lord, the tenants, and such as had rights of common.[3] The Bill was dropped; but had it become law, it is possible that enclosures would have been much more numerous, and the intensive changes which began after 1760 might thus have been anticipated.

As well as draining and enclosing, there was also an increasing interest in the potentialities of the land, and many later innovations were foreshadowed in the books and pamphlets of the time. Earlier in the century the rotation of crops had been studied by such writers as Markham, who had suggested a ten or twelve years' sequence, with three or four years of grass.[4] Some writers advocated fertilizers, one improvement being that of 'denshireing' or charring the surface soil and scattering the ash as a fertilizer; other devices suggested were flooding and irrigating. Another improvement was that of preparing the seed before sowing, either by soaking in a liquid, sometimes brine, or by

[1] *Modern Reports*, ii. 104.
[2] e.g. *English Reports*, xxi (Chancery), 501 and 912.
[3] 1665–6, *H.M.C. Rep.* vii, app. 178–9, *MSS. of the House of Lords*.
[4] Ashley, *The bread of our forefathers*, 32–3.

dusting it with lime,[1] a measure probably intended to secure greater fertility as well as immunity from birds and vermin. More important was the advocacy of new crops, such as lucerne, clover, turnips, and sainfoin, originally recommended by sir R. Weston after his travels in Flanders. Weston was perhaps the first Englishman to perceive the double value of the turnip as a cleaning crop and as a winter food for cattle; but in his lifetime it remained merely a root for domestic cultivation. Worlidge, one of the best of these semi-scientific writers, recommended French tares or vetches as a cattle food,[2] and saxifrage on pastures where cheese was made; he thought also that the buckwheat might profitably be grown. The potato was recommended by another writer[3] who, aware of the popular dislike of it, prescribed numerous recipes for making bread, paste, puddings, and custard from this tuber, so that its taste might be disguised as much as possible.

These books and pamphlets are evidence of at least some public interest in agriculture. A more striking proof of this interest is provided by the investigations which the Royal Society commenced in 1664, when a 'Georgicall Committee' was appointed, which resolved to compose a general history of agriculture, and to make inquiries into its practice in contemporary England. The scope of this investigation[4] was directed mainly to the kinds of soil, the manures employed, the types of plough in use, the distribution of different kinds of crops, and the yield per acre; on these and other points questions were compiled and sent to prominent agriculturists in different parts of England; and the replies show that at least in some districts husbandry was by no means the haphazard and hide-bound occupation sometimes supposed to have preceded the scientific culture of the eighteenth century. In particular, there is evidence that the new grasses such as clover and trefoil were being grown, though there is little yet about the turnip; for the ploughs, horses were being used as

[1] *A direction to the husbandman* in Bodley, Ashmole, 1672.
[2] *Systema Agriculturae* (1669); reprint in D. Macdonald, *Agricultural Writers, 1200–1800* (1908), 116.
[3] J. Forster, *England's happiness increased* (1664).
[4] For this see R. V. Lennard, *English agriculture under Charles II; the evidence of the Royal Society's enquiries*, in *Economic History Journal*, 1932.

much as oxen; manuring by dung and sea-sand was commonly resorted to, and was generally combined with liming or marling; while in districts such as Dorset, Kent, Gloucestershire, and the East Riding the folding of sheep was practised on the 'corn ground' of the hilly country. The paring and burning of ground are also alluded to in several reports; and in most of the replies, wheat, oats, barley, peas, beans, and rye are mentioned. Hemp and flax appear in the Devon and Cornwall returns; tares and vetches are specified for Kent and some of the southern counties. There appears to have been a general recognition of the advantage of using seed grown on another soil, and all the reports describe methods of soaking or otherwise preparing the seed before planting; in one county (Dorset) a sieve was used for separating good from bad seed. The usual rotation of two crops and a fallow seems to have been followed; but in some cases there is mention of a seven years' rotation. Finally, the returns show the importance attached to convertible husbandry and the breaking up of pasture; they show also that meadows were improved by the mowing of nettles and rushes. Only in root crops does there appear to have been little progress.

But, on the other hand, while there was this recognition in the most enlightened quarters of the scientific nature of agriculture, there was not yet in existence a landlord class with sufficient money and enterprise to put the new ideas into effect. Still more, 'improvements' were sometimes openly derided, and in the Commons a landlord declared that they were a mischief, because by increasing production they lowered prices, and consequently rents.[1] Nor was the tenant always favourable to improvements, since these might provide a pretext for increased rent; hence the Berkshire proverb: 'he that havocs may sit, he that improves must flit.'[2] So far, therefore, as the land was concerned, the later seventeenth century was a period of beginnings and suggestions rather than of achievement; but agriculturally, it was an increasingly prosperous age, mainly because of the steadily enhanced demand for corn,[3] and this helped to create the capitalist landlord who was to be the mainspring of progress in the next century.

If England was behind some continental countries in root

[1] Speech of col. Titus, Feb. 8, 1673 in *Parl. Hist.* iv. 517.
[2] *V.C.H., Berks.* ii. 213. [3] See *infra*, 66.

crops, she was not behind in orchards. French influence after
the Restoration may account for the greater vogue of the plum,
the pear, the peach, the nectarine, and the melon; but this
influence could not have modified the culture of the apple, in
which England was supreme. Attention was directed to the
Herefordshire orchards as early as 1657, when they were feelingly
described by one who combined practical experience with
aesthetic appreciation of the varied and seasonal beauties of an
orchard country.[1] In Worcestershire cherries and pears were
grown to greatest perfection. Of economic importance, because
of the great consumption of cider, orchards and the propagation
of fruit trees were a source of increasing delight to men of means
and leisure, whose experiments helped to increase the attractiveness of English country life, and to provide a profitable as well
as aesthetic diversion. So there grew up a literature of Pomona,
and if a man failed to grow apples profitably, he might nevertheless write about their culture with acceptance and even applause.
To literature also silviculture owes a debt, for its study was promoted by the publication of Evelyn's *Sylva*, and by the printed
recommendations of such 'improvers' as Blith.

With the cultivation of the tree went that of the flower.
Chaucer and Shakespeare showed a deep knowledge and appreciation of English flowers, both having been endowed with
an eye for the minute detail of natural life; the philosopher Bacon
had commended gardens, and his praise was to be confirmed by
that of Temple. As we owed some new fruits to the French, so to
the Dutch we were indebted for the introduction of the tulip,
possibly also of the lily of the valley and the carnation;[2] the rose
species was enriched by the coming of the Provence and the
Jericho rose; but these new-comers did not lessen the popularity
of such old favourites as the gilliflower (the wallflower), the
violet, the red hyacinth, the madonna lily, the daffodil, and the
fritillary. Most of the guides to husbandry contained instructions
for gardening, and Parkinson's classic, *Paradisi in Sole*, was supplemented by new publications.[3] As great houses of the nobility

---

[1] I. [John] B. [Beal], *Herefordshire Orchards a Pattern*, 3.

[2] *Present state of England*, pt. iii (1683), 253 sqq.

[3] For the bibliography see the section General Agriculture, in G. Davies,
Bibliography of British History, Stuart Period.

were built or rebuilt, special pride was taken in the decoration of open spaces with fountains, avenues, statues, canals, fishponds, orangeries, and orchards, all of which provided opportunities for the landscape gardener; and already the formal English garden was to be found at such great country houses as Euston, Ham, Althorp, Cassiobury, Swallowfield, and Clieveden,[1] where the decorative arts were employed with such effect that, in comparison, the older mansions of Hatfield, Nonsuch, Audley End, Knole, and Badminton seemed uncouth or antiquated. The same instinct which sought for new flowers and for their more effective display welcomed also the addition of new trees and shrubs. The mulberry had been introduced early in the century; from Virginia came the red cedar, the tulip tree, and the American plane; and other new-comers soon to be acclimatized were the Aleppo pine and the Lebanon cedar.[2] To the upper classes at least, the reign of Charles brought a keener and more educated appreciation of a well-ordered estate or a colourful garden; and his reign marks an important stage in that evolution whereby the English country-side became the most varied and attractive in the world.[3]

Such an improved estate would be self-sufficing, providing its owner and his guests with food and sport distinguished for quality and simplicity rather than for variety or extravagance, an object realized by the almost patriarchal existence of the duke of Beaufort at Badminton, as thus described by Roger North:[4]

He had above £2,000 per annum in his hands which he managed by stewards, bailiffs and servants: and of that, a great part of the country, which was his own lying round about him, was part, and the husbandmen were of his family, and provided for in his large, extended house. He bred all his horses, which came to the husbandry first colts, and from thence, as they were fit were taken into his equipage. . . . He had about two hundred persons in his family, all provided for: and in his

[1] These were respectively the country houses, either new or rebuilt, of Arlington, Lauderdale, Sunderland, Essex, Clarendon, and Buckingham. Much information about these and other English gardens will be found in Evelyn, *Diary, passim.* See also R. Blomfield, *The formal garden in England.*

[2] J. E. Gillespie, *Influence of over-seas expansion on England*, 97.

[3] In the autumn of 1680 the French ambassador noted with some surprise that there were few people in London, as so many had gone into the country (*Baschet*, 146, Aug. 23/Sept. 2, 1680).

[4] *The Lives of the Norths* (Bohn ed.), i. 171.

capital house, nine original tables, covered every day: and, for the accommodation of so many, a large hall was built, with a sort of alcove at one end for distinction: but yet the whole lay in the view of him that was chief. The women had their dining table also and were distributed in like manner. The method of governing this great family was admirable and easy, and such as might have been a pattern.... No fault of order was passed by. Soap and candle were made in the house: so likewise the malt was ground there: and all the drink that came to the duke's table was of malt sun-dried on the leads of the house....

Beaufort was carrying out on an exceptional scale what many landed Englishmen were doing or attempting to do. Of these the dramatist Shadwell wrote:[1]

> Give me the good man that lives in his own grounds,
> And within his own bounds,
> Has room for his hawks and his hounds,
> Can feast his own tenants with fowls and with fishes
> And from his own store with good store of dishes,
> And not with damned wine, but with good English ale,
> O'er their faithful hearts can prevail,
> And nothing to others does owe
> But from his own house hears his own oxen low.

These things would have been impossible of attainment in a country of small holders; nor would white bread have become so common in English dietary if a stream of capital had not been continually poured into the land.[2] Much of that capital came not from crops, but from trade and the profits of office; and many of the great landed families began not as agriculturists, but as graziers, tradesmen, contractors, merchants, state officials, and tax-farmers. Primogeniture helped to keep the large estate intact; another device which helped to secure, as far as possible, the perpetual association of the family name with broad acres was the 'strict settlement', devised by lord keeper sir Orlando Bridgeman (1606–74), whereby it was made possible for the heir, generally at his marriage, to settle the estates for one more generation. In this way the ownership of land lost much of that insecurity which had detracted from its social value in Tudor times and in the

[1] Shadwell, *Epsom Wells*.
[2] For an interesting discussion of this see W. J. Ashley, *The bread of our forefathers*.

Civil Wars; accordingly, in Restoration England many things combined to make land a specially desirable object of property.

Such, in brief outline, was the land. It is now necessary to turn to some of its products, and to its main industries.

3. THE CHIEF ECONOMIC COMMODITIES

Of natural products corn was the most important. Not yet was there any scientific study of hybridization, but English farmers were familiar with at least a dozen varieties of wheat, most notably with the pollard wheat, sown on stiff lands, and the flaxen and lammas wheat on light and poor soils. Seed was generally planted in the autumn, and was thought to fare best in a wet season; that sown on enclosed land was said to be liable to mildew —the only agricultural objection to enclosures.[1] The best bread was made from good wheat with a proportion of salt. Wheaten cakes were also made under the ashes of the fire, and a hard, coarse bread was made from rye; indeed rye provided about 40 per cent. of the bread corn in the later years of the century.[2] Grain was put to numerous other uses. Wheat meal and oat meal were given to horses and poultry; barley served for malt and for fattening pigs; and from even 'musty wheat' was made a crude spirit, which was mixed with water and sugar 'to make it more pleasant for women'. The Commons, anxious to find a substitute for French brandy as an export to the plantations, were interested in this commodity; but as it became 'ropy' on voyages, it could not be shipped abroad.[3]

The Restoration legislature gradually evolved a definite Corn Law policy.[4] In the Book of Rates of 1660[5] a duty of 2s. per quarter was imposed on imported wheat when the price at the port of landing did not exceed 44s. per quarter, and 4d. per quarter when the price exceeded that amount. These rates were subsequently increased, as by the Act of 1670[6] which laid an almost prohibitive scale of charges on imported corn where the

[1] N. Bailey, *Dictionarium Rusticum* (ed. 1704), s.v. 'wheat'.
[2] W. J. Ashley, *The Bread of our Forefathers*, 14–15.
[3] *Grey*, i. 225: also the evidence in *H.M.C. Rep.* viii, app. i. 145–6.
[4] For this see N. S. B. Gras, *Evolution of the English Corn Market*, and Lipson, *Economic History*, ii. 448–64.
[5] 12 Car. II, cap. iv.   [6] 22 Car. II, cap. xiii.

home price was below 80s. One effect of this policy was to provide almost complete protection to the home producer, since
foreign corn was kept out by a high tariff wall. In regard to
exports also there was a notable development. The Book of Rates
established the duty on exported wheat at 1s. per quarter; in
1663 export was explicitly permitted when the home price did
not exceed 48s., provided the duties were paid; and by the Act of
1670 the price restriction was removed, in order to encourage
tillage. Three years later[1] a system of bounties was instituted
whereby, when wheat was at 48s. or less, 5s. was paid for every
quarter of wheat exported, with smaller sums for rye and barley.
England's withdrawal in 1674 from the third Anglo-Dutch war
led to an increased demand for the native grain, notably on the
part of Holland; and under this bounty system an export trade
in grain was rapidly developed. The bounties, which lapsed in
1681, were revived in 1689 and remained a characteristic feature
of the old mercantilist system, their effect being not so much to
raise the price of corn, as to keep the price steady, and in this
way they helped to provide an incentive for the development of
arable farming in the eighteenth century. This artificial stimulus
may, as Adam Smith contended, have been harmful to the community, but at least it benefited English agriculture and brought
more land into cultivation.[2]

Contrasted with grain there are products and commodities the
demand for which has changed over a long period. These might
be grouped according as their utility has increased or diminished.
In the former category was cotton-wool, used with a proportion
of flax in the making of Lancashire fustians, but still known to
many Englishmen as an absorbent material for use in ink-horns.
Iron might be included in this class; for it was not yet used in
structural work, and served mainly for implements, ordnance,
and ornamental ware; but there were increasing opportunities
for its application, and in Worcestershire the Foleys and Dudleys
were building up an iron industry; while in Staffordshire and
round Birmingham the trade in small-arms was rapidly extending. An alloy of tin and lead was used for making pewter, an
industry in which England was pre-eminent; but, though the
uses of these metals has greatly extended, the lead mines of the

[1] 25 Car. II, cap. i, par. xxxi.   [2] Lipson, op. cit., ii. 455.

Peak[1] are extinct, and many of the Cornish mines[2] are now derelict. Coal had not yet displaced wood for fuel, but it was coming to be more generally used; moreover, an export trade in coal to Portugal and the Mediterranean was being built up. Silk and linen were both in increased demand, and were threatening the supremacy of the native broadcloth, but our silk and linen industries could not compete with the French until, with the increased immigration of Huguenots after 1680, new processes were introduced; and thereafter English manufacturers were able to hold their own in these textiles.

In the same category, that of commodities for which the demand has increased, are sugar, glass, tea, and coffee, all of them at first luxuries, or curiosities which soon became necessities. Sugar supplemented the native honey, and helped to provide a more varied diet. Glass works were established near London, and in Restoration England the glass window was to be found not only in the 'gilt coaches' of the rich, but in the cottages of the poor. This almost universal use of the window-pane must have been of revolutionary importance in English life; for only with adequate illumination can there be pride in the interior of one's house. Another stimulus in the same direction was supplied by the increased imports of porcelain from the east and mahogany from the west, thereby providing women with opportunity for the exercise of a refinement never attainable in the old 'parlor', with its benches of oak or deal, and its lingering odours of beer and tobacco. Three women make a market; with a pot of tea and a set of china they become a drawing-room. But not until the next century was this evolution accomplished.

Of the second category, that of commodities which have suffered a diminution in comparative importance, an example is leather. The raw hide was the basis of one of the most extensive industries of the period; like English wool, the native leather was considered superior to the foreign product, and English craftsmanship was seen at its best in the manufacture of boots, shoes, and saddlery. Old boots were either used for fuel or exported to France.[3] At first Charles II's government extended to leather

---

[1] See *infra*, 79–80.   [2] See *infra*, 78–9.
[3] H. Belasyse, *An English traveller's first curiosity* (1657), in *H.M.C. Rep.*, *Various Collections*, i. 200.

the same protection as was already given to wool, namely, prohibition of export.[1] But this policy was speedily reversed, and for a characteristic reason: because it was thought that, in consequence of the embargo, raw hides had fallen in price, thereby discouraging the breeding of cattle, and so causing a fall in rents. Free export was therefore allowed,[2] avowedly in the interests of the landlords. By this the grazier probably benefited; but the removal of the restriction was said to react unfavourably on the leather trade; for the best raw material was supposed to be sent abroad, leaving the poorer qualities to be worked up at home, thereby injuring no less than twenty-six allied trades. This decline was intensified by the fact that the plantations, which, earlier in the reign, imported large quantities of wrought leather, soon employed artificers of their own; in consequence the leather industry was held in 1685 to be in a state of impoverishment.[3]

A clearer illustration of this diminution in the economic importance of a commodity is provided by spice. Earlier in the century no kitchen was complete without its supply of the native saffron, or imported pepper, nutmeg, cloves, and cinnamon, all liberally used in the flavouring of dishes at a time when few vegetables were consumed. They were also utilized in pharmacy, each having a reputed medicinal quality, and when burned they served as fumigants. Owing to their small bulk and comparatively high price, spices were a most profitable article of import from the east; indeed one of the main objects of Anglo-Dutch rivalry was to secure control of the Spice Islands, an object which, despite their most strenuous efforts, the English East India Company never succeeded in achieving, and so the Dutch retained an almost complete monopoly. How much importance they attached to this trade may be deduced from the fact that, in the peace concluding the second Anglo-Dutch war, the small Spice Island of Pularoon was considered adequate compensation for the loss of the New Netherlands. But already the fashion was beginning to change; for sugar was becoming an established article of dietary, the odour of coffee was displacing that of cinnamon, and

---

[1] 14 Car. II, cap. vii.   [2] 19–20 Car. II, cap. x.
[3] *H.M.C. Rep.* xi, app. pt. ii. 312, *MSS. of the House of Lords*: petition of the shoe-makers and leather manufacturers, June 4, 1685.

tobacco smoke (poured out in denser volumes after the Plague) was establishing itself as a universal disinfectant. In some cases the better quality of meat (through feeding on the new grasses) may account for this change of taste; and in 1674 Anthony Wood[1] noted that spices were seldom served with meat, and that the trade was declining. There were remote but important consequences of English failure to capture the spice trade. Expulsion from the profitable islands drove the English to the Indian mainland, and so added to the Company's trading activities the responsibilities of empire. This was one of the two accidents which indirectly paved the way for British dominion in India, the other being that, of the competitors for a marriage alliance with Charles II, the Portuguese were best supplied with ready money. That Bombay was part of the dowry did not seem a great inducement; for some educated Englishmen thought that Bombay was a fort in Brazil.

Among the material needs of Restoration England to which a special importance was then attached are timber, wool, fish and salt, tobacco, beer. Each will be considered briefly in turn.

Timber. In 1660 about an eighth part of England was said to be wooded, and there were nominally sixty-eight royal forests, but it should be noted that the word forest was often used of treeless wastes such as can be seen to-day in the Scottish deer forests. Three royal preserves—the New Forest, the Forest of Dean, and that of Alice Holt (Hampshire)[2]—supplied some of the needs of the Navy. Timber had not been conserved during the Commonwealth; and the naval wars, together with the rebuilding of the city of London, forced the problem of its supply on public attention. Accordingly, the government bestirred itself; new sources were tapped, and in 1666 an agent was sent to Scotland, where he contracted for 2,000 fir trees to serve as masts.[3] Yarranton the 'improver' suggested that timber should be brought from Ireland.[4] Nor were these the only expedients. A part of the Forest of Dean was enclosed in order to provide a nursery for young

---

[1] *Wood*, ii. 300.
[2] For this see R. G. Albion, *Forests and Sea Power*.
[3] *Carte MS.* 222, f. 85.
[4] Yarranton, *England's Improvement* . . ., 39.

trees,[1] and some improvements were effected in the management of the New Forest.[2] Even the Navigation Acts had to be modified to permit free importation of Baltic timber, as the difficulty was that English ships were not adapted to the stowage of great lengths of wood,[3] and the Dutch had already established themselves in the Baltic trade.

In spite of these efforts there was a serious shortage, most serious after 1679, when unseasoned wood had to be used, responsible perhaps for the large toadstools which Pepys collected from the interior of ships' hulls.[4] Greatest of all difficulties was that of procuring what the ship-wrights called 'compass oak', that is the large pieces required for the stern post (sometimes 40 feet long and 2 feet thick) and for the stem and knees; indeed, for oak of these dimensions, the Navy had to draw mainly from a single source of supply—the privately-owned forest of Ashdown, where the heavy Sussex clay produced the best oak in England. Foreign oak provided fewer pieces of the requisite size or shape, and so had to be used mainly for planking, for which purpose beech and elm were also used, but they were inferior. In addition to the hull there were the masts and rigging, and one full-rigged ship would consume a large supply of fir, pine, or spruce, varying in length from the mainmast of a first-rate (about 100 feet) to the fore-top-gallant yard of about 20 feet.[5] The straight, elastic fir needed for masts and spars was then obtained from the southern Baltic, that of Riga having the preference; but after 1652 masts began to be imported from New England, and when her charter was in danger, Massachusetts attempted to conciliate the home government by a present of masts. But an imperial policy in regard to timber was impossible so long as England insisted on taking all her best oak from Sussex; nor was there any recognition of the enormous resources of the American forests. Inadequacy of timber-supply helped to limit English achievement in the last two Anglo-Dutch wars, and of this period it is specially true that

[1] 19–20 Car. II, cap. viii, and *Cal. Tr. Bks.*, *1667–8*, 131, 200.

[2] By paying the keepers in money instead of wood a saving of £3,000 a year was effected. *Cal. Tr. Bks.*, *1669–72*, 1120.

[3] For English shipping see *infra*, 232–4.

[4] S. Pepys, *Memoires of the Royal Navy* (1690), ed. with introduction by J. R. Tanner (1906), 47.

[5] A. Moore, *Seventeenth-Century Rigging*, in *Mariners' Mirror*, ii, no. 9.

naval supremacy was dependent on oak—of hulls almost as much as of hearts.

Wool. Our misquotation of the old adage 'to spoil the sheep for a ha'porth of tar', and the frequency of the name 'Ship Street' in our inland towns, serve to prove that sheep and wool have suffered a diminution in national importance. Throughout the fifteenth and sixteenth centuries wool had proved a most profitable article of speculation, and the churches of the Cotswolds and East Anglia were built mainly by men who had made fortunes from the rich pastures there. Over-production and deterioration in the breed of sheep diminished its importance in the seventeenth century, leading to a considerable fall in price; moreover, there was increasing competition from Spanish wool which, after 1648, found a ready market in Holland and the Low Countries;[1] and, later in the century, Ireland was added to the number of wool-exporting countries. In spite of the threat of a glut at home, the Restoration government renewed the old prohibition of export,[2] from a conviction that the English product had special advantages over the foreign, and that free export would endanger the native cloth trade by providing the foreigner with good material on which to work. The legislators were here voicing the popular view, a view justified by one economic consideration, namely, that England had unique advantages not so much in the quality as in the variety[3] of its wool, which might be middle, fine or superfine, short or long, coarse as in Suffolk or of superlative fineness as in the Leominster district of Herefordshire.[4] From the long wool were made the worsteds, and from the shorter was made an endless variety of cloth; so the English craftsman had at his disposal a wider choice in the length and texture of his material than could be found on the Continent, where there were mainly two types—the very fine wool of Spain, so short and fragile that often it was difficult to work, and the coarser wools of France, Holland, Flanders, and Germany. For this reason the English material was eagerly sought after, and the fact that so much of it was

---

[1] *Add. MS.* 32094, f. 243.
[2] 12 Car. II, cap. xxxii, and 14 Car. II, cap. xviii.   [3] See *supra*, 35.
[4] *Cal. S.P. Dom.*, 1675–6, 373 sqq. Also *England's Interest by Trade Asserted* (1671). For evidence regarding foreign use of English wool see *H.M.C. Rep.* viii, app. pt. i, 127–8, *MSS. of House of Lords.*

smuggled abroad gave some support to the views of those who wished to retain the prohibition on its export. From this smuggled material France was able to make worsted stuffs and stockings, which were re-exported to England, a trade lucrative for the French but responsible for some of the Gallophobia so intense in the latter half of the century.

Until the nineteenth century this trade was jealously safeguarded by the legislature, since it was that which gave employment to the maximum number of persons of both sexes and all ages in practically every corner of England.[1] Change of fashion threatened to destroy its supremacy, and the native homespun had to face the competition of materials such as calico, muslin, and silk; but, with the Revocation of the Edict of Nantes (1685) and the increased immigration of Huguenots, there was developed in England not only a silk industry, but an improved woollen industry, especially in those processes where an admixture of silk could be employed. New methods of dyeing were also adopted through the example of French immigrants. At the same time fresh efforts were made to promote the use of English wool. Already there were Acts that shrouds should be of woollen only;[2] in 1685 it was proposed to make compulsory the lining of coaches with wool, and to require women under the degree of gentlewoman to wear hats of the same material.[3] After 1678 the price of the raw material rose from the lowest point touched in the century (5d.–6d. per pound), a rise due to various causes, including increased exports to Spain and Portugal,[4] and the creation of what was practically a free market by smuggling.

Fish and Salt. For England of the later seventeenth century salt-water fish meant mainly herring caught in the North Sea, pilchards from the Devonshire or more often from the Cornish coast, salmon (obtainable in many English rivers), mullet from

[1] For this see *infra*, 81–2.

[2] 18–19 Car. II, cap. iv; 30 Car. II, cap. iii; 32 Car. II, cap. i. A certificate to this effect had to be signed by the relatives.

[3] *C.J.* ix. 733, June 12, 1685.

[4] In the period 1670–1700 English exports to Portugal, consisting mainly of provisions and cloth, are said to have trebled in value [V. M. Shillington and A. B. Chapman, *Commercial Relations of England and Portugal* (1907), 213]. It was the adverse balance of trade against Portugal which led to an increase in the export of Portuguese wines to England after 1678 (ibid. 220).

the Sussex coast, and sprats. The red herring, which abounded near the east coast and was cured at English ports, was regarded as a distinctively national commodity, and was assigned special place in the all-comprehensive triumvirate—'fish, flesh and good red herring'. To the legislator, fish was associated with shipping and naval supremacy, many of the earlier Acts for the encouragement of the Navy being little distinguishable from Acts for the promotion of fishing; to the divine, the consumption of fish was linked with abstinence on Fridays and in Lent. Both therefore agreed in advocating a fish dietary, and the methods of preserving then employed ensured the imposition of an appreciable degree of self-mortification on the consumer. Economically also, barrelled fish was a necessity in the winter, when little fresh meat could be obtained, and it was a profitable article of export; indeed, it might without great exaggeration be said that, while in the sixteenth century western Europe was divided between the warring camps of Protestant and Catholic, in the succeeding century the two leading Protestant nations were fighting each other in order to capture the profitable trade of supplying salted fish to Catholic countries. The fact that shoals of herring were to be found near the English coast induced Englishmen to make a bid for the trade;[1] but these efforts were unsuccessful, because the Dutch, with their large fleets, their unrivalled methods of packing, and their wonderful organization, had already made this trade their own.[2] The herring was therefore one of the main causes of Anglo-Dutch hostility, and the herring-buss was the foster-mother of the iron-clad.

Hence the importance of salt. Among the varieties in repute were that from Cape Verde and that from Setubal (near Lisbon), the last-named being extensively used by the Dutch, who experimented in the blending of salts. Of the native sorts, those from the brine-pans at South Shields and from the pits of Staffordshire, Cheshire, and Worcestershire were the most widely used.

---

[1] For this see *infra*, cap. vi.
[2] In an undated memorandum (*S.P. For.*, *Holland*, 219) it is estimated that the annual value of the Dutch herring exports to Elbing, Staaten, and Danzig was £620,000; to Denmark, Sweden, and Norway, £170,000; to Hamburg, Bremen, and Emden, £100,000; to Russia, £27,000; to Germany, £440,000; and to France £1,000,000.

Evaporation over coal or wood fires was the method commonly
employed, the aim being to separate the bittern or lye from the
kern or crystals; efforts were also made to procure as large crystals
as possible, free from the bromine of the bittern.[1] Cheshire salt
had a bad colour, possibly because it was clarified by unsuitable
substances; Staffordshire salt was more slowly crystallized, and
the use of white of egg gave it a better appearance; but nevertheless the salt used in England must at times have been an unsavoury article, and may have added a flavour to the substances
which it purported to preserve. The best results were obtained
from 'salt upon salt', that is, the granules of brine evaporated in
the sun, refined by boiling with salt-water to eliminate dirt, sand,
and bittern.[2] In these processes the Dutch were supreme; moreover they paid more attention to sorting and barrelling.

Tobacco. There was a steady increase in the social and economic importance of tobacco. With the exception of Charles II,
the Stuarts disliked the weed, and already James I had blown
heavily on its reputation in his *Counterblast*, wherein he demonstrated that the taking of tobacco was an ignoble habit, reducing
a man to the level of a chimney, and rendering him liable to
melancholia. This aversion was reflected in the earlier Stuart
policy towards the colonies; for repeated efforts were made to
induce the planters of Virginia to turn their attention to commodities more useful than tobacco; and high impositions were
levied on the imported article, the effect of which was to cause
Englishmen to grow their own supplies. Hence, small plantations were established in many counties, notably Gloucestershire,
Herefordshire, Worcestershire, and Warwickshire, where there
was little difficulty in growing the crops; but the methods of
curing were unsatisfactory, as the leaves had to be suspended on
strings in the autumn sun, and owing to cold nights were never
properly ripened. During the Commonwealth, these plantations
were seldom interfered with (though the industry was forbidden
by Ordinance), possibly because it was thought that the English
planter, from the seasonal character of his work, with its long

---

[1] J. Houghton, *Collection for the improvement of husbandry and trade* (1727 ed.),
ii. 62 sqq.

[2] There is a contemporary account of these processes by John Collins,
F.R.S., *Salt and Fishery* (1682).

periods of comparative idleness (and consequent debauchery), was likely to be a suitable object for royalist propaganda.[1] English tobacco was said to be harmful to its partakers, for much of it rotted in the maturing process;[2] and adulterations, such as starch and coal-dust, made further heavy demands on the robustness of the native taste.

The Restoration inaugurated a consistent and vigorous policy towards tobacco. Smoking had now established itself as a social habit, and although as late as 1664 an attempt was made to encourage the export of pitch and tar from Virginia and Maryland,[3] it was at last recognized that these plantations were specially adapted for a crop from which a large fiscal revenue could be obtained. Accordingly, colonial tobacco was included in the 'enumerated' raw materials of which England was becoming the staple, a staple whence native consumer and European importer drew their supplies on payment of a duty. A necessary corollary to this policy was the suppression of tobacco-growing in this country. Several prohibitory statutes were therefore passed,[4] one of which provided an exception in favour of the 'Physick Gardens' of the universities, and 'other private gardens for surgery', where not more than half a pole might be grown for experimental or medicinal purposes. But the general prohibition was difficult of enforcement, and companies of dragoons had to be employed to root up the plants.

Thus tobacco had its justification in the revenue which it provided, and in the amount of English shipping required for its import and re-export. In 1671 this trade employed about 140 ships of between 150 and 500 tons, and the Customs benefited by about £100,000 per annum.[5] In this way England was awakened to the fact that the plantations, so far from being burdens, were potential sources of profit. Consequences of almost equal importance attended the spread of the tobacco habit at home. Medicinal qualities were at first attributed to it; and when coupled with psalm-singing the weed was supposed by some to be a cure

[1] C. M. MacInnes, *The early English tobacco trade*, 96–102.
[2] For tobacco-growing in England see W. J. Hardy, in *Archaeologia*, li (1888). 			[3] *Cal. S.P. Dom., 1664–5*, 113.
[4] 12 Car. II, cap. xxxiv; 15 Car. II, cap. viii; 22–3 Car. II, cap. xxvi.
[5] *H.M.C. Rep.* ix, pt. ii. 10, *MSS. of the House of Lords.*

for melancholy;[1] moreover, its smoke was held to provide in a volatile and therefore more powerful form the virtues of two substances specially favoured by the alchemist—sulphur and nitre.[2] Smoking thus commended itself to an age of alembics and distillations, providing a counterblast to rival aromas; but it came to be more than a protective against the unsavoury, because its narcotic qualities helped to foster that spirit of compromise which, more perhaps than any other quality, helps to distinguish our age from the eras of religious strife.

Beer. Beer was commended by the chemists and physicians because, by 'decoction and fermentation', the cold 'dampness' of the water was removed, leaving it 'brisk and sparkling with the airial life and richness of spirit'. 'Waters', it was said, 'are best to be taken when the sun hath exhaled the damp and cold fog therefrom, and their bowels are warmed with the benevolent rays thereof, for to be sure what Nature does not in this case, Art must.'[3] The virtues of fermented substances were therefore contrasted with the evils of 'raw' or cold water. But, in truth, English beer needed no commendation, as it was then a national drink, more widely used than is tea to-day. It was an essential part of the people's dietary, and great harm was done when army and navy contractors profited by supplying the Navy with bad beer, from which source there were several deaths in the third Anglo-Dutch[4] war. It was also the standard drink at elections, and gained in comparison with coffee; for the oriental beverage by keeping men awake was said to make them seditious, while the more somnolent beer kept them loyal. 'Plotting and Sotting' were among the earliest divisions of English party politics, and the tories, faithful to the native brew, satirized the 'syrop of soot and old shoes'[5] imbibed in whig coffee-houses, imputing to their opponents a degree of wakefulness inconsistent with the full requirements of seventeenth-century loyalism.[6] The earliest accusation against the whigs was their sobriety.

[1] This prescription was offered to George Fox and rejected: *Journal* (Everyman ed.), 4. [2] R. Thorius, *Hymnus Tabaci* (translation of 1651).
[3] *Cervisiarii Comes* (1692), 28. [4] *Cal. S.P. Dom.*, *1672–3*, viii.
[5] Quoted by sir George Sitwell, *The First Whig*, 122.
[6]   'And better it is to be honestly sotting
    Than live to be hanged for caballing and plotting.'
        (*The Pot Companions*, in *Bodley*, *Wood*, 417, xciii.)

To the legislator, beer was the ideal object of taxation because (a) both the ingredients and the taste for it were almost constant factors; (b) it was a necessity, in the sense that it was served at every meal, including breakfast; and (c) it was a luxury, in the sense that water could be used instead. Accordingly, revenue from the Excise on beer possessed a uniformity and dependability not to be found in any other form of taxation. Wine would fiscally be less certain, because it was a foreign and much more varied commodity; face-powder or perruques would be a precarious source of revenue, since the fashion might go out as quickly as it had come in. The duchess of Portsmouth, ignorant of English ways, was content to have the security for her pension assigned on the wine licences, not foreseeing the day when England would prohibit the import of French wine; but lady Castlemaine, more astute or better informed, had her pension placed on the Excise as 'the more secure and legall fonds'.[1] When, by a silent but momentous revolution, the tenants of the crown by knight service divested themselves of their feudal dues and obligations, the burden was transferred to the substance best able to bear it, namely, beer.[2] The same liquid contributed to the stability of the two greatest financial institutions in the country—the National Debt and the Bank of England; for each originated as a national loan, and the security for the payment of interest on both loans was placed on the most reliable fiscal basis—the Excise.[3]

4. THE CHIEF OCCUPATIONS: MINING AND METAL-WORKING; TEXTILES; AGRICULTURE

Mining and metal-working were important industries of Restoration England, but their distribution was not identical with that of to-day; for, while most of them relied on water-power, on the other hand they were less dependent on coal. Coal was, however, an essential element in the iron-making in the Forest of Dean, where a pliable metal called sow iron was smelted from iron-stone and from the mounds of cinders reputed to have been left by the Romans. This industry, which is said to have employed 60,000 men, involved the consumption of both coal and wood; the

---

[1] *H.M.C. Rep.* vi, app. pt. i. 473.   [2] See *infra*, 159.
[3] 4 Gul. et Mar., cap. iii, and 5 Gul. et Mar., cap. vii respectively.

products were sent to the forges of Worcestershire, Shropshire, Staffordshire, and Warwickshire to be made into bar iron.[1] The forges in the Forest were leased from the crown; and both miners and colliers were a monopolist community, having their own court at St. Briavel's, where questions of debt, trespass, and right-of-way were determined. A share of the profits was paid to the crown and to the lords of the soil. Mining was here an ancient 'mystery'; the right of working the pits and sinking new shafts was confined to those born within the bounds of the Forest; nor might any 'foreigner' come to see 'the practices of our sovereign lord the King in his mines'.[2] Crown rights do not appear to have been so long respected in mines outside the Forest of Dean; but this was compensated by the Customs receipts from the increasing exports of coal.[3] Among other places, coal was obtained from the shallow pits of Atherstone and Nuneaton, from some parts of Shropshire, but most extensively from the mines of Durham. It may be said generally of the northern coal industry that, in Restoration England, it was becoming more specialized; for the workings were deeper, and mining was ceasing to be a part-time occupation; moreover, as it generally cost about £1,000 to sink a new shaft, capital was essential, and there was also the expense of way-leaves, of special importance because the mine-owner rarely possessed the freehold.[4] Frequent flooding of the pits was another difficulty; in consequence, coal-mining was a highly speculative enterprise. But it was still possible to make profit even from the shallow mines, because the inferior coal found near the surface could be sent to the salt-pans at South Shields, while the better variety from greater depths was shipped in Newcastle colliers to the markets in the south.

The tin mines of Cornwall were then in full activity, providing irregular and often sweated employment to ten or twelve thousand tin-miners, who lived in hovels and worked in short shifts (often by candle-light), engaged in an unhealthy occupation,

[1] Yarranton, *England's Improvement* . . ., 57, 59, 60.

[2] There is a good account of their laws and usages in H. G. Nicholls, *Ironmaking in the Forest of Dean* (1886), 65 sqq.

[3] Coal was assessed in the Book of Rates at £8 per Newcastle chaldron.

[4] For this subject generally see J. U. Nef, *The Rise of the British Coal Industry 1550–1700*, 2 vols. (1932).

which suffered the additional disadvantage of decreasing wages, due to diminished demand. Moreover, the miners were often at the mercy of the tin factors; nor did they have any by-occupation such as weaving to supplement their variable earnings.[1] Tin-mining included a number of processes. The ore, having been brought to the surface, was first broken up in a stamping mill, after which it was taken to the blowing house, where it was melted and cast into blocks of from 300 to 400 pounds weight. The owner having set his mark on them, the blocks were taken twice yearly to the coinage towns—Truro, Lostwithiel, Helston, and Liskeard, where they were assayed or 'coined' by cutting off a corner ('coin'). These terms must not be taken to imply the existence of substantial buildings, since the blowing houses were merely structures of rock or turf having thatched roofs which were burnt down every few years in order to salve the tin blown into the thatch.[2]

More favourable conditions prevailed in the lead-mining of the Mendips and the Peak, where the miners worked individually or in small partnerships, and there were fewer complaints of exploitation by middlemen. The heart of the Forest of Mendip was the manor of Cheddar, once part of the ancient demesne of the crown; in the neighbourhood, and especially at Chewton, lead was extracted from the unenclosed common, and when this was worked out, other metals such as calamine and manganese were mined. Here, as in Cornwall and the Forest of Dean, there were courts and laws to regulate the relationship between the miner and his mates on the one hand and the lord of the soil on the other.[3] There was a similar jurisdiction in the most important of lead-bearing districts in England—the Peak district of Derbyshire.[4] By custom, a prospector who found ore in the district freed his claim by giving a 'dish' of lead to the lessee of the royal

---

[1] G. R. Lewis, *The Stannaries*, 217, 220-1.   [2] Ibid. 17.

[3] For the Mendip mines see J. W. Gough, *Mendip Mines and Forest Bounds*, in *Somerset Record Society*, xlv (1931).

[4] For the Derbyshire mines see *Bygone Derbyshire* (ed. W. Andrews, 1892); *The compleat mineral laws of Derbyshire* (1734); *The rhymed chronicle of Edward Manlove* (original ed. 1653; edited with notes by T. Tapping, 1851); also W. Hardy, *The miner's guide* (1748). Miscellaneous information will be found in *Add. MSS.* 6681 and 6682. The subject is worthy of a modern monograph.

rights; and in order to obtain full title and possession he applied to the barmaster who, with at least two of the jury, marked out the 'meers' of ground, each containing about 30 square yards. By custom also if a miner left his 'grove' (the shaft leading down to his mine) for nine weeks he forfeited it, unless it was proved to be unworkable because of wind or water; so too his wife might lose her dower, if the 'grover' or miner left his holding unworked for want of 'stows', or pulleys for drawing up the ore in tubs. The crude ore was first dressed with a chipping hammer, and then taken to a 'bing place' where it was crushed; it was then sold by the standard measure of the 'dish'—a receptacle 28 inches long, 6 inches wide, and 4 inches deep.[1] At Wirksworth a barmote court was held twice a year to regulate the conduct of this primitive and almost self-contained community:

And two great courts of Burghmoot ought to be
In every year upon the minery,
To punish miners that transgress the law,
To curb offenders and to keep in awe
Such as be cavers,[2] or doe rob men's coes,[3]
Such as be pilferers, or doe steal men's stows:
To order grovers, make them pay their part,
Joyn with their fellows, or their grove desert,
Or work their meers beyond their length and stake,
Or otherwise abuse the mine and rake,[4]
Or dig or delve in any man's bing place,
Or do his stows throw off, break or deface:
To fine offenders that doe break the peace,
Or shed men's blood, or any tumults raise
Or open leave their shafts, or groves or holes
By which men lose their cattle, sheep or foles.[5]

Tin and lead were essential for the pewter industry; but the increased production of gold and silver-ware helped to relegate pewter to the kitchen, and this process was contemporaneous with a falling off in the exports of tin and lead to the Mediter-

---

[1] *The compleat mineral laws of Derbyshire* (1734).
[2] Men wandering about the mines to beg or steal.
[3] Coes were the sheds in which miners left their tools.
[4] A wide vein lying perpendicularly between two shafts.
[5] *The rhymed chronicle of E. Manlove*, ed. T. Tipping.

ranean and the East. Increasing use was, however, being found for copper, which was obtained from various mines, including one at Keswick and another at Ecton Hill (Staffordshire); these were under the nominal control of an old monopolist company —the Mines Royal. The smelting of brass was in the hands of another monopoly—the Society of the Mineral and Battery Works.[1] These two companies were obliged to lease out their mines and works to capitalists and partnerships; but the latter company had premises in various parts of Nottinghamshire, and brass foundries at Isleworth and Rotherhithe, where it gave direct employment to wage-earners. In general, therefore, smelting and brass-making were capitalist ventures conducted on a factory system; but the products, such as iron and brass wire, with copper and brass sheets, were the bases of many domestic industries, including the making of pins, nails, kettles, wool-cards, and hardware, that could be carried out by small men working singly or in partnership.[2] In this domestic industry there was a characteristic relationship. The brazier (except where he was a direct employee of the Mineral and Battery Works) obtained his raw material from the company and sold it through the middleman; between these two his status was that of debtor and creditor rather than of buyer and seller.

This relationship is to be found also in the textile industries, of which the most important was the making of woollen cloth. Every part of England contributed to this basic industry, each district supplying a distinctive variety, such as the 'flanions' of Essex and Suffolk, the kerseys of Hampshire, Surrey, and Devon, the worsteds of Norfolk, and the varieties classed as the New Draperies, all subject to minute control and inspection in order to ensure conformity in size, material, and workmanship. There was such a multitude of statutes regulating their manufacture that the wit of man could not comprehend them all; and, for centuries, scarcely a year of parliamentary activity had passed without the addition of some fresh enactment to the Statute Book. The national character of this industry was emphasized by the fact that workers were not dependent on the wool of their neighbourhood; on the contrary, there was much transit of raw

[1] For this see H. Hamilton, *English brass and copper industries to 1800*.
[2] Ibid. 85.

material, and varieties from a distance might be combined; thus the wool of the West Riding was used locally only for the coarsest cloth, and was supplemented by the finer products of Rutland, Warwick, and Oxfordshire.[1] So too there was multiplicity in the occupations brought into existence by the working-up of wool, because, from the moment of leaving the sheep's back, the raw material passed through a hierarchy of craftsmen—the spinner who made the yarn, the weaver who wove the cloth, the fuller who thickened and felted it, the shearman who dressed it, and the dyer who coloured it.[2] In the older England there were few villages where no yarn was spun; is not every unmarried English woman a spinster? Throughout the ten thousand parishes of England the women in their cottages were preparing the material on which English maritime trade was built; for it was mainly by her exports of cloth that England paid for her imports.

In several districts, notably Yorkshire, there existed what has been termed the 'clothier' or 'commission' system, whereby the employer bought the raw material, 'put it out' to cottage workers, and then marketed the finished piece; but this agency was not fully specialized, since the same man might be wool-buyer, weaver, and cloth-seller; or these activities might be shared among a few relatives or friends. Only where operations were conducted on a large scale would the master clothier be solely a capitalist agent.[3] It was in Wiltshire and the south-west of England that this specialization had proceeded farthest; for there large-scale production made possible a division of labour. In addition to the clothier-employer, there was the middleman whose business was to go round the country buying wool from the farmer and selling it to the clothier, in accordance with local needs. The reputation of these middlemen was bad, as they were said to engross the market; and their increased number provides evidence of the part played by capitalist enterprise in the clothing trade.

Capital was playing a similar part in the development of the Lancashire cotton industry; for, in the course of the century, there had grown up bands of venturers who brought Cyprus cotton to

[1] H. Heaton, *Yorkshire woollen and worsted industries*, 118.
[2] E. Lipson, *History of the English woollen and worsted industries*, 27.
[3] Heaton, op. cit. 91–2.

Lancashire and marketed the finished product in London;[1] here indeed, even more than in woollens, the worker was dependent on the capitalist, and was completely cut off from both the consumer and the source of his raw material. The custom was to advance on credit a supply of cotton and yarn to the various types of worker, whether farmer-weavers or small-scale employers, and in this way the industry was manipulated by a number of dealers, equipped with capital of very diverse amounts, many of them Puritans or Presbyterians,[2] and all of them characterized by northern enterprise, such as eventually transformed Manchester, Bolton, and Rochdale into busy centres of linen-weaving and cotton-spinning. Individualism was therefore more prominent in these textiles than in the older and more fully regulated clothing industry; moreover, as these newer developments lay mostly outside the corporate towns, the new-comers did not have to force their way against the vested rights of which the privileged towns were such staunch upholders.[3] Of the more free commercial centre thus created a good example was Rochdale, a town then consisting of little more than a church, a few streets, inns, woolshops, warehouses of clothiers, mercers, drapers, with fulling mills and dye-works on the river; here was a centre for a wide area of workers and distributors, most of them occupying small holdings and cottages in the local country-side.[4] Thus linen and cotton not only threatened the old monopoly of wool, but gave rise to industries free from the restrictions which still regulated the production of cloth.

But even in the clothing industry there are evidences of greater freedom in the conditions of labour. In the corporate towns it was sometimes difficult to enforce the conditions of apprenticeship, and this difficulty was greater in the country, where the master did not have the backing of a municipal authority.[5] Moreover, the justices had ceased to assess the maximum rates for craftsmen,[6] and so there was somewhat greater bargaining power. But

[1] A. P. Wadsworth and J. de L. Mann, *The cotton trade and industrial Lancashire, 1600–1780*, 36.

[2] For this see R. H. Tawney, *Religion and the rise of capitalism*, ch. v.

[3] A. P. Wadsworth and J. de L. Mann, op. cit. 53–5.

[4] Ibid. 55. [5] Ibid. 60.

[6] R. H. Tawney, *Assessment of wages by justices of the peace*, in *Vierteljahrschrift für Sozial- und Wirthschaftsgeschichte*, xi. 544.

the wage problem was totally unlike that of to-day, because the town- and village-workers were mostly in a stronger position, as they generally had the support of subsistence farming; some of them, notably the village weaver and the joiner, often sold direct to their customers; and in general there was no large class of men dependent solely on wages. In consequence the government was concerned not so much with wages as with prices and usury.[1] Where there was conflict of interest, it was sometimes due to the introduction of labour-saving devices, such as the Dutch small-wares loom in place of the old single loom. There were weavers' riots in 1675 from this cause, and it is notable that the attorney-general was ordered to consult with the judges in order to determine whether the arrested rioters could be charged with high treason.[2]

These facts support the view that there were numerous local differences in the conditions of labour prevailing in the mining, metal-working, and textile industries; consequently all generalizations about economic conditions in the strongly provincial England of the Restoration must be made and received with caution. This is equally true of husbandry; for just as there were innumerable gradations between the exceptional extremes of the capitalist employer and the wage-earning employee, so on the land there were many types intermediate between the landlord and the agricultural labourer. The word 'husbandman' has been used of a composite class—the small copyholder, obliged to supplement his meagre profits by working for wages, generally in time of harvest. This class was very large. Unfortunately its members were silent; they rarely kept accounts; they wrote neither memoirs nor letters; few of them were even lay preachers, and they left behind them little more than the interrogation: how did they make ends meet? For the poorest of them, and for all dependent solely on wages, the answer was sometimes provided by the high rate of mortality, but nevertheless, it should not be assumed that conditions were specially harsh for these men in the reign of Charles, since the later seventeenth century compares favourably with the early nineteenth, so far as the workers on the land were concerned.

[1] R. H. Tawney, op. cit. 537.
[2] *Cal. S.P. Dom.*, *1675–6*, 250–60, quoted in A. P. Wadsworth and J. de L. Mann, op. cit. 101.

Even thus, the fact still remains that for the majority of the inhabitants of the country-side life was hard and precarious; sometimes it was hopeless. As an illustration of the narrow margin on which the wage-earner had to live, take the wage assessment of the Worcestershire justices in 1662.[1] For a bailiff, the rate was £4 per annum; for a chief hind, £3 6s. 8d.; for a husbandman, £2 10s.; for a labourer, without meat and drink, 7d. per day; with meat and drink, 3d., and 1d. per day more for the period between Candlemas and Harvest. It has been calculated that the average rate for the ordinary agricultural labourer as assessed at Quarter Sessions was 3½d. per day in winter, and 4½d. in summer, with meat and drink;[2] and what this meant may be seen by comparison with the bare cost of living as estimated from the allowances made for poor relief: namely, 4s. to 5s. per week for an adult.[3] It is true that the labourer's wife and family sometimes earned wages, but these rarely amounted to 10s. per week; with the result that while all other classes generally showed a balance, however small, of income over expenditure, this class shows a deficit; and neither contemporary nor modern economists can explain how they lived. A significant proof of the difficulty of the problem is provided by the fact that in many parishes the overseers and church-wardens strictly excluded from settlement all who were wholly dependent on agricultural wages. Indeed this class was considered by many a social danger, because it seemed to be not an essential part of the old economic system, but an excrescence on it.

This problem is by no means confined to the seventeenth century. The worker on the land is the most elusive of all personalities, and evidence about him, particularly for England of the Restoration, is difficult to obtain. About the more substantial copyhold tenants, however, some information can be gleaned from the records of 'progresses', a medieval institution still retained by a few collegiate and scholastic corporations, for such records illustrate the relations between the manorial lord and the copyhold tenant, and generally possess a human element not to be found in manorial accounts. The progress was primarily the rent-collector's visit; but it entailed other duties, because timber

[1] *H.M.C. Rep.*, *Various Collections*, i. 323.
[2] A. Clark, *Working life of women in the seventeenth century*, 66.
[3] Ibid. 69.

and premises were inspected, courts were held, and human contact was established by visit or the receipt of hospitality. There was an element of risk about the progress, since rent-collectors, especially if heads of colleges or ecclesiastics, were good game for highwaymen; and so blunderbusses had to be carried; or pirates might even have to be reckoned with, as when a warden of Winchester College was spirited away from the shore and held to ransom by a hovering band of buccaneers.[1] Business, charity, adventure, and social entertainment were thus harmoniously blended in the itinerary of the manorial lord.

From the three volumes of Progress notes made by Michael Woodward, who was warden of New College from 1659 to 1675, it is possible to conjecture what may have been the relations between the lord of a manor and his copyholders. Woodward, who was not distinguished for learning, was a good administrator of the older type; and, as a parish rector in Berkshire, he had already acquired an intimate knowledge of many matters relating to agriculture. As warden of New College, he was required by the statutes to combine two sets of duties not usually associated, but still performed by his successors—the presidency of a large college[2] and the management of scattered estates. Accompanied by one of the fellows as outrider and by the steward of the manors, he visited, in spring and autumn, properties in Oxfordshire, Buckinghamshire, Cambridgeshire, Essex, and Norfolk, and also tenements in the city of London: these, for the most part being the original endowments of the college.

His first visit was to Tingewick (Bucks.) in April 1659. Court was held at 10 a.m.; in the afternoon the warden had some discourse with the villagers about the enclosing of their common, and by riding round it he observed its bounds, and noted how much was to be allowed to each township. The inspection completed, he then asked the men of Tingewick whether they would abide by the decision of two commissioners chosen by them, a proposal which they rejected, because they 'would not be tied to any man'; nor would they alter what they had already decided

---

[1] For this see an account by Mr. Herbert Chitty in *The Wykehamist*, no. 512 (1913), 115. The incident occurred in the Isle of Wight, and a ransom of £1 was paid for the warden. I owe this reference to Mr. Chitty.

[2] For this see *infra*, ii. 699–701.

at their meetings. There then ensued a spirited contest between warden and villagers, with custom as the umpire. On his side, the lord of the manor had to see to it that a reasonable proportion was assigned to the college and the college farm, in support of which apportionment he cited the copyholders' consent thereto in his predecessor's time; whereupon his tenants required written evidence. Accordingly the warden promised to bring at the next progress a survey of Tingewick, with documents concerning it; and eventually the enclosure was effected by four commissioners, two representing the college and two the inhabitants.

Much time was spent at Tingewick and elsewhere in the inspection of the woods and granting allowances of timber. The warden himself marked and priced the trees that were to be cut down, the prices of whole trees varying from 5s. to 16s. each, the bark being generally valued at 2s. 4d. per lb. 'To one Johnson, a poor cottager to repair his house on the common—20 feet' is a characteristic entry. The most substantial tenant in Tingewick was allowed 500 feet for his new house, but an extra tree or two for lathes was refused. When warden Woodward found that men from a neighbouring village had stolen a 'stick' for a may-pole he required them to come into court in order to pay for it—20d. for the college and 4d. for the bailiff. Stealing wood for may-poles was a constant matter of anxiety to the warden, who was forced to ask his 'man' to procure an attorney of Buckingham to take out process against the offenders unless they would compound for it in court and pay for the trespass as well. Another great source of dispute was the 'lopp and topp' of trees. In 1662 the court had to determine whether the woodman of Tingewick was entitled to this as one of his perquisites, a demand which led to an investigation of college archives, and the production of a paper signed by the 'ancient men' of the village testifying that they had never heard of such a custom. So the woodman's petition was dismissed. 'Lopp and topp' was demanded also by villagers to whom trees had been granted, on the ground that others had already been given it with their timber; very unwillingly did the warden yield to this, the strongest argument in village economy. When Woodward's successor, Nicholas, made his first visit to Tingewick, he was met with the claim that copyholders could sell timber growing on their land, a claim supported by the contention that it was customary, and that the oldest villager had known it to be done; but the steward countered this plea by reminding them that, according to the custom of the manor, they might cut timber only to repair, not to sell.

The formal business at these courts related mainly to the renewal of copyholds, when a few pounds were extracted in fines and rents; occasionally there was no business 'save the making of a constable', as at Oakeley in May 1663; at other times the warden drew a complete blank, for instance at Radcliffe, in April 1660, when 'there was no money in the place, not so much as to discharge the regards'.[1] The more serious work included applications for permission to divide copyholds into smaller lots, a division generally held responsible for pauperism.[2] Half a yard-land[3] appears to have been regarded as the economic minimum; while the full yardland was possibly the largest unit that might profitably be worked by one man, his family and plough team, the yearly value of such a holding varying from $£4$ to $£12$. Exceptionally, however, consent was given to the division of half a yardland into two, where there was already a house on each portion, and the petitioners were not dependent on agriculture for a livelihood. Sometimes also the court would intervene in order to protect the inhabitant against the moneyed intruder. Thus at Radcliffe (Bucks.) an outsider wished to buy the reversion of a copyhold for his friends and so put out the 'ancient' family: a request refused by Woodward, unless the family in possession would come into court and acknowledge their consent; for a life or two the stranger could buy, but the reversion belonged to the ancient possessors. There were also special circumstances in which the court might allow a villager to carry away his house, provided it was not made of college timber. For example, a man built a wooden cottage of his own material, paying 4s. per annum rent. At his death he left two daughters, of whom the elder had married a miller, an out-parishioner. This woman was sum-

[1] The gratuities paid to the servants at the houses where the Progress received hospitality.

[2] For the development of sub-leases and the redistribution of holdings see R. V. Lennard, *Rural Northamptonshire under the Commonwealth*, in *Oxford Studies in Social and Legal History*, no. v.

[3] The yardland was nominally about 30 acres, but in practice was generally much less.

moned to court and informed that she might take away the house; she was then sent back to her husband by a warrant, this giving her protection against arrest for vagabondage.

Control might also be exercised over the character of the repairs undertaken by the tenants; as when wood was granted originally for the purpose of building a chimney, a stipulation might be added that the chimney should be built of stone, and the wood put to some other use. There was also the veto which might be exercised over the marriages of tenants. This was rare in Woodward's day, but he noted of the manor of St. Walerick (Essex) that no woman might marry outside the 'homage',[1] the only instance of this inhibition which he records.

As lord of the manor Woodward acted at times in a manner which would now be considered high-handed. In 1667, at Radcliffe, a Quaker asked permission to make an affirmation instead of an oath for the reversion of his copyhold. This the lord refused, with the threat that if the Quaker did not conform, the reversion would be granted to Woodward's 'man' Paul Symmonds. The warden then induced Symmonds to undertake that, at the next court, he would offer £7 for the reversion, while the price for the Quaker (if he took the oath) was to be £8, the difference to be paid to Symmonds in consideration of his resigning his interest. This unholy contract was contested by the 'homage', not on the ground that it was immoral, but that it was a breach of their custom, an objection parried by the steward, who declared that in copyholds of inheritance the lord could grant the reversion to whomsoever he pleased. So the Quaker, having taken the oath, paid the enhanced fine; the commission of £1 was given to Symmonds, and thus at one stroke the lord penalized the Nonconformist, confuted the village lawyers, and made his man-servant's position one of greater emolument and trust.

Another instance was at Steeple Morden (Cambridgeshire). In May 1665 the old village midwife came to Woodward with an offer to sell her holding, consisting of one tenement, a barn, an acre of land, and a little close. She first asked for £50, afterwards coming down to £30, for she might, she said, live for another twenty years, in which case the college would be making a good bargain. The steward offered her £20, which she declined; he

[1] The homage consisted of all who owed suit to the manorial court.

then refused more than four years' purchase, that is £15 or £18. At successive courts the steward renewed his efforts to induce the old lady to accept these somewhat niggardly terms; but she refused, and had her revenge by allowing the premises to fall into dilapidation; and so, five years later, Woodward was obliged to direct that from her rent props should be bought to support the house, which by then threatened to fall down. This expense was to be incurred 'until such time as the old hagge should die, for shee will not mend it'. She continued to be a source of anxiety to her economical landlord, who did not succeed so easily with her as with the Quaker of Radcliffe.

Some of the villages visited on progress were still unenclosed, as Great Horwood (Bucks.), where the villagers were very poor. Their allotments were in widely scattered areas, and their common was encroached upon by more enterprising neighbours. Subject to the consent of the lord, they continued to regulate the routine of village economy by common agreement, and in 1671 they asked the warden to approve their plan for 'stinting' of the cattle in the common fields. Their scheme was as follows:

> An order of the inhabitants, coppieholders of Horwood Magna for stinting of Commons. Made Oct. 24, 1670, to which many have set their hands and seals.
> For every eight acres of arable with hades,[1] one rother[2] beast.
> For every three acres of sound[3] ground, one horse or cow.
> For one acre and a half or arable with hades, 1 sheep.
> For one acre of sound ground, 2 sheep.
> For four poles of meadow as much as an acre of sound ground.
> Every cottage to keep 2 beasts and 5 sheep.

On examining this scheme Woodward objected that it would prejudice the college demesnes in the village, which, by decree, were allowed common for a yardland. As these demesnes consisted of four closes and about five acres of arable, on the above allotment common would be allowed for only five acres of arable, that is, three sheep. 'It is cunningly penned', said the outrider, 'with intent to wheedle the lord into subscription.' 'Latet anguis in herba,' noted the warden (one of his few classical allusions).

---

[1] The transverse strips of land on which the plough was turned at the end of the furrows.
[2] i.e. horned beast.   [3] Drained and cleared.

The diary, though a business record, contains items not without interest. When in the country, Sunday was amply occupied with sermons, prayers, and catechizings; and the warden himself sometimes officiated in the pulpit. In London (he lodged at the Red Lion in Holborn) the host brought to his reverend guest books suitable for his calling, these including 'Dr. Boyes his Postilles' and 'Edmund Calamie's *Godly Man's Antidote* with Eliz. Moore's *Evidences for Heaven* in one book', possibly hotel copies. At this hostel the warden sometimes dined on 'a dish of steakes', eating what he thought good and leaving the rest for his man-servant; but when unexpected visitors arrived, the remains of the 'steakes' were retrieved from the servants' quarters and supplemented with a dish of mackerel. In these visits he saw something of social London, as when, in 1667, he dined at Exeter House with the Spanish ambassador Molina, who had lodged in the college at the time of the Plague, and had presented to his hosts a large gilt cup. Less enjoyable were his visits to his immediate superior the bishop of Winchester, Visitor of the College, as on one occasion when he waited on him at Westminster at seven in the morning, and was obliged to occupy himself until eight, an hour which he spent in reading Butler's *Hudibras* ('a false author' he noted). When at last the bishop (George Morley) appeared, he rated the warden in true medieval fashion because of the great cost of the college organ—'an ornament' he styled it. After hearing the warden's defence, the Visitor insinuated that the college must be in evil plight, because in fifty years it had produced few learned men and only one bishop. Thereupon Woodward pleaded the vicissitudes of the times and the poverty of the college, for its total income was but £1,700 per annum, and the fellowships were worth only £8 per annum.

At the college house in Mugwell Street, occupied by a merchant, the warden was introduced to some of the refinements then rapidly spreading among the well-to-do.

We went to our house in Mugwell Street which Mr. Cripps hath made very handsome. I was led by his wife into all the rooms of itt, and being come downe wee had a collation, viz, a dish of pickled oisters and glasses of old and new sack out of the Butt. She gave us also a box of Spanish marmerlade, and when shee perceived that I was putting itt upp into a paper to keep what I could not eate, she gave unto me not only the remainder of the first box, but also another box, both which, about three days before were brought out of Spaine. The box that was whole I presented unto My Lady Smith, being invited by sir Will. Smith to dine there.[1]

On his next visit to this house in 1666 he found that it had been completely destroyed by the Fire; but so far from wasting sentiment over it, he ordered the rubble to be cleared away, and measurements of the property made, so that there should be no dispute about boundaries in the rebuilding. In the country, the hospitality enjoyed by the Progress was simpler, but more abundant. Sometimes the 'hard meats', such as pigeon pie and westphalia ham, caused the warden sleepless nights; in hot weather he once took too much 'cooling sillabub', but he was prepared for emergencies and, as he laconically notes, 'my strong waters cured me'. He was careful to avoid accepting hospitality at the hands of those tenants from whom it was not expected, as a precedent might thus be established. Unusual occurrences in these progresses were noted with the fidelity of a Pepys. In April 1675 at Radcliffe (where the Progress were the guests of sir William Smith) the party, consisting of the warden, the outrider, the steward, the vicar, the schoolmaster, and the outrider's 'mate', Mr. Morshead, went into a withdrawing room by the parlour 'to drink a pipe of tobacco'. At a late hour, Mr. Morshead, 'to show his nobleness and slight of money, took out a purse of gold and gave it freely and frankly to Mr. Outrider Hobbs, who divided the said gold among the rest of the company there'. There is no record that Mr. Morshead repented of this unusual action, nor did his associates appear to experience any qualms about accepting the gift. Illness occasionally obliged the warden to prolong his stay, as when a 'sore leg' detained him in a Buckinghamshire village until the medical fellow of the college was sent from Oxford to assist the ministrations of his hostess.

Warden Woodward's memoranda have here been cited not as typical manorial documents of the period, but as illustrations of the difficulties and opportunities confronting a manorial lord determined to retain the prerogatives of the corporation which he represented. He might quite well have allowed many claims

[1] Sir William Smith was a burgess for Buckingham and one of the college tenants at Radcliffe.

to fall into desuetude, or have acquiesced in the gradual encroachment of a new, more commercial type of landholding; but he preferred to insist on those details of rule and custom which constituted the essence of the older relationship between landlord and tenant. His notes give a passing glimpse of remote villages where life, it is true, was hard, but tempered by personal contact with a superior who, himself amenable to higher jurisdictions (the Visitor and the College), was seeking not his own profit, but that of a religious, charitable and educational foundation. Moreover, the villagers with whom he dealt were not the landless cottagers of to-day, but mostly small-holders, habituated to a knowledge of their rights, and sometimes prepared to extend them. Frequently in these progresses he was solicited by tenants for his voice in the nomination of boys to Winchester; and though there were more applications than places, the link connecting our oldest public school with the soil was maintained, and so something of the spirit of William of Wykeham still survived. Woodward as landlord may sometimes appear harsh; this is perhaps because he was possibly the only manorial lord of his times who left a full account of his stewardship.

To conclude. On the land, Restoration England retained, from the medieval past, something of an older, less commercialized economy; while in her natural products and industries, she was finding material for a rapidly expanding overseas trade. It was by this harmonious alliance of the old with the new that England was soon to attain her unique position among European powers.

III

THE PEOPLE: THEIR SOCIAL PROGRESS

1. THE DEVELOPMENT OF SOCIETY

THE progress of English civilization in the reign of Charles II was rapid. Before enumerating the more noteworthy of the classes which constituted English society, it is necessary first to describe some of the institutions which promoted social progress.

London was the most important of these institutions. The city, with a population estimated roughly at half a million, was a densely packed community (broken here and there by the gardens attached to large houses), situated mainly on the north bank of the Thames, and was still officially bounded by its ancient gates: Ludgate and Newgate on the west; Aldersgate, Cripplegate, Moorgate, and Bishopsgate on the north; and Aldgate on the east.[1] Outside of Southwark there was little population south of London Bridge, for Bermondsey, Newington Butts, and Lambeth were villages, while Peckham and Vauxhall were rural resorts. To the north of the old city were the fields round Islington, with their cow-sheds and outhouses; to the east, the Mile End Road became a country lane immediately beyond Whitechapel; to the west, one might walk past gardens as far as Westminster; and farther north, the suburbs did not extend beyond the modern Trafalgar Square and Charing Cross Road. By destroying most of the medieval city, the Great Fire made possible the creation of a new and larger London, with wider streets and spacious squares, such as Bloomsbury and Leicester Squares, and that of Covent Garden (with its porticoes); another breathing space was left in Lincoln's Inn Fields. Already fashion was moving west-

---

[1] Among contemporary accounts of the city are J. Brydall, *Camera Regis* (1676) and *The Present State of England* (1683), pt. iii, 109 sqq. This third part of *The Present State* is not very commonly met with, and is not by Chamberlayne, the author of the other parts. There is a large modern literature, including sir Walter Besant's *London in the Time of the Stuarts*, and R. R. Sharpe, *London and the Kingdom*. For a map see *Map of Seventeenth-Century England* (Ordnance Survey, 1930).

ward, and before the end of the century the aristocratic district of St. James's had come into existence, with its town houses of the nobility.[1] Several bishops, including those of Ely, Gloucester, Lichfield, and Lincoln, still retained official lodgings in the metropolis; at Lambeth and Fulham the archbishop of Canterbury and the bishop of London had their respective head-quarters.

Divided into twenty-six wards, the city was governed by a lord mayor, assisted by a recorder, sheriffs, a town clerk, a common serjeant (who acted as counsel for lord mayor and aldermen), and a deputy coroner and constables. The pageantry maintained by the lord mayor never failed to impress visitors; but his powers were no less than his pomp, for he was principal in the commission of felony in the city, a conservator of the Thames, chief coroner of London, chief butler to the king at his coronation, and chief magistrate of a capital city rapidly becoming a decisive power in European politics and international trade. Before the close of the Middle Ages, the city had accumulated a great number of privileges and customs. Thus the lord mayor and aldermen could make ordinances and by-laws; every shop was deemed a market except on Sundays and holy days; execution could not be levied on the husband for the torts of his wife trading as a merchant on her own account; and there was a special fund for the maintenance of the orphans of freemen. In order to enjoy full civic privileges, a man had to become free of a city company, which he might do in one of three ways: by birthright, if he were the son of a freeman; by service, that is by apprenticeship to a freeman; and by 'redemption', or order of the court of aldermen. The city suffered only one notable disability, namely, that it was the least adequately represented constituency; for it sent only four members to parliament, or about a tenth of the total number returned from Cornwall. On the other hand, Middlesex and Westminster each returned two members.

The Thames provided the most common avenue of transport, and, as the city was then spread out like an arc imposed on one of its banks, no point in it was far distant from the river. In 1676 there was said to be 2,000 men plying their wherries on the Thames. For some time these watermen had complained of the competition from hackney coaches, complaints with which the

[1] For this see A. I. Dasent, *The History of St. James's Square.*

government was in sympathy, because the watermen contributed to the personnel of the Navy, whereas the hackney coachmen were said to be worse than useless to the State, as their horses consumed provender, and their vehicles merely pandered to the comfort of the lazy; accordingly, one of the earlier Stuart proclamations had required that they should be used only for a trip of three miles or more.[1] But in spite of such discouragement, hackney coaches became an established feature of Restoration London, providing a more easy means of communication, and intensifying also the problem of street accidents. Streets were roughly paved; ditches, like the Fleet Ditch, were not railed off; in consequence, there were many upsets, and as pavements were narrow or non-existent, pedestrians were sometimes killed by coaches or drays. On these occasions the drivers were generally tried for manslaughter, of which charge they were usually acquitted, but their vehicles were sometimes confiscated as *deodands*.

Civic amenities were improved by a gradual realization of the need for scavenging arrangements. In 1662 an Act appointed commissioners for this purpose.[2] They were to meet at the Office of Works in Scotland Yard; they were authorized to make vaults, sewers, and drains, and for this purpose they were empowered to levy a rate. The same Act forbade the inhabitants to throw ashes or refuse in front of their houses, and ordered them to retain the rubbish until the scavengers arrived. These measures, coupled with the rebuilding after the Great Fire, prepared the way for the London of modern times, but the human occupants of the streets continued to give life and colour to the changing metropolis; for the alleys echoed with the strident calls of the vendors of 'small cole' or 'grand scissors'; there were men selling beef and women selling glass; occasionally a Scotch pedlar would penetrate to these recesses with his load of linen or cloth; but all these pursued their trade at the risk of being arrested for vagabondage or as forestallers of the market. In the shops of the Strand, Fleet Street, Ludgate, and Cheapside there was to be had an increasing variety of wares—pottery, musical instruments, tobacco pipes, barometers, clocks, guns, lacquered cabinets, and mathematical instruments, in addition to the miscellaneous wares classed as

[1] 1636, *Steele*, i. 1713.　　　　[2] 14 Car. II, cap. ii.

haberdashery; there was also gold- and silver-ware, in which the standards of taste and workmanship were extremely high.

One illustration of the city's advance at this time is provided by the establishment of an intelligence bureau.[1] This office was at *The Pea Hen*, opposite Somerset House, and was conducted by one T. Mayhew, whose objects were to keep a register of the names of persons going beyond seas (so that fugitive husbands could be traced), to publish a list of lands and goods for sale, and to provide information where 'artists of all sciences' were to be found. By his organization and intelligence, Nonconformists and Papists would be unable to take themselves and their treasure out of the kingdom; soldiers and seamen might thus be prevented from serving foreign princes; runaway servants, as well as lost and stolen horses, would be restored to their masters. Mayhew proposed also to give information about new books, about curios and interesting sights, and clients in the country were to receive weekly bulletins, so that they could keep in touch with all that was stirring in the metropolis. It is not known how far this scheme succeeded in its avowed objects of keeping in their place all who wanted to leave it, and supplying the others with miscellaneous information. A similar scheme, proposed by a captain Douglas in 1688, was the establishment in London of a central office, open day and night, in control of a band of scouts patrolling the roads throughout the country. These scouts were to have authority to arrest deserters and highwaymen; the funds were to be provided by levies on the counties for every highwayman or deserter captured, and the profits of the enterprise were to accrue to its proposer.[2]

It was from London and the Court that fashion was dictated; but in the evolution of English society other influences have also played their part, and it should be remembered that Charles's Court was much more French than English. Accordingly, illustration of the characteristics of English society in the wider sense may be sought for outside Whitehall, and might be chosen from an infinity of subjects. The selection here adopted is intended to show points of resemblance as much as points of contrast between English civilization then and now; with this

---

[1] *The register's intelligence and advertisement office* (probably about 1680), in Bodley, *Pamph.* 276 a, ccxc.   [2] *Rawl. MS.* A 171, f. 41.

object, a choice has been made of these topics: sermons, coffee-houses, stage coaches, games and pastimes, health resorts, quack medicines, speculation and office-holding, and, finally, the literature of deportment.

Sermons have never been such an important institution in England as in Scotland; but during the Interregnum the standards of ecclesiastical oratory in the south were comparable with those in the north. It was because so many Cromwellians had been lay preachers that the Restoration statesmen kept a strict eye on sermons, since these had recent associations with republicanism; it was therefore concluded that a sermon was a good thing in the authorized place, namely the parish church, but elsewhere it was presumably dangerous. This explains why an unfortunate man was imprisoned for several months because he read printed sermons to friends in his own house.[1] Even over the conforming clergy some control had to be exercised lest they might be carried away by eloquence; and, after the passing of the Act of Uniformity (1662), Convocation addressed itself to the task of securing a general standard of reverence, decency, and order in churches. The result was a circular letter[2] enjoining rules for sermons, whereby pastors were adjured to assert the doctrine and discipline of the Church of England with 'modesty, gravity and candour', and to avoid abstruse and speculative notions, such as 'the deep points of election and reprobation'. Free grace and predestination, over which so much ecclesiastical blood had been shed, were therefore taboo; sermons thenceforth were to be catechetical rather than controversial; they were to emphasize the moral duties of the individual, as churchman and citizen, and not to perplex him with the intricacies of speculative theology.

But English academic education was still influenced by an older system in which lucid exposition might be sacrificed to dialectical subtlety. On the strength of an elementary knowledge of Latin syntax, many poor boys who might have been better employed as craftsmen were sent to the universities as sizars where, instead of liberal reading, they encountered Aristotelian logic, a narrow range of classical authors, and a great mass of theological polemic. Accordingly, as priests, they sometimes pre-

---

[1] *Cal. S.P. Dom.*, *1664*, 487.

[2] E. Cardwell, *Documentary annals of the church of England*, ii. 253.

ferred the pulpit to the lectern since, if Eachard[1] is to be believed, they were better at embroidering a text than pronouncing successfully the more difficult names of the Old Testament. When the reading of the lessons was left to some 'Ten or Twelve Pound Man' the discredit was complete; but congregations were not always very critical, and unintelligibility in the preacher was sometimes charitably construed as profundity.

If he springs forth now and then in high raptures towards the uppermost Heavens, dashing here and there an all-confounding word; if he soars aloft in unintelligible huffs, preaches points deep and mystical, and delivers them as dark and phantastical; that is the way of being accounted a most able and learned instructor.[2]

Of the styles of preaching, Eachard distinguished two, the familiar and the metaphysical, the former finding its similes in the wares of the general dealer (as in the famous Scottish example, 'O Lord, thou art a goose, aye dreeping'), the latter soaring high above earthly parallels, as in this example:[3]

Omnipotent All: Thou art only: because Thou art All, and because Thou only art. As for us, we are naught, but we seem to be, and only seem to be; because we are not; because we are but mites of Entity and crumbs of something.

The same truths were supposed to be expressed by the Presbyterian preacher thus:[4]

Lord, we know Lord, O Lord we do, that Thou Lord kno'st good Lord, that we know nothing: and we thank Thee, O Lord, O Lord, I say with ingemination; we return Thee thanks that Thou hast been pleased of Thy great goodness and mercy to make us sensible of our Nothingness.

Eachard was guilty of exaggeration, but his strictures were not without effect, for they prompted the compilation of a practicable set of rules for preaching.[5] The parson was advised to leave alone certain difficult things, such as obscure texts, or baffling problems, as how Adam who was created perfect came to be tempted, or abstruse books, as those of Daniel and the Revela-

---

[1] Eachard, *The ground and occasion of the contempt of the Clergy.*
[2] Eachard, op. cit. (1705 ed.), 33. [3] Ibid. 47.
[4] *Presbytery truly displayed* (1680).
[5] J. Arderne, *Directions concerning the matter and style of sermons,* 1671.

tion. This was good advice, because in that age many Englishmen and most Scotsmen had each his own interpretation of the more mystical books of scripture. 'Choose sermons suitable to the state of the people you address.' 'Choose words wholly English.' Divide the sermon into three parts—proposition, in which the text is laid bare; confirmation, in which it is illustrated and amplified; and finally inference, or the practical conclusions to be deduced, in which, it is hinted, a somewhat heightened oratory is permissible. It was well that the sermonizings of Charles's reign were tempered by the sarcasms of Eachard, by the instructions of Arderne, and by the example of Tillotson; for there were so many evidences of God's wrath—there were War, Fire, and Plague, there was unheard-of debauchery in high places, there were Presbyterians and Nonconformists, not to mention the Papists and the Whore of Rome—all of these such insistent themes of animadversion, that the pulpit cushion, from its weekly cuffings, was the one piece of church furniture totally devoid of dust. Throughout the reign of Charles, and especially during the Popish Plot, the sermon was one of the most potent influences on the masses, and the vogue of attendance on popular preachers increased. There was even an Anglican revivalist movement, when a renowned orator, the German-born Anthony Horneck, was induced in 1671 to preach at the Savoy, where his sermons were so thronged that his parish was said to extend from Whitechapel to Whitehall.[1] St. Michael's, Cornhill, was also much frequented by those who appreciated the earnest ministrations of William Smythies, and at the neighbouring church of St. Peter's could be heard the eloquent Beveridge, afterwards bishop of St. Asaph. These men were probably too disturbing for Pepys, who was an assiduous taster of the more mature vintages. Charles II showed sound taste in sermons, for he disliked 'wrangling about forms and gestures',[2] and appreciated the thoughtful discourses of the learned and pious Isaac Barrow.

In order to express his own views, the Coffee House was the best place of resort for the layman, since by assiduity of atten-

[1] For the influence of preachers on the growth of religious societies see G. V. Portus, *Caritas Anglicana*.

[2] Cf. Charles's letter to the archbishop of Canterbury, Oct. 1662, in Cardwell, *Documentary Annals* . . . ii. 253.

dance and eloquence of discourse he might there create for himself a niche almost as sacrosanct as the pulpit itself.

Coffee houses [it was said] make all sorts of people sociable; the rich and the poor meet together, as also do the learned and the unlearned. It improves arts, merchandize and all other knowledge; for here an inquisitive man that aims at good learning may get more in an evening than he shall by books in a month. He may find out such coffee-houses where men frequent who are studious in such matters as his enquiry tends to, and he may in short space gain the pith and marrow of the others' reading and studies. I have heard a worthy friend of mine who was of good learning (and had a very good esteem of the universities) say that he did think that coffee-houses had improved useful knowledge as much as the universities have.[1]

But not all contemporaries were agreed on this point. In 1678 Anthony Wood, in answer to the question why serious learning had declined in Oxford, said that it was owing to the increase of coffee-houses and taverns, where seniors and juniors passed a great part of the day.[2] These two views are not incompatible, because while it is true that coffee-houses were responsible for great waste of time at the universities, they helped to open up a new world of speculation and inquiry to men not endowed with learning. In this process of levelling, they bridged the gulf which hitherto had separated the learned from the unlearned, and conferred on the humbler ranks of society an acquaintance with the terminology of debate, as well as a keen interest in public affairs.

It was for this reason that coffee-houses were regarded with disfavour by the government. As early as 1671 they were officially considered to be nurseries of sedition,[3] and in 1675 an order for their suppression was issued.[4] But the proclamation does not appear to have been enforced, and thereafter the government directed its energies to the exclusion of newspapers from these places of public resort. In September 1677 twenty coffee-house keepers were summoned before the Council for having admitted this literature into their premises; their licences were not renewed,

[1] J. Houghton, *Collection for the improvement of husbandry and trade* (1727 ed.), iv. 132.

[2] *Wood*, ii. 429.   [3] *Cal. S.P. Dom., 1671*, 581.

[4] Dec. 29, 1675. *Steele*, i. 3622. By proclamation of Jan. 1676 their suppression was postponed till the following June, and their proprietors had to give security that they would not introduce scandalous papers.

and the king was highly incensed against these 'sordid mechanick wretches who, to gain a little money had the impudence and folly to prostitute affairs of state indifferently to the views of those that frequent such houses, some of them of lewd principles, and some of mean birth and education'.[1] A few years later, when petitioning was the method of appeal adopted by the unenfranchised, signatures were easily obtained at the coffee-houses, the rate, according to L'Estrange, being 4s. per hundred names.[2] So too, as party distinctions emerged, these houses reflected the politics of their patrons, the whigs favouring Kid's Coffee-house (the 'Amsterdam'), where the full-throated blasphemies of Titus Oates could be listened to, and the tories resorting to Jonathan's in Exchange Alley, and Gray's Inn Coffee-house.[3] The government employed at least one coffee-house spy.[4] It was in these schools that voteless Englishmen learned the rudiments of politics.

Like the coffee-houses, the stage-coaches[5] had at first to face considerable opposition. There were many economic objections. As substitutes for riding, they caused loss to the trades of saddler and smith, never compensated by the demand for provender created by the coach horses; they were also held responsible for diminished Excise revenue because (it was argued) their passengers stopped at the inns less frequently than did horsemen. Their use was a symptom of effeminacy; they were also noisome and uncomfortable.[6]

What advantage is it to a man's health to be called out of their beds into these coaches an hour before day in the morning? to be hurried in them from place to place till one, two or three within night? Insomuch that, after sitting all day in the summer time stifled with heat, or choked with the dust, or in the winter time starving and freezing with cold, or choked with filthy fogs, they are after brought into their inns by torchlight when it is too late to sit up to get a supper, and next morning they are forced into the coach so early they can get no break-

---

[1] H. Thynne to T. Thynne, Sept. 19, 1677, in *Add. MS.* 32095, f. 38.

[2] R. L'Estrange, *Citt and Bumpkin in a dialogue over a pot of ale* (1680).

[3] Sitwell, *The First Whig*, 126.

[4] Dangerfield (Sitwell, op. cit. 126). For the subject generally see J. Walker, *Secret service under Charles II and James II*, in *Trans. R.H. Soc.*, series iv, no. xv.

[5] For this subject see Joan Parkes, *Travel in XVIIth-century England*.

[6] *The grand concern of England explained.*

fast. What addition is it to men's health or business to ride all day with strangers, oftentimes, sick, ancient, diseased persons, or young children crying, to whose humours they are obliged to be subject, and many times are poisoned with their nasty scents and crippled by the crowds of boxes and bundles? Is it for a man's health to travel with tired jades, to be laid fast in the foul ways and forced to wade up to the knees in mire, and afterwards sit in the cold till teams of horses can be sent to pull the coach out? To travel in rotten coaches, and to have their tackle, or perch or axle tree broken, and then to wait three or four hours, sometimes half a day to have them mended again? Is it for the advantage of business that a man when he sets out on a journey must come just at their hour or be left behind?

There was little effeminacy about such a method of travel. It displaced riding and sailing as a means of penetrating to provincial England. The mails were carried at the rate of 2d. for one sheet up to 80 miles, and it was possible for a passenger to travel from London to Exeter, Chester, or York in from 3 to 5 days at a cost of about 40s. in summer and 45s. in winter.

For long, this method of transport was impeded by the unsatisfactory state of the English roads. Local responsibility for their repair and upkeep was introduced by a statute of 1555, which required every parish to appoint two surveyors,[1] but numerous indictments at Quarter Sessions show that this statute was frequently ignored. An Act of 1662 empowered the surveyors to levy an assessment of 6d. in the £1 on real property, and required that narrow roads should be widened to a width of 8 yards.[2] In the following year was passed the first Turnpike Act, whereby toll gates were established in the counties of Hertfordshire, Cambridgeshire, and Huntingdonshire, but the tolls were easily evaded;[3] indeed the multiplicity of regulation and indictment suggests that the upkeep of the roads was neglected, a deduction confirmed by records of travel, which show that many of the chief highways were frequently impassable, and that elsewhere communication was maintained by tracks and paths. Even in comparatively populous counties, such as Sussex, the ruts were so deep that it was impossible to drive in double harness;[4] sometimes

[1] For the roads see S. and B. Webb, *The King's Highway*.
[2] 14 Car. II, cap. vi.
[3] 15 Car. II, cap. i; see also Jackman, *Development of transportation in modern England*, i, ch. 2.   [4] *Grey*, i. 233.

gravel would be dug from a road by a farmer, leaving a pit which, after heavy rains, would fill with water and engulf a whole horse and cart. The old maxim 'Bad for the rider, good for the abider' summarized the association of sticky roads with good soil. These things made travel a matter not of daily habitude, but of almost pioneer adventure. There were also the terrors of darkness and highwaymen. At Wokingham a bell was rung at night in order to guide travellers to the town, and at Maidenhead the parson received a supplement to his stipend because his duties required him to pass a thicket frequented by highwaymen who infested the Bath road.[1] The commercial and social development of England was for long impeded by the unsatisfactory condition of the roads.

Stage-coaches, by diminishing the necessity for outdoor exercise, may have helped to impress on Englishmen the value of games; but these did not play the same part in national life as they do to-day, when fewer drugs are used, and there is a more general appreciation of the efficacy of fresh air and cold water. There had long been, however, a recognition of the need for exercise; 'any exercise whereby sweat is procured is good.... Old men must walk while they are able'—such was the advice of a medical writer in the earlier part of the century.[2] Of distinctively open-air exercises (in addition to riding) there was hunting of the stag, buck, boar, otter, fox, and hare, pursuits now coming to be monopolized by the gentry, under the protection of the Game Laws, and with the help of a new functionary—the Gamekeeper.[3] Fowling, with nets or guns, could be engaged in throughout the land, for on the coasts were the chough, the gull, the puffin, and the gannet, and in marsh lands were to be found the hoop, the dottrel, the wild goose, and the bustard.[4] These occupations at least habituated their votaries to the open air, an advantage thus described by a huntsman:[5]

What innocent and natural delights are they when he seeth the day breaking forth those blushes and roses which poets and writers of romances only paint, but the huntsman truly courts? When he heareth the chirping of small birds pearching upon their dewy

---

[1] *V.C.H., Berkshire*, ii. 214.   [2] W. Vaughan, *Directions for Health*, 1633.
[3] 22–3 Car. II, cap. xxv.   [4] *Present State of England* (1683), pt. iii. 21.
[5] N. Cox, *The Gentleman's Recreation* (1677).

boughs? When he draws in the fragrancy and coolness of the air? How jolly is his spirit when he suffers it to be imported with the noise of bugle horns and the baying of hounds, which leap up and play round about him.

In highest repute was Angling, the contemplative man's recreation, the pastime which attracted to the backwaters some of the finest spirits when they wearied of the heat and noise of the highway. English fishermen had reason to be proud of their rivers, for nowhere else could be found streams so varied or accessible, reflecting on their surface a landscape in which quiet gradations of colour mingled harmoniously with the forms of mill, or bridge, or spire. In John Taylor our waterways had a poet whose inspiration, it is true, was dilute, but his love for the stream was sincere. Fish abounded in these unpolluted sources and may have been less shy of artificial bait, for anglers might then easily acquire

> that good fashion,
> Not to catch fish with oaths, but contemplation.

The noble Trent, with its thirty distinct kinds of fish, was hailed as 'Great Britain's Hellespont' by one who loved the mellow quiescence of its then secluded stream—'Heaven and Earth', he wrote[1] of the Trent landscape, 'are here correlates, which duly to contemplate poises our passion and baffles our pride.' For the true devotee, angling was almost devotional; his attire was not to be light or dazzling,[2] but 'sub fusc'; and whether baiting his hook or watching his float, he must consider himself the exponent of a semi-mystic cult. Was not the first English writer on Angling a nun?[3] Were not four of the twelve apostles fishermen? 'Angling is an art', wrote Izaak Walton, 'and an art worth learning; the question is whether you be capable of learning it.' The personal requirements were exacting, for the true angler must be 'a generall Scholler and well seene in the liberall sciences. He should have sweetness of speech, strength of arguments, knowledge in the Sun, Moone, and Starres. He should be a good

---

[1] R. Franck, *Northern Memoirs* (compiled in 1658, published in 1694), xxiii.   [2] N. Cox, op. cit., iv. 7–12.

[3] Dame Juliana Berners, *The art of fyshynge with an angle*, first printed in 1496 by Wynkyn de Worde. For the question of Juliana's authenticity see an excellent article, s.v. 'Berners' in *D.N.B.*

Knower of countries.'[1] Neither the educational ideals nor the methods of travel in vogue to-day are favourable to the development of such aptitudes, and as civilization advances men become less knowledgeable in streams.

With persons of 'promiscuous quality' ball games were popular. Cornishmen, distinguished for their skill as wrestlers, were noted also for their 'hurling play', which was conducted thus.[2] Having chosen twenty to twenty-five for each side, and having selected suitable objects to serve as goals, one of the players came forward with a leather ball, small and hard, which he tossed into their midst. The player who caught it rushed towards the enemy goal, wrestling with opponents on his way, or throwing the ball to one of his own side. This game was therefore not unlike our modern 'Rugger', but it was possibly even more strenuous, because there were mounted horsemen on the field, whose stirrup a player might seize and be pulled along at a breakneck pace. A church was sometimes used as a goal; sometimes also the teams were very large—as many able-bodied men as the village could produce. Parish played against parish; but the great sporting event of the west was the match between Cornwall and Devon, when the best efforts of the Cornishmen were stimulated by the fact that they were playing against 'foreigners'.

Other pastimes included Archery and Bowls, the former often coupled with Fencing as an essential part of a gentleman's education; while the latter, so far from being considered a sedate game, was then said to cause expenditure of time, money, and curses—'a school of wrangling' was a contemporary's[3] description of a bowling alley, where men, after contorting their bodies into extraordinary shapes, argued themselves hoarse over a hairsbreadth. On the other hand, Billiards was 'a gentle, cleanly and most ingenious game', played with a short, bent cue, raised over the shoulder,[4] and there were few towns of note without a billiard table. Tennis was popularized by the strenuous example of Charles II, who built new courts at Whitehall; there were courts

---

[1] *The Secrets of Angling*, by J. D. Esquire, 1613 (in *Bibliotheca Curiosa*, xxvii. 1886).

[2] There is a contemporary description by J. Ray in his *Memorials* (1846 ed.), 193–4.   [3] *The Compleat Gamester* (1680 ed.), 35.

[4] Ibid., the woodcut illustration.

also at the Gaming House in the Haymarket.[1] In a different category is Cockfighting, which then enjoyed the national pre-eminence since accorded to fox-hunting, the hound among beasts and the cock among birds being considered emblems of English valour; and there was even an attempt to introduce Bull Fighting, but in the agitation which followed the Rye House Plot the scheme lapsed.[2] For Hobby Horses a utilitarian value was claimed by a showman named Wells, who established his 'Academy' in the fields between Leicester Square and Soho. Here was provided entertainment from morning to night; on the artificial horses in perpetual motion a man might learn to ride, to shoot a pistol, to carry a lance, to run at the ring, and, in fact, acquire all the accomplishments taught in the academies of the nobility. The price of admission was one shilling, and there were several sorts of musical instruments 'befitting the subject'.[3]

Outdoor games and fast days benefited national health, but the latter were ceasing to be observed; and, as society developed, increasing resort was made to mineral spas,[4] notably Bath, Epsom, and Tunbridge. Not all the visitors went for their health; for example, at Tunbridge the groves and the feminine fashions were among the attractions:

> The Grove dos cast an advantagious gloome,
> And nothing of their wardrobe's left at home.[5]

The waters of Bath were supposed to be good for the figure, and were patronized by the more prominent ladies of Charles's Court when personal influence was found to fluctuate with physical outline. Epsom waters were laxative. Those who believed in sulphur visited Harrogate, where the water was brought into private rooms by servant girls whose faces 'shone like bacon rine —the sulphurous waters had so fouled their pristine complexion'.[6] Other places, such as Astrop in Northamptonshire, Enstone in Oxfordshire, and Brill in Buckinghamshire, have lost the old

---

[1] J. Marshall, *Annals of Tennis*, 90. [2] *P.C. Reg.* 70, July 25, 1683.
[3] The prospectus is in *Bodley, Wood*, 276 a, cxxxiii.
[4] For a full and interesting account see R. V. Lennard, *Englishmen at rest and play* (1931).
[5] *Add. MS.* 34362, f. 86.
[6] Baskerville, *Journey*, in *H.M.C. Rep., Portland MSS.* ii.

reputation of their waters. At the more fashionable resorts a strange medley congregated, for instance at Tunbridge Wells.

Loretto was scarce haunted with such swarms of pilgrims as our health-restoring places, nor Rome more crowded in a Jubilee than we were. Three families not seldom dwelt in one chamber scarce as big as a taffity tart, and lovingly pigg'd it together. Strangers from remote regions came in guilt coaches. We shall never forget these jolly days, how we have been frequented by the noble and the gay, the fine and the fair, the roaring fopps and the still, sly formal cocks-combs; the swaggerers in buff and the venerable in satin; the flaming lassies and the simpering dames, those that help others and those that help themselves, the witts and the jilts, the fond husbands and the more foolish maintainers, the miserly fathers and the generous sons and the free sporting daughters, the hectoring bullies and the snuffling precisian, the long hair and the over-grown ears, Whigg and Tory, Trimmer and all were every mother's son our constant customers.[1]

The popularity of the Spa helped to change the traditional attitude to cold water; but old prejudices died hard,[2] and the majority of Englishmen maintained a conservative attitude, avoiding complete submersion except in very special circumstances, or when exceptional results might be expected therefrom. Baths and bathing had been sources of immorality in pagan times, and were roundly denounced by the best medieval opinion; accordingly, when consulted on these things, the College of Physicians counselled strict precautions against their abuse.[3] To salt water the objections were even more serious. No one wanted to live by the sea; for its air caused agues, dropsies, rheumatism, and 'consumption', because of 'saline effluvia';[4] nor did normal persons bathe in the sea, though a few pioneers were starting the cult. Since the days of Anglo-Saxon literature the sea had disappeared from the sources of literary inspiration; for it was scarcely known to landsmen, even poets; nor, after Canute, did the sea-shore interest any of our kings until George III, by frequenting Wey-mouth, inaugurated the era of coast resorts. Thus the appeal of the sea, like that of the mountain, is of comparatively modern date.

[1] An exclamation from Tunbridge . . . (1684), in Bodley, Ashmole, F. 5. cix a.
[2] But see R. V. Lennard in op. cit. 73 sqq.
[3] H.M.C. Rep. viii, app. 230, MSS. of the College of Physicians.
[4] C. Leigh, Natural History of Lancashire (1700), 6.

After all, the spa could have been frequented by only a small part of the population, and so a much wider appeal was made by the sale of quack medicines, a trade of venerable antiquity, based on a knowledge not of the human body but of human psychology. The invention of printing, the development of newspapers, the increasing proportion of sedentary occupations, and the use of a more ample and varied diet all helped to foster the business both of the qualified physician and his charlatan rival; and it was in the reign of Charles II that the widely advertised secret remedy established itself as an institution. Advertisements of these concoctions show a sound knowledge of the basic principles of quack publicity. To quote a few examples. The 'Never Failing Cordial' of T. Hinde[1] was 'agreeable to nature'; for its operations were performed 'as nature would have it'. It had cured its inventor, who was now anxious both to share his good fortune with his fellow men, and to warn them against imitations. Suitable for every constitution, the Cordial dispelled gout, stone, gravel, 'melancholy drooping spirits', surfeits, vapours, coughs, colds and wheezings; it could be taken by a child; and the cost was only 3s. per half pint. The advertisement was accompanied by a list of persons (with addresses) who had been cured. A somewhat truculent advertisement was that published by Charles Peter 'the surgeon' from his Bathing House in St. Martin's Lane.[2] Mr. Peter announced that his authority was quite sufficient to guarantee his Cordial Tincture or, indeed, anything else; moreover he had been cured by it, and was influenced only by motives of benevolence. His Tincture was a sovereign remedy for all the usual complaints. 'Take seven or eight spoonfuls as soon as the fit takes you, and if you have not ease in half-an-hour take seven or eight spoonfuls more, and then depend upon it.' This remedy therefore worked by faith and perseverance. It was best combined with a visit to Mr. Peter's bathing establishment, where the patient was advised to prepare for the waters by taking a good dose, followed by another after the bath 'to remove ill effects'.

But these nostrums were insignificant in comparison with the 'True Orvietan' discovered by Cornelius à Tilbury and sold by His Majesty's special licence. Cornelius, a worthy descendant of

---

[1] Advertisement in *Bodley, Wood*, 276 a, xxxiii.
[2] In *Bodley, Ashmole*, 1036, iii.

that Alexander of Abonuteichos immortalized by the satire of Lucian, set a high standard in his profession. According to his own account[1] he swallowed a large dose of poison in the royal presence and then took a dose of his Orvietan, with such satisfactory results that Charles appointed him one of his surgeons-in-ordinary (presumably without salary). Nor was royal patronage the only advantage which Cornelius could boast over his rivals; because his remedy could be used for the diseases of cattle as well as of human beings, and as it stifled poison, so it must stifle disease. The popularity of such remedies disturbed both physicians and apothecaries, who complained in 1670 that 'crowds for the most part follow quacks';[2] but this was not surprising, since medical science was still comparatively undeveloped, the surgeons had not long been separated from the barbers, nor the apothecaries from the grocers. Moreover there were so many rival schools of opinion that the layman was perplexed. Wherever a patient did resort to both physician and apothecary, his death would often be the subject of dispute between these two; but if he survived, he might well provide one more proof of the robustness of the human body.

Quack medicines have here been quoted not as an extraordinary feature in English life, but as a normal one. Another perfectly normal characteristic was speculation. The cautious man would either hoard his savings, or deposit them with the Goldsmiths; or, if he were more venturesome, he might invest in one of the great chartered companies such as the East India Company. He was even invited to lend money to the State, but events did not always show this investment to be a sound one;[3] nor, until the reign of William III, did the government succeed in establishing public confidence in national loans. Meanwhile there were two gambles for the speculator, sharply contrasted in the demand which they made on his patience—the Tontine and the Lottery. The first of these was invented about the middle of the century by an Italian named Tonti, and was on several occasions adopted by the French Treasury as a source of revenue. Briefly, the scheme was as follows. Groups were formed, composed of men or children, the ages within the groups being nearly equal; each member of the group subscribed the same sum, or was credited with a sum sub-

---

[1] *Bodley, Ashmole*, xxii.   [2] Ibid. xxxii.   [3] *Infra*, ii. 442-9.

scribed by a parent or friend; in this way, the State immediately received a sum of ready money. The capital did not have to be paid off until only one survivor of the group remained, when the whole sum, with or without interest, was paid to him, either in a capital sum or in an annuity. So far therefore as the State was concerned, the critical moment was postponed as long as humanly possible; from the point of view of the investor, the critical moment came when he was left competing with only one other rival, by which time the interest of the gamble was likely to have been transferred to his sons or nephews. Tontines for young children were rendered particularly speculative by the high rate of infantile mortality. An optional scheme of tontined annuities was included in the National Debt as organized by Charles Montagu in 1692, but in Charles's reign they were private or civic gambles, one example of the latter being the scheme approved in 1674 by the lord mayor and council of the city of London.[1] In this tontine, subscriptions of not less than £20 were invited, subscribers to be arranged in ranks, according to age; the youngest rank was from 1 month to 7 years, the oldest from 63 to 70. Six per cent. interest was paid, and as members of each rank died off, their shares were transferred to the survivors, until the last survivor took all the stakes. 'What is the hazard of losing £20', asked the author of the prospectus, 'in comparison to the great advantage that may be obtained by survivorship?' By having a plunge in a tontine, family affection, it was alleged, would be strengthened, for relatives would now cherish each other all the more—'in taking the greater care of preserving their mutual healths'. In effect, therefore, a new crime was invented, namely that of keeping alive an aged relative when he ought to be dead. Nor was this all; for if one's own chances in the contest seemed slight, one might make the investment on behalf of a suitable person, preferably one of 'a temperate and sober conversation', likely to prove a winner in the longevity stakes.

The advantage of the lottery was that the gambler did not have to wait so long for the result. A monopoly of lotteries was assigned at the Restoration to the Loyal and Indigent Officers, as a reward for their devotion,[2] but in practice the profits of these speculations

---

[1] *Proposals for subscriptions of money*, 1674, in *Bodley*, G.P. 1119.
[2] *Infra*, 164.

appear to have been captured by enterprising members of
Charles's Court. The government did its best to popularize
lotteries. Secretary Williamson sent repeated requests to the
corporation of Bristol for permission in favour of licensees to
exercise their monopolies at local fairs; in one instance, the civic
authorities, in signifying their assent, insisted on excepting the
Royal Oak lottery which, it was said, 'broke half the cashiers in
Bristol at its last visit'.[1] Pepys attended a lottery in which many
who risked £10 received only a pair of gloves, but their hopes
were stimulated when a more fortunate investor won a suit of
hangings valued at £430, 'or near it'; and a financier insured
about 200 persons against drawing blanks by charging a premium
of 1s. per person.[2] In 1682 the jewels of prince Rupert's estate
were disposed of by a lottery, Francis Child acting as trustee, but
by then the public had become suspicious of these devices for
raising money, and it was not till the reign of William III that
some degree of honesty was introduced into the exercise of this
government monopoly.

A lottery [wrote sir William Petty[3]] is a tax upon unfortunate, self-
conceited fools. . . . Because the world abounds with this kind of fool,
it is not fit that every man that will may cheat every man that would
be cheated, but it is ordained that the Sovereign should have the
guardianship of these fools, or that some favourite should beg the
sovereign's right of taking advantage of such men's folly.

In other words, this means of raising money was part of the
crown's prerogative custody of idiots.

There were other and more genteel methods of speculation.
Most dignified of all, for either sex, was the well-planned marriage;
here the desideratum was generally an estate in an eligible part
of England. One reason why Evelyn disliked the suit of sir
Gilbert Gerrard for his daughter's hand was that most of the
suitor's estate was in coal pits, some of them as far off as Newcastle; moreover, these pits were on lease from the bishop of
Durham, who might grant concurrent leases.[4] So too, the mar-

---

[1] J. Latimer, *Annals of Bristol*, 327. The Royal Oak lottery was said to
be a swindle; see J. Ashton, *History of English lotteries*, 32 sqq.

[2] *Pepys*, July 20, 1664.

[3] Petty, *Treatise of taxes and contributions* (1667), ch. viii.

[4] *Evelyn*, March 1, 1686.

quess of Huntly was not considered a good match for the daughter
of an English peer, because the Scottish marquess had an estate
of only £1,500 per annum, 'all in oats and sheep', and as his house
was in the wilds of Scotland, four days from Edinburgh, the lady
was 'condemned to that sad place for ever, a strange disposing
of a handsome lady'.[1] There was also the practice of securing or
granting a life annuity by private negotiation. The great lord
Halifax did considerable business of this nature, his usual terms[2]
being nine years purchase for a man of 26. One proposal made
to him in 1677 was that of a person aged 47, with a wife of the
same age who offered £1,500 for £200 per annum for their joint
lives; on the death of one, the survivor to receive £100 per annum,
'which is the considerable part of the bargain'. Some members
of the Manners family entertained similar proposals; £1,600 on
a life of 52 for £200 per annum, and £4,000 for £500 per annum
on a life of 56 were among the offers.[3]

This element of speculation predominated in several spheres
from which it is nowadays excluded. It was to be found in most
offices, which were often valued not for their salaries, but for
their perquisites and indirect facilities for making gains; moreover, a government might make money by creating new offices
and selling them, a practice never so common in England as
in France, where it became almost a normal means of raising
revenue. Nevertheless it was not unknown in this country. Thus,
for the sale of coal, Charles appears to have appointed twelve
'coal-meters', who had purchased their places by paying a twelfth
'of the benefit of their coal meting'. In 1663 he appointed three
more, with the consent of the lord mayor and aldermen of the
city of London, to whom he gave his assurance 'on the word of
a king' that no more coal-meters would be created, and that the
salary of those already appointed would be guaranteed by the
revenue from coal, the sale of which was increasing rapidly.[4] In
some of the higher offices, there was an element of purchase and
sale. Thus, outgoing secretaries of state generally required a large
price from their successors; even judges were not above suspicion,

[1] Lady Chaworth to lord Roos, Oct. 19, 1676, in *H.M.C. Rep.* xii, app. v.
30, *MSS. of the Duke of Rutland.*

[2] *Savile Correspondence* (*Camd. Soc.*), 58.

[3] *H.M.C. Rep.* xii, app. v. 23.   [4] *Cal. S.P. Dom., 1663–4,* 79.

and in 1676 there was fastened to the gates of Westminster Hall a sarcastic notice that several judges' places were to be sold, for which tenders from young lawyers were invited.[1] Pepys was told by his master Sandwich that 'it was not the salary of any place that did make a man rich, but the opportunity of getting money when he is in place'.[2] An illustration of this principle is provided in the written contract[3] whereby the diarist secured from Povey a lease of the office of treasurer to the commissioners for Tangier. Of this post the nominal fee was £300 per annum, but from one source and another, including the payments to contractors for building the mole, 'certain consideration hath been and probably will be continued to the treasurer'. Povey was to resign the exercise of this office to Pepys, reserving for himself four-sevenths of these 'rewards or considerations', the other three-sevenths passing to Pepys, who undertook to keep his partner informed of all matters relating to Tangier. The effect of this agreement appears to have been that for all practical purposes Pepys stepped into Povey's shoes, so far as the office was concerned, but was bound to pay to his sleeping partner a portion of the spoils. But in 1672 Povey complained that the diarist had not carried out his part of the bargain; nor did Pepys's 'tedious accounts' satisfy Povey that all the commissions paid by the contractors had been accounted for, and so an acrimonious correspondence followed.

It should be recalled, however, that, especially in the departments of the secretaries of state, many payments were made to officials which to-day would be effected by means of government stamps or fees; hence perquisites were often an essential and legitimate part of a government servant's salary. This fact may have influenced the Commons when (in 1675) they rejected a Bill incapacitating members of parliament from holding office during the sitting of parliament; for it was contended that the proposed measure would change the constitution from a monarchy into a commonwealth, and that the service of the crown would be made incompatible with service in parliament.[4] A similar fate overtook two Bills intended to effect improvement in office-holding; one,

[1] H.M.C. Rep. vii, app. 494.
[2] Quoted in R. G. Albion, Forests and Sea Power, 48.
[3] Rawl. MS. A 172, f. 100.
[4] Parl. Hist. iv. 695–8.

of 1667,[1] would have imposed on holders of offices pertaining to parliament and the courts of justice an oath that they had not given any consideration for their offices; the other, a Bill[2] of 1678, was designed to prevent the lord treasurer, the commissioners of the Treasury, and the lord lieutenant of Ireland from making any undue advantage of their places. These illustrations suggest that an office was then regarded not as a place of trust, but rather as a freehold, capable of a lease or a reversionary interest, and forfeitable only through gross neglect, in the same way as the right to vote, whether for a scholar or fellow of one's college, was often considered a right, for the exercise of which a money payment might sometimes be expected. If modern civilizations have sacrificed many of the theological convictions which pervaded the whole life of the past, they may yet have acquired some compensation in the greater sense of personal responsibility which characterizes the public life of to-day.

The above topics have been cited to prove the comparatively high level achieved by English civilization in the later seventeenth century. That society in the widest sense was habituating itself to the greater amenities available for its use is shown by the rise of a type of literature to be found only when humanity has reached a high degree of sophistication—the literature of deportment. If the courtesies of good society had not been acquired by training in early life, they might now be learnt from books; accordingly there were published a number of manuals (some of them translations from the French) intended either to equip the studious aspirant for the performance of a particular vocation, or to guide his conduct on the thousand-and-one occasions when good breeding can be distinguished from bad. As many of these were written specially for women, they help to illustrate the status assigned to the female sex.

Of the vocational type of guide an example is *The compleat servant maid, or the young maiden's tutor*, of which the fourth edition was published in 1685, a book which showed how highly skilled and responsible were the duties of domestic service when adequately performed. The accomplishments required of the woman who wished to be a waiting gentlewoman to a person of quality

[1] *H.M.C. Rep.* viii, app., pt. i. 112. Sale of Offices Bill, Oct. 23, 1667.
[2] Ibid., *Rep.* xi, app., pt. ii. 119.

were five in number: to dress suitably, to be skilled in the art of
preserving perishables, to write a legible hand, to have skill in
arithmetic, and to carve well. For each of these were provided
explicit instructions, and the successful student of this book must
have been a very superior member of the household; for she had
to be courteous and modest, humble and submissive, sober in
countenance and discourse, able to write in both Roman and
Italian hand, qualified in both addition and 'substraction', a
reader of good books and an attentive listener to sermons; varying
the daily bill of fare by selection from such edibles as turkey,
goose, beef, marrow pie, veal, game, neat's tongue, duck, rabbit,
fried oysters, with the accompaniment, in season, of asparagus,
'sallets', strawberries, and artichokes. In addition to this, she
must know how to disjoint a quarter of lamb, to display a crane,
unbrace a mallard, wing a partridge, disfigure a peacock, thigh
a woodcock, and lift a swan. Few could hope to reach such a level
of accomplishment; but though the book was obviously intended
for the class now known as lady-housekeeper, a ray of hope was
directed to a very different stratum of society—the 'under cook
maids'. These domestics, if they desired preferment, were advised
to watch the cook, so that they might qualify themselves in
cookery, and thus improve their station in life; for, as it was truly
remarked, 'everyone must have a beginning'.[1]

In general, women were advised to content themselves with
their domestic and family duties, virtue and modesty being the
characteristics most befitting their sex; moreover, as there were
no facilities for divorce, a greater demand was sometimes made
on the virtue of resignation. 'Every young lady should be like the
watch in her pocket; if it be not wound up morning and evening,
it is false and unprofitable.'[2] Among the books specially recommended for their reading were Artemidorus's *Interpretation of
Dreams*, Sidney's *Arcadia*, Taylor's *Holy Living and Holy Dying*,
and a lurid old compilation entitled *God's revenge against murther*.
It may be noted that the women of Restoration England were
distinguished more for the latitude of their orthography than of
their reading, but on the other hand their domestic duties were
often more extensive than those of to-day; for these included a

---

[1] *The compleat servant maid* (1685 ed.), 135.
[2] *Youth's behaviour or decencie in conversation* (1661), pt. ii. 133.

knowledge of spicery, the distilling of perfumed waters and cordials, candying and preserving, dairying and spinning; moreover
they were expected to have an elementary skill in surgery and
physic. Some women were credited with 'a strange sagacity as
to the curing of wounds', acquired not by the precepts of books,
but by 'excogitancy'. An example was the wife of William
Houlder, who (when his surgeons had failed) cured Charles's
injured hand by the application of a poultice.[1]

In the guides to deportment, women of honourable descent
were counselled, when in difficulty, to bear in mind their lineage,
and to ask of any proposed course of conduct: 'is this according
to the laws and rules of honour?' or: 'according to the example of
so many excellent ladies from whom I am descended?'[2] Thus the
responsibilities entailed by good birth were wisely insisted upon.
So too, in her relations with the other sex, the lady was adjured
to preserve strict modesty. If a spinster entered into company,
she was to curtsy twice, and, if women were present, she was to
offer her respects in some 'quaint compliment'; but if she were
alone with men, then the initiative fell to the other sex. For such
occasions, models of opening conversations were provided, according to the needs or intentions of the male. If he were a suitor,
he might elect to play a *giuoco piano* game, with such an opening
move as one of these: 'I wish you all joy and prosperity', or 'I am
Your Ladyship's most affectionate servant'; but a more daring
player would choose one of the gambits: 'I am an honourer, I
wish I could say an imitator of your vertues', or the still more
hazardous 'I bless the moment that gives me an opportunity to
enjoy your company'. With a widow, fewer moves were required
'once the ice is broke'.[3] Such manuals, containing also directions
for carving and for the interpretation of dreams, could be obtained
at the shops on London Bridge.

2. SOME CLASSES OF SOCIETY

For the purpose of this section a selection has been made of the
following: prisoner, pauper, vagabond, merchant and tradesman, lawyer, parson, peer, and king.

---

[1] *Aubrey*, i. 405.   [2] *New additions to youth's behaviour*, ch. 33.
[3] These examples are from *Rules of civility or the art of good breeding* (*Bodley,
Wood*, 69).

The prisoner. English prisons have no historian, but glimpses into life in seventeenth-century gaols may be obtained from contemporaries, especially from Quakers who suffered imprisonment. George Fox thus describes the experiences of a convert: In the year 1655 he was committed to Colchester Castle, where he endured great hardships and sufferings, being put by the cruel jailer into a hole in the Castle wall, called the Oven, so high from the ground that he went up to it by a ladder which, being six feet too short, he was obliged to climb from the ladder to the hole by a rope that was fastened above. And when Friends would have given him a cord and basket to draw up his victuals, the inhuman jailer would not suffer them, but forced him to go up and down by that short ladder and rope to fetch his victuals. At length his limbs being much benumbed by lying in that place, yet being constrained to go down and take some victuals, as he came up the ladder again with his victuals in one hand and caught at the rope with the other he missed the rope and fell down from a very great height upon the stones; by which fall he was exceedingly wounded in his head and arms, and he died a short time after.[1]

But not all contemporary references to prison life are quotable. Nor were the prisoners invariably of a hardened type, likely to endure their surroundings with equanimity; for many were prisoners for debt, with no hope of release until the debt was paid, while others were political or religious dissentients. But before the end of the century there was printed one of the earliest pleas for prison reform—*The Cry of the Oppressed*,[2] by Moses Pitt, a book containing a collection of evidence from men who had experienced imprisonment.

The only respect in which the legislature attempted to provide amelioration was in favour of prisoners for debt. In 1670–1 a measure[3] was passed which rehearsed that, by reason of the recent calamities, so many were in prison, and so noisome was their condition that they were likely to spread plague and disease. Accordingly, the statute enacted that justices might summon imprisoned debtors, and tender to each an oath that he was not worth more than £10 in real or personal estate. If the debtor took the oath, then notice was to be served on the creditor to appear at the next Quarter Sessions when, if the truth of his

[1] *Journal of George Fox* (Everyman ed.), 90.

[2] 1691.   [3] 22–3 Car. II, cap. xx.

certificate was uncontested, the prisoner might be released without fee. Alternatively, if the creditor insisted that his debtor should remain in prison, the former was to provide an adequate weekly allowance for the continued maintenance of the latter in gaol. This Act also required that prisoners for debt should be kept separate from felons, because (as the statute rehearsed) in Newgate and elsewhere many distressed gentlemen and tradesmen were kept awake at night by the foul language of felons and the clanking of their chains. Lastly, the Act ordered that investigation should be made into what charitable legacies and bequests were available for imprisoned debtors, a list of which was to be hung up in every gaol. Thus, even to that most impersonal of all historical sources, the Statute Book, there penetrated some hint of what the prison walls concealed.

There was still an element of private ownership in the management of many prisons, some of which were conducted as speculative enterprises. A gaoler might be possessed of the freehold of his premises, and for that reason might try to elude the supervision of the county which, not being a body politic, had no remedy at law; in practice, however, there appears to have been a compromise between the keeper as lessee of the king, and the sheriff as custodian of the county.[1] The keeper had also his regular fees; he might easily make a profit on the food, and he could expect a substantial ransom for each prisoner exported to the plantations. For instance, when a rich Jamaican planter, Christopher Jeaffreson, went to London in 1681 for a supply of convict labour he knew that the supply would be plentiful; but he had to pay 40s. to 50s. to the chief gaoler of Newgate for each of the 300 convicts allowed him, a sum shared with the Recorder of London and the keepers of other prisons from which supplies were obtained.[2] Moreover, there were great differences in gaols and gaolers. Among the latter was one lady of title—Mary, lady Broughton, keeper of the King's Prison of the Gateway in Westminster; so too there was the comparatively comfortable Fleet prison, 'a caravanserai kept by a landlord who was a life tenant',[3]

---

[1] *H.M.C. Rep.* viii, app. 150, Worcester Gaol Bill, in *MSS. of the House of Lords.*

[2] J. C. Jeaffreson, *A young squire of the seventeenth century* (1878), 141.

[3] *The Œconomy of the Fleet* (Camd. Soc. 1879), Introduction.

wherein rooms were shared by only two or three persons, and the women had a department of their own. Accommodation could be had in this prison for twopence per night; there was also a beggars' ward and a dungeon for the refractory; in this penal hostelry life may not have been unlike what was afterwards experienced there by Mr. Pickwick. But the Fleet was exceptional; for elsewhere there were hard usage and intolerable conditions, as well as the exaction of exorbitant fees, this last a frequent subject of complaint from county gaols. In reply to such a petition, the Shropshire magistrates[1] ordered a list of authorized fees to be hung up in the premises.

The pauper. Elizabethan legislation had laid down the foundations of a system of poor relief; important additions were made by the Acts of 1662[2] and 1666–7.[3] By the former of these Acts, the justices were authorized to remove to his place of last settlement any one coming into a tenement worth less than £10 per annum who seemed likely to fall on the rates, place of last settlement being defined as the parish where the immigrant was last domiciled as a servant, apprentice, householder, or sojourner for the space of forty days. This was an old principle, still enforced by the authorities of many corporate towns. In the preamble to the Act it was alleged that, taking advantage of the Poor Law system, people were in the habit of moving from one parish to another where there was the best stock, or the most extensive commons, on which to build cottages; such men, having consumed the stock, moved on to the next parish offering similar advantages, and so a race of sturdy vagabonds was growing up. No evidence has ever been adduced in support of this contention; indeed the preamble to the Act attempted to prove too much; because if vagabonds settled in cottages, that alone was likely to restrain them from roving. Moreover, the Act was specially unjust because, while purporting to inhibit rogues and vagabonds, it really penalized the poorer type of cottager, and so helped to accentuate the problem of poverty. By the same Act, there were created Corporation Workhouses for London and Westminster, governed by a president, deputy, and treasurer; similar institutions were to be established within the weekly bills of mortality in Middlesex and

---

[1] *Shropshire County Records* (ed. Wakeman and Kenyon), 108.
[2] 14 Car. II, cap. xii.   [3] 18–19 Car. II, cap. ix.

Surrey, the officials of which (appointed by the justices) were empowered to apprehend rogues and vagabonds and set them to work. Justices in Quarter Sessions were ordered to report to the Privy Council the names of such rogues as they thought fit to be transported. By-laws could be made by the governing bodies of these institutions and they were permitted to levy a rate. Lastly, this Act of 1662 authorized the payment of a reward of 2s. to any one apprehending a rogue, vagabond, or sturdy beggar, and empowered the churchwardens to seize the chattels of putative fathers or mothers likely to desert their child. This Act was supplemented by that of 1666–7 which, having recited that insufficient stock had been provided for setting the poor to work, required the justices in Quarter Sessions to provide a sufficient stock, and to appoint and pay efficient overseers for the direction of the labour of the poor.

From these Acts it may be seen that the poor law enactments of Charles's reign attempted to amplify the Elizabethan system, which was based on the principle of providing relief for the impotent, work for the able, and punishment for the idle poor. Only in the last of these objects does the law appear to have been effective. For the impotent the State provided no institution, leaving them to the almshouses, or to the charity dispensed by churchwardens or private persons; or they might receive small sums from the overseers of the poor, who often distributed charity in money or kind to the sick and aged. 'To John Unworth in his sickness, 2s.; item, more to his burial, 3s.' is a characteristic entry.[1] If the pauper was not bed-ridden he might apply to a Justice for a licence to beg, but in such instances the distress or disability had to be fairly serious, as in these examples of licensed persons who received grants of from 3d. to 2s. 6d. from the churchwardens— 'a seaman cast away', 'a tonglis [tongueless] man', 'a man that had been in slavery', 'a man, wife and five children undone by an earthquake', 'two women and children burnt out of all they had', 'a man that his leg did rot'.[2] As relieving officers, the churchwardens were sometimes indiscriminate in their charity—generally 6d. to the small fry with their tale of woe and the justice's

[1] *Durham Parish Books* (Surtees Society), 238.

[2] Most of these are examples from the Churchwardens' Accounts of Puddlehinton (Dorset).

licence, a larger sum to the Huguenot refugee or the Protestant ejected from Ireland, and the maximum to the 'decayed gent', whose aristocratic origin was revealed by the linen which he still wore.

The comparative immobility of poorer labour was one of the harshest characteristics of the older system, for a stranger entering a parish was allowed to settle there only if he had four acres to his cottage;[1] he might be driven back to his place of settlement if his premises were of less value than £10 per annum, or if he showed signs of indigence. Moreover, the travelling poor were not seeking for districts where there were higher rates of pay, because the Elizabethan Statute of Artificers, by empowering the justices to regulate these rates, helped to maintain comparative uniformity throughout the country; the itinerant labourer might therefore be seeking not profit, but work. This immobility reacted also on the disabled poor, for there were still many charitable trusts throughout the country, some villages being well endowed, while others knew only the mercy of justices and overseers; in consequence, the intensity of pauperism varied considerably. Nor was there any attempt to consider poverty in relation to unemployment, for the accepted view was that a poor man out of work must be a rogue, unless he could prove the contrary; in consequence, legislation was mainly repressive in character, and in the last resort the only outlets for the unwanted were transportation, the gaol, and the gallows. These evils were intensified by the Anglo-Dutch wars, which not only caused economic dislocation, but turned loose on the country-side many seamen who could not obtain their pay.

Even thus, the legislation might have had some justification if work had been provided for the willing poor, but in this it appears to have failed; for in few parishes at this time was there available a stock of raw material, such as flax or wool, on which the poor could be set to work.[2] Nor did the workhouses always succeed in providing such material. It is true that they supplied a small amount of canvas for the Navy,[3] but the employment was irregular, and in some cases was limited to young paupers. Thus, after

[1] 31 Eliz., cap. vii.
[2] For this subject see E. Leonard, *Early history of English poor relief*, 275–6.
[3] *Cal. Tr. Bks.*, *1667–8*, 47.

the passing of the Act of 1662 a start was made with the erection of a workhouse in London. The initial capital available was £4,445, of which about £4,000 was spent in building a hostel, wherein were housed about 40 youths, between the ages of 7 and 16, fetched from the parish of St. Giles; and, with the curious explanation that it was neither a hospital nor a nursery, the custodians appear to have turned away all persons not within these ages. Its inmates commenced tapestry work for hangings; but this was interrupted by the Plague, when the institution was used as a hospital, and about 150 diseased persons had to be accommodated. The Governors then made a bargain with a doctor to pay him 20s. for each person who recovered, and nothing if he died; on this contractual basis, 56 recovered. When the Plague had subsided, fresh funds were necessary; and so a rate was levied by consent of the justices, producing £675, augmented by a gift of £1,000 from the king and £50 from the archbishop of Canterbury. Later references suggest, however, that all was not well with the workhouse. In 1669 it was rumoured that the funds had been embezzled by one of the officials, who had since gone to the Indies, and the Governors were accused of taking in people from the highways and keeping them prisoners. The sick house, it was alleged, had been converted into an ale-house; and the poor, it was said, were maintained not by the Governors, but by the private charity of London merchants, especially sir Robert Viner.[1]

In this failure of both legislature and parish authorities to cope with the problem of poverty, there was left some initiative for the philanthropists. Among those who attempted to devise schemes for the employment of the poor were sir Matthew Hale and sir Josiah Child;[2] of more practical importance were the activities of a London draper named Thomas Firmin, who in 1665 began to employ the poor on cloth-making. Later he started a linen factory in Little Britain, where 1,700 persons are said to have been kept at work; children as young as three years of age were admitted and taught to read and spin. Firmin conducted this

---

[1] Evidence before the House of Commons, March 16, 1670, in *Grey*, i. 403–5.

[2] For this see B. Kirkman Gray, *History of English Philanthropy*; and S. and B. Webb, *The Old Poor Law*.

enterprise on an economic basis, on the view that the steady and trained employment of the poor was not only philanthropic but profitable,[1] and he left on record an account of his principles. If he had £100 a year to settle on a poor parish, he wrote,[2] he would do it thus: £20 a year to an able and honest woman to teach the poorest children to read, and spin flax and hemp; £5 for the rent of the school; £25 for buying stock; £40 for payment of the children's labour; £8 for wheels and reels; and £2 for an annual dinner to the trustees. For adult mendicants he had no sympathy. In his opinion they were a people who came from the 'suburbs of hell itself'.

The vagabond. In contrast with the depressing subjects of gaol life and pauperism, roguery and vagabondage have a rich litera-ture of their own,[3] for already the picaresque novel of Spain was finding imitators in England, and the rogue, long known to the legislator, the constable, and the justice, was now coming to interest the man-of-letters. The age-long contest between wit and circumstance, between the plausible, cunning vagabond and the stolid mass of respectable and stationary society has never been without a certain fascination; it reflects itself in the popular-ity of the 'crook' and detective story of to-day, as in the seven-teenth century it inspired descriptions of the travels and cheats of draw-latches and sneak-thieves. These heroes of adventure were members of a separate civilization, having its social divi-sions, its distinctive language, and its code of honour; contrasted with them were the 'honest and painfull' pedlars and chapmen, for the licensing of whom James I had created an office. This was granted to Killigrew and other patentees, who derived some profit from the fees.[4]

There were several types of rogue. The 'upright man' was the elected head of a pack, sometimes equipped with a truncheon; the 'ruffler' was one who, pretending to be an old maimed soldier, sought out former royalist commanders and claimed to have served under them; the 'anglers' went about with a rod, having

---

[1] S. and B. Webb, op. cit. 106; and T. Firmin, *Some proposals for employing the poor* (1681).   [2] Firmin, op. cit. 9.

[3] For a good bibliography see F. W. Chandler, *The literature of roguery*; also C. J. Ribton Turner, *History of vagrants and vagrancy*.

[4] *P.C. Reg.* 65, March 22, 1676.

a hook at the end, which they inserted into open windows at night on the chance of a catch; the 'priggers of prancers' were horse-thieves, who carried a small pad saddle and bridle for any chance mount. They could change the colour of a horse's coat, and by adding an artificial star to its forehead they made identification more difficult. 'Polliards' and 'clapperdogeons' used children, either their own or borrowed ones, in order to stir the sympathy of the charitable; 'fraters' were men who, by a forged patent, collected money for a hospital; 'Abram men' or 'Tom o' Bed-lams' added ribbons or fox's tails to their clothing and pilfered under the guise of madness; the 'Whip Jack' was the counterfeit mariner who went about with his 'mort' or woman-companion, whom he claimed to have saved from shipwreck; 'dommerars' were men who pretended to be dumb; 'kynchen coves' were orphans who had taken to the highways; 'strowling morts' were pretended widows, generally working with a ruffler hidden in the background; the 'quire birds' were those who had sung in Newgate or Bridewell and had escaped the gallows. Lastly, the 'patricio', or strollers' priest, 'married' couples over a dead horse; the man and his 'mort' shook hands over the carcass and were thereupon pronounced man and wife.[1]

In the freemasonry of the road there was a distinctive language from which colloquial English has not disdained to borrow: thus, a 'toppin cove' was a hangman, 'fencing cully', a receiver, 'rum mort' meant curious wench, 'to tip' was to give. A picturesque vocabulary was therefore at the disposal of rogue literature, which was based mainly on the antithesis between the happy-go-lucky stroller and his grim destiny in the background, an antithesis prompting such a lament as this, that of a wench who had lost her rogue to the hangman.

> Now my little rogue is gone,
> By the highways begs there none
> In body both for length and bone,
> Like my clapperdogeon.
>
> Dumb and madman thou could'st play,
> Or a drivelling fool all day,
> And like a poor man thou could'st pray,
> Yet scaped with passes sealed away.

[1] R. Head, *The Canting Academy* (1673), 58 sqq.

When the evening hath been wet,
For fire the hedges down did'st beat,
Me then with stolen duck did'st treat,
Or else a fat goose was our meat.

Mallards then I could not lack,
Bacon hung always at my back,
Nor corn wanted in my sack,
With good milk pottage I held tack.

To thy dog and dish adieu,
Thy staff and pass I ne'er must view,
Though thy cloak was far from new,
In it my rogue to me was true.[1]

The merchant and tradesman. It might seem strange to associate these two, and still more strange to place them in such close proximity to the vagabond. But the categories of to-day do not always coincide with those of the seventeenth century; for human occupations were not then so highly specialized, and one man might engage in several occupations now carefully kept apart. Thus, a man would manufacture fustians or woollens and carry them round the country as a chapman, in which last capacity he might have to prove to the constables or justices that he was not a rogue; so too he might serve an apprenticeship as a goldsmith, and combine efficiency in this craft with the lending of money on pledges, and thus become a banker. Now that commercial travellers are employed, neither merchant nor manufacturer need be itinerant; just as with the establishment of banks, pawnbrokers are no longer the sole money-lenders. The first class, that of the chapman-merchant-manufacturer, includes such honoured names as that of Humphrey Chetham (1580–1653), the great benefactor of Manchester; the second class, that of the men who were first goldsmiths, then pawnbrokers, and finally bankers, is well represented by sir Francis Child the elder (1642–1713), whose ledgers demonstrate this process of evolution. Hence there was still some association between pedlar and manufacturer, between craftsman and merchant; but after 1660 a greater measure of specialization may be traced.

This increasing differentiation can be seen in the history of

[1] R. Head, op. cit. 16. The above is Head's translation from the original.

the great City Companies of London.[1] As chartered institutions these Companies had to endure the assaults levelled at their franchises by the Corporation Act of 1661 and by writs of *quo warranto*;[2] some of them became impoverished, but most of them continued their charitable and educational work, maintaining almshouses and schools throughout the country, and combining these benevolent activities with solicitude for the welfare of their craft. Already also they had acquired exalted connexions; for many noble families traced their origin to a Draper, a Tailor, or a Haberdasher, and even kings had not disdained to be made free of their mysteries; for example, Queen Elizabeth was a Mercer, and Charles II had this much in common with William III that he was a Grocer. These facts make terminology somewhat difficult. When it is added that, later in the reign, the Companies exercised political influence, it will be seen that they were becoming corporations of merchants and capitalists, conscious of the prerogatives attached to wealth and civic status. Their liverymen had mostly begun life as craftsmen or tradesmen; they were ending it as city magnates. It was here that money exercised a direct influence, without the intervening medium of land. The three Anglo-Dutch wars of the seventeenth century emphasized these potentialities of wealth; since the government, having no facilities for credit, was obliged to resort to the man who could provision the fleet from his own funds, or supply ready money on the security of the taxes; hence the increased opportunities for the capitalist-victualler and the goldsmith money-lender. Examples of the first class include William Penn the younger (1644–1718), founder of Pennsylvania; Thomas Papillon (1623–1702), descendant of a French family (a Mercer), and a burgess for Dover; sir Josiah Child (1630–99), a governor of the East India Company, whose fortune was estimated at £200,000; and William Kiffen, a cloth merchant and baptist minister, who refused to accept James's Indulgence in 1687. Of the second class the most distinguished representative was sir R. Viner (1631–88), goldsmith, lord mayor, and banker to Charles II.

Many of the great merchants were Nonconformists; some, like Papillon and Dubois, were Huguenots; the majority of them

[1] For these see W. Herbert, *History of the great livery companies.*
[2] *Infra*, ii. 517–19, 634–6.

provided a substantial backing for the whig party, and by the Revolution of 1689 they had become an estate of the realm which no government could afford to ignore. Probity, thrift, and Protestantism were the qualities which served to contrast them with the men whom the later Stuarts delighted to honour, a contrast which had some influence on the early history of party politics. Charles II, who sometimes accepted their hospitality, succeeded in suppressing their political aspirations; but they proved eventually to be stronger than the Stuarts themselves. Nevertheless, these facts should not obscure the jurisdiction which the City Companies still exercised on the craftsmen within the bounds of the city. They limited the number of apprentices that might be taken by wardens, liverymen, and masters; disposed of apprentices on the death of their master, and prescribed the conduct of the apprentice on Sundays and holy days. Fines were imposed on the idle and the recalcitrant.[1] Over workmanship there was a similar supervision. Thus the master, wardens, and assistants of the Paviors' Company were authorized to conduct a 'search and view' of pavior work;[2] the Company of Pewterers enforced the rule that 'turn wheels' or unskilled labourers should not be initiated into the practice of the craft, but only journeymen and apprentices; a freeman might be fined because of the bad quality of his spoons,[3] or because his standishes were not of the required degree of fineness.[4] The Companies still maintained close contact with the practice of their craft or trade.

But in this respect it is noticeable that an increasing number of journeymen left London after they had served their indentures; possibly because they could not pay the fees for admission to the livery of a Company, or perhaps because in the country they had more opportunity or more freedom. This migration may have helped to restrict somewhat the scope of the Companies' prerogatives, or to emphasize their social and benevolent character. Parallel with this was the process whereby, in many crafts, there was evolved a sharper contrast between the capitalist manu-

---

[1] For examples of this disciplinary control see *Records of the Worshipful Company of Carpenters* (ed. B. Marsh), i, Apprentices' Entry Books, 1654–94.

[2] C. Welch, *History of the Worshipful Company of Paviors*, 51.

[3] C. Welch, *History of the Worshipful Company of Pewterers*, ii. 145.

[4] Ibid. 134.

facturer and the workman without capital, to the exclusion of the small master. This may be seen from the Clothworkers' organization, where the original line of cleavage was between the mercantile and the industrial interest, between the merchant-exporter on the one hand and the employer and worker on the other; after the Restoration the latter class, composed mainly of small masters, was being displaced by the larger employer and the journeyman; and in this way the interests of capital and labour were brought into clearer definition. Before the end of the century there is even evidence of combination among journeymen.[1] This specialization of capital helped further to produce differentiation; for the Feltmakers separated themselves from the Haberdashers, the Clothiers from the Drapers, and the Printers from the Stationers; and so an increasing number of workers were severed from the capitalist and benevolent institutions of which they had once formed an essential part. Hence it is possible to trace in the later seventeenth century an increasing distinction between the merchant and the craftsman or tradesman. The first was realizing new opportunities for money; the second was nominally bound by the regulations of Company or Gild, though these were becoming more difficult to enforce.

There was also the control exercised by the State. Tradesmen and craftsmen were still subject to the Elizabethan Statute of Artificers (1563), which enacted the statutory periods of apprenticeship, and empowered the justices to declare rates of wages; but this latter restriction appears to have been maintained only for the agricultural worker. For each occupation there were statutory regulations. A baker could not sell his bread of less weight than the due assize, that is, in proportion to the price of corn in the market; moreover he had to put his proper mark on the bread, and could not sell more than thirteen to the dozen. The miller had to regulate his toll for grinding corn according to the strength of the water driving his mill; the vintner had to import his wine in casks of the regulation size and sell it according to the Chancery price list; tanners were limited in the choice of the substances they might use for raising hides, and must have their leather examined and sealed before sale; the

[1] For this see G. Unwin, *Industrial organisation in the XVIth and XVIIth centuries*, ch. viii.

shoemaker could not mix his leathers; the cooper must use only barrels of the prescribed size. 'Beaver makers are to make beaver hats and the felt makers felt hats; there is to be no mixing'; such was the spirit of regulation in an age when almost every human activity was subject to minute control. But these rules had been most effectively enforced only under the early Stuarts, and though they survived both Commonwealth and Restoration they were gradually being replaced by a more elastic order of things; indeed, before the end of Charles's reign the principles of economic individualism were beginning to be enunciated.[1]

The lawyer. A similar process of specialization may be seen in the development of the modern professions, which became more clearly differentiated in proportion as the old ecclesiastical immunities were destroyed. This process was commenced by the Tudor legislatures and was continued by the early Stuarts. Highwaymen[2] and pirates[3] were the first to lose their benefit of clergy, and were thus obliged to recognize the purely secular character of their activities. So too with the other occupations. As the beaver merchant must stick to beaver, and the felt merchant to felt, so the surgeon must no longer practice barbery nor the barber surgery;[4] nor might the pawnbroker disguise his usury by calling himself a broker, as if his were an honest or lawful trade, whereas he was really no broker but a mere 'friperer'.[5] In this legislative rearrangement of men there were some inequalities; for, while the cook appears to have lost his medieval pre-eminence, the physicians suddenly leaped into high status by their incorporation into a royal college, and by the rule that aspirants for the medical profession must first satisfy the bishop of London, who, for examination purposes, was assisted by a panel of experts.[6] The clergy themselves became professional by this legislation, because their pluralities were cut down,[7] they were forbidden to exercise a trade[8] or to keep a tavern,[9] and they had to be resident. It was decreed also that bakers, brewers, surgeons, and scriveners were no longer to be accounted handicraftsmen, as their calling was a superior one.[10]

---

[1] *Infra*, 225–6. [2] 23 Hen. VIII, cap. i. [3] 27 Hen. VIII, cap. iv.
[4] 32 Hen. VIII, cap. xlii.   [5] 2 Jac. I, cap. xxi.
[6] 3 Hen. VIII, cap. xi.   [7] 21 Hen. VIII, cap. xiii.
[8] Ibid.   [9] Ibid.   [10] 22 Hen. VIII, cap. xiii.

The lawyers were the strongest and oldest of the secular and learned professions. As in no other country, the common lawyers were a national institution; their jurisprudence was the one thing which had survived unscathed the upheavals of Renaissance and Reformation, thereby giving fresh colour to their claim that English common-law traditions stretched back to the mists of Saxon antiquity, a tradition zealously fostered by centuries of insular practice and experience. Moreover their system might claim to be national, because it was studied not in cosmopolitan universities, such as medieval Oxford and Cambridge, nor in foreign cities, such as Pavia or Bologna, but in the heart of London, at the Inns of Court, where congregated the younger sons of many of the best families for exercise in what Maynard called the *Ars Bablativa*, and for initiation into the pleasures of the metropolis and the gossip of the courts. It was a momentous change when such men were tempted to seek the suffrage of the boroughs and introduce themselves into politics; for they possessed, as did no other body, ambition, social influence, determination, collective cohesion, and individual pertinacity. Legal training qualified them to be both critical and remorseless in debate. They were pedantic, but on the other hand they were never academic, and so were not debarred from an active part in public life. Their jurisprudence, in which were combined medieval methods of pleading with accumulations of statute and custom, still contrived to serve the needs of English society. Leaving wills and divorce to the Church, and wreck and salvage to the Admiralty; they shed their barbarous French, but retained a sufficient number of technicalities and obscurities to baffle the unqualified, and to provide a profitable as well as honourable career for the man of acute mind and ready tongue.

Francis North, lord Guilford, may be cited as a specially favourable product of the system. The third son of Dudley, lord North, he was admitted a fellow commoner of St. John's College, Cambridge, in 1653, and two years later moved into 'a moiety of a petit chamber' at the Middle Temple. There he engaged in liberal studies, application to the law, indoor and outdoor games, with unlimited social intercourse of a kind likely to aid him in his profession. In vacation, he took boxes of books with him into the country, his favourite reading being the Year Books, which,

he held, combined instruction with diversion. At noon and night
in the common hall of the Middle Temple he took part in debates,
and became noted as an admirable 'put case'; this readiness in
argument was sharpened by frequent moots. He digested all he
read into commonplace books, and developed a lawyerly love for
the abridgement; his vast reading and much of his observation
were therefore summarized and indexed for immediate use.
Visits to family estates enabled him to go 'court keeping', that
is, presiding in manorial courts, where his skill in reasoning the
'homage' into paying fines for essoigns[1] and other technicalities
won the admiration of the family steward. This gave him some
knowledge of 'the humours and subtleties' of country people.
As a student he frequented the Common Pleas, where 'all the
suits were drawn forth upon the ancient and genuine process of
the Common Law', in preference to the King's Bench, where
'more news than law is stirring'.[2] From every flower he gathered
honey and he kept on good terms with the 'cocks of the circuit';
then he was assisted by sir Geoffrey Palmer, attorney-general, and
eventually attained to the office of lord keeper. His success he
owed to aptitude, application, and social influence; also to his
subservience to the prerogative. High personal qualities can be
traced also in the careers of sergeant Maynard and chief justice
Hale; but these men were notably honourable examples of their
class, for it was under the later Stuarts that the English Bench
reached its lowest depths.

More is heard of the attorneys and solicitors. In 1683 a complete guide for their use was published, the reader being assured
that no one need despair of becoming a solicitor 'whom God and
Nature have blest with a competence of wit, memory, and judgement, and inclinations and industry suitable to the profession'.[3]
Neither Stuart legislators nor Puritan reformers had any doubt
regarding the inclinations and industry of these men; for so
numerous were the misdemeanours of the dishonest among their
ranks, that a statute of James I attempted a drastic weeding-out
by confining the profession to 'those who have been found by
their dealings to be of skilful and honest disposition'.[4] Equally
ineffective were the later attempts to diminish the opportunities

---

[1] Excuses for absence from court.   [2] *Lives of the Norths*, i. 28.
[3] *The Compleat Solliciter* (1683).   [4] 3 Jac. I, cap. vii.

of the attorneys, and in 1673 Chief Justice Vaughan told a committee of the Commons that complaints were rare because they 'are terrible upon the people'.[1] The truth is that as society developed, and sin became more variegated, the business of the speculative lawyer increased, and when life in the capital became more hectic it may have become more colourful:

> These are the busie days when the Green Bag
> At Westminster about the Hall doth wag;
> The effects whereof (Brethren and Friends) are double,
> The lawyers get the coin, clients the trouble.[2]

The same iridescent quality is revealed in a contemporary biography of a 'cheating solliciter' named Richard Farr, who probably stood to his brother practitioners in the same relationship as did Bunyan's Mr. Badman to his fellow tradesman, that is, a synthesis of all the sins possible in one occupation.

And now if any wrangling, controversy, law-suit or business of difficulty arose among the neighbourhood, who but Mr. Farr for a Solliciter? If, as the livelihood of that end of the town [Long Acre] depends much on lodgings, any person, having taken a large house wanted hangings and other furniture, who but Mr. Farr for a Broker? If any wanted a sum of money on good security, who but Mr. Farr for a Procurer? Now did he appear in his plush coat, and sometimes with his pantaloons and muff; now had he his variety of shapes and apparel suitable to the designs he intended. Now did his friends court him and his enemies stand in awe of him.

Mr. Farr was stated to have forged title-deeds, received stolen goods, and sold 'bottle ale'. He was at last hanged for burglary. As a bird of prey he had lived; as a bird of plumage he died, dressed in a purple gown and a vermilion waistcoat, having left 20s. for a sermon on the text *Blessed are the dead which die in the Lord*, afterwards amended by the chaplain to the more appropriate *Except ye repent ye shall all likewise perish*.[3]

The parson. 'The two plagues of the nation', wrote the Fifth-Monarchy man, John Rogers,[4] 'rose up from the bottomless pit

[1] *H.M.C. Rep.* ix, app., pt. ii. 20. *MSS. of the House of Lords.*
[2] *A yea and nay almanac*, in *Bodley, Douce*, A 581.
[3] *The cheating solliciter cheated* (1665), in *Bodley, Wood*, 372.
[4] Quoted in E. Rogers, *Life and Opinions of a Fifth-Monarchy Man* (1867).

and are the priests and the lawyers.' This adequately summarizes
a view, widely held in the seventeenth century, regarding the
origin of these professions. The parson, generally the product of
one of the two universities, was as distinctively professional as the
lawyer, and expounded a theology which, in virtue at least of its
compromises, might claim to be characteristically English.

As a career, the Church was not lucrative. Then, as now, its
wealth was unevenly distributed, ranging from the well-endowed
bishopric of Durham, with the revenues of its palatine jurisdiction and profitable leases of coal pits, to comparatively poor
bishoprics like Hereford and Exeter. There was the same disparity in the livings, because the value of the tithe varied from
parish to parish; and this, together with fees and offerings, was
the source of the parson's income. Tithe was regulated by a
heterogeneous body of rules and customs, and was levied on corn,
on timber (when cut and sold), and on pigs; beasts of the plough
were exempt, but if oxen were fattened on grass, tithe might be
levied on the herbage. Milk was tithed—on every tenth day, but
not throughout the year; so also wool, on 'Shear Day'. If a
parishioner had ten lambs, he paid one to the Rector; if nine, he
paid one and received in return a halfpenny, and so in proportion. Three eggs were exacted for each cock and drake, and for
each hen[1] and duck. So even the cocks and hens were not without
their historical importance, and the stipends of the established
ministers of religion might fluctuate with the volume of crowings
from the farm-yards. This dependence on agriculture helped to
forge the links uniting squire and parson in the dyarchy of the
country-side, a union strengthened by the contrast between the
poverty of the average living and the comfort enjoyed by many
merchants and tradesmen in the towns; for a rector was fortunate
if his living was worth as much as £40 a year; and the stipends of
Oxford and Cambridge dons (also derived from agricultural endowments) seldom exceeded £10, unless supplemented by chap-
laincies or lectureships. In consequence, even the poorest of
college benefices were eagerly sought after, and vacancies were
the occasion of expert negotiation. Preferment was solicited by
methods more direct than those of to-day; and in 1681 Charles
had to signify his pleasure that applications should be sent not

[1] *English Reports*, xxi (Chancery) 1107–8 and xxii. 617–21.

to him, but to the archbishop of Canterbury and the bishop of London.[1]

Of the social status of the Church at this time, it is more difficult to generalize. The ecclesiastical life does not appear to have attracted a high proportion of men from old or distinguished families, nor did the limitations of parochial life make easy of attainment a high standard of either culture or social well-being on the part of those who had found in the Church an avenue towards an improved status. Exceptions, such as Compton, bishop of London, are so often insisted on that they help to confirm faith in the older generalization, that the social position of the later Caroline clergy was considered low by contemporaries.

But neither pedantry nor undistinguished origin prevented the clergy from playing a part of unique importance and value in the evolution of English society. Then, as now, much of the best pastoral work was done by men of whom least was heard. The black-sheep and the sycophants were notorious, but they were easily outnumbered by the men who, in poverty and obscurity, maintained at least a glimmer of spirituality in a country-side almost completely insulated from the outside world. Parson and parish church often stood out above the sordid acrimonies of the old English village as emblems, at least, of more permanent things. Nor was this all. More perhaps than any other class, the clergy were the fathers of men who achieved eminence in every field of public activity and intellectual pursuit; for, like the younger members of many county families, the sons of the rectory and the manse had to go far afield for a career, achieving their ambition in naval or military service, or in the secular professions, or in exploration, or in the administration of the colonies and dependencies, and so providing a select body of men, mostly endowed with the advantages of frugal home-training, good education, social eligibility rather than social position, and the incentive of comparative poverty. Both England and Scotland have been rich in this type. One illustration was provided as early as the reign of Charles II. In 1678 the king issued a patent for the erection of a corporation to grant relief to poor widows and children of clergy. Of the governors of this corporation, all sons of clergy, there were two bishops (Rochester and Carlisle), a judge (sir

[1] Cal. S.P. Dom., 1680–1, 187.

Wm. Dolben), a notable parliamentarian (sir T. Meres), a secretary of state (sir Joseph Williamson), and sir Christopher Wren.[1]

The peer. As the parson was the expounder of divine purpose
revealed to man in the Creation, so the peer was the living embodiment of that purpose; for as God only can make an heir, the
existence of a landed aristocracy was obviously a proof of intelligent design in the shaping of the universe. This view was voiced
by Anglican and Presbyterian alike. 'Peers of noble birth and
education', wrote Prynne, 'are more generous, heroic spirits, and
not so apt to be overawed by regal threats, nor seduced with
inward and private ends from the public good,'[2] a view identical
with that expounded as early as 1621 by Peacham in his classic
The Compleat Gentleman, where he affirmed that there are 'certain
sparks and secret seeds of virtue' innate in the progeny of noble
personages, 'from which grows fruit more early and more vigorous than that which the industry of the vulgar can produce'.
Personally and collectively the peers had remarkable attributes,
but contact with exalted personages caused Pepys to note (with
surprise) that they were just like ordinary mortals.[3]

As lords of parliament the peers represented themselves; it was
therefore a matter of national expediency that they should be
supported in their estates, for only if backed by landed influence
could they fulfil their allotted place in the constitution. With
some justice, Shaftesbury claimed that the English peerage was
the only alternative to a standing army,[4] because, in the absence
of this hereditary bulwark, the crown would be at the mercy of
factions, and without an army would quickly fall into a republic.
This national necessity for their well-being entailed a number of
important privileges. The last act of the Long Parliament of the
Civil War was a declaration asserting that the rights of the lords
should be safeguarded; throughout the reign of Charles II these
rights were frequently affirmed, and in some cases extended.[5]
Their houses could not be searched for arms except by special
warrant from the king;[6] peers in hereditary offices were not

---

[1] In *Bodley, Wood*, 276 a, 38.
[2] Prynne, *A Plea for the Lords* (1648).   [3] *Pepys,* July 26, 1665.
[4] Speech of Nov. 20, 1675, in *Parl. Hist.* iv. 796.
[5] For their distinctive privileges as Lords of Parliament see *infra*, ii. 463–6.
[6] 14 Car. II, cap. iii.

obliged to take the oath against transubstantiation imposed in 1673;[1] they could not be imprisoned by attachment out of Chancery;[2] they could not be committed for misdemeanours.[3] As a witness, the peer gave evidence not on his oath, but on his honour, because all peers are of 'known integrity';[4] at common law any one slandering a peer could be punished by the pillory and loss of his ears.[5] When indicted of a criminal offence, he might put himself on his peerage, that is, claim the right to be tried by his peers acting as a jury under the presidency of a Lord High Steward; and, if convicted, he might claim benefit of clergy, even if he could not read. If he were convicted a second time, he could not again plead clergy, but as one of the king's hereditary advisers he might hope for a special exercise of the royal clemency in his favour. In effect, therefore, there was a reasonable chance that, after two murders, he would remain unhanged.

Few law suits could be contested by a commoner with a peer on equal terms. Thus, in 1667 one Carr, clerk to a troop of Life Guards, refused to pay to his commanding officer, lord Gerard of Brandon, £2,000 a year in excess of what was due to him. For this, lord Gerard threatened to kill Carr, and assaulted his wife and children. Carr petitioned the House of Commons 'to consider his lot, which may be that of any commoner under a great lord'. When the Lords were informed that such a petition had been presented to the Commons, they summoned Carr to their chamber, ordered him to be fined £1,000, to be set in the stocks, and imprisoned in the Fleet; and his petition was given to the hangman for public burning.[6] It is noteworthy of this instance that, though Carr had brought his petition to the Commons, they did not dare to interfere in a matter concerning the personal privilege of a peer. This lord Gerard was in later life one of the Monmouth conspirators, and is said to have advised his tool to murder the duke of York. In 1676, in a drunken frolic, his son killed a foot-boy in St. James's Park, but no proceedings were taken. Father and son were buried in Westminster Abbey. A more extreme instance was that of the seventh earl of Pembroke.

---

[1] 25 Car. II, cap. ii.   [2] *L.J.* xii. 122, Oct. 22, 1667.
[3] Sir R. Sawyer in the Seven Bishops' Case.   [4] *Grey*, ii. 447.
[5] *Modern Reports*, ii. 162; see also *infra*, ii. 465.
[6] *H.M.C. Rep.* viii. *MSS. of the House of Lords*, 115, Dec. 16, 1667.

In 1678 he was found guilty of manslaughter by the court of the Lord High Steward, but on pleading benefit of clergy, he was discharged. In 1681 he was again indicted for manslaughter, but some of his fellow peers presented a petition on his behalf, with successful results. These are the only recorded instances where he was brought to trial for his assaults, but in the coffee-houses he was credited with no less than twenty-six homicides.[1]

Considering the great extent of their legal immunities, and the character of the life at the Court of Charles II, it is surprising that so few peers committed manslaughter; indeed the record of the English peerage compares very favourably in this respect with that of other countries. Pembroke and the Gerards must not be taken as typical examples, but as extreme instances of how far a vicious man might press the privileges incident to his rank. About the personnel of the Restoration peerage it is impossible to generalize, for heredity appears to have created the same diversity to be found in any miscellaneous body of men. Thus the Cecil and Percy families were not producing their best scions, nor were any of the Howards distinguished for either character or ability; on the other hand both prince Rupert and the duke of Buckingham were possessed of brilliant endowments, though they squandered them. One of the greatest names in the history of science is that of Robert Boyle, son of the first earl of Cork; in politics, Shaftesbury was one of the most dynamic of forces in English history, while Ormonde and his son Ossory were preeminent in their integrity and high sense of honour. But it was of particular importance that the English peerage never became a caste. Many of the eldest sons of peers sat in the Commons, a practice which strengthened the power and prestige of the Lower House; younger sons sometimes went into trade, the great chartered companies providing good opportunity for both adventure and profit. Except in their freedom from arrest for misdemeanours,[2] the children of peers were not distinguishable in law from commoners; moreover, by marriage and social intercourse

[1] *Impartial account of the misfortune that lately happened to the Rt. Hon. the earl of Pembroke* (1679).

[2] Report of the committee to consider privileges of peers, Feb. 11, 1674, in *L.J.* xii. 633.

they mingled more freely with their social inferiors than did the high-born children of continental countries.

The king. Charles II brought English kingship to its highest point of power, almost immediately before the application of devices intended to make it fool-proof. In comparison, the prerogative wielded by the Tudors was simpler, as it had fewer religious sanctions, and Englishmen were then less critical; Charles, on the other hand, came to England on the crest of a great wave which, sweeping away every vestige of republicanism or political experiment, revealed the divinely-planned foundations on which the earlier Stuarts had attempted to construct their power. It was the industrious and conscientious James who, in record time, succeeded in destroying these foundations, thus eliminating the religious element altogether, and bequeathing to parliament such effective control over a limited and safeguarded kingship that opportunities for royal genius or even individuality became thenceforth more rare. This is the central point of interest in the history of England between the Restoration and the Revolution; for in these years one king demonstrated how long he could retain control of a delicately-adjusted but dangerous mechanism, while his brother showed in how short a time he could be destroyed by it.

Religion and mythology, law and tradition had each contributed to the building of the wonderful edifice into which Charles stepped on May 25, 1660. The crown was thought of, not as an office having definitely allotted powers, but as constituting in itself the life-blood of the State. The king was not a functionary at the head of a pyramid, but was himself the stone and mortar of the structure, clearly discernible on every side of it, filling minute crannies and cracks scarcely discernible by the human eye, and holding the edifice together by that supernatural power derived from unction and consecration. He was the source of life in the State, for every legitimate enterprise had ultimately its origin and sanction in him. As fountain of honour, he made peers, who are perpetual legislators; by his charters he enfranchised boroughs, and these appointed temporary legislators; as wielder of the power formerly exercised by the pope, he created bishops and they priests; he made sheriffs and they juries; he appointed judges *durante bene placito* to administer his laws in his courts of justice, and lords lieutenant to transmit his orders to his Militia. His Navy he directed through his lord high admiral. He declared war and made peace; he could do no wrong, though his ministers might. He might plead and demur, that is, argue on both fact and law; he could choose his action, and sue in whatever court he might elect; he could make a lease to commence from a date passed; he had a right to unclaimed property; nonuser could never be pleaded against him, for *nullum tempus occurrit regi*. He could invade any man's freehold to search for saltpetre; the earth yielded to him a portion of its precious metals; the sea washed up treasure for his use, and in receding left land of which he claimed a part. He alone could profit, without effort, from the wrongdoing, the folly, and the superstition of his fellow men —from their wrongdoing, as when he received a portion of the fine or forfeiture attached to the infringement of a statute; from their folly, in his monopoly of lotteries; from their superstition, in his right to confiscate all lands and rents bequeathed for the maintenance of an anniversary or obit to help to save the soul of a donor from purgatory. The extent of his privilege was the measure of the subject's obligation, and he was the one exception in reference to which the normality of other men could be both measured and enforced.

Secular vocabulary provides a poor medium for a description of these powers. As God's lieutenant on earth the king was a priest, and so must not give reasons for what he said or did. He was the centre from which radiated zones of good and evil; for through his hands he transmitted the healing power;[1] but alike in the fire of his displeasure and the frost of his indifference there was death. He must not be cursed in public or private; his power of pardon was unlimited; even in the presence of death he was an exception; for as it was treason to think of his death, so nothing might be spoken or written wherein his decease was expressed or implied. It was for him to declare when men shall mourn and when they shall rejoice, for he had taken upon himself the person of the state; in Hobbes's imagery he was the mighty leviathan, in

---

[1] For a contemporary work on the healing power see J. Browne, *Charisma Basilicon* (1684); the best modern account is R. Crawford, *The King's Evil*. For the subject generally see Frazer, *The Golden Bough*, i, and M. Bloch, *Les Rois Thaumaturges*.

whose belly cowered his subjects, as did Jonah, sharing whether they would or not in all the movements of the whale, risking the possible dangers of digestion in order to avoid the certain death which lay in the waters outside; as mere passengers unjustified in offering even a suggestion regarding the navigation, but, as intimate parts of the monster's anatomy, incurring in the eyes of the outside world a corporate responsibility, not to be evaded, for the gyrations, however eccentric, of the organism into which they were merged.

But there was an anti-climax; for Charles II was the only man in his kingdoms obliged to beg in public for an increase of his inadequate salary.

3. THE RESTORATION AS SEEN BY SOME CONTEMPORARIES

Such, in brief, were some of the social characteristics of the people over whom Charles was to rule. At this point it might well be asked whether the Restoration elicited any expression of opinion in regard to the possibilities suddenly opened up by this momentous event in national history. What hopes for the future of English civilization were raised by the peaceful but drastic change from republicanism to monarchy? For the surviving regicides there was the prospect of punishment; for all who had not kept pace with events there was a chance of disqualification or ostracism; for the returning exiles there were hopes of office or reward; for the majority of men the Restoration appears to have brought a sense of rejoicing and expectation. 'I stood in the Strand and beheld it and blessed God' was Evelyn's[1] comment on the entry of Charles into London on May 29. This was the general feeling: thankfulness that an age of experiment and anarchy was ended. But this could not last for long, and soon men were eagerly examining the real implications of Charles's return.

Among the more thoughtful of these men was Edward Hyde, the great lord Clarendon, who in the exile which he shared with the king had carefully followed the course of events in England, and afterwards in a second exile was to record his impressions of English society at the moment of the Restoration.[2] He noted the almost miraculous suddenness of the change, how it thrilled England with joy, and was followed by a 'revolution in the

[1] *Evelyn*, May 29, 1660.   [2] *Clar. Cont.* i. 320–6, 336–56.

general affections of the people' almost as momentous as that
which it had succeeded. To explain how this change came about
was one of the main purposes of the *Continuation*. The root causes
he found in the manner by which the Restoration itself had been
effected; for Monck, having given a lead to the Presbyterians, had
encouraged them to raise hopes which could not be fulfilled; his
army had reason to think that they had been cheated by their
leader; and, in addition to these sources of discontent, there was
the actively hostile element among the followers of Lambert and
in some of the Sects. On this considerable section of the community the Restoration had, in a sense, been foisted. More serious,
the Royalists did not have the moral stamina for a proper use of
the opportunities placed within their grasp. Many had become
impoverished; others, in the course of long exile, had become un-
English in habit and sentiment; among them generally was a
loosening of the moral ties, and relapse into bickering, effeminacy,
and vice. In only two royalist nobles, the marquess of Hertford
and lord Southampton, were the pristine virtues of English
loyalty to be found. Hence, according to Clarendon, a canker
had bitten deeply into the very foundations of the throne itself.
Cromwell had from policy encouraged this association between
monarchy and debauchery in order to discredit both; Charles
was obliged to acquiesce in this association because he wished
to give himself as little trouble as possible. So the royal ship of
state started her voyage with a heavy list, and the captain did
not have the strength of mind to order the jettisoning of any part
of the cargo.

Such was the spirit of Clarendon's commentary on the Restoration as an epoch in the history of English society. We know that
he was idealizing the past, and that to some extent he was out
of date; but there is nevertheless much truth in his criticisms. A
more optimistic tone may be traced in the complete manual of
advice[1] drawn up for the guidance of Charles by one well entitled
to his opinions and accustomed to expressing them—William
Cavendish, earl of Newcastle, famous as the victor of Adwalton
Moor, the patron successively of Ben Jonson and Dryden, the
royalist who, having spent a million pounds in the cause of the

---

[1] *Clar. MS.* 109. See also S. A. Strong, *A catalogue of letters and other historical
documents exhibited in the library at Welbeck.*

king, was rewarded in 1665 with a dukedom. He was old enough to remember the glories of Elizabeth's reign; he had known James I and Charles I intimately; he was superior to both personal and party interests; and, as a famous horseman and horse-breaker, he was entitled to give advice on how to govern subordinates. He was no statesman; he was probably even more out of date than Clarendon; but he had this advantage, that his age and experience qualified him to draw for purposes of comparison upon a considerable period of English history, and so enabled him to set the social and political problems of the Restoration in sharper definition against the background of the older régime.

His advice may be thus summarized. He thought that the immediate danger to the newly-restored monarchy came from the towns, especially from the metropolis; London should therefore be disarmed and controlled by two forts, one on each side of the Thames. These precautions, with a well-fortified Tower, would serve to keep the commercial classes in their place, and in the provinces the same object would be promoted by regiments of dragoons. The next thing to be set in order was religion. Lay preaching must be discouraged; schoolmasters should be such only as the bishops license; the parson is to preach weekly from a printed sermon, this being the work either of a bishop or of a person approved by him. The episcopate thus provides the ruler with intermediaries through whom he can exercise control over both clergy and laity; but this is not the sole advantage of the Church of England for the purposes of statecraft, because that Church enjoins only a moderate number of holy days, whereas the Papists waste too much time in processions and pilgrimages, and the Presbyterians are prodigal of energy in extempore prayer and ranting. Religion, in fact, must be the first concern of the statesman, because the enthusiasm of the common people breeds revolution—'the Bible in English under every weaver's and chamber-maid's arms hath done us much hurt.' So too with the institutions from which the Church draws its supplies. There are too many students at the universities, and if the colleges had but half their numbers these would be better fed and better taught. The same is true of the grammar schools, where syntaxes are well thumbed, while horse and plough are neglected;

consequently, the schools should limit their numbers, for their only justification is that they serve the needs of the Church and (to a less extent) those of the Law and the Merchants. Education has its uses but, like everything else, there can be too much of it. The duke was writing at a time when it had not yet become fashionable for statesmen to commend the study of the classics.

With the help of the Church and the Law, Englishmen would be kept in order, and a recurrence of such an episode as the Interregnum made impossible. Thus, the bishops in their dioceses should act as 'intelligencers', reporting to the government on Papists, Presbyterians, and Schismatics, while in the universities there should be spies to search out the unorthodox and the seditious. The Star Chamber might well be revived in order to deal with riots, and the Court of High Commission for morals. Criticism of these and other prerogative courts had come, wrote the duke, not from the people, but from the common lawyers, whose opposition was not disinterested, because they were, he considered, concerned only with the threat to their fees implied by the business of these special jurisdictions. There were other spheres in which there might well be revivals of older practice. Gentry ought to serve on juries—they were now become too proud for that, and so this privilege had been usurped by the lower orders; moreover, the king himself might well preside occasionally in one of his courts of justice, if only to check the corruption of judges. The lawyers generally must be 'lookt to', for they had a deep hand in the initiation of the late troubles; moreover, the diminution of their numbers was in itself a social advance, and this could best be done if fewer people were taught reading and writing. Lawsuits consume vast sums of money; nearly every case eventually finds its way into Chancery, 'and God knows how many years it may be there'. Salaries and profits of the great officers of state should be reduced; and the king must remember that in the last resort it is with an army, not with the lawyers, that the sovereign controls multitudes.

As for commerce, the duke stated that when everything is cheap, there is scarcity of money, and when everything is dear, then there is plenty of money. It might therefore be deduced that it is good policy to keep prices, and therefore rents, high. The kingdom would be full of money if exports exceeded imports.

No attempt was made to adjust or reconcile these economic axioms. The study of trade was, he thought, an essential part of politics, and he cited 'old Burley' to demonstrate that a man cannot be a statesman unless he understands commerce. The duke added some shrewd criticism of English fiscal practice, condemning such things as monopolies and frauds in the farming of the Customs; he also suggested that subsidies were yielding less than formerly because the most substantial men in the counties were appointed commissioners, in which capacity they under-assessed themselves, leaving their poorer neighbours to make up the difference. Excise he considered the ideal tax, because it fell on every one. Tradesmen, he thought, were responsible for an economic grievance, since by engrossing money in their hands and letting it out at high rates, they were damaging the interests of landowners; for instance, when money is at 10 per cent., land is at 15 years' purchase, whereas at 8 per cent. land is at 20 years' purchase; interest should therefore be stabilized at 8 per cent., a rate sufficiently low for the advantage of the landlord, and sufficiently high to induce foreigners, especially Dutch, to invest money in this country. It was also of economic as of social importance that the laws against vagrants should be strictly enforced; and for this purpose the counties should be patrolled by troopers, officered by younger sons of good family. It may be added that these are not exceptional opinions; on the contrary, the duke was here voicing the opinions of the average squire.

'Ceremony and order, with force, governs all and keeps every man and everything within the circle of their own conditions.' This was the key-note of Newcastle's social philosophy. His Majesty was adjured to follow queen Elizabeth in this respect, who used to appear in public gorgeously attired, pronouncing her benediction: 'God bless you, my good people'—words of no great matter, 'yet I assure Your Majesty it went far with the people' and it cost nothing. Hence class distinctions must be kept clear, and the privileges of the nobility maintained. 'The worst in the nobility is but to pull down one king and set up another, so that they are always for monarchy; but the commons pull down root and branch, and utterly destroy monarchy.'

Referring to recent disorders, the duke claimed that their main cause was the king's lack of money. 'A parliament which bargains with you is not a free parliament.' Parliaments are justifiable only if you are able to control them. Here again Elizabeth's reign provided the example. The second error committed by the earlier Stuarts was the creation of too many peers; whereas Elizabeth was sparing in this respect, and 'there was no joining with the House of Commons in those days'. It was bad policy to try to pacify a man by making him a peer. Thirdly, the subjects were allowed to dispute the king's prerogative in Westminster Hall and in parliament. Fourthly, too many privy councillors were appointed, and both lawyers and merchants were admitted too freely into the royal counsels. The fifth mistake was allowing parliaments to sit too long—'a parliament will never want work', so it should be held to a strict time limit. The permission of weekly news-sheets was the sixth default of Charles's predecessors, for these journals filled the minds of the ignorant with their inflammatory domestic and foreign intelligence, whereas the discourse of men should be mainly about 'hunting and hawking, bowling and cocking'. Lastly, and worst of all, evil had come on the nation from the mixing of classes. In Elizabeth's day, a gentleman would put his younger son to the university, then to an inn of court, afterwards to wait on an ambassador, then to be his secretary, or possibly a secretary of state. 'But when great favourites came in, they jostled out this breed of statesmen: whosoever would give £1,000 more for the place, would have it.' The gentry, seeing this, have put their sons into trade, or other private careers, and so the crown was deprived of the support of that class pre-eminently fitted for state service.

As for the king himself, the duke's advice was explicit. He must entertain; he must have frequent masques at Whitehall, invitations to which are to be issued with the greatest circumspection. His Majesty should appear publicly in the tilt-yard; he should run at the ring, and ride horses of 'manège' to demonstrate his horsemanship (Charles preferred to ride as a gentleman jockey at Newmarket). The king should frequently attend at Newmarket, 'the sweetest place in the world', where he would have the additional advantage of a sermon on Sunday by a Cambridge divine. Other permissible recreations were 'Tennis, Pall, Walies and Goffe'. For the 'meaner people' there were the playhouses and Paris Garden in London; in the country, May games, morris dancing, the fool, the hobby horse, with carols and wassail at Christmas. The duke commended dancing, and noted king James's approval of that exercise. Are not poisonous humours sweated out in a tarantelle?

The duke of Newcastle was describing a civilization which by 1660 was becoming little more than a reminiscence; but in England survivals are long-lived, the sentiment for the past is deeply rooted, and an age is to be judged not alone by the wisdom of the statesman or the originality of the pioneer, but by the less articulate conservatism of the 'ordinary' man. Within little more than a generation there was to emerge a new England, endowed with a constitutional monarchy, divided by a party system; tolerant but critical, devoting her best energies to maritime and commercial expansion, and committed to a policy of active intervention in European affairs; an England more serious of purpose and more conscious of its potentialities than any of which the earlier Stuarts had dreamed. How great was this change can be measured only against the weight of opinion which resisted innovation. But the change was an insensible one, and the duke's dissertation has this value, that it depicts that attachment to tradition which at times has proved a silent but powerful force in the evolution of the English nation, a sentiment to be illustrated in the events which form the theme of this book.

It is at least certain that the counsels of the dissertation had no influence on royal policy; for its extreme length precludes the hope that Charles ever read it.

IV

THE RESTORATION SETTLEMENT

THE restored king was thus described by one who knew him:

He is somewhat taller than the middle stature of Englishmen; so exactly formed that the most curious eye cannot find any error in his shape. His face is rather grave than severe, which is very much softened whensoever he speaks; his complexion is somewhat dark, but much enlightened by his eyes, which are quick and sparkling. Until he was near twenty years of age the figure of his face was very lovely, but he is since grown leaner; and now the majesty of his countenance supplies the lines of beauty. His hair, which he hath in great plenty is of a shining black, not frizzled, but so naturally curling into great rings that it is a very comely ornament. His motions are so easy and graceful that they do very much recommend his person when he either walks, dances, plays at pall mall, at tennis, or rides the great horse, which are his usual exercises. To the gracefulness of his deportment may be joined his easiness of access, his patience in attention, and the gentleness both in the tune and style of his speech; so that those whom either the veneration for his dignity or the majesty of his presence have put into an awful respect are reassured as soon as he enters into a conversation.[1]

Personal attractiveness was matched by varied accomplishment. His French was fluent; he understood Italian and Spanish; Mathematics he had studied so far as it concerned fortification; he had read 'choice pieces' from the *Politics* (of Aristotle); he was skilled in Navigation, and knew something of Modern History. Most of these things were part of the formal training of a prince; but of one unusual subject he had made a special study, that of reading character from the face. He was keenly interested in books treating of this topic,[2] and his career amply illustrated the measure of his proficiency in the art. To the patriotism, moral courage, and self-sacrifice which have been eulogized by his more recent biographers he made no claim.

[1] Sir Samuel Tuke, *A character of Charles II* (1660).
[2] He read with interest the *Physonomia* of G. B. della Porta (*Miscellanea Aulica*, 124).

Charles II was built on simple and straightforward lines rendered elusive and mystifying by the cynicism engendered of experience. He might well have endorsed the avowal of Bunyan's *Mr. Lustings*: 'I was ever of opinion that the happiest life a man could live on earth was to keep himself free from nothing that he desired . . . and I have never been false at any time to this opinion of mine.'[1] This quality of frankness, with his mental alertness and unfailing shrewdness, he may have derived from his grandfather Henry IV of France, while from his father Charles I he appears to have inherited little more than a supreme sense of the dignity of kingship. So far as he had any religious convictions, he respected Roman Catholicism for its authoritative traditions, and because the ministrations of its priests appeared to provide a spiritual hygiene suitable to a temperament such as his; indeed, like his old fellow exile, cardinal de Retz, he may have thought that, if a man must have a religion, he should choose a 'decent' one. Fond of novelty, lazy and intolerant of routine, he succeeded in combining kingship with comfort and even amusement at a time when there was no cabinet to bear the responsibilities of policy, thereby mingling decision and inactivity with such exact balance as both to strengthen the prerogative and postpone the revolution. As a man and as a Stuart he was a remarkable exception. As a Stuart, he was able to abide tobacco,[2] he had a sense of humour, and he knew when to yield; as a man, he had the gift then known as second-sight, and after thirty years of age he had nothing more to learn. His jests served to disarm his associates, as his intuition enabled him to read their minds; where others excelled in cleverness, industry, or virtue, he concealed instinct, determination, and a sound political sense. Such were his assets; his most serious liability was his brother James.

Of the king's ministers the greatest was Edward Hyde, created lord chancellor in 1658 and earl of Clarendon in 1661. In his autobiography he drew this pen-portrait of himself in earlier years:

He rather discoursed like an epicure than was one. He was in his nature inclined to pride and passion, and to a humour between wrangling and disputing, very troublesome, which good company

---

[1] Bunyan, *Holy War*.   [2] *Savile Correspondence* (*Camd. Soc.*), 196.

in a short time so much reformed and mastered that no man was
more affable and courteous. His integrity was ever without blemish
and believed to be above temptation. He was firm and unshaken
in his friendships.[1]

This character-sketch is somewhat nebulous, and indistinctness
still clouds the vision of posterity as it views Clarendon in the
long line of English statesmen. His personality was certainly
more complicated than that of Wolsey or Burghley, who were
framed in coarser, or at least simpler moulds; on the other hand
he was lacking in the richer humanity of Walpole and Chatham.
The suppression of passion to which he confessed may account
for a certain rigidity of temperament, as the irritability of his
later years was probably caused by gout. His real character[2]
can be as little determined from his own eulogy as from the
diatribes of his opponents.[3]

Lack of vision and lack of sympathy were probably the chief
defects in Clarendon's character. He showed the one by his
comparative indifference to the problems of colonial administration, and by his supine acquiescence in a foreign policy which
subordinated the English Court to France; the other defect was
reflected in his attitude to the nonconformists; indeed, he was
completely unsentimental in regard to that which stirred most
deeply the passions of his contemporaries, for he believed religion to be not a spiritual experience, but a social cement, binding
the subject tightly into his place in this world. These defects
might have been compensated for by agility; but in this respect
the Clarendon of 1660 was no match for the younger men who
were then wriggling out of obscurity. He had a genius for friendship, but not enough imagination to see an opponent's point
of view; as he himself admitted[4] he was 'uncounsellable', and
this impenetrability hardened with years and change. His
eminent gifts were best suited for a static world where rigid
economy would not be counted for avarice, nor high-handed-
ness for corruption; a world where dignity was a virtue and

---

[1] *Clar. Cont.* i. 77–8.

[2] For a brilliant character-sketch see sir Charles Firth's *Edward Hyde, earl
of Clarendon* (1909).

[3] For a collection of these see G. Agar Ellis, *Historical enquiries respecting the
earl of Clarendon* (1827).　　　　[4] *Clar. Cont.* iii. 170.

change a vice. He had brought the chosen people out of the wilderness; it might have been a kinder fate for him and for England had he been withdrawn at the moment of achievement, since his almost patriarchal austerity served only to reveal the contrast between the old world and the new. Aloof from the petty meanness of his personal enemies, he retained his statuesque composure in defeat as in success; and he could at times retreat from turmoil into a concealed and ordered inner life. These were his 'vacations' in which he reflected on his actions. The first of them was when he lived in Jersey before the prince of Wales went into France; the second was his two years' embassy in Spain (1649–50); the third was his banishment.[1] The last of these retreats was fruitful; for to it we owe the completion of the *History of the Rebellion* and the *Autobiography*.

Among the relatives who had shared in the royal exile were James, duke of York and Albany, three years younger than Charles, on whom were conferred the offices of lord high admiral and warden of the Cinque Ports; the king's mother Henrietta Maria, aged 51 in 1660 and still, so far as was in her power, a baleful influence on the House of Stuart; his sister Henrietta Anne ('Minette'), 16 years old, afterwards duchess of Orléans; the only one of his surviving relatives for whom Charles had any affection. Of the great officers of state, the most notable was Monck, appointed captain-general of the Forces, lord-lieutenant of Ireland, master of the horse, and duke of Albemarle; James Butler, lord steward of the Household and marquis, afterwards duke of Ormonde; Thomas Wriothesley, earl of Southampton, lord high treasurer, one of the most devoted and respected of the king's entourage. None of these men was over 52 at the Restoration; but they were mostly somewhat older than their years, and all of them were temperamentally unlike the king, who was more than twenty years their junior. Only Monck and Southampton, neither of whom had spent an exile abroad, could claim to be distinctively English in training or outlook, but neither had any considerable influence on policy; and so, from the outset there was a foreign or at least un-English element in Charles's innermost counsels.

Abroad, the restored monarchy was represented by Henry

[1] *Clar. Cont.* iii. 458–9.

Jermyn, earl of St. Albans, a close confidant and possibly the husband of Henrietta Maria; in Portugal and afterwards in Spain by the poetic sir Richard Fanshawe; in Holland by the wily George Downing, noted for his dislike of the Dutch, his knowledge of finance, and his ingenious explanation of his earlier republicanism.[1] Others who helped to maintain some continuity between Commonwealth and Monarchy included sir John Maynard (now an active prosecutor for the crown) and Arthur Annesley, soon to be earl of Anglesey. Successful transition was also illustrated by Anthony Ashley Cooper, baron Ashley and chancellor of the Exchequer after 1661; and by Edward Montagu, earl of Manchester, lord chamberlain of the Household. Among the younger generation were George Villiers, duke of Buckingham, privy councillor and gentleman of the Bedchamber, and Henry Bennet, recalled from the embassy at Madrid to be keeper of the Privy Purse. Administrative aptitude and personal integrity were embodied in sir Edward Nicholas and sir William Morrice, the two principal secretaries of state. Nicholas, now nearly a septuagenarian, was specially noted for the faithful service he had rendered to Charles I; Morrice has already been referred to for his part in promoting the Restoration.[2]

Before the king's return to England, the main terms of a settlement had been announced by the advisers of the exiled Court. In his letter to the House of Commons Charles had expressed the hope that the Commons would be as circumspect regarding the royal honour and authority as of their own liberty and property; in the Declaration of Breda he had declared a general pardon to all (except to such as should be excepted), and had promised a 'liberty to tender consciences', coupled with a willingness to assent to an Act for securing these objects. To parliament also was referred the vexed question of grants and purchases of lands. In so far as the Restoration was conditional, these were the conditions. They were acceptable to a majority of the nation. The Presbyterians were thereby encouraged to think that room might be found for their system in an established church, either by a 'comprehension', or by a compromise, to be achieved by concessions on both sides; so too the plundered

---

[1] He attributed this to his training in New England.   [2] *Supra*, 26.

Cavaliers awaited the reward of sacrifice, and the soldiers hoped that their titles to land acquired during the Usurpation would be confirmed. In the background was the Court, gratified that the Restoration had been effected on the minimum of commitment, and that these vague concessions were subject to parliamentary ratification.

It was first necessary to establish some measure of continuity with the past. On June 1, 1660, Charles gave his assent to Bills intended to secure this continuity. By one of them,[1] the Long Parliament of 1640 was declared to be fully dissolved and determined, and the Lords and Commons then sitting at Westminster were proclaimed to constitute the two Houses of Parliament, notwithstanding the absence of the king's writ at their summons. By another statute,[2] judicial proceedings were to be continued, so that writs and processes already issued under any of the Commonwealth styles might still be acted upon. This latter Act retained two legal reforms of the Commonwealth—that whereby English was made the language of the courts and the law books,[3] and that enabling the tenant or defendant to enter the general plea of Not Guilty, and so join issue at once without the preliminary production of evidence in bar of the action.[4] Continuity of legal process was made still more effective by a statute, generally called the Act for Confirming Judicial Proceedings,[5] which provided that no fines, verdicts, or judgements (other than sales of estates by ordinance of pretended parliaments) made since May 1, 1642 should be void for want of legal authority in the courts wherein they had originated; but the right of appeal against the decision of a Commonwealth court was safeguarded. Throughout this law-making the Convention acted on the assumption that whatever had been decreed by one or both Houses without the participation of the king was illegal; but, on the other hand, a certain proportion of Commonwealth legislation was embodied in that of the Convention and later parliaments.[6] It was the Cavalier Parliament which, by its first statute, annulled all Acts or Ordinances for levying troops, raising money

---

[1] 12 Car. II, cap. i.   [2] Ibid., cap. iii.
[3] *Acts and Ord.* ii. 455–6, Nov. 22, 1650.
[4] Ibid. ii. 442–4, Oct. 23, 1650.   [5] 12 Car. II, cap. xii.
[6] For this see sir Charles Firth in *Acts and Ord.* iii. xxxi sqq.

or imposing oaths to which the royal assent had not been given.[1]

In these measures parliament mingled moderation with expediency, and avoided the enunciation of abstract principle. More debatable was the legislation directly resulting from the promises laid down in the Declaration of Breda, for the consideration of which document the Commons appointed a committee[2] on May 3. The result of this committee's deliberations was the Bill of General Pardon, Indemnity, and Oblivion introduced to the House on May 9. Its terms were debated with steadily increasing acrimony. The first resolution was that the surviving regicides should be secured, and that, of those who had sat in judgement on Charles I, 7 should be excepted in life and estate. Of the 67 'regicide judges' 44 were still alive; the designation of 'regicide' was, however, extended to include those 11 who had taken part in the trial, but had not signed the death warrant.[3] Four, namely Bradshaw, Ireton, Cromwell, and Pride, were posthumously attainted (May 14); of the living, the 7 already doomed were soon increased to 12 by the addition of 3 officials at the trial and the 2 (unknown) executioners. Still unappeased, the Commons decided to select for death 20 persons, not actually regicides, but notable for their part in the Usurpation; and thereupon the patience of Charles and Clarendon was sorely tried by long delay while the House, egged on by Prynne, selected its victims. Not till July 11 was the Bill ready for the Lords, who, even more merciless than the Commons, proposed capital punishment for all the king's judges, whether they had signed the death warrant or not.[4] But as the more judicious counsels of Clarendon prevailed, they abandoned this demand.

The Bill of Indemnity[5] received the royal assent on August 29, 1660. It bestowed a general pardon for all treasons, felonies, and numerous other offences committed since January 1, 1637, by any 'colour of command' from the late king Charles, or from the present king, or by any pretended authority derived from either or both Houses. All acts of hostility between king and parlia-

[1] 13 Car. II, stat. i, cap. i.
[2] *C.J.* viii. 8.
[3] Masson, *Life of Milton*, vi. 33–8.
[4] *Parl. Hist.* iv. 84.
[5] 12 Car. II, cap. xi.

ment were to be consigned to perpetual oblivion; and any one guilty of reproaches tending to recall the memory of the late differences should, if a gentleman, forfeit the sum of ten pounds; if of lesser degree, forty shillings. The Bill excluded by name thirty living persons, together with the two (unknown) executioners; in addition, twenty-four deceased regicides were attainted as to their estates, and six of the surviving regicides were excepted for punishment other than capital. In another category were placed nineteen living regicides, who were also excepted from the general pardon, but with a proviso that, in the event of their being attainted for high treason, their fate should be suspended until the king, by advice and assent of both Houses, ordered their execution. Lambert and Vane were nominally excepted, but there was an informal undertaking to petition the king on their behalf. Against Milton, proceedings were threatened because of the literary aid which he had lent to the Commonwealth; these, however, were abandoned through the private intervention of Clarges, Morrice, and Annesley.[1]

More urgent than revenge was the problem of finance. At the moment of the Restoration, the total amount of national indebtedness amounted to about three million pounds, for none of which did the legislature accept complete responsibility. There were the public and private debts of Charles I; the borrowings of Charles II in exile, and also the accumulated arrears of Commonwealth and Protectorate administration. The Convention was not unwilling to honour the first two classes of liability, but failed to find a means of doing so; succeeding parliaments evaded the question, leaving Charles to settle as much of his father's and his own obligations as he could from his normal revenue.[2] Of the third group, the most urgent consisted of arrears of pay due to the military and naval forces at the time of the Restoration, amounting by November 10 to £680,000;[3] in addition to which there was a standing Navy debt, estimated in March 1660 at £694,112.[4] As the immediate necessity was disbandment, parliament ordered the levy of assessments

[1] Masson, *Milton*, vi. 187.

[2] *Cal. Tr. Bks.*, *1660–7*, xvi–xviii, Dr. Shaw's introduction.

[3] Ibid. xii.   [4] *Cal. S.P. Dom.*, *1659–60*, 383.

at the rate of £70,000 per month for a total period of eleven months, together with a Poll Tax, estimated to yield £210,000. The greater part of the revenue from these taxes, amounting in all to nearly a million pounds, was assigned to paying off the forces, a process not completed until February 1661, when 18 regiments of foot, 13 regiments of horse, and 59 garrisons had been paid off.[1] To each non-commissioned officer and man an additional week's pay was given, and the Act providing for their dismissal facilitated their re-entry into civil life by absolving them from the customary requirements of apprenticeship, a concession modelled on a precedent set during the Usurpation.[2] Monck's Life Guards and his regiments of horse and foot remained on a permanent but somewhat informal establishment.[3] To the bravery and discipline of the disbanded troops Clarendon paid an eloquent tribute, coupled with the somewhat elusive statement: 'the only sure way never to part with them is to disband them'.[4] This proved to be the real difficulty; they were disbanded, but not parted with; hence the frequently reiterated proclamations ordering their departure from London, where they had many associates, with whom they were said to be concocting republican plots. More than any of the religious bodies, these ex-soldiers were a danger to the re-established monarchy, and their activities can be traced in all the movements directed against it.

There was still the problem of providing an adequate revenue for the crown. In regard to one of the sources of this revenue, the Convention had already made up its mind; for early in May the Commons indicated that they proposed to confirm the abolition of the Court of Wards; while, on his side, Charles expressed a willingness to forgo the large arrears in respect of wards, licences on alienation, purveyance, and respite of homage.[5] Having settled this preliminary, a committee of the Commons proceeded to examine the sources of royal revenue in

[1] The order of disbandment was determined by drawing lots at successive meetings of the Privy Council. *P.C. Reg. 54*, Sept. 14, 1660.

[2] *Acts and Ord.* ii. 1006–7.

[3] C. Walton, *History of the British Standing Army*, 3 sqq.

[4] Clarendon's speech at the adjournment, Sept. 13, 1660, *L.J.* xi. 174.

[5] *C.J.* viii. 107, July 13, 1660. The Court of Wards had already been abolished by Ordinance of the Commonwealth.

order to formulate proposals, and the surviving minutes[1] of its meetings reveal the extraordinary mixture of fact and aspiration on which Charles's revenue was assessed. It was first thought that a total hereditary grant of £864,586 might be raised by taking the yield from the Customs at £400,000 per annum (the usual parliamentary estimate): Excise, £250,000; Crown Lands, £100,000; Post Office, £21,000; the remainder to come from a number of small miscellaneous items, including a very conjectural £18,600 from the compositions of recusants. On the expenditure side the committee was agreed (and the Commons accepted their figures) that the yearly cost to the crown of the peace-time administration would amount to £1,200,000. How was the difference (more than £300,000) between estimated yield and expenditure to be made up? With this problem the committee reinvestigated its figures. Having examined the Customs returns as far back as 1642, they found that for the current year these might amount, not to £400,000, but to £354,176; they thought, nevertheless, that the higher figure could be raised 'if new powers be given for the due collecting of them' [the Customs]. So too with the Excise; only 'if better collected' would it yield £250,000. The discussion was then (July 20) transferred to the whole House in committee. It was there resolved to advance the Excise to £400,000, 'if it be now short of that value'; but even thus it was clear that some new tax had to be devised. A proposed imposition on salt was rejected; it was then thought that 'paper and parchment' might be taxed, and it was decided that Bills should be brought in for regulating wine licences and the office of post-master. The proposed tax on paper and parchment took effect later in the Law duties;[2] wine licences[3] and the post office[4] each contributed a small revenue; but these three sources together did not make up more than a fraction of the deficiency between the Commons' generous estimate of the yield from the hereditary sources and the sum of £1,200,000 which they admitted to be necessary for the civil administration. On

---

[1] *Shaftesbury*, xxxiv, no. 20, June 27–July 23, 1660. See also Dr. Shaw's introduction to *Cal. Tr. Bks., 1660–7* for the subject of Charles's revenue in general.

[2] 22–3 Car. II, cap. ix.   [3] 12 Car. II, cap. xxv.

[4] 12 Car. II, cap. xxxv, and 15 Car. II, cap. xiv.

their own figures, they recognized a gap of at least £300,000; the experience of the first seven years of the reign showed it to be nearly £400,000 per annum.[1]

There was another obscurity in regard to the king's revenue, never wholly dispelled The estimated £1,200,000 did not allow for extraordinary expenditure, such as that entailed by war. As late as 1678, when the Commons insisted that the crown should embark on war with France, one of the best-informed members of the Commons, sir T. Lee, contended[2] that, from his peace-time revenue Charles should defray the costs of this proposed war. Moreover, as mismanagement and increasing debt charges diminished still further the inadequate allowance thus provided, the inevitable consequence for the crown was bankruptcy, and for the legislature confusion and suspicion. But in 1660 no one could have foreseen that, with the development of English industry and commerce, the revenue from Customs and Excise would eventually reach such a figure as to make Charles and his successor independent of parliament.

The net result was that Charles could depend for life, and independently of parliamentary grant, on two main sources of revenue—the Customs and Excise, together yielding at first between £600,000 and £700,000 per annum, and later in the reign an average of about a million per annum. The remainder of his non-parliamentary revenue was derived from sources some of which were more picturesque than profitable. He was soon to have a fluctuating return from a tax on hearths; as a substantial but decaying landlord he still received about £15,000 yearly from the duchy of Cornwall (which cost £5,000 to collect),[3] and a revenue of about £50,000 from fee-farm rents (most of which were soon to be sold).[4] He continued to derive variable sums from the tin and logwood farms, the transport of skins, the sale of alum, the carrying of water to Westminster, and the postage of letters. Institutions such as the Society of Music, the Company of Frame-Work Knitters, and the Company of Tobacco Pipe Makers paid him a small annual sum; and though, by the abolition of the Court of Wards, he parted company with the wards

---

[1] *Cal. Tr. Bks.*, *1660–7*, xxxv.

[2] *Grey*, v. 27.   [3] Ibid. i. 266.

[4] 22 Car. II, cap. v. See also *infra*, ii. 431–2, and *Cal. Tr. Bks.*, *1672–5*, xii–xiii.

and widows, he was left with the custody of 'natural fools' or idiots, from which he derived a modest fee.

These matters were further complicated by their association with an event having an even wider historical interest—the statutory abolition of the Court of Wards.[1] In compensation for all the emoluments hitherto accruing from this source, it was resolved to settle one-half of the Excise perpetually on the crown[2] (a moiety assumed to have a value of at least £100,000 per annum), while the other half was settled on Charles for life.[3] This had not passed the Commons without debate, as some members were hotly opposed to the Excise, while others thought that it would be better to retain and regulate the Court of Wards than to impose an increased tax which might need an army to enforce it.[4] The fiscal effect of the new arrangement was that, in place of income derived from landowners holding of the crown, there was substituted an additional tax on beer, cider, and tea, falling on rich and poor alike. There were also social consequences. The preamble to the Act taking away the Court of Wards and Liveries recited that this court, as well as tenure by knight service of the king, had become more burdensome to the kingdom than beneficial to the crown; that, moreover, since the intermission of the court (i.e. since 1645) many persons had disposed by will and otherwise of lands held by these tenures; for these reasons the Statute abolished the Court of Wards with tenure by knight service (of the king or of others),[5] and converted that tenure into free and common socage. The Act did not affect rents or heriots from crown lands due in respect of tenements other than those held by knight service; nor did it abolish tenure by grand sergeanty nor tenure by copy of court roll; but purveyance, with provisioning and pre-emption for the royal household was taken away.

In this way statutory effect was given to a change, first proposed in the reign of James I, and carried into effect by the

---

[1] 12 Car. II, cap. xxiv.   [2] Ibid.
[3] Ibid., cap. xxiii.   [4] *Parl. Hist.* iv. 148.
[5] There was at least one instance of this. In 1672 the Treasury compounded with John, earl of Dover, for his losses consequent on this abolition. His tenants of the manor of Conisborough had held of him by knight service. *Cal. Tr. Bks., 1669–72*, 1287.

Ordinance of 1646. By the institution of the Court of Wards Henry VIII had preserved from threatened desuetude the feudal dues and services owing by his tenants-in-chief, and had thereby capitalized the surviving incidents of medieval allegiance. To the tenants of the crown by military service, great and small, the change must have been welcome; since it relieved them from disabilities thus described by Blackstone:[1]

The heir, on the death of his ancestor, if of full age was plundered of the first emoluments arising from his inheritance by way of Relief and Primer Seizin; and, if under age, of the whole of his estate during infancy. And then, as sir Thomas Smith very feelingly complains, 'when he came to his own, after he was out of wardship, his woods decayed, houses fallen down, stock wasted and gone, lands let forth and ploughed to be barren', to reduce him still further, he was yet to pay half a year's profits for suing out livery, and also the price or value of his marriage. Add to this the untimely and expensive honour of knighthood to make his poverty more completely splendid; and when by these deductions his fortune was so shattered and ruined that perhaps he was obliged to sell his patrimony, he had not even that poor privilege allowed him without paying an exorbitant fine for a licence on alienation.

The tenures so abolished were, it might seem, mere anachronisms; for land, once a unit of jurisdiction, had for long been an object of investment and development. Military service was now only an ornamental relic; 'feudal' bonds survived only at coronations and ceremonial occasions; and so, by sweeping away all these *disjecta membra* of the past, the statute might well seem merely to have abolished what was already dead. But it is possible that full justice has not been done to the historical importance of the change. Its immediate effect was that the crown, by the loss of purveyance, had to pay from £70,000 to £120,000 more for household expenses.[2] There were more important consequences. The Court of Wards was not a 'feudal' but a Tudor institution, having for its purpose not to enforce military service, but to extract money from and to exercise personal control over a large proportion of the landed classes. That Court had levied what was tantamount to an elaborate system of death and succession

[1] Quoted in Digby, *History of the law of real property*, 4th ed., 391–2.
[2] *Cal. S.P. Dom., 1663–4*, 420.

duties, with the difference that these fell entirely on one class—the landed class, whose emancipation was thus achieved by spreading their burden over the community in general. This was not all. Enforced sale of fee-farm rents completed the severance of the sovereign from the land, and thereby the older conception of monarchy was exchanged for one which, while still biblical in sentiment, was ceasing to be territorial, and had not yet become official. The full extent of these sacrifices was concealed behind the consummate skill with which Charles wielded this changing and anomalous prerogative; but nevertheless the Statute Book bears eloquent witness to the gathering strength of that landed class which was soon to dictate to the crown. Nor should it be forgotten that, in his manorial courts, the landlord continued to enforce the personal supervision from which he had himself escaped.

More difficulty was experienced in settling the questions of the Land and the Church. During the Usurpation many territorial families had been displaced by a host of new-comers, and it was in land that the Royalists had had to pay for their loyalty. An edict[1] of 1644 had inaugurated a system whereby all of royalist inclinations, even if they had not taken up arms, were obliged to compound for their estates. The owner had to make his terms with the Committee for Compounding, the fines varying from two-thirds to one-tenth of the value; nor, until the whole fine was paid, was he free from the threat of sequestration. Throughout the fifteen years during which this policy was intermittently enforced, many estates had been divided or sold in order to provide money for the fines, with the result that great quantities of land were thrown on the market, and so the price was depressed. Beteeen 1643 and 1649 alone the money received from sequestrated estates amounted to £209,547.[2]

Independently of this compounding, whether voluntary or enforced, were the sale of royal goods and land, and the large fines on wealthy peers and commoners. With the increasing financial difficulties of the Commonwealth, still larger measures of confiscation had to be carried out, and three Acts of Sale,[3] promulgated in 1651–2, vested in trustees the estates of 719 named

---

[1] Printed, *in extenso*, in *Calendar of Committee for Compounding*, V. vi–ix.
[2] Ibid. V. xxxii.   [3] *Acts and Ord.* ii. 520, 591, and 623.

persons, including the duke of Buckingham, the earl of Newcastle, the earl of Worcester, the earl of Derby, the marquis of Winchester, lord Craven, and sir Edward Hyde. These enforced sales were afterwards considered in a different light from the sacrifices of those persons who had sold in order to compound. There was still another class of confiscated estate—the lands of the Church, estimated at the capital value of £2,400,000.[1]

Early in July 1660 a Bill, drafted in the interests of the purchasers of crown and church lands, formulated some general principles of a land settlement. As it was opposed by the Royalists, the Commons agreed to omit from its scope all the crown lands, and refer the amended Bill to a committee of the whole House.[2] Nothing further was heard of it. The only legislation on the subject consisted of two somewhat vague clauses in the Act of Indemnity and the Act for the Confirmation of Judicial Proceedings, of which the first provided for the immunity of bona-fide purchasers of lands, not being church or crown lands, nor lands sold or given for the delinquency or pretended delinquency of any person in the period January 1, 1641–April 25, 1660; while the second Act contained a clause to the effect that sales of estates in virtue of any parliamentary ordinance since May 1, 1642, were neither nullified nor confirmed. All that could with certainty be deduced from these clauses taken together was that crown and church lands must be restored; there was less certainty in regard to land sold by parliamentary ordinance; and no legislative provision whatever for land sold 'voluntarily', that is, under economic or other pressure. Further proof of the inadequacy of the legislation is supplied by the fact that some of the more notable Royalists, such as the marquis of Newcastle, lord Gerard of Brandon, and lord Culpeper, were specially provided for in private Bills, a course which would not have been necessary if the statutory enactments had been clearly defined. What appears to be certain is that purchasers of crown lands were dispossessed altogether; those who had bought church lands were either ejected or retained as tenants; those who had sold their land in order to help the royal cause, or to pay the heavy fines imposed

---

[1] Sir C. H. Firth, in *Cambridge Modern History*, v. 95.

[2] *Parl. Hist.* iv. 80. There does not appear to be any evidence of the terms of the Bill.

on their loyalty received no compensation. Purchasers of land which had actually been confiscated by the state did not have a valid title, but they do not appear to have stirred until moved by civil action or by special petition to the Lords.[1] So far, therefore, as there was any principle in this settlement, it was to restore crown and church land to its rightful owners; to confirm possession acquired by private contract, and to secure complete restitution for certain favoured persons.

No formula could have satisfied all parties. The Convention legislators may have acted on the principle that the settlement was best which entailed least dislocation; for wholesale restitution would have penalized many 'under-purchasers' who had acquired their land in good faith, and had paid for it nearly as much as its value on the best title. Nor was it always a simple matter of purchase and sale; for the question was entangled with marriage settlements, trusteeships, and mortgages; whole streets of new houses in London had been built where formerly there was royalist land; many copy-holders had surrendered their old estates for lives or years, and had bought the freehold in order to give a title to their sons.[2] Among the discontented were two main classes—the purchasers ejected from crown lands, and the impoverished Royalists whose sacrifices went unrewarded because 'voluntary'; but on the other hand a large new class of landowner was confirmed in possession—the tradesmen, merchants, and soldiers who had bought estates, large and small, with their savings. The entry of this new class into English life broadened the basis of allegiance to the crown;[3] it also altered the character of English landownership by introducing into its ranks men who, in the Usurpation, had acquired a habit of restiveness under another man's yoke, a concerted and not unintelligent restiveness, occasioned by high principles rather than by high spirits, and calling for a readjustment of relations between driver and team. Whiggery may have begun when lay-preachers acquired real estate.

For the 'loyal and indigent officers' who had served under

---

[1] For this see the numerous petitions to the Lords in *H.M.C. Rep.* vii, app., pt. i. 86 sqq. *MSS. of the House of Lords.*

[2] *Considerations offered to public view* (1660) in *Bodley*, p. 1119.

[3] K. Feiling, *History of the Tory Party*, 101.

Charles I and had remained faithful to his son a slender provision was made by the legislature. A sum of £60,000 was ordered to be divided among such of them as had no means of livelihood, their claims to be determined by commissioners appointed for each county.[1] For those able to work, some prospect of employment was held out in the Act[2] licensing hackney coachmen, a clause of which gave preference to 'ancient coachmen' and to those who had suffered in the royal cause, a concession which proved of little value; because, after paying £5 for their licences the ex-sufferers found the streets of London filling with unlicensed drivers.[3] A like fate seems to have overtaken the monopoly of lotteries granted for six years to the 'Truly Loyal Indigent Commissioned Officers'; for these men complained that the commissioners appointed to administer the lotteries on their behalf had defrauded them of the profits,[4] and that the crown ignored their monopoly by granting lotteries to other persons.

As Clarendon was blamed by the plundered Cavaliers for the land settlement, so he was blamed by the Presbyterians for the church settlement.[5] Having contributed notably to the reinstatement of the king, and having some claim to establishment, or at least a desire for it, the Presbyterians never forgot that Charles had signed the Solemn League and Covenant; and as he commenced his reign with no less than ten Presbyterian chaplains (all strictly rationed in their sermons) it might at least be presumed that he did not publicly reject the efficacy of Calvinist ministrations. In archbishop Ussher's 'Model' there already existed a plan for union, based on the surrender by the bishops of their claims *jure divino*, and their reduction to the status of

[1] 14 Car. II, cap. viii, and 15 Car. II, cap. iii.

[2] 14 Car. II, cap. ii.

[3] *Rawl. MS.* A. 185, f. 229. Complaint of the Hackney Coachmen.

[4] *P.C. Reg.* 64, Oct. 21, 1674.

[5] The original documents relating to the settlement will be found in *Documents relating to the Act of Uniformity* (1862). See also E. Cardwell, *Documentary annals of the Church of England* (1839 and 1844), and *A History of Conferences* . . . (1840). For a very full modern account see J. Stoughton, *The Church of the Restoration* (1881). There is a good account of the subject in both R. Lodge, *Political History of England* (1660–1702), and G. M. Trevelyan, *England under the Stuarts*. Among excellent monographs relating directly or indirectly to the subject is that of F. Bate, *The Declaration of Indulgence* (1908).

presidents of synods; a scheme of mitigated episcopacy which, had it been accepted, might have combined the moderate Presbyterians of the Commonwealth with the Anglican clergy of the Restoration in one latitudinarian and non-prelatical body. Indeed, it was hoped by many that the troublous times of Laudian episcopacy were gone for ever, and that common ground might be found in that Elizabethan Protestantism wherefrom Anglicanism and Presbyterianism had first become differentiated.

In the Convention there were no advocates of a Laudian episcopacy. Many were for bishops, but no one was for 'lords bishops'; others contended that it was impossible to tell what was the discipline of the Church of England 'according to law'.[1] Eventually, the fundamental issue was laid aside, and the Commons contented themselves with a Bill for settling and restoring ministers to their livings.[2] This Act, while providing no protection for 'intruded' ministers, attempted to minimize the opportunities for eviction; and its terms show the willingness of the Convention to compromise. A similar spirit appeared to be reflected in the royal Declaration on Ecclesiastical Affairs,[3] issued on October 25, 1660, wherein it was announced that differences of opinion in regard to ceremonies were to be left to the determination of a national synod; and, in the meantime, no one was to be denied the Lord's Supper because he refused to kneel; nor was any one to be obliged to bow at the name of Jesus, or to use the cross in baptism; there was also to be liberty in the use of the surplice. This temporary latitude, pending the settlement of differences, was to extend to all churches, other than royal, cathedral, and collegiate churches.

The Declaration was discussed by the Commons[4] after their recess (Nov. 28) in order to embody its principles in a Bill. To some, it appeared to grant too large a measure of toleration; others were for leaving it as it stood, for reasons of expediency. The latter opinion was that expressed by secretary Morrice, on behalf of the government; time, he said, rather than legislation would do what was desired; in other words, the Court did not wish to make good the royal promises. To this view a majority of the Commons was won over, partly (it is said) by the personal

---

[1] Parl. Hist. iv. 82–3, July 16.   [2] 12 Car. II, cap. xvii.
[3] In Parl. Hist. iv. 131–41.   [4] Parl. Hist. iv. 153.

intervention of Charles himself.[1] So ended the deliberations of the Convention on ecclesiastical matters. They had passed an Act protecting beneficed clergy, provided they were not intruders; but the vital question of religious settlement they left untouched. In this they were the victims of circumstance. They were suspicious of the very generous terms of the Declaration, the verbosity of which may well have detracted from its effectiveness; moreover, had they drafted their Bill in accordance with its terms, it is doubtful if it would have passed the Lords.

In these ways the Convention Parliament succeeded in formulating a settlement which, by postponing debatable points, enabled the monarchy to entrench itself once more in English life. But, within the few months of its commencement, a notable change can be detected. At their first meetings, it might have been possible to make terms which would have embodied some of the hard-won achievements of the Long Parliament. Of this there was at least a hint when, on May 29, the Commons read and committed a Bill for the confirmation of the privileges of parliament, of Magna Carta, of the 'Statutum de Tallagio non Concedendo', and of the Petition of Right;[2] they also discussed a Bill for abolishing the titles conferred by Charles I after his retreat to Oxford.[3] On August 10 they debated whether the Poll Bill should precede the Indemnity Act; until, wheedled by secretary Morrice's taunt that they were afraid of their own fears, they acted on his suggestion that confidence was their greatest obligation, and presented the Money Bill first, in spite of long parliamentary precedent to the contrary.[4] They even discussed a motion that the king should be urged to marry a Protestant; but were reminded that, according to Elizabethan traditions, royal marriages were not the affair of parliaments.[5] As they were suspicious of Roman Catholics, so they were suspicious of the crown's military resources, and in November they objected[6] to a Militia Bill that it seemed to have 'martial law' in it. On all points, however, except prohibitions of Sabbath-breaking and profanity, the Presbyterian element in the Convention was

[1] Report of Ruvigny, Oct. 21–Nov. 1, 1660 in *Baschet*, 108.
[2] *Parl. Hist.* iv. 54.
[3] Bordeaux's report, May 21–May 31 in *Baschet*, 107.
[4] *Parl. Hist.* iv. 93–4.   [5] Ibid. iv. 119.   [6] Ibid. iv. 145.

defeated, and as the session neared its end the two notes of revenge on republicans and devotion to the crown became louder. Early in December 1660 it was resolved that the carcasses of Cromwell, Ireton, Bradshaw, and Pride should be drawn on a hurdle to Tyburn and there hanged up in their coffins;[1] a few days later money presents were voted to two persons who had assisted the king's flight from Worcester. These things symbolized the rising tide of devotion to the crown. On that tide were to be returned to Westminster men who had none of the qualities of circumspection and restraint wherewith the Commons of the Convention had effected one of the most remarkable changes in the history of England.

Of that transition neither Statute Book nor record of parliamentary debate can give more than a shadowy impression. The fugitive press and the drama are almost totally deficient as evidences of the national upheaval which followed the return of Charles Stuart; Pepys is clear but limited; of literature to which one might look for guidance there is a lack of everything except printed sermons. But from the thousands of petitions[2] which poured in on king, council, and parliament one may infer what the Restoration meant for many Englishmen. In one class were the petitions of those old servants of the king who expected restoration to their former offices; in this category were sergeants-at-arms, king's printers, a master of the posts, a master of the barges, and the purveyor of wax for the Grand Seal. In another class were applications for restitution to college fellowships and headships, and city recorderships. Ecclesiastical promotions, governorships of forts, and revenue offices fill another class of petitions. For special provisos in the Act of Indemnity there were about seventy applications, and the Act for Confirmation of Judicial Proceedings accounted for another fifty.[3] There were collective petitions, as from cripples who had sacrificed their limbs in His Majesty's service; from six hundred impoverished

---

[1] *C.J.* viii. 197.

[2] These will be found in many sources, notably in the *Calendars of State Papers, Domestic*, from 1660 to 1662. For a classification see *Cal. S.P. Dom., 1660–1*, 83 sqq. See also, for the petitions to the Lords, *H.M.C. Rep.* vii, app. i. 79–175. *MSS. of the House of Lords.*

[3] *H.M.C. Rep.* vii, app. i. 95–100.

Protestants who had lost their all in the Irish Rebellion; from 'many thousand' distressed prisoners for debt; from cities and boroughs complaining of the encroachments of men who had risen high in municipal politics during the time of troubles. Personal solicitations made to the king were legion, constant interruptions in his walks which may have trained Charles to develop that 'woonted large pace'[1] whereby he outdistanced petitioners, and so spared himself these public appeals to his generosity.

While England was settling down under the new dispensation, the Restoration settlement was being effected in the kingdoms of Scotland and Ireland, and in the plantations. The varied character of its reception in the plantations showed that some of the old leaven was still working. In Virginia and Rhode Island, where the loyalist party was in a majority, the king was speedily proclaimed; more tardy were Connecticut and New Plymouth, where devotion to the crown was not so intense. To scarcely any two colonies did the Restoration mean quite the same thing; thus, in Barbados there was ended that measure of dominion status which the island had enjoyed during the Commonwealth,[2] and the old Carlisle patent was revived; in Baltimore (Maryland) there was also a resumption of proprietary rights (in favour of the Calvert family). Massachusetts, on the other hand, did not fit into the categories of crown or proprietary colony; it was not only an anomaly in the American plantations, but was the enterprising leader of a confederacy of almost independent states, all of them incarnating the austere morality and uncompromising independence of early Puritan republicanism. Accordingly, there was both difficulty and delay in securing the proclamation of Charles Stuart in Massachusetts. 'It is not unknown to you', wrote an English agent,[3] 'that they [the New Englanders] look on themselves as a free state . . . there being too many against owning the King, or their having any dependence on England.' Not till August 1661 was the king proclaimed in Boston, and then without enthusiasm, because of the threat of peremptory orders from the English Privy Council.

---

[1] *Diary of Henry Teonge* (1805 ed.), 232.   [2] V. T. Harlow, *Barbados*, 127.
[3] *Clar. MS.* 74, f. 228, March 11, 1661.

More was to be heard of this claim to independence; and the reign of Charles II, though fruitful of experiments in colonial administration, brought with it problems of imperialism incapable of satisfactory solution on the principles of seventeenth-century statesmanship.[1]

Ireland, more inert than the western possessions, was secured mainly by the efforts of two old servants of the Commonwealth —Charles Coote (afterwards earl of Mountrath), president of Connaught since 1645; and Roger Boyle, afterwards baron Broghill and first earl of Orrery, who commanded in Munster. Since the fall of Richard, these two men, sinking their differences, had co-operated in order to secure a safe passage for the returning monarch, and on May 14, 1660, Charles was proclaimed in Dublin. The Irish Celts had no reason to regret the end of the Cromwellian régime; and the English soldiery who controlled them appear to have made the same assumption as did Monck's troops—that they would be confirmed in their lands. This hope was not completely fulfilled, and accounts for most of the troubles that followed from the Restoration in Ireland.

The settlement was conducted mainly from London and by the Irish committee of the Privy Council. Lords Justices (including Coote and Broghill) and a Chancellor (sir Maurice Eustace) having been appointed, the executive was entrusted to Coote and major William Bury in their capacities of commissioners for the government of Ireland. The lord-lieutenancy was conferred on Monck, but as he was an absentee, a deputy (lord Robartes) was appointed, who also withheld his presence from Dublin and accepted the office of lord privy seal. For some time, therefore, there was considerable difficulty in determining who were responsible for the government of Ireland. The expressed intentions of the English privy council showed a desire to increase the efficiency of the Army, to maintain a higher standard of honesty among officials and to develop trade—provided this did not conflict with English interests. The expert knowledge of Ormonde and of Bramhall, bishop of Derry, was utilized in dealing with the great avalanche of petitions which poured in.

The Church was first restored. This was not difficult, because,

[1] For the Navigation Acts and the plantations see *infra*, 235–245; for the colonies and plantations generally see *infra*, ii, cap. xviii.

except in Ulster, episcopacy was the system most acceptable to the Protestants. John Bramhall, an old enemy of Presbyterians, was promoted archbishop of Armagh and primate of Ireland; in January 1661 ten of the surviving bishops were consecrated in St. Patrick's Cathedral. There then followed a settlement reflecting that carried out in England. By the Irish Act of Uniformity (1662) the Revised Prayer Book was imposed; benefices were restricted to those who had received episcopal ordination; oaths of non-resistance, conformity, and repudiation of the Covenant were required of all clergy and of all teachers, whether public or private. As for Roman Catholics, they were to suffer more from disability than from persecution. Their cause was represented by archbishop Peter Walsh, who strove to remove the ostracism from which they suffered, and succeeded in obtaining the release of a number of imprisoned clergy. An attempt was also made to induce the priests to sign a loyal remonstrance repudiating the right of any foreign power to absolve them from their allegiance; but the response to this appeal was poor, and so Ireland continued in her divided obedience. With the native Irish Charles and many of his Court were in sympathy, and their interests were ably sustained by Ormonde; but they remained a class apart, regarded with increasing suspicion by the English administration.

The land settlement was by far the most difficult question.[1] This was because there were so many claimants, and because, since the Irish rebellion of 1641-3, there had been so many dispossessions, beginning with the eviction of Roman Catholics, and followed by the confiscations and resettlements of the Commonwealth. Most of the best acres were occupied by two classes known as the Soldiers and Adventurers. Of these, the Soldiers held land in lieu of pay for their services in conquering Ireland from the Irish, while the Adventurers derived title from their loans of money to facilitate that object, in return for which land had been mortgaged to them on very favourable terms. Both classes of claimant derived their rights from a period anterior to the Usurpation, and could cite in their favour Acts of Parliament to

---

[1] For this see *Ormonde*, iv. 42–66; *Cal. S.P. Ire.*, *1660–3*, Introduction; Bagwell, *Ireland under the Stuarts*. For a clear summary of a complicated matter see R. Lodge, *Political History of England, 1660–1702*, 44–52.

which Charles I had assented; but on the other hand these men had co-operated in Cromwell's Irish policy, and so were deemed an unsuitable type of Irish landlord, because undistinguished by personal connexion with the Court, and tainted with the venom of Commonwealth individualism. A nation of small free-holders would be difficult to govern on the standards of Clarendon. Of the other claimants there were the Roman Catholics and the Courtiers; in the end the Courtiers fared best.

By a Declaration issued on November 30, 1660, the Adventurers and Soldiers were confirmed in lands held by them in May 1659. The chief exceptions were church lands, which were to be restored to their former owners; also lands obtained in virtue of decrees in Cromwellian courts, and the lands of those who had opposed the Restoration. Provision was made, mainly in Wicklow, Longford, Leitrim, and Donegal, for officers who had served in Ireland before June 1649; and such officers were to be given preference in their claims to forfeited houses within walled towns; in this way it was hoped that the 'Forty-Nine Men', as these old loyalists were called, would provide the nucleus of a well-disposed population. Next, dispossessed Protestants who had not been in rebellion were to be restored, and wherever their reinstatement involved dispossession of Soldiers and Adventurers, these latter were to be compensated elsewhere. Lastly, the 'innocent' Papists, that is those who had not joined in the rebellion of 1641–3, were to give up their lands in Connaught and Clare, and to be 'reprised' from the lands of those Soldiers and Adventurers who had dispossessed them of their original holdings. These two last clauses obviously modified the grant of confirmation to Soldiers and Adventurers contained in the first clause.

The execution of this Declaration was committed to a body of thirty-six persons, most of them having private interests in Irish land, and there then ensued an interminable process of petitions, influence, and jobbery. First of all, the scope of the phrase 'innocent Papist' was restricted so as to exclude all who held their estates within the area occupied by the rebels during the first two years of the Rebellion, unless they could prove that they had been driven there for refuge. Then special provision was made for Monck, the Coote and Allen families, lord Massarene, and lord Cork. The commissioners next detailed the order in which claims were to be settled—Protestants before Papists; those who had accepted compensation lands in the west after those who had not. The Adventurers had to give proof of title, by survey, if necessary; arrangements had also to be made for the collection of outstanding rents; concealed lands and forged titles were to be investigated. Throughout these resettlements there was continual conflict of Protestant and Catholic, English and Irish, Loyalist and Cromwellian, Episcopalian and Dissenter, all parties besieging the commissioners with claims which no human justice could have satisfied even had Ireland enlarged to twice its size. The general result was that, in spite of Charles's well-known inclinations in their favour, the Papists lost as against the Protestants, and the Cromwellian settlers had to give way to the Courtiers. It has been computed that of the 8,000 Roman Catholics who had formerly held land in Ireland about 1,300 were restored, and possibly as much as a fifth part of the ten million acres available was once more owned by Catholics.[1] The Catholic interest in Ireland was to be ruined not by the settlement of the Restoration, but by that of the Revolution.

Monck's resignation of the lord-lieutenancy in November 1661 was followed by the appointment of the one statesman who knew Ireland intimately and was capable of ruling it with sympathy and justice—the duke of Ormonde. He first signified the royal assent to the Act of Settlement passed by the Protestant parliament assembled in Dublin, an Act whereby lands forfeited since the Rebellion were declared to be vested in the crown for distribution according to the terms of the Declaration of November 1660. The same parliament granted subsidies from the clergy and laity, together with a hereditary revenue from the Excise and from Tonnage and Poundage. A hearth tax was substituted for the old feudal dues. Thus far the Soldiers and Adventurers, who formed a majority in the Irish House of Commons, had signalized their loyalty and their gratitude for the promises of confirmation held out by the Declaration and embodied in the Act of Settlement. But the difficulties inherent in that settlement, and the limitation in the number of Irish acres, became more distressingly obvious as the innumerable claims were adjudicated. In England it was soon felt that too much had been conceded to the Soldiers and

[1] W. F. T. Butler, *Confiscation in Irish History*, 198–200.

Adventurers; and the increasingly Papist character of Charles's entourage prompted a modification of the settlement which, while securing the Protestant interest, discriminated more definitely against those Protestant claimants whose careers savoured of Cromwellianism. Accordingly, after the Irish Parliament had been carefully packed, an Explanatory Act was passed in 1665, the main provision of which was that the Adventurers and Soldiers were to be confirmed in only two-thirds of their lands, and that Adventurers claiming on the 'doubling ordinance' of 1643 were to have land, not of twice the value of their subscriptions (as allotted to them by that ordinance), but of only two-thirds of that value. In order to effect a readjustment on these terms, a new Court of Claims was instituted. These provisions did not redress the balance in favour of Papists; but their execution, at the expense of Soldiers and Adventurers, increased the amount of land at the disposal of the crown, and the absentee Irish landlord thus became an institution.

In both England and Ireland the Restoration settlement showed a moderation when contrasted with that in Scotland. The northern kingdom could boast a more general devotion to the Stuarts than could her southern neighbour; for she had produced neither Sectaries[1] nor Regicides; ever since 1648 most of her native leaders had parted company with the English parliamentarians, and had exerted themselves on behalf of the royal cause; moreover, many of them had fought at Worcester on Charles's behalf. Throughout the Cromwellian domination the country had suffered in sullen poverty, hoping for the return of her crowned and covenanted king. Cromwell had taken the Scots into partnership in a legislative union; hence a Stuart would be at least as sympathetic to Scottish interests. The Declaration of Breda had encouraged the English Dissenters to hope for special consideration; much more, therefore, might the Scottish Presbyterians look for toleration in a country where they were in a majority. These hopes were doomed to speedy disappointment. The Union was tacitly abandoned, and the Navigation Acts excluded Scotland from the plantation trade; soon her only over-seas connexion, that with Holland, was to be ruined by

[1] The word Sectary was generally applied by contemporaries not to Presbyterians but to the numerous other exponents of dissent.

Anglo-Dutch hostilities. Even more, many of Charles's Scottish advisers (having forgotten their earlier Presbyterianism) turned on their mother church with vindictive energy, and attempted to destroy the one vigorous Scottish institution—the Kirk. It was in Scotland that Stuart principles of government had first suffered discredit; the lesson was to be repeated at the expense of the same kingdom.

In England the Restoration had commenced with the summoning and assembling of a representative parliament; in Scotland it began when Charles nominated the members of his privy council. The chancellorship was conferred on William Cunningham, earl of Glencairn, one of the 'Engagers' of 1648. He had suffered a term of imprisonment in Edinburgh Castle after an unsuccessful rising in 1654. The presidency of the Council was conferred on a more striking but less respectable person, namely, John Leslie, earl and afterwards duke of Rothes, then an ardent courtier of thirty, with a short term of imprisonment to his credit. His handwriting suggests immaturity, but in the accomplishments fashionable at the Restoration he was highly developed; and he had a boyish love for soldiers, or, as he himself expressed it: 'he lyked sogeris above all other wayes of living'.[1] As the Scottish equivalent for Buckingham (without Buckingham's wit) he had to be provided for; so when, in 1667, he had to be removed from the administration, he was consoled by his appointment to the chancellorship for life, in spite of almost total illiteracy. The post of lord high commissioner to the parliament of Scotland was conferred on John Middleton, first earl of Middleton, once a major in the covenanting army, but now remembered for his services at Preston and Worcester, and known to be zealous for the restoration of that episcopacy against which he had once fought. On John Maitland, second earl and afterwards duke of Lauderdale, was conferred the secretaryship of the Council. Descended from the adroit Maitland of Lethington, Lauderdale had once been an ardent Covenanter; but on the other hand he had suffered continuous imprisonment since Worcester fight, and was now securely established in the royal favour as a convenient instrument for Stuart policy in Scotland. For this he was well qualified by a combination of characteristics seldom found together; for

[1] Quoted in Dalton, *The Scots Army, 1661–88*, 15.

he was a Hebrew scholar, a dexterous manager, and an obsequious courtier; of a breed, in fact, quite unknown south of the border. He was also a convenient butt for the more obscene of Charles's practical jokes, and his virtues, but never his abilities, were steadily corroded by contact with his king.

The Scottish Church was divided into two parties, differing not so much in doctrine as in their attitude to the Stuarts. One party, known as the Engagers or Resolutioners,[1] was the more moderate and seemingly the more politic of the two; they believed that a Stuart might tolerate Presbyterianism. For some of these, the acceptance of episcopalian Presbyterianism was not difficult, since they were the party of accommodation and compromise. The other party, known as the Remonstrants or Protesters, had already (1650) rejected Charles Stuart until he should give better evidence of true allegiance to the Covenant; they were considered much the more bigoted, but they proved to be the more clear-headed. This party was strongest in the south-west, notably in Ayrshire and Dumfriesshire, where Calvinist Presbyterianism was to be found in its pristine rigidity. Both parties were soon dealt with. The Committee of Estates, which exercised executive functions pending the meeting of parliament, ordered the imprisonment of a body of Protesters, and prohibited conventicles; while the Resolutioners were invited to read between the lines of Charles's letter to the Presbytery of Edinburgh (Sept. 3, 1660): 'We do resolve to protect and preserve the government of the Church of Scotland *as it is settled by law.*'

A select body of representatives of the nobility and royal boroughs, known as the Scottish Estates, met on January 1, 1661, under the presidency of Middleton. In its first session of six months the record number of 393 Acts was achieved. Coupled with the usual prohibitions of swearing, drinking, and sabbath-breaking was a legislative surrender, by which the power of choosing ministers, summoning and dissolving parliaments, and making war and peace were unreservedly conferred on the crown;[2] this, together with the grant of an annual revenue[3] of

---

[1] So called because they supported a resolution to receive back those who had lapsed from the Covenant and were repentant.

[2] *Acts of the Parliaments of Scotland* (1819), vii. 10, Jan. 1661.

[3] Ibid. vii. 78, March 1661.

£40,000 which the country could not afford to pay, proved the loyalty but not the moderation of Scotland's effusive and sometimes unbalanced statesmen. To make the surrender of the constitution more complete, by an Act Rescissory[1] all the proceedings of the Scottish parliaments since 1640 were cut away as by a pair of shears. The Church was soonest to experience the effect of these changes. In terms of the Act Rescissory, the phrase 'the Church of Scotland as it is settled by law' must mean that Church which Charles I had attempted to impose upon the country, a conclusion made explicit in September 1661 when Glencairn and Rothes brought back to Edinburgh a royal letter signifying the intended restoration of bishops. A few months later James Sharp was nominated archbishop of St. Andrews, Fairfoul archbishop of Glasgow, Leighton bishop of Dumblane, and Hamilton of Galloway.

Robert Leighton (1611–84), afterwards archbishop of Glasgow, was a very favourable representative of those Scottish Presbyterians who had assimilated some of the best elements in French culture; for he had studied at Douai; he was a scholar and linguist; moreover he had close links with the Jansenists. His outlook was therefore free from provincialism, and he accepted the restoration of episcopacy as not inconsistent with the views of the more moderate Presbyterians; unwillingly he accepted also a bishopric. By nature pious and conciliatory, he was one of the few good influences on the Scottish episcopal bench. Very different was the Primate, James Sharp(1613–79), whose education had been of a more restricted character. His quick shrewdness had won for him Cromwell's description, 'Sharp of that ilk'; he was esteemed by Monck, and he had done some propaganda work on behalf of the Restoration; from a politic 'resolutioner' he had become a courtier episcopalian. His selection as Primate was probably intended to lull the suspicions of his co-religionaries; but the choice was unfortunate, because Sharp believed that the views which he himself had adopted from self-interest could be imposed on his fellow countrymen by force. He was not a Scottish Laud, for he was a time-server and a renegade. Soon he was busy with the campaign for the enforcement of episcopacy. In May 1662 it was enacted[2] that ministers

---

[1] *Acts of the Parliaments of Scotland*, vii. 86–7.　　　[2] Ibid. vii. 372.

not presented by their lawful patrons, nor collated by their bishops, should resign their livings; to enforce which Act, the privy council ordered parishioners to refuse payment of stipends to those clergy who had not so qualified themselves. Nearly three hundred ministers left their manses rather than comply, and so about a third part of the Scottish Church was forced into non-conformity. By 1663 the Restoration in Scotland was complete, in the sense that the Stuart king was absolute; he nominated his privy council as he nominated his bishops; parliament was a clique of subservient nobles and burgesses, and an episcopalian church was in progress of imposition on old opponents of prelacy.

A notable incident of the Restoration in Scotland was the execution of one of the greatest nobles, the eighth earl and first marquess of Argyle. Somewhat less than justice has been done to him by either contemporaries or posterity. His stand on behalf of the religion of his countrymen in the First Bishops' War has brought on him the accusation of Presbyterian bigot; his reputation has suffered also from the fact that his enemy and rival was the knightly Montrose. He placed the crown on Charles's head at Scone, but did not take part in the expedition which ended in defeat at Worcester. He strove to secure joint action between the parliaments of the two countries, but in the contending sects and factions of his day there was no room for a policy of caution; and those of his clan who claimed supernatural vision foresaw the end, revealed to Argyle himself in the *sortes Vergilianae*:[1]

Inque humeros cervix collapsa recumbit.

Having presented his court to Charles at the Restoration he was arrested and dispatched to Edinburgh on an indictment of high treason. At the trial, early in 1661, the charge of complicity in the execution of Charles I could not be proved, and an acquittal seemed inevitable, when Monck sent private letters, written to him by Argyle during the Commonwealth, in which were expressions that might be construed to mean approval of the Usurpation. On the strength of these personal confidences he was convicted, meeting his death with fortitude at the Cross of Edinburgh on May 27, 1661. On July 23, 1663, Johnstone of

[1] R. Law, *Memorialls* . . . (ed. C. K. Sharpe, 1818), 116.

Warriston was executed on grounds equally paltry. A noted Remonstrant, he was guilty of having accepted office under Cromwell. He and Argyle had incurred the personal resentment of Charles, and the Scottish courts of justice could be depended upon.

The comparative innocence of Scotland in the events of Charles's execution and the subsequent Usurpation may account for the small number of Scottish judicial victims. In England the number was greater; but there was the same discrimination between those who had been in time to worship the rising sun and those who had not. Proceedings against the regicides and others who had been excepted by the Act of Indemnity commenced on October 6, 1660, at Hick's Hall, when sir Orlando Bridgeman, in his charge to the grand jury, defined treason in terms wide enough to include several of those who sat on the bench with him; for the essence of treason, he maintained, consisted in the 'wicked imagination', even though not followed by 'treason apparent'.[1] The grand jury, having been instructed that levying war against the king's authority is as much treason as levying war against the king's person, had no difficulty in bringing in true bills against the accused persons, and on the following day the trials commenced at the Old Bailey.

Sir Heneage Finch, solicitor-general, conducted the prosecution; counsel was allowed to the accused only on points of law, it being in the discretion of the court to determine what was a point of law. Hugh Peters, though not a regicide, was indicted because he did 'consult about the king's death'. There were two witnesses to prove that he had compared the king with Barabbas;[2] there was proof that he had taken up arms; that he had called the day of the king's trial a glorious day, resembling it to the judging of the world by the Saints—surely, it was argued, no man could have contrived the king's death more than this wretch had done. Had he not been the principal person to induce the soldiery to cry out 'Justice, Justice'? Hugh Peters was doomed before he was tried. In all, twenty-nine of the accused were sentenced to execution by hanging and quarter-

---

[1] *The manner of the arraignment of those 28 persons who were appointed to be tried at the Sessions House in the Old Bayly* (1660), 9–10.   [2] Ibid. 153–4.

ing,[1] of whom ten suffered this sentence, namely, Harrison, Carew, Cook, Peters, Scott, Clements, Jones, Axtell, Hacker, and Scroop. 'A bloody week', noted Pepys on Saturday, October 20, a week in which he had been to see the executions, and had busied himself in arranging his book-shelves.

This did not end the work of revenge. Lambert and Vane were in a special class—they were technically excepted from mercy, but both Houses had petitioned that in the event of their being attainted, their lives should be spared. Charles granted the petition.[2] The trial of Vane began in the King's Bench on June 2, 1662, when evidence for the prosecution was directed mainly to establishing his activities at meetings of the Council of State. In his defence, Vane asked to have counsel assigned to him on several points of law, such as whether the collective body of parliament could be impeached of high treason, and whether any person acting by authority of parliament could commit treason within the limits of that authority. To this it was replied that privilege of parliament was no shelter for breach of the peace, much less for treason; and that, moreover, the sitting of a few persons within the walls of parliament did not constitute a parliament. The prisoner might well have replied that, if he was guilty, his guilt was shared by many for whom the Restoration had brought not prosecution but advancement; he preferred, however, to base his defence on broad grounds of abstract justice.

When new and unheard-of changes do fall out in the kingdom, it is not likely that the known and written laws of the land should be the exact rule; but the grounds and rules of justice contained and declared in the Law of Nature are and ought to be a sanctuary in such cases. The Law of Nature thus considered is a part of the law of England. . . . There is no precedent that ever both or either House of Parliament did commit treason.

Such was his defence, argued with courage and eloquence; and he properly urged that the case argued against him was of such general importance that it ought to be taken before the High Court of Parliament.[3]

Vane probably realized that this vindication of parliamentary

---

[1] The 28 accused persons had been increased to 29 by the addition of William Hewlett, a supposed executioner of Charles I.

[2] *L.J.* xi. 163.   [3] *Trial of sir Henry Vane at the King's Bench* (1662).

sovereignty would cost him his life. Having been found guilty on June 6, he was sentenced to death on the following day. On that day Charles wrote to Clarendon:

The relation that has been made to me of Sir Henry Vane's carriage yesterday is the occasion of this letter, which if I am rightly informed was so insolent as to justify all he had done, acknowledging no power in England but a parliament. If he has given new occasion to be hanged, certainly he is too dangerous to let live, if we can honestly put him out of the way.[1]

This was Vane's death-warrant. He was executed a week later on Tower Hill, and men could not but contrast his heroic idealism with Stuart perfidy.

His trial had coincided with that of Lambert, whose submissive behaviour, coupled with his refusal to justify his actions, secured for him a respite from execution. The remainder of his life was spent in moderately indulgent confinement in Guernsey, where he died a prisoner in 1683, having lost his memory some years earlier. To the end, his name remained on the lips of plotters, and the romance which it conjured up was heightened to its last gleams in the cloud of witness raised by Titus Oates.[2] Of the remaining notables, Ludlow was in exile in Switzerland; Hesilrige died in the Tower; Richard Cromwell survived until 1712, his taste for landscape gratified by his practice of drawing in water-colour. Fleetwood, most fortunate perhaps of all, took a third wife and settled in the seclusion of Stoke Newington, where he was an assiduous attendant on the ministrations of the Rev. Dr. Owen. But Restoration vengeance was not confined to the living. The bodies of four great regicides had already been exhumed and gibbeted; in September 1661 the bones of twenty-one persons were removed from Westminster Abbey and buried in an adjacent pit. Among these were the remains of Pym, Blake, and the mother of Cromwell.[3]

There remained only Coronation and Marriage to complete the Restoration settlement.

---

[1] *Lansdowne MS.* (B.M.), 1236, f. 132.

[2] If the plot had succeeded Lambert was to be Adjutant-General of the Forces (Titus Oates, *A true narrative of the horrid Plot*, 1679).

[3] *Clar. MS.* 75, f. 186.

Preparations for the Coronation were conducted on a scale which ensured that nothing should be wanting in its antique splendour. A special commission, presided over by lord chancellor Hyde was appointed to arrange the ceremony, and to decide on the many claims from persons professing the right to perform service thereat. There were two claimants for the office of lord high chamberlain; namely, Aubrey de Vere, earl of Oxford, and Montagu Bertie, earl of Lindsey; judgement was given in favour of the latter. Edward Dymock's right to be champion was uncontested. The dean and chapter of Westminster were to instruct the king and assist the archbishop of Canterbury; but, owing to the great age and infirmity of archbishop Juxon, his part was modified and curtailed. The earls of Pembroke and Northumberland were to bear the spurs; the earl of Shrewsbury the sword; Henry Howard, as seised of the manor of Farnham, was to support the king's right arm; the barons of the Cinque Ports were confirmed in their claim to carry the king's canopy: the mayor and citizens of London had the privilege of serving the king with wine in a golden cup, while the mayor and citizens of Oxford made themselves responsible for the butlering. All the picturesque incidents of the old personal allegiance were thus revived; and though the crown had been placed on an economical, almost penurious allowance, nevertheless it had lost nothing of its old splendour.[1]

These preliminary arrangements were accompanied by the conferment of honours. On April 10, 1661, sixty-eight knights of the bath were created; ten days later six earls and six barons were added to the peerage by special creation. Lord chancellor Hyde became earl of Clarendon; Arthur Annesley, earl of Anglesey; sir J. Grenville, earl of Bath. Baronies were conferred on sir Anthony Ashley Cooper (baron Ashley), sir George Booth (lord Delamere), and Denzil Holles (lord Holles). These, with the already ennobled Monck (duke of Albemarle) and Montagu (earl of Sandwich), represented the more notable of Restoration honours. St. George's Day, April 23, 1661, was selected for the supreme event.

On the morning of the 23rd Charles walked on blue cloth

[1] For the details see *Cal. S.P. Dom., 1660–1*, 584–6; Masson, *Milton*, vi. 152; L. G. W. Legg, *English Coronation Records*, 276–86.

through Palace Yard to the Abbey, where the throne had been erected. There, Gilbert Sheldon, bishop of London, turning to south, west, and north, called on the people to say whether they accepted Charles as their sovereign; the answer was vociferous; in their turn, the nobility gave an answer as emphatic. After the anthem, the king, surrounded by the nobility and bishops, proceeded to the altar, on which were placed the regalia; there the king knelt and a bishop prayed. Then followed a sermon by Morley, bishop of Worcester, on Proverbs xxviii. 2: 'For the transgression of a land many are the princes thereof: but by a man of understanding and knowledge the state thereof shall be prolonged.' Sheldon then tendered the Coronation Oaths, while Warner, bishop of Rochester, requested, in the ancient formula, that the king would preserve the privileges of the Church and the Bishops. These were among the preliminaries to the Anointing, for which solemnity the king removed some of his vestments, while the holy oil was poured from a bottle into a spoon. First the palms of the hands, then the breasts, next the back and shoulders, then the 'bowings of the arms', and finally the head, were anointed by the archbishop, and never did inunction prove more efficacious; for Charles was to effect more cures for the King's Evil than any other sovereign in recorded history. When the king had been girt with the panoply of state, St. Edward's crown was brought from the altar and placed by the archbishop on the royal head; at which, the supreme moment, shouts of 'God save the King' resounded through the Abbey, while salvoes of guns from the Tower signified the completion of the essential part of the ceremony. Through these long and solemn hours Charles bore himself with stateliness and decorum; but his thoughts may well have wandered to that very different ceremony of ten years before in the church at Scone, when he was crowned with the 'tottering crown' of Scotland, and after a sermon[1] which emphasized the need for his personal reformation was sent forth in a hopeless attempt to win his southern kingdom by force of arms.

Charles's marriage must be considered in relation to the place of Restoration England in European diplomacy. With both France and Spain Charles was on not unfriendly terms, and the

[1] *Coronation of Charles I at Scone* [Jan. 1, 1651] in *Bodley, Godw. Pamph.* 1371.

war with the latter was ended by a proclamation[1] of September 10, 1660. With Brandenburg[2] and Denmark[3] relations were regulated by treaties, neither of which was destined to have lasting effect. With Holland the negotiations were more complicated. By the treaty of Westminster (1654) the spice island of Pularoon was to be surrendered by the Dutch; but this was never done, and the various pretexts for refusal served to endanger Anglo-Dutch relations. A royal warrant for taking over the island was issued on December 22, 1660; but as Charles would not recognize a Commonwealth treaty, no mention was made of the treaty of Westminster, and so one more excuse was provided for withholding the island. Ever since the first Anglo-Dutch war there had been accumulating a long list of claims by the English East India Company against the Dutch Company, the English being as determined to trade in the Spice Islands as the Dutch were to exclude them, and soon this bitter rivalry was extended to West Africa. It was in order to adjust these claims that Dutch ambassadors arrived in England in October 1660, and though these efforts at compromise eventually resulted in the treaty of September 4/14, 1662, the claims of the English Company were never satisfactorily settled. Hence from the moment of Charles's restoration, relations with Holland steadily became more strained.[4]

With Portugal, relations were more cordial. Engaged in a struggle against Spain for independence since 1640, Portugal had assumed a position of triangular importance in European diplomacy; for she succeeded in maintaining the old alliance with England during the Interregnum, in spite of the execution of the brother of one of her ambassadors; she was also a unit in

[1] Steele, i. 3254.

[2] By a treaty of July 20/30, 1661, with the Elector of Brandenburg England undertook to support the Elector's claims to Cleves and Jülich in return for assistance to England in the North Sea and Baltic; there was also to be free commercial intercourse between the two countries. (Dumont, vi, pt. ii. 364.) See also C. Brinkmann, Relations between England and Germany in E.H.R. xxiv.

[3] By a treaty of Feb. 13/23, 1661, England and Denmark undertook to resist the enemies of the other, both having common interests on the west coast of Africa. (Dumont, vi, pt. ii. 346.) See also H. L. Schoolcraft, England and Denmark, 1660–7, in E.H.R. xxv.

[4] See infra, cap. vi. For Anglo-Dutch relations generally in this period see N. Japikse, De Verwikkelingen tusschen de Republiek en Engeland 1660–5.

the calculations of French diplomacy, in so far as she could be subsidized to maintain her struggle with Spain; thirdly, she had succeeded in preserving the friendship of the exiled Stuarts. Still commercially important because of her overseas possessions, Portugal needed man-power in order to continue the fight for her independence, and seemed able to pay for assistance, whether from her imports, or supposed imports, of bullion, or by transfer of her undeveloped territorial possessions. Abstractly, therefore, there were several good reasons why England should secure a Portuguese alliance; for thereby the old commercial connexion would be strengthened; employment would be found abroad for Englishmen who had survived their usefulness at home; and a share might be acquired in the disintegrating Portuguese empire. The alliance would be favoured by France, because thereby one of her allies would have a stiffening of Anglo-Saxon manhood against Spain. To cement this alliance, there was available a Portuguese princess—Catherine of Braganza. It was a matter of popular supposition that this bride would bring neither good looks nor a child, objections which caused Clarendon to hesitate before recommending the match.[1] Numerous other alliances were warmly recommended to Charles, and the nation would have preferred a Protestant; but financial and diplomatic considerations combined to favour the Portuguese marriage; and, by appearing to dally with rival candidates, the Portuguese terms were forced up. In the state of Charles's finances ready money was a consideration. Batteville, the Spanish ambassador, was profuse in promises, but ill supplied with funds; De Melho, the Portuguese agent, had £10,000 for distribution. This fact was not without influence on the final decision.[2]

[1] According to *Ormonde*, iv. 108, Clarendon, Southampton, and Ormonde tried to dissuade Charles from this match. Clarendon's own account is that when he first heard of the proposal, he asked the king if he had given over all thoughts of a Protestant wife. When Charles said that he saw no objection to the Portuguese match, Clarendon suggested that the matter be referred to a committee. This committee, which included Clarendon, Ormonde, Southampton, and Nicholas, unanimously agreed that there was no *Catholic* princess whom the king might more advantageously marry than the Infanta of Portugal. (*Clar. Cont.* i. 493–5.)

[2] Report of Giavarina, July 20/30, 1660, and of Quirini, Venetian agent

The project of a Portuguese marriage had preceded the Restoration; its achievement was partly the work of Monck. Acting on the assumption that the cause of his country had been abandoned by Mazarin, the Portuguese ambassador in England, Francesco de Melho, tried to negotiate a treaty with the Council of State;[1] and when Monck became the real executive, De Melho transferred his solicitations to him, telling him that, if Charles should be called back to England, the Spaniards would stop him in Flanders in order to exact security for the restoration of Dunkirk and Jamaica. This is said to have caused Monck to advise Charles to move his headquarters from the Spanish Low Countries. The ambassador then suggested to Monck a marriage of the Infanta with Charles, the dowry to include Tangier, Bombay, and three million cruzados. Tangier, it was urged, would give England control of the Mediterranean, and Bombay would provide a base from which the trade of the Indies might be secured. A treaty was eventually signed (April 18, 1660) whereby Portugal was allowed to enlist English troops for her defence, but this treaty was not ratified. At the time, therefore, when Monck was quietly preparing the way for restoration, his thoughts were also being directed to the highway leading to British supremacy in the Mediterranean and in India.[2]

These negotiations were conducted mainly through two men, Morrice, afterwards secretary Morrice, and Russell, the English secretary to the Portuguese embassy. The proposed marriage was suggested to Charles shortly after his arrival in England; and meanwhile the whole weight of French diplomacy was directed to the completion of the Anglo-Portuguese alliance, in order that English troops might be used against Louis XIV's enemy, Spain. For this purpose an agent, La Bastide, was sent on a secret mission to England, where he had many conversations with Clarendon, to whom he intimated that his master

in Spain, Feb. 20/March 2, 1661, in *Cal. S.P. Ven., 1660–1*, 177 and 253, respectively.

[1] Proceedings of the Council of State, July 28, 1659, in *Rawl. MSS.* A. 134.

[2] For this see Southwell's account in *Add. MS.* 20722; also *Ormonde*, iv. 101 sqq.; and *S.P. For. (Portugal)*, the letters of Don Alfonso and De Melho to Charles, Nov. 1660. Modern accounts will be found in E. Prestage, *The diplomatic relations of Portugal with France, England, and Holland*, and Feiling, *British Foreign Policy*, 44 sqq.

Louis had himself thought of marrying the Portuguese princess;
but 'for better perfecting the peace with Spain' he had been
obliged to marry a Spanish lady and desert Portugal.[1] Louis
would provide funds for a vigorous onslaught on his father-in-
law Philip IV, but the matter must, of course, be kept absolutely
secret. Moreover, according to La Bastide, this secret association would effect another good object—it would keep the Dutch
in their place.[2]

Considerable sums passed in the course of these negotiations.
Two hundred thousand crowns[3] were handed over at Havre in
February 1661, the greater part of which was paid to Carteret
for the Navy;[4] two months later Clarendon suggested a loan of
£50,000 from Louis, but was informed that the Portuguese
marriage must come first. On May 2, 1661, the chancellor was
able to report that the wedding was definitely agreed upon,
and eight days later the Council ordered a proclamation to be
issued embodying its unanimous consent to His Majesty's marriage with the Infanta. The £50,000 from France being now
assured, Louis promised Clarendon that the Franco-Spanish
alliance would be publicly honoured, and that he would pretend
indifference to the Portuguese match. Thus French influence
and money turned the scale in favour of a policy giving England
immediate advantages, and helping to bring Charles within the
elaborate net-work radiating from Versailles; and it is to Clarendon, more than to Charles, that the initiation of a policy of
dependence on France must be attributed.

The marriage treaty,[5] signed on June 23, 1661, and ratified
two months later, engaged Charles to use his power to effect a
solid peace between Portugal and the Dutch and, in the event
of warfare, to guarantee the defence of the Portuguese East
Indies; also to supply 10,000 auxiliaries for the defence of

[1] *Clar. Cont.* i. 517.

[2] This correspondence will be found in *Clar. MS.* 75, notably ff. 99–103,
and f. 393.

[3] The French crown or écu was just under 5*s.* in the English money of
the period. The livre was nearly 1*s.* 8*d.* These are average amounts for the
reign of Charles II, deduced from equivalents in the *Calendar of Treasury
Books.*   [4] *Clar. MS.* 76, f. 20.

[5] For the first drafts of the treaty see *Clar. MS.* 75, ff. 213–17. For the
taking over of Bombay see P. B. M. Malabari, *Bombay in the making*, ch. 3.

Portugal against Spain. In return were ceded to him the port and island of Bombay, the port of Tangier, and two million cruzados[1] in sugar, Brazil wood, and money. These were attractive terms for England, and probably no other matrimonial alliance was of such consequence as this; for, while its immediate pretext was diplomatic, its real significance was that England took over some of the remnants of a great colonial enterprise from a power no longer able to fulfil its world-wide commitments. This union was destined to bring to England first sugar and mahogany, followed later by wine; more important, the treaty gave to England an even greater interest in the Mediterranean, and, by opening up the Indian Empire to her commercial enterprise, more definitely turned the directions of English policy to the wider horizons of maritime empire.

The assistance or neutrality of our man-power appeared to be the most obvious of English assets in the later part of the seventeenth century. Portugal was willing to pay for the former; later, France was anxious to purchase the latter. But continental conditions did not at that time elicit the best qualities of Englishmen as auxiliaries; moreover, the men sent to the assistance of our ally were considered a good riddance by those who arranged for their transportation. There soon followed difficulties about food, drink, and pay. While English soldiers were accustomed to twelve months' pay in the year, the Portuguese had only seven or eight, and at a lesser rate; hence it was contended that payment of the English contingent on their standard would cause the French and Portuguese troops to mutiny. This was an inauspicious start. By April 1663 the situation was such that the English troops, so far from being 'profitable' to their employers, were alleged to be 'a considerable damage to the kingdom'.[2] Their pay was then in arrears, and so the Portuguese government was asked either to pay them or send them back. But already the English alliance was redressing the balance in the peninsula; for, in the spring of 1663, an English squadron secured the safe entry into harbour of the Brazil fleet, and in June of that year the English soldiers, under the leadership of Schomberg,

[1] Two million cruzados amounted to about £330,000—*Cal. Tr. Bks.*, *1660–7*, 407. Payment of the money was not completed until 1670, ibid., *1669–72*, 373. [2] *Clar. MS.* 78, f. 118, and 79, f. 165.

helped to win the battle of Ameixial, and with it Portuguese independence. Soon English diplomacy was to complete what English arms had begun; because solicitude for Portuguese interests influenced the subsequent English negotiations with Spain; and it was partly owing to pressure from England and Holland, united in the Triple Alliance of 1668, that Spain was induced to recognize the independence of Portugal.[1] So the advantages of Charles's marriage were not all on one side.

The last act of the Restoration settlement was the wedding of Charles with the Infanta. Under the escort of Sandwich, Catherine and her retinue of ladies and priests reached Portsmouth on May 13, 1662, where they were joined by the bridegroom a week later. There were two ceremonies at Portsmouth on May 21, the one, according to Roman Catholic rites, being performed by the abbé d'Aubigny; the other, in conformity with the English service, by Sheldon. On the morning of his wedding-day Charles wrote thus to Clarendon:[2]

Her face is not so exact as to be called a beauty, though her eyes are excellent good, and not anything in her face that in the least degree can shoque one . . . and if I have any skill in visiognimy, which I think I have, she must be as good a woman as ever was borne. Her conversation, as much as I can perceave is very good, for she hath wit enough, and a most agreeable voyse. You would wonder to see how well we are acquainted already.

Clarendon certainly needed reassuring on the 'acquaintance' of bride and bridegroom; for he knew that already lady Castlemaine was exercising her spell, and when he protested against the latter's appointment as one of the Queen's waiting-women, he received from Charles a letter[3] written in very different vein:

If you will oblige me eternally, make this businesse as easy to me as you can, of what opinion soever you are; for I am resolved to go through with this matter, let what will come of it. . . . And whosoever I find to be My Lady Castlemaine's enemy in this matter, I do promise on my word to be his enemy as long as I live.

Thus early in his reign was Charles, like Solomon, advised by strange women.

[1] See *infra*, 334.
[2] *Lansdowne MS.* 1236, f. 124.   [3] Ibid., f. 128.

V

THE ADMINISTRATION OF CLARENDON
1661–4

IN the years immediately following the Restoration Charles relied on the experience and prestige of Clarendon; and in their range the chancellor's activities extended to every corner that could be reached by an active and solicitous administration, activities radiating from the privy council. Clarendon's theory of government was based on a clear-cut distinction between the spheres of executive and legislative, according to which the former was vested solely in Council, while the latter was committed to king in parliament.[1] Over the king he exercised a tutelage[2] which became more galling with years, and from which Charles at last emancipated himself with the help of the chancellor's enemies.

When Charles's privy council assembled for the first time in England on May 31, 1660, its composition showed a strange mixture of Royalists, Presbyterians, and old servants of the Commonwealth. In the first class were Clarendon, Southampton, Ormonde, Somerset, Lindsey, and Dorchester; in the second Northumberland, Anglesey, Say and Sele, Holles, and Robartes; in the third class were Albemarle, Sandwich, and Charles Howard, first earl of Carlisle. Its numbers steadily increased from 27 to 40 and even 50, at which point it became unwieldy. It is difficult to describe the extensive scope of the Council's administration. Contemporaries such as Pepys deplored the amount of time spent by the king and the full Board over trivial suits;[3] an inspection of the Registers shows that the criticism was not unjustified. At one meeting, the business might be of national importance, as when, in 1669, a letter was drafted to the governors of the plantations requiring them to take the oath enjoined by

---

[1] For this see E. I. Carlyle, *Clarendon and the Privy Council* in *E.H.R.* xxviii.

[2] For the communications between Clarendon and Charles at privy council meetings see *Notes which passed at the meetings of the privy council*, ed. W. D. Macray (Roxburghe Club, 1896).

[3] *Pepys*, July 3, 1667.

the Navigation Acts,[1] or when, in 1674, Lauderdale was heard in defence of his policy;[2] sometimes its business was that of a law court, as when it adjudicated in a matter of wardship,[3] or decided a disputed assessment,[4] or heard a complaint by a lady of ill-usage from her husband;[5] at other times its edicts were little more than police regulations, as when it prohibited public burials during the Plague,[6] or issued an order for the eviction of malefactors seeking sanctuary in Scotland Yard.[7] The powers of the Council were so extensive because they were undefined. It was a nebula from which the separate ministerial departments were afterwards evolved, a great clearing-house of government, presided over by a king for whose personality and ability there was still much scope. It was a personal rather than a public institution; its proceedings could not be divulged,[8] and its decisions might be restricted by the absence of those greater lords to whose opinion the king was known to attach weight; conversely, it was a matter of principle that a mere quorum could not reverse a decision made at a meeting where these lords had been present.[9] In debate the youngest spoke first.[10]

Chairmanship of such an assembly was no formal matter, since the king was sometimes asked to act as arbiter in questions which to-day would be referred to a high-court judge. For example, in June 1681, after counsel had been heard on both sides in a dispute between the East India and the Levant Companies regarding their claims to Mocha, it was agreed to refer the issue to Charles's determination.[11] Few kings were so well endowed with the ability to weigh conflicting evidence in a technical suit, or to give a ruling that would satisfy the requirements of equity; and the records of both treasury[12] and privy council in the reign of Charles bear witness to the exercise of an aptitude far more valuable to the state than unintelligent industry.

The privy council gave formal approbation to treaties, and had an indeterminate share in drafting them; but in the last

[1] P.C. Reg. 62, Jan. 20, 1669.   [2] Ibid. 64, May 27.

[3] Ibid. 59, May 16, 1666.   [4] Ibid.   [5] Ibid. 65, Jan. 21, 1676.

[6] Ibid. 59, May 16, 1666.   [7] Ibid. 64, May 15, 1674.

[8] On one occasion the king complained that information had been revealed in Muddiman's News-letters. Cal. S.P. Dom., 1676–7, 356.

[9] Ibid. 1680–1, Oct. 5, 1681.   [10] P.C. Reg. 60, Feb. 12, 1668.

[11] Ibid. 69, June 30, 1681.   [12] For an instance see infra, ii. 425.

resort treaty-making lay with the king, and Charles never sacrificed this element in his prerogative.[1] Nominally also, Bills sent up from parliament were examined in Council, and in the years immediately following the Restoration, considerable time was devoted to their inspection;[2] but this vigilance did not last long; for Charles's Council became less effective as it grew larger, so that much of its work consisted in the hearing of petitions and their reference to the proper authority. Thus, to the lord chancellor were referred all petitions for reviews of judgements and stoppage of grants: to the treasury, matters concerning Customs, Excise, and pensions: to the attorney-general everything relating to charters, outlawries, points of law, and Irish legislation. Litigation over revenue, notably Excise, was frequently interfered with, and justices who had given a decision adverse to Excise farmers were constantly summoned to answer before the Council, a practice which the Commons voted a grievance in November 1675.[3] There was one other sphere of activity. Proclamations, usually drafted by the attorney-general, were passed under the Great Seal by the advice and consent of the whole Board. Of the proclamations of Charles's reign, the majority enforced existing laws, and so were reminders of those things in the Statute Book which, from time to time, it was deemed specially expedient to enforce.[4] Lent proclamations continued until 1664; fast-days, sabbath-observance, and prohibitions of the export of wool were old and well-tried favourites; Quakers were sometimes ordered by proclamation to be released, and Jesuits to be expelled the kingdom; and at national crises such as the Popish Plot government was conducted mainly by these instruments. They well illustrate the solicitous paternalism of Stuart government. The monetary value of gold coins;[5] the manual of political science approved by the government;[6] the use of gilt by coachmakers;[7]

---

[1] For the development of the conduct of foreign policy see K. Feiling, *British Foreign Policy*, 19–22; also E. R. Turner, *The Privy Council in the XVIIth and XVIIIth centuries*, ii. 117–19.

[2] Turner, op. cit. ii. 130.   [3] *Grey*, iii. 443.

[4] For a good general account of the scope of these proclamations see *Steele*, i, Introduction.   [5] *Steele*, i. 3324, Aug. 26, 1661.

[6] *Steele*, i. 3371, Dec. 5, 1662. The manual was *God and the King*, originally drawn up by or for James I. It is a very dull book.

[7] Ibid. i. 3335, Nov. 20, 1661.

the sweeping of streets in Westminster;[1] the spreading of false news, as that the king was about to dissolve parliament[2]—all these were deliberated by the privy council and each provided matter for a proclamation. There was no special tribunal for the enforcement of these edicts; nor were they questioned, except in so far as they assumed a dispensing power. They serve mainly as an indication of those offences which the subject persisted in committing.

Such were the chief activities of the full council. In practice many duties had to be 'committed' to specified 'committees', some of a very temporary character. In 1668 it was resolved that nothing should be decided in council until it had been considered by a committee; nor was anything to be referred to a committee until it had received preliminary consideration at the Board.[3] In the opening years of the reign there were about thirty committees,[4] of which two—that for naval affairs and that for plantations—were standing committees; but late in 1660, on the advice of Thomas Povey (who had served in the Commonwealth Council for the Colonies), two permanent bodies were established —a Council of Trade and a Council of Foreign Plantations. Both bodies included privy councillors, merchants, traders, representatives of the mercantile companies, and government officials. The Council of Trade, which met at Mercers' Hall, was designed to consider English commerce primarily as affected by our relations with foreign powers;[5] it heard petitions from traders and companies; expressed its opinion on such abstract questions as the export of bullion, and proposed convoy routes.[6] The Council of Foreign Plantations was commissioned mainly to investigate conditions in the colonies—their laws, government, and customs; to inquire into the execution of the Navigation Acts, and to deal with all matters concerning emigration and the propagation of the gospel in the colonies.[7] Both councils obtained their informa-

---

[1] *Steele*, i. 3366, July 17, 1662.   [2] Ibid. i. 3595, May 2, 1674.

[3] *Add. MS.* 38861, f. 18. Order for establishing a future regulation of committees of Council, Feb. 12, 1667/8.   [4] For a list see *Add. MS.* 37820, f. 65.

[5] For the minutes of the Council of Trade see *Add. MS.* 25115. The records of this Council and of that for Plantations do not extend beyond 1664–5.   [6] *Cal. Tr. Bks., 1660–7*, 245–6.

[7] For a good account see E. I. Carlyle, *Clarendon and the Privy Council* in *E.H.R.* xxvii.

tion by interview and correspondence; they included experts, such as Povey, who, in 1661, was made receiver-general for the rents and revenues of the American and African plantations; but their powers and duties to some extent overlapped; moreover they soon became too large for efficiency. Their responsibilities were extended by grants of charters to new commercial companies and colonies. As scarcely any two colonies were similar, and as plantations were developed in different latitudes of North America, while dependencies were erected in the Mediterranean and in the East, these committees had to deal with the problems of a rapidly developing empire. In this, they were not greatly assisted by Clarendon, from whom, as the real head of the administration, they might justifiably have expected a lead. The colonies were 'crying aloud for the authority of the crown'; by 1660 their progress had reached a stage when some general principles of colonial administration might have been formulated; but the chancellor, confined to bed by gout during the greater part of each winter, was not interested in colonies, and so no attempt was made to realize a golden opportunity.[1]

In 1668, when the committees of Council were reorganized,[2] plantations were grouped with commerce in a new Committee for Trade. This body, which included Robartes, Buckingham, Arlington, Lauderdale, Ashley, Clifford, and Carteret, met once a week, any three members constituting a quorum. But Arlington and Ashley—both of them more concerned than Clarendon in colonial administration—soon felt the need for a less formal council, and accordingly in October 1670 there was created a new Council for Plantations, the special purpose of which was to consider colonial affairs in relation to English trade.[3] This Council, strengthened by the inclusion of several London merchants, undertook a direct investigation of the working of the Navigation Acts. The link between commerce and colonization was again recognized by the erection, in 1672, of the Council for Trade and Plantations, of which Shaftesbury was president, and John Locke one of the clerks.[4] Commissions

---

[1] P. L. Kaye, *English colonial administration under Clarendon*, 17.
[2] *P.C. Reg.* 60, Feb. 12, 1668, and *Add. MS.* 38861, f. 18.
[3] Its instructions will be found in *Shaftesbury*, xlix, no. 8.
[4] Ibid., no. 27.

and instructions for colonial governors were drafted by this council, and a measure of co-operation and efficiency was introduced into the administration of the colonies. Shaftesbury's downfall was fatal to this body, of which he was the guiding spirit, and in March 1675 its duties were merged in the committee of Council for Trade and Plantations, better known as the Lords of Trade. For over twenty years this remained a standing committee for the government of the colonies; it usually acted with knowledge and promptitude, and was responsible for the handling of every colonial question as it emerged.[1]

In the rearrangement of February 1668 three other committees were regulated—that for Admiralty, Navy, Military Affairs and Fortifications; that for Complaints and Grievances; and that for Foreign Affairs. Of special importance was the last. Ever since June 1660 foreign affairs had been considered by a committee composed of Albemarle, Clarendon, Southampton, Ormonde, and the two secretaries, a committee formal only in the sense that all its members were privy councillors. In so far as Charles sought guidance in foreign policy, it was to this cabinet or cabal that he referred himself. Its existence was formalized in the rearrangement of 1668 by its inclusion among the four great standing committees, when its members were prince Rupert, Arlington, Ashley, Buckingham, Albemarle, Ormonde, and secretary Morrice. The wide scope of its duties may be inferred from the reference to it of correspondence with justices and local officials regarding the temper of the kingdom, and its tenders of advice on such matters as Charles did not reserve for his personal initiative. Until 1679 this Committee for Foreign Affairs was recognized as a cabinet or junto; thereafter it became less a Council committee and more an informal committee of king's friends; some of its more formal duties, such as drafting instructions for ambassadors, or regulating complaints of infraction of treaties, being assigned to a Committee of Intelligence. This latter was one of the formal committees which Charles frequently attended.[2]

The secretariat of the privy council had acquired increased importance from both Cromwellian experience and French

---

[1] For this see G. L. Beer, *The Old Colonial System*, i. 249–58.
[2] Its minutes (1679–82) are in *Add. MS.* 15643.

influence.[1] Unless overshadowed by a great chancellor, such as Clarendon, or a great treasurer, as Danby, secretaries might, as did Arlington and Sunderland, take upon themselves many of the functions now performed by a prime minister. Primarily a household official, the secretary generally had a seat in the Commons where, on the one hand, he would be expected to facilitate the passage of measures approved by the executive; and, on the other, to face his responsibilities as an ordinary member of the House. 'As a privy councillor', said secretary Coventry in 1677, 'I have taken my oath, but as a parliament man I have my opinion.'[2] It was not always easy to fulfil this dual function; for while, in the earlier years of the reign, the secretary was like a spring, facilitating easy communication between executive and legislature, he later became a buffer, forced to sustain the impact of a body of men increasingly conscious of their strength. Thus in the height of the *Shirley* v. *Fagg* controversy the two secretaries, Williamson and Coventry, desired the leave of the House to go out, but they were not allowed to do so until after a debate.[3] Three years later (Nov. 1678) Williamson, on acknowledging that he had countersigned several commissions for popish recusants, was committed by the infuriated Commons to the Tower, not as a servant of the king, but as a member of the House; he was promptly released by Charles's order, not as a member of the House, but as a servant of the king.[4] The position was so difficult that the released secretary stayed away from Westminster for several days.

The two principal secretaries of state were almost always members of the committees of Council, and were the only councillors who could never be regarded as merely ornamental; since, in Clarendon's words,[5] they were 'for service and intelligence'. Moreover, the office had valuable perquisites; it offered vast opportunities for the ambitious man, and was therefore

[1] For an excellent monograph on this see F. M. G. Evans (Mrs. C. S. S. Higham), *The principal secretary of state.*

[2] *Grey*, iv. 385.　　　　　　　　　　[3] *Grey*, iii. 254.

[4] Before taking this step, Charles consulted the Committee of Intelligence. For what passed there see the separate minute dated Nov. 19, 1678 in *Add. MS.* 15643: also F. M. G. Evans, op. cit. 143.

[5] Quoted by F. M. G. Evans, op. cit. 237.

eagerly sought after, its purchase price rising to as much as £8,000. Claiming the powers of a justice of the peace, the secretary examined suspected persons and committed them to custody; he co-operated with Chancery in the exercise of the prerogative of mercy; by the Press Act of 1662 he had authority to license books; he issued passports, corresponded with governors of plantations, and had a large share in the direction of home defence; military commissions and correspondence with senior officers passed through his office. Under his charge was a 'Paper Office' in which he might be required to search for precedents.[1] In foreign affairs there was a geographical division of duties between the two principal officials; for example, in 1662, when sir Henry Bennet (Arlington) succeeded Nicholas as one of the secretaries, France and Portugal were in the southern province, while the Empire and the German states were grouped in the northern province. Throughout Charles's reign, the southern was the more important of the two, and, while responsible for this sphere Arlington was exercising the powers of a modern minister of foreign affairs.[2] The secretary's activity in military administration was somewhat lessened by the appointment, in 1683, of William Blathwayt as secretary-at-war, by whose energy and ability this was made an office of importance.

Clarendon could not have foreseen that the institution which seemed to him traditional and static was destined to prove both dynamic and progressive. Nowhere else can the steady expansion of English administrative needs be seen so clearly as in the records of the privy council; in no other body could have been found the elasticity and versatility essential for handling the daily-increasing problems of an adolescent kingdom and a juvenile empire. If the principles of constitutional monarchy were not conceded in Charles's reign, at least its framework was being pieced together; and the monarch who appeared to trouble himself least with the details of government presided over a Council which was already utilizing the services of the expert and specialist. With the steady progress of English maritime enterprise, the creation of new institutions, the exigencies of two wars,

---

[1] *P.C. Reg.* 68, Oct. 10, 1679.

[2] For a full contemporary account of the geographical division see *H.M.C. Rep.* iv, app. 230. *Coventry Papers.*

and an awakening interest in the public conduct of the nation's affairs it came to be realized that the science of government is both complicated and difficult, dependent not only on the aptitude of its agents, but on the collection and interchange of intelligence. Already under the later Stuarts the foundations of a modern and efficient administration were being laid.

During this part of Charles's reign there was almost complete harmony between executive and legislature. His second parliament, the Pensionary Parliament or Long Parliament of the Restoration, met on May 8, 1661, when a full House of Commons was returned, containing a proportion of members from the Convention and the old Long Parliament.[1] Its complexion may be deduced from the king's greeting: 'I know most of your names and faces and can never hope to find better men in your places.' The chancellor was equally gracious. 'It is the privilege,' he said, 'if you please, the prerogative of the common people of England to be represented by the greatest and learnedest and wealthiest and wisest persons that can be chose out of the nation; and the confounding of the Commons of England, which is a noble representative, with the common people of England was the first ingredient in that accursed dose which intoxicated the brains of men with that imagination of a commonwealth.' On his side, the Speaker (sir Edward Turner) assured His Majesty that he was the greatest monarch in the world, and expressed the wish that this announcement might reach to Spain and the Indies. Seldom have the walls of the Parliament House echoed such a concord of harmony.[2]

This unison was ominous for Dissenters and Republicans. On May 20 the Commons obliged themselves to take the Sacrament according to the rites of the Church of England, and ordered the Solemn League and Covenant to be burned.[3] Setting quickly to work, they added a series of measures to the Statute Book of such a character as to create a second Restoration settlement far more uncompromising than the first. The earliest of these was a comprehensive Act for the safety and preservation of His Majesty's

---

[1] For its composition see *infra*, ii. 472–3.
[2] *L.J.* xi. 241–4, 246–8.
[3] *Parl. Hist.* iv. 209.

person,[1] which imposed the penalties of high treason on the expression by printing, writing, or preaching, of any doctrines subversive of the king's royal estate, or likely to encourage the levying of war on the king. Disqualification from office was the punishment for all who declared the king heretic or papist, or asserted that he was trying to introduce popery; and the penalties of *praemunire* were prescribed for every one who maintained that the parliament begun on November 3, 1640, was not dissolved, or that there was an obligation on any person to endeavour a change of government, or that parliament had a legislative power without the king. An exception was made in favour of privilege of debate in parliament. Then followed an Act[2] partly repealing that Act of 1640 which had both disabled persons in Holy Orders from exercising temporal jurisdiction and had abolished the Court of High Commission. By this repealing Statute of 1661 the spiritual peers were restored to their places in parliament, and ecclesiastical courts, with the exception of the Elizabethan High Commission, were revived.[3]

Next, by an Act against tumultuous petitioning,[4] it was made illegal to obtain more than twenty signatures to a petition, or for more than ten persons to present one to parliament. A Militia Act[5] declared the supreme control of the Militia and of all military and naval forces to be vested in the crown; this Act, by its recognition of military forces other than the Militia and the Navy, gave some statutory colour to the institution of a standing army. Lastly, an Act for regulating Corporations[6] authorized commissions to be issued for the better government of all corporate towns, and imposed no less than five obligations on all mayors and officials within these franchises; namely, (1) the oath of allegiance, (2) the oath of supremacy, (3) the taking of the Sacrament according to the practice of the Church of England, (4) a non-resistance oath, and (5) a declaration against the validity of the Solemn League and Covenant. The activities of the commissioners appointed in terms of this Act were not to extend beyond March 25, 1664; but the powers conferred on the

---

[1] 13 Car. II, stat. i, cap. i. See *infra*, ii. 513–14.   [2] Ibid., cap. ii.
[3] Ibid., cap. xii.
[4] Ibid., cap. v.   [5] Ibid., cap. vi. See also *infra*, ii. 470.
[6] Ibid., stat. ii, cap. i. See also *infra*, ii. 517–19.

crown were to be most fully exercised in the great drive against the charters that began in 1681. These Acts are evidence of the passionate outburst of loyalty on the part of a youthful and inexperienced House of Commons.

There was one problem yet to be settled—the fulfilment of the promise of toleration held out in the Declaration of Breda. The Convention Parliament had evaded this question; but Charles's Declaration[1] of October 25, 1660, had promised a national synod for the determination of differences, and on April 5, 1661, this synod met at the Savoy, under the presidency of Sanderson, bishop of Lincoln. Failure was inevitable from the start, because the bishops were once again in the Lords, immeasurably strengthened by their cult of the martyred king; and now that the Restoration was safely achieved, they felt that there was no need to make concessions to those who had helped to bring it about. To make matters worse, Baxter and Calamay, who led for the Dissenters, helped to obscure the real issues under non-essentials, such as the use of 'Lord's Day' for 'Sunday', 'Minister' for 'Priest', and the retention of obsolete words in the Psalter. Kneeling at communion and the gift of prayer by laymen added fuel to the theological fire. More important was the Puritan demand that in the Liturgy there should be used no phrases implying that the congregation was in a state of grace. Here was something more vital than vestments or kneeling. To the Puritan, religion was a personal relationship between God and Man; and Man, overweighted by original sin, was certain to be doomed unless saved by grace; to the Anglican and the Catholic, on the other hand, baptism did regenerate, and the Church with its sacraments fulfilled an essential part in the process of salvation. The Presbyterian-Puritan would confine salvation only to those elected thereto by divine decree; his opponent, less concerned with the solution of celestial probabilities, was as deeply concerned with the spiritual side of existence, but aimed at securing, by the well-ordered ritual of the parish church, a reiterated acquiescence in the established order of things. Both Baxter and Calamy were grievously out of date in thinking that Elizabethan Calvinism was still an essential element in Anglicanism; indeed the Savoy Conference was an

[1] See *supra*, 165–6.

anachronism, reminiscent of 1643 rather than of 1661; for while it was sitting Convocation began its sessions, and its pronouncements were indirectly the reply to the Puritan demands.[1]

The Savoy Conference ended on July 23, 1661; in November a committee of the two houses of Convocation proceeded to the revision of the Prayer Book of 1559. A last appeal for compromise was made in the Lords by the earl of Northumberland, who pleaded that this Book might be confirmed without alteration; but he was answered that it was too late, for letters-patent ordering revision had already been issued.[2] As a result of the committee's labours, about six hundred changes were effected, and several new prayers were added, including that for all sorts and conditions of men (drawn up by Gunning, bishop of Ely). The changes, based mainly on the preliminary work of Gunning and Cosin (bishop of Durham), emphasized the priestly character of the ministry, the regenerative effects of baptism, and the commemorative functions of the Lord's Supper. The Thirty-nine Articles, with their affirmation of the doctrine of Predestination, remained unaltered; otherwise the revised formulary succeeded in rejecting everything considered distinctively Puritan or Papist, and theological difficulties were safely navigated by steering between them. 'It hath been the wisdom of the Church of England', declared the preface, 'to keep the mean between the two extremes of too much stiffness in refusing and of too much easiness in admitting any variation from it.' The revised book was accepted by Convocation on December 20,1661, and by both Houses of Parliament in April 1662. So far as it is permissible for the inexpert layman to have an opinion on these matters, it may be said that the revision emphasized the native catholicism of the Church of England, and stereotyped a liturgy remarkable for both purity of diction and the absence of the dogmatic or provocative.[3]

Now that the liturgy of the Church of England was amended and restored, it remained only to establish the monopoly of a state

---

[1] An account of the deliberations at this conference will be found in *Documents illustrating the Act of Uniformity* (1862).   [2] *Clar. Cont.* ii. 129.

[3] For this subject see E. Cardwell, *A history of conferences and other proceedings connected with the revision of the Book of Common Prayer* (1840); F. Proctor and W. H. Frere, *A new history of the Book of Common Prayer.*

church on the basis of penal legislation. The Act of Uniformity,[1] which received the royal assent on May 19, 1662, imposed the revised Prayer Book, and ordered all deans, lecturers, pastors, and schoolmasters to sign a declaration in which were embodied three things: a repudiation of the Solemn League and Covenant, a denial of the right to take up arms against the king, whether on his (pretended) authority or not, and an undertaking to adopt the liturgy of the Church of England as now established by law. The statute further enacted that, after St. Bartholomew's Day (Sunday, Aug. 24) 1662, every one then in possession of a benefice and not already in holy orders by episcopal ordination should (unless meanwhile he submitted to such ordination) be disabled and deprived. There is some contemporary evidence that, in the Lords, Clarendon opposed the harsher measures embodied in the Bill;[2] by his own later account, however, he thought that once the measure was passed it should be enforced, and he discouraged the king from seeking expedients whereby its penalties might be mitigated.[3] In the Council, some urged that the Presbyterian ministers should be continued in their livings, as the Declaration of Breda had appeared to promise them; but Sheldon, on behalf of his colleagues, made it known that he would comply with no resolution inconsistent with the Act of Uniformity, and that therefore the Presbyterian incumbents must go.[4] So the bishops had their pound of flesh.

By the Act of Uniformity the ministry of the Church of England was confined to persons having fulfilled three conditions: (1) ordination at the hands of a bishop, (2) unfeigned assent to everything in the new Prayer Book, and (3) subscription to a doctrine of non-resistance, together with a repudiation of the view that the Solemn League and Covenant had binding force on any one, including those who had sworn to observe it. Much was therefore asked of candidates for Anglican Orders, and much was undertaken by aspirants thereto. But the Act had certain more immediate and more easily-assessed consequences; for by its

---

[1] 14 Car. II, cap. iv.

[2] *Rawdon Papers*, 137; also Feiling, *History of the Tory Party*, 105, n. 1.

[3] *Clar. Cont.* ii. 142–9.

[4] *Carte MS.* 32, f. 3. Letter to Ormonde regarding the debates in Council (received Sept. 3, 1662).

terms a large number of beneficed clergy were automatically dispossessed if they failed to conform by St. Bartholomew's Day. There are conflicting estimates of the number so affected. A reliable estimate[1] is that about 2,000 men, or about a fifth part of all the beneficed clergy, were deprived during the weeks immediately following the 24th of August 1662. While it is true that a small proportion conformed in order to avoid expulsion, it is certain that the Church lost heavily by this unnecessary sacrifice of many of its best clergy, who were thereby forced into penury and embittered dissent, some of them taking to the plough or to menial occupations, others maintaining a precarious livelihood on little more than bread and water. Most of them helped to strengthen the cause of nonconformity by personal influence and example. Equally serious was the loss of conscientious laymen who followed their dispossessed pastors. By making the Church of England more Erastian and less Protestant, the Act of Uniformity attempted to render the faith immune from the liberal tendencies already manifest in contemporary thought; and so the decline of the Anglican Church, not stemmed until the nineteenth century, may be dated from the moment when this Statute welded into one common ostracism all the different shades and degrees of dissent.

But at the moment when the Cavalier Parliament appeared to have secured the Restoration settlement on the basis then regarded as the soundest, namely religious uniformity, there were becoming evident in king and Court certain indications of leaning to Rome. Charles appears for a time to have toyed with Roman Catholicism and with the project of its partial recognition in England. It is not known what negotiations[2] took place, but,

---

[1] There is a list of dispossessed persons by E. Calamy (in *Bodley, Tanner*, 780). Cf. A. S. Matthews, *Calamy Revised* (1934).

[2] Ranke, *History of England*, iii. 396–8. The document to which Ranke refers is in *Aff. Étr. (Angleterre)*, 81, f. 29, and is dated Feb. 1663. It is entitled: 'Oblatio ex parte Caroli Secundi pro optatissima trium suorum regnorum Angliae, Scotiae et Hiberniae cum Sede Apostolica reunione.' In this document Pius II's Confession of Faith is accepted, with the decisions of the Council of Trent and other Councils; also the decisions of the last two Popes on the Jansenist controversy, but reserving the *stabilita jura et consuetudines* of the English Church. The regimen of the English Church is to remain in archbishops and bishops; married bishops are to retain their wives, but to

whatever they were, nothing came of them. On this very slender evidence a mass of legend has been constructed; and if Charles had had the opportunity of reading what was afterwards to be written on this subject, it is doubtful by which he would have been the more amazed—by the religious enthusiasm attributed to him, or by the Jekyll-and-Hyde career of his reputedly eldest son, James de Cloche.[1] Such authentic correspondence between the Court and Rome as has survived relates mainly to an application for a cardinal's hat on behalf of a relative, the sieur d'Aubigny, uncle of the sixth duke of Lennox, a man summarily described by Burnet as 'a very vicious man, though maintaining an outward decency'.[2] Charles's mother took part in the correspondence, and assured the Pope that, as both the king and a number of his ministers were favourable to the Roman Catholics, an attempt would be made in parliament to obtain some relief for them.[3]

Among the ministers to whom the Queen Mother was referring, it is possible that even Clarendon was included; for he was still leaning, on the one side, to a suspension of the Act of Uniformity in favour of Presbyterians, while, on the other, he had relations with the Catholics through his secretary Bellings;[4] and so, in spite of the categoric statements in his *Autobiography*, it may be inferred that in 1662 the chancellor had no religious policy at all. Events may have forced him to make up his mind. On December 26, 1662, Charles boldly issued a Declaration in which, having alluded to his promises from Breda and the settlement of the Church by the Act of Uniformity, he announced that he would try to induce parliament to concur in securing legislative sanction for the exercise of that dispensing power which he conceived to be inherent in himself.[5] To this proposal the Speaker of the

be succeeded by celibates. Belief in Purgatory is accepted. There is no evidence to connect Charles II with this document.

[1] For some forged letters to and from Rome on this subject see Boero, *Istoria della converzione alla Chiesa Catholica di Carlo II*. See also Andrew Lang, *The Valet's Tragedy*. This mysterious son of Charles was entered in the baptismal registry of Jersey not as James de la Cloche, but as James de Cloche du Bourg de Jersey.

[2] *Burnet*, i. 243.   [3] *P.R.O. Rome Transcripts*, 99, f. 41.

[4] K. Feiling, *Clarendon and the Act of Uniformity* in *E.H.R.* xliv.

[5] *Parl. Hist.* iv. 257.

Commons replied[1] in no uncertain terms (Feb. 27, 1663): 'We have considered the nature of Your Majesty's Declaration from Breda and are humbly of opinion that Your Majesty ought not to be pressed with it any further, because it is not a promise in itself, but only a gracious declaration of Your Majesty's intentions to do what in you lay, and what a parliament should advise you to do.' This step having failed, the king's friends now introduced into the Lords a Bill enabling the king by letters patent or otherwise to dispense with the Act of Uniformity. This Bill, the drafting of which was done mainly by the Presbyterian Robartes, was attacked by Clarendon[2] and was lost in committee; rightly or wrongly to Clarendon was attributed this failure to embody in law the royal preference for toleration.

Clarendon's opinions may have been influenced by the fact that the Declaration of 1662 was penned by one whom he regarded with intense dislike—sir Henry Bennet, afterwards lord Arlington. From the moment when, in October 1662, Bennet succeeded Nicholas as one of the secretaries of state, the authority of Clarendon began to be undermined; for even thus early, Charles was turning to younger men, and was seeking ministers more accommodating in disposition than the chancellor. It might therefore be possible at this point to distinguish two parties in embryo: the one, youthful and enthusiastic, convinced that the king was now so firmly settled in the saddle as to justify a canter in the direction of Rome, or to whatever quarter the rider's fancy took him; the other, older and more experienced, afraid that the steed bestridden by Charles was waiting the first opportunity to throw him, and must therefore be held firmly in check. Clarendon, of necessity, came to be more closely associated with leadership of the latter party, and his caution was soon discredited by what seemed to many contemporaries a mercenary surrender. This was the sale of Dunkirk. In August 1661 the question of its transfer to France had first been mooted, when Clarendon[3] informed D'Estrades that its garrison and maintenance had cost the king, since his return, about £400,000. Of those who advised the sale, the foremost was Sandwich, who

---

[1] *Parl. Hist.* iv. 261.

[2] *Lister*, ii. 211–12 and iii. 243, Clarendon to Ormonde, March 1663; and *Clar. Cont.* ii. 347.   [3] *Clar. S.P.* iii, supplement, xxi–xxv.

considered that the harbour was exposed to storms and liable to be silted up; it was argued also that the fortress was weak on the land side; that the cost of its upkeep (£120,000 per annum) was disproportionate to its value; and also that its retention might involve England in continental war. Some thought that the acquisition of Tangier made Dunkirk unnecessary as a naval base, and that the finances did not permit the upkeep of both places. At the Council Board only the earl of St. Albans opposed the proposed sale;[1] its possible value for the herring fishing does not appear to have been considered.[2] After much bargaining, conducted mainly by Clarendon and D'Estrades, a sum of five million livres was agreed upon, and the transfer was effected late in October 1662.[3] Part of the purchase price was to be used by Charles for the active support of Portugal, the French ambassador being instructed to see that this condition was fulfilled.[4] This speedy sacrifice of one of Cromwell's most valued acquisitions could not but have had its influence on public opinion; and, quite unjustly, to Clarendon was imputed not only the initiative in this transaction, but a share in the purchase price. His house, in course of erection in Piccadilly, was nicknamed Dunkirk House.

Clarendon's decline may be dated from the summer of 1661, when the implications of the Restoration Settlement had become revealed; for by Catholic and Nonconformist alike he was held responsible for the denial of toleration; by the Courtiers, he was thought to be the agent whereby parliament had made insufficient financial provision for the crown; by the Cavaliers, he was blamed for the land settlement, and for the insufficient reward to loyalists.[5] By 1663 he might well have been removed from the royal favour had it not been for the rashness of one of the Catholic hot-heads—the earl of Bristol, who took upon himself the leader-

---

[1] *Clar. Cont.* ii. 248. Clarendon thought that by opposition St. Albans designed to bring the negotiation into his own hands.

[2] Cf. the memorial on this point in *Sloane MS.* 2444.

[3] *Lister*, ii. 173.

[4] *Instructions Donneés (Angleterre)*, i. 318. For the disposal of the Dunkirk money see *Cal. Tr. Bks.*, *1660–7*, 459 and 493. £70,000 was paid to the Navy; £30,000 to the Guards; £36,000 to the Household; £14,000 to Tangier.

[5] For the cabals against Clarendon in August 1661 see D'Estrades's report in *Baschet*, 109, Aug. 19/29. For May 1662 see *Rawdon Papers*, 164–5.

ship of the chancellor's enemies. Bristol, knowing Charles's secret inclinations, appears to have utilized this knowledge in a manner suggestive of blackmail.[1] Having assured Charles that he had sufficient influence in the Commons to raise there a party which would be more solicitous of his revenues, he then attacked Clarendon from his seat in the Lords; and on July 10, 1663, brought forward articles of impeachment. Seldom has a more ridiculous venture been made in parliament. The accusations, wherever they were not matters of hearsay or gossip, were easily refutable untruths; and when the Lords referred the articles to the Judges, the latter reported that, even if the charges were substantiated, there was no treason in them; nor might a charge of high treason be originally introduced into the Lords by one peer against another. So ignominious was the collapse of the prosecution that Bristol absconded, and Clarendon's influence was, for the time, restored; but with this difference, that while hitherto he had relied mainly on his personal influence with Charles, he must henceforth depend on his churchmanship, and on his alliance with the bishops and the intolerant element in the House of Commons.

The result was seen in the measures which followed the Act of Uniformity, a series of statutes to which the name Clarendon Code has been given—an attribution justified only in the sense that, after 1663, Clarendon was the most notable exponent of the view that sedition and dissent were inseparable. He was not the author of the legislation which passes under his name, yet he was one of the most influential of those who professed belief in its necessity, and his complete acquiescence in it was the price he paid for retaining power. It is certain at least that the Clarendon of 1663 was not the free agent who in 1660 had helped to draw up the Declaration of Breda; for he was now dependent on the Anglican Commons against the king, and on national intolerance against his crypto-Catholic enemies. From this point, therefore, the flood of legislative revenge had free course. The Conventicle Act (1664)[2] made illegal all assemblies of five or more persons over 16 years of age under colour of religion; for the first offence, a fine of £5 was imposed, and, after a third conviction, the penalty was transportation to a plantation other than Virginia or New

---

[1] *Clar. Cont.* ii. 258–62, and *Lister*, ii. 222 sqq.   [2] 16 Car. II, cap. iv.

England. The Act for restraining nonconformists from inhabiting corporations,[1] commonly called the Five Mile Act (1665), reaffirmed the obligation of all in holy orders to take the prescribed oaths, and forbade all preachers and teachers refusing the oaths to come within five miles of a corporate town, or of the parish where they had taught or preached. All such persons, as well as those who failed to attend the parish church, were forbidden, under a penalty of £40, to teach, whether as schoolmasters or private tutors; and thus the legislature did its best to deprive the educated dissenter or ejected minister of one of his most natural means of livelihood. By a later Act (1670)[2] persons permitting conventicles to be held in their houses were to be fined £20, and constables were authorized to break into enclosed premises in search of conventicles. This Act was followed (May 1670–April 1671) by an intensive campaign[3] against the sects, when the Militia was called upon to disperse conventicles, and offenders were dealt with summarily at Quarter Sessions. In the course of this campaign, informing became a lucrative profession. Relief eventually came, not from the adoption of enlightened views such as Ashley was maintaining, but from a change in the international situation whereby the flood of vindictiveness was diverted from the Dissenters to Papists.

Such was the legislation—most of it imposed on Charles as the price of supply. It is difficult to determine how far it was enforced, for much depended on the temperament of the justices; moreover England was still a country of segregated provincialism, and just as equity was as long as the chancellor's foot, so mercy was as warm as the justice's heart. In towns where there existed large communities of Dissenters, as Bristol, Gloucester, Taunton, Canterbury, Norwich, Dover, and Yarmouth, offences against the Code were frequently winked at, and in these places the grand juries sometimes refused to indict Quakers or Dissenters. In Lewes, conventicles were reported to be as frequent as in Oliver's time;[4] Bath was famous for these gatherings, and Charles may himself have seen them when he went there with his consort in the summer of 1663. At Hereford, Roman

---

[1] 17 Car. II, cap. ii.   [2] 22 Car. II, cap. i.
[3] F. Bate, *Declaration of Indulgence*, 68.
[4] *Cal. S.P. Dom.*, 1663–4, 293.

Catholics were more frequently indicted than Nonconformists.[1] Moreover, the royal clemency was sometimes exercised, as when in January 1663 a warrant was issued ordering the release of all conventiclers in Newgate, provided they were not seditious.[2] But sometimes the law was enforced to the ruin of its victims. Bunyan suffered twelve years close confinement, and throughout the State Papers of the reign will be found many instances where the law was rigorously applied.

In a sense, the so-called Clarendon Code was panic legislation, explained not so much by zeal on behalf of Anglican doctrine or discipline, as by a form of national hysteria which did not find its full expression until the Popish Plot. These Acts were passed when the air was heavy with rumours of rebellions and insurrections; it needed only a few authentic plots to justify such fears in the minds of the legislature. One of the earliest was in December 1660, when an old Cromwellian soldier was arrested and, on being questioned by the king, confessed that there was a design to murder Monck and march on Whitehall. Sixty suspects were captured as a result of his disclosures, including colonel Overton.[3] Hence the fear entertained by the government that the disbanded troops were planning an insurrection, and hence also the numerous proclamations[4] ordering their departure from London. In January 1661 a fanatic cooper named Venner, accompanied by fifty men, proceeded to set up in the streets of London the Fifth Monarchy or reign of Jesus Christ on earth. This was instantly suppressed; Venner and others were hanged, but, unfortunately, from the truth that the Fifth Monarchy men were extremists was deduced the unwarrantable opinion that all Dissenters were politically dangerous. In September of the same year another rising was thought to be imminent from headquarters at Wrexham, 'the most factious town in England', the leaders of which were said to be in communication with the exiled Ludlow;[5] and September 3, the

---

[1] *Cal. S.P. Dom.*, *1663–4*, 293.

[2] Register of Royal Warrants, 1661–5, *Add. MS.* 35117, f. 74.

[3] Report of Bartet in *Baschet*, 108, Dec. 17/27, 1660.

[4] e.g. the proclamations of Dec. 1660; April 1661; Nov. 1661; March 1664; Nov. 1664 (in *Steele*, i. 3270, 3296, 3339, 3397, and 3404).

[5] *Cal. S.P. Dom.*, *1661–2*, 80.

anniversary of the battles of Dunbar and Worcester and of Cromwell's death, was regarded as the most likely date of the rising.

The instructions issued at frequent intervals to the lords lieutenant show that the Privy Council attached great weight to these rumours. At such moments of panic the measures taken for increased security consisted in calling out the Militia, occupying places of strength, imprisoning scare-mongers, and enforcing more strictly the laws against rogues and vagabonds.[1] On at least one occasion these rumours proved to have some foundation. In October 1663 so insistent was the talk of a rising in Yorkshire that the leading Dissenters were put under restraint; musketeers were placed in populous boroughs, and the Militia was concentrated at Ferrybridge.[2] The talk was not without foundation. A plot of northern Presbyterians and Anabaptists was foiled through information having been intercepted (notably by bishop Cosin),[3] and so the government was able to arrest many of the ringleaders before the day planned for the rising. Ludlow was to have held Wales with 10,000 men; Fairfax also was named as a possible leader, and there was a design of inducing the troops returning from Portuguese service to serve as auxiliaries. Of this plot, sometimes called the Derwentdale Plot, the objects were said to be (1) capture of Whitehall, and the seizure of Clarendon, with the dukes of York and Albemarle, in order to oblige the king to implement his promises given at Breda, (2) abolition of Excise and Hearth Money, and (3) restoration of a gospel ministry. Fairfax and Manchester disowned the use made by the plotters of their names. The seriousness of this project, together with the large proportion of the population supposed to be in sympathy with its objects, may have served in some measure to justify the extreme measures taken by the legislature to bridle dissent.

That the surviving regicides on the Continent were awaiting an opportunity of returning to England in order to overthrow the monarchy was the conviction of every one in touch with the intelligence department organized by the secretaries of state.

[1] An example of these instructions will be found in *P.C. Reg.* 56, July 6, 1662.   [2] *Cal. S.P. Dom.*, *1663-4*, 298-380.
[3] Rev. H. Gee, *The Derwentdale Plot* in *Trans. R. H. Soc.*, series iii, xi.

Special vigilance had therefore to be exercised—in the north, and at all the ports; also among the soldiers and sailors who had served the Commonwealth. There was constant interception of mails from abroad, particularly Holland; the exiles Sidney and Ludlow, the 'old Army' in Ireland, and even persons 'strongly neuter' were alike the objects of inquiry and supervision. As late as 1671, Richard Cromwell, the most innocuous personality of his age, was considered so dangerous that orders were given to search houses in London where he was thought to be concealed. There was no limit to the extent of these fears; indeed, even such a national affair as the Second Dutch War was considered by some to have originated as a 'court diversion', intended to provide an enterprise for keeping the people occupied and quiet.[1] In consequence, Charles's government regarded all concourses of men as dangerous—whether they were conventiclers worshipping in cellar or on the hill-side; or London apprentices 'rambling' on an afternoon holiday; or talkative gatherings in coffee-houses; or dinners of city companies, where men might become heated by injudicious toasts. The fact that Charles died peaceably in his royal bed has led posterity to under-estimate the element of precipitancy and anxiety from which no statesman of his reign could altogether escape.

While its monopoly was being assured, the work of reconstruction proceeded steadily in the Church of England in the years immediately after the Restoration.[2] Churches and episcopal palaces were restored, mainly by the munificence of great ecclesiastics such as Cosin, Morley, and Sheldon; the old territorial possessions were regained, and the activities of archidiaconal and consistorial courts were renewed. The High Commission with its *ex officio* oath was gone; but on the other hand the church courts were busier than ever with defaulting laymen.[3] In these years of consolidation the Anglican theologians were also busy, and in their writings can be detected the drift from the grim

[1] Memoir on the origin of the war between English and Dutch, in *Aff. Étr.* (*Angleterre*), 82, printed in Japikse, *De verwikkelingen tusschen de Republiek en Engeland*, bijlage xv.

[2] For this see J. Stoughton, *The Church of the Restoration*, ii. 198 sqq. For a more distinctively Anglican interpretation of the subject see W. H. Hutton, *The English Church from the accession of Charles I to the death of Queen Anne.*

[3] For this see *infra*, ii. 495–9.

dogmatism of sixteenth-century formularies to more liberal and eclectic doctrines. Examples are Herbert Thorndyke (1598–1672), Peter Heylyn (1600–62), George Bull (1634–1710), and Jeremy Taylor[1] (1613–67). Thorndyke, a fellow of Trinity College, Cambridge, succeeded in evolving doctrines so oecumenic in character as to receive the commendation of cardinal Newman. He definitely rejected the Calvinism which had been given a temporary lodging in the necessitous Elizabethan Church, and proclaimed that a man's will is determined by his own acts. Heylyn, as parson of Alresford, had vindicated the principles of his church even during the Usurpation; later, though debarred from promotion by ill health, he perpetuated in his books a scholarly but somewhat querulous Laudianism, particularly acceptable to churchmen who held Calvinist theology in abhorrence. George Bull, bishop of St. Davids, wrote with such enlightenment on the necessity for good works that his countrymen thought him a Socinian, and Bossuet thought him a Papist, a misconception which was cleared up by Bull himself in his *Corruptions of the Church of Rome*, by far the most popular of his works. Most memorable of these writers was Jeremy Taylor, who, in his devotional writings, explored the vast resources of the English language in sonorous periods that have survived the controversies which first inspired them. His *Holy Living* and *Holy Dying*, while never profound nor even incisive, have always held the attention of readers by their convincing exposition of the duties of a Christian, and to his sermons, his books, and his personal example the devotional element in Anglicanism owes much.

On the fringes of the Church of England stood the pioneers of a liberal and mystical Protestantism, men collectively known as the Cambridge Platonists.[2] Composed mainly of scholars and college tutors, this school had some personal affinities with the Puritan Emmanuel College, but in temper it was more Anglican than Nonconformist. They were the true continuators of Hooker, Falkland, and Chillingworth. Among the more notable of them

[1] There is a good account of these theologians in Stoughton, op. cit. ii. 268 sqq.; see also W. H. Hutton, *A history of the English Church, 1625–1714.*

[2] For this subject see J. Tulloch, *Rational Theology and Christian Philosophy in England in the seventeenth century* (1872).

were Benjamin Whichcote and Henry More. Whichcote strove
for the reinstatement of reason in theology: 'Man', he wrote,[1]
'has as much right to use his own understanding in judging of
truth, as he has the right to use his own eyes'; also, 'those who
differ upon reason, may come together by reason'. These were
remarkable views in an age slowly emancipating itself from the
opinion that religion, like knowledge, is finite, and already fully
revealed. Henry More tried to reinterpret for his contemporaries the lessons he had derived from a study of Plato, Ficino,
and Descartes, lessons in which philosophic doubt was harmonized with lofty idealism and mysticism. Though educated a
Calvinist, he liked the Church of England for 'its decent gran-
deur and splendour';[2] and he revered the pristine Anglicanism
of Hooker. No one explored more deeply than did he the inner
workings of fancy and enthusiasm in the life of the spirit. 'Walking abroad after his studies,' wrote his biographer, 'his sallies
towards Nature would be often inexpressibly enravishing and
beyond what he could convey to others.'[3] To these 'notional
apprehensions' of high matters he joined a probity of life and
demeanour well according with them, and he has enriched our
literature with apocalyptic treatises wherein he very nearly succeeded in explaining his semi-spiritualist beliefs. By his life and
teaching he helped to restore the soul to religion, and he is one
of the few theological writers of his age who can still be read.

If our common necessities and duties are the same [wrote Stilling-
fleet];[4] if we have the same blessings to pray and to thank God for
in our solemn devotions; why should we think it unlawful or un-
fitting to use the same expressions? Is God pleased with the change
of our words and phrases? Can we imagine the Holy Spirit is given
to dictate new expressions in prayers?

In their moderation and reasonableness these words are characteristic of the appeal made by the more educated exponents of
the later Caroline Church. That Church could at least expect
the allegiance of by far the greater part of the nation; for, in a
population estimated at nearly five millions, there were probably
not more than 150,000 Dissenters, and only 15,000 to 20,000

[1] Tulloch, op. cit. ii. 100.   [2] Ibid. ii. 338.
[3] R. Ward, *Life of Henry More* (1710), 54.
[4] Stillingfleet, *Ecclesiastical Cases* (1698), 41.

Roman Catholics.[1] Articles of inquiry presented by bishops and archdeacons testify to the minute control exercised by the Church over the daily lives and opinions of the flock; and by investigation and punishment, these custodians strove to expel blasphemy, atheism, and immorality. So too they insisted on belief in the Scriptures, as containing everything necessary for salvation; in the Church of England, as a true and apostolic church, a true member of the Catholic Church; in the ritual of that Church, as neither popish nor idolatrous; in the baptism of infants, as lawful and necessary, and in the doctrine that the king has the same authority in causes ecclesiastical 'as hath been given always to all godly princes by God himself'.[2]

Such were the more formal ministrations. At the universities, where some speculation was permissible, learned men debated whether original sin was transferred from Adam; whether the 'pseudo-Roman Catholic Church' was idolatrous; whether Christ would reign one thousand years on earth before the Day of Judgement; whether faith should be kept with heretics; were all the Apostles equal? are good works necessary to salvation? is marriage forbidden to bishops, priests, and deacons *jure divino*?[3] Less disturbing were the printed directions provided for the guidance of laymen; such as *Catechetical Questions*,[4] where problems were reduced to question and answer; or *Directions about preparing for Death*,[5] a book of eminently practicable morality, containing a suitable list of passages from scripture; or *The Communicant Instructed*,[6] consisting of eleven chapters of exacting questions for the ordeal of self-examination. The number and tone of these books suggest that the older, dogmatic theology was slowly

[1] For estimates see Stoughton, op. cit. ii. 207–8. In the spring of 1676 Danby, with the help of the Church, attempted a census of religions in England. For the province of Canterbury the number of adult Roman Catholics was estimated at 12,000, and of adult Nonconformists, 93,000. The province of York was assumed to contain a sixth of these totals. (A. Browning, *Life and Letters of sir T. Osborne, earl of Danby*, i, ch. x.)

[2] Articles of visitation and inquiry in the diocese of Ely, in the second episcopal visitation of Peter [Gunning], 1679.

[3] These were the theological *Quaestiones* debated at Oxford in the Act of 1661. *Bodley Fol. Θ* 659.

[4] By S. Lowth, 1673.

[5] By T. B., 1669.

[6] Anon., 1668.

being replaced by a faith emphasizing the duties of the Christian as churchman and subject.

There was also much spiritual activity outside the bounds of the Church. Of that more moderate English Presbyterianism which was forced by legislation into the camp of active dissent Richard Baxter may be taken as an example. In boyhood he 'searched the Scriptures' and conducted his own education, a process in which he became earnest but uncompromising. He thought that kneeling might be lawful, but he had doubts regarding the surplice and the use of the cross in baptism. He composed long, sad books, all in a minor key; and his ministry in Kidderminster coincided with a period of spiritual regeneration in a town then considered of dubious reputation. At the Savoy Conference he had led his cause with courage and ability, but that cause might have been better served by one more diplomatic and less conscientious. Like Calamy, he had declined a bishopric at the Restoration; and whatever name may be applied to his principles, it is clear that they were in no way subversive of the state; for his followers were not Quakers, nor Anabaptists, nor Fifth Monarchy Men, all of whom incurred the suspicion generally aroused in that age by the novel or the original; on the contrary, Baxter and Calamy taught a Protestantism which claimed to be as old and as authoritative as that professed by the Church of England. Their moderate Presbyterianism might well have joined forces with moderate Anglicanism, and so Nonconformity would have been narrowed down to the Sects, which ultimately would have been discredited by their own excesses.

The disciples of Baxter, often spoken of as Presbyterian, were latitudinarian and evangelical rather than Calvinist, representative not so much of definite dogmas as of those vaguer spiritual questionings in which English dissent had found its beginnings. One reason why the more formal Presbyterianism failed to make much headway in England was the difficulty of finding a competent body of men to act as ruling elders. Pride's Purge and the abolition of the House of Lords had destroyed the strength of the party in parliament, and prevented it from obtaining any footing during the Usurpation; there was a brief revival in the weeks immediately preceding the Restoration, and even a hope of comprehension in the Establishment, but the Cavalier reaction thrust even the aristocratic type of Presbyterianism into the abyss of social and political disability, and the term came to be used loosely of dissent, whether extreme or moderate, religious or political. While Roman Catholics were penalized, Presbyterians were ostracized, a difference thus explained in Crowne's *Sir Courtly Nice* (1685):

Testimony (A Fanatic): Friend, if you be a Papist, I'll ha' you before a justice.
Hothead (A Zealot): Sirrah, if you be a Presbyterian, I'll kick you downstairs.

It is probable that after 1660 many Presbyterians went over to Anglicanism, thus providing the nucleus of a Low-Church party; but a greater number may have joined the Independents, who were the true exponents of native nonconformity, the legitimate inheritors of the Wycliffite tradition, and among the progenitors of Wesleyanism and Congregationalism. The Independents were to be found throughout England; but they were strongest in London, in the weaving villages of East Anglia, and in the towns of the south-west, in Gloucestershire and in Bedfordshire. Rejecting altogether the institutional conception of the church, they dissociated religion from the state; they thought of each congregation as a distinct entity, responsible for its own organization; and from the Bible they derived both the inspiration and the confirmation of the pettiest acts of human existence. By this substitution of individual judgement for definite dogma and ordered worship, they offended all the best seventeenth-century canons, particularly as they were mostly 'small' men, pursuing mechanical occupations in crowded little towns, and therefore thought to be in special need of control and supervision. In the New England colonies Independency found its fullest expression; for there its emotionalism accorded well with the needs of men thrown back on themselves for the perpetuation of their civilization; producing pioneers, ruthless and indomitable in their leadership, and a chosen people, jealously safeguarding those religious and civil convictions which they had brought with them into the wilderness.

Thus English Independency acquired some influence and

cohesion by contrast with the more formal Presbyterianism. The same is true of the Society of Friends,[1] founded by George Fox (1624–91), the son of a Leicestershire weaver, and on his mother's side a descendant of martyrs. He received a 'call' at the age of 19, but, as his doubts were not dispelled by consultations with the clergy, he began his ministry by the most spontaneous of all methods—by brawling in church. His personal emaciation and his gift of second sight made him tolerant of blows, and both candid and trenchant in his utterances, which had a simplicity and directness that would have been destroyed by book-learning; for he was 'one of Nature's originals, being no man's copy', a creature of complete spontaneity and impulse, more likely to remove his boots than his hat. At first he consorted mainly with Baptists, from whom he recruited many followers; these converts, first named Children of the Light, were afterwards called Truth's Friends, and in 1650 they were termed Quakers. Soon the society was reinforced by admission of the more visionary of the Sectaries, whose almost corybantic enthusiasm was soothed and regulated by Fox's discipline of silence; indeed it was by this mingling of emotionalism with quietism that Fox wielded his influence over contemporaries. This dualism has influenced the later history of Quakerism. In 1668 it was noted that, because of the severity of the law against them, they began to be respected,[2] and by 1669 they may be considered an organized body; for they commenced their yearly meetings in that year; and thereafter they were purged and welded in the fires of persecution which, for George Fox, were tempered by his absences on missionary work in Scotland, Holland, and North America.[3] With other Nonconformists the Quakers enjoyed a brief respite from persecution between 1672 and 1675; but in 1684–5 the rigour against them was renewed for a short period, and nearly 1,400 were confined in gaol.[4] On

---

[1] There is a large literature of the subject. Reference should be made to Fox's *Journal*; also, W. C. Braithwaite, *The beginnings of Quakerism* and *The second period of Quakerism* (1660–1725); also E. B. Emmott, *The story of Quakerism*, and M. E. Hirst, *The Quakers in peace and war*.

[2] *Grey*, i. 128.

[3] For a survey of Quaker life and organization see C. E. Whiting, *Studies in English Puritanism*, ch. v.

[4] Braithwaite, *The second period of Quakerism*, 84, 109.

both English and American civilization they have left their mark; for they were among the earliest opponents of dynastic wars; they have always consistently advocated national development by peace rather than aggression, and their deep convictions have generally been linked with personal integrity and business aptitude. The Quakers were the dynamic force in English dissent.

The Baptists are said to have derived their first inspiration from John Smith, a vicar of Gainsborough, who in 1608 fled with some of his parishioners to Amsterdam, where he founded a church. He believed that baptism could regenerate the adult alone, and only after he had made a personal confession of faith. He held also that the true apostolic succession had been lost, and that the Church must be restored to a primitive and apostolic model. By 1644 two forms of Baptist worship were established in England—the General Baptists who, like the Arminians, believed in a universal atonement for all men; and the Particular or Calvinist Baptists who limited regeneration to the Elect. They both issued confessions of faith in 1677–8 and held several general assemblies in the later years of the century. They were strongest in Kent, Leicestershire, Lincolnshire, and Buckingham, but practically non-existent in the north of England, and it was in North America, rather than in England, that they achieved their fullest development. General Harrison, though classed as a Fifth Monarchy man, professed adherence to their principles; John Bunyan,[1] though often regarded as a typical Baptist preacher, repudiated the name, and cannot be definitely allotted to any one sect.

But this enumeration fails to do justice to the rich variety of English dissent.[2] When Cosmo III, grand duke of Tuscany, travelled in England he was astounded by the number and diversity of the recognized religious beliefs.[3] There were the Brownists, a congregational sect; the Fifth Monarchy Men, who awaited Christ's reign of a thousand years, and believed that women should be admitted to the ministry; the Sabbatarians,

[1] For Bunyan see *infra*, ii. 738–41.
[2] For a full account see C. E. Whiting, *Studies in English Puritanism*.
[3] L. Magalotti, *Travels of Cosmo III* (1821); also Whiting, op. cit., ch. vi, 'The Minor Sects'.

who kept the Sabbath with Jewish rigidity; the Muggletonians, who were alleged to believe in the efficacy of cursing and swearing; the Libertines and Antinomians, who distinguished between the sins of the wicked and the sins of the Children of Light; the Ranters, who burnt bibles; the Adamites, who rejected clothing; the Anabaptists, who rejected infant baptism; and the Familists, who rejected all but love. Such at least were some of the distinctive tenets imputed, rightly or wrongly, to these sects. For adequate commentary on these rejections and expectations resort must be made to the famous box, from which James II extracted the mysterious documents[1] penned by his royal brother. 'It is a sad thing to consider', announced the oracle from the box, 'what a world of heresies are crept into this nation; every man thinks himself as competent a judge as the very apostles themselves. If the power of interpreting Scriptures be in every man's brain, what need have we of a church?'

But these multi-coloured products prove a native vigour in the garden of English religion, constantly fortified by the pruning of legislator and justice, and impervious to the icy blasts of sarcasm and ridicule. Englishmen were less sensitive than Frenchmen to the ludicrous or the bizarre; hence *Hudibras* never achieved the success of the *Satyre Menipée*, and the 'good nature' which Clarendon noted as a characteristic of Englishmen[2] helped gradually to foster a tolerance of personal opinion. As nowhere else, men acquired the habit of thinking for themselves. Insistence on uniformity served only to strengthen disagreement; and to Clarendon may be attributed some responsibility for the entrenchment in our national life of the one native institution which no foreigner can hope to copy—the nonconformist conscience.

Such, in brief, was the direction given to Restoration England by the administration of Clarendon. Abroad, there were soon to be fought the last two Anglo-Dutch wars. For an understanding of the causes and the course of these wars it is necessary to interpose two chapters, one on our commerce, the other on our fighting services.

---

[1] *Sloane MS.* 3251, ff. 12–14.
[2] Clarendon's speech, Sept. 13, 1660, in *L.J.* xi. 174.

VI

COMMERCE AND TRADE

THE surveyor of Charles II's England would have learned much about its commerce from ships and cargoes. Thus, in the coasting trade, carried on by ships of seldom more than 40 tons burthen, there was conveyed a great number of goods which to-day would be transported by road. Provisions, raw hides, horses, cattle, malt, saddlery, soap, iron, tin, and pewter-ware were then transported by sea, these humble cargoes being seldom without a consignment of highly flavoured spices such as aniseed and caraway. Inspection of the larger ships entering English ports might reveal a cargo of 'sea cole' from Newcastle, or iron from Stockholm, salt from France or Scotland, brandy and wine from Bordeaux, canvas from Brittany, wine from Cadiz and the Canaries, deal planks and resin from Norway, spices, carpets, and oriental ware from Smyrna, the Levant, or the East Indies. Mixed cargoes would include Flemish soap, spruce deals, flax, potash, whale-fins, Scotch salmon, pipe-staves, and wrought silk.[1] Outward-bound ships might have coal[2] for Lisbon; hemp-seed, barley, oats, and wheat for Dutch ports; 'decayed pease' for Norway; or sprats for Rotterdam; but all these exports yielded in importance to the vast quantities of manufactured cloth and woollens which then found a ready market abroad. Ships sailing to the Mediterranean were sometimes (owing to the danger from pirates) mustered into fleets —a practice facilitated by the seasonal character of some of the trades. For example, the earliest pilchard ships generally sailed from Plymouth in August, and might pick up in the Channel a fleet of cloth ships bound for Turkey; late in October these ships started their homeward voyage with cargoes of currants

---

[1] Information derived from the *Port Books* (*P.R.O.*).

[2] For the state of the coal trade in 1671 see *H.M.C. Rep.* ix, app., pt. ii, where a petitioner stated that English coal was sold cheaper abroad than at home. It appears to have been exported mainly to Ireland, Portugal, and the Plantations. For the difficulties consequent on the inequality of Customs duties on English and Scottish coal see *Carte MS.* 34, f. 170 (Apr. 1665).

and oil. In November the latest pilchard ships were sent out, and, after landing their wares at Venice, Zante, Smyrna, and Messina, returned with the last consignments of oil and fruit.[1] Occasionally these fleets were convoyed.

Evading the Customs was reduced by some shipmasters to a fine art. Thus a ship from Holland, France, or Flanders with 'fine and high-customed goods' might unlade these at sea into a collier, which would smuggle them in under its coal; or the richly-laden ship might manage to press in with a fleet of colliers and so escape unnoticed; sometimes also brandy, wine, linens, silk, and spices were concealed under apples or onions, which took so long to sell in port that, after about a week, the tidesmen were discharged, and the more valuable commodities could then be landed; or a ship coming from Norway, supposed to have nothing but heavy and large goods such as timber, might have taken in a cargo at Amsterdam before sailing to a Norwegian port.[2] Occasionally goods were smuggled in warships.[3] In order to cope with these evasions, the legislature was obliged to strengthen the powers of the Customs officials,[4] and though smuggling was never stamped out, it was carried on under greater difficulties.

From these observations it might have been deduced that England had a large trade with Portugal, Brazil, the Canaries, and Madeira in sugar, 'speckled wood' (mahogany), fruit, and sack; with France, in canvas, linen, brandy, and wine; with the Baltic, in ships' stores; with the Mediterranean, in spices, silk, fruit, and oil. In exchange for these were exported commodities such as fish, tin, lead, and manufactured goods, mainly cloth. It would be noted also that many of these imports were re-exported, and that England was becoming a staple for tobacco, most of it from Virginia and Maryland, and of sugar, notably from Barbados. Further investigation would have shown that the balance of our trade with Flemish ports was favourable, our exports being estimated at twice the value of our imports;[5] that

---

[1] Proposals touching convoys, in *Memoirs of the English Affairs, chiefly naval* (1729), 196.

[2] Proposals for advancing His Majesty's Customs, in *Shaftesbury*, xxx, no. 67.   [3] For evasions of the Navigation Acts see *infra*, 243–4.

[4] See *infra*, ii. 422.   [5] *H.M.C. Rep.* ix, app., pt. ii. 11, Mar. 1671.

with Portugal, the balance was becoming increasingly favour-able,[1] owing to our increased exports of coal, cloth, corn, fish, lead, and tin, commodities which were paid for in bullion, sugar, mahogany, fruit and wine; and that Spain also was a good 'vent' for our products, though her colonial empire was still closed to English trade. France, on the other hand, was respon-sible for a heavy balance against us, estimated in 1674 to be nearly a million pounds per annum.[2] English opinion was in-fluenced by these facts, in so far as they were known. Patriots, however, were concerned not only with the disparity between the values of our exports to France and our imports therefrom, but with the supposed effeminate character of these latter, con-sisting as they did mainly of silk, claret, and fancy goods. Had the patriots been in possession of all the facts, they might have found still further cause for indignation; because in the course of the reign there was a steady increase in luxury imports, espe-cially from France. In 1680 they included green tortoise-shell from Jamaica, wrought silk from Leghorn, hair and periwigs from Rostock, tobacco boxes, 'marmerlade' boxes, children's daggers and rattles from Bilbao, singing birds from Rotterdam, 'diaper napkening' from Hamburg, and from France (the inter-dict on her wines, linen, cloth, silk, salt, and paper had been imposed in 1678) there were commodities which must have shocked any sober-minded Saxon—cucumbers, hair-powder, chocolate, preserved ginger, almonds, looking-glasses, tooth-brushes, and even paving pebbles.[3] It was in our ports that was most clearly evidenced the great development of wealth and luxury in the reign of Charles; and the parliamentary debates of the reign might have been even more acrimonious had our politicians been in the habit of frequenting the docks.

England was comparatively late in entering the race for mari-time supremacy. By 1660 the United Dutch Provinces had made serious inroads on the monopoly of colonial empire formerly divided between Spain and Portugal. Her scattered plantations in the west, together with her trading interests in the Mediterranean and in the east, forced England into the

---

[1] Ibid. 11–12.   [2] Ibid. 14, 33.
[3] *Port Book*, 95 (London, 1680).

contest; but internal troubles prevented a good start, and much lee-way had to be made up; for, by their industry and concentrated effort, the Dutch had already entrenched themselves in the East Indies, where their island empire could be best defended by their ships; in the New Netherlands they had a wedge dividing our North Atlantic possessions, and they had built up a world-wide carrying trade, with which no rival could hope to compete.[1] In this they had been helped by certain racial and geographical advantages. When other nations were dreaming of military glory or religious uniformity, they were creating a wealthy civilization based on toleration, enterprise and penetration. They had abundance of cheap capital, and Amsterdam was soon to become the world's money market. Situated at the confluence of great rivers, they had convenient transport, supplemented by so many canals that few of their greater storehouses were more than a hundred yards from navigable water. Indeed they were universal in their activities, producing little themselves, but exploiting and transporting the products of others; 'for do they not work the sugars of the west? the timber and iron of the Baltic? the lead, tin, and wool of England? the hemp of Russia? the yarns and dyeing stuffs of Turkey? To be short, in all the ancient states and empires, those who had the shipping had the wealth.'[2]

In comparison, England at the moment of the Restoration was poor and unprogressive. The yield from the Customs was little different from that of 1640. The old chartered companies had difficulty in providing adequate outlets for the export of English goods; the Merchant Adventurers were in debt; the Levant Company was suffering from the frauds of its factors

[1] Cf. Dryden, *Annus Mirabilis*:

> For them alone the heavens had kindly heat,
> In eastern quarries ripening precious dew;
> For them the Idumaean balm did sweat,
> And in hot Ceylon spicy forests grew.

> The Sun but seemed the labourer of the year;
> Each waxing moon supplied her watery store,
> To swell those tides, which from the Line did bear,
> Their brim-full vessels to the Belgian shore.

[2] Petty, *Political Arithmetic* in *Economic Writings of Sir William Petty* (ed. C. A. Hull), i. 258.

and its rivalry with the French; the Greenland Adventurers were ceasing to pursue the whale; the African Company was barely able to hold its own against the Dutch on the west coast of Africa; the East India Company was bombarding the privy council with complaints against its Teutonic rivals in the East Indies; the herring in British waters were being caught and marketed by foreigners with an assiduity exasperating to helpless spectators. A pleasure-loving king and a government in continual fear of republicanism and dissent completed this unpromising outlook for English commercial development. These were the obvious disadvantages; deeper down were other impediments, such as the acute Petty[1] enumerated—namely, the great differences in colonial legislatures and the anomaly of the New England confederacy, so marked an anomaly 'that 'tis hard to say what may be the consequences of it'; the bitter differences about questions of royal prerogative and parliamentary privilege; the want of real union with Ireland; the levy of taxes on capital, especially land, and the loss to the revenue from tax-farmers; the inequality of shires, dioceses, and the representation of the people in parliament, 'all which do hinder the operations of Authority in the same manner as a wheel irregularly made and eccentrically hung'; and, lastly, the division of power whereby the rights of raising money and of making war were in different hands. All of these impediments, thought Petty, were artificial, and their removal would promote commercial expansion.

But England had certain latent advantages for the race in which she was about to take part. Co-operation between committees of the privy council and merchants shows how the administration fully realized the need for technical advice; specialists such as Povey and Downing were given abundant scope. Constantly were matters of trade and commerce discussed by parliamentary committees, where evidence was heard from persons likely to be affected by proposed legislation, and where witnesses often emphasized the relative advantages possessed by the Dutch—their thrift, small ships, low duties, low interest, banks, mercantile law, inland navigation, easy admission of burghers, encouragement of fishing, good poor laws, religious

[1] Ibid. ch. v.

liberty, and high average education.[1] Some Englishmen thought
that these things were inconsistent with monarchy, and that their
adoption would cause the crown to fall into a republic; others
on the contrary held that everything was to be gained by following the Dutch example. Our statute book shows a few traces of
the latter view; for the legislature passed an Act[2] against the
taking of excessive interest, limiting the legal rate to 6 per cent.;
attempts were made to amend the laws of bankruptcy[3] and of
marine assurance;[4] the measures of corn and salt were standardized;[5] the herring fishing encouraged;[6] and the packing of butter
was subjected to definite rules,[7] in order to prevent fraud and the
use of defective casks. Even more, however, than this administrative and legislative activity, there was this advantage for England
that the right human material was available; because the best
families did not disdain to enter trade, as is shown in the histories
of the Finch, Reresby, and North families. There was also the
contribution of Protestant nonconformity, a contribution marked
by the qualities of industry and integrity, reinforced by the skill,
capital, and enterprise of the Huguenot refugees, whose migration
to England, begun in Elizabeth's reign, reached its maximum
in the years 1680–90.[8]

Concurrently with these developments, there became manifest
a more general recognition of the fact that commerce is an affair
of state, 'because it conduces more to a universal monarchy than
either arms or territory'.[9] Public interest in the subject was also

[1] *H.M.C. Rep.* viii, app., pt. i, 133–4. Minutes of committee to consider
fall of rents and decay of trade, Oct. 28, 1669.

[2] 12 Car. II, cap. xii.

[3] The Statute 14 Car. II, cap. xxiv, excepted from the bankruptcy legislation all investments in the East India Company, the Guinea Company, and
any joint stock for the fishing trade.

[4] By 14 Car. II, cap. xxiv, the lord chancellor might authorize standing
commissioners to hear disputes between merchants regarding marine
assurance.   [5] 22 Car. II, cap. viii.

[6] See *infra*, 230–2.   [7] 14 Car. II, cap. xxvi.

[8] The increased immigration of Huguenots into England after 1680 was
fostered by Henry Savile, English envoy in Paris. For this see *Savile Corre-*
spondence (*Camd. Soc.*); D. C. Agnew, *French Protestant Refugees*; and W. A.
Shaw, *Letters of Denisation and Acts of Naturalisation . . . 1603–1720* (Huguenot
Society, xviii).

[9] Considerations about the commission for trade in *Shaftesbury*, xlix, no. 27.

shown by the publication of numerous pamphlets, in some of which an attempt was made to elucidate the laws governing international trade. While most of these books condemned the importation of French silks and wine as economically and morally indefensible, others maintained that all commercial restraints are intrinsically injurious, and that there can be no sound objection either to the French trade or to the East India Company's exports of bullion in return for luxuries, because, with variety of markets, there is greater wealth and elasticity than in restricted and protected markets.[1] One writer, Samuel Fortrey, while deploring our unduly large imports from France, contended that if the monopolies of the privileged companies were taken away, our commodities would sell at better rates, and our imports would be distributed at cheaper prices.[2] Later in the century, Dudley North went so far as to declare that no trade advantageous to the merchant could be injurious to the public, for 'no laws can set prices in trade, which must and will make themselves'.[3] Money he defined as a merchandise whereof there might be a glut as well as a scarcity; his declaration that any special favour to one trade is 'an abuse, and cuts so much of profit from the public' is an anticipation of later doctrine. 'A swap hurts not a nation' was a more concise expression of the same view.[4]

In one respect English legislation reflected this association of prosperity with commercial freedom. Late in 1660 the Council of Trade considered the question of export of bullion, and acted on advice of which a record has been preserved. 'The balance of trade (by which is understood the proportion that the commodities exported have in value to the commodities imported) is the main cause of exportation and importation of bullion' —such was the pronouncement of the Council;[5] it was deduced from this definition that restriction of the export of bullion was an interference with the balance of trade, and was therefore

---

[1] Cf. *England's great happiness* (1677), printed in J. R. McCulloch, *Literature of political economy*. Mun's tract *England's treasure by foreign trade*, written early in the century, was printed in 1664.

[2] *England's interest and improvement* (1663).

[3] *Discourses upon trade* (1691).

[4] J. Houghton, *Collection for improvement of husbandry and trade* (1727 ed.), ii. 474.

[5] There is a copy of their minute in *Rawl. MS.* A. 478, f. 80.

injurious. In spite of a protest by the Lords[1] this advice was given legislative effect in the comprehensive Act for the encouragement of trade.[2]

But against these considerations in favour of open competition, there was at that time a stronger case in favour of regulated trade. In the opinion of the majority, national prosperity was subordinate to national security; and the minute control extended over the citizen at home should, it was held, extend in some measure to the merchant trading abroad. Hence the crown, vested with the prerogative of regulating the course of foreign trade, maintained that control by the grant of exclusive monopolies and charters. The privileges of at least five companies were therefore confirmed; new ones were established, and accordingly the main arteries for the circulation of English exports were the East India Company, the Levant Company, the African or Guinea Company, and the Canary Islands Company, together with the old Merchant Adventurers (trading with Germany and the Netherlands in cloth) and the Eastland Company (importing naval stores from the Baltic). A Royal Fishery Company was formed in the hope that England might derive some benefit from the abundance of herring in her own waters, and a Hudson's Bay Company was founded to exploit the furs and skins of the Hudson's Bay territory.

Each of these companies has a distinctive history.[3] One of the first to lose its monopoly was the Merchant Adventurers, which was a Regulated company, having no joint stock; consequently it was obliged to pay the interest on its loans by a levy on cloth. This caused dissatisfaction, and, moreover, the company was unable to free itself from debt, which in 1664 amounted to £75,000. Its decline was hastened also by the diminution in the

---

[1] *L.J.* xi. 571, July 24, 1663.   [2] 15 Car. II, cap. vii.

[3] For this see Cunningham, *Growth of English Industry and Commerce, Modern Times*, pt. i (4th ed.), 214–79; Lipson, *Economic History of England*, ii, ch. 2. For the separate companies see M. Epstein, *Early history of the Levant Company*; A. C. Wood, *The English embassy at Constantinople* in *E.H.R.* xl. 1925; G. F. Abbott, *Under the Turk in Constantinople*; G. F. Zook, *Company of Royal Adventurers trading into Africa*; S. A. Khan, *The East India Trade in the seventeenth century*; H. B. Morse, *The Chronicles of the East India Company trading to China*. There is a vast amount of information in W. R. Scott, *Joint Stock Companies* (3 vols., 1912).

exports of undressed cloth, owing to improved methods in dyeing and dressing at home.[1] Another of the Regulated companies that failed to exclude free traders and interlopers was the Eastland Company, whose privileges were seriously curtailed by the Act of 1673 which opened up the trade to Sweden, Norway, and Denmark, and conferred the right of membership on all persons paying an entrance fee of forty shillings.[2] This left only the eastern coast of the Baltic as its monopoly, and thereafter the Company existed in little more than name. So too, the old Russia Company, at first a joint stock enterprise, was unable, after the Restoration, to secure its former privileges in Russia, and thereafter survived in the Regulated form, as a loosely knit body of merchants having irregular Russian sailings. Not till the eighteenth century did this trade become extensive.[3] In contrast with these companies was the Hudson's Bay Company, which resulted from the repeated, earlier attempts to find a North-West passage. Originally a French-Huguenot venture, the enterprise was taken over by an English Company, and with the help of prince Rupert a charter was obtained in 1670. Superiority in shipping enabled the Company to hold its own against the French, and as the greater part of the capital came to be concentrated into few hands, it was possible to maintain a certain continuity and consistency of policy.[4]

The East India Company was the most important of these privileged organizations. Originally a Regulated company, it had long been conducted on a joint stock basis, whereby losses on hazardous and lengthy voyages were distributed among the shareholders, who were now trading on the sixth of their successive stocks—a sum of £400,000 raised in 1657, estimated ten years later to be worth £1,200,000. During the earlier years of Charles's reign this trade was conducted by a fleet of about 28 ships, of between 250 and 600 tons burthen, of which about 14 were sent out each year. These ships, large and well built, were turned over into other trades after seven years' use, where they were generally thought to be good for another thirty years'

---

[1] Scott, op. cit. i. 268.
[2] 25 Car. II, cap. vii; Lipson, op. cit. ii, 325.   [3] Lipson, ii. 332–3.
[4] For the early history of this company see R. E. Pinkerton, *The Hudson's Bay Company*.

service;[1] indeed, until the advent of steam, the East Indiamen
were the finest and fastest ships of the mercantile marine. The
Company had gained a footing in China, with head-quarters at
Amoy, and had trading connexions with Persia. In India, a
number of factories were established; and the acquisition of
Bombay[2] from the crown added the responsibilities of civil jurisdiction to the privilege of trading monopoly.

The chief imports from the east were indigo, raw cotton, raw
silk, porcelain, saltpetre, and calicoes. Pepper was imported,
but often at a loss, a policy persevered in to prevent the Dutch
from monopolizing this trade. Tea began to be imported in considerable quantities in 1678. Calicoes and chintzes were to be
found in almost every cargo, and at East India House were
stored a great assortment of eastern fabrics with such recondite
names as sallompores, percellaes, moorees, ginghams, izzarees,
romalls, mullmulls, and sarnoes. In return for these the Company exported bullion, cloth, lead, iron, and quicksilver. It has
been asserted that in the last ten years of Charles's reign a total
of about four million pounds of coin and bullion was exported,[3]
but, concurrently with this, great quantities of manufactured
cloth were sent out, and a considerable proportion of the imports
was re-exported. The Customs also benefited, the amount
derived from this source in 1681 amounting to £60,000.[4] Large
dividends were paid by the Company, not always warranted by
trading profits. In the years 1663–5 these averaged 40 per cent.;
there was a drop during the Dutch wars, followed by fluctuations
from ½ per cent. in 1678 to 50 per cent. in 1680, with averages of
about 25 per cent. thereafter.[5] Numerous loans to Charles II
enhanced this reputation for prosperity, over £80,000 in the
years 1660–7 and a total of £324,000 in the period 1660–84.[6]
There were about five hundred shareholders, including the king,
the duke of York, and many courtiers. Strict economy, even to
cheese-paring, and rigid enforcement of its monopoly were the

---

[1] Williamson's notes about the East India Company, in *Cal. S.P. Dom.*,
1677–8, 363.   [2] See *infra*, ii. 659–62.
[3] S. A. Khan, *The East India trade in the seventeenth century*, 169.
[4] Ibid. 172.   [5] *Rawl. MS.* A. 245, f. 1.
[6] Khan, op. cit. 150. Information compiled from Court Minute Books of
the East India Company and Calendars of Treasury Books.

watchwords of its directors, in pursuit of which policy they had the assistance of some of the best business men of the period, including the two Childs, the merchants Papillon and Dubois, sir Samuel Barnardiston, and alderman sir John Moore. But its finances were not so sound as the figures implied. In 1681 the Company owed more than half-a-million pounds,[1] and after the Revolution its stability was further weakened by the increasing activities of interlopers. For Charles II it was a useful money-lending corporation, and in return he was obliged to make the protection of its interests a matter of national policy, even where the defence of these interests might not be in accord with economic principle; for England it was a national institution, essential to the maintenance of commitments and trading posts in the east.

The Levant Company, a Regulated enterprise, wherein each merchant traded with his own capital, was destined to a less successful career, mainly because of French rivalry in the eastern Mediterranean, and because the Company's agent in Constantinople, obliged to combine ambassadorial with commercial duties, had to pacify each of a rapid succession of temperamental Grand Viziers. It needed natural as well as material gifts to cope successfully with Turkish officialdom.[2] At sea, the Company's fleets were often at the mercy of Mediterranean pirates, while in the east the subsidized French company, with its shorter sea-passage from Toulon or Marseilles, and a more ancient association with the Ottoman, served to place the English Turkey merchant in a position of disadvantage. English cloth was the staple article of export, in return for 'currans', dates, carpets, and a medley of Levantine goods. A new charter was granted in 1661, and a short period of comparative prosperity ensued; but this was precarious, as so many factors in the east traded on their own account; while at home the Company had to face the criticism that it 'rigged the market' by fixing the prices at which cloth was sold abroad and imports at home.[3] In 1754 the trade was thrown open, and in 1825 the Company surrendered its charter.

[1] Khan, 172.
[2] Many illustrations are provided in the career of sir John Finch. See G. F. Abbott, *Under the Turk in Constantinople*. For Dudley North's dealings with the Turk see his biography in *The Lives of the Norths*.   [3] Lipson, ii. 342.

Sir John Finch and sir Dudley North were the greatest of the Turkey merchants in this period, both of whom excelled in diplomatic finesse, a quality abundantly exercised during their stay in the east.

Earlier in the century a number of adventurers had attempted to develop the West African trade, and in 1663 the duke of York and prince Rupert lent their aid to the foundation of a joint-stock enterprise, the Royal African Company,[1] intended to exchange English manufactured goods for gold and ivory, and to maintain a supply of negroes for the plantations. Starting with a nominal capital of about £120,000, of which £20,000 was privately borrowed and £44,000 unpaid,[2] the Company sent twenty-five ships to the African coast, and from the gold which they brought back were minted guineas. But from the first the Company had to contend with serious difficulties. A large percentage of negroes, packed into the vile-smelling holds of the west-bound ships, persisted in dying; there were constant disputes about the price of the survivors, most of them weakened or diseased by the voyage; and when a figure of £17 or £18 a head had been agreed upon, the Company usually had difficulty in collecting the money from planters, accustomed to living on the credit of long-term 'chits'. Even more serious was the persistent opposition of the Dutch, who mapped out the whole trade of the Ivory and Gold Coast for their own, and did not scruple to incite the native to attack the English in isolated forts. In consequence, the Company was soon in a precarious position; the raids of De Ruyter accounted for eight of their ships, and left them with only one fort—Cape Corse; trading licences were granted to private persons, and what remained of the Company's fleet was turned over to the king's service. The more enterprising members of the Company traded separately, and in 1669 a body of them was formed into the Gambia Adventurers, with a monopoly of the trade of northern Africa for seven years.[3]

But the most exasperating failure of all was that of the Royal Fishery Company. This was no new venture. In August 1661

[1] The shareholders included the king, queen, duke of York, prince Rupert, and 107 others. For their names see *Rawl. MS.* A. 478, f. 4.

[2] G. F. Zook, *The Company of Royal Adventurers trading into Africa*, 16–18.

[3] Zook, op. cit. 23.

letters patent[1] touching the 'Royal Fishery' were issued, which, after reciting the fact that 'great plenty' of fish were to be found in English estuaries, appointed commissioners with powers to make regulations for the Fishery industry and to employ officials. The king was declared 'Protector' of the new association, and fishermen were accorded exceptional privileges—they were to be amenable only to the Council of the Royal Fishing; neither they nor their boats might be arrested for debt; they were to be exempt from jury service, and were to have favourable treatment from the Customs authorities. The Company was incorporated by letters patent dated April 8, 1664, with the duke of York as governor, assisted by a directorate of peers and ministers. As there were no funds, money was to be obtained by assigning certain lotteries for the exclusive benefit of the enterprise (at the expense of those needy veterans The Loyal and Indigent Officers), and by the issue of a brief for the collection of offerings in parish churches. Innkeepers were ordered to take a minimum number of barrels of the native fish; wharves, quays, and storehouses were to be erected; fishing busses and pinks were to be built; and Englishmen were at last to eat herring caught and salted by their compatriots. With the help of an organizer named Simon Smith the principles of deep-sea fishing were promulgated in an official pamphlet entitled *The Royal Herring Buss Fishing*.[2]

The total amount raised from the offerings in parish churches amounted to £818 6s. 4½d., which had cost about £500 to collect.[3] There is an ominous silence[4] about the amount received from the lotteries. Nevertheless a start was made; ten fishing boats, costing about £900 each, were built, and a subsidy was promised to builders of herring boats. But the exalted persons who controlled the destinies of the Company were not deeply interested, and rarely met; in consequence, even this modest enterprise speedily declined, and the Dutch could well afford

[1] *Stowe MS.* 325, f. 152. For the earlier attempts to establish a herring industry see J. T. Jenkins, *The Herring and the Herring Fisheries*, 81 sqq.

[2] Proclamation of July 23, 1660. *Steele*, i. 3235.

[3] J. R. Elder, *The Royal Fishery Companies*, 99.

[4] Broken by a reference from Pepys (Oct. 18, 1664), who was ashamed that so noble an object was dependent on such a base means.

to ignore the amateurish English effort. It needed only war at sea to end the experiment, and by 1667 the Royal Fishery Company had ceased to exist. A new company was formed in 1676 under the nominal leadership of York and Danby, with a capital of about £10,000. There was an element of irony in the fate of this company. As English ship-builders were slow to adapt themselves to the building of the type of craft required for this industry, the Company had to have its ships built in Holland, and some of them were even manned with Dutch crews. For this reason they were seized by the French in their naval warfare with Holland. Moreover, insult was added to injury; for while the Dutch were the most eloquent advocates of freedom of the seas in home waters, they were acting on the opposite policy in the East Indies and on the African coast; thus having it both ways, and so irritating defeated rivals.

In this maritime contest the vital thing was the ship. That this was fully realized by the legislator is seen in the statutory attempts to encourage ship-building; thus, an Act[1] of 1662 imposed extra Customs duties on ships engaged in the Mediterranean trade having less than two decks, and granted a relaxation of one-tenth of the dues to all who, in the seven years after March 25, 1662, should build in His Majesty's dominions a ship of two decks or two-and-a-half decks with a forecastle and 30 pieces of ordnance. An Act[2] of 1670–1 provided that if a master delivered up to pirates a ship of not less than 200 tons and 16 guns he should thereafter be incapable of command. There was also the pressure of opinion. Repeatedly was this conclusive argument adduced in favour of a particular trade, that it would employ a larger amount of shipping than a rival trade; for example, the English sugar-refiners, when presenting their case for brown against white sugar, argued that the former needs thrice the amount of shipping used by the latter, owing to greater bulk.[3] So too when, in 1671, it was proposed to increase the duty on plantation tobacco, the planters contended[4] that the trade employed yearly 140 sail of ships averaging between 150–500 tons, and paying about £100,000 annually in Customs duties; the extra duty, they held, would mean a smaller demand and so a falling

[1] 14 Car. II, cap. xi.
[2] 22–3 Car. II, cap. xi.
[3] *H.M.C. Rep.* ix, app., pt. ii, 11–12.
[4] Ibid. 10.

off in shipping employed and Customs paid. It was maintained also that a trade employing English ships in long voyages was intrinsically better than one conducted in shorter passages; hence Downing argued against the linen and canvas trade with Brittany, in favour of the salt trade with Portugal, on the grounds that French trade 'sucks the marrow of our bones', and that the longer passage to Setubal would benefit our shipping.[1] Other evidence of the steadily increasing importance of shipping is seen in the beginnings of marine insurance.[2]

In ships and ship-building the Dutch had great advantages.[3] They possessed abundant and cheap capital; their merchants could avoid the middleman by a network of foreign agencies; the ship-builder had his timber floated down to him on navigable waters; wages were lower and there was less wastage of material. In addition, more up-to-date methods and machinery were employed, with the result that it was possible to build at a cost of £4 10s. per ton, whereas in England the cost was £7. By mass-production methods our rivals were able to build quickly great fleets of single-decked fly-boats of 200–500 tons, long in proportion to beam, easily-worked, and presenting a very small freeboard when fully loaded. But the material was not so good; they did not last so long as did English ships, and they broke up when they went ashore. Hence English ships, as then built, could not compete in trades where bulky commodities had to be transported quickly without regard to the needs of defence, that is, in the seas from the Garonne to Archangel, where the cargoes were mainly wine, salt, fish, grain, timber, and iron. England, therefore, could not hold her own in the Greenland,

[1] *L.J.* xii. 496.
[2] By 14 Car. II, cap. xxiii, commissions might be issued out of the Admiralty Court for the examination of witnesses abroad. In 1662 a colonel Russell proposed to raise a fund of £100,000 as capital for a maritime insurance company. (*Cal. S.P. Dom., 1661–2*, 446.) The report thereon by the Council of Trade will be found in *Stowe MS.* 325, f. 184 *b*. In 1680 there was an office at the Royal Exchange where policies and charter parties were issued: the first notice of Lloyd's is in 1688. (F. Martin, *The History of Lloyd's and marine insurance in Great Britain*, 59.)
[3] For this subject see an excellent article by Prof. V. Barbour, *Dutch and English merchant shipping* in *Economic History Review*, ii. This has been extensively used in the above paragraph.

North Sea, and Baltic trades. On the other hand, in the 'rich' trades of the East Indies, Levant, Madeira, and Guinea, where the cargoes were valuable in proportion to bulk, and the consideration of self-defence paramount, English shipping had the advantage. Our shipwrights could build a man-of-war, or a great merchantman easily convertible into a warship, or a fast frigate or even a yacht; but they were chary of modifying design, and hesitated to attempt a dogger, a whaler, a herring buss or a pink; whereas the Dutch adapted design to trade, and aimed chiefly at maximum stowage, with ease of handling. Our maritime failures have sometimes been attributed to unwise legislation, but it is possible that our overseas trade has been conditioned as much by our ships as by our laws.

The inadequacy of the Navigation Act of 1651 has helped to obscure some of the earlier attempts to obtain for England a share of the carrying trade. Though enforced in home waters, the Act of 1651 could not have excluded the Dutch from the American trade, so long as they were in possession of the New Netherlands, and so long as there was no machinery for enforcing the restrictions. But that the Act failed does not prove the motive behind it to have been impossible of achievement. A carrying trade can best be developed when one's neighbours are at war on the sea, and one's ships full of 'neutral' goods. Prior to 1648 the main combatants at sea were Spain and Holland; and so England, comparatively free from naval warfare, began tentatively to derive advantage from this unusual state of affairs by providing neutral transport for continental goods. A 'composition trade' was started at Dover, enriching the port with dues and English ships with freights. The practice in this trade was for merchants in Holland and Flanders to obtain advices of ships sailing from London for southern ports; these ships picked up at Dover the cargoes sent by foreign exporters, and so, by the payment of harbour dues and transhipment charges, belligerents were able to secure safe transit for their wares. This profitable trade appears to have been monopolized by Dover, because of its strategic position; and it is noteworthy that some foreign merchants preferred this method of transport owing to the reputedly greater safety of English ships. It was revived even in a year of European peace (1661) when the Council of

Trade imposed duties of 1 per cent. on Rate Book values of cargoes imported, with ¼ per cent. on their exportation; the privilege was then granted for three years, and it was proposed to extend it to Plymouth, Harwich or Newcastle, and Deptford. In 1674 when England withdrew from the Third Anglo-Dutch War leaving France to carry on hostilities, there was a return of conditions specially favourable to the composition trade, and Dover again obtained a renewal of the privilege. Already, however, England had embarked on a policy of obtaining freights not by trading quietly as a neutral, but by challenging the greatest sea-power of the century.[1]

When on September 13, 1660, the Act for encouraging and increasing of shipping and navigation was presented to the Sovereign, the Speaker of the House of Commons announced that the Bill would enable His Majesty 'to give the law to foreign princes abroad ... and it is the only way to enlarge Your Majesty's dominions all over the world, for so long as Your Majesty is master at sea, your merchants will be welcome wherever they come'. This was one of a series of measures to which collectively the name of Navigation Acts has been given. These Acts renewed and extended the Act of 1651, the basic principles of which had been:

(1) That no goods were to be imported from Asia, Africa, or America but in English ships.

(2) That goods from Europe could be imported only in English ships or in such foreign ships 'as do truly and properly belong to the people of that country or place of which the said goods are the growth or manufacture'.

The Act of 1660 (12 Car. II, cap. xviii) is so important that its clauses may be set forth in detail. The preamble described the purpose of the Act as 'the increase of shipping and encour-

---

[1] For the composition trade see *Stowe MS.* 325, f. 174–80; *Rawl. MS. A.* 172, f. 114; *Cal. Tr. Bks. 1672–5*, 245, 250. For the rules laid down by the Privy Council when the trade was renewed in 1661 see *P.C. Reg.* 55, June 10, 1661. On this occasion a special dispensation of the Navigation Act was made by a *non-obstante* in the privy seal authorizing the renewal of the trade. At the same time it was ordered that the plantations be not admitted into the Trade. It was left to the Lord Treasurer, the Chancellor of the Exchequer, and the late Farmers of the Customs to determine on what points the Navigation Act would have to be dispensed with.

agement of the navigation of this nation, wherein . . . the wealth, safety and strength of this Kingdom is so much concerned'. Then followed these clauses:

I. No goods may be imported to or exported from English possessions in Asia, Africa or America but in ships actually owned by Englishmen or Irishmen, whereof the master and at least three-fourths of the crew are English, under penalty of forfeiture of vessel and cargo.

II. No alien may exercise the office of merchant or factor in the Plantations.

Governors of Plantations are to take an oath for the strict observation of these provisions.

III. No goods of the growth or manufacture of Africa, Asia or America shall be imported into England or Ireland or the Channel Islands save in ships belonging to Englishmen or Irishmen, or belonging to denizens of His Majesty's territories in Asia, Africa or America, the master and crew to be qualified as above.

IV. Foreign goods brought into England or Ireland or the Channel Islands in English-built shipping must be shipped direct from their countries of origin, or from places whence they were usually first shipped.

V. Double aliens Customs duties are to be imposed on all dried or salted fish, oil, blubber, whale-fins and whale-bones imported in vessels whereof the owners had neither caught, cured nor extracted these commodities.

VI. Only ships owned by Englishmen or naturalized Englishmen and manned by the requisite majority of Englishmen may engage in the coasting trade of England or Ireland.

VII. All relaxations and abatements provided in the Book of Rates for goods imported or exported in English-built or Plantation-built shipping are to be granted only where the nationality qualification of the crew is fulfilled.

VIII. Naval stores, sugar, oils, grains, wines and spirits are to be imported only in ships owned by the original exporters and manned by the required proportion of Englishmen. Currants and commodities from the Levant are to be imported only in English-built ships, manned as aforesaid, with an exception in favour of foreign ships built in the country or place where the cargo was first shipped, provided master and crew conformed to the nationality qualification.

IX. French and Rhenish wine are to be deemed aliens' goods unless imported in English-owned and English-manned ships. Naval stores, oil, grain, sugar, potash and spirits, together with all Russian and Levantine commodities imported in other than English-owned and manned shipping shall be deemed aliens' goods.

X. Certificates are to be granted by Customs Officers to shippers who attest that they are the bona-fide owners of the ships in respect of which the certificate is granted.

XI. Customs officers and governors of Plantations who grant the privileges of English shipping to foreign vessels, other than those conforming to the ownership and manning qualifications specified in the clauses of the Act appropriate to each particular case, shall be deprived of their offices.

XII and XIII. Provisos for transhipment of goods in favour of the Levant and East India Companies.

XIV. Goods are to be freely imported from Spain, Portugal, the Azores, Madeira and the Canary Islands in English-owned and manned ships.

XV. The Act shall not extend to Bullion.

XVI. Aliens' duty shall not be imposed on corn, salt or fish imported from Scotland in Scotch-built ships, whereof the master and three-fourths of the crew are Scots, nor on seal oil from Russia imported in shipping owned by some one at the place of export and manned by Englishmen.

XVII. A duty of Five Shillings on each ton of merchandise imported into England in French ships.

XVIII. Sugar, tobacco, cotton-wool, indigo, ginger, fustick and other dyeing woods of the English Plantations are to be shipped only to England or Ireland or other English Plantations.

XIX. English ships sailing for the Plantations shall give sureties (£1,000 for ships of less than 100 tons, £2,000 for ships of greater burthen) that if they ship in the Plantations any of the goods enumerated in clause XVIII, they will land them at English or Irish ports only, 'the danger of the seas excepted'. Ships from other places trading with the Plantations by permission of this Act shall give bond to the Governor of the Plantation that enumerated articles in their cargoes shall be landed only in ports of England, or Ireland or another English Plantation.

This Statute united a number of intentions, of which these may be definitely distinguished: (1) to benefit English shipping by giving it a monopoly in the plantation trade; (2) to keep aliens out of the plantations; (3) to secure the co-operation of the plantations in the scheme by imposing an oath on governors; (4) to extend a principle already applied to tobacco, namely, that of 'enumeration', whereby certain specified raw materials were to be landed in England or Ireland only—afterwards amended to England only; in this way, England would become the staple for those sub-tropical commodities at that time most in demand; (5) to retaliate against those carriers, notably the Dutch, who shipped into English ports commodities which they had not themselves produced. An Act combining such a diversity of objects was bound to have only a qualified success; for example the first and last, as above defined, proved to be incompatible, because the effect of the 'last was to throw the Baltic trade in timber and ships' stores into the hands of Dutch and Danes, who were thus able to create a monopoly, whereby the price of these materials was raised for the English builder; and so the immediate effect was to make English shipbuilding more costly.[1] Formerly, English importers had used foreign-built ships for their imports from the Baltic; this they could no longer do, and as English ships were unsuitable for the stowage of timber, the immediate effect of the Navigation Act was to drive the English importer from the Baltic trade. The second object, to keep aliens out of the plantations, was not always economically defensible; because some of the colonies, notably Barbados,[2] had materially benefited from Dutch capital; moreover, to compel the plantations to confine themselves to the English market was to do them an economic injustice. The third object, that of inducing the colonial governors to co-operate by obliging them to take an oath, proved difficult of execution, but served at least to provide one common element in colonial administration. Lastly, the concentration of the 'enumerated' articles in England for redistribution created a partial monopoly in these articles, and so provided special protection for a limited class of importer.

There was nothing in the Act to prevent a direct trade between the plantations and European ports in colonial ships. This omission was remedied in the Act[3] for the Encouragement of Trade (1663) which enacted that European goods for the plantations must be shipped in England and in English ships,

---

[1] Lipson, *Economic History*, iii. 131.

[2] V. T. Harlow, *Barbados*, 42.

[3] 15 Car. II, cap. vii.

the reason cited for this inhibition being that it was the custom of other nations to keep their colonial trade to themselves. The exceptions in which there was permitted direct trade with Europe were salt for the Newfoundland and New England fisheries, Scottish and Irish horses and provisions, and wine from the Portuguese possessions of Madeira and the Azores. The system was made still more complete by Acts[1] of 1670–1 and 1673, of which the first excluded Ireland from the privilege granted by the Act of 1660 whereby enumerated goods might be landed there (with a saving clause for stress of weather), while the second imposed export duties on the enumerated goods when shipped from one plantation to another. The object of this last provision was to prevent leakage of these commodities into European trade from inter-colonial trade. Except that rice, molasses, and copper were later added to the list of enumerated goods, the Act of 1660, with the supplementary Acts of 1663, 1670–1, and 1673, remained the basis of the old Navigation Policy.

Assuming that defence is more important than opulence, the Navigation Acts were, wrote Adam Smith,[2] 'perhaps the wisest of all the commercial regulations of England'. The exclusion of foreign capital from our colonial trade reduced the total amount of capital available for that trade, thereby lessening competition and increasing profits on the restricted amount of capital so employed. Profits in this trade were therefore higher than they would have been in conditions of free trade. But this reacted unfavourably on those trades wherein English capital did not have protection, compelling us to buy dearer and less, and sell cheaper and less; so reducing production and consumption in trades for which England had natural advantages but no artificial monopoly. In effect, therefore, high profits on a portion of national capital and high wages for labour at home were counterbalanced by the underselling of English goods in foreign markets. Nor was this the only element of artificiality enforced by legislation; for the Navigation system transferred a considerable portion of our capital from a direct foreign trade into a round-about one, whereby this country paid for her continental

---

[1] 22–3 Car. II, cap. xxvi, and 25 Car. II, cap. vii.
[2] *Wealth of Nations*, bk. iv, ch. ii.

imports, not by the export of her own goods, but by the re-export of that amount of the 'enumerated' articles (notably tobacco and sugar) not required at home. Small direct foreign trades with quick returns were the alternative to this indirect trade with slow returns; but the latter policy appeared to benefit English shipping, and so was adopted even at the expense of penalizing an appreciable proportion of English capital.

Such were the ultimate effects of the Navigation Acts as expounded a century later by Adam Smith. His views had already been anticipated. Writing in 1671 Roger Coke contended that, on the whole, the system had injured English trade, and that Dutch prosperity had increased in spite of it. He showed how the retaliatory clauses had forced the Baltic trade into foreign-manned and foreign-owned ships.[1] Sir Josiah Child[2] maintained that, while the Acts had secured for us our trade with the plantations, and a good part of the direct Levantine, Italian, Spanish, and Portuguese trades, they had caused (mainly through high interest on scarce capital) the loss of the Greenland, Eastland, Scottish, Irish, and Guinea trades, the East India trade in spices, and the Norwegian trade in timber; the last to the Danes, most of the others to the Dutch. 'The Dutch low interest', he wrote, 'has miserably lessened us in all trades of the world not secured to us by laws, or by some natural advantage.' For example, we have natural advantages for the trade in red herring, because these abound off our coast; they must be brought fresh on shore and dried over wood fires. So too, we have the Newfoundland fisheries to ourselves, but if the Dutch with their cheap capital once obtained a footing there, they would soon drive us out. Our rivals, he argued, could always beat us in open market by buying dear and selling cheap; they were bound to reap advantage from the colonies of others, provided the trades of these colonies were not monopolized by the parent countries. Child attributed our high rate of interest to the trade of 'bankering', and consoled his readers with the assurance that England still retained her supremacy in wool,

[1] R. Coke, *Reasons of the increase of the Dutch trade.* For a very able and lucid investigation of the effects of the Navigation Acts see Lipson, op. cit. iii. 116–53.

[2] J. Child, *A discourse about trade* (1690, probably written about 1666).

cheap fuel, victuals, red herring, pilchards, the Newfoundland cod-fishing, and the lead and tin mines.

Discussion of the effects of the Navigation Acts has sometimes been obscured by the assumption that these Acts were intended to secure one definite object. So far as that object was to knit the plantations into a scheme whereby their interests were subordinated to the supposed interests of the mother country, the Acts may be said to have succeeded; they also provided freights and long passages for English shipping. But it is more difficult to say whether they achieved their avowed object of encouraging shipping. On the one hand, it is indubitable that there was a steady increase in our mercantile tonnage;[1] but it would be rash to attribute this to Navigation legislation, because it may have been due to that development of commerce which proceeded irrespective of laws, and perhaps even in spite of these laws. The increase might, it is true, have been even greater in conditions of free trade, but this is in the realm of conjecture. It is possible that the most definite effects of the Navigation Acts may be traced not so much in the increasing volume of English trade as in its changed direction.

This change of direction may have been intentional on the part of those who framed the Acts. Their calculations were influenced by this consideration, that in the forty years preceding the Restoration our trade had altered in at least one respect, that there was a serious diminution in exports of woollen manufactures to the Hanse and Baltic towns; there was also a threat that the Dutch might drive us out of the Mediterranean trade, as they already, in effect, excluded us from the African trade and the spice trade of the East Indies. It was therefore not in an atmosphere of statistics or economic speculation, but under the threat of a menace to English political security and economic existence, that the legislators of the Restoration acted. They were faced with this alternative—either to restore the old trade with northern and eastern Europe; or to redress the balance by securing, as firmly as laws would permit, the still

[1] In sir R. Temple's *Revenue Collections* (*Stowe MS.* 324, f. 13) there is a list of ships entering the Thames that were large enough to be boarded by tidesmen. In 1672 these numbered 1,055; in 1676, 1,550; in 1680, 1,535; in 1685, 1,764.

unexplored resources of the North American colonies. So they took a decisive and momentous step. They surrendered the hemp, pitch, and tar of New England on which earlier legislators had set so much store; they ignored the pepper and cacaonuts of Jamaica and the white flax of Virginia, for which a ready market might have been had at home, and they set themselves both to encourage and to monopolize commodities for the production of which it seemed that the empire had special advantages not shared by other colonial empires, namely tobacco, sugar, cotton, and dyeing woods. In return for these, English shippers would send out, not cloth, but iron, tin, and leather manufactures, with provisions and re-exported wines—commodities for some of which we had practically no European market. By exchanging our manufactured goods (other than cloth) for sub-tropical raw material, much of which might be re-exported, a diversion would be created from the old continental trade conducted mainly from ports on the eastern coast of England.

Other consequences were hinted at by contemporaries. The diversion to the west helped to develop ports such as Liverpool, Plymouth, and Bristol, and so relieved the congestion in London docks. Even more, by this closer dependence of the plantations on the home country, Englishmen increased 'the limits of their dwelling', adding not only the trade of one climate after another, but 'joining the countries themselves and the inheritance of them to these His Majesty's dominions; laying a just foundation for the making them an affair of state, and of far greater care, weight and import to the crown than others'. The more commodities we could obtain from the plantations, the more employment we should find for our colonists; and by multiplying the English stock in these outposts 'the empire of England is rendered more august, formidable and considerable abroad'.[1] In this way a contemporary attempt was made to justify the Navigation Acts on broad grounds of imperial as well as economic policy. Such a defence does more than justice to the legislators of 1660; but at least it suggests how the Navigation system may have appeared to the more open-minded of the Englishmen who first studied its effects.

[1] These extracts are from a MS. treatise of the late seventeenth century, *The advantages of trading with our plantations*, in *Rawl. MS.* A. 478, f. 65.

On the plantations, the immediate results of these Acts can be more definitely assessed. There were not enough ships within the category of English-built and English-manned to cope with the trade; consequently great quantities of produce, notably tobacco of Virginia and sugar of Barbados, were sometimes left in the hands of planters, for want of legally qualified ships. Hence an accentuation of the evils consequent on gluts—the most serious difficulty experienced by the producers of the enumerated products. It was not surprising, therefore, that in the colonies many attempts were made to evade the Acts. In the New England states the loss to the English Treasury on this score was said to be £100,000 per annum; in Maryland there was occasional difficulty in interpreting the intricacies of the system, causing disputes between the proprietor lord Baltimore and the English Customs officials; in Virginia, a councillor might sometimes be also a collector, and as such might have to inform himself of those laws which, as a trader, he had violated; but in his capacity of judge of the supreme court he could give a ruling thereon, thereby saving much friction, but still further increasing the loss to the Customs.[1] Evasion, especially in the earlier years of the system, was not difficult. Thus a Scottish ship would call at an English port for a cargo of 'slight goods', and would then return to a Scottish port for a great quantity of linen, which would be landed in a colonial port under cover of the English certificate.[2] Foreign Jews soon found a way out. One of a group, having obtained naturalization in England, would act there as an agent and cover for the cargoes of his unnaturalized brethren (mostly in Holland); or, by collusion with an English merchant, would pass off goods (assembled at Amsterdam or Rotterdam) under fraudulent entries.[3] Agents for these purposes were to be found at several ports, notably Dover, Cowes, and Falmouth. The Jewish settlement in Barbados, by its English and Dutch agents, was able to undersell legitimate merchants by 20 per cent.[4] Indeed, in August 1662 Downing complained to Clarendon that commodities of all

---

[1] P. A. Bruce, *Institutional History of Virginia*, ii. 360–1.

[2] T. Keith, *Commercial relations of England and Scotland*, 120 sqq.

[3] S. Hayne, *Abstract of Statutes concerning aliens trading in England* (1685), 8 sqq. [4] V. T. Harlow, *Barbados*, 262.

sorts were being carried from Holland to England and Ireland as if there were no Navigation Act.[1]

These evasions necessitated the establishment in the colonial ports of a preventive service; a necessary measure, but possibly responsible for more resentment than the Navigation Acts themselves, because involving conflict between colonial trader and English official. In 1669 the privy council ordered the Customs farmers to maintain, at their own charge, one or more persons in each plantation to administer the oath to the governor, and to prevent abuses in the collection of the Customs.[2] This control was not imposed without difficulty. Colonies, such as South Carolina, founded at a date later than the Navigation Act of 1660, claimed exemption; in Maryland, a collector of Customs was murdered by a member of the Council;[3] in Massachusetts, where the laws were sometimes openly defied, there was growing up a direct trade in plantation goods with European ports conducted in ships owned by New Englanders.[4] In 1671 the Customs farmers were displaced by commissioners of Customs, who directed special attention to tobacco smuggling in Virginia and Maryland, and by 1678 collectors of Customs had been appointed in all the colonies, these officials being concerned not only with the exaction of dues, but with the maintenance of the system by the colonial administrators, from the governor down to the subordinate clerks. The enforcement of the Navigation Acts therefore helped to engender friction between the crown's representatives, that is governor and council on the one hand, and the treasury representatives, that is the surveyors and collectors on the other;[5] and it was a misfortune for the later history of the empire that the Englishmen with whom the colonists most usually came into contact were the agents responsible to the home country for the maintenance of a repressive economic system.

The restrictions had to be relaxed on several occasions, notably during the two Dutch Wars when it was imperative to secure naval supplies. One of the earliest relaxations was that

[1] Quoted in Japikse, *De verwikkelingen tusschen de Republiek en Engeland*, 55.
[2] *P.C. Reg.* 62, Jan. 20, 1668/9.
[3] G. L. Beer, *The old colonial system*, ii. 173.
[4] Ibid. ii. 251.   [5] Ibid. i. 286 sqq.

for the free importation of spices, pending the surrender of Pularoon.[1] In January 1666 foreign mariners were allowed to be shipped at Ostend for service in English ships;[2] in the preceding year the trade with the Baltic in hemp, pitch, tar, masts, saltpetre, and copper had been practically thrown open. The reconstruction of London after the Fire of London made the shortage of timber even more serious, and led to further breaches in the system.[3] There were also instances of special concessions made to Scots, notably to Scottish sugar-refiners, who undertook to bring their cargoes back to either Scotland or England; and in the colonies there was a general demand not only for Scottish provisions but also (notably in Barbados and Jamaica) for Scottish settlers.[4] Scotsmen, it is true, could settle in the colonies, but as most of their trade therewith was vetoed, emigration was discouraged. So too, the exceptions in favour of Ireland did not help to conciliate opinion there. The Act of 1660 was welcomed because it did not distinguish between Irish and English shipping, and permitted the import of plantation goods, including the enumerated articles; but the Act of 1663 limited Irish exports to horses and provisions, and the Act of 1670–1 prohibited the import of the enumerated goods to any ports but English. In practice, this was often evaded by ships entering Irish ports under pretended stress of weather; and so long as provisions could be exported, Irish trade did not suffer so much as did that of Scotland. Irish resentment was directed not so much against the Navigation Acts as against the prohibition of Irish cattle in England.

Thus the Navigation Act was an essential part of the Restoration settlement, and involved two things destined to prove of consequence: a re-orientation of trade in the direction of the Atlantic, and a challenge to the Dutch monopoly of the carrying trade. The consequences of the second had speedily to be faced, and it is now necessary to outline the successive stages in the commercial conflict which led to war.

---

[1] Proclamation of Dec. 20, 1662. *Steele*, i. 3374.
[2] *Cal. Tr. Bks. 1660–7*, 714.
[3] See *infra*, 305.
[4] T. Keith, op. cit. 128.

The exchange of courtesies at the Restoration served merely to mask the rivalry and antipathy between the two peoples.[1] Charles had been extended a warm welcome in Holland, and, but for the Navigation Act, he might soon after his accession have obtained a loan from the Dutch; if, moreover, the commercial aims of the two countries had been reconcilable, it is possible that Englishmen would have welcomed an alliance with their co-religionaries against the French. There were half-hearted attempts at compromise. In October 1660 the Dutch ambassadors arrived with powers to negotiate a commercial treaty on the basis of the Magnus Intercursus of 1496—that is, free trade and equal fishing rights for both countries; but, with their restricted fleets, English commercial interests were not anxious to renew these privileges. There was also an old tradition, revived and amplified by Selden, that the seas round Britain were not free, and that England had prescriptive rights in the Channel, the North Sea, and the Atlantic as far west as America. Did not the Dutch themselves admit this when they dipped the flag? The English pretension was an absurd one, and was not so easily enforceable as were the Dutch claims to exclusive monopoly in the isolated and thinly-manned forts of West Africa and the East Indies; but this academic myth served nevertheless to sustain public opinion. In December 1660 a Bill was introduced into the Commons to provide means for preventing the Dutch from fishing off the English coast. The Bill was not passed, and could never have been enforced; but the mere threat was enough, for the States General were determined to maintain this fishing by war if necessary. Irritation was also caused by the Dutch failure to surrender the valued spice island of Pularoon; and so by April 1661 it seemed clear that there could be no commercial agreement between the two countries.

The Anglo-Portuguese marriage alliance of June 1661 helped further to complicate the situation. It served to justify Charles's offers of mediation between Portuguese and Dutch; but when, after De Witt's acceptance of English mediation, Downing was restored to his post as resident at The Hague, a fresh irritant was introduced into Anglo-Dutch relations; because Downing,

[1] Cf. Prof. Schoolcraft, *The capture of New Amsterdam* in *E.H.R.* xxii.

one of the most successful 'climbers' of the Restoration, was a keen business man, after the standards of his day, and was personally unacceptable to the equally astute business men of Holland. Though nominally a mediator, he directed his efforts to obtaining the elimination from the proposed Dutch-Portuguese treaty of everything that might conflict with English commercial interests.[1] Hence the Portuguese agent Miranda was soon placed in an impossible position. On the one hand he was being pressed by the Dutch to concede to them all the trading privileges already granted to the English, including preference in the salt trade of Setubal;[2] while, on the other, he had to satisfy Downing that the proposed concessions were not inconsistent with the terms of the Anglo-Portuguese treaty of 1654. From this apparent impasse Miranda easily extricated himself by suggesting the insertion of a clause to the effect that the concessions granted to the Dutch should be without prejudice to those already granted to the English. Clarendon, who did not wish to press matters, was willing to accept this, and indeed there was little support in England for Downing's peremptory attitude; and so the Dutch-Portuguese treaty was at last signed in July 1661. By this treaty the Dutch were placed on terms of equality with the English in the Portuguese trade, and were given preferential treatment at Setubal. Thus the Hollanders had obtained their privileges in the Portuguese empire by an inexpensive treaty; while England's admission into that empire had been at the expense of a diplomatic marriage. Moreover, it was noted that this treaty was not ratified by the States General until December 1662, nor published in Batavia until March 1663, an interval which enabled the Dutch to obtain possession of the Portuguese pepper trade of south-west India.[3]

Charles, who had no love for the rule of the commoner De Witt, resented his exclusion of the young prince of Orange from office; but neither he nor Clarendon was anxious for hostilities; and they may have been mollified when (with the connivance

---

[1] For the correspondence of Downing with Clarendon see *Lister*, iii, *passim*.

[2] Setubal, sometimes referred to as St. Eves and St. Ubas, is 10 miles south-east of Lisbon. It was the source of a specially fine salt.

[3] *Court Minutes of the East India Company* (ed. E. B. Sainsbury, with introductions by Sir W. Foster), 1660–3, xl.

of De Witt) Downing was able to arrest the regicides Okey, Barkstead, and Corbet, and send them over to England for execution (April 1662). At the same time, De Witt scored a diplomatic feat—an alliance[1] with France, signed April 17/27, 1662, whereby each promised to aid the other in a European war, provided the other was not an aggressor. Here was the reply to English talk of expelling the Dutch herring fleets from British waters; since, with France as an active ally, Holland had little to fear from English threats. The addition of England herself to the list of De Witt's friends might well have seemed to remove the last obstacle to Dutch penetration. By the treaty of Westminster, September 4/14, 1662, the two nations bound themselves to aid each other against their rebels; the Dutch undertook to strike flags and lower top-sails on meeting an English man-of-war in British seas; and they promised once more to restore Pularoon to any one bringing a commission from Charles under the Great Seal. The European trade of each was to be open to the other. January 10/20, 1659, was agreed upon as the limiting date for claims arising from damage sustained in the Indies, the acceptance of Pularoon being taken as a cancellation of all claims prior to that date; for claims arising from damage in any other part of the world, March 4, 1654 was taken as the limit. Disputes of later date were to be submitted to commissioners, with the exception that claimants in respect of the ships *Bona Ventura* and *Bona Esperanza* were to proceed in their suits.[2] Thus the settlement of Anglo-Dutch disputes was merely postponed.

These consecutive alliances with Portuguese, French, and English were triumphs for Dutch diplomacy; for thereby the natural enemies of Holland had (diplomatically at least) been transformed into the firmest friends of the Republic. The Dutch had obtained official admission into the Portuguese empire; they had secured in Louis XIV a powerful ally, pledged to come to their support if attacked in European waters, and they appeared to have momentarily pacified England by again promising to surrender Pularoon, and by referring to commissioners the more recent cases of dispute. Of their new friends, Portugal

[1] *Dumont*, vi, pt. ii. 422.

[2] For a full account of this litigation see Feiling, *British Foreign Policy*, 108–11.

had been generous of privileges, some of which had already been granted to England; England still remembered Amboyna and, though unprepared for war, was committed to a policy which, if successful, must undermine the basis of Dutch prosperity. Most dubious of De Witt's associates was the French king. As the Catholic lion of the world he was genuinely anxious that the heretic dogs England and Holland should weaken themselves by conflict; but, if he had to choose between them, he would prefer the English dog, because it had a pedigree, and might be more easily adapted to serve the lion's purposes than the continental animal. The lion was now committed to assist the Dutch dog, but was not sure that faith need be kept with such a creature; and even if he had to join in the fray, he could do so in such a way as not to assist his ally overmuch. Behind this diplomatic smoke-screen, the only substantial things were the wealth, the energy, and the organization of the Dutch navies and mercantile marine; they were the only European forces ready for naval war.

Even thus, it might have been possible to avoid war if the terms of the Anglo-Dutch treaty had been possible of fulfilment, but many of the disputes arising from seizures of ships and cargoes were really incapable of satisfactory solution. Thus the two ships *Bona Ventura* and *Bona Esperanza* had been seized[1] as long ago as 1643 when the two nations were at peace. While sir Paul Pindar, an assignee of the owners, was suing the Dutch East India Company for damages, Courteen, heir of one of the owners, agreed in 1649 to compromise the suit by accepting 850,000 guilders. Meanwhile Pindar's suit was pressed by his heirs, and even the arbitration of the Swiss cantons failed to effect a settlement. The longer the case lasted the more complicated it became, and as the original parties died off, a series of young and vigorous heirs joined the fray. The Anglo-Dutch treaty had declared that the *lis incoepta* was to proceed; presumably the *lis incoepta* was this suit between private parties, but Downing was explicitly informed that this was not the English interpretation; the phrase, he was told, meant the dispute between him, as English envoy, and the States General.[2]

---

[1] On a voyage from Goa to China. Several of the crews were killed.

[2] Additional Instructions to Downing (n.d.) in *S.P. For. (Holland)*, 219.

Thus these almost legendary ships sailed out of the seas of litigation into the shoals of diplomacy, where they were soon joined by the *Hopewell* and the *Leopard*, driven from the Malabar coast. Other complaints were raised into affairs of state. The East India Company had a bill for damages amounting to more than £200,000; the Turkey Company claimed to be unsatisfied creditors for about half that amount; these, with the claims of private merchants, brought the total up to about £700,000. The loss sustained by the withholding of Pularoon was estimated at more than four millions.[1] As early as 1661 the Council of Trade had recommended the East India Company to the king's special protection, since otherwise their stock of £800,000 would be lost,[2] and it soon became obvious that royal charters granted to trading companies were valueless if the state could not guarantee exercise of the rights conceded. Opinion was hardened by the fact that not only did the Dutch fail to restore Pularoon, but in 1664 they devastated it so thoroughly that, if it had to be given up, the plantation would be valueless for many years.[3]

In the earlier months of 1664 the English clothiers added their complaints to the swollen burden of protests against the Dutch, and on April 22 both Houses of Parliament called upon Charles to provide redress.[4] A start had already been made. On March 12, 1664, a patent was issued to the duke of York granting to him and his heirs the strip of land enclosing the Hudson river, known as the New Netherlands. This act was not one of impulse. For long, the English inhabitants of Long Island had complained of damage done to them and English interests by the Dutch, complaints investigated by a special committee of Council which included sir John Berkeley, sir George Carteret, and William Coventry, the duke of York's secretary. In consequence, it was determined to seize the New Netherlands. Equipped with a royal charter and a grant of £4,000 for the expenses of conquest, James conceded the district between the Hudson and the Delaware to Carteret and Berkeley. An expedition under captain Nicholls captured New Amsterdam in August

---

[1] *L.J.* xi. 599; *H.M.C. Rep.* vii, app. 176; *Court Minutes of the East India Company, 1664–7*, v. sqq.

[2] Khan, op. cit. 108.   [3] *Court Minutes, 1664–7*, v. and ix.

[4] *C.J.* viii. 548, and *L.J.* xi. 600.

1664, in spite of a firm stand made by the governor, Stuyvesant.[1] This act has been condemned as a flagrant violation of international morality, since war had not yet been declared; but on the other hand it should be recalled that outside of Europe the two nations had for some months been in a state of virtual warfare.

There was activity also on the west coast of Africa. Early in 1664 captain Robert Holmes seized Goree, one of the most important centres of the Dutch West India Company, and followed this by the capture of several stations from which the English had already been expelled, including Cape Coast Castle, Anta, Anambo, and Adia.[2] By this time it was obvious that European hostilities were imminent, and it was therefore assumed that both nations would retain their battle-fleets in home waters. Knowing this assumption, De Witt secretly ordered De Ruyter from the Mediterranean to African waters, and in October 1664 the great Dutch admiral recaptured Goree and expelled the English from their forts, delivering their stores and munitions to the agents of the Dutch Company.[3] One fort only was left—that of Cape Corse, which De Ruyter left alone because of its strong position. The English had indeed, as Pepys expressed it, been 'beaten to dirt at Guinny'.[4] The secrecy with which De Ruyter's expedition had been planned and the effectiveness of its achievement startled even the Dutch; for De Witt had not taken all the Provinces into his confidence, and he had caused irritation by his attempted concealment of the design from the Orange party in Zeeland.[5] Thus, by swift action, De Witt replied to the challenge already thrown down by the English capture of the New Netherlands, and so committed the heterogeneous Dutch Provinces to a war for which they were not unprepared, but on which they were not all anxious to embark. The Dutch polity was such that it prospered best by neutrality in the warfare of other nations; but they were now called on to vindicate their commercial supremacy by force of arms.

[1] For details see Prof. Schoolcraft's article in *E.H.R.* xxii. 674.

[2] Early in July 1664 the Dutch West India Company made its complaint to the States General of the loss of these places. *Colenbrander*, i. 130.

[3] G. F. Zook, *The Company of Royal Adventurers trading into Africa*, 61.

[4] Pepys, Dec. 22, 1664, quoted by Zook, op. cit. 61.

[5] *Colenbrander*, i. 147.

VII

THE FIGHTING SERVICES

NEITHER the merchants who pressed for war nor the government which embarked upon it were fully informed of the preparedness of England. The Fighting Services consisted of three forces—the Militia, the Standing Army, and the Navy. Of these, the first two were of almost negligible strength, while the last abounded in good material, but was not yet adequately organized for the strain of contest with a great maritime power. The wonder is not that England fared so badly in her contests with the Dutch, but that, in spite of mismanagement and enforced economy, she fared so well.

By the Act[1] of 1661 the Cavalier Parliament vested supreme control of the Militia and all the armed forces in the crown, and so abandoned a safeguard which had been fought for in the Puritan Rebellion. The state of the military forces at the Restoration suggests that the sacrifice may not have been a great one. By his commissions of lieutenancy the king authorized select members of the landed gentry to charge all persons having a minimum property qualification with the supply and equipment of horsemen and foot-soldiers. Once a year was held the General Muster of the regiments of Militia, a county function lasting four days; training and exercise were conducted four times a year, on each occasion for not more than two days. The Acts of 1662–3 and 1663[2] prescribed the standard rates of pay—2s. 6d. per day for a trooper and 1s. for a foot-soldier—and the regulation arms; namely, for horsemen, a back, breast, and pot; for footmen, a musket having a barrel at least 3 feet long, a sword and a 'collar of bandeleers'; for pikemen, a pike of ash not less than 16 feet long, with back, breast, headpiece, and sword. By statute also the king was empowered to raise by Assessment funds for the maintenance of the Militia; but no statute gave him power to transport these subjects out of the kingdom, as the Militia constituted the old territorial army for home defence.

[1] *Supra*, 198. [2] 13–14 Car. II, cap. iii, and 15 Car. II, cap. iv.

Additional instructions were provided for the lords lieutenant by the privy council at moments when, as in the winter
of 1661–2, there seemed danger of disturbance from Dissenters
or Republicans; or when, as in the Dutch Wars, there was the
possibility of an enemy landing. Thus the instructions sent on
the 2nd of August 1662 to lord Herbert of Ragland (lord lieutenant of Gloucestershire) ordered him to divide his effectives
so that one-twentieth part of the Foot might always be on duty,
except in time of harvest and in mid-winter; and so that no man
would serve in all more than fourteen days in the year. A portion of the Militia was to be placed in walled towns, for there
the Dissenters abounded; the Horse were to be kept ready for
dispersing conventicles.[1] Other miscellaneous duties imposed
on these functionaries were those of providing pick-axes and
spades for land forts, and drawing off the cattle from Romney
and Pevensey marshes.[2] When the Militia was called out in the
summer of 1666 they were concentrated on three points, Maidenhead, St. Albans, and Northampton;[3] and in the course of the
Second Dutch War they proved of some service as coast-watchers
and trench-diggers.

The men thus mustered were the only troops in the country
having a full parliamentary sanction. But they did not, when
under arms, sacrifice any of their legal rights as civilians; and
in practice the Militia was important not as a military body,
but as one of the institutions of local government, for at times
it exercised police functions; while at elections, both lord
lieutenant and his numerous deputies were concerned mainly
with the tactics of the polling booth.[4] Its inadequacy was most
clearly demonstrated at the Sedgemoor campaign, when many
of the companies showed sympathy with the rebels, a fact which
provided James II with at least an excuse for a professional
army. Almost equally ineffective, but much more provocative,
was the standing army,[5] composed in Charles's reign of a few

---

[1] *Carte MS.* 130, f. 281.

[2] *P.C. Reg.* 59, July 3 and July 4, 1666.

[3] Ibid., June 30.   [4] For this see *infra*, ii. 474–6.

[5] There is a good account of the standing army in this period in C. Walton,
History of the British Standing Army. For the Coldstream Guards see G. Davies,
The early history of the Coldstream Guards. Also, G. C. A. Arthur, *The story of
the Household Cavalry*; F. W. Hamilton, *The origin and history of the First or*

regiments of Guards. These included the Foot and Life Guards recruited at the Restoration from regiments which had served the king in exile, and the Coldstream Guards, made up from Monck's regiments. The Royal Horse Guards, or Blues, were established after the suppression of Venner's rebellion; there were also the Royal Scots, consisting of Scots in French service who returned to France in 1662, and were recalled in 1678; and, after 1683, there was the Tangier regiment, the 'lambs' of captain Kirke, who came to England as the Second or Queen's Regiment of Foot, and were pitted against Monmouth's peasants in 1685. The Cavalry regiments raised for Tangier were later merged with the First Royal Dragoons; a second regiment of Dragoons, the Scots Greys, was formed in 1681. These regiments, with the Yeomen of the Guard, composed the bulk of Charles's standing army; and the total number of effectives, including garrison troops, did not usually exceed 7,000 men; but their number was at times increased, notably in the Third Dutch War, and in 1678, when the Commons urged a war against France. Of the volunteer companies the most notable was the Honourable Artillery Company, formed in 1537.

The Navy calls for more detailed notice. Reference must first be made to institutions which, directly or indirectly, served the maritime interests of England. Among these were the great trading companies, notably the East India Company,[1] the Newfoundland Fisheries[2] and the fleets of Newcastle colliers, all of which provided training in seamanship, and so made available a skilled personnel for the fighting-ships; indeed, without her mercantile marine England as a naval power would have been negligible. At least one of these institutions, the East India Company, maintained (at Poplar) an almshouse for its old seamen.[3] At Deptford three almshouses were established by Trinity House, a corporation founded in the reign of Henry VIII. In these retreats were housed old and indigent masters of ships or their widows, to each of whom was allotted a pension, with firing and gowns. Shipwrecked mariners, and 'sick and decayed

Grenadier Guards; J. C. Leask and H. M. McCance, The regimental records of the Royal Scots.

　[1] For the East India Company see supra, 227–9, and infra, ii. 661–3.
　[2] See infra, ii. 668–9.　　　　　　　　[3] Rawl. MS. A. 183 a, f. 189.

seamen' were also among the recipients of this charity;[1] and for those seamen or their widows who were able to work, oakum was supplied for picking, at the rate of one shilling per hundred-weight.[2] But charity was only a small part of the activities of Trinity House. Its main duties were to assess rates for pilotage, to appoint fitting pilots, to maintain a number of lights on the coast, and to superintend the placing of buoys and beacons in channels and estuaries.[3] Unfortunately, its control in these matters was not complete; for several lights were leased out to private persons, who found the lighthouse a good speculation, and were tempted to economize in the wood or coal fires which then supplied the illumination. Thus in 1662 a patent of light-houses on the North and South Foreland was granted[4] to sir J. Meldrum, who was authorized to collect one shilling on each ton of regular shipping passing the lights, and two pence on foreign ships, the money to be collected at the first port of call. As the lease was for 50 years at £20 per annum, it is clear that sir J. Meldrum enjoyed the favour of the Court. In November 1666 Meldrum's lights were so dim that several ships were endangered, and others had to remain hove-to all night.[5]

With such an imperfectly organized system of lights, coast-wise sailing at night must have been a trying ordeal. In the daytime a course might be set by taking a bearing from some well-known landmarks, such as church spires, landmarks made inviolate by a sixteenth-century statute;[6] or shoals might be avoided by altering course when such a mark came into sight, for which purpose the ship's boy was sent aloft to keep a look-out. This was how sir William Petty, ancestor of the Lansdowne family, began his service at sea. He was sent up the rigging to give notice of a steeple which indicated a shoal; but as he was

---

[1] Ibid., f. 209. A fourth almshouse for 18 pensioners appears to have been erected by 1681.

[2] H.M.C. Rep. viii, app., pt. i. 250. MSS. of Trinity House.

[3] Rawl. MS. A. 185, f. 74. [4] Steele, i. 3360.

[5] Cal. S.P. Dom., 1666–7, 104–5. An abstract of all the crown grants of lighthouses may be seen in Rawl. MS. A. 171, f. 22, Sept. 12, 1688. These included three lights at Winterton and two at Orfordness (three being candle lights); the Harwich Fire Lights, and the Spurn Fire Light. The last had been granted to Justinian Angel and his heirs for ever at a rent of £5 per annum. [6] 8 Eliz., cap. xiii.

very short-sighted, the captain saw the steeple before the boy, and just missed disaster; so Petty's maritime career had a painful ending at this point.[1] As the chronometer had not yet been invented, there was no method of determining the longitude with precision, hence the reckoning had to be made with instruments which to-day would be considered primitive; and in days before the patent log, sailors sometimes calculated rate of progress by walking aft at such a speed as to keep pace with some light object thrown overboard.[2]

There was also the difficulty that charts were not always accurate, and passengers might sometimes dispute their interpretation with the navigator.[3] That some latitude of opinion was possible may be inferred by reference to one of the sailing directions then in use. Thus for the Thames estuary, where there are numerous sand-banks, this was the direction for distinguishing between the Kentish Knock and the Long Sand:

When you are near the Knock, you shall see the land of the North Foreland very plain; but when you are at the Long Sand head, you will hardly see the land, except it be very clear weather or you go up the shrouds.[4]

Even the names of these shoals and channels were supposed to suggest something of their danger; for there were the Black Deeps and the Shivering Sands; there was the Shipwash 'which has washed many a ship away', and the Galloper 'because ships gallop away from it'. No study of the Anglo-Dutch naval hostilities can have any meaning without reference to these shoals on the chart or the map.[5] The charts then in use were commonly called 'Dutch Waggoners', from their compiler the Dutch geographer Wagenaar; but in 1671 a proclamation[6] ordered that, in their stead, there should be used the charts compiled by John Seller, the hydrographer-in-ordinary, which together

[1] *Aubrey*, ii. 146. Although he did not again serve at sea, Petty was interested in things maritime and invented a double-bottomed ship. See *infra*, 734. [2] *Pepys' Naval Minutes* (*N.R.S.* ed. Tanner), 159.

[3] For an example see the incident recorded in *Journals and Correspondence of S. Pepys* (ed. J. Smith), ii. 39.

[4] J. Seller, *Description of the sands, shoals, buoys, beacons, roads, channels and sea marks on the coast of England* (n.d.), in *Bodley*, B. 3, 15 Art.

[5] The approximate position of some of these is shown on the map opposite p. 388. [6] *Steele*, i. 3543.

with unofficial *Plats*[1] and *Descriptions*, provided the mariner with sailing directions. Sometimes survey work was entrusted to the captains of His Majesty's ships, and a diary[2] kept by Sandwich in 1661–2 shows the minute records kept by the more efficient naval officers; moreover it is not without interest that before the Revolution extensive soundings had been made and recorded of the Straits of Gibraltar.[3]

From those seafaring men who plied their dangerous and generally thankless occupation in the coasting and deep-sea trades the Navy derived its sailors and sometimes its officers; it therefore had good human material on which to draw. Organization presented a more difficult problem. At the Restoration, the existing Admiralty and Navy Commissioners were temporarily retained in office; and that there was no drastic breach with the past is shown by the retention of such old parliamentarian officials as Penn, Batten and the members of the Pett family, who now worked harmoniously with Royalists such as sir R. Slingsbie, sir George Carteret, and lord Berkeley of Stratton. With the possible exception of Berkeley, who was a soldier, all these men had special qualifications for the work of naval administration. Thus Penn had rendered good service at sea, though his reputation had suffered from failure to capture San Domingo in 1655; sir William Batten had served as second-in-command to Warwick in 1642 and was now, as surveyor, exercising an office first held by him twenty-two years before. The Pett[4] family had been building ships since Tudor times. Carteret, commencing his sea service in 1632, had commanded privateers against parliamentarian ships; Slingsbie was also an old royalist seaman. Lastly, there was Pepys, who, though the only civilian and landsman among these experts, had already, in the service of Sandwich, laid the foundations of a knowledge of ships and seamen the most profound in the annals of the British admiralty. This policy of entrusting

---

[1] e.g. that in *Bodley, Wood*, C. 13.

[2] In the possession of J. P. R. Lyell, Esq.

[3] e.g. sir H. Shere's *Discourse on the currents in the Straits of Gibraltar* (1674–5) in *Bodley MS.*, *Smith*, 22.

[4] *Autobiography of Phineas Pett* (*N.R.S.* ed. W. G. Perrin, li), xxi. See also A. W. Johns in *Mariners' Mirror*, xii, no. 4.

control of the Navy mainly to men having some technical qualifications was continued by the later Stuarts.[1]

The most notable naval revival at the Restoration was that
of the office of lord high admiral, and its exercise by a prince
who was both soldier and seaman—the duke of York. His
administrative duties included those of rendering to the king,
whenever required, an account of the state of the Navy, and of
consulting at least once a month with the principal officers of the
Navy at their place of meeting, in order to inform himself of
their proceedings; he was also nominally responsible for the
choice of officers. His judicial functions were exercised by the
admiralty court in London and in vice-admirals' courts in
the maritime shires, these tribunals having adjudication of
prizes of war and salvage of ships, together with authority
to prepare indictments at Quarter Sessions for piracy, and to
proceed against persons guilty of embezzling naval stores or
stealing from wrecked ships. The vice-admirals conducted this
jurisdiction with the help of 'discreet persons in the Civil Law
dwelling within the circuit of their office . . . or, for want of a
civilian, one expert in the Common Law'. A quarterly general
session was held in the chief town of each circuit, and there were
also general courts of inquiry, convened as occasion required.
This judicial prerogative of the lord high admiral was a source
of considerable profit.[2]

The principal officers with whom the lord high admiral had
to consult were Carteret (treasurer), Slingsbie (controller),
Batten (surveyor), and Pepys (clerk of the acts). These officials
acted in conjunction with the Navy commissioners Berkeley,

[1] For naval administration in this period, the most important contributions are those by the late J. R. Tanner, including those in *E.H.R.* xii; his
introduction to the *Catalogue of Pepysian MSS.* (*N.R.S.*); and his edition of
Pepys's Naval Minutes (*N.R.S.* lx). Extensive use of these sources has been
made in this chapter. For a good bibliography see G. E. Mainwaring,
Bibliography of English Naval History (1929).

[2] For the duties of the lord high admiral and the prerogative of the
admiralty courts see MS. 2874, f. 43 and f. 153 in the Pepysian Library,
Cambridge. Also *Stowe MS.*, 327, f. 2, and *Add. MS.* 38861, f. 16. The lord
high admiral's badge of office was a whistle (see J. Corbett, in *Mariners'
Mirror*, iii, no. 12). For the relations of the lord high admiral to the Navy
Board see W. G. Perrin, ibid. xii, no. 2, and for his administration generally
see E. S. de Beer, ibid. xiii, no. 1.

Penn and Peter Pett, a fourth commissioner, William Coventry,[1] being appointed in 1662. Together, these men constituted the Navy Board, or the lord high admiral's advisory council, its powers defined within the terms of the lord high admiral's instructions. It made contracts, paid ships' companies, regulated rates of pay, selected candidates for commissions, and supervised dockyards and naval ship-building. Collectively, the Board was endowed with summary jurisdiction over dockyard employees and over seamen committing riots on shore.[2] Individually, their duties were these: the treasurer to pay estimates and obtain his funds from the treasury; the controller to keep duplicate accounts and supervise victualling; the surveyor to keep himself informed of the state of ships and dockyards; while the clerk of the acts served as secretary, and kept minutes and records.[3]

The system had this advantage, that it associated the personal initiative of a lord high admiral such as the duke of York with the competence and energy of men like Pepys. But an important change had to be introduced in the Third Dutch War, when the Test Act obliged James to give up his office. His powers lapsed to the king, who delegated a share of them to a commission which included prince Rupert, Shaftesbury, Osborne, Anglesey, Buckingham, Monmouth, and Lauderdale, a board not distinguished for maritime experience, nor likely to provide an adequate counterpart to the still surviving Navy Board. Of these lords commissioners Pepys was appointed secretary in June 1673. A dualism was thus created; for there was now an Admiralty Board, having supreme executive and military functions, but without technical knowledge, working with a Navy Board, which possessed considerable administrative experience, but little or no executive authority. These two bodies might well have supplemented each other; but in practice they generally overlapped. In spite of his exclusion from office, however, James continued to wield considerable influence until 1679, when the agitation of the Popish Plot caused him to

---

[1] William Coventry was the duke's private secretary and a friend of Pepys. He was also an effective speaker in the Commons and contributed to the downfall of Clarendon. Unfortunately there is no biography of him.
[2] 16 Car. II, cap. v.
[3] J. R. Tanner, *Introduction to Catalogue of Pepysian MSS.* (*N.R.S.*), i. 186.

remove himself altogether from naval affairs. The commissions for executing the office of lord high admiral were revoked in 1684, when Charles resumed the office to himself, delegating the duty of inspecting the Navy to his brother; and the years 1679–84, when commissionerships were given to men without naval experience, were years of neglect and decline in the English Navy.[1] In June 1684 Pepys's office of 'secretary for the affairs of the admiralty' was constituted by letters patent. Finally, when James succeeded to the throne he reassumed the office of lord high admiral.

Throughout these years the main difficulty in naval administration was want of money. English legislators, more familiar with 'crops than ships, showed an imperfect realization of the expense of an adequately maintained fleet, and still more of the enormously increased cost in time of war; nor did the higher officials succeed in taking advantage of periods of peace in order to have the ships ready for emergencies. The ordinary charge of the peace-time Navy at the Restoration was estimated at £400,000 per annum—or one-third of the total revenue which parliament thought necessary for the national services and failed to provide. By 1670 this cost had risen to £500,000.[2] The first two years of the Second Dutch War (Sept. 1664–Sept. 1666) cost over three millions, almost all of it on account of naval expenditure, leaving a deficit of nearly one million,[3] in spite of special parliamentary grants. With the coming of peace, the rate of increase of debt was lessened, but there remained a large permanent debt, which was considerably reduced in the reign of James.

This shortage of money had disastrous consequences, especially in the Second Anglo-Dutch War (1665–7). Not only were the seamen unpaid, but supplies had to be bought at prices heightened by as much as 40 per cent. owing to the abnormally low level of government credit.[4] Bargains had to be sacrificed

---

[1] For evidence see Pepys, *Memoirs relating to the state of the royal navy of England* (1690). Later edition ed. J. R. Tanner (1906).

[2] Lord Keeper Bridgeman's *Narrative of the state of public affairs*, Oct. 24, 1670, in *Parl. Hist.* iv. 456.

[3] For this see Dr. Shaw's introduction to *Cal. Tr. Bks., 1667–8.*

[4] *Grey,* i. 267.

because there was no ready money; ships had to be kept in commission because the crews could not be paid off, or put out of commission because there was no money for repairs; pressing for seamen became more difficult in proportion as it was realized that semi-starvation and penury were even more likely incidents of naval service than death or wounds. Hence the creditors of the government were often in desperate plight; many of them were sent to prison for debt; and it is probable that, but for the signing of peace (1667), the Stop of the Exchequer (1672) would have come earlier.

The seamen were the chief victims. A system of payment by credit-notes or tickets was introduced in May 1665;[1] but, as there were frequent delays and difficulties in cashing these coupons, a trade in tickets at the expense of the seamen speedily came into existence. Discharged sailors, obliged to find lodgings at some distance from their home, often parted with their tickets (at a considerable discount) to brokers who thronged the dockyard gates; the brokers then sold them to agents, who were able to redeem them at face value in the Navy Office. Sometimes even the tickets were withheld, and discharged men were ordered to other ships without pay. There were long arrears also in the pittance of a few pence per day allowed for hospital maintenance to the sick and wounded, who were landed (sometimes naked) on the beach; and even so late as June 1668 there was still a sum of £290,000 owing for wages of seamen.[2] Similar distress prevailed among the workmen in the yards, causing a desertion of rope-makers in the summer of 1665; and the conditions at Portsmouth induced a commissioner to declare that, for want of board-wages, men were being turned out of doors by landlords, and forced to perish in the streets more like dogs than men.[3] There is evidence that some of the naval carpenters and labourers died of starvation.[4] In the summer of 1667 a tardy attempt was made to remedy these abuses when the duke of York and twelve others were appointed to receive complaints from seamen and others as to the exactions practised on them,

---

[1] *C.J.* ix. 49 sqq.   [2] *Cal. S.P. Dom., 1667-8*, 443.
[3] Ibid., *1664-5*, 522.
[4] *Further Correspondence of S. Pepys* (ed. J. R. Tanner), 171.
[5] *Cal. S.P. Dom., 1667*, lx.

a step which may have been a sequel to the discovery that 3,000 English and Scottish seamen were serving in the Dutch fleets, and that others were engaging daily, in spite of the certainty of hanging when captured by their compatriots. A scapegoat for this mismanagement was found in Carteret, who was induced to exchange his office for that of deputy-treasurer of Ireland.

Connected with the financial difficulties was the collapse of the victualling arrangements. At the beginning of the Second Dutch War the entire victualling of the Navy was entrusted to one man, Denis Gauden; but he was unequal to this herculean task, and in October 1665 Pepys as 'the fittest man in England' was appointed Surveyor General of Victualling, an office for which his optimism and energy were the best qualifications. A temporary improvement followed. Gauden continued to supply victuals, but in conjunction with two responsible persons; and, in August 1668 (when £176,000 was owing to him), he undertook to provision the fleet at the rate of 6d. per day per man in harbour, and 8d. at sea.[1] The Third Dutch War brought a renewal of complaints, intensified by the Stop of the Exchequer, whereby the Navy contractors, sir T. Littleton, Josiah Child, and T. Papillon, were forced to expend large sums of their own money on the necessities of the Fleet. This, however, did not completely justify their provision of bad beer, mouldy bread, and meat from animals which had died natural deaths;[2] but they may have acted on the supposition, not extinct, that sailors can live on refuse. There was some improvement after the last of the Dutch wars, and in 1678 a new contract was entered into whereby three victuallers supplied provisions on a scale which allowed to each man, *per diem*, 1 gallon of beer, 1 lb. of wheaten biscuit, 2 lb. of salt beef (or bacon and pork as substitutes), one-eighth of a full-sized North Sea cod, 24 inches long, or a sixth part of a haberdine, 22 inches long, or 1 lb. of 'Poor John', with 2 ounces of butter and 4 ounces of salted cheese.[3] The victuallers were also to supply an allowance of ready money—9d. per man per month in ships of 60 men or under, and 6d. in ships carrying more than 60 men; wine in lieu of beer was allowed on ships sailing south of the thirty-ninth

---

[1] *Cal. S.P. Dom., 1667–8*, xviii.
[2] Ibid., *1672–3*, viii. sqq.   [3] Tanner in *E.H.R.* xiii. 31.

parallel. The contract system was superseded in 1683 by a state victualling department administered by commissioners.[1] Even thus, however, the dietary of the Fleet was not a varied one, and was responsible for the 'calentures' and 'scarbots' nowadays mitigated by daily tots of coarse lime-juice. A seaman who sailed under sir John Harman in 1669–71 on a Mediterranean expedition thus expressed himself:

> Our beef and pork is very scant,
> I'm sure of weight, one half it want:
> Our bread is black, and maggots in it crawl,
> That's all the fresh meat we are fed withal.
> When we these things to Sir John Harman say,
> Our purser mends the matter for a day,
> Thinking to make us weary of complaining,
> But he upon our bellies still is gaming;
> A little rice we get instead of fish,
> Which to you well is known, but a poor dish,
> Except good spice to put in it you had,
> For with a good sauce a deal board is not bad.
> Our drink it is but vinegar and water,
> Four-shilling beer in England's ten times better,
> So that when sailors gets good wine
> They think themselves in Heaven for the time.[2]

From the point of view of the lower deck there was an even more serious cause for complaint than deficiencies of pay or food. This was the system by which most of them were forced to enter naval service. Any man having sea experience might be requisitioned; homeward-bound merchant ships might be stopped at sea, and a proportion of their crews 'impressed' (i.e. pressed). Certain privileged vessels were, in theory at least, exempted from the press, including colliers, fishing boats, transports, and the barge of the archbishop of Canterbury; but in practice this distinction was not always maintained. Contingents of seamen, sometimes very juvenile,[3] were also obtained from Watermen's Hall, which licensed the wherries on the Thames. Constantly were the maritime counties scoured in search of men who by their appearance suggested some association with salt-

---

[1] Tanner in Introduction to *Pepysian MSS.* (*N.R.S.*), i. 180.
[2] J. Baltharpe, *The Straights Voyage, or St. David's Poem* (1671).
[3] *Cal. S.P. Dom., 1667–8*, 364.

water, and the leaving of tickets at their houses left them a choice between service and gaol. Had the press-gangs 'imprested' only seafaring men, the system might have been less iniquitous; but so great was the shortage of crews during the Dutch Wars, especially that of 1665-7, that farmers and teamsters were sometimes seized, generally after being well plied in an ale-house;[1] and among the victims were men of 50-70 years of age, who as soon as found to be unfit were sent away destitute.[2] Occasionally a certificate from the churchwardens that a man's wife and children would be left on the parish was tried as a means of securing exemption;[3] or men might try to escape by taking refuge in inland towns, such as Oxford, where the college authorities were required to search for fugitives.[4] As a deterrent, capital punishment was suggested, and a Navy commissioner proposed that gibbets should be erected on the Portsmouth road on which to hang every one in ten deserters.[5]

The result of this shortage was that in the Second Dutch War sixth-rate ships had to be dismanned in order to provide for the larger vessels,[6] and never did the English Navy have such motley crews as during that war; for several consignments of pressed men were said to be fit only for spreading vermin; some were composed of mere children; many were in rags, others were sick, with the marks of the Plague on them.[7] An observer noted, after the Four Days Battle of June 1666, that many of the Englishmen seen swimming or floating in the water were dressed in the black Sunday clothes worn by them when captured by the press outside the church door.[8]

There was some improvement in the Third Dutch War, when an attempt was made to secure voluntary enlistment by giving a bounty of six weeks' pay and a certificate to all who joined of their own accord.[9] But even thus England was at a disadvantage when compared with Holland. Our country was maritime in the sense that she was dependent on her Navy and Mercantile Marine, but not in the sense that Holland was maritime; for every Dutchman had at least seen a ship, and among

---

[1] *Cal. S.P. Dom.*, *1672-3*, ix and 376.   [2] Ibid., *1664-5*, 240.
[3] Ibid., *1664-5*, 429.   [4] Ibid., *1671-2*, viii.   [5] Ibid., *1664-5*, 192.
[6] Ibid., *1665-6*, 543.   [7] Ibid., *1667-8*, 207.   [8] *Colenbrander*, i. 396.
[9] *Cal. Tr. Bks.*, *1672-5*, 39, and *Shaftesbury*, vii. 570.

his countrymen there was a great reserve supply of trained men available for active service; whereas the English merchant sailor was not regarded as a national asset at all, and there were at least a million Englishmen who had never even seen the sea. It is true that England had great naval traditions, that her empire necessitated the exercise of sea-power, and that her later Stuart kings were fond of the sea; but, on the other hand, England was by temperament agricultural; her naval forces were only in process of organization, and she was dependent for the humbler personnel of the Fleet on a despised and completely unorganized merchant service. Neither press-gang nor pay-ticket was likely to elicit the best from her seafaring men. The Dutch, it is true, were not ruled by a yachtsman; nor did they insist on rigid social distinctions between their Navy and Merchant Service; but they valued their mercantile sailors, and paid for their services. This is one reason why they were so powerful at sea.

Nevertheless, the history of the Navy under the later Stuarts shows both specialization and progress. First of all, there were the improvements in the building of ships.[1] The Dutch two-deckers carried their lower tier of guns four feet from the water-line; in similar English ships the distance was three feet; consequently, sir Anthony Deane, with other English shipwrights, built an improved type of vessel, carrying its lowest guns four feet above the water, and allowing greater room for stowage. From the French also we learned to make our ships more beamy and more manageable in a sea-way.[2] A third improvement experimented with was that of sheathing, generally with copper or lead; but this method of preserving the lower part of the hull from corrosion was not generally successful, because of the galvanic action set up. On the whole, English builders maintained their own with the Dutch. The greater depth of water round our coasts enabled us to build ships of deeper draught;

[1] His Majesty's ships were classified according to their gun-power, ranging from 90 to 100 guns for a first-rate to the 14–18 guns of the sixth-rate. In practice it was usual to speak of all ships above fourth-rates, or having more than 50 guns, as capital ships. First-rates such as the *Sovereign*, the *Prince*, and the *Charles* of the Third Dutch War mounted 110 guns, had a tonnage of about 2,000 tons, and crews of nearly 800 men.

[2] A. W. Laird Clowes, *History of the Royal Navy*, ii. 242.

less 'floaty' than the Dutch models, but faster when close-hauled because of their greater 'sharpness' and depth of keel; on the other hand, when sailing 'large', that is, before the wind, the Dutch had the advantage. Hence ours were better adapted for tacking and manœuvring, and so the English fleets were more often successful in securing the weather-gauge.[1]

In tactics the Restoration admirals profited by the experience of Cromwell's 'Generals at Sea'; indeed the fighting instructions issued by the duke of York at the opening of the Second Dutch War were based on those issued in 1654.[2] A distinction was, however, introduced between defence against an attack from windward and against that from leeward; in general also, greater mobility was aimed at. But it is easy to over-estimate the scientific element in the maritime tactics of the period. Naval warfare was conditioned by the severe limitations of the square-rigged ship. The primary object of a fleet was to sink or capture the enemy, by gun-fire, or fire-ships, or by boarding, or by forcing him on a shoal; and the preliminary considered requisite for the attainment of these primary objects was to obtain the weather-gauge of the enemy—that is, get to windward of him and retain this tactical advantage throughout. That the windward position was to be striven for is one of the few axioms of seventeenth-century naval tactics; and for these reasons, first, because the fleet to windward had the initiative, since it could come down on the wind and attack; second, the gunners on the windward ships had a clear view, unimpeded by the smoke enveloping the leeward ships; and third, the advantage of the wind was most obvious in the use of fire-ships, which could be drifted down the wind towards the enemy. These were the most dreaded engines of naval warfare, and their effective use was the most concrete advantage of the weather-gauge.[3] On the other hand the windward position had this disadvantage, that, particularly in the earlier type of English ship, the lower tier of guns on the lee side might be under water in a stiff breeze, and so could not be brought into use at all.

---

[1] Mr. Shere's answers to some queries of Mr. Pepys regarding ships (1680), in *Rawl. MS.* A. 175, f. 328.   [2] *Fighting Instructions* (*N.R.S.*), ed. Corbett, 110.
[3] For a set of instructions to fire-ships lying on guard at Sheerness see Perrin in *Mariners' Mirror*, x, no. 1.

Once having gained the toss of the weather-gauge there were no clearly defined principles to follow.[1] But the general practice in the later Dutch wars was for each fleet to file past the other, firing into the enemy hulls and rigging; the ships in the van, having fired their volleys, then bore round to take up position behind the rearmost ships so as to repeat the attack. This was continued until the order of battle was broken,[2] when there was likely to be a general mêlée in which the disabled ships might be boarded or burnt by fire-ships. The English were distinguished for the precision with which they kept their line; they did not have roving free-lances, like the younger Tromp; nor were their fleets divided by political differences, such as sometimes interfered with the effectiveness of the Dutch, where there were Orange and De Witt factions. Moreover, having great faith in their gunners, the English placed less reliance on boarding the enemy than did the French. Our gunners found the great Dutch hulls a good target, as the proportion of unseasoned wood in these hulls made them specially vulnerable; in their turn, the English ships presented a smaller and more substantial free-board, and so their masts and rigging were most likely to be aimed at. The Dutch were credited with the occasional use of 'stink-pots' for projection into enemy ships; but these were not frequently utilized, because of the danger to their users.[3]

Two schools of English tacticians have been distinguished—that of York, Sandwich, and Penn, or the 'formal' school, having faith in rules, and prepared to spend much time in manœuvring for position, and the more 'dashing' school, represented by Monck and Rupert, who were credited with a belief in hard fighting and a willingness to take risks in order to secure an advantage.[4] The time spent in manœuvring at the battle of Lowestoft (June 1666) and failure to press the advantage of the

[1] *Remarks of sieur Arnoul on the English and Dutch Navies* (1670) in *Colenbrander*, ii. 7–128.

[2] The expedient of 'breaking the line' has sometimes been acclaimed as a tactical principle, and has been attributed as such to Lawson and De Ruyter. It had already been practised in the First Anglo-Dutch War. J. C. de Jonge, *Geschiedenis van het Nederlandsche Zeewesen* (3rd ed.), ii. 108.

[3] *Remarques sur la marine d'Hollande, par le sieur Arnoul* (1670) in *Colenbrander*, ii. 19.

[4] *Fighting Instructions* (ed. Corbett, *N.R.S.*), 134.

weather-gauge once it had been obtained, served for a time to
discredit the 'formal' school, and may account in some measure
for the supersession of York and Sandwich by Rupert and
Monck. But the difference may have been one of personal
temperament rather than of military principle. Manœuvres
that were followed by failure have generally been condemned
as mistakes so palpable that they can be understood even by
the untutored landsman; but the same manœuvres followed by
success are often hailed as subtle strokes of strategy, to be understood by the initiated alone.

In combat each man had his allotted place. The captain,
standing by the sailing master, gave his orders from the poop.
In capital ships the first lieutenant commanded the first battery
with the master gunner, the second lieutenant stood by the
second battery, and the third lieutenant controlled the forward
guns. The captain gave general orders, such as for firing or
manœuvring; the sailing master gave the more detailed orders
for effecting the manœuvre. Midshipmen stood by the yards
and braces ready for the order to go about: they were available
also as skeleton crews for prizes. The boatswain stood by the
anchors: the carpenter and his crew were down in the bilges
ready to execute temporary repairs to the hull; the surgeon
with his instruments was generally in the cockpit, accompanied
by the chaplain.[1] Fleets fought in three squadrons—the Red,
White, and Blue, each generally controlled by an admiral, vice-
admiral, and rear-admiral respectively. In theory the White
was the van and the Blue the rear; while the greatest strength of
ships and guns, with the supreme command, was centred in
the Red. Nominally also the White led the attack, the Red
seconded and engaged the enemy Admiral, while the Blue
followed with supplies and succour for distressed ships. But in
practice these distinctions were not preserved. Orders were
communicated by a code of signals agreed upon before combat,
these including the firing of guns and the hoisting of flags.

The intelligence service was hampered by the bad state of
the English roads, and much time might be lost when important
information had to be sent by land; moreover, as official orders
had to be countersigned by a secretary of state, there might be

---

[1] *Mémoire sur la marine d'Angleterre* (1672) in *Colenbrander*, ii. 56.

delay if he was not awakened in the night.[1] Equally serious was the fact that in neither of the last two Dutch Wars was there any real unity of command.[2] In a modern naval war there would be recorded at the Admiralty all the general instructions issued to the fleets; but in the seventeenth century there was no such system. Little harm might have resulted if the commander-in-chief at sea had been left to his own initiative; this was not always so, however, as Charles sometimes sent suggestions which, though not actually orders, were bound to have some influence on the conduct of their recipient.[3] On at least one occasion when he sent orders he allowed them to be modified if the admiral thought fit.[4] On their side the Dutch were influenced, especially in the Second Dutch War, by political dissensions; and their various Admiralties did not always work harmoniously together.

Specialization under the later Stuarts is to be seen more notably in material and personnel. Thus, the Navy was more definitely dissociated from the Mercantile Marine. No one was to fly the Jack without a licence from the lord high admiral; merchant captains were to fly the red ensign only, and were threatened with imprisonment if they used one of the distinctive naval flags.[5] So too with His Majesty's stores. These were now to be marked with the broad arrow, and all ropes used in the Navy were distinguished by a white strand in order to aid detection if stolen.[6] Acts of 1664 and 1671 increased the power of the judiciary to punish those who embezzled naval stores;[7] but pilfering appears to have been inevitable wherever these were concerned, and was never stamped out. Thus, in the yards, if the sawyers left any wood in the pits overnight it would be gone in the morning;[8] at Woolwich, some tradesmen acted as receivers and thereby acquired considerable estates;[9] and so in an age when every one, including the moral Pepys, had his perquisites,

---

[1] For an instance see *infra*, 298–9.

[2] There is an interesting note on this subject in *Rawl. MS*. A. 195, f. 64.

[3] Examples are in *Harleian MS*., 7006, f. 164 sqq.

[4] Charles to the duke of York, July 27, 1672, in *Lansdowne MS*. 1236, f. 139.

[5] Proclamation of Nov. 19, 1661, and Sept. 18, 1674, in *Steele*, i. 3333 and 3599.   [6] *Steele*, i. 3333.

[7] 16 Car. II, cap. v, and 22–3 Car. II, cap. xxxiii.

[8] *Cal. S.P. Dom.*, *1667–8*, 443.   [9] Ibid., *1672–3*, 258.

it was not surprising that workmen had generous views of the
size of 'chips'. The extent of this wastage was dramatically
realized when the Dutch sailed up the Medway; for oak planks
could not be found on which to mount the guns[1] (though it was
known that they ought to have been in store), and the unsatisfactory substitute of deal planks had to be used.

In matters of personnel the general policy was to make
naval service more professional. To this the legislature lent its
aid, and the disciplinary code in force during the Commonwealth was embodied in a Statute[2] passed in 1661 whereby
espionage, sedition, mutiny, and embezzling of stores were made
statutable offences, and captains at sea were authorized to conduct courts martial. A further distinction from the civilian was
introduced when officers serving in His Majesty's ships were
exempted from service as constables, surveyors, or churchwardens.[3] Of similar consequence was the custom, begun in
1661, whereby one volunteer was to be entered on each ship, to
have the pay of a midshipman, and 'to have such kindness as
you shall judge fit for a gentleman', together with suitable
accommodation, and opportunities for instruction in navigation and seamanship.[4] This reform, the work of the duke of
York, was the beginning of the evolution of the modern naval
officer. Technical qualifications were soon to be required of
him. In December 1677, after receiving complaints from sir
John Narbrough, then serving in the Mediterranean, the king
and lords of the Admiralty decided to introduce an examination for the post of sea-lieutenant, a test to be taken after three
years' experience at sea.[5] Four years earlier a step in the same
direction had been taken on the personal initiative of the king;
for in August 1673 he established in Christ's Hospital a foundation of forty boys, to be known as the Children of the New Royal
Foundation, who were to be educated in mathematics and
navigation with a view to service in the Fleet.[6]

Even thus the sailor, like the soldier, did not lose his civilian
status when in service, and several misdemeanours which would

---

[1] See *infra*, 311.   [2] 13 Car. II, cap. ix.
[3] Order in Council of Aug. 28, 1663.
[4] Tedder, *Navy of the Restoration*, 59–60.
[5] Tanner, in *E.H.R.* xiii. 48 sqq.   [6] *Cal. Tr. Bks.* iv, 1672–5, 379.

now be tried by courts martial were then cognizable by the justices in Quarter Sessions. Sometimes also a disciplinary case would be referred to the Admiralty for decision, if justice could not be obtained elsewhere; as for example the complaint of purser Trevor against captain Vittels, which was adjudicated by Pepys and Dartmouth in January 1688. The matter arose thus.[1] Trevor, purser of the *Suffolk*, was going ashore at Chatham on Michaelmas Day 1685, when Vittels, captain of the *Britannia*, ordered him to give assistance in securing some ships which had dragged their anchors. Trevor refused, on the ground that he was going ashore on higher authority; he was thereupon assaulted by the captain with a boat-hook. Trevor laid information before a justice, and sought damages at common law, but as a settlement could not be reached, both parties eventually agreed to abide by the decision of Pepys and Dartmouth, the king having ordered Vittels to give satisfaction to the complainant. At the hearing in the Admiralty office, medical certificates and testimonials of character were produced on both sides, and witnesses gave sworn evidence of what each party had said about the other before and after the incident. The two arbiters awarded the purser damages of £50 against the captain.

This case shows that the province of the courts martial was not yet clearly defined. But certain things were invariably referred to these courts; for instance, incompetent handling of one of His Majesty's ships. Pepys records such a trial in 1673 when the pilot of H.M.S. *Fairfax* was tried by a panel of nine captains for running his ship aground in the Thames. The pilot was acquitted.[2] The same tribunal tried the captain of the *Fairfax*, who was absent from his ship without leave at the time of the grounding; his sentence was the very moderate one of dismissal from his then command.[3] In the following year, a similar moderation was shown in the sentence inflicted on captain Haddock, formerly commander of the fire-ship *Ann and Christopher*. Having lost company with his superior officer in the Mediterranean, captain Haddock stayed for several days at Malaga, where he took in some merchantable goods for a

---

[1] *Rawl. MS.* A. 177. For a similar adjudication in the quarrel between sir John Berry and sir Wm. Booth see ibid., f. 78.

[2] *Rawl. MS.* A. 181, f. 172.   [3] Ibid., f. 174.

commission. He was sentenced to disburse all his profits on the transaction, and to be suspended from his command for six months.[1]

The Navy then included a proportion of 'gentlemen' captains; a class not, at that time, easily amenable to discipline. There was a distinction between the discipline imposed on men selected on account of good birth, and that enforced on those not so fortunately endowed; indeed, that gentlemen were the natural leaders of other men was axiomatic in the seventeenth century, and is still a principle of modern armies and navies, with the amendment that some training is now considered necessary to supplement the in-born valour. At that time, the comparative simplicity of naval tactics and the absence of a technical literature of strategy appeared to justify a commander of rank in manœuvring a ship within the limits imposed by the laws of navigation and the competence of a professional sailing master; for while the first of these could not be court-martialled, the second could. Other things helped to confirm the prerogative of the amateur. Monck, when commanding at sea, had often caused laughter[2] among his ship's company by shouting from the poop such orders as 'Right Wheel', or 'Left Wheel'; but then the great Generals at Sea had had 'a special presence of God with them' which raised them above the trivialities of maritime terminology. After the Restoration, when providential co-operation was again restricted, the case for pedigree was confirmed by the prowess of the duke of York and prince Rupert, who, like Monck, had acquired their training in land service; and so these were the golden days of the 'gentleman' captain. But those, like Pepys, who knew the Navy best, deplored the giving of commissions to titled incompetents, who thus displaced the 'tarpaulings of Wapping and Blackwall, from whence the good commanders of old were all used to be chosen';[3] and the diarist kept a sharp look-out in Whitehall for gentlemen captains overstaying their leave.

This dualism between the 'gentleman' captain and the mercantile sailor is as old as the English Navy. Drake, in his circumnavigation of the world, was obliged to order a cessation of 'stomaching between gentlemen and sailors';[1] even to-day, the few men who receive naval commissions from the merchant service or the lower deck have to justify their advancement not only by efficiency but also by tact. The chief sufferers were those qualified officers of the mercantile marine, such as mates, pilots, and sailing masters, who, when pressed into service, might be assigned the quarters of ordinary seamen; while the 'gentleman' captain took over the greater part of the accommodation for his servants, volunteer friends, his barber, or his 'decayed kindred'; claiming 'the steerage for his grandure, the quarter deck for his jarrs and pidgeons, and oft time all abaft the mainmast upon the upper deck'.[2] Other contemporary accusations against those officers who had not graduated from sea service were that they spent too long in harbour; that they preferred fighting in line and out of gun-shot of the enemy; and that when they were grappled by an enemy ship they did know how to get clear. Both Charles and James were for gentlemen commanders,[3] and one reason why the former disliked the Dutch was because so many of them were merchant sailors; but, on the other hand, neither of these kings could complain of the conduct of those of their admirals who had begun as professional seamen; for these included Lawson, Myngs, Harman, Tiddeman, and Berry. In justice also to the lower deck and Mercantile Marine it should be recalled that Drake, Frobisher, and Hawkins (none of whom began his service at sea as a 'gentleman' or naval officer) represent that class of seaman which the later Stuarts despised. On the whole, seventeenth-century sailors preferred a 'tarpaulin' captain because, though he might be taciturn, he was not likely to be arrogant; an illustration of this is to be seen in the affection with which sir Christopher Myngs was held by his men. Sandwich was the best of the 'gentlemen' officers, Buckingham the worst. The duke served as a volunteer under Albemarle (Monck) in the fight off Lowestoft in June 1666. As the fight waxed hotter Albemarle proclaimed that he would pistol himself rather than surrender; whereupon Buckingham announced that, before such a serious state of

---

[1] Quoted in *Life and Works of sir H. Mainwaring*, ed. G. E. Mainwaring and W. G. Perrin, ii. 280.

[2] R. Gibson's *Collections on the Navy*, in *Add. MS.* 11602, f. 27.

[3] Ibid., f. 71.

affairs was reached he, with other gentlemen volunteers, would throw the commander-in-chief overboard.[1] Fortunately he did not have to stretch his prerogative so far; but he never went to sea again.[2]

Whatever dubiety there may have been regarding the comparative merits of these two types of officer, there can be no doubt that over the men, while at sea, a much stricter disciplinary code was enforced, a code attributable to the duke of York. In 1663 he issued printed instructions to naval commanders, and these were afterwards amplified into a comprehensive code of forty-four articles by the commissioners who later executed his office.[3]

This code, not unlike a miniature of the modern King's Regulations and Admiralty Instructions, included these rules: divine service was to be conducted twice a day by the whole ship's company according to the liturgy of the Church of England; on appointment, the captain was at once to proceed on board his ship, and send a weekly report while she was fitting out; he was obliged always to be on board his ship during his command. The crew were to be mustered weekly, and were to be discharged by ticket only when absolutely necessary; quarters and duty were to be assigned to each man, and a schedule thereof hung up in the steerage. In conjunction with master and boatswain, the captain was to determine who were to be inferior officers, able seamen, ordinary seamen, grommets, and boys; no merchandise was to be carried; when seizing a prize the hatches were to be spiked up, and tobacco was to be taken in the forecastle only over a tub of water. For the maintenance of these rules the captain was responsible.

There were also orders affecting the crews, a copy of which was hung up in steerage or forecastle; these enjoined the following penalties:

1. For swearing and drunkenness, forfeiture of one day's pay.

---

[1] Lady Burghclere, *George Villiers, second duke of Buckingham*, 145.

[2] From trembling at sea when not a gun roared,
And then steal ashore by breaking our word,
With Dammee if ere you'll catch me aboard,
    Libera nos Domine.

        The True Protestant's Litany.

[3] There is a copy in *Rawl. MS.* A. 181, f. 215.

2. For telling a lie, able-bodied seamen and inferior ratings were to be hoisted on the main-stay, having a broom and shovel tied to their backs, and to remain in this posture for half an hour; while the ship's company cried out 'A liar, A liar'.
For ratings above that of able-bodied seamen, forfeiture of one day's pay.
3. For theft, the culprit to be towed ashore, and the amount made good out of his wages.
4. For going ashore without leave, two days' pay.
5. Neglect of watch, one day's pay.
6. Defiling the decks, not more than twelve lashes.

These rules were to be read out to the assembled ship's company once a month, and it may be observed that the penalties were more lenient than those afterwards enforced. It may be noted also that life on board a Stuart warship was much more informal than that of a modern man-of-war. An immoderate number of healths were drunk; on the most trivial pretext, great quantities of ammunition would be expended in salutes. Women friends of the crew were not only allowed on board, but sometimes remained on as passengers until they were disembarked; and when they were at last seen safely over the side, it was to the accompaniment of appeals such as 'Loath to depart', or 'Maids, where are your hearts?', strains dispensed by the ship's band, then known as 'the complete noise'—a technical, not a derogatory term.

Inadequate pay and the absence or uncertainty of a pension contributed to the difficulties experienced in making naval service fully professional. The average rates of pay[1] varied from 50s. per day for a Fleet vice-admiral to 14s. 3d. per month for a grommet, and 9s. 6d. for a boy. The captain of a First Rate had per month £21; of a Sixth Rate, £7; the lieutenant ranged between £4 4s. and £2 16s.; the master, between £7 and £4; the boatswain had slightly less than the lieutenant; gunner, purser, and carpenter had £4; the surgeon £2 10s.; the cook £1 5s.; the able-bodied seaman £1 4s.; and the ordinary seaman 19s. These were the rates in force at the end of the reign of Charles II. An allowance was sometimes made in lieu of prize-money, at the rate of 10s. per ton of enemy ships captured, and £6 13s. 4d. for every piece of ordnance;[2] these amounts being divided among ship's

[1] *Add. MS.* 9307, f. 225.   [2] *Steele*, i. 3402, Oct. 28, 1664.

companies. No regular provision was at first made for widows or dependants; but in 1665 there was instituted a scheme whereby small payments were made to children and widows of officers, varying in accordance with rank from £15 to £300;[1] and, for the relatives of seamen, from £2 to £10. In 1672 a system was adopted whereby disabled officers who had completed fifteen years' service were given pensions; but these were cut down in 1679, a fit prelude to a period of naval decline.[2] A system of half-pay for officers not actually engaged in service was initiated in 1674,[3] but this does not appear to have extended beyond commanders of First and Second Rates and captains of flag ships. To complete a somewhat haphazard system, deductions were made from naval pay for the provision of a chaplain and barber, and also for the upkeep of Chatham Chest, a fund from which were made payments to sailors in respect of wounds. In 1684 the scale was a life pension of £6 13s. 4d. for the loss of an arm or leg, £13 6s. 8d. for two arms or legs; £4 for loss of an eye, and £5 for a disabled arm. Persons having a lesser disability were viewed by the surgeon acting for the Chest and recommended for an appropriate amount. Pensioners had to call in person or by deputy to receive the money, and as this was impossible for the majority of Scottish and Irish sailors, these men were obliged to compound for the pension—the amount allowed by the Governors of the Chest being a capital sum equal to twice the annual value.[4]

Sporadic attempts were made to deal with the question of the sick and wounded. In 1664 a temporary commission for this purpose was instituted on the model of that of 1653.[5] Of this new commission Evelyn was the most active spirit, but his activities were impeded by lack of funds. The commissioners appointed for the last of the Dutch wars were ordered to distribute the sick and wounded throughout the few available hospitals, and failing such accommodation, to billet them on private persons. There were then no naval hospitals and the resources of the London institutions were more than taxed during these wars. Some improvement was effected by securing closer co-operation between

[1] *Add. MS.* 9320, f. 28, Sept. 1665.   [2] *P.C. Reg.* 68, Dec. 21, 1679.
[3] *Add. MS.* 9307, f. 96.   [4] Ibid., f. 198.
[5] Tanner in *E.H.R.* xii. 64.

the Admiralty and the medical profession by means of the surgeon-general of the Navy, who was required to assist the governor of Surgeons' Hall in the work of procuring suitable surgeons and their mates for service at sea. Inspection of medical chests, visiting the sick and wounded and certifying the nature of the officers' wounds were among the other duties of the surgeon-general.[1] An effort was also made on behalf of those Cinderellas of the service, the chaplains. In the Stuart navies chaplains were sometimes paid at the same rate as seamen; many of them had gone to sea in order to get away from trouble; for almost all of them their position on board ship was ignominious in the extreme.[2] The chaplain was scarcely recognized as an officer; and when he addressed the ship's company he sometimes did so standing in the steerage, surrounded by lumber, as did Henry Teonge when he preached his first sermon in the *Assistance* (June 1675) to a congregation of sailors and sea-sick women.[3] So long as he could not himself ring the bell for service, it was generally left to the commanding officer to decide whether or not there should be any service at all. A slight change for the better was introduced in 1677, when it was ordered that naval chaplains should be such only as had the approval of the bishop of London. It was a slender qualification, but at least it was a start.

Such, in brief, were some of the characteristics of the Restoration Navy. But the fierceness of the European hostilities about to be described should not obscure the world-wide extent of the duties already entrusted to English sailors. Our possessions in the West Indies would have been lost but for the energy and skill of seamen, notably sir John Harman (an old lieutenant of Blake's), who in 1667 decisively defeated the French off Martinique.[4] It was during the Third Dutch War that St. Helena was finally recaptured from the Dutch.[5] These events signified the emergence of England as an oceanic power. To this period also may be assigned the rapid development of English sea-power in the Mediterranean, enhanced by the acquisition of Tangier. An illustration of the use

---

[1] *Rawl. MS.* A. 171, f. 208.
[2] Memo addressed to Pepys regarding naval chaplains (undated), in *Rawl. MS.* A. 171, f. 1.
[3] *Diary of Henry Teonge*, 9.
[4] See *infra*, 307-8.
[5] See *infra*, ii. 663.

of this power was seen in 1678 when sir John Narbrough's fleet
was able to keep immobilized the French admiral Duquesne, a
pressure which led directly to Louis XIV's evacuation of Sicily.[1]
In general, however, Tangier did not serve any very definite
naval purpose; it was a bad harbour and was not a frequent
resort of His Majesty's ships. But there was a base of operations
at Port Mahon, where a naval depot was established by the connivance of the governor;[2] and at Gibraltar a start had already
been made, for Charles was given permission to build barracks
outside the walls, and store-houses and sheds appear to have been
set up for the convenience of English men-of-war visiting the
port. 'It is certainly a most convenient port', wrote an English
naval agent there, 'whenever His Majesty has a war with any of
the governments of Barbary,' adding the story that the Turks had
decided not to have a war with the French because of their
bomb-boats, nor with the English, because the Spaniards had
allowed them the use of Gibraltar.[3] It 1683 there was a rumour
in Holland that lord Dartmouth had taken possession of the port
in virtue of a treaty between England and Spain;[4] and it is clear
that in English official circles great importance was attached to
the securing of a foothold on the western outpost of the Mediterranean.[5] But when in 1686 an attempt was made to extend the
scope of this primitive naval base, and to obtain stores and houses
within the town, the Spanish government refused to allow any
further enlargement on the ground that this would cause difficulty with other powers.[6] Tangier had already been lost because
its maintenance was made a party question; but it had scarcely
left our possession before a beginning had been made on the
other side of the Straits.

It was against the corsairs of Barbary, Tripoli, and Algiers that

[1] J. S. Corbett, *England in the Mediterranean*, ii. 103.

[2] *Cal. S.P. Dom.*, *1671*, xxviii.

[3] *S.P. For.* (*Spain*), 72, letter of Wm. Soanes to lord Lansdowne, Gibraltar,
March 12/22, 1686.

[4] *H.M.C. Rep.* vii, app. 293, lord Preston to Jenkins, Nov. 3/13, 1683.

[5] Cf. Pepys's memorial touching Gibraltar, in *Rawl. MS.* A. 266, f. 105,
Feb. 14, 1685/6.

[6] *S.P. For.* (*Spain*), 72, Spanish memoir of May 17, 1686. Lord Lansdowne
(ibid. May 23) thought that the Spanish government gave its refusal because
it feared a similar demand from the French.

English naval force in the Mediterranean was mainly directed. The plight of English captives in Algiers, soon to be the concern of war-ships, was at first left to private charity. In February 1662 300 English captives petitioned for the raising of a fund to effect their ransom; to this appeal the response was good, a sum of £4,000 being raised, supplemented by a government grant of £20,000, and a committee was appointed to supervise the redemption of captives.[1] From the funds thus provided the English consul at Algiers was able to secure the release of several English slaves; and considerable sums appear to have been devoted to this object; for example, when an Algerine ship took refuge in Harwich, the five English captives aboard were ransomed by the government at a total cost of £378.[2] The usual ransom was about £40 per man; and the parish records of England abound in testimony to the charity of the poorest villagers who contributed for these ransoms. Another fund for this purpose was deposited in the Chamber of London; but it proved inadequate, and in March 1684 it contained only about £300.[3] The method of redemption by purchase had broken down.

Negotiation was also tried. Treaties were signed in 1662 with the Bassa and Divan of Algiers,[4] and with the Bassa and People of Tripoli;[5] a treaty with Algiers concluded by sir T. Allen in October 1664 stipulated that all British subjects then in slavery were to be released, and that henceforth no British subjects were to be enslaved.[6] But the corsairs soon forgot their commitments, and a change for the worse came in 1671, when a band of Janissaries obtained control of Algiers. Two years earlier the Turkish conquest of Candia had released for other service a band of Salee Rovers; soon these pirates were dictating their terms, prescribing the style of passes to be carried by English merchant ships, and extracting a percentage from the auctions of slaves for the profit of the new government and the upkeep of harbours and mosques. A new period of aggression commenced, and the services of the

[1] Cal. S.P. Dom., 1661–2, 285.
[2] Rawl. MS. A. 139 b, f. 39, n.d., but probably reign of James II.
[3] P.C. Reg. 70, March 12, 1683/4.
[4] Dumont, vi, pt. ii. 420.   [5] Ibid. 431.
[6] Ibid. vi, pt. iii. 31.

Mediterranean fleet had to be called in. Accordingly, in October 1674 sir John Narbrough was sent out with a squadron which blockaded Tripoli and destroyed several frigates; the blockade forced the Dey to come to terms, which included the release of about 450 English captives and a promise of compensation.[1] No sooner had Narbrough returned to England than the piracies were resumed with fresh vigour. In 1677, therefore, he was again employed in blockading the nests of the sea rovers, and after a vigorous campaign he returned to England in 1679, leaving vice-admiral Herbert to continue the work. In the course of these years many Moors and Turks were captured and sold at Tangier, Majorca, Genoa, and Cadiz.[2] Only by this policy of reprisals were the evils of piracy and slavery mitigated; and thus the English Navy performed in the Mediterranean the functions of a maritime police.

In conclusion it may be noted that the period of the later Stuarts was one of the most formative in the history of the Navy; for there was steady improvement in administration, and there was accumulated in the hard struggles with the Dutch a great fund of experience for the service of the future. One illustration of this progress is to be seen in the increase of tonnage. Between 1660 and 1673 there were added to the 156 ships in existence at the Restoration a total of 147 vessels, an increase representing more than 60,000 tons, 20,000 men, and 4,000 guns.[3] Losses incurred in the Dutch wars were more than made good, and in 1675 Pepys could boast that more ships had been built since 1670 than in any other five years of English history.[4] But this expansion was not continuous, and was sometimes counterbalanced by periods of retrenchment and severe economy, such as the period commencing early in 1667 and continuing until 1670, and that which, beginning in 1679, lasted until the Revolution. In the reign of James the administration was good, and the Navy was less deeply in debt; but there was a decline in the number of ships from 162 to 143, a diminution of about 5,000 tons.[5] This was not very serious in itself, but it was part of a dangerous policy of economy at the expense of the greatest fighting service of the

[1] *Cal. S.P. Dom.*, *1675–6*, 12.
[2] *Rawl. MS*. A. 177, f. 164.
[3] Tanner in *E.H.R.* xii. 57.
[4] *Parl. Hist.* iv. 774.
[5] Tanner in *E.H.R.* xiv. 268.

state, and it was not without its influence on the fate of the House of Stuart.

An illustration of this economizing just before the Revolution is provided in a memoir of Pepys preserved in the Pepysian Library.[1] On Tuesday, May 8, 1688, the Navy Board met at Chatham in sir Peter Pett's house to consider what to advise the king regarding the security of his great ships in Chatham harbour. The Board had already suggested that all the fortifications between Sheerness and Upnor should be put in a serviceable condition, that the boom and chain by Upnor Castle should be fixed and made ready, and that all the third- and fourth-rate ships should be manned and victualled (necessitating between six and eight thousand men). These measures the Board considered necessary in view of the fact that the Prince of Orange was fitting out a fleet; but, as James refused to believe that there was any such danger from Holland, and as he thought these measures would entail too much expenditure, the Board had met in order to devise a second-best plan. Accordingly they agreed to recommend the fitting out of guardships and fire-ships, and that the land fortifications should be made serviceable, their main concern being 'to make the charge as easy to the king as might be'. These measures, with the manning of 10 third-rates and 2 fourth-rates at a cost of £30,000 they thought the irreducible minimum. As the king was due to visit the yard on that day, the Board asked Pepys to open the matter to His Majesty.

At 1 p.m. the king arrived with the prince of Denmark and lord Dartmouth. His first act was to proceed on horseback to review 'a foot regiment that was drawn up on the backside of the brick wall'. He then listened to the representations of Pepys. His reply was that he did not think the Dutch had so great a fleet as was reported; however, he would have some new batteries erected and would have the old ones repaired—that being 'the properest and best security to his Navy'. Next day he went so far as to consent to the manning of two third-rates and three fourth-rates 'with the lowest complement of men'. After discourse about lead sheathing and the preservation of timber, James gave directions regarding flags and colours to be used by flag officers, and expressed dissatisfaction at the amount of money spent on healths

[1] *Pepys MS.* 2879, f. 913 sqq.

and salutes. So ended the royal visit. On that evening, Pepys with Deane and Hewer went to visit the ships in Gillingham reach, and then on board the *Britannia*, where the purser regaled them with a bowl of punch and 'a fine, cold treat'. Then they visited Gillingham fort, 'whose condition as to carriages and platforms is better to be silent than to say anything'. Thence they walked home through the woods, so terminating a day in which a sailor-king of England had won his point, that shore fortifications are the best defence of the Fleet.

But the James of this incident was a very different person from the James who, as duke of York, performed such great naval service as to induce Englishmen to take a deeper interest in the Navy and the Sea. The next chapter treats of this more heroic period in the history of himself and of his country.

VIII

THE SECOND ANGLO-DUTCH WAR
1665–7

THOUGH he disliked the Dutch and wished to see the young prince of Orange rule in the place of Pensionary De Witt, Charles was not anxious for war. This is true also of the two senior Restoration statesmen, Clarendon and Southampton, who had the caution of experience; and even the East India Company, though solicitous for the redress of its grievances, was not convinced that this could best be secured by naval contest, because in such a struggle the English might be driven altogether out of the East Indies. At The Hague Downing thought that the Dutch would yield rather than fight; at Versailles Louis XIV, pledged by his Franco-Dutch treaty of 1662, hoped that hostilities would be avoided. The war party in England was led by three of the younger and rising school of politicians—Henry Bennet, Thomas Clifford, and William Coventry, of whom the first two, at the request of Charles, had been admitted to Clarendon's informal committee of parliamentary management.[1] There was also the duke of York, round whom clustered young and ardent men, anxious for the opportunities brought by a national crisis. So far as there was antithesis between the war party and that of Clarendon, the former possessed this advantage for Charles, that it had youth, change, and enterprise on its side.

This party could depend on a House of Commons which contained many men of immature years. Already in April 1664 the Commons had concurred with the Lords in a vote desiring the king to take steps for the protection of English trade against the Dutch.[2] In his speech at the opening of the fourth session of the Cavalier Parliament (Nov. 24, 1664) Charles, after narrating the events of the summer, disavowed having given a commission to captain Holmes for the seizure of the Dutch fort at Cape Verde, and drew the attention of his auditory to the significance of De

---

[1] *Clar. Cont.* ii. 208–10.
[2] *C.J.* viii. 548, April 21, 1664, and *L.J.* xi. 600, April 22.

Ruyter's expedition to Guinea,[1] whereupon both Houses voted their thanks to the king. Thanks were also voted to the city of London for its financial assistance,[2] and the only doubt remaining was whether the Commons would give a grant sufficient for a war in which they were assuming a considerable degree of initiative. Bennet and Coventry thought that only as much should be asked for as would ensure committal to hostilities, but Clarendon and Southampton rightly concluded that now was the time to take advantage of the bellicose temper of the Commons and so, at the Chancellor's instigation, sir Robert Paston, a Norfolk squire, was prompted to move for a grant of £2,500,000, which he did on the 9th of February 1665.[3] To the surprise of the parliamentary managers the vote was carried, the money to be raised by an assessment spread over a period of three years. Even thus, however, England was at a disadvantage as compared with the United Provinces, where Holland experienced more difficulty in refusing than in finding money.[4] The declaration of war on the States General followed on February 22, 1665.

English preparations had begun in the preceding October. Rupert had at first been ordered to follow De Ruyter to the Guinea coast, but this was countermanded when it was learnt that the Dutch were making preparations for hostilities in European waters; orders were therefore given for the immediate fitting out of forty ships, including the first-rates *Royal Charles* and *Royal James*. As lord high admiral the duke of York supervised the preparations. An embargo was placed on all ships in English waters, except coasting and fishing vessels, East India ships and vessels having a special permit. The justices were instructed to compile lists of seamen in their districts; 1,200 soldiers were ordered to be mobilized for service in the Fleet; a commission was issued for the care of the sick and wounded; accommodation was taken over at St. Bartholomew's and St. Thomas's Hospitals, and encouragement was given to the import of pitch and tar by the removal of customs duties on those commodities when ex-

[1] *L.J.* xi. 624–5.
[2] For the loan of £100,000 for one and a half years see *Cal. S.P. Dom., 1664–5*, 43.
[3] *Clar. Cont.* ii. 309–10.
[4] *Colenbrander*, i. 175, May 21, 1665.

ported by Virginia or Maryland.[1] Orders for the auction of goods taken from enemy ships and for the payment of an allowance to Dutch prisoners of war completed the preparations of the duke of York.

On March 23, 1665, he took over command at the Gunfleet, and ordered his flag-officers to meet every morning on board the *Royal Charles*, so that a definite order of battle might be devised; for this war, it was asserted, would be won not merely by the valour for which the Cromwellian Generals at Sea had distinguished themselves, but by adherence to a definite system of tactics.[2] The ships were said to be better manned than they had been in the First Dutch War; indeed it was a fleet of which the nation might well be proud, for it consisted of 98 men-of-war, including 3 first-rates, 11 second-rates, 15 third-rates, 32 fourth-rates, and 11 fifth-rates with 26 merchantmen, accompanied by fireships and tenders. When, early in May 1665, this armada put to sea, the Red was commanded by the duke, admiral of the fleet, flying the royal standard at the main, with Lawson his vice-admiral and sir William Berkeley his rear-admiral; the White by prince Rupert, vice-admiral of the fleet, flying the union flag, with sir Christopher Myngs his vice-admiral and Robert Sansum his rear-admiral, and the Blue by the earl of Sandwich, with sir George Ayscue his vice-admiral and Thomas Tiddeman his rear-admiral. Early in May this fleet cruised between Scheveningen and Texel within sight of the Dutch ships, which they could not induce to come out; and for some time there was a fear in England that the enemy would avoid a decision in European waters, where the rival fleets were more evenly matched.

Delay by the Dutch was owing to a number of good causes. There was difficulty in obtaining the full quota of men and munitions from each of the states; and the main fleet, when it did have its complement of men, was prevented by contrary winds from joining the Zeeland fleet. De Witt went to and fro among ths ships encouraging the sailors with promises of good pay and provision for dependants;[3] indeed, during these weeks of tense expectation and postponements it was by the energy and optimism

---

[1] *Cal. S.P. Dom.*, *1664–5*, 113 sqq., Dec. 16, 1664.

[2] J. S. Clarke, *Life of James II*, i. 405.

[3] *Colenbrander*, i. 175.

of the great Pensionary that co-operation and obedience were
secured in a composite force which included many Orangists; but
even thus, it was feared that the contingents of Zeeland and Frisia
were not whole-hearted in enthusiasm for the Republic.[1] The
Dutch were at some disadvantage also in this respect, that De
Ruyter, their best admiral, was not then in European waters; on
the other hand in Obdam (admiral of the fleet), John Evertsen
the elder (admiral of the Zeeland squadron and second in command), and Tromp they had naval commanders of exceptional
ability and experience. They at last succeeded in mustering 110
war-ships and 10 fireships, most of them having at least 50 guns;[2]
and so in gun-power the enemy had the advantage over the English. In the last fortnight of May 1665 the Hollander was waiting
till the wind veered east-south-east or north-east in order to come
out.

On Sunday, May 28, the frigates *Bonaventure* and *Sapphire*
brought news to the Gunfleet that the Dutch were at sea; this
news was followed closely by Downing's letter intimating that
Obdam had orders to seek the enemy even into the Thames.[3] To
obtain more sea room, the English fleet weighed on the morning
of Tuesday, May 30, and proceeded in the direction of Southwold
Bay; two days later, the look-out on prince Rupert's ship sighted
about 100 sail in the offing, whereupon the fleet stood to the south,
the wind being then north-east and the Dutch to windward at
east-north-east. Thursday afternoon and the whole of Friday
were spent in manœuvring for position on courses east and
east-by-north of Southwold, the distance between the fleets gradually decreasing, but the Dutch still preserving the weather
gage.[4]

By nightfall of Friday, June 2, the fleets were within two leagues
of each other, and this sailing contest was illuminated by the
accidental firing of a Dutch fireship. That night, when about
eight leagues east of Lowestoft, the wind veered to south-west, so

---

[1] *Colenbrander*, i. 212. Tromp is said to have told the prince of Orange
that they would fight better under his auspices, ibid. i. 241. Downing was
accused of secretly acting against De Witt on behalf of Orange, ibid. i. 240.

[2] Ibid. i. 188.

[3] Downing to Arlington, May 23/June 2, 1665, in *Colenbrander*, i. 181–3.

[4] Sandwich, *Journal* (*N.R.S.*), lxiv. 221–3.

enabling the duke to obtain the windward position. At 2 a.m. there began some long-range firing which proved more noisy than effective; the dawn of Saturday, June 3, brought 'a fine chasing gale' at south-south-west, and at 4 a.m. when the fleets were approximately eleven or twelve leagues east of Lowestoft, sailing south-east, the Dutch put about; and, as their ships sailed past in a westerly direction close-hauled on the port tack, they poured broadsides into each English ship in succession. Not all the English ships were in line, as some had luffed to get to windward of their companions.[1] Three times the two lines appear to have filed past each other, exchanging shots with each ship in turn; but in spite of desperate efforts, the Dutch failed to get to windward; and by 10 a.m. they and the English were sailing approximately south-east, on the starboard tack,[2] engaged in a running fight, in which the enemy 'knocked it out with us', sometimes close, sometimes far off. But, with the advantage of the weather gage, the duke steadily bore down on the Hollanders, Rupert and Myngs with the White in the van, and Sandwich with the Blue in the rear; until by 1 p.m. the Dutch line was broken, and a general mêlée ensued, the two flagships *De Eendracht* and *Royal Charles* fighting almost broadside on, while John Evertsen pounded the *Plymouth*, commanded by captain Thomas Allin, who afterwards recorded laconically in his log: 'I presently stood in so near as not to shoot in vain, and plied my gunners very hard for two hours.'[3] As guns were silenced, and masts and rigging fell overboard, disabled ships drifted from their places in line; and by the afternoon it became obvious that the Dutch were becoming disorganized by long-range, well-placed shots.

In the dense smoke it was difficult to see what was happening, but the losses on both sides were heavy. The critical moment came when shots fired into her hull ignited the magazine of the Dutch flagship, causing an explosion in which Obdam and about 400 men were killed. By 6 p.m. the Dutch were in flight for their harbours, led by Evertsen the elder and the Zeeland squadron;

---

[1] Ibid. 224.

[2] The evidence for this stage of the battle is confusing. See the narrative in *Harleian MS.* 7010, f. 566, printed by *Colenbrander*, i. 188 sqq., and Sandwich's *Journal*.

[3] Allin's log is in *Bodley, Tanner MS.* 296 (no foliation).

and when at 11 p.m. the duke turned in, he left orders that the pursuit should be continued throughout the night. There then occurred an incident typical of Stuart history. The duke had his secretary on board, Henry Brouncker, confidant and gamester, to whom his master showed a fidelity as firm as that of his grandfather to the first duke of Buckingham. Brouncker, convinced that he had had enough fighting, pretended to have come from the duke's cabin with an order to shorten sail. Captain Harman, believing that the order was genuine, took in sail, and at dawn the duke was just in time to see the enemy escaping through the shallows into the Texel.[1]

Leaving some fourth-rates as scouts on the Dutch coast the duke returned to the Gunfleet in order to refit. His losses included Lawson, vice-admiral of the Red, who died of wounds, and about 800 officers and men. The Dutch had suffered heavier casualties, namely, four admirals, including Obdam, and about 5,000 officers and men; moreover they had lost 12 men-of-war. Both nations hailed the battle of Lowestoft as a victory, but when the extent of their defeat came to be known, the indignation of the Dutch knew no bounds, and a mob threw John Evertsen into the sea, from which he was rescued in order that he might answer for his conduct to the States General. 'A greater victory never known in the world' was Pepys's comment;[2] indeed the diarist was so elated that he distributed four shillings among the boys in the street. In his stately prose, Dryden[3] thus recorded how the sound of the guns was heard in London:

While these vast floating bodies, on either side, moved against each other in parallel lines, and our countrymen, under the happy conduct of His Royal Highness went breaking by little and little into the line of the enemies; the noise of the cannon from both navies reached our ears about the city, so that all men being alarmed with it, and in a dreadful suspense of the event which we knew was then deciding, everyone went following the sound as his fancy led him; and, leaving the town almost empty, some took towards the Park, some across the River, others down it, all seeking the noise in the depth of silence.

---

[1] J. S. Clarke, *Original Memoirs of James II.* The account in this source is confirmed by the parliamentary debates of 1667–8; *infra*, 319–20.

[2] *Pepys*, June 8, 1665.   [3] *Essay of dramatic poesy.*

The defeat off Lowestoft helped to strengthen the Orange party in Holland, and imposed an increasing strain on Dutch allegiance to De Witt; moreover it made French assistance more than ever necessary, though Louis XIV was still engaged in a show of mediation. Near at hand also was the menace of a new enemy— the turbulent bishop of Münster, whose agent signed on June 3, 1665, an offensive alliance with England, by which the bishop undertook (in return for a subsidy) to invade Holland, his pretext for intervention being a claim to sovereignty over Borkeloo in Guelderland.[1] This ecclesiastic has the distinction of being the only potentate to receive a subsidy from Charles's resources; but the subsidy proved to be a waste of money; for the bishop, an early exponent of mechanical invention in war, though he invaded Dutch territory, achieved as little by his incendiary projectiles as by his military bravado. It was evidence of the failure of English diplomacy that this was our only ally; and moreover even he was soon to be detached, leaving England alone against an increasing number of enemies. In a long contest, initial victory is not always the best guarantee for ultimate success, and so it proved in this war, because England was tempted thenceforth to under-estimate her enemy, while the Dutch redoubled their efforts to regain supremacy at sea. Throughout their recuperation in the late summer of 1665 they were at least able to avoid disaster, while the English lost by their precipitancy.

This was illustrated in the disastrous attack on Bergen. As the king was anxious that neither the duke of York nor prince Rupert should again risk his life in naval combat, supreme command was entrusted to Sandwich, who, with Penn, was ordered to cruise about the Dogger Bank in order to intercept De Ruyter and the rich fleets from the Indies and Smyrna which were taking the homeward voyage by the north of Scotland. The conduct of Sandwich in this command was not judicious. Through the agency of the English envoy at Copenhagen, sir Gilbert Talbot, he was negotiating an arrangement with the king of Denmark whereby the latter, for a half-share in the spoils, was to permit the English fleet to attack the Dutch merchant ships in the neutral port of Bergen, and thereby gain more wealth 'than

[1] For this alliance see C. Brinkmann, 'Charles II and the bishop of Münster', in *E.H.R.* xxi, and Feiling, *British Foreign Policy*, 150–7.

perhaps his crown was worth'.[1] Relying on verbal assurances,
Sandwich, late in July 1665, when he was in latitude 58° N., detached Tiddeman with fourteen ships for this enterprise. Tiddeman entered Bergen on July 31, where there ensued a contest
between the admiral and the governor, the former in haste to
plunder the Dutch ships before the expected arrival of De Ruyter,
the latter urging delay until more definite instructions were received from Copenhagen. In the midst of this dispute, Tiddeman's squadron attacked the Dutch ships in harbour (Aug. 2),
but the guns of the shore forts were turned on the English ships,
and, after suffering more than three hours of bombardment, the
English admiral had to retire. He had lost no ships, but 118 of
his men were killed, including Sandwich's son.[2] As the wind was
in the south, the English could not use fireships against the Dutch
merchantmen; and this retreat from Bergen was disastrous, not
only for national prestige, but because it helped to range Denmark against us. Another misfortune was that De Ruyter
managed to slip past the English cordon and, sailing by Jutland
and Heligoland, came safely to anchor in the Ems,[3] to the general
rejoicing of the Dutch, whose spirits were further raised when De
Witt himself proceeded to sea and escorted home the Bergen
merchantmen. At The Hague, Downing found the Dutch
'huffed up to the skies'.[4]

When it seemed clear that the Dutch would not risk another
fleet action in the summer of 1665, English efforts were concentrated on the attack on Dutch trade. Putting to sea on
August 28, Sandwich succeeded in capturing nine East Indiamen
under convoy, the total value of the prizes being estimated at
£200,000.[5] This success was marred by a rash act on the part of
one who in the course of a brilliant career had aroused some enmities. Before obtaining permission, and without communication with the lord high admiral, who was then in Yorkshire, where
a rising of the Sectaries was feared, Sandwich proceeded to 'break
bulk' in the captured cargoes, and to distribute to his flag-officers

---

[1] Sandwich, *Narrative* in *Colenbrander*, i. 257; F. R. Harris, *Sandwich*, i,
ch. viii.   [2] Tedder, *Navy of the Restoration*, 133–4.
[3] He arrived at Delfzyl on July 27/Aug. 6, 1665. P. J. Blok, *Michiel
Adriaanz de Ruyter*, 219.   [4] *Colenbrander*, i. 282.
[5] *Cal. S.P. Dom.*, 1664–5, 558.

a portion of the spoils. This gave to his enemies Albemarle and sir William Coventry a much appreciated opportunity. The admiral narrowly escaped impeachment, and was sent off to Madrid on a special embassy; not till 1672 did he return to sea service. Such was the dubious ending to the hostilities at sea in the first year of the war. On the whole, fortune had favoured the English, but they had not succeeded in pressing home their initial advantage; nor did their finances permit the maintenance of a vigorous offensive. In September a number of ships were paid off, and others were kept in commission only for convoys. There was also mismanagement. Funds intended for the sick and wounded were diverted; only by pawning goods could money for these sufferers be obtained, and even the patient Evelyn was moved to wrath by the wretched plight of those who had risked all in their country's cause.[1]

Plague soon provided a sinister companion for war. There were few years in the seventeenth century in which no deaths from this cause were reported, and in the opinion of some medical writers an epidemic was overdue.[2] A few cases occurred in November 1664; then followed a hard, black frost, succeeded in 1665 by a hot summer and sultry autumn, prolific in flies and insects; indeed on July 3, 1665, the hardy Pepys noted that the season was a sickly one. Prevalence of 'spotted fever' since 1658, the increase of pleurisy and pneumonia in the winter of 1664-5, and over-indulgence in fruit during the hot summer of 1665— each of these was suggested as a pre-disposing factor in this, the last great epidemic in England. Later writers have cited the insanitary conditions of London and some of the greater towns such as Norwich, where there were populations and odours of oriental density and savour, providing hotbeds for the intensive cultivation of germs. But the Great Plague of 1665, bubonic in character, was brought by the rat and circulated by the flea. In its pneumonic form it was most deadly, and was spread by the breath of infected persons.

The infection is said to have come from the Levant by way of Holland in bales of merchandise.[3] It was first noticed in May 1665 when there were 43 deaths from this cause, followed in June

[1] *Cal. S.P. Dom.*, *1664-5*, 571. Evelyn to Pepys, Sept. 23, 1665.
[2] Creighton, *History of Epidemics*, i. 653.   [3] N. Hodges, *Loimologia*, 30.

by nearly 600; in July the deaths were counted in thousands, and the epidemic reached its height in September, when there was a recorded total for the month of more than 30,000 deaths. In a population estimated at just under half-a-million nearly 70,000 perished from this cause in the year 1665. After September the pestilence subsided, and for the whole of the succeeding year there do not appear to have been more than about 2,000 fatal cases. The plague spread to the provinces, appearing notably in Norwich, Southampton, Portsmouth, Sunderland, and Newcastle; the comparative immunity of Oxford is difficult of explanation. It was a true *morbus pauperum*, for it visited mainly the poor, very few of the upper classes being affected, and it called forth scenes of sacrifice and heroism in which many of the clergy, doctors, and magistrates distinguished themselves. Sheldon, Albemarle, Craven, and the lord mayor remained in the city; but the Court betook itself to Salisbury and then to Oxford, where parliament met in November. There the courtiers shocked both university and city by an indecency foreign to English standards.[1]

As both medical science and public health were in their infancy, little could be done either to cure the sufferers or stay the progress of the disease. In May the College of Physicians was asked by the privy council to send prescriptions, which it did.[2] These were probably herbal, as were most of the remedies or antidotes suggested; for example, there was the popular prophylactic made of sage, rue, buttercup-root, angelica-root, snake-root, and saffron, infused in malaga; and, for an external ointment, a paste made of bay salt and castile soap.[3] Of the medical men who devoted themselves to the care of the plague-stricken one of the most assiduous was Nathaniel Hodges, who safeguarded himself from infection by burning a disinfectant over hot coals in the houses of his patients, and by draughts of sack after the ordeal of a crowded consulting-room. He acted on a definite theory which attributed both health and disease to the 'nitrous spirit' which exhales from the bowels of the earth. By this 'nitro-aerial' substance, diffused through the air by sun and vapour, all plant and animal life was preserved; but its balsamic

[1] For illustrations see *Wood*, ii. 68.
[2] *H.M.C. Rep.* viii, app., pt. i. 230. *MSS. of the College of Physicians.*
[3] *A directory for the poor against plague*, in *Shaftesbury*, iv, no. 140.

quality might, he thought, be corrupted by natural causes, as undue heat or moisture, whereby it degenerated into a 'pestilential miasma', such as may be detected after earthquakes and near the sea-coast. He condemned quacks and apothecaries, their nostrums doing more harm than good; and, as a prophylactic, he recommended the use of oily substances—'to cover over the stomach with a plaister, to guard it against corrosive effluvia'. He also commended diaphoretics, to produce acrid perspiration, and saline substances, to keep the internal ferments from contagion. These last two remedies may have had some efficacy, but not necessarily for the virtues which he attributed to them.[1]

As there were no hospitals for the accommodation of the infected, and as the pest-houses were completely inadequate, the victims were isolated in their houses, thereby imposing what was tantamount to a death-sentence on the other inmates of the house. There was not enough lime for use in the churchyards, where the shallow graves were covered with crows and ravens except when the diggers were at work;[2] and the melancholy of London in the Plague year was deepened by 'the horrible crowd and lamentable moan of the poor seamen, that lie starving in the streets for lack of money'.[3] Beyond insisting on isolation, and prohibiting the holding of the great fairs, the government did little, though the usual remedy of a fast-day was invoked;[4] nor until May 1666 was a definite system of regulations imposed. This code[5] included these rules:

1. No household goods coming from a place supposed to be infected are to be received in any city, village or hamlet.
2. All public meetings are prohibited where there is suspicion of plague.
3. Fires in movable pans are to be used at all necessary public meetings and disinfectants are to be burnt thereon.
4. No unwholesome food is to be exposed for sale.
5. No swine, dogs, cats or tame pigeons are to be permitted to walk about infected streets.
6. No more ale-houses are to be licensed than are absolutely necessary.

[1] N. Hodges, *Loimologia*, 37–47.
[2] *Cal. S.P. Dom.*, *1665–6*, 538.
[3] *Pepys*, Oct. 7, 1665.
[4] *Steele*, i. 3426, July 6, 1665.
[5] *Steele*, i. 3461, May 11, 1666.

7. Each city is to provide a place remote from its boundaries where a pest-house, huts or sheds may be erected.

8. Monthly fasts and public prayers on Wednesdays and Fridays are to be strictly observed. Collections are to be made for the relief of the poor in infected places.

These rules had already been supplemented by the regulations based on those issued in the Plague year 1625 and enforced in London by lord mayor and aldermen.[1] Examiners were appointed for each parish who were to find out what houses were infected; such houses were to be shut up, and two watchmen, one by day, the other by night, were to prevent ingress or egress. Women searchers, assisted by surgeons, were ordered to report on evidence of plague on the bodies which they searched. Heads of households, on noticing any botch, pimple, or swelling, or any sudden sickness in members of their families, were to give notice to the examiners; after death or cure these households were placed in quarantine for a month. All these closed houses were marked by a red cross, one foot in length, with the inscription: 'Lord, have mercy upon us.' To the inmates necessaries were supplied by the constables. Burials were conducted by night, and the relatives and friends were forbidden to attend.

Such rules help to convey some idea of what the Plague must have meant to the poor of London. Of the visitation there was no chronicler, though our literature was afterwards enriched by Defoe's *Journal*, which compensates for historical inaccuracy by imaginative truth.[2] More important, this, the last of the greater seventeenth-century epidemics, was followed by increased interest in the science of Public Health. There was reissued Dr. Francis Herring's *Preservatives against the Plague*,[3] in which the policy of burying in churches and crowded churchyards was condemned, and the removal of rubbish from ditches in the suburbs was advocated. A further impetus was provided by the statistical observations of captain John Graunt, a Fellow of the Royal Society.[4] It

[1] Quoted by sir Walter Besant in *London in the time of the Stuarts*, 255–9.

[2] But see R. Crawfurd, *Plague and pestilence in literature and art*.

[3] First published in 1625.

[4] It was believed by some contemporaries, including Evelyn, that sir William Petty was the author of this book. Petty's biographer, lord Fitzmaurice, believes that there was joint authorship (*Life of sir William Petty*, 180).

had been customary, since at least as early as 1625, to publish bills of mortality recording burials within the parochial cemeteries of the city, together with a note of the disease accounting for death. As these records were compiled not by doctors but by searchers, many of them persons of limited capacity, the information provided was often unreliable, and rumour took the place of evidence; but even had such statistics been compiled by medical men, they would still have only a limited value, for many diseases were not yet differentiated, and in doubt the favourite cause of death was 'a consumption'. But that they might have a great value was demonstrated by John Graunt (1620–74), who showed[1] how essential are statistics in determining the prevalence and fatality of disease; and in this way he laid the foundations of the scientific study of mortality on which modern life insurance is based. From his observations, he concluded that 7 per cent. of Londoners lived to 70; that the proportion of lunatics was 158 in 229,250; that of 100 births, 36 died before the age of 6, and only one lived to 76; that one person in a thousand died of gout, but that gouty people were mostly long-lived; and, finally, that rickets was becoming the most prevalent disease of the age. The bills of mortality had themselves originated from the disaster of plague; it was owing to the epidemic of 1665 and to Graunt's observations that the science of medical statistics was inaugurated.

Plague and financial stringency help to explain why England failed to maintain the success which had followed her entry into the war. There were other factors. Throughout the earlier part of 1665 the attitude of France was uncertain, and Louis had gone so far as to send to England the *célèbre ambassade* composed of three envoys with a mission to secure, if possible, an eleventh-hour reconciliation of English and Dutch.[2] To some, it seemed that France would not keep faith with her ally, and that Louis would either remain neutral or engage in war only in order to effect the occupation of the Spanish Low Countries; this, at least, appears to have been the opinion of Henry Bennet, created lord Arlington,

---

[1] *Natural and political observations on the Bills of Mortality.* The sixth edition appeared in 1676.

[2] For this see J. J. Jusserand, *A French ambassador at the court of Charles II.* See also *infra*, 324.

the English minister now most closely associated with foreign
policy. Anxious to form an alliance with Spain, Arlington professed to regard the representations of the *célèbre ambassade* as
bluster.[1] Eventually (November, 1665) a preliminary treaty[2]
between England and Spain was signed. It was little more than
a commercial convention, but it might one day lead to an offensive and defensive alliance, on the basis of peace between Spain
and Portugal. It is true that Spain was unlikely to provide England with effective help; but neither (it was thought) did Louis
intend to give any active assistance to the Dutch; so the one
alliance seemed to balance the other. French bluff was to be
countered by English bluff.

The results of this amateurish diplomacy were seen by the
autumn of 1665 when England became completely isolated.
Her one ally, the bishop of Münster, was a menace rather than a
help, since his conduct threatened to embroil us with the princes
of Germany, and his military exploits against the Dutch were
incommensurate with even the attenuated subsidy which reached
his coffers.[3] Neither Sweden nor any of the German states showed
a disposition to take up arms against the increasing threat from
France, mainly because French diplomacy and French money
were being employed to such good purpose; and Spain proved
herself powerless to resist French designs in the Spanish Low
Countries. In November 1665, when hostilities with France were
seen to be imminent, Arlington made an ineffective effort to
dispose the Dutch to peace by negotiating with the Orange
opposition to De Witt;[4] and, as the winter of 1665–6 advanced, the
futility of English foreign policy was more clearly demonstrated.
Attempts to bring in on our side Brandenburg, Mainz, and
Neuburg failed because, while all of these powers were willing
to see French power lessened, they were equally anxious to spare
the Dutch.[5] The Anglo-Spanish *rapprochement* failed to separate
France from Holland, in spite of the common interests of Spain
and Holland in the Low Countries; Denmark had been our
enemy ever since the Bergen incident; Sweden might have been

---

[1] V. Barbour, *Arlington*, 84 sqq.   [2] See *infra*, 324–5.
[3] Feiling, *British Foreign Policy*, 155–7.
[4] With the help of Henry de Coulant, lord of Buat. Barbour, op. cit. 90,
and Feiling, 195–201.   [5] Feiling, op. cit. 163.

willing to join with England, but would not declare against France; even in Madrid French counsels were once more reinstated, and so the mere threat from France served to negative all Arlington's efforts to procure allies. In January 1666 France and Denmark declared war on England; in April, the bishop of Münster made his peace. 'The subject is too vexatious to discourse any more upon,' wrote Arlington[1] to Temple; 'I am glad the farce is at an end.' By October 1666 the Dutch had as allies France, Denmark, and Brandenburg.[2]

When naval hostilities were renewed in the summer of 1666 the enemy had a slight superiority in ships and gun-power; they had also the advantage of the services of De Ruyter, and at least the diplomatic benefit of the French alliance. At first it seemed that the French fleet would give active assistance. On April 19 the duc de Beaufort, in command of the French Navy, left Toulon for the purpose of effecting a junction with either the Dutch fleet or the French ships at Brest and La Rochelle;[3] but this scheme was changed when it was learned that sir Jeremy Smith, with the Mediterranean squadron of 26 ships, had returned to Plymouth, and that the Dutch would not be able to put to sea until June.[4] Accordingly, Louis ordered Beaufort to take his fleet into the Tagus, lest it might be attacked by the English, and *par une infinité de raisons* it was necessary to conserve the French fleet.[5] The importance of this change lay in its secret execution, since for some time the English intelligence service believed that Beaufort was hovering off the mouth of the Channel in order to join forces with his ally. In the Four Days' Battle of June 1666 the English suffered heavily for this mistake.

The Dutch in 1666 were therefore a more formidable enemy than they had been in the previous year. In April the young prince of Orange was officially taken under the protection of the State, and an effort was made to safeguard him from Stuart and English influence, measures which served to pacify feeling in Zeeland and to secure more active co-operation between the

---

[1] *Letters of Arlington to Temple* (1701), 74–7. April 27, 1666.
[2] *Dumont*, vi, pt. iii, 122.
[3] *Instruction au duc de Beaufort*, Feb. 26, 1666, in *Colenbrander*, i. 298.
[4] *Instructions* of April 30/May 10 in *Colenbrander*, i. 306.
[5] Ibid. i, 307.

Dutch admiralties; indeed the outlook for our enemy was so much more hopeful that the king of England was advised 'to mix some water with his wine'.[1] There were even rumours that, while the Dutch engaged the English, the French would carry out a landing in England or Scotland;[2] and though the Hollanders were still uneasy regarding French support, they spared no effort to fit out a great fleet, which eventually consisted of 84 warships, 13 frigates and 4 fireships. It was the finest fleet, said De Witt,[3] that was ever seen in Dutch harbours, and certainly more united than that of the previous year.

In joint command of the English force of about 80 ships were prince Rupert and the Duke of Albemarle (Monck), appointed by commission of the duke of York. On May 29, 1666, in obedience to orders sent from London, prince Rupert sailed into the Channel with 20 ships in order to join 10 ships off Plymouth and intercept Beaufort, then supposed to be entering the Channel.[4] Albemarle, at anchor in the Downs, was doubtful whether to risk his diminished force in a contest, or return to the Gunfleet for reinforcements; but a decision lay in his power, and he appears to have been hopeful of success, handicapped as he was. Setting sail on Thursday, May 31, he came to anchor about 5 leagues south-east of the North Foreland, the wind blowing a fresh gale at south-west.[5] Next day he stood northwards, and at 6 a.m. Dutch scouts were reported to the north-east. A council of flag-officers which met at 7 a.m. (June 1) on the flagship *Royal Charles* was not unanimous that an engagement should be sought; we had the weather gage, it was true; but such a stiff breeze was blowing that it would not be possible to use the lower tiers of guns. Albemarle, however, to use what may well have been his own expression 'resolved to bear with them', and sent a message to the duke of York, who ordered Coventry to prepare orders for the return of Rupert. Coventry contented himself with sending the signed order to Arlington for his counter-signature; but as

---

[1] *News letter* in *Colenbrander*, i. 303.
[2] *Add. MS.* 32094, f. 75, May 30/June 9, 1666.
[3] Blok, *De Ruyter*, 245–6.
[4] Prince Rupert's narrative in *C.J.* ix. 10 sqq.
[5] *True narrative of the engagement, published by command*, in *Carte MS.* 222, f. 103.

Arlington was in bed when the missive arrived, and could not be disturbed until next morning, valuable time was lost.[1]

By noon of Friday, June 1, the Dutch fleet of 84 sail was seen at anchor off Ostend, the English being then about a league to windward. Keeping out of range of the Dutch van and centre (commanded by Evertsen the elder and De Ruyter respectively), Albemarle bore down on the enemy rear, led by Tromp, then lying to the south-east of the Dutch centre. Tromp at once slipped his cables and stood off on the same tack as his opponents; that is, towards south-east, the wind blowing hard from south-west, and so for several hours Albemarle, followed by his best ships, was sailing on the starboard tack hotly engaged with Tromp before Evertsen or De Ruyter could come into action. It was a bold stroke, and very nearly demoralized the Dutch; but unfortunately the heavier guns on the leeward side of the English ships could not be used, as their ports were awash; while Tromp, standing to leeward, could bring to bear the full force of his starboard broadsides. Moreover, this tack led them both close inshore, and so Albemarle had to go about before engaging again with Tromp.[2] Accordingly the English rear became the van; and when De Ruyter and Evertsen were able to come into action the re-formed English line was caught between two fires, with the result that several units were surrounded, including the *Swiftsure*, flagship of sir William Berkeley, who fell dead in his cabin after showing a courage rendered reckless by the unjust imputation of faint-heartedness under which his reputation had been clouded. In another of the surrounded ships, the *Henry*, rear-admiral sir John Harman maintained a heroic resistance, though his sails and rigging were on fire. Only his guns were left in action, and he met the Dutch demand to surrender with a broadside which killed the Dutch admiral Cornelius Evertsen (the younger). Tacking twice again, Albemarle tried to break the enemy line, losing the *Swiftsure*, the *Seven Oaks*, and the *Loyal George* in the attempt. At dusk the fleets separated, Albemarle standing west-north-west, and De Ruyter south. The night was spent in mending rigging.

---

[1] *Clar. Cont.* iii. 72. Clarendon, who was no friend of Arlington's, noted that this unwillingness to disturb his slumbers was 'a tenderness not accustomed to be in the family of a secretary'.   [2] Blok, op. cit.

The fight was renewed on the morning of Saturday, June 2, in a variable wind, each fleet sailing past the other in line and on opposite tacks, until the rearmost ships of each were clear, with about an hour's respite, while the vans put about on the other tack. There were now little more than 40 ships on the English side against nearly 80 Dutch; the wind had fallen somewhat; and when, by skilful manœuvring, Monck gained the weather gage its advantage to him was greater than it had been on the previous day. Attempts by Tromp and other Dutch leaders to pursue independent tactics caused some disorder in the enemy line; but the English commander, anxious to retain the windward position, did not have sufficient ships to risk a spirited onslaught. Three times did the fleets pass each other on opposite tacks; on the third occasion Albemarle, realizing the inadequacy of his forces, continued his course towards the English coast, the disabled ships in the van, and the larger vessels covering the rear. This justifiable retreat was conducted with great skill. The Dutch followed all night, but a calm on the morning of Sunday, June 3, prevented both fleets from making headway. On the afternoon of Sunday (the third day of the fight) Rupert's squadron was sighted returning from its fool's errand in the Channel, and when rejoining the main fleet the pilots took their ships over the Galloper Sands, leaving the *Royal Prince* with sir John Ayscue on board an easy prey to the pursuers, who took Ayscue prisoner and burned his ship. Albemarle then boarded Rupert's flagship, the *Royal James*, and in conjunction with other flag-officers resolved to attack the enemy next morning. On the English side there was now a total of about 58 ships against the Dutch 78.

On the morning of Monday, June 4, the fourth day of the battle, the wind strong from south-west, the two fleets again engaged, both sailing on the starboard tack, the Dutch to windward. At the end of two hours' firing both lines were in confusion, and some of the English ships pierced through the Dutch line to windward. Among these were several of the van led by sir Christopher Myngs, who bore up and engaged the enemy admiral De Liefde, the two fighting broadside on; and as the Dutch ship was dismasted, Myngs attempted to burn her with a fireship. When De Ruyter brought support to the hard-pressed De Liefde, Myngs was in the centre of an inferno; but he continued to give his orders though part of his throat was blown away and he had to stop the gap with his fingers. A bullet through his neck ended the career of one of the most courageous sailors in the history of the British Navy. Four times the English fleet passed through the Dutch, plying them with broadsides as they passed; but De Ruyter concentrated his fire on the *Royal Charles* and *Royal James*, and with Tromp firing from the other quarter, the mainstay and main topmast of the *Royal James* came 'all by the board', while the rigging of her sister ship was so badly damaged that she could no longer tack. At last the whole English fleet succeeded in running through the gauntlet to the windward position, but by then there was complete disorder, and neither side had enough strength to continue the contest, which had been fought until the ships above water were badly mauled and tattered, and the surviving crews completely exhausted. According to the Dutch account, the English were saved from annihilation by the sudden descent of a fog. At the firing of a gun De Ruyter made off to his coast, leaving the English too weak to attempt pursuit. So ended the Four Days' Battle. For neither side did it secure a decision or even a strategic advantage.[1]

Dutch exploits in this contest were sung by Vondel and were commemorated by the striking of a medal. Their losses have been variously estimated from 4 to 7 ships, with 2,000 officers and men killed and wounded. Among these were two admirals. English losses were heavier: namely, admirals Berkeley and Myngs (killed), Ayscue (captured), about 20 ships destroyed or taken, and about 8,000 killed, wounded, and prisoners. In tactics the battle discredited somewhat the more formal plan of adhering rigidly to formation, and confirmed the necessity of breaking the line;[2] otherwise it proved merely that a larger fleet could inflict more damage on a smaller fleet than that which the larger one sustained, and De Ruyter himself admitted that his opponents might well have won the battle because of the valour and tenacity with which they fought.[3] Both sides gave proof of seamanship and

---

[1] For the sources see *Colenbrander*, i, *passim*; Narrative of the engagement June 8, 1666, in *Add. MS.* 32094, f. 137: the official English account in *Carte MS.* 222; Hans Svendsen's journal in *Colenbrander*, i. 356 sqq.; W. Laird Clowes, *The Royal Navy*, ii. 267–77; A. W. Tedder, *Navy of the Restoration*, 159–65.   [2] *Colenbrander*, i. 371.   [3] Blok, *De Ruyter*, 254.

courage. The French had not come to the aid of their ally, but there had been a rumour of their intention to do so; hence the order which detached Rupert's squadron was given in good faith; indeed the division of the fleet, condemned as it is by naval historians, was explicable on the information available for the English intelligence service. A risk was taken which, in other circumstances, might have been rewarded with success, and it remains true that in warfare there is an element of chance which not even the most scientific strategy can eliminate.

Within a few weeks English superiority in fighting quality was illustrated. Repairs were effected on both sides with such rapidity that by the end of July the Dutch had formed a fleet of over 90 ships, and had again a slight advantage over the English. The two fleets sighted each other off the mouth of the Thames on July 24, 1666, the enemy being to the north-east and to windward, between Orfordness and the North Foreland. Next day sir Thomas Allin approached with the White at the head of a well-kept line, and at 10 a.m. the battle commenced, when Allin attacked the Dutch van led by John Evertsen, forcing it to give way and bear up before the wind. Meanwhile the English centre under Monck and Rupert engaged De Ruyter, while Tromp separated himself from his fellows in a descent on the English rear commanded by sir Jeremy Smith. At 2 p.m. the Dutch van began to give way; but the contest between the centres was more stubbornly contested, and not till 4 p.m. did De Ruyter call in his stragglers and retreat. This retreat was continued during the night of the 25th; but next day the fight between Tromp and Smith was renewed, until the former had to take refuge in flight. As this battle was fought on St. James's Day (July 25, 1666) it is generally referred to as the St. James's Fight. It was indubitably an English victory, the enemy losing about 20 ships and 7,000 killed and wounded including Evertsen the elder (killed); while the English lost only the *Resolution*, several fireships, and a small number of men, reckoned at 500. For some time feeling in Holland was bitter against Tromp, whose independent action had served in effect to divide the fleet.[1]

It was now the turn of the Dutch to fear invasion. Hovering

[1] Contemporary accounts in *Colenbrander*, i. 302–53; also W. Laird Clowes, op. cit. ii. 278–82.

off the enemy coast, English scouts obtained intelligence of the existence of valuable stores for the States and East India fleets on the islands of Vlieland and Ter Schelling. At a council held on board the flagship by Albemarle and Rupert it was resolved to attempt a raid on these stores, and for this purpose a body of 900 soldiers and sailors was detached in a squadron of nine ships commanded by sir Robert Holmes. Early on the morning of August 8 this force anchored off the entrance to the Vlie. Meanwhile prince Rupert's pinnace the *Fan Fan*, which had been reconnoitring behind the island, reported the presence of about 150 merchantmen, mostly homeward bound, waiting for an opportunity of making their harbours. As these were protected by only two men-of-war Holmes decided to deal with them first; so he transferred his flag to the *Fan Fan* in Ter Schelling roads, and sent in the *Pembroke* with fireships to attack the merchantmen. The two Dutch warships were first destroyed; then fresh ships were sent in, and soon the vast mercantile fleet was feeding an enormous bonfire, from which only a few units escaped by sailing up a creek. The attackers destroyed but did not plunder; a landing party burned some of the stores on the island next day.[1] With the loss of about a dozen men Holmes inflicted on the Dutch losses valued at a million pounds.

The year 1666 is notable for another great conflagration—the Fire of London. A number of accidents combined to make this a disaster of exceptional magnitude. It occurred in the autumn, when many merchants were gone to the country, and tradesmen were at fairs or were away collecting their rents; it broke out in a street where there were stores of combustible material, such as pitch, tar, and cordage; an east wind blew it towards the centre of the city, and the water-engine at the north end of London Bridge happened at the time to be out of order.[2] The Fire started in Pudding Lane early on Sunday morning, September 2, and was carried by the wind down Thames Street, where many old buildings were soon alight; within a few hours there was a blaze

---

[1] Estimates of the number of Dutch merchantmen differ. J. C. de Jonge (*Geschiedenis van het Nederlandsche Zeewesen*, ii. 146–7) gives the number as 114. For a contemporary account by one of the English landing-party see *Navy Miscellany* (*N.R.S.* lxiii), iii. 23.

[2] Besant, *London in the time of the Stuarts*, 248.

a mile long devastating Fish Street Hill, Canning Street, Grace-church Street, Lombard Street, and Cornhill, and extending to Fenchurch Street. In this, the earliest stage, the Royal Exchange and many churches were burned down. By Cheapside, the devastation then spread to Newgate Street, Holborn Bridge, Ludgate Hill, and the Inner Temple, where its course was arrested. The Custom House was destroyed; St. Paul's was a smouldering ruin above ground, and in the cellars beneath St. Faith's church there was great havoc where the Stationers had placed their stores of books. Dr. Taswell, then a Westminster schoolboy, saw the burning of St. Paul's at night, when the illumination was so great that he was able to read from a small pocket edition of Terence; as late as Thursday he found the pave-ments near the smouldering ruins so hot as to scorch his shoes.[1] The suburbs of the city, namely Strand, Covent Garden, Hol-born, and Clerkenwell, all escaped narrowly; but even in remote districts some of the effects were experienced. 'Had you been at Kensington', wrote a resident in that borough, 'you would have thought for five days that it had been Doomsday, from the fire, and cries and howlings of the people. My gardens were covered with ashes of papers, linens and plaster-work blown there by the tempest.'[2] Half-burnt papers were carried by the wind as far as Eton, and in Oxford people observed that the rays of the sun were tinged with an unusual redness.[3]

As the season was dry and the wells at their lowest the fire blazed unchecked for several days. The Tower was saved by destroying the neighbouring houses with cannon; similar measures were resorted to in order to prevent a westward spread by the Thames. When after five days the fire was at last quenched, the city was found to consist for the most part of heaps of stones which reminded a north-countryman of his native fells,[4] and the Thames could be seen from what was once Cheapside. On foot and on horseback the king, accompanied by the dukes of York and Albemarle, made a round of the ruins twice a day, giving

[1] *Autobiography of William Taswell* (Camden Miscellany, ii. 1853), 10–13.
[2] *Cal. S.P. Dom., Addenda, 1660–70*; anon. to lord Conway, Sept. 8, 1668.
[3] Taswell in op. cit. 13.
[4] A. Fleming to his brother, Sept. 6, 1666, in *Fleming MSS., H.M.C. Rep.* xii, app., pt. vii, 41.

directions and assisting the work of salvage. The victims saved what they could, but carts could not be had save at 'inhuman' prices, and many of the homeless were obliged to camp out on Moorfields, where ship's biscuits were served out to them.[1] There was little loss of life directly due to the fire; there was enormous material damage, however, for not only had the greater part of the old medieval London ceased to exist, but large quantities of goods were destroyed. Gresham's College was hastily utilized for an Exchange and Post Office, and the magistrates met in Leadenhall, as the Guildhall had been burnt out. By the 8th of September, when the ruins could at last be surveyed, the government had one more task to perform—that of rebuilding the capital of the kingdom.

After the preliminary investigation, the two surveyors reported that the fire had begun early on the morning of September 2 in the house of a baker, and continued till September 6, consuming 373 acres of the 450 acres within the walls, and 63 acres outside. 89 parish churches and 13,200 houses were certified as destroyed.[2] So vast was the work of reconstruction that the Navigation Acts had to be relaxed in order to allow the free import of timber.[3] The character of the rebuilding was determined by a Statute which sanctioned four kinds of new house,[4] namely, (1) the least sort fronting by-lanes, (2) those fronting streets and lanes of note, (3) those fronting 'high and principal streets', and (4) mansion houses, not fronting one of the three former ways.[5] The lord mayor was empowered to declare what were streets and lanes; the houses were required to be built of brick or stone, and the

---

[1] Of these refugees Dryden wrote:

> The most in fields like herded beasts lie down
> To dews obnoxious on the grassy floor,
> And while their babes in sleep their sorrows drown,
> Sad parents watch the remnant of their store.
>
> *Annus Mirabilis.*

[2] *H.M.C. Rep.* vii, app. 464. Certificate of Jonas Moore and Ralph Gatrix, surveyors.

[3] *Cal. S.P. Dom.*, *1667–8*, 295, March 18, 1668.

[4] 18–19 Car. II, cap. viii. This Act raised money for the rebuilding by an increased Customs levy on coal.

[5] For illustrations of surviving representatives of these types see W. G. Bell, *The Great Fire of London.*

roofs of the first three sorts were to be uniform; also, the first story of each house was to have a height of ten feet, the smallest sort to have two stories, the next in size three stories, and the next four. Prices of bricks, tiles, and lime were to be set by two judges of the King's Bench; wages were to be declared by the lord mayor and aldermen. The maximum number of new churches was fixed at thirty-nine, and a pillar was ordered to be set up to retain in memory 'for ever' the desolation of September 1666.

It was fortunate that in this enforced rebuilding the city had the services of sir Christopher Wren, who left the stamp of his genius on the new metropolis which gradually took shape. But he did not have a free hand, and some of his schemes were put aside from lack of money; even his plans for St. Paul's were interfered with,[1] and only in the city churches does he appear to have had full scope. The number of buildings attributed to his master-hand has been over-estimated. An attempt, however, was made to build on a definite plan. A court sitting in Clifford's Inn determined boundaries and rents; party walls and piers were set out under the supervision of surveyors, and an attempt was made to adhere to rules probably too minute for enforcement. The level of the ground near Fleet Street was raised by using stone from the ruins of St. Paul's; Holborn Bridge was enlarged; buckets and brass squirts were placed at stations throughout the city; and shops, provided with doors and glass windows, took the place of the old stalls. A duty on coal was allocated to the re-building; but even thus the city had to borrow money to pay for the new Guildhall, which was not completed until 1675; seven years earlier the first stone was laid of the first pillar of the new Royal Exchange. The private enterprise of the Livery Companies, which had lost 44 halls, provided a stimulus, for they soon began reconstructing, and they built with taste.[2]

One good result can be attributed to the Fire—that in destroy-ing the old sunless hovels and alleys a sanitary improvement was effected, and to that extent the chances of a recurrence of an epidemic such as that of 1665 were rendered more remote. A second result was that many transferred their homes to what were

[1] W. G. Bell, in op. cit. 262.

[2] Cal. S.P. Dom., 1667–8, xlvi. 144; W. G. Bell, op. cit. 269–70; Besant, London in the time of the Stuarts, 256.

English detachment then captured Cayenne in Surinam, bu
efforts to recapture St. Kitts proved fruitless. The French West
India Company suffered heavily from the raids of English ships.[1]

Meanwhile, by the winter of 1666–7 England had become
tired of the war, and the Commons were increasingly anxious
about its cost. Peace negotiations were accordingly instituted;
lord St. Albans was sent to Paris in January 1667, and the Dutch
were invited to come to terms. An understanding with France
was first established, Louis undertaking to surrender his West
India conquests, provided Charles gave a written promise that
on the conclusion of peace he would enter into a close alliance
with France; or that, alternatively he would refrain for one year
from all alliances contrary to the French interest. On February
12, 1667, Charles signed an engagement of neutrality on the
basis of the latter alternative.[2] There was more difficulty in
dealing with De Witt; but at last, in March 1667, Breda was
agreed upon as the place for the peace congress. It was known
that the Dutch in the spring of 1667 were making active preparations for another campaign;[3] but Englishmen were no longer
in a mood for warfare, and so the peace negotiations continued.

Charles's advisers now appear to have assumed that peace was
assured. They knew that Louis was anxious to detach himself
from the Dutch and to secure English neutrality for his designs
on Flanders; but none of them appears to have realized that
French desertion, so far from making the Dutch more anxious
to end the war, might make them more determined to continue
it. In this mistaken feeling of security drastic retrenchments in
the English Navy were initiated. On May 24 Charles instructed
the duke of York to maintain only such a squadron as would
distract the enemy and disturb his trade.[4] In accordance with
this order many third-rates and all ships requiring extensive
repairs were paid off. Sir William Coventry and Arlington, who
had been most forward in precipitating the war, were now the
most zealous promoters of economy, Coventry advocating re-
ductions of crews on fireships;[5] while Arlington, in his instruc-

---

[1] W. Laird Clowes, op. cit. ii. 431–3; La Roncière, *Histoire de la marine
française*, v. 465–7; S. L. Mims, *Colbert's West India Policy*, 126–42.

[2] *Mignet*, ii. 45.   [3] *Cal. S.P. Dom.*, *1667*, 9, 62–3.

[4] *Cal. S.P. Dom.*, *1667*, 118.   [5] Ibid. 130–1.

then the suburbs, and with the genesis of a greater Lond
overcrowding in the city was relieved. A third effect
salutary may be suggested. The Fire had followed immed
on the Plague, both occurring in a fiercely contested w
which France was ranged with our enemies. Men drew
conclusions from the concurrence of these events. Plague
a divine visitation, but the Fire had been contrived by hu
agency. Men had been seen (so it was afterwards repor
throwing fire-balls into cellars; if these miscreants were
Frenchmen or Dutchmen, they were probably Papists, an
these days commemoration of Guy Fawkes was something n
serious than a pleasant annual ritual.[1] A populace which k
the terrors of Plague and Fire fell an easy victim to the Po
Plot.

The stirring events of this, the *Annus Mirabilis* (1666), were
confined to Europe; for Louis XIV, though he showed li
inclination to assist the Dutch, proved that he was anxiou
attack English power in the West Indies. The island of St. Kitr
was the first to experience the menace from this source. Th
centre was occupied by the English, the French having set
ments at both extremities. In April 1666, in spite of assista
from Jamaica, the English settlers were defeated in a pitc
battle, and the planters (to the number of about 8,000)
deported to other islands, notably Montserrat and Jamaica.
the help of nearly 1,000 Irish the French now ruled in St.
This success was speedily followed by another, for in Nove
the French commander La Barre captured Antigua, and
pelled its evacuation by the inhabitants. Montserrat wa
taken (February 1667), and soon it appeared likely that
England was fighting it out with the Dutch her possessi
the West Indies would change hands. But in April 1667 si
Harman arrived with a strong force, and with Nevis as h
he inflicted great damage on a combined fleet of Fren
Dutch in an action fought off the island on May 20. In the
ing month he decisively defeated the French fleet off Mar
These were the only naval battles of the war to which th
decisive can be applied, for they saved the West Ind

---

[1] Cf. *Pyrotechnica Loyolana* (1667), with its wood-cuts depicting
and Jesuits as incendiaries.

tions for the defence of the eastern and southern coasts, adjured the lords lieutenant 'to make the greatest show you can in numbers . . . more especially of horse, even though it be of such as are otherwise wholly unfit; horse being the force that most discourage the enemy from landing'.[1]

But if Arlington was showing symptoms of an equine intelligence, the Dutch were still thinking in terms of ships and salt water. In April they had sailed up the Firth of Forth and attacked Burntisland; a month later they had a fleet of over 100 sail ready for a descent.[2] On May 20/30, 1667, it was secretly resolved by the States General to attempt 'something notable'; and John de Witt induced his admirals to undertake a hazardous attempt on the Thames.[3] On the same date (June 7) that Henry Coventry landed at Dover bearing the preliminary articles of peace from Breda, a fleet of 50–60 Dutch ships was sighted off the North Foreland, and at 8 p.m. it was seen to anchor in the Gunfleet.[4] Realizing at last that something definite was intended, but still guessing where the blow[5] would fall, the government ordered the Navy commissioners to prepare fireships, and sent a large contingent of Militia to the Isle of Wight. At Bridlington, Plymouth, and Portsmouth there was feverish work on the fortifications, and the anxious inhabitants of Margate were further perplexed by the strange accent of a Scottish regiment quartered in their midst. When at last it was seen that De Witt was planning a blow at the very heart of the nation, sir Edward Spragge was posted with several fireships in the Medway, while Dutch prizes and other vessels were moved further up the river. Ships were also placed at Gillingham for the purpose of defending the chain across the Medway.

On the night of June 7 De Ruyter anchored in the King's Channel; the secret instructions were read, and the final dispositions of a carefully-laid plan were completed. Accurate

[1] Ibid. 145–6. [2] Ibid. 116. [3] Blok, *De Ruyter*, 275.
[4] *Cal. S.P. Dom., 1667*, 156–7, and Blok, op. cit. 277.
[5] Among the sources for the disaster of the Medway, reference may be made to the contemporary accounts in *Colenbrander*, i. 533–91; *Cal. S.P. Dom.*, Introduction (specially valuable) and *passim* in the documents; W. Laird Clowes, op. cit. ii. 288–94; J. C. de Jonge, *Geschiedenis van het Nederlandsche Zeewesen*, ii. 175–205; Blok, *De Ruyter*, 272–85; Tedder, *Navy of the Restoration*.

soundings of the estuary had been made, so that the Dutch
pilots knew it as well as their own waters; and the recent attacks
on the Firth of Forth and north-east coast by Van Ghent's
squadron had helped to conceal from the English the real
objective of the main fleet. The enterprise was timed so that
advantage could be taken of a spring tide. De Ruyter now
divided his fleet, retaining the larger portion by him at the
mouth of the Thames as a covering force, and sending Van
Ghent with a squadron of 17 warships accompanied by 24
auxiliaries and fireships to the Medway in order to perform
there what Holmes the year before had effected in the Vlie.
Accompanying Van Ghent was Cornelius De Witt, brother of
the Pensionary; it was Cornelius as much as De Ruyter who
stirred the Dutch to undertake what seemed to some of their
officers an impossible feat.[1] For a few days contrary winds
delayed the expedition, and a Dutch landing party in Thanet
was beaten off by the Scots; but on Tuesday, June 11, the
invaders, having bombarded Sheerness, landed 800 men on the
island of Sheppey, and on the morning of Wednesday, June 12,
Van Ghent appeared off the Medway.

There was neither time, material, nor organization for adequate defence. Albemarle, who had arrived at Gravesend on
Monday, found very few guns mounted there; at Tilbury he
discovered the same state of affairs. Next morning he saw the
topsails of the Dutch ships in the river; so he hurried on to
Chatham, where he found the workmen in the yard in a state
of panic. Even boats could not be had, for most of the small
craft had been used to take away personal belongings;[2] nor was
there any ammunition, except a small store in the *Monmouth*.
A train of ammunition intended for Gravesend had therefore
to be diverted to Chatham and arrived there on Wednesday.
Defence of the chain was Albemarle's next concern; but here his
difficulties began in earnest; for the stores had to be broken into
in order to procure tools; and when at last these were obtained,
he had to send off a detachment for the defence of Upnor Castle.
He had then to deal with the delay and incompetence of commissioner Pett, with whose tardy help he caused ships to be

---

[1] Blok, op. cit. 277.

[2] Report of sir John Mennes, June 16, 1667, in *Colenbrander*, i. 555.

sunk on each side of the chain, which was eight feet ten inches deep and was held by pulleys.[1] Albemarle's hastily improvised arrangements revealed a state of mismanagement and disorganization unparalleled in our history. For his batteries he was dependent mainly on volunteers; the trouble, however, was not that the gun crews were amateurs, but that for the mountings there were no oak planks to be had (they had been pilfered), with the result that thin deal planking had to be used instead, and at each shot the gun wheels sank through the planks into the ground. In truth the great naval base of Chatham was found to be indefensible against a single ship; the outer defence at Upnor Castle was without ammunition and was a place of entertainment; the powder was mostly too bad to be used. Something of Stuart nonchalance and indifference had penetrated into the greatest of our naval arsenals; and the Dutch, had they had the mind to, might safely have gone as far as London Bridge and from there bombarded the capital.[2]

The greater part of the English fleet, including the flagships *Royal Charles* and *Royal James*, was then in Chatham dock, all the ships denuded of their crews and in some cases dismantled. The outer defence of the Medway was Sheerness, the guns of which had already been silenced; there remained the inner defence, consisting of Upnor Castle, and the chain stretching across the river at Gillingham reach. On the eve of the Dutch attack (Wednesday, June 12, 1667) the chain was defended by sunken ships and by the guardships *Charles V* and *Mathias*; these with the *Monmouth* were destroyed by the invaders, and a passage was forced through. Upnor Castle was in charge of major Scott, supported by a mixed company of seamen, foot and gunners, with a few guns; while sir Edward Spragge was on the eastern side of the chain. In Chatham dock an entrenchment had been hurriedly made by Albemarle, and 14 guns were placed in position; there were also 10 field-pieces hidden behind hedges on the slope of the hill. Such was the situation of the defence on

[1] *Rawl. MS.* A. 195, f. 128.
[2] *Carte MS.* 35, f. 478. For contemporary accounts of the conditions at Chatham see *Colenbrander*, i. 548 sqq.; *Cal. S.P. Dom., 1667*, Introduction and text, *passim*; the duke of Albemarle's narrative of the miscarriages of the war in *C.J.* ix. 10 sqq.

the morning of Thursday, June 13, after a night spent by the Dutch in clearing a passage through what remained of the boom. With the flood tide of Thursday the Dutch again approached the chain, exchanging shots with Upnor Castle and Spragge's batteries; they then sent fireships into the dock, which destroyed the *Royal Oak*, the *Loyal London*, and the *Royal James*. While the fireships were engaged in the harbour completing their work of destruction, Albemarle's guns replied vainly from the shore; and as one helpless ship after another fell a victim to the audacious intruder, his cheers could be heard even in the din of explosions and cracklings. 'Nooit grooter victoria voor Nederland,'[1] shouted a Dutch chaplain, syllables which must have been intelligible to the Englishmen who heard them. Only when they had used up all their fireships did the invaders retire, taking with them the *Royal Charles* and the *Unity*. The most ignominious sight of all was to see the great flagship of the fleet taken away by 'a sorry boat and six men'.[2]

The enemy carried out this exploit with surprisingly little loss; indeed their estimate is 30 men and 2 fireships, but probably this is an under-estimate.[3] English loss of life was not heavy, but of ships and prestige incalculable. Our fleet had been found in a state of almost complete defencelessness; our blockhouses wanted guns, platforms, and ammunition; some of them had bullets too large for their cannon, and a lurid light had revealed embezzlement and mismanagement in our greatest naval dock-yard. But for the defence hastily organized by Albemarle, and ably seconded by train bands, volunteers and a few seamen, the English Navy might well have been completely destroyed. Not unnaturally, there were great rejoicings in Holland. A medal was struck; Antonides van der Goes commemorated the exploit in his *Thames on Fire*, and Vondel once more broke into song.[4] De Ruyter, Van Ghent, and Cornelius de Witt were the heroes of the hour; to them, the States General presented golden goblets, not for their reward but for the remembrance of posterity.

[1] J. C. de Jonge, op. cit. ii. 196.
[2] Sir E. Spragge's evidence, in Diary of J. Millward, *Add. MS.* 33413, Oct. 22, 1667.
[3] These are the figures given by Blok, op. cit. 283.
[4] Blok, op. cit. 285.

In England there was a torrent of recrimination. The sale of Dunkirk was recalled, and the trees outside Clarendon's house in Piccadilly ('Dunkirk House') were pulled up by the mob. Spragge was attacked as an Irish papist; naval paymasters had to shoulder the blame for the long arrears of seamen's pay; neither king nor court was spared the abuse of critics. Charles and the duke of York vehemently repudiated responsibility for the policy of laying up the fleet; and to conciliate popular opinion, which could not but contrast this Stuart disgrace with Cromwellian achievement, twelve new regiments of 1,000 men each were raised and placed under the command of old Parliamentarians such as Manchester and Fairfax, while the governorship of Windsor Castle was taken from the noted royalist lord Mordaunt. But this was only adding fuel to the fire, since it raised the suspicion that a standing army was intended. This distrust was reflected in the parliament which met by proclamation on July 25, when the Commons passed a resolution that His Majesty be desired to disband the newly raised troops as soon as the peace was concluded. In reply, Charles protested that he was too much of an Englishman to think of governing by a standing army.[1] Parliament was then prorogued until October 10.

Meanwhile peace[2] with both France and the United Provinces was signed at Breda on July 21, 1667. The main principle adopted in the treaty was that of surrender of conquests; in this sense the contest had been a drawn one. Its effect, therefore, was that Louis restored the English portion of St. Christopher's, together with Antigua and Montserrat; in exchange, England ceded Acadia to France. This surrender to France of the whole of Acadia took no consideration of the Scottish province of Nova Scotia. The treaty with the Dutch provided that each should refuse refuge to rebels against the other; that free entry should be permitted into each other's ports in stress of weather; and, in spite of the Navigation Acts, the Dutch were granted the privilege of importing into England all merchandise originating in Germany or Holland. For the purposes of the salute at sea, the Dutch succeeded in narrowing the area denoted by 'British Seas' to the English Channel, and a ship was held to enter the

---

[1] *L.J.* xii. 114, July 25, 1667.   [2] *Dumont*, vii, pt. i. 40 sqq.

Channel when Scilly bore north-north-west. Except for this, however, the question of the flag was left undetermined.

Most important of the results following from the treaty was the retention of New York and New Jersey by England; of Pularoon and Dutch Guiana by Holland, and of Acadia and French Guiana by France. In West Africa we lost everything except Fort James and Cape Coast Castle. It is clear, therefore, that England had not achieved the objects with which she embarked on war. The East India Company still wanted Pularoon; nothing was said in the treaty about the Company's claim for damages, and the whole question of entry into the East-Indian and West-African trade was left undetermined. In fact the treaty of Breda may be said to have intensified the commercial rivalry between the two nations and to have led directly to the Third and last Dutch War. Within a few months the East India Company was again petitioning the Council against the Dutch policy of debarring the English from direct trade with natives; and the old questions of compensation for damages and entry into the spice trade were soon revived in their wonted intensity. But the Third Dutch War was to be conducted under auspices very different from those which had preluded the Second; for already suspicion of the executive had entered into the minds of the legislature, and the gathering menace from France was to force on Englishmen a realization of the common interests which they shared with the Dutch.

For the humiliation of the Medway and the inconclusive peace a scapegoat was needed: it was provided by the chancellor. Throughout the course of the war he had been steadily losing ground with both king and nation. At Court his austerity was a matter for ridicule, and his tutelage was becoming more and more distasteful to the sovereign; in the Commons was a band of young and ambitious politicians scheming to displace him. To the uncritical multitude he was the villain of the Dunkirk episode and the author of an unpopular war. Most serious of all, he had made no secret of his opinion that the Commons should be kept within rigid bounds, and the House had now taken upon itself to criticize and control the administration which Clarendon regarded as sacrosanct. As a result of these disagreements, he had in 1666 suggested a dissolution of parliament, in the hope that a more tractable House of Commons would be returned; he was accused also of having said that the Commons were of use only to raise money, and were not fit to meddle with affairs of state.[1] It was not difficult to twist his casual remarks into allegations that he wished to dispense with parliament altogether; moreover, his suggestion at the time of the Medway disaster of an imposition on the maritime counties in order to provide for adequate military defence was easily construed into a design for a standing army. The conclusion of the war left him a solitary target for ammunition which had been accumulating since the Restoration.

The influence of lady Castlemaine confirmed Charles in his determination to be rid of him. When, on August 30, secretary Morrice went to him with a royal demand for the Seals, he complied; but he refused to act on hints that he should leave the country. At the opening of the seventh session on October 10, 1667, both Houses thanked the king for his removal of the chancellor; in reply, Charles gave his assurance that he would never again employ Clarendon in public affairs.[2] Articles of impeachment were hastily collected, and by November 6 no less than seventeen counts were reported from the committee to which the duty had been delegated. He had, it was alleged, designed a standing army; he had said that the king was a papist; he had obtained money from the grant of patents; he had procured the imprisonment of English subjects in remote islands and garrisons; he had corruptly sold offices; he had farmed the customs at less than their proper rates; he had received bribes from the vintners for enhancing the price of wine; he had advised and effected the sale of Dunkirk; he had, in an arbitrary way, examined divers subjects at the council-table concerning their lands and chattels, and had stopped proceedings at law relative thereto, by order of the Council; he had extorted money by the threats of *quo warranto* against many corporations after their charters had been confirmed by Act of Parliament; he had received great sums for bills of settlement in Ireland; he had deluded and betrayed His Majesty in foreign treaties and had divulged his secret counsels to the enemy; and,

[1] Diary of J. Millward, *Add. MS.* 33413, Oct. 26, 1667.
[2] *L.J.* xii. 125, Oct. 26, 1667.

lastly, he was the author of the division of the fleet in the late war.[1]

With the exception of the count that he had betrayed the king's counsels to his enemies, none of these charges amounted to treason. Many of them were mere hearsay; the accusation that he had called the king a papist was almost common form, and the other allegations, where they were true, merely implied that Clarendon was high-handed and avaricious. There was a strong personal element in the attack, illustrated in the speech made by sir Thomas Osborne, afterwards earl of Danby; a speech thus recorded in the staccato notes of Anchitel Grey:[2]

The king ready to change his religion—no money remaining—no person in employment but who can buy it—we are upon our last legs—no man ever had more employments—threatens any man that gave advice—no vessel to swim without his hand at the rudder—no money issued out of the Treasury without his approbation—if any other men had the thoughts they had not the power—he has no pique against him, but he is one of the four hundred (of the House of Commons) thought by the chancellor useless and inconsiderable.

These were the real grievances against the chancellor. The formal indictment was taken to the Lords by Seymour, with a request that they would order the committal of the accused; but this the Lords refused, on the ground that no particular treason had been assigned. This refusal led to a prolonged dispute between the two Houses, somewhat embittered by the duke of York's support of his father-in-law; but the Lords refused to give way, leaving to the chancellor's enemies, Buckingham, Arlington, and Bristol, the slender satisfaction of recording their protest[3] in the Journals. At last on November 29 the ex-chancellor, still protesting his innocence, withdrew from England, leaving behind him a long petition to the Lords in which he attempted to vindicate himself. The two Houses ordered the petition to be burned, and passed an Act of Banishment[4] in which it was declared that, having been impeached and having then withdrawn himself, he was to suffer lifelong exile and to be per-

[1] *C.J.* ix. 15–16.   [2] *Grey*, i. 23.

[3] *L.J.* xii. 141–2, Nov. 20, 1667. Albemarle was also among the dissenting peers.

[4] 19–20 Car. II, cap. ii.

manently disabled from holding office. Clarendon endured this sentence until his death at Rouen in 1674.

Throughout the session of 1667–8 the Commons continued their debates on the two vital topics—the financial administration and the mismanagement of the war. As early as the autumn session of 1666 they had called for accounts from the officers of the Navy and Ordnance in order to see how much of the money raised by the two Aids remained unspent. Hitherto the legislature had been dependent for information on the speeches of those members of the administration who had seats in the House; and this calling for accounts was an important stage in the process whereby the Commons acquired complete cognizance of the expenditure of revenue. But the Lords, acting in what they thought were the interests of the crown, vetoed the Commons' demand for a joint committee of inspection by the quibble that their precedents related to conferences, not committees; whereupon the lower House tacked to its Poll Bill a proviso empowering a small committee to examine into the accounts on oath. But, by bringing in the loyalist members, the Court succeeded in procuring an amendment which separated the proviso from the Bill. So the king got the supply[1] without the onerous condition originally attached thereto. The Commons then (Dec. 1666) passed a Bill for taking account of the sums voted for the war; but the Lords countered this by petitioning the king to name his own commission, as an act of grace. Charles complied, and his commission was appointed by letters patent of March 1667. In this contest of wits, therefore, the Commons had been 'dished'. But the events of the summer of 1667 suddenly transformed the farce into drama, and Charles was the first to realize the expediency of making concessions; so the Commons' Bill[2] for taking accounts was allowed to pass into law, and hence one of the results of the Dutch invasion of the Medway was that the Lower House vindicated its claim to inspect national accounts by its own committee.[3]

The report of the Commons' commission (communicated to the House in Nov. 1669) provides a commentary on the financing

---

[1] 18–19 Car. II, cap. i.   [2] 19–20 Car. II, cap. i.
[3] For a full account of this see the very able and emphatic introduction of Dr. W. A. Shaw to *Cal. Tr. Bks.* 1667–8.

of the war, and the complete confusion surrounding the provision made for the crown's normal peace-time revenue. On the one hand, opponents of the Court such as sir T. Meres estimated that nearly seven million pounds had been provided for war expenditure, of which one million was still unspent; on the other hand Williamson, on behalf of the executive, contended that, while the Dutch had spent eight millions on the war, we had not spent half that sum.[1] There was similar confusion in the investigations of the commission. It was required to report on the sums actually voted for the war; these being the Royal Aid of March 1665, the Additional Aid of October 1665, the Three Months' tax for the Militia granted in 1661-2, the Poll Bill of October 1666, and the Eleven Months' Assessment of January 1667. From all these sources the total yield by the end of 1668 amounted to £4,355,047, and as the commission was satisfied that at least £4,335,244 had actually been spent on the war, the accounts may in a sense be said to have balanced.[2]

Unfortunately, seventeenth-century book-keeping was not so simple as this. As funds were kept in water-tight compartments, and as receipts might come in long after the date on which they were nominally due, the commission did not have at its disposal the materials requisite for an adequate balance-sheet. Moreover the matter was complicated by the addition of two large supplementary sums, one on each side of the account. On the receipt side they added a total of about £1,169,880 received from Customs, Excise, Hearth Money, Prizes and Dunkirk Money, which Charles had voluntarily applied to the purposes of the war, though not bound to do so, since these were mostly part of his hereditary revenue, and were required for the purposes of ordinary administration. By diverting these large sums from the already inadequate crown revenue, the debt on the civil administration was increased, and the inevitable bankruptcy was brought within nearer view. On the other side of the account, the expenditure side, the commission introduced two items which it refused to pass—£698,357 paid to the earl of Anglesey, treasurer of the Navy, and not yet accounted for; and £780,139, most of which had been paid to Carteret, Anglesey's predecessor, and was supposed by the commission to have been

---

[1] *Grey*, i. 186-7. [2] Shaw, in op. cit. lxiv-lxv.

applied to purposes other than the war. On the one hand, therefore, Charles had contributed a sum which he need not have
contributed; on the other hand there was a larger sum about
the disposal of which there remained some dubiety; and so
royal generosity was more than balanced by popular suspicion.
These facts were destined to be of great consequence in the
adjustment of relations between crown and legislature. But
meanwhile there remains the question: how did England manage to conduct this war so cheaply? By withholding pay from
the seamen and stinting their diet; by laying up ships, and leaving the smaller fry of contractors to be forced into bankruptcy.
This economy might have been acceptable if all had shared
alike, and in this respect a good example was set by the Court
musicians, who, though their pay was more than three years in
arrear, continued to supply wind for their instruments. But
money could always be found for the courtiers, the courtesans,
and the hangers-on who battened on Charles's good nature;
and no balance-sheets, however plausible, can eliminate the
enormous expenditure which these entailed.[1]

As the Commons criticized the financing of the war, so they
criticized its management. In his evidence of October 22, 1667,
sir Edward Spragge said that Albemarle had advised the sinking
of great ships to protect the boom; but instead, only a few small
ones were sunk, through which the Dutch forced a passage. As
to the dividing of the fleet before the Four Days' Battle of June
1666, this was attributed by Spragge to false intelligence that
the Dutch would not be out for six weeks.[2] Secretary Morrice
then gave an account of this incident within the limits of publicity allowed to one sworn of the king's counsels. His information
of the Dutch movements was derived, he said, from a paid agent
in Holland; whereupon the Commons resolved not to press for
documents, since by so doing they might prejudice the Dutch
spy in the employment of the English government. Prince
Rupert's version was next given (Oct. 31). According to him
the separation was founded on intelligence of some French ships
being at Belle Isle, and others expected at Brest; there was also
news that the Dutch were not likely to be out for some weeks;
accordingly, it was thought that he might be spared to look after

[1] *Infra*, ii. 446-8.   [2] Millward's Diary, *Add. MS.* 33413, Oct. 22, 1666.

the French, in case they were minded to do damage in the Channel. Stress of weather, he said, had forced him into St. Helen's Roads, where he had learned that the Dutch were out. In this evidence Rupert made a general complaint of the lack of provisions in the fleet, and the delay in fitting out the greater ships. Albemarle then followed with his testimony. According to this, on May 14 he had been visited by sir G. Carteret and sir W. Coventry with a request that he would spare 20 ships to fall on the French; then, after detaching Rupert and these ships, he received from Arlington on the 27th a letter dated the 24th informing him of the report that the Dutch would be out 'suddenly'. Two days later he received (at 10 p.m.) orders to proceed to the Gunfleet. His evidence therefore shows that an interval of three days had elapsed between the dispatch and receipt of Arlington's all-important letter. Albemarle concluded his evidence with an account of the chaotic conditions at Chatham when he went there to organize the defence.[1]

As a result of these investigations, articles of impeachment were brought in against commissioner Pett and sir W. Penn[2] (for neglect of duty), but the charges were not proceeded with. The divisions of the fleet, neglect in fortifying Sheerness, and payment of sailors by tickets were each condemned.[3] Brouncker was questioned about his conduct in the battle off Lowestoft, when he brought pretended orders to sir John Harman, commanding him to shorten sail; for this he was dismissed the House in disgrace.[4] These proceedings showed that, while still in the dark regarding the working of the administration, and still unaware of the inadequacy of their grants both for the war and for the royal revenue, the Commons were nevertheless awakening to a sense of the magnitude of their duties. Only six years had elapsed since their enthusiastic surrender of constitutional safeguards to the executive; now, the acid of disaster and disgrace had eaten away much of the tinsel and gilt with which the Cavalier Parliament had once been decked; nor, until these ornaments were removed, could parliament realize the great traditions of which

---

[1] *C.J.* ix. 10–30.
[2] Ibid. ix. 42–3, Dec. 19, 1667; 85, April 21, 1668.
[3] Ibid. ix. 49–53, Feb. 14, 1668.
[4] Ibid. ix. 85–86, April 21, 1668.

it was the custodian. In 1661 the House of Commons was a house of courtiers; by 1667 it was becoming a house of critics. It needed only the Third Dutch War to make them party politicians. Behind it all was the bogey of Popery, its menace becoming more sinister with each year that passed.

IX

CHARLES II AND LOUIS XIV, 1668–72

Of the two royal cousins whose inter-relations were of such consequence, Charles had obtained most of his knowledge of diplomacy from continental travel and intimate acquaintance with men; whereas Louis, except at the head of invading armies, never passed his frontiers, and was dependent for information on the reports of a host of agents. The English king governed a state long divided by religious differences, and soon to be embroiled in political faction; but the *Grand Monarque* was assured of the devoted loyalty of his subjects and, after 1685, of their religious uniformity. Nor were these the only differences; for, while Charles was lazy, immoral, and impecunious, Louis was industrious, respectable, and rich. Temperamentally, also, they presented a striking contrast. For every conceivable contingency Louis had an oriental profusion of cunning expedients, and so was able to do many things at once; while Charles, who was obliged to wait on events, preferred to settle one problem before tackling another. The elaborate calculations of Louis and his heavy investments in the House of Stuart were based on the assumption that if he could be sure of the English Court, he could be sure of the English nation.

Since the commencement of his personal rule (March 1661) Louis had assigned to England an important place in the network of policy with which he covered the civilized areas of the globe. From the point of view of Versailles, it appeared that England might be educated for the place she was destined to fill in a French world. Her heresies she would probably live down, since Reformation doctrines were not only ceasing to find fresh converts, but were becoming discredited by their mutual antagonisms; her strange constitution, with its talk of personal liberty, could easily be adjusted by a capable monarch brought up on the right principles; her Stuart kings, Christians and gentlemen like the Bourbons themselves, might serve as willing subordinates in the campaign for Gallic glory about to be inaugurated. Even her Saxon population, though naïve and uncouth, were not

unhopeful subjects for proper education, since their island existence had preserved them unspoilt, and whatever their minds
might be, their bodies were worth something, because they provided good seamen and soldiers, with a reputation for tenacity
and endurance, qualities admirably fitted to supplement the
dash and brilliance of the Frenchman. Louis was sure that he
and Charles ought to be friends, and he had money with which
to pay for friendship.

A long and distinguished series of French ambassadors was
accredited to the English Court. The acceptance by Charles and
Clarendon of subsidies for the Portuguese marriage augured well
for the Bourbon-Stuart goodwill, which was further promoted
by the comte de Cominges, who was sent over late in 1662;[1] but
Louis had heard rumours of republicanism in England, so he
instructed Cominges not to commit his master to the giving of
help against Charles's rebellious subjects, since difficulties at
home would make the English king more grateful for French
support. Cominges was, however, to inform himself fully of
the economic and political conditions of the country, and of its
literature and men of letters; for Louis affirmed a determination
to utilize this information 'for my service and my glory'. He
added that a supply of English convicts would be welcome, as
they would make good galley-slaves.[2]

Having secured the Dutch by the defensive alliance[3] of April
1662, and in the assurance of the friendship or at least the
neutrality of England, Louis could wait patiently for the death
of his father-in-law before demanding all or part of the Spanish
inheritance. His association with England, Portugal's ally,
helped to guarantee the diplomatic isolation of Spain. The first
interruption of these amicable relations came with the imminence
of Anglo-Dutch hostilities, a threat which placed Louis in a
position of some difficulty, because it was an unforeseen diversion
of European policy from the lines which he had so cleverly laid
down. The difficulty came from two sources: first, if England
provoked Holland into a war, France would be obliged, in
accordance with the treaty of 1662, to come to the help of the

---

[1] For his instructions see *Instructions Données*, i. 314–40.

[2] J. J. Jusserand, *A French ambassador at the Court of Charles II*, 133.

[3] *Supra*, 248–9.

Dutch; and secondly, a war between these two maritime powers would probably result in leaving one of them supreme at sea, and therefore a menace to France. Charles assured Louis that, as the Dutch were really the aggressors, Louis might honourably absolve himself from his obligations;[1] but the French king was not convinced, and even at the eleventh hour he tried to obviate hostilities by diplomacy. So in April 1665 the *célèbre ambassade*, consisting of Henri de Bourbon, duc de Verneuil, and Cominges, was dispatched to England with instructions to combine with ambassador Courtin, and allay the war fever of the English House of Commons, with bribes if necessary. Charles dealt with the *célèbre ambassade* in terms which showed an appreciation of Louis's scruples and difficulties. It was not he but parliament which wanted war; he was sorry, he said, that the king of France should ally with a power against which England had so many grievances; moreover it was not an edifying spectacle to see the Most Christian King associated with Dutch republicans—'vous le devez à la royauté contre la république'.[2] The thrust may have gone home, but nevertheless Louis honoured his engagement and both kings went to war.

Thus the attempt to divert English policy had failed, but Louis was too great to feel personal resentment against Charles on this score. Throughout the Second Dutch War the king of France showed how tender might be his enmity when incurred by his friends, and how worthless his alliance when secured by his enemies, thereby introducing into diplomacy complications of a subtlety hitherto undreamt of. He combined two things apparently impossible of unison—he kept his faith with the Dutch, and at the same time he prevented either side establishing supremacy. The war was an interruption in his calculations, and so was disposed of in a manner that left things as they were. But if his sailors were idle, his diplomats were not; for he was conducting an intensive campaign against Spain, whose possessions he hoped to monopolize or partition. Already in November 1665 the English agent Fanshawe had signed the protocol of a treaty with Spain by which England was to be accorded the commercial advantages enjoyed by French and Dutch;[3] but by

---

[1] *Mignet*, i. 415.
[2] July 1665. Jusserand, op. cit. 172.
[3] *Mignet*, i. 433.

the beginning of 1666 France was nominally at war with England, and so it was imperative for Louis that England should share in the diplomatic isolation of Spain. Accordingly, the full force of French activity was directed against the Anglo-Spanish entente. The French ambassador in Madrid was directed to inform the Spanish government that, if the alliance with England were perfected, the French king would consider himself absolved from the treaty of the Pyrenees, since England was now his enemy. This threat was accompanied by an offer of mediation with Portugal. Meanwhile, the efforts of Fanshawe and Southwell to obtain the goodwill of Portugal were rebuffed, the Portuguese expressing a preference for French mediation; and the marriage of Alfonso VI with Mlle de Nemours (Feb. 1666) served still further to counterbalance English influence in Lisbon, and to consolidate the alliance of France and Portugal at the expense of Spain.

The substitution of Sandwich for Fanshawe in May 1666 did not bring the projected Anglo-Spanish treaty any nearer, and Spain succeeded neither in securing peace with Portugal, nor active alliance with England. But a commercial Anglo-Spanish agreement[1] was eventually concluded (May 13–23, 1667) which was later to be of great value to English commerce, since it allowed our colonial produce to enter Spanish ports duty-free. For the moment, however, in this game of snatching immediate advantages success lay with the French.[2] Louis completed his diplomatic triumphs with the Franco-Portuguese alliance[3] of March 1667, whereby he detached our oldest ally, and left helpless the power which he intended to master. Elsewhere English diplomacy was defeated by the insistent penetration and forethought of France. Neither Carlingford in Vienna nor Henry Coventry in Stockholm was able to secure an ally; in April 1666 the bishop of Münster had been detached from our associates when France induced the elector of Brandenburg to declare war on him; and at the same time Frederick III of Denmark was added to our enemies. Charles would have to pay for his refusal of French mediation; and though in European waters he was spared the attacks of the French Navy, he must see in the falling away of his friends and the increasing number of his enemies

[1] *Dumont*, vii, pt. i. 27.   [2] Feiling, op. cit. 233.
[3] *Dumont*, vii, pt. i. 17.

convincing proofs of the heavy effects of Bourbon displeasure. The lesson for the king of England was that he must accommodate his policy to the behests of Versailles, no matter what his subjects or House of Commons might think.

Thus by methods almost as devious and inscrutable as those of Providence Louis paved the way for the fulfilment of his designs. He had separated Portugal from both Spain and England so that he could use it against either of these two; he assured himself against the Emperor by alliances with the German princes; by influence and money he entrenched himself behind the ramparts of alliance or neutrality, and continued to deceive his hereditary enemy with the pretext of negotiation.[1] It remained only to detach England in order that the helplessness of Spain might be complete. This he achieved even before the cessation of Anglo-Dutch hostilities; for in April 1667 he secured Charles's written promise 'on the word of a king' that he would not ally with an enemy of France for the space of one year, and that during this year he would take steps to effect a close co-operation (*une liaison étroite*) with France.[2] Having obtained these advantages for the major operation which he contemplated, Louis could afford to be conciliatory at the Breda conferences which closed the minor operation standing in the way of his vaster designs; indeed, he did not wait for the conclusion of hostilities before startling Europe with a declaration of his real intentions. In the *Traité des droits de la reine* . . . he came forward not as an aggressor, but as the defender of abstract justice, anxious to confer the benefits of French civilization on territories which, 'by the unanimous consent of all the famous universities' 'devolved' on his consort. In May 1667 Turenne quickly captured Charleroi, Armentières, Tournai, Douai, and Lille. Thus, even before the signing of the treaty of Breda, the European situation completely changed—a change full of menace for the Dutch and of interesting possibilities for England.

In the shaping of foreign policy Charles had the help of advisers,

---

[1] As late as March 1667 Louis instructed his agent in Madrid to talk of an alliance with Spain for the purpose of driving the English out of the West Indies. (*Mignet*, i. 520.)   [2] *Mignet*, ii. 45.

while Louis had servants; consequently the former king was sometimes obliged to cheat not only his enemies but his ministers, and to that extent he was handicapped. For some time before the fall of Clarendon, Charles had begun to admit to his counsels a number of men having collectively no official status, and known to history from the word formed by the initials of their names, as the Cabal. It was not the first junto or informal cabinet council in England; but what little cohesion it possessed arose from the fact that all its members had, in different degrees, been enemies of Clarendon, and had risen by his fall; a second and equally negative characteristic was that none of them was devoted to the Anglican Church; for Clifford was a Roman Catholic, Arlington a crypto-Catholic; Ashley and Buckingham had links with the Dissenters, and the ex-Presbyterian Lauderdale would willingly have enforced any form of state religion on his fellow Scots. Thirdly, they were all opportunists, and were therefore both useful tools and good game for a monarch even more unscrupulous than themselves. The Cabal was only one of a series of rapidly changing groups of men who enjoyed some measure of royal confidence, and its dissolution was as obscure as its origin.

Chief of these men was sir Henry Bennet, created baron Arlington in 1663 and earl in 1672. From Eton and Christ Church he brought some reputation for scholarship; from the Civil Wars he brought a scar on the face as permanent proof of his loyalty. He had the gift for making the right friends and discarding them at the right moment; but as he lacked courage he never rose to real greatness among the bad men of Charles's Court. As Stuart agent at Madrid before the Restoration he had acquired a knowledge of Spanish and the habitude of diplomacy; to these he added a certain precision and formality of manner. In October 1662 he had succeeded Nicholas as one of the secretaries of state; with the decline of Clarendon he acquired more of the king's confidence by his suppleness and assiduity, and because as linguist and methodical worker he had two of the technical qualifications requisite in a minister of foreign affairs. Always civil and obliging, his chief talent was that of anticipating and fostering what he thought to be the secret wishes of his royal master, a slippery path for one having 'the pedantick carriage of a true penman'.[1] He was credited with having urged England's entry into the Second Dutch War; but his marriage to a Dutch lady made it difficult for him to maintain a reputation for patriotism, or even consistency; nor did he succeed in achieving his cherished project of an alliance with Spain, because that would have involved the abandonment of Portugal. His nominal Anglicanism and his secret sympathies with Roman Catholicism further enhanced his usefulness for Charles. He repudiated the insinuation that he was a 'premier minister'.[2]

Chief of the satellites clustering round Arlington was Thomas Clifford, created first lord Clifford of Chudleigh and lord high treasurer in 1672. As a member of the House of Commons he had been among the first to enrol himself among the King's Friends, and was rewarded with a Tellership in the Exchequer and several commissionerships; he also performed good though irregular service at sea in the Second Dutch War, when he acted as Arlington's agent. In September 1665 he co-operated with Henry Coventry at Copenhagen in the attempted reconciliation with Denmark; and thereafter his promotion was rapid, a privy-councillorship being followed (on the death of Southampton) by a commissionership of the Treasury. As he had been Arlington's confidant in the Navy, so he was his right-hand man in the Commons, where he acted always on behalf of the Court. These rapid promotions caused some justifiable surprise among his contemporaries. But there was some consistency in his conduct. As an ardent Catholic he desired toleration for his co-religionaries; he disliked the Dutch; he dreaded everything that savoured of republicanism, and he believed that Charles should rule by a Tudor despotism. In him therefore Charles found a warm advocate of the policy which led to the secret alliance with France and the third war with the Dutch. He was an anomaly among Restoration statesmen—a believer in his horoscope, a warm-hearted friend, and a passionate enemy. He died by his own hand.

[1] Ailesbury, *Memoirs* (ed. 1890), 14.

[2] Conway to sir J. Finch, Feb. 1668, in *Cal. S.P. Dom., 1667–8*, 258. For an unsympathetic character-sketch see *Clar. S.P.* iii, Appendix lxxxi; for a sympathetic one see Feiling in op. cit. 76–80. For a good biography see Prof. H. Barbour, *Henry Bennet, earl of Arlington*.

In striking contrast with him was Buckingham, son of the favourite of James I and Charles I, endowed with vast estates, brought up like a prince, distinguished by the most national of all English names—George; the most convincing personal proof that birth and brains are inseparable. As the only one of Charles's ministers who pursued a career for amusement he had a special place in Charles's affections; but he frequently transgressed the wide limits of royal tolerance, and set a standard of ducal independence and vagary never since approached. His personal dislikes were the sole incentives in his political career, and his failures were caused by this, that even Restoration England was not educated up to his standards of excess and indecency. Probably from a dislike of Anglican respectability he favoured the cause of the Dissenters, and was therefore useful as a possible agent in the policy of toleration; but he was a dangerous tool, because he had no compunction in committing treason; and he was an enemy to be feared because of his vast resources of ridicule. Henry VIII would have sent him to the block; but Charles preserved him as a curio having unique ornamental possibilities if handled with circumspection. He was like Clarendon in this, that circumstances had imposed him on the king, and like Clarendon also, he was set aside when he had served his purpose. His Mastership of the Horse and privy councillorship gave him his official status at Court; his ready wit blended well with Charles's conversational sallies, and his character of bully and adulterer made him an acceptable agent in the negotiations with Versailles.

Of the two remaining members of the Cabal Lauderdale, who had successfully lived down his Presbyterian associations, gave Charles the longest and the most devoted service as his secretary for Scottish affairs. His 'Saracen fiery face' and his 'high Scotch' pronunciation[1] added a touch of variety and colour to Charles's more intimate councils. He spoilt the good stories of his colleagues in the telling of them, and he retailed his own coarse jests as specimens of wit. His Hebrew scholarship was all that remained of a somewhat faded ecclesiasticism, and he was the crudest but most dependable tool in the Cabal.

Lastly, there was Anthony Ashley Cooper, vigorous in mind

[1] Ailesbury, *Memoirs*, 14–15.

and weak in health, an enigma even to those contemporaries who knew him best. Within the loose limits of the category 'parliamentary Presbyterian' he had won the guarded esteem of Cromwell, who could never quite trust a man with a middle name, since two names were then thought sufficient for an honest man. Ashley had kept pace with the movement which led to the king's recall; and, as he was known to have business aptitudes, he was appointed to the then subordinate post of chancellor of the Exchequer, and created baron Ashley in 1661. A certain liberalism in his outlook led him to oppose the ecclesiastical policy associated with the name of Clarendon; while his instinct for accommodation led him to join forces with Bennet, who had only success to counterbalance his obvious inferiority of mind and character. Diligence and talent were the qualities which made Ashley of service to the enemies of the chancellor; and as treasurer of Prizes in the Second Dutch War he was able to commend himself to Charles. With these activities he combined colonial enterprises in the new world wherein he hoped to realize those visions of toleration and self-government unattainable in the old;[1] indeed the strands of idealism and scruple are closely woven into the texture of his career. He might have stepped out of one of Mr. Gladstone's cabinets into the Cabal, and out of the Cabal into a conclave of Whitechapel desperadoes; he was the Jekyll and Hyde of English politics, alike an apostle of enlightenment and progress, and an agent of force and falsehood, all the more formidable because his frame was small and his spirit unquenchable. He introduced into politics the new elements of advertisement and publicity, as Danby introduced those of organization and party management; on the bases of Oates's perjuries and Monmouth's pretended legitimacy he created a great political party distinguished for personal independence and exalted principle. In judging between him and Charles posterity may have to be content with the king's reference[2] of the question to the Day of Judgement.

This portrait gallery would be incomplete without at least a bust of Will Chiffinch. In 1668 he succeeded a respectable brother in the office of page of His Majesty's bedchamber, and

---

[1] For this see *infra*, ii. 673–6.
[2] Charles's frank statement of the case will be found in *Burnet*, ii. 300.

he died just in time to avoid the deluge of 1688. As confidential agent, procurer-general, and pawnbroker-in-chief[1] to the king, he handled many thousands of pounds; and so extensive was his private information that, had reputations been commonly assessed in money, he could have blackmailed more than half the court of his royal master. Pepys, who sometimes dined with him on pickled herring, always found him 'civil'. Under his skilled management, eavesdropping became a profession and the backstairs a political institution. His functions were thus described by Roger North:[2]

The back-stairs might properly be called the spy office where the King spoke with particular persons about intrigues of all sorts. . . . Chiffinch was a most impetuous drinker and, in that capacity, an admirable spy; for he let none part from him sober, if it were possible to get them drunk; and his great artifice was pushing idolatrous healths of his good master. Nor, to make sure work, would he scruple to put his master's salutiferous drops (which were called the King's, of the nature of Goddard's)[3] into the glasses; and, being a Hercules, well-breathed at the sport himself, he commonly had the better, and discovered men's characters which the King could never have obtained by any other means.

Chiffinch performed a great and honourable service to the Stuarts by *not* writing his memoirs.

Such were the councillors most closely associated with Charles when, with the French invasion of the Low Countries (May 1667) and the conclusion of hostilities at Breda (July 1667), entirely new problems of policy presented themselves. Louis now called upon the States General to co-operate with him in compelling Spain to recognize his rights by 'devolution', reminding them of the sacrifices he had made on their behalf; while to Charles he explained frankly the unfortunate circumstances which had obliged him to declare war on England in January 1666. The declaration of war, he confided, was really no more than a scrap of paper (*un parchemin*), and in the ensuing war he had used his fleet, not to assist the Dutch, but to escort a bridal procession, that of Mlle de Nemours to Lisbon, for her marriage with Alfonso VI. Moreover

[1] For an example see *Cal. Tr. Bks., 1681–5*, 251–2.
[2] *Life of Francis North, Lord Guilford* (1742), 210.
[3] For the 'drops' of Dr. Goddard see *D.N.B.*, s.v. Jonathan Goddard.

he had ceased from even the pretext of war in European waters two months before peace was signed.[1] In order to reinforce these arguments, the ambassador Henri de Ruvigny was sent to England in August 1667. On his side, Charles, warmly seconded by Buckingham, made no secret of the fact that his heart had always been for a French alliance; but unfortunately there were few of his opinion either in council or parliament. He hinted that Spain had made him tempting offers, but France would have the preference.[2] Louis then offered one of two things—a league of mutual support (against rebellious subjects), or a joint enterprise against the Spanish West Indies.[3] Louis added that as the Dutch were likely in the near future to do something that would absolve him from keeping his ever-memorable engagement of 1662, Charles would have an opportunity of wiping off old scores against his commercial rivals, without fear of French intervention on their behalf.

Charles knew that in its exhausted state England could not for some time engage in hostilities, even in conjunction with an acceptable ally; accordingly, he suggested a policy of neutrality, and on this basis the negotiations were lengthened out into the winter of 1667–8. Arlington and the pro-Spanish party profited by this delay to further the design of an alliance with the Dutch against France; and an agent named Meerman was sent to England by De Witt for the encouragement of this proposal. The anti-French party in England also tried to make capital of the fact that the exiled Clarendon was in refuge at Rouen; but Louis promptly deprived his opponents of this weapon against him by ordering the expulsion of the ex-chancellor from France. For a time, therefore, Charles dallied with two sets of negotiations—that with De Witt and that with Louis.[4] The former led to immediate results. Sir William Temple, then agent at Brussels, saw that the success of France in the Low Countries might well force the Dutch into the arms of the French; these fears he communicated to Arlington, who, on November 25, 1667, instructed Temple to ascertain if De Witt would enter into a defensive alliance with the English for the security of the Spanish Nether-

[1] *Mignet*, ii. 508. [2] Ibid. ii. 517.
[3] Ibid. ii. 518–19, Oct. 9, N.S. 1667.
[4] Ibid. ii. 540–5, Dec.–Jan. 1667–8.

lands. De Witt, though surprised by this sudden change of front, expressed willingness to enter a compact of joint mediation and defence. In order to conclude such a treaty,[1] Temple, about whose sincerity and friendship for the Dutch there could be no doubt, was, at the request of Arlington, sent to The Hague in January 1668.

The Triple Alliance, to which Sweden adhered conditionally in January and definitely in May, was signed on January 13/23, 1668, and consisted of three compacts. By the first, Charles and the States General engaged in a defensive alliance whereby each promised to provide armed assistance if the other were attacked. The second and the third, the one public, the other private, defined the terms of mediation between France and Spain, in which Sweden was invited to participate. These terms were identical with those[2] which Louis had himself proposed in September 1667, namely, that Spain would adopt one of two alternatives—either confirm Louis in his Flemish conquests of 1667, or transfer to him all Spanish rights in either Luxemburg or Franche Comté, together with Cambrai, Douai, St. Omer, Bergues, Furnes, and Linck. Charles and the States General bound themselves to employ their efforts to induce Spain to accept these terms, and to oblige the two crowns to accommodate their differences on this basis. By the secret clauses England and Holland undertook to do their utmost to establish peace between Spain and Portugal, and they agreed that, in the event of France failing to restore peace on the alternatives specified, they would wage war on France by land and sea until France was reduced to the limits defined in the treaty of the Pyrenees.[3]

Thus, by the terms of the Triple Alliance Louis's enemy and ally of a few months before were both now ranged against him, but in such a manner that the threat of hostilities was secret, and the French king was publicly invited merely to give effect to terms which he himself had suggested. The contracting parties hastened to assure Louis of their good intentions, Charles explaining to Ruvigny that the alliance made no difference in their relations; and in a personal letter he assured Louis that he had

[1] The 'tenor mandati' is in *Dumont*, vii, pt. i. 66.
[2] In his Memoir for the comte d'Estrades, *Mignet*, ii. 492.
[3] *Mignet*, ii. 549–55.

acted in his (Louis's) best interests. As the Triple Alliance was popular in England, and seemed likely to effect its object, Arlington boasted that he was its author, while Temple suddenly leaped into fame as the champion of Dutch interests. From this point, therefore, may be dated the beginnings of that change in English sentiment, whereby commercial rivalry with the Dutch was subordinated to hatred of France and jealousy of her political ambitions. The mingling of the currents can be seen in the Commons' debates during the earlier months of 1668. Having announced the formation of the Triple Alliance, Charles asked parliament for two things—a supply in order to fit out the Fleet, and the consideration of means to secure unison among his Protestant subjects.[1] In response, the Commons voted the sum of £310,000 to be raised by an imposition on wine and spirits, a levy intended to fall heavily on French imports;[2] in regard to the second request there was some difference of opinion, for while a majority petitioned the king to issue a proclamation against conventicles, several members of the Commons expressed a desire for comprehension or toleration.[3] Here was the beginning of that process whereby Protestant Englishmen were to be welded together in the fire of hatred against France and the Papists.

Charles's policy was thus a well-timed bid for the support of English opinion, and also a hint to Louis that a good price must be paid for English support. Another effect of the Triple Alliance was that Spain, realizing her impotence at last, agreed to come to terms with Portugal; accordingly, the latter country was detached from France, and her independence achieved, a measure facilitated by a revolution which occurred late in 1667, when the insane Alfonso VI (a protégé of Louis) was deposed and replaced by his brother.[4] On February 3, 1668, was signed the treaty by which Spain treated Portugal as an independent power, and so was ended a struggle which had lasted for more than twenty years. Thus the members of the Triple Alliance could congratulate themselves on the efficacy of their intervention. Louis also could congratulate himself; for in January 1668 he had signed with the Emperor Leopold a treaty dividing the Spanish

<hr>

[1] L.J. xii. 181.
[2] 19-20 Car. II, cap. vi.
[3] Grey, i. 110-15.
[4] Mignet, ii. 565 sqq.

empire between them. But, as if this were not enough, in February he sent Condé into Franche Comté, which he speedily occupied. This conquest Louis restored to Spain by the treaty of Aix-la-Chapelle (April 1668), retaining only, from his captures of May 1667, some frontier towns, such as Lille, Douai, and Charleroi, a magnanimity which astonished Europe, for nothing could have resisted the force of French arms; and since Louis was not noted for moderation, there must have been some reason for this act of generosity. Surely the Triple Alliance was the cause that the travailing mountain had produced no more than a mouse? Or was Louis making a public demonstration of both his military force and his political morality? That the French king held the latter view may be inferred from his Memoirs.[1]

The surrenders made by Louis at the treaty of Aix-la-Chapelle were so obviously inconsistent with his military successes that the treaty was unpopular even in France; and in spite of his secret arrangement with the emperor, the French king eventually came to the conclusion that in reality he had been duped. Charles had not kept his 'word of a king'; the Dutch, for whom he and his ancestors had sacrificed themselves, had returned friendship with betrayal. It was not the treachery of Charles that rankled in his mind, for the English king was only secretly his ally, but the treachery of his public and traditional allies, the States General. At this point there was superimposed on French political strategy the consideration of economic policy. France had important overseas possessions; but what advantage were they? The furs of Canada were traded not by Frenchmen but by Dutch and English; at French Senegal, the same Protestant powers were in control of the export trade in negroes; in Martinique, the Frenchman grew sugar with the help of Dutch capital and exported it in Dutch ships; only in unhealthy Madagascar were the French colonists unencumbered by these foreign traffickers. Already, England had passed Navigation Acts to keep the Hollander out of her overseas trade; and by her treaty of 1667 with Spain had obtained just enough footing in the Spanish empire to make possible a profitable trade in contraband

[1] It was stated in the Memoirs compiled for Louis that by these concessions he wanted to establish confidence among small states. (*Œuvres de Louis XIV*, ed. 1806, ii. 369.)

and logwood. It was Colbert who had first awakened to the facts.[1] He realized that by their penetration the Dutch were obtaining cargoes and markets where they had no territorial responsibilities, and accordingly he set himself to do for France what the English legislature was attempting to do for England. In 1664 he founded the West India Company with the express object of transferring the sugar freights to French ships, and in 1667 he imposed such a severe tariff on imports into France that the Dutch themselves had to admit the prospect of ruin.

Not content with the economic advantage already secured to him by tariffs, Colbert urged a war of extermination against Holland, apparently on the assumption that he could transfer Dutch industries and ships *en masse* to France. This was one of the few aberrations in the policy of an otherwise enlightened statesman, and he had to pay for it; for by the treaty which ended the war of 1672 he was obliged to surrender his tariff of 1667, and so restore to the Dutch their economic advantage. If Colbert erred so grievously in trying to obtain better conditions by war than he already possessed by peace, the attitude of Louis XIV may well be understood; for at least he was not thinking in economic terms at all (there is scarcely any mention of such things in his correspondence); he was occupied not with tariffs but with higher things—with religion and glory. It was characteristic of the juxtaposition of two entirely different policies that while the two kings were considering a political and religious alliance, their ministers were negotiating a commercial treaty designed to give specially favourable terms to the imports from each country, and intended to complete the work of the tariffs by uniting England and France in a Customs union against the Dutch;[2] it was characteristic also that while the first of these

---

[1] For this see Lavisse, *Histoire de France*, vii, pt. i. 233 sqq., and S. L. Mims, *Colbert's West India Policy*, 51 and 69.

[2] The first draft of this treaty was sent by Arlington to Colbert late in August 1669. It provided free entry and trade in the ports of the other on terms afterwards to be arranged; each was to export cloth and silk to the other; French wine was to be freely admitted, but not French fancy goods. Tariffs were to be reduced to conform with the moderate ones imposed by France in 1664. It was objected in France that the advantages of this treaty were all on the English side; especially as French fancy goods were prohibited; and the project never materialized. For an account of the

alliances was completed, the second was not. There was added a peculiar psychological element. Louis admitted privately that in the second Dutch War he had, in spite of his alliance, made no sacrifice whatever on behalf of the Dutch; but nevertheless he was genuinely indignant that they had forsaken him. Charles had also played false, and might again do so; yet somehow it seemed to Louis that the infidelity of a Stuart differed fundamentally from that of a Dutchman. At Versailles, therefore, righteous indignation was superimposed on economic motive; but the two did not harmonize, and it was the higher of these impulses which really stirred Louis, especially as it was linked with the establishment of Catholicism in England. So the negotiations with Whitehall were resumed, and the cordial relations between the two kings were speedily restored.

Charles Colbert de Croissy (younger brother of the great Colbert) came to England as ambassador in August 1668, with instructions to the effect that Spain was no longer the enemy, but the States General. He was warned against Lisola, the active Imperial agent in England, and against Arlington, the man with a Spanish heart and a Dutch wife; but Arlington might be bribed, and a *buffet de vaisselle d'argent* of the value of 100,000 écus was suggested as the probable limit of his price.[1] The envoy found both king and duke of York anxious for a French alliance, and that Buckingham was the most active agent for this policy, while Arlington was its chief opponent; but the Frenchman may have had reason to conclude that the cause of his country was as much hampered by the advocacy of its friends as by the opposition of its enemies; for Buckingham was striving to remove every friend of the Dutch from office, while Arlington was scheming, with the help of Temple,[2] to create a great anti-French league composed of the States General, the Swiss Cantons, Brandenburg, Luxemburg, and Saxony. There could be no hope, therefore, that a definite policy would crystallize from the mixture of personal jealousy and suspicion which constituted the substance of English diplomacy in 1668. Enmity between Buckingham and Arlington

---

treaty see P. de Ségur-Dupeyron, *Histoire des négociations commerciales du règne de Louis XIV*, 246–54.

[1] *Instructions Données*, ii. 53. For the relative value of the écu at this time see *supra*.   [2] Temple, *Memoirs*, ii. 369.

helped to neutralize their rival principles; the Cabal was held together only by fear of the exiled Clarendon; commercial jealousy of the Dutch was still so strong that Clifford hinted at another war, and the rapid development of the French Navy and Mercantile Marine under the supervision of Colbert conjured up visions of a menace to England even greater than that from Holland. In these uncertainties Charles was more than usually evasive. To his sister he explained his difficulty in accepting the French alliance. The commercial interests in England were, he explained, becoming alarmed by the extension of French enterprise, and he personally was bound by a treaty with the Dutch—a restraint which, he hinted, would be appreciated by Louis, who had proved himself 'a martyr to his word'.[1] If Charles was so cryptic in a private letter to his sister, it may readily be understood that his ministers failed to divine his intentions.

Charles may at last have been induced to make up his mind by an event within his own household. Early in 1669 the duke of York began to doubt whether his membership of the Church of England was consistent with salvation, and recourse to a Jesuit father confirmed these misgivings. Not only did James decide to avow the Catholic faith, but he discoursed freely on this subject with two Catholics in his entourage, lord Arundell of Wardour and sir Thomas Clifford, and also with the undeclared Catholic, Arlington, all of whom knew of the king's religious inclinations. Now that the brother had openly declared himself, there seemed an opportunity not only of inducing the sovereign himself to avow the faith, but to take measures for its promotion in England. On January 25, 1669 (anniversary of the conversion of St. Paul), Charles interviewed the duke and his three sympathizers, and after expressing his sorrow that he could not at that time avow his religious convictions, he asked for their views on the best means of promoting the Roman Catholic religion in England. If the duke of York's biographer is to be believed, Charles shed tears as he discoursed on these solemn topics.[2] The decision of this secret conclave was said to be a resolve to seek the support of France, and with this object the negotiations with Louis were resumed. These were committed to lord Wardour,

---

[1] *Mignet*, iii. 50.
[2] J. S. Clarke, *Life of James II*, i. 440 sqq.

Henry Jermyn (lord St. Albans), and sir Richard Bellings, and were not at first communicated to the French ambassador.

Arlington was now readily won over to the project of a French alliance, and as lady Castlemaine regarded it with favour she was confirmed in the cause by judicious presents.[1] The agents employed by Charles were well chosen. Henry Jermyn, lord St. Albans, was admirably fitted for the post of ambassador-extraordinary in France; for he was by temperament more French than English, and combined the qualities of prudence and parsimony with the gambling instinct. As the confidant and possibly the husband of the queen-mother he was the elderly representative of the family interests. Sir Richard Bellings, private secretary to Queen Catherine, and lord Arundell of Wardour represented ardent, native Catholicism, and their comparative obscurity was an advantage in an affair requiring the utmost secrecy. While the real negotiations were being conducted by these men, Colbert de Croissy and Buckingham were kept busy with the long-projected commercial treaty,[2] which now served as a blind to the more serious commitments of the two monarchs.

By October 1669 the main principles of agreement had been reached, these being that France would undertake to assist Charles in two separate designs—the restoration of Catholicism in England, and the renewal of hostilities with the Dutch. It was now thought necessary to bring Colbert de Croissy into the secret; he was admitted to at least a version of it. In an interview with him early in November, Charles admitted that the project of restoring Catholicism in England might seem utter folly; but nevertheless he was convinced that, with the help of Louis, he could do it; for he was assured of the devotion of his troops; the governors of several of his garrisons were Catholics, and the Sectaries hated the Anglicans more than the Catholics. He was now convinced of the necessity of publicly confessing his Catholicism; not merely for spiritual reasons, but because only on this foundation could he restore the monarchy. The ambassador did his best to moderate this religious zeal in the English monarch,

---

[1] *Mignet*, iii. 87.

[2] Dispatch of Colbert de Croissy to Louis XIV, Nov. 13, 1669, in *Mignet*, iii. 100–6.

warning him of the danger of kindling tumult; for religion is a 'fire of brimstone and nitre', consuming everything in an instant; and moreover, with 20,000 ex-Cromwellian soldiers in London, it would be suicide to commence with the religious part of the compact. Why not begin with the war on Holland, since that would commend itself to English desires; and then, after a successful campaign, Charles could garrison the places allotted to him abroad with troops of whose obedience he was not certain, while at home he could depend on his veterans and new levies to enforce the change of religion? His subjects, satisfied with the material results of the war, and confronted with a king well armed for defence and attack, both at home and abroad, would thereupon acquiesce in the royal will, and subsidies could be obtained from parliament on the pretext that they were needed for war against the Dutch. These were the views of Louis, as communicated to the king by the ambassador. Charles concluded by saying that after all it might be best to begin with war on the Dutch; but he himself was impatient to launch the great spiritual enterprise. Louis expressed approval of the arguments which his agent had used to cool the religious ardour of Charles.[1]

During the breathing space of the long parliamentary recess (May 9, 1668–October 19, 1669) Charles ordered a review of his financial situation in order that he might determine how far he was dependent on parliamentary support. It was estimated that the total proceeds from the hereditary sources amounted to £1,030,000; and it was thought that by strict economy the Civil List might be reduced to £996,476. The lords commissioners of the Treasury were ordered on July 22, 1668, to put this report into execution.[2] It might have been possible to do so if provision had been made for clearing away existing debt, or making good the deficits in the Customs, Excise, and Hearth Money due to unforeseen causes, and if Charles had been able to limit his private expenditure to the moderate dimensions specified in the scheme of retrenchment. But it was soon obvious that the scheme was satisfactory only on paper, and that Charles was still

[1] *Mignet*, iii. 106.
[2] *Cal. S.P. Dom.*, *1667–8*, 499. For full details see *P.C. Reg.* 60, July 22, 1668.

dependent on the generosity, or rather the reasonableness of the Commons, and on the demands of those who ministered to his assiduous and indiscriminate proclivities. A second alternative had to be considered—that of summoning a new parliament which, it was assumed, would contain a considerable proportion of Dissenters, who might be willing to make substantial grants in return for toleration. But even Albemarle was against this project, because of the disorder which it might excite; nor was Charles willing to be at the mercy of men who were still marked by the stigma of republicanism. The Cavalier Parliament was suspicious, niggardly, and quarrelsome; but at least it would retain the monarchy by force rather than compromise; moreover, its intolerance was helping to maintain Protestant disunity, and so was of indirect service to the duke of York and the Catholic members of the Cabal. It was of service also to Buckingham, who encouraged its suspicion of the prerogative in order that he might make Charles more amenable to his influence.

It seemed inevitable, therefore, that Charles must submit to the yoke of his legislature. When parliament reassembled in October 1669 he announced[1] that the grant of £310,000 made early in 1668 had been wholly spent on the Navy, and on the special naval expenditure entailed by England's participation in the Triple Alliance. He earnestly desired his listeners to make some provision for the payment of his debts; at the same time a project for reuniting England with Scotland was recommended for favourable consideration. In their reply, the Commons showed that these things did not touch them deeply. They were more concerned about their privileges, as involved in the dispute *Skinner* v. *The East India Company*,[2] than about the danger of the executive falling into bankruptcy; more important for them than union with the northern kingdom were the accusations of embezzlement against sir George Carteret, formerly treasurer of the Navy, who after several heated debates was suspended[3] from the deliberations of the House by a narrow majority on December 10. At the same time it was proposed to impeach the earl of Orrery for fraud in the administration of Munster, and it was resolved to petition the king to allow witnesses to come over from Ireland.[4] Thus, instead of granting a supply, the Commons showed a dis-

[1] *L.J.* xii. 251–2. [2] See *infra*, ii. 469. [3] *Grey*, i. 214. [4] *Parl. Hist.* iv. 434–9.

position to investigate the administration of the finances in both England and Ireland, and the talk of impeachment recalled memories of the days of Strafford. On December 11 Charles suddenly prorogued both Houses until February 14, 1670. He had experienced nothing but disappointment and vexation from this session.

This prorogation coincided with the completion by Bellings of the first[1] draft of the secret treaty with France, a draft shown to Colbert de Croissy on December 18. Briefly summarized, its proposals were these. For his declaration of Catholicism Charles demanded £200,000 sterling, together with more money and armed assistance (at the charge of France) in the event of the announcement of Catholicism causing a rebellion in England ('ce qu'on ne croit pas'). A subsidy of £800,000 per annum was to be paid for English participation in the joint attack on Holland, the avowed purpose of which was to destroy the government of the States General. In Dutch territory England was to have the islands of Walcheren and Cadsand, while Flushing was to go to the prince of Orange, whose interests were to be safeguarded. Charles undertook to abide by the treaty of Aix-la-Chapelle, but in the event of Louis arranging a partition of Spanish territory, England was to have Ostend, Sluys, Minorca, and the Spanish American possessions, together with French help to take over these possessions. The declaration of Catholicism was to precede the war on Holland.

In suggesting these terms Charles may have over-estimated the generosity of Louis. The latter did not think that £200,000 was an exorbitant price for inducing Charles to enter the Catholic fold publicly; but he agreed with Colbert de Croissy that the £800,000 annual subsidy for the war was 'a thunder-clap which took his breath away'.[2] Charles reduced the amount to £300,000, but refused to concede the supreme command of the allied fleets to the French. While these negotiations were proceeding, he was quietly strengthening his position so as to increase his bargaining power in relation to both parliament and Louis XIV. Through Lauderdale, his lord high commissioner, he succeeded in persuading the Scottish estates to pass an act giving him power to

---

[1] *Mignet*, iii. 117–23.
[2] Colbert de Croissy to Louis XIV, Dec. 30, 1669, in *Mignet*, iii. 127.

use the Scottish militia outside their frontiers,[1] and at the same time he secured Ireland, after Ormonde's recall (March 1669), by appointing as lord lieutenants first the Presbyterian Robartes, who was known to be in sympathy with the king's toleration policy, and then (May 1670), after Robartes's dismissal, lord Berkeley of Stratton, who was entirely dominated by Catholic personages, including his secretary sir Ellis Leighton.[2] The treaty of Dover was thus preceded by changes in Scotland and Ireland intended to make it more possible for Charles to use these countries against England.

In thus playing one party against another Charles showed consummate skill; never indeed throughout his reign was he more actively employed than in the earlier months of 1670, when at last there seemed a prospect that he might one day free himself from the institution which trammelled his actions. The members who reassembled on February 14, 1670, may have been vaguely conscious that the situation was altering insensibly in favour of the executive; for they showed themselves more compliant than they had been in the previous autumn. Not only did they consent to erase from their records all entries relating to the case of Skinner and the East India Company,[3] but they hastened the consideration of supply, and voted an additional levy on wine and vinegar for seven years, estimated to produce about £400,000 per annum.[4] They even shelved the question of further research into the financial administration of Carteret; and when he adjourned them on April 11, Charles could with truth assure his Lords and Gentlemen that 'he was very well satisfied with the results of the meeting'.[5] The Dutch were also pleased; for the tax on wine and vinegar fell most heavily on French imports; and it was clear that the legislature did not favour commercial reciprocity with France. In this vote Louis might have detected an illustration of English sentiment towards his country; but neither economic considerations nor national opinion had any place in the great schemes which he was patiently perfecting.

With this accession of financial strength and popular goodwill Charles was in a better position for bargaining; and early in 1670 he enlisted the support of his sister, the duchess of Orléans, in his

[1] *Infra*, ii. 413.   [2] *Infra*, ii. 396–7.   [3] *Parl. Hist.* iv. 444.
[4] 22 Car. II, cap. iii.   [5] *L.J.* xii. 351.

efforts to secure the largest possible subsidies, a move probably made by the duke of Buckingham, who wished the two kings to negotiate as 'gentleman to gentleman'. From the point of view of the French monarch, Madame might be useful if she could induce her brother to undertake the war before the announcement of Catholicism, and a personal interview seemed the best expedient to effect this purpose; but many weeks were spent in obtaining the consent of the duke of Orléans, who was jealous lest his wife should acquire glory for herself, and so emancipate herself from his tutelage. The Dutch, moreover, were now convinced that some secret business was on foot, and Arlington had much trouble in keeping the insistent van Beuning at arm's length. At last the scruples of the duke of Orléans were overcome, and on May 16, 1670, Madame was at Dover, where she interviewed Charles. She may have repeated the French arguments for completing the war before the conversion; or she may even have suggested that the two might be combined;[1] but in any case it is doubtful whether she could have exercised much influence on her brother, who always kept his own counsels, and knew the conditions in England much better than she did; indeed, Charles probably welcomed the interview at Dover, not because it enabled him to discuss high policy, but because it provided the opportunity of meeting the only relative for whom he had any affection.[2] Six days later (May 22, 1670) the secret treaty of Dover was signed by Arlington, Arundell, Clifford, and Bellings for England, and by Colbert de Croissy for France.

The preamble to the secret treaty of Dover recited that only by a perfect union between their persons could the kings of England and France procure entire felicity for their subjects. Then followed these clauses:[3]

1. For the perpetual union and friendship between the two kings and their states articles so secret and advantageous to both monarchs have been agreed upon that a treaty of similar importance can hardly be found in any period of history.

[1] This is suggested in one of her letters; see K. Feiling, *Henrietta Stuart and the origins of the treaty of Dover* in *E.H.R.* xlvii.

[2] In Dec. 1661 Charles welcomed his sister's proposal of a meeting at Dunkirk. (*Aff. Étr. Angleterre*, 26, f. 17, Dec. 16, 1661.)

[3] For the text see *Mignet*, iii. 187–97.

2. The King of England, being convinced of the truth of the Roman Catholic religion is resolved to declare it, and to reconcile himself with the Church of Rome as soon as the state of his country's affairs permit. He has such confidence in the fidelity and affection of his subjects that none of them, not even those who (as yet) have been denied a full outpouring of divine grace, will fail in their due obedience to their sovereign. But as there are always unquiet spirits who mask their designs under the guise of religion, the King of England, for the peace of his kingdom, will avail himself of the assistance of the King of France, who, on his part, as he is anxious to contribute to a design glorious not only for the King of England, but for the whole of Catholic Christendom, promises to pay to the King of England the sum of two million livres tournois, the first half payable three months after ratification of the present treaty, the other half three months later. In addition, the King of France undertakes to provide, at his own expense, 6,000 troops for the execution of this design, if they should be required. The time for the declaration of Catholicism is left entirely to the discretion of the King of England.

3. The King of France will never violate the peace which he has concluded with Spain, nor will he do anything inconsistent with the terms of the treaty of Aix-la-Chapelle; so that it will be possible for the King of England to act in conformity with the conditions of the Triple Alliance.

4. If the King of France should acquire any fresh claims or rights on the Spanish dominions, the King of England will assist him by land and sea to enforce these rights.

5. Each of the contracting sovereigns has a sufficiently large population to justify their joint resolution to humble the pride of the States General, and to destroy the power of a people which has not only shown ingratitude to those who have helped it to create its republic, but has had the insolence to set itself up as a sovereign arbiter among other states. Accordingly both sovereigns will jointly declare war on the States General, and neither will engage in a treaty or truce without the other. All treaties between the States General and either of the contracting parties (except the Triple Alliance) shall be considered void.

6. In the joint hostilities agreed upon the King of France will defray all the expenses of the campaign by land, the King of England agreeing to supply at his charge 6,000 foot.

7. For the war by sea the King of England will arm at least 60 men-of-war and 10 fireships, to be joined by a French auxiliary

fleet of at least 30 good ships, the whole to be under the command of the duke of York. To assist the King of England to defray the costs of the campaign, the King of France undertakes to pay him each year the sum of three million livres tournois, for so long as the war may last. The English share of the conquests from the Dutch shall be Walcheren, Sluys and Cadsand. Both sovereigns undertake to exert themselves to procure that the Prince of Orange shall find his interests in the continuation and conclusion of the war.

8. Each sovereign shall do his utmost to persuade the kings of Sweden and Denmark to join in the war against the Dutch, or at least to remain neutral; an attempt will also be made to secure the participation of the electors of Cologne and Brandenburg, the house of Brunswick, the duke of Neuburg, and the bishop of Münster.

9. After the King of England has made the declaration specified in article 2, it will be free for the King of France to decide the time for the joint declaration of war.

10. Should there be found in any treaty of either crown with another state any clause inconsistent with the terms of this treaty, such clause shall be null and void.

11. In order to unite the interests of the subjects of both crowns, it is agreed that the treaty of commerce on foot[1] shall be brought to a conclusion as soon as possible.

The first difficulty confronting the execution of this secret treaty was that it had been signed by only two of the king's ministers and was unknown to the Protestant members of the Cabal, of whom Buckingham might prove the most troublesome if he found himself entirely excluded from confidence. It was resolved, therefore, to negotiate a second treaty identical with the first, except as regards the king's declaration of Catholicism. A convenient starting-point for the fictitious treaty was found in the visit of the marquis de Bellefonds to London in July 1670 on a mission of condolence on the death of Charles's sister.[2] The duke was anxious to be entrusted with the duty of returning this visit of courtesy and affection, a mission for which he was specially qualified; because he had been mainly responsible for bringing Madame into the negotiations, and he had been induced by Madame to enter into some kind of reconciliation with Arlington.

[1] See *supra*, 336–7.
[2] The duchess of Orléans died within about eight days after her return to France from Dover.

Louis agreed to play his part in the comedy. He interviewed Buckingham early in August, talked of his passionate desire to combine with Charles against the Dutch, and then instructed Lionne to draw up a treaty embodying his desires, adding that he would insist on Charles appointing the duke to command the English expeditionary corps. Louis was interested in Buckingham, whom he regarded as a typical English aristocrat; and at parting he gave him a present of 10,000 livres for his paramour, the countess of Shrewsbury.[1] George returned with this draft of the treaty, specially intended for him, and to a less extent for Lauderdale and Ashley; and Charles was pressed to expedite the conclusion of the 'Protestant' version of the alliance, since Louis wished to commence hostilities early in 1671. At the same time Charles (somewhat unnecessarily) was again adjured not to avow his Catholicism before the declaration of war, since that would have a bad effect on the German Protestant princes whose support was being sought.

Delays in the completion of the bogus treaty helped to confirm the impression of its genuineness. The three Protestant members of the Cabal insisted on better terms; in particular, they demanded Goeree and Woorne in addition to Cadsand and Walcheren; and when Colbert de Croissy found Charles ready to support this demand of his uninformed ministers, he must have felt, as had some of his predecessors, that the English were indeed 'drôle'. Arlington's natural indecision on these points confirmed Buckingham's opinion that his colleague was a knave as well as a fool. At last Louis consented to give up Goeree and Woorne; and so conquests which he had not yet made were disposed of in a treaty set on foot mainly to keep Buckingham out of mischief. But most enigmatic of all was Charles's conduct as a prospective convert. His religious zeal seemed suddenly to have cooled, and he declined Louis's offer to negotiate with the Papacy through a French prelate, as he would rather have an English intermediary. When Colbert de Croissy pressed the conclusion of the business by the method of Charles's own choice, a fresh objection was found: namely, the pope (Alexander VII) was old and ill; consequently it would be impolitic to entrust such an important secret to a moribund pontiff.[2] Throughout these

---

[1] *Mignet*, iii. 221–2.   [2] Ibid. iii. 237–42.

difficulties and delays the French monarch showed a patience and forbearance to which his biographers have not yet done justice.

Misunderstandings were not ended until December 1670 when at last (Dec. 21/31) the bogus treaty was signed on behalf of France by the French ambassador, and of England by all the members of the Cabal. Its terms were identical with those of the secret treaty except that the clause relating to the king's conversion was omitted; the payment on behalf of the 'Catholicité' was transferred to the first year of the annual subsidy for the war; Goeree and Woorne were added to the English share of Dutch territory, and the date for the declaration of war was fixed for the spring of 1672. Louis was anxious that the simulated treaty, as soon as sealed, should be annulled by a secret declaration signed by the two kings and the negotiators of the original treaty; but Charles, knowing the additional advantages secured for him in the bogus instrument, refused his assent, on the ground that the latter was the only agreement to which he could give public effect.[1] He undertook, however, to sign a declaration that the two millions accorded in the secret treaty were solely for the conversion, so that he could not claim this money in addition to the composite sum granted in the public document.[2] Thus, at the moment when Louis had accomplished what was apparently a great stroke of policy, there was a certain amount of obscurity in the conditions imposed on his tributary state; for there were two treaties, both valid; the first subsidizing Charles for his conversion, payment for which was to be made at a definite time, but the date of conversion was left to the discretion of Charles; while in the second treaty the reference to the conversion had to be omitted altogether, and its price was transferred to the first year of the annual subsidy for the war. On this important point of Charles's defection to Rome, and with it the hoped-for conversion of England, Louis was committed to pay the money; but Charles was not so clearly bound to fulfil his obligation, since the vagueness of his promises in the first treaty was capped by his complete silence in the second.

A more serious criticism of the treaty, from the *French* point of view, is that Louis thereby enlisted English help not for the main

[1] *Mignet*, iii. 255.   [2] Ibid. iii. 266.

object of his policy (to dismember the Spanish Empire), but for a secondary and subsidiary object, inspired not so much by high policy as by personal resentment, namely, to humiliate the Dutch. It is true that, if he annihilated Holland, Louis might more easily lay his hands on the Spanish Netherlands, but in view of the immense superiority of his army this was not necessary, a fact which had already been demonstrated in the campaigns of 1667; consequently, the Dutch war did not hold an essential position in the logical development of French designs. But it was otherwise in English policy. The first two Anglo-Dutch wars had left undetermined the question of maritime supremacy; and in 1665 Louis had been convinced of the danger to France that one of the sea-powers might obtain a definite superiority, so convinced indeed that he had exerted all his skill to prevent these powers seeking a decision.[1] Now, however, in 1670 his feelings towards the Dutch were so bitter that he was willing to pay England to join with him against them; though it was obvious that, until France was powerful enough at sea to challenge the two maritime powers, the defeat of one of these must redound to the advantage of the other. The attack on the Dutch, therefore, was a dangerous diversion in French diplomacy, but a perfectly legitimate development in English policy. Its execution did much to diminish indirectly the menace of Dutch rivalry, and so helped to make possible the great commercial and maritime expansion of England in the last decades of the seventeenth century. Without that development Chatham could never have challenged the Bourbons. That this initial advantage was obtained with the help of French money at the expense of a small state is the reason why Charles's conduct has always been unpopular in England, where considerations of policy are frequently subordinated to considerations of decency. Charles's guilt lay in this, that from Louis's ardent piety he obtained money; his merit, in that from Louis's indignation against the Dutch he obtained an advantageous offensive alliance against the commercial rivals of his countrymen; his skill, in obtaining a double set of terms, in both of which the obligations of France were clear, while his were easily capable of dispute. Adopting the methods of his French partner, he showed that he could beat him in a game which, by general

[1] See *supra*, 324.

consent of historians, is regarded not as a test of immorality, or low cunning, but of supreme intellectual ability.

When the two Houses met again on October 24, 1670, for their resumed ninth session, they were treated to a lengthy review of the state of foreign affairs by lord chancellor Bridgeman, in which credit was taken for Charles's participation in the Triple Alliance, 'which league produced that effect that it quenched the fire which was ready to set all Christendom in a flame'. Reference was also made to treaties into which England had entered with Savoy, Denmark, and Spain.[1] Attention was then drawn to the increasing maritime development of both Holland and France. Since 1660 the average annual cost of the English Navy had amounted, according to Bridgeman, to £500,000; a sum of £800,000 would be required to equip a fleet adequate for English commitments, or capable of contesting supremacy with our rivals.[2] The Commons responded with surprising alacrity. They granted a subsidy estimated to yield £800,000 to be raised by a levy on incomes and on personal and real estate;[3] an additional Excise on beer and ale,[4] and a new tax (for nine years) on proceedings at law.[5] Throughout the winter of 1670–1 this concord between legislature and executive was maintained; but on March 10, 1671, an ominous note was sounded when both Houses presented a petition against the growth of popery, which was attributed to the great numbers of priests and Jesuits frequenting London and Westminster, and to the laxity with which the law was administered.[6] Meanwhile the Bills of Supply had passed both Houses but had not yet been presented to the crown. Charles, now sure of the supplies, sacrificed the Catholics. He

[1] The treaty with Savoy (Sept. 9/19, 1669, *Dumont*, vii, pt. i. 119–20) granted entry for English ships into the Mediterranean port of Villefranche. The treaty with Denmark (Nov. 19/29, 1669, *Dumont*, vii, pt. i. 126–30) bound each party to assist against the other's enemies. The treaty with Spain, sometimes known as Godolphin's Treaty, was signed at Madrid on July 8/18, 1670 (*Dumont*, vii, pt. i. 137–9) and was intended to stop the depredations of both English and Spanish in American waters. Each country undertook to disavow piracy, to cease issuing letters of reprisal, and to open its harbours to refugees from pirates and storms. See *infra*, ii. 667.

[2] *L.J.* xii. 352–3.

[3] 22–3 Car. II, cap. iii. For the taxes generally see *infra*, ii, ch. xii.

[4] 22–3 Car. II, cap. v. It was for six years.

[5] Ibid., cap. ix.   [6] *C.J.* ix. 205–6; *L.J.* xi. 449–52.

appeased his parliament by a proclamation[1] requiring all Jesuits and Romish priests to leave England before May 1, 1671, and ordering all judges to put into force the laws against popish recusants. This was a curious commentary on the secret treaty which he had just signed. Having obtained this concession in return for their supplies, the Commons then threw their energies into a dispute with the Lords on their right to amend Money Bills.[2]

These events were of some importance in the evolution of Charles's policy. Hitherto, the intolerance of the Commons had been directed against the Dissenters, and in that intolerance Charles had been obliged to acquiesce; but meanwhile the secret inclinations of the king and the ardent propaganda of the duke of York had encouraged the activities of priests and Jesuits in high places, where their presence was bound to be noted; and moreover, the comings and goings between France and England had raised a crop of rumours, though the secret was still well kept. The Commons' address against Papists had served to impress on Charles the necessity for coming to a decision. Hitherto he had yielded in order to obtain supplies; but even thus the supplies were insufficient to enable him to pay his creditors; and there was now a prospect that parliament would force him to sacrifice not the Dissenters, but the Papists, in return for such inadequate grants. So on April 22, 1671, he thanked the two houses for their votes, assuring them that the money would be spent in paying his debts;[3] and by successive prorogations he suspended their meetings until February 4, 1672-3. In the interval of nearly two years he committed acts which had a profound reaction on the fate of his dynasty and the history of his country.

The determination of personal responsibility for these acts is one of peculiar difficulty, because Charles was as much at the mercy of his friends as of his enemies, and he preferred to arrive at his objective by indirect means. The most pressing question was the debt of his administration, amounting to about two million pounds, and the inevitability of bankruptcy unless some new source of income were added to those originally assigned to him by parliament. As an offset against this, there was the sum

---

[1] *Steele*, i. 3545, Mar. 23, 1671.
[2] *Infra*, 471-2.   [3] *L.J.* xii. 516.

to be paid by France to support his conversion to Catholicism, irrespective of when he avowed his Catholicism; and the promise of subsidies for a war which, it might well be supposed, parliament would approve and consequently support. Louis XIV had been convinced of Charles's religious zeal, and he had undertaken to pay the money not only in order that Charles should become a Catholic, but that he might restore Catholicism in England, by force if necessary, with such toleration for Protestants as was then considered due to them by established Catholic monarchs—that is, none.[1] Catholicism, as understood by European rulers, was not merely a system of personal beliefs, but a theory of government, based on tradition, order, and effective control; of this system Protestantism seemed the negation. Charles, as much as Louis, was convinced of this fact. He was pressed by the duke of York, and to a less extent by Clifford, to take the plunge, and, beginning with the avowal of Catholicism, to restore all of the royal prerogative that had been usurped by parliaments. Ever since the fall of Clarendon he had ruled by ministers fundamentally opposed in temperament and policy to the emphatically expressed wishes of the Commons; and there was every reason to think that, if he took the decisive step urged by his brother and paid for by his cousin, he would carry with him the support of the Cabal. A revolution might therefore very well have taken place in the years 1671–2. In that period parliament did not meet, and Charles was being asked not to do something novel, but to restore the traditional faith, to resume the old prerogative, to eliminate an institution which had proved the bane of his House, and bring England into line with the respectable Catholic monarchies of the Continent.

Had James been king, the revolution would have taken place. But Charles possessed intuition, which often served him better than the combination of industry and cleverness which wins admiration for monarchs. He was enough of an Englishman to realize that the country could not be ruled on the French pattern; moreover, he well knew that the debauchery of his own Court was not a true index of the state of England. Though pressed by friends and confidants he remained solitary among them all, committing his real thoughts to neither memoirs nor relatives,

[1] The Huguenots were still tolerated in France, but this ceased in 1685.

and deluding even his paramours into a belief in their influence. So he put off the declaration of his Catholicism indefinitely, knowing, as few of his advisers knew, the dangers of such a declaration; and he attempted a compromise for which there seemed a reasonable hope of success. When that compromise failed, he extricated himself with a quickness and dexterity which confounded his associates.

The middle way consisted in making active preparations to carry out one half of the bargain with Louis—that of the war with the Dutch; while, as regards the other half, he proposed to exercise a power supposed to be still inherent in the prerogative because never definitely surrendered; namely, that of suspending the enforcement of statutes where the forfeiture or part of it was the king's. At this time nothing in English law was 'more loose and disprincipled' than the suspending and dispensing power.[1] These were among the prerogatives of early kingship; but medieval thought had introduced the distinction that the king could neither suspend nor dispense with the laws of nature and the laws of God. Hence the distinction of *mala prohibita* and *mala in se*. Then came the additional complication—the ecclesiastical supremacy as defined in the reign of queen Elizabeth, which seemed to extend this residuary power of the crown; but Coke tempered it with the new doctrine that the king could not dispense with statutes relating to religion. By this time, the distinction between *mala prohibita* and *mala in se* had, as lord Guilford said, been reduced to a skeleton, since no two periods of history would be found in agreement regarding the categories of offences to be comprised in this distinction.

The earlier opponents of the prerogative such as Eliot had made much of the 'law of nature', by which inborn reason determines what is honest and what dishonest. Consequently, the king could not break his contracts; hence also, the royal rights of abrogation would apply only to civil laws, and not to those 'in which there is a divine and natural right';[2] in other words, the

---

[1] *Add. MS.* 32520, f. 3. Lord Guilford's papers. For a discussion of the dispensing power in ecclesiastical matters see E. F. Churchill in *Law Quarterly Review*, xxxviii, July and Oct. 1922. See also, for a good account, Holdsworth, *History of English Law*, vi. 217–25.

[2] Sir John Eliot, *De Jure Majestatis*, in *Works* ed. Grosart, i. 97.

king could suspend or dispense only where neither religion nor private property was concerned. But as natural rights appeared to have died a natural death at the Restoration, there was this to be said for the suspending and dispensing power, that neither in statute nor in common law did there exist anything very definite against their exercise. The first had hardly been used by Tudors or early Stuarts, but the second had frequently been invoked, and appeared to be limited only by the decision in the *Case of Monopolies* (1602–3) that a dispensation to defeat the spirit of an Act of Parliament was void. At the Restoration, such wide powers were attributed to the crown that it was thought possible to obtain revenue by granting toleration to those who would pay for licences, or compound for fines; indeed so natural seemed this assumption, that the committee for assessing Charles's revenue had made an estimate of how much might be derived from this source.[1] But as soon as Anglicanism was firmly established, it was found impossible to confirm the king's dispensing power by Statute;[2] accordingly, as the legislature refused to come to its aid, the crown would have to fall back on those older rights, the existence of which was tacitly recognized by the Commons themselves when they insisted on the insertion of the word 'nuisance' into the Bill prohibiting Irish cattle; for it was generally accepted that the king could not dispense with a law prohibiting a common nuisance. By exercising a branch of the power thus indirectly recognized, the crown only would suffer, since the forfeitures would be sacrificed; by a general suspension of the penal laws, Dissenters would benefit as well as Papists, and so there might be a large measure of popular support. The experiment, therefore, seemed worth trying. But it is evidence of the great advance or change in English opinion that what might have been effected with profit in 1660 could not be effected gratuitously in 1672.

Accordingly, on March 15, 1672, Charles issued his Declaration of Indulgence wherein, on the authority of his supreme power in ecclesiastical matters, he suspended the execution of all penal laws against nonconformists and recusants. The Declaration secured Roman Catholics from molestation provided they worshipped in their own houses, and allowed the dissenting

---

[1] See *supra*, 157.

[2] For the Bill of 1662–3 see *H.M.C. Rep.* vii, app. 167–8.

ministers to worship in public provided they obtained a licence.[1] Two months earlier (Jan. 20) had occurred the Stop of the Exchequer;[2] and so in the earlier months of 1672 Charles's government, already in partial bankruptcy, was staking everything on the last card of war against a Protestant power. Herein was the difference between the Second and the Third Dutch War. The former was waged at the solicitation of parliament on behalf of the mercantile interests, and might therefore be called national; the second was little more than a gamble, with Catholicism as one of the stakes.

With such dubious preliminaries Charles proposed to carry with him into the Third Dutch War a nation still mindful of the shame of the Medway, and resentful of Dutch prosperity, but now awakened to a suspicion of the real drift of royal policy. Before war was declared, the Dutch, thanks to French diplomacy, were surrounded by a ring of enemies which included the elector of Cologne and the bishop of Münster. The Emperor was neutral; the Swedish nobles were bribed to undertake an attack on any German prince coming to the help of the Dutch. Only to Spain or Brandenburg could Holland look for assistance. French money had secured this position that, whether from expectation of future rewards or from jealousy of each other, no combination against France seemed possible of formation, and whatever Louis could not win over he had sterilized. It remained only for his ally to find some plausible pretext for declaring war. In the summer of 1671 Temple was recalled from The Hague, and as the yacht *Merlin* conveying lady Temple passed through a Dutch fleet, the English captain fired because he was not saluted. Here was the required pretext. In December Downing 'le plus grand querelleur de la diplomatie britannique'[3] was sent to The Hague with orders to insist that the Dutch should lower their flag in the presence of even a single English warship. The reply of the Dutch was conciliatory; they would adhere to the

---

[1] For nearly a year these licences were issued. The number granted to Presbyterians was 848, to Independents 368, to Baptists 201; altogether more than 1,500 licences were issued. Many of the imprisoned, including about 500 Quakers were released. *Cal. S.P. Dom., 1672–3*, xxxvii–lx; F. Bate, *The declaration of indulgence*, 79 sqq.; W. C. Braithwaite, *The second period of Quakerism*, 81–6.

[2] *Infra*, ii. 448–9.   [3] Quoted in *Mignet*, iii. 694.

treaty of Breda which bound them to salute English ships, but not single English ships; nevertheless they were willing to discuss some regulation for avoiding confusion.[1]

As the *Merlin* incident failed to produce the required effect, stronger measures were resorted to. Early in March 1672 Holmes, with an inadequate force, was ordered to intercept off the Isle of Wight the large Dutch Smyrna fleet which was escorted by eleven warships. Holmes carried out his instructions, and engaged in a running fight on the afternoon and evening of March 12; but though he made a few captures, his own ships were so badly disabled that he had to give up the attempt. This seemed good enough, so on March 17, 1672, two days after the issue of the Declaration of Indulgence, Charles declared war on the States General.

[1] *S.P. For. (Holland)*, 188. Boreel to Charles II, Jan. 28/Feb. 7, 1672.

X

THE THIRD ANGLO-DUTCH WAR, 1672–4

AT the moment when war was declared neither of the aggressors thought that hostilities were likely to be prolonged; for the Dutch must, it was thought, succumb to the joint naval and military offensive launched against them. Louis XIV professed that the war was a semi-divine punishment on a recalcitrant race; to Charles, the episode was part of a personal bargain, the execution of which was not without advantage to his subjects; to the Dutch, the war brought disaster, revolution, and a heroic struggle for national existence.

The terms of Anglo-French naval co-operation were formulated[1] on February 5, 1672. It was arranged that at least 30 French warships and 8 fireships were to fit out at Brest so as to join the duke of York by April 25 as the White squadron, its precedence to be immediately after the Red, which together with the Blue was to comprise at least 50 English ships. Facilities for repair and refit of French ships were to be provided at English ports; interchange of intelligence was to be effected by means of fast frigates. Supreme command was entrusted to the duke of York, flying his flag in the *Prince* (100 guns), having as his immediate subordinate the French vice-admiral D'Estrées, whose renown originated from land exploits.[2] Serving under D'Estrées was Duquesne, between whom and his chief there was rooted antipathy. On the English side there were several notable officers, such as Sandwich, admiral of the Blue (*Royal James*), sir Joseph Jordan (*Sovereign*), sir John Harman (*Royal Charles*), sir John Kempthorne (*St. Andrew*), and sir Robert Holmes (*St. Michael*). To these allied leaders it seemed likely that the Dutch would avoid attack and take shelter behind their sand-dunes; but Charles made no secret of his belief that De Ruyter and his lieutenants were formidable antagonists, likely to take advantage of every opportunity; he suggested therefore that the

---

[1] In *Colenbrander*, ii. 79 sqq.

[2] For his character see La Roncière, *Histoire de la Marine française*, v. 549–51.

French ambition of boarding enemy vessels might be deferred until the enemy was in disorder.[1] On his side Louis issued instructions showing solicitude about salutes, and a desire that French sailors would prove their superiority to the English in valour.[2] On May 3, 1672, Charles himself inspected the French naval contingent at Spithead, where he may have noted that our allies were lacking in fast frigates, and that their smaller craft were scarcely fitted for the storms of the North Sea. Such were the auspices of Anglo-French co-operation in the Third Dutch War.

In ships, guns, and men the French and English had a clear superiority over the Dutch, for together they had about 98 warships to the enemy's 75; the former carrying 6,000 guns and 34,000 men, while the enemy strength was 4,500 guns and 20,000[3] men. So far from being alarmed at the size of the forces arrayed against them, the Dutch, from their experience of the French, thought that England would derive little help from her associates; some indeed thought that they would prove an embarrassment rather than a help. Dutch preparations were at first impeded by difficulty in securing effective co-operation with the Zeeland contingent; but under De Ruyter's command there was eventually attained a greater unity of action than had been possible in the preceding war, and the dramatic events which followed in quick succession gave to the Dutch defence a unity and heroism which the combined forces of England and France could not break.

The immediate tactical object of De Ruyter was to fall on the English fleet before its junction with the French, for which purpose he cruised, late in April, between Sole Bay and the North Foreland. Failing to meet with enemy ships he entered the Channel, but could not proceed far owing to contrary winds and fog. He then sailed to the Flemish coast in the hope of luring the enemy there. There was even talk among the Dutch of repeating the attack on the Medway, but this was abandoned when it was learnt that Sheerness was well defended.[4] Mean-

---

[1] La Roncière, *Histoire de la Marine française*, v. 531–2.
[2] Instructions to D'Estrées, March 4, 1672, in *Colenbrander*, ii. 85.
[3] Clowes, *The Royal Navy*, ii. 301, and De Jonge, *Geschiedenis van het Nederlandsche Zeewesen*, ii. 286. [4] Blok, *De Ruyter*, 318–19.

while, having joined forces at Spithead on May 3–4, the allied fleets put to sea, and on the 19th came upon De Ruyter off the coast of Zeeland. The enemy tacked towards the land, followed closely by the allies, but a thick fog next day prevented the fleets coming to action. As fresh water was running low, English and French put into Southwold Bay (Sole Bay) on the Suffolk coast.

On May 27, when the wind came easterly, Sandwich advised putting to sea lest they might be caught on a lee shore; but this advice was overruled by the duke of York, who thought that the Dutch were intent on hiding behind their shoals. Next day the wisdom of Sandwich's opinion was verified; because at 2.30 a.m., while the duke's ship was still on the careen, firing was heard to windward, and scouts brought news of the approach of De Ruyter. This took the allies by surprise. The wind was now east by south, and the combined fleets were anchored parallel with the shore, the French (the van) being to the south, and the rear (Sandwich) to the north. Having righted his ship the duke ordered the fleet to weigh, and by sunrise he could see the enemy ships bearing north-east from him.[1] As the allies stood north to engage (in some disarray, for all the ships had not yet joined) the French van became the rear—a fact which may have had some influence on their subsequent conduct. The Dutch, sailing on the starboard tack, were in two divisions, line abreast; the advanced division consisting of about 18 units, followed by the main fleet in three squadrons, commanded by Van Ghent (right), De Ruyter and Van Nes (centre), and Banckers (left); their total armament amounting to 61 capital ships, 14 frigates, 22 scouts, and 32 fireships.[2] De Ruyter, accompanied by Cornelius De Witt, flew his flag in the *Seven Provinces*.

By 6 a.m. the Blue and the Red were engaged with Van Ghent and De Ruyter respectively, all sailing north-north-east, parallel with the coast, the allies not yet completely recovered from the disorder of their sudden departure. D'Estrées's instructions from the duke were 'to keep his wind as much as possible'; but for some reason he disobeyed this order by putting round to the

[1] The duke of York's account of this battle is in the Pepysian Library, MS. 2873, f. 137 sqq. See also Clarke, *Life of James II*, i. 463 sqq.

[2] Clowes, op. cit. ii. 303, and Blok, op. cit. 321.

port tack and sailing south-east by south, on which course he
was followed by Banckers and a portion of the Dutch left.
Subsequent recrimination with his captains did not help to
redeem D'Estrées's conduct, and though some of his ships fought
well in this battle, the French contingent did not have the chance
of justifying the hopes of their king that they would prove superior
in valour to the English.[1] It was an early demonstration of the
value of the French alliance.

Meanwhile English and Dutch were hammering it out with
a ferocity of which earlier conflicts had given ample evidence.
As the Dutch were to windward and had a large supply of fireships, the duke, to prevent panic, ordered that no man should
mention the word fireship, and that notice of the approach of
one should be referred to only in a whisper.[2] De Ruyter chose
York's flagship as the special object of his attack, and came up
so close that he seemed determined to board her; but changing
his mind he luffed, and directed his energies to disabling the
English ships as a preliminary to burning them. By the time,
however, that he was ready to use fireships the wind had dropped
so much that they had to be towed, and were then beaten off
without difficulty. But with De Ruyter on her bow and Van
Nes on her quarter the plight of the royal flagship was soon
desperate; by 10 a.m. her rigging had been shot away and 200
of her crew killed, so that the duke had to shift his flag to the
St. Michael. When close to the sand-banks off Lowestoft the
St. Michael had to put about, and on her port tack to the south-
east was obliged to pass through the gauntlet of the Amsterdam
squadron to windward and De Ruyter to leeward, whereupon
several third- and fourth-rates 'very seasonably' got ahead of
her, and with five feet of water in her hold the new flagship
just managed to keep afloat. Simultaneously, the contest between Sandwich (*Royal James*) and Van Ghent (*Dolfin*) was
being fought to a finish. The Dutch admiral was killed; the
Royal James, set on fire by a fireship, blew up, leaving hundreds
of her crew struggling in the water, many of whom were rescued
by the *Dartmouth*. Sandwich, who had fought magnificently,
got away from his sinking ship in an overcrowded rowing boat,

[1] For the French account see La Roncière, op. cit. v. 535 sqq.
[2] Clarke, op. cit. i. 465.

but it capsized, and he was drowned. Several days later his body was recovered and given burial in Westminster Abbey.[1]

The heroic resistance of Sandwich and the death of Van Ghent served for a time to put the Dutch out of action, thus enabling what remained of the English Blue to come to the support of the Red in the fight with De Ruyter. At 5 p.m. sir R. Holmes informed the duke that the *St. Michael* could no longer remain in the line, so the royal commander-in-chief transferred his flag again, this time to the *London*, taking an hour to row from one ship to the other. By 6 p.m. when some kind of formation had again been resumed, both fleets stood south in order to join with the roving D'Estrées and the hovering Banckers; but by dusk the fight was at an end, and both fleets returned to their coasts. De Ruyter confessed that this was the most obstinately contested battle in his experience.

Like most drawn battles, that of Sole Bay was claimed as a victory on both sides.[2] It had been marked by great feats of gallantry, and by heavy losses in men and ships, the English casualties being estimated at 2,500 men.[3] De Ruyter had added to his laurels by skilful handling of the weaker side; but earlier in the fight he had not fully utilized the advantage of the weather gage, nor had his fireships (of which 11 were destroyed) done all that was expected of them. The action was decisive, however, in this sense that it prevented the English from obtaining mastery of the North Sea, and so made a landing on the Dutch coast a very problematic enterprise. Had the Dutch been completely defeated, the war might have come to an end at this point; for they could not have withstood disaster on both flanks; it was therefore her sea-power that preserved the independence of the United Provinces. For France, the battle served as an apprenticeship in the art of naval warfare;[4] for England, it accentuated that hatred of the French which was soon to supersede dislike of the Dutch.

[1] F. R. Harris, *Sandwich*, ii, chs. xv and xvi.

[2] According to the Dutch account they had lost three men-of-war, 1,700 men, and about 900 mortally wounded. Seven of their ships had to be towed in. They had fought the English on their coast, and the enemy had gone away from them (Major Scott's news from a Zeeland deputy, in *S.P. For.* (*Holland*), 189, June 3).

[3] Clowes, op. cit. ii. 308.   [4] La Roncière, op. cit. v. 534.

The battle coincided with the launching of a devastating attack by Turenne and Condé. On May 30 Louis XIV crossed the Rhine; the province of Utrecht was speedily evacuated, and Over Yssel was occupied by the combined troops of the duke of Luxemburg, the elector of Cologne, and the bishop of Münster. From Bodegrave the prince of Orange maintained a persistent defence with small detachments of troops; but the States General were forced on June 16 to ask Louis on what terms he would grant peace. So humiliating, however, were the terms proposed that, desperate as was their plight, the States refused them. Yielding to the popular demand, the States General rescinded the edict of 1667 whereby the Stadholderate had been abolished; and on June 30 the prince took the oaths as Stadholder of Holland and Zeeland. Within a few weeks the De Witt brothers were assassinated and for a time Orange dictatorship was superimposed on the burgher federalism of the Dutch.

These events quickly following on each other produced a complete change in the diplomatic situation. Having survived the first shock of the attack, and having set their house in order, the Dutch were now concentrating on the maintenance of an obdurate resistance, and the breaking down of the diplomatic isolation in which the activities of Louis had placed them. At first, even Charles failed to keep pace with events; for he was still thinking in terms of the secret treaty of Dover. He made a bid for the retention of Spanish neutrality by confiding to the queen of Spain his secret intention of avowing the true faith and restoring it in England,[1] while to Colbert de Croissy he intimated that he was about to send a priest to Rome for definite advice regarding the 'Catholicité', towards which pious object he hoped the French clergy would be willing to make a contribution.[2] Thus, while his contemporaries were thinking of little else than guns and offensive treaties, the king of England was trying to extract still more juice from the over-ripe orange of religion. But suddenly the overthrow of the two De Witts and the advancement of his nephew opened up a new possibility, since negotia-

[1] *Aff. Étr. (Angleterre)*, 103, f. 138. Colbert de Croissy to Louis XIV, March 14, 1672: quoted in V. Barbour, *Arlington*, 188.

[2] *Aff. Étr. (Angleterre)*, 103, f. 213. Colbert de Croissy to Louis XIV, May 9, 1672; quoted in V. Barbour, *Arlington*, 188.

tions might, he thought, be concluded with William, profitable to both parties and not unacceptable to Louis. By such negotiations Charles would keep the British public 'amused' by hopes of peace, and so prevent demonstrations in England against the French or in favour of the Dutch.

Buckingham was an obvious tool for this enterprise; with him was coupled Arlington, whose devotion to Charles sometimes outran his discernment. These two were commissioned on June 21 to treat for a peace with 'the States General or any other princes and states concerned in the present war'.[1] The bases on which the commissioners were empowered to treat included (1) recognition of England's claim to the salute, (2) payment of a subsidy for war expenses, (3) the cession of cautionary towns such as Flushing, Sluys, and Brill, with a subsidy for maintenance of garrisons there, (4) favourable conditions for the prince of Orange, (5) an annual subsidy for the herring fishing, (6) adjustment of trade in the East Indies, and (7) a year's grace for the departure of Englishmen from Surinam.[2] With these instructions the plenipotentiaries landed at Maeslandsluys on June 23, where they were met with shouts of 'God bless the king of England, God bless the prince of Orange, and God confound the States', and there they witnessed scenes reminiscent of the burning of the Rump. Proceeding with his colleague to the prince's camp, Buckingham attempted to dazzle that youth with hopes of sovereignty under English and French patronage, the alternative being annihilation;[3] but these threats made little impression on the hard-grained Stadholder, who had already inaugurated his life-long campaign against Louis XIV. After this failure, they proceeded to Louis's camp near Utrecht, where they concluded the treaty of Heeswick, whereby England and France undertook not to treat with the Dutch except on conditions which, for France, were identical with those already rejected by the States and, for England, were similar to those enumerated in the original instructions to the two plenipoten-

[1] Instructions quoted in *Colenbrander*, ii. 141 sqq.
[2] Surinam in Guiana. It had been restored to the Dutch by the treaty of Guiana.
[3] Monmouth, Buckingham, and Arlington to Clifford, June 24, in *S.P. For. (Holland)*, 189.

tiaries. These combined terms were forwarded to the prince of Orange, who communicated them to the States General, by whom they were rejected; this public refusal was dispatched to the English envoys as the prince's reply to their offer. Arlington and Buckingham next proceeded to Antwerp, where they attempted, by threats of war, to bully the Spanish viceroy into neutrality, under-estimating the Spanish sense of honour, as they had already under-estimated the Dutch pride of independence.

Thus the English embassy had failed in its mission, and Charles remained committed to a war becoming every day more unpopular. The turning-point came early in July 1672 when a storm dispersed from the Texel an allied fleet which was awaiting an opportunity of putting ashore a landing party. Meanwhile the French army, dispersed over scattered garrisons, could attempt nothing decisive in what remained of the summer of 1672, and was forced to sit still in the hope that winter frosts would make possible further penetration into Holland.

As the time for the autumn session of parliament approached, the cleavage of opinion among Charles's advisers became more acute. Arlington, now aware of the realities of the situation was anxious for peace, knowing as he did that the war was unpopular, and that English demands would have to be moderated. Even more, he realized that the Dutch were certain to make the most of the difficulties likely to be created by parliamentary criticism of the war.[1] That these fears were well grounded was shown by the visit to England in January 1673 of two Dutch agents Gerbrandt Zas and William Arton, who were commissioned to investigate and influence opinion in England. They were sent to the Tower as spies,[2] and the suspicion that they were in the pay of William of Orange served to demonstrate that the prince was not likely to be detached from his countrymen by a separate Anglo-Dutch peace. An empty treasury and Louis's refusal to grant a loan (in addition to the subsidy) reduced Arlington to the impotence of despair. In Clifford, now lord treasurer, and other survivors from the Cabal, Charles found more buoyant supporters; so when parliament eventually did

[1] V. Barbour, *Arlington*, 200.
[2] They were tried by a special commission and ordered to be shot. *P.C. Reg.* 63, Feb. 15, 1673; also *Cal. S.P. Dom., 1672–3*, 428, 483–4, 605.

meet (Feb. 4, 1672–3), Charles, having declared that he was resolved to adhere to his Declaration of Indulgence, boldly demanded a supply. Shaftesbury followed suit with his famous *Delenda est Carthago* speech, which was intended to persuade the Commons that this war like its immediate predecessor was their war. 'The States of Holland', he declared, 'are England's eternal enemy both by interest and inclination.' Still ignorant of the secret treaty of Dover, he waxed eloquent on the king's concern for Protestantism, and repudiated the insinuation that the forces raised for the war were to be directed against the liberties and property of Englishmen. The chancellor gave to parliament his verbal guarantee that English institutions were absolutely secure.[1]

The Commons concerned themselves at first, not with the great issues raised in the speeches of king and chancellor, but with a violation of their privileges. During the vacation Shaftesbury had issued writs for the election of thirty-six members to fill vacancies created in the prorogation of nearly two years. Eight of these were in Dorset, where his family influence was strongest; and there was good reason to suppose that, here as elsewhere, the chancellor had used his connexion in order to obtain fresh supporters for the Court. Having first unseated the thirty-six members so elected, the Commons affirmed the principle that the issue of writs rested solely with their House.[2] They then (Feb. 17), somewhat to the surprise of the court, voted an eighteen months' assessment of £70,000 per month, a vote sufficient not only for securing a peace, but for continuing the war. But before proceeding further with this tempting bait, the Commons took up that part of the king's speech where Charles had declared his policy to be unchangeable—the Declaration of Indulgence. They presented an address (Feb. 14, 1673) declaring that penal laws in matters ecclesiastical could be suspended only by parliament; this they coupled with a resolution to bring in a Bill of Relief for Protestant dissenters, a proposal which was narrowed in committee to 'ease for Protestant subjects that will subscribe to the doctrines of the church of England and take the oaths of allegiance and supremacy'.[3]

[1] *L.J.* xii. 524–6, Feb. 5, 1672–3. [2] *C.J.* ix. 248, Feb. 6.
[3] Ibid. ix. 252.

Meanwhile (Feb. 22) no answer had yet been received by the Commons to their protest against the attempt to exercise the suspending power. In debate on the question whether to press the king for a reply, a rudimentary distinction of parties was clearly demonstrated; indeed, when sir T. Meres spoke on behalf of 'a few plain, country gentlemen who, though rude and unmannerly, had as good hearts as the best of their fellow members', he was suggesting a distinction between those who were honoured with the confidence of the Court and those who were not, a distinction at once dismissed as unparliamentary by secretary Coventry, who contended that there was no reason to discriminate between the loyalty of these two sections of the House.[1] At last, on February 24, came the king's long-awaited answer to the Commons' address. He was troubled, he said, that his Declaration should be the cause of such disquiet, and that the Commons should question his power in ecclesiastical matters, a prerogative never challenged in the reigns of any of his predecessors. He made no pretence of suspending laws where the properties, rights, or liberties of his subjects were concerned; nor had he presumed to alter anything in the established doctrine or discipline of the Church of England; but nevertheless he would concur in any Bill for securing the ease of Dissenters and the peace of Church and Kingdom.[2]

But this did not content the Commons. They objected that the reply left untouched the question of the suspending power; and after a prolonged debate, led by sir T. Meres and sir William Coventry, they presented a second address (Feb. 26) submitting that the king's answer was not sufficient to clear any apprehensions that might remain of a royal right to suspend penal statutes in matters ecclesiastical 'wherein Your Majesty has been much misinformed'.[3] A further stage towards the Test Act was reached two days later when it was resolved that all refusing to take the oaths of allegiance and supremacy and to receive the sacraments according to the Church of England should be incapable of any public employment, military or civil.[4]

For a time the storm-centre was transferred to the Lords. On

---

[1] *Grey*, ii. 52–3. For the name Country Party and the names whig and tory see *infra*, ii.   [2] *C.J.* ix. 256.
[3] *Grey*, ii. 62.   [4] *C.J.* ix. 260.

March 1 Charles addressed them[1] with a complaint of the messages he had received from the Commons, and solicited their advice. Clifford defended the Declaration in a wild speech which, in the opinion of Charles, who was present to hear it, did more harm than good to the cause of the prerogative. Of the king's advisers, Arlington alone believed that Charles would be obliged to surrender; on the other hand, Buckingham and Lauderdale advised insistence on the Declaration and dissolution of parliament. Shaftesbury had at first been of their opinion; but, always quick to detect a change of wind, he perceived that the Lords might stand by the Commons in a matter which appeared to trench on the integrity of the Church of England; and moreover, he may have been won over to Arlington's opinion by the latter's revelation to him at this time of the terms of the secret treaty of Dover. The French ambassador was in favour of Charles's withdrawal from the false position in which he had placed himself; only Clifford and the duke of York were totally opposed to compromise. Thus the issue was becoming narrowed to the alternatives of Protestantism or Revolution—Protestantism as understood by the Anglican House of Commons, and Revolution, as hinted at in the secret commitments of Charles, the purport of which could be guessed from the pages of a pamphlet, *England's appeal from the private cabal at Whitehall to the Grand Council of the Nation*, which was widely circulated in England in March 1673. This pamphlet, attributed to the authorship of one of William of Orange's paid agents, hinted at the 'liberality' of Louis XIV and its possible connexion with the displacement from Charles's counsels of men having Protestant sympathies, such as Ormonde.[2]

Had Charles been assured of the support of the Lords at this crisis he might have defied the Commons, but he was speedily disillusioned of his hope that the Lords would accept his invitation to join him against the Lower House; for the Peers responded to his appeal by assuring him that his answer, in referring the points in question to parliamentary procedure, was good and gracious.[3] The courtesy of the answer could not conceal its

---

[1] *L.J.* xii. 539.
[2] Barbour, *Arlington*, 210. The pamphlet is in *State Tracts* (1688).
[3] *L.J.* xii. 542, March 4, 1672–3.

significance. Toleration must, the message implied, come in only by a parliamentary way; the king must therefore abandon the Declaration and leave the Commons to proceed by Bill. On March 8, 1673, Charles took a step which no other male Stuart would have taken—he cancelled the Declaration of Indulgence.[1] Public rejoicings in the streets of London signalized this, the most important royal surrender of the century. A week later the Money Bill was ordered to be engrossed.

In addition to the Money Bill (i.e. an Assessment)[2] two measures were now before the Commons—a Bill for granting ease to the Dissenters, and another for preventing the dangers that might arise from popish recusants. The former, having been read a third time on March 19, was sent to the Lords, where it was mangled by amendments, and eventually wrecked by the prorogation of March 29. The other Bill had a very different fate. At its third reading, a proviso was accepted for a clause renouncing the doctrine of transubstantiation, in spite of secretary Coventry's indignant protest,[3] 'will you exclude God?'; and with this proviso the Commons believed they had a test so watertight that not even the pope could find a leak in it. This measure, which passed both Houses and received the royal assent on March 29, is better known as the Test Act.[4] Briefly summarized, it incapacitated from offices and places of trust under the crown all persons refusing to take the oaths of allegiance and supremacy, together with the sacrament according to the Church of England. All persons taking the oaths were required to subscribe this declaration:

I declare that I believe that there is not any Transubstantiation in the sacrament of the Lord's Supper, or in the elements of Bread and Wine at or after the consecration thereof by any person whatsoever.

Refusal to take the oaths and subscribe the declaration incapacitated not only from public office but also from the prosecution of any suit in law or equity, the guardianship of children

---

[1] *C.J.* ix. 266.

[2] 25 Car. II, cap. i. This was a grant of £1,238,750 to be raised by an eighteen months' assessment. [3] *Grey*, ii. 97, March 12, 1673.

[4] 25 Car. II, cap. ii. Sometimes referred to as the Test Act, no. i, in distinction from that of 1678 which imposed affirmations of religious belief on members of both Houses.

or the fulfilment of an executorship. The Act was without prejudice to the rights of peers in hereditary offices, and the drawing
of pensions or salaries granted by His Majesty for valuable
consideration. Incapacity extended also to Protestants by birth
who brought up their children in the popish manner.

So far, therefore, as oaths and declarations could do so, the
Test Act confined the privileges of full citizenship to those communicants of the Church of England who conscientiously rejected the doctrine that the elements of the sacrament were
turned into something other than bread and wine by the priest's
blessing; and thus office-holding was in effect confined to the
public professors of both the Erastianism and the Protestantism
of the Church of England. Charles must have known that it
was a heavy price for the parliamentary grant; but he had little
choice, and he had been pressed by Colbert de Croissy to
acquiesce. It was the clearest possible repudiation of the tentative efforts at toleration which, with fluctuations, had influenced
Charles's policy ever since the Declaration of Breda; moreover,
its terms were formulated in such a way as to exclude the
crypto-Papists. At a time when definition and authority were
of paramount importance in politics and religion alike, the Test
Act provided something which served both as a religious formulary and a written constitution, and its maintenance came
to be indelibly associated with the security of the English
Monarchy and Anglican Protestantism.[1] Its strength lay in its
intolerance and exclusiveness, a fact which came to be appreciated by English Catholics and Dissenters; because, in place of
the shifting sands of latitude and compromise, it substituted the
rock of rigid dogma, and transformed a Reformation doctrine
from a spiritual conviction into a national safeguard.

The spring session of 1673 concluded in a manner which
recalled the Long Parliament of 1640. On March 25 two
addresses to the king were adopted by the Commons. The first
was a request that no Papist should be employed as soldier or
commander in Ireland; the second was that the proclamation[2]
of December 4, 1672 might be withdrawn, because its provisions for dealing with disorders committed by soldiers appeared to exempt them from the ordinary course of justice.[3]

---

[1] For this see *infra*, ii. 516–17.   [2] *Steele*, i. 3576.   [3] *C.J.* ix. 276–7.

Complaints of abuses in the pressing and billeting of soldiers, and the demand that all soldiers should be immediately disbanded on the conclusion of hostilities, revealed the nature of the fears prompting the address. These requests, which were not presented as conditions preceding supply, met with Charles's non-committal answer that he would consider them, and that before their next meeting he would take care that no man should have reason to complain. There then followed (Mar. 29) a debate on whether these addresses should be printed. Secretary Coventry compared the practice to the Remonstrances of the Long Parliament; sir Richard Temple condemned the proposal as an appeal to the people; while Mr. Swynfyn thought that they should be printed 'in order that a countryman should have something to show'.[1] It was eventually recognized that the Licensing Act made the proposal impracticable. In the afternoon, while the Lords were still debating amendments to the Bill for ease of Dissenters, the king came to the House and passed eight public Acts, including the Money Bill and the Test Act. The remaining six included an Act which, when received from the Lords by the Commons, had been passed with some demur, a Bill for a general pardon of all crimes, including high treason, murder, and perjury, not otherwise excepted, before and up to March 25, 1673.[2] Parliament was then adjourned to October 20, 1673. Thus, though Charles had been forced to yield to the Commons in the matter of the suspending power, he had nevertheless secured an unexpectedly liberal supply; and he had obtained a measure of legal immunity for the advisers who had co-operated in his secret policy.

The immediate result of the Test Act was that the duke of York had to retire from public life (June 1673); the office of lord high admiral was put into commission, and the command of the fleet was entrusted to prince Rupert. Ormonde was again admitted to a share of the king's confidence, though he remained out of office until 1677. Churchmanship, stability, and respectability—these were now the requirements of statesmanship. Arlington, Buckingham, and Shaftesbury had to be retained as ostensible representatives of Protestantism, but their tenure was precarious; for the versatility of the first two made

[1] *Grey*, ii. 174–6.   [2] 24–5 Car. II, cap. iv.

them suspect to the Commons, and the gyrations of the third were beginning to trouble Charles, not because they were gyrations, but because they were always explained on the ground of high principle. As events forced Charles to work with ministers rather than conspirators, he quietly adapted himself to the change, accepting parliamentary domination under compulsion, but still intent on that system of government in which neither parliament nor public opinion had any place.

These few weeks of parliamentary activity in the spring of 1673 clearly reflected the strange conflict of fear and impulse through which England was passing. There still remained the old commercial jealousy of the Dutch, but it was yielding to hatred of aggressive France. There was the public policy of Charles, ostensibly national because anti-Dutch; but there was increasing suspicion of the secret policy, which subordinated Whitehall to Versailles. Concern for Protestantism was intensified by our war against a state where the Protestants were in a majority, especially as we were joined with a Catholic ally; but were the Dutch so very religious?

> What injuries soe'er upon us fall,
> Yet still, *the same religion* answers all;
> Religion wheedled you to civil war,
> Drew English blood, and Dutchmen's now would spare;
> Be gulled no longer, for you'll find it true,
> They have no more religion, faith, than you.[1]

It was characteristic of this confusion that two entirely different policies were pursued. On the one hand there was propaganda, assisted by secretary Williamson, for the purpose of inciting hatred of the Dutch. The government appears to have supplied information for Henry Stubbe's *Justification of the present war against the United Netherlands*.[2] Marvell's sarcastic *Character of*

---

[1] Dryden, prologue to *Amboyna*.

[2] This may be the book which was licensed by express order from Arlington (*Cal. S.P. Dom.*, *1672-3*, 629). For Stubbe's communications with Williamson see *Cal. S.P. Dom.*, *1672*, 284, 319, 323. It is noteworthy that Stubbe drew up an *Enquiry into the spiritual supremacy of the kings of England*, but this does not appear to have been printed (*Cal. S.P. Dom.*, *1672-3*, 350). For another example of war propaganda see *The Dutch Usurpation, or a brief view of the behaviour of the States General* (1672), published over the name (possibly pseudonymous) of W. de Britaine.

Holland was freely circulated; the massacre of Amboyna became an inspiration of literature not disdained by Dryden,[1] and its details were rehearsed on an open stage at Charing Cross[2] in company with farces and drolls. On the other hand, there was an attempt to induce Dutchmen to transport themselves and their possessions into England in accordance with the royal proclamation of June 1672.[3] Ireland, it was thought, would benefit specially from these thrifty immigrants; Dover and Yarmouth would profit by the naturalization of foreign fishermen, who would bring their boats and gear. In the Commons a Bill for the naturalization of foreign Protestants was debated,[4] but did not survive the adjournment; nevertheless, a number of Dutchmen were naturalized,[5] and a small community of Dutch weavers settled in Somerset.[6] England began her second year of war with the Dutch in the midst of attempts to induce them to come and settle among us.

There were delays in fitting out the fleet, delays mainly caused by the division of duties between the Navy Board and the Board of Admiralty commissioners appointed to carry out the duties of the lord high admiral. Sir Robert Holmes was not given a command because of his interest with the duke of York; sir Edward Spragge could not hoist his flag until he had returned from his mission to France, where he was consulting with D'Estrées on the general plan of campaign. As a result of these consultations it was decided that the French squadron, instead of forming the van, should be placed in the centre, where, as Colbert explained[7] to Louis, it would sustain 'the fiercest shock of the attack'. The French monarch was not informed of another reason for this change—namely, to prevent a repetition of D'Estrées's tactics at the battle of Sole Bay. Had the allies been ready for vigorous action in April 1673 they might well have effected a landing on the coast of Zeeland, as the Dutch

[1] In his *Amboyna, or the cruelties of the Dutch to the English merchants* (1673).
[2] *Cal. S.P. Dom.*, *1672–3*, 148, Nov. 11, 1672.
[3] *Steele*, ii. 2361, June 22.   [4] *Parl. Hist.* iv. 577–9.
[5] W. A. Shaw, *Letters of Denization and Naturalisation for aliens in England and Ireland* (Huguenot Society Publications, xviii), 109 sqq.
[6] *P.C. Reg.* 64, April 25 and May 9, 1673. They appear also to have settled in Wilts., ibid., July 28, 1675.
[7] Colbert to Seignelay, in *Colenbrander*, ii. 230.

fleet was then dispersed and unprepared; but it was not until May 14 that a junction of the two fleets was effected. The French squadron, forming the centre or White and composed of 27 warships, 2 frigates, and 18 fireships, was commanded as before by D'Estrées; while the English contingent of 54 warships, 8 frigates, and 24 fireships was led by Rupert (Red) and Spragge (Blue). Against this joint force the Dutch could muster only 52 ships of the line, 12 frigates, and 52 fireships. Of necessity the defensive was forced on them, and accordingly in May De Ruyter took up station off the Schonveld, thereby covering Flushing and Middelburg; he had also the advantage that he was surrounded by almost inaccessible sandbanks. On May 14 a proclamation by William of Orange was circulated, calling for supreme sacrifice in the defence of the fatherland.[1]

The allied plan of campaign was to break down Dutch resistance by attack from two sides; and while Louis was forcing the surrender of Maestricht, his ships were to co-operate with the English in the landing of an expeditionary force in Zeeland. Accordingly, about 8,000 troops under the command of Schomberg were stationed at Yarmouth, and on May 20 the allied fleet put to sea. Five days later the Dutch were sighted at anchor off the Schonveld; on the 28th a light squadron was sent in to draw them out. De Ruyter came out more suddenly than was expected, whereupon the allies were surprised into action. For some time the fleets sailed parallel with the shore, the wind being at south-south-west, thus giving to the allies the advantage of the weather gage, by which, however, they could not fully profit because of the danger of running on the shoals.[2] Tromp, as usual, acted with vigour and independence, holding his own with 11 ships against 28. He changed his flagship three times and was saved from disaster only by the consummate skill of De Ruyter. All the combatants fought valiantly, and though few ships other than fireships were lost, the death-roll was very heavy. For once, the French enjoyed the opportunity of boarding the enemy. Captain Tivas, of the *Conquérant*, who had sworn in a La Rochelle cabaret that he would board Tromp, brought his ship alongside the Dutch admiral's *Gouden Leeuw*, put 100 of

[1] Blok, op. cit. 339.
[2] Clowes, op. cit. 311–12; La Roncière, op. cit. 554–62.

the Dutch crew out of action, and was prevented only by a bullet from fulfilling his ambition. Two flag-officers were lost in this indecisive action, which ended at nightfall when De Ruyter anchored off West Kapelle, with English and French about two miles north-west of him.

For some days the attackers remained on the coast to be ready for a Dutch sortie, while De Ruyter made use of the interval to effect repairs at leisure and choose his time. When, on June 3, the wind was at north-east he came out, again surprising the enemy; and after some long-range firing the squadrons engaged each other in what D'Estrées called *une grande escarmouche*.[1] At dusk the fleets separated and returned to their coasts. On all sides, about 1,000 men had been killed and wounded in these two engagements; many of the greater ships were damaged, but none lost. While neither action of the Schonveld was decisive, both demonstrated the power of the Dutch to maintain their defensive tactics and prevent a landing.

During what remained of June 1673 both sides were employed in fitting out as large fleets as possible, the allies anxious to force a decision, the Dutch determined to maintain their defensive. At a council of war held (July 16) on board the *Royal Sovereign* (attended by Charles) orders were given to Rupert to sail to the Flemish coast, and, after showing himself to De Ruyter at the Schonveld, proceed to the Texel, in the hope that he would be followed there, and that so a combat would take place where there was more sea-room.[2] As Rupert did not wish to be hampered with the troop transports, these were ordered to be left behind at Yarmouth until a decision at sea had been reached. On July 17 the allied fleet of 92 ships proceeded to sea, the French being placed in the van, as experience had shown that the centre was the proper place for the commander-in-chief. De Ruyter appears to have been sighted on the 20th. The allies then took up position off Scheveningen, the sight of their ships causing terror to the populace, hundreds of whom fled. 'All the beacons on the coast', wrote an observer, 'were fired last night, and fires upon all the steeples and jangling their bells and drums to call the country in. . . . Some few persons are said to have

---

[1] La Roncière, v. 563.

[2] *Colenbrander*, op. cit. ii. 288.

been killed upon the strand about Skeveling this day by great shott from the fleet.'[1]

Rupert meanwhile was hampered by his instructions, which were no more definite than that he should await further orders before engaging the enemy; nor was he to attack the Dutch East India fleet except between Dogger Bank and Texel, as otherwise the English coast might be left exposed.[2] With these somewhat vague directions he sailed north towards the Texel, followed by De Ruyter from Scheveningen, and about midday August 10 the two fleets sighted each other, the wind being then at north-east.[3] By 4 p.m. Rupert had obtained the windward position, standing south-east, the Dutch course being approximately north. Both fleets tacked in the night, Rupert avoiding a combat in the dark because he had so many raw seamen in his ships, and when the wind veered to east and east-by-south the Dutch succeeded in obtaining the weather gage.

The engagement opened early on the 11th of August off Kijkduin, between Petten and Camperdown, and is described by the Dutch as the battle of Kijkduin. De Ruyter at once bore down on Rupert;[4] the Zeeland squadron held D'Estrées and the allied van, while Tromp attacked the allied rear, commanded by Spragge. The French, ordered to continue course towards the south so as to weather the enemy van, completed this order; but Banckers, seeing the danger of being caught between two fires, turned and broke through the French line in order to rejoin his chief. Meanwhile, the French admiral, having become separated from the main fleet in his execution of the duty entrusted to him, utilized this as a pretext for not supporting Rupert, who was now being pressed by both De Ruyter and Banckers, while Spragge was fighting it out with Tromp. As the French stood off to the south-east, fog and rain at first prevented this separation from being noticed, and meanwhile two titanic struggles were proceeding—that between Spragge and Tromp, and that of Rupert against De Ruyter and Banckers. Spragge and Tromp fought until the sea around was littered with wreckage and bodies; both admirals had to

---

[1] News-letter from Rotterdam, printed in *Colenbrander*, ii. 293.
[2] Charles to Rupert, Aug. 3, ibid. ii. 297.
[3] *True relation . . .* in *Colenbrander*, ii. 301.   [4] Blok, op. cit. 349.

transfer their flag three times, and at the third change of flag
Spragge was killed. 'It was all fire and flame,' said one of the
crew of the *Seven Provinces*.[1] Meanwhile Rupert, firing broadsides to windward and leeward, managed to edge over to his
rear-admiral (Chicheley), and by 4 p.m., followed by De Ruyter,
he succeeded in joining the Blue, badly mauled in the fight with
Tromp. Ketches and sloops were sent out to bring in the windward vessels so as to concentrate the fleet, and prevent De
Ruyter from capturing the lame ships. At 5 p.m. there was a
short and final encounter between De Ruyter and Rupert, the
latter using fireships effectively, a contest which might have
terminated in a decision if the straggling D'Estrées had been
induced to join. But the French admiral lay off to windward,
a *spectateur immobile*[2] of the combat, though ordered by signal to
bear down on the enemy:

It was the plainest and greatest opportunity ever lost at sea. The
fight continued until the day was neere spent: the sun was just
setting, when I edged off with an easy sail, so as to carry off the
disabled ships. The Dutch also laid their heads to the eastward and
soe the battle ended, when came a messenger from Comte d'Estrées
to receive orders and to know the meaning of the blue flaggs being
on the mizzen peak, which I wondered at, since there was no instruction playner to be understood or more necessary amongst the
general instructions for fighting which he had layd before him; and
besides it wanted neither signal nor instruction to tell him what he
should then have done; the case was so plaine to every man's eye
in the whole fleet.[3]

In these blunt words prince Rupert described the conduct of
the French admiral. The battle of the Texel added one more
to the list of indecisive engagements, but it marked the end of
attempts to land troops, and it freed the coast of Holland from
blockade. Both English and Dutch came out of it with an
enhanced reputation for dogged courage. It was the last important engagement between the two races who, in a sense, had
fought each other to a finish. The lesson of the French desertion was not lost on England, where a fickle associate was held
in greater dislike than a determined enemy.

[1] Blok, op. cit. 349. [2] La Roncière, v. 573.
[3] Prince Rupert's account in *Colenbrander*, ii. 308–9.

Negotiations for a separate peace had been proceeding during these hostilities. As early as September 1672 the Swedish Regency had endeavoured to fulfil its obligations to both France and the States General by offering mediation, but without effect. As the war proceeded, it was feared in Sweden that the total defeat of the Dutch might leave the English in supreme control of the commerce of northern Europe,[1] and eventually, in the course of the winter of 1672–3, this proffered mediation was accepted by both France and England, the discussion being then diverted to the choice of a town suitable for the peace congress. Cologne was decided upon, and in April 1673 the earl of Sunderland, associated with the envoys Jenkins and Williamson, was chosen to represent England. Discussions commenced early in June 1673. Louis had every reason to suppose that Charles would stand by him,[2] because the English king had rejected offers of a separate Dutch peace. Nor was there any slackening of the English demands, which differed little from those which Buckingham and Arlington had presented in 1672; while the French terms were hardened by Louis's capture of Maestricht in June 1673. Meanwhile the war assumed a very different aspect when, in August 1673, the Dutch secured the co-operation of the Emperor, Spain, and Lorraine, a diplomatic success followed in September by William's capture of Naarden. Thus, by the autumn of 1673 the whole aspect of the war had changed. From the agent of divine justice commissioned to punish an upstart race, Louis found himself merely one of several belligerents, faced with the prospect of a lengthy war, and having for his only ally that country where his race and religion were held in deep dislike. Soon it was clear that peace could no longer be discussed on the basis of the terms proposed in the summer of 1672.

Continuation of the war was made more difficult for Charles by a domestic event. The duke of York's first wife, Anne Hyde, had died in March 1671, leaving two daughters. The royal widower was eager to marry again, and soon this matter became the subject of anxious inquiry. Claudia Felicitas, archduchess of Brunswick, was first suggested; but her marriage to the emperor Leopold caused James to look elsewhere, and he

[1] *Mignet*, iv. 140.   [2] Ibid. iv. 176.

naturally turned to the universal provider, Louis XIV, who devoted himself to this question with customary conscientiousness. It must be a French lady, or one in French interests, and there must be an heir. Madame de Guise was first recommended; she was no great beauty, it is true, but her fruitfulness could be guaranteed,[1] and for some time she remained on the select list kept by the duchess of Portsmouth.[2] Meanwhile, negotiations between Colbert and the dowager duchess Laura of Modena resulted in the selection of the latter's daughter, Mary Beatrice of Modena, for whom Louis promised a dowry of 400,000 crowns; the pope (Clement X) added his solicitations, and in July 1673 the earl of Peterborough was sent to ask for the consent of the intended bride. There was need for haste, because parliament would soon be in session; moreover, earlier in the year there had been talk of another bridegroom, namely Charles himself. The royal physician was reported to have informed the king that his queen was in 'consumption' and could not live more than a few months; but, apart from his consort's health, Charles was being urged by the enemies of the duke of York to divorce Catherine and marry again.[3] He gave some encouragement to these solicitations by interesting himself in the choice of a bride, and announcing that he would trust no more to portraits;[4] but while Charles was talking and his ministers quarrelling, James was acting. On September 30 his marriage contract was sealed, and the wedding completed by proxy. The haste with which these negotiations were conducted served to emphasize the fact that of all within Charles's entourage, the duke of York was the only man with a definite policy and the will to carry it out.[5]

When parliament met on October 20, 1673, the Commons showed a temper even more uncompromising than that of the preceding March. Unaware of the ceremony at Modena, they voted an address that the marriage of the duke with the princess

[1] Letter of Louvois, Sept. 29, 1671, quoted in H. Forneron, *Louise de Querouaille*, 57.

[2] Report of Colbert de Croissy, July 24, 1673, in *Baschet*, 128.

[3] Ibid. Feb. 10/20.

[4] Ibid. Feb. 10/20, 1673.

[5] In Aug. 1676, when acknowledging a present of ear-rings for the duchess from Louis XIV, James told the French ambassador that he regarded his bride as the daughter of Louis (*Baschet*, 133, Aug. 3/13, 1676).

of Modena should not take place, and that he should marry a Protestant. Charles's reply was to prorogue parliament for a week.[1] On their reassembly the king informed both Houses of the failure of the Cologne negotiations; he also asked for supplies to continue the war and to provide for repayment of his debt to the goldsmiths.[2] Shaftesbury followed with a disquisition on the necessity of securing the dominion of the seas and a subsidy from the Dutch for the herring fishing; these objects, with the establishment of the prince of Orange against the Lovestein faction and the adjustment of the East India trade, were, he claimed, legitimate reasons for the continuation of hostilities. The Commons responded by debating not the grant of a supply, but the refusal of one; the pope, it was said in the House, had expressed approval of the progress of French arms; at the battle of the Texel, English and Dutch had been gladiators and the French spectators; this was not their war; and Sacheverell hinted at the dark designs of the 'villainous councillors' who had persuaded the king to embark on it. Sir William Coventry attacked the French alliance as destructive of both trade and religion; other members deplored this joining with the most insidious enemy of our wool monopoly (France) and enmity with the best customer for our woollens[3] (Spain). A touch of humour was added to the debate when sir Robert Carr, moving that they proceed in a parliamentary way, suggested that they should present their grievances (if they had any) 'and the king will give you redress' (*laughed at*).

The result was an address against the duke's marriage, and the refusal of supply before the expiration of the eighteen months' assessment granted in the previous session, unless it should appear that the obstinacy of the Dutch rendered it necessary; nor would a further supply be granted until the country was effectually secured from the dangers of popery and popish counsels.[4] The grievance of a standing army was next discussed, many members showing a certain hyper-sensitiveness in regard to the troops for whose maintenance they had themselves voted supplies. Abuses in the billeting of troops, martial law for soldiers, and the inevitable debauchery which must inevitably follow the arming of youth were all expatiated on by sir T. Meres, who induced the

[1] *L.J.* xii. 587. [2] *L.J.* xii. 589–90.
[3] *Grey*, ii. 198–214. [4] *C.J.* ix. 284–5, Oct. 30–1, 1673.

Commons to pass a resolution that a standing army was a grievance, in spite of secretary Coventry's distinction between an army and a standing army.[1] When on November 4 sir R. Thomas added 'evil councillors' to the list of grievances, Black Rod's tap at the door was heard, and parliament was prorogued to January 7, 1674. November 4 was indeed an ominous date for prorogation, as was revealed next day, when all London flocked to a great pope-burning, where there was the additional attraction that the effigy of a Frenchman could be shot at by spectators.[2]

These debates showed how untenable was Charles's position, and how unpopular were some of his ministers. Most of them were busy plotting against each other; nor could good counsel be expected from men inspired mainly by personal enmities, and concerned chiefly about their own safety. Charles talked of 'gaining time'; James said it was 'losing time'.[3] Government was brought to such a pitch, noted the Venetian ambassador, that the king called a cabinet council for the purpose of not listening to it, and the ministers held forth so as not to be understood.[4] A new fear had entered into English statecraft—fear of parliament and of something vaguely called the nation; in consequence there could be neither secrecy nor freedom in the king's councils. Against the emphatic opinion of the majority of the privy council Charles refused to dissolve parliament, though he was reminded of the fate of his father;[5] it was also insinuated that his failure to take decisive action was cowardice. He was pressed by his brother to take drastic steps with the opposition leaders; indeed the duke sent for Shaftesbury and told him to his face that he was a madman. The one genuine Protestant in high office—Shaftesbury—was removed on November 9, the seals being given to Finch. 'It is only laying down my gown and putting on my sword,' said the dismissed chancellor as he stepped from office into opposition. Arlington, ever playing for safety, advised Charles to yield now, as he had yielded over the Declaration of Indulgence, for compliance seemed the only alternative to national revolt.

As the English executive wavered, the French king hastened to supply under-props. Ruvigny was sent to England nominally in order to congratulate the duke of York on his marriage, but

---

[1] *Grey*, ii. 222.　　　　[2] *Ven. Trans.*, 14/44, Nov. 7/17, 1673.
[3] Ibid., Nov. 5/15, 1673.　　[4] Ibid., Dec. 12/22.　　[5] Ibid., Nov. 7/17.

really to reinstate Buckingham in the French interest and, if possible, add other supports thereto. For this purpose he was accompanied by the marquis de Sessac,[1] who, having been detected cheating at cards, was now in need of a vacation wherein to restore his honour. Buckingham soon convinced Sessac that he had enough influence with the Commons to induce them to confirm the (public) Anglo-French alliance; whereupon Sessac proposed the obvious solution of the difficulty, namely, that the king should show this public treaty to the Commons and keep the secret treaty up his sleeve.[2] While these subsidiary negotiations were proceeding, Charles was explaining his predicament to the French ambassador—how his revenues for 1674 were already fully anticipated, and he would need at least £1,400,000 for next year's campaign. Colbert de Croissy thought this an over-estimate, but asked Louis to authorize him to advance up to £500,000. The extra subsidy was granted early in December, together with an extra £10,000 as a bait for Shaftesbury;[3] but in spite of these lavish grants Louis now realized that he must prepare himself for a separate Anglo-Dutch peace. In his desperation he would do anything to retain Charles's co-operation —he would increase the subsidy by two million livres and would even diminish the size of his fleet in order to soothe English maritime jealousy. But in spite of the combined efforts of the two French envoys, overtures for a separate peace with the Dutch were negotiated through Spain.[4]

Colbert de Croissy and Ruvigny now directed their attention to those of Charles's advisers and ex-advisers, namely Arlington, Buckingham, Ormonde, and Shaftesbury, who were supposed to have a following in the Commons. Through these intermediaries Englishmen were to be persuaded that the sole object of the war was a good peace, that Charles had no intention of changing the constitution, and that Louis was far from suggesting such counsels. The large sums required for this propaganda were to be supplied by Sessac on his own credit, and distributed by Buckingham; but

---

[1] For his career see Germain Martin, *Histoire du crédit en France sous le règne de Louis XIV*, i. 201.   [2] *Baschet*, 130, Jan. 1/11, 1673/4.

[3] On Buckingham's suggestion, Ruvigny had asked for this sum in order to bribe Shaftesbury. *Instructions Données (Angleterre)*, ii. 125–6.

[4] *Mignet*, iv. 251.

none of this fund was to be given to Charles or Arlington, who, if they applied for a grant from this source, were to be assured that Sessac was advancing the money on his own risk, in the hope of rehabilitating himself at the French Court.[1] The recruits obtained from this campaign were neither numerous nor promising—lord Ogle, son of the duke of Newcastle, lord Berkeley, lord Bristol, and sir Robert Carr. Buckingham reported that he had agreed with Osborne to induce Charles to make public the fictitious treaty of December 31, 1670, in order to calm the fears of parliament. Charles and Louis were persuaded to consent to this piece of deception, while Colbert de Croissy, wearied of the comedy and of the increasing hatred of Catholicism in England, was recalled at his own request, the Huguenot Ruvigny being appointed in his stead. To the departing ambassador Charles gave a receipt for all the French money he had received since December 1670—eight million livres tournois, or about £600,000. By the end of 1673, therefore, the position was this—if parliament could be fooled by the bogus treaty, Charles might be able to continue his amicable relations with France; Arlington, then negotiating a separate treaty with the Dutch, would be 'dished', and Buckingham's influence would be established on a secure French basis. But as the date of the reassembling of parliament approached, Charles became more and more dubious of the success of the intended ruse.

These fears were amply justified when parliament met on January 7, 1673–4. In his speech from the throne[2] Charles assured both Houses that it was impossible for him to doubt their affection, especially at such a crisis as this. In order to obtain peace without dishonour supplies were needed; 'a cheerful aid is now more necessary than ever'. As there were rumours of secret engagements with France he would willingly show his treaties with that power to a committee of both Houses 'without any the least reserve'. It was noticed that he fumbled at these words.[3] Parliament responded ominously by a request for a public fast 'to seek a reconciliation at the hands of Almighty God', a request readily granted.[4] The Commons then fell to their grievances—

[1] *Instructions Données*, ii. 138. [2] *L.J.* xii. 594–5.
[3] Conway to Essex, Jan. 10, 1674, in *Essex Papers* (ed. O. Airy), i. 161.
[4] Jan. 16, 1674, *Steele*, i. 3587.

men had been pressed to serve overseas; the war was bad for trade; the king should have consulted with parliament before engaging in hostilities. By 191 to 139 it was decided to thank the king for his speech, and it was then resolved to take measures for suppressing popery and removing popish and dangerous councillors. A beginning was made with Lauderdale, who was accused of raising 20,000 foot and 2,000 horse in Scotland for a pernicious design to alter the English constitution; an address for his removal was passed unanimously. Then came Buckingham's turn. A carefully prepared list of questions and accusations was compiled.[1] He had broken the Triple Alliance by his negotiations in 1672; he had raised troops in Yorkshire; he had visited the king of France; he had referred to Charles as an arrant knave, and he was guilty of crimes so heinous that they were unmentionable, even in Rome. Arlington came next. Nothing, it was said, had passed but through his hands, including the raising of an army and the Declaration of Indulgence; he was the 'great conduit pipe', and it was freely reported abroad that he was a Papist.[2] On January 15, 1674, articles of impeachment against him were brought in. These alleged that he had obtained commissions for Papists; he had lodged a priest in his household; he had embezzled the treasure of the kingdom for his own greatness; he had advised the king to enter on the war before he was out of debt. In vain did secretary Coventry protest that these were vague charges; that Arlington had acted on the king's orders, and that the Commons had not defined their phrase 'popishly affected'.[3]

Buckingham's vindication of himself before the Commons (Jan. 13, 1674) was a forensic masterpiece. The real culprit, he explained, was Arlington. So far from breaking the Triple Alliance he had taken the chief part in making it. He had gone to Holland in 1672 in order to prevent De Witt joining with the French; he had endangered his career because of his consistent reverence for the House of Commons. A tragic victim of circumstances, he could hunt with a pack of hounds, but not with a pair of lobsters;[4] he therefore desired leave to sell his office of Master of the Horse, and concluded by commending himself and his

[1] *C.J.* ix. 292 sqq.   [2] *Grey*, ii. 271.   [3] *Grey*, ii. 273.
[4] i.e. either the king and the duke of York or prince Rupert and Arlington.

actions to the good construction of the honourable House.[1] His listeners, who did not quite know what to make of this mixture of innuendo and fooling, had no better success with their question-naire, which was intended to extract answers implicating Arling-ton. Two days later Arlington also defended himself before the Commons. He had always, he said, been for moderate courses, Buckingham for exorbitant ones. He had had only a sum of £10,000 and an estate of £1,000 per annum out of Ireland. As this defence seemed the more convincing, it was decided by a narrow majority not to petition for his dismissal; but they asked for Buckingham's removal, and delegated to a committee the duty of finding out if he were impeachable.

Criticism of his ministers by the Commons must have been as galling to Charles as their enforcement of the Test Act had al-ready proved. One encroachment on the prerogative was being followed by another; earlier parliamentary history appeared to be repeating itself, and the crown itself might again be over-whelmed by an avalanche such as that of 1648–9. At the same time both York and Osborne tried to discredit the Commons with the king. The majority of the members, they said, were per-sons of no consideration, many of them subsisting on the royal charity; if parliament were dissolved, a number of these men would die naked in debtors' prisons. The House, they argued, was exceeding its powers; not satisfied with being consulted about supply, the members were claiming to examine the causes of taxation, and were setting up for regents of the crown.[2] But once again Charles's intuition served him in good stead. For a second time he would yield, but his recoil, when it came, would be all the stronger. Neither House had taken advantage of his invita-tion to inspect the treaties; as this ruse had failed, he must proceed with the separate treaty which Temple, with the help of Spain, was then mediating. To Louis he could explain his defection by attributing its origin to a proposed marriage alliance between William and the princess Anne.[3] On January 24 he took the unusual step of submitting to both Houses a letter from the States General, intimating the terms on which they would agree to make peace. The letter, with a memorial from the French ambassador,

---

[1] *Grey*, ii. 249–50.   [2] *Ven. Trans.* (14/44), Jan. 23/Feb. 2, 1674.
[3] Ibid., Feb. 6/16, 1674.

was read to the House by secretary Coventry, and on this basis
the Commons advised Charles to proceed to a *speedy peace*, the
word *honourable* being purposely omitted, lest its retention might
occasion a further demand for supplies.[1] By February 11 the
negotiations were completed, and Charles was then able to announce that he had made an honourable peace. Intimating that
he had sent home the Irish troops, he now asked that money be
supplied for a larger fleet, in order that England might not lag
behind other nations.[2]

Having thanked him for this announcement, the Commons
turned at once to the dangers from popery; the military establishments of Scotland and Ireland; illegal imprisonment of subjects;
and the threat of a standing army. 'This army',[3] said colonel
Birch, 'though of but sixteen hundred is able to make the kingdom jealous.' 'Plymouth', said sir Nicholas Carew, 'is well fortified by land, but not by sea.' In vain secretary Coventry protested against the ambiguity of the word 'grievance' as applied
to the armed forces of the crown; moreover, once people suspected
that every man in a red coat was a grievance, bloodshed was bound
to follow.[4] In spite of this reasonable protest on behalf of the
government, it was voted on February 7 that the continuing of
any standing forces other than the Militia was a great grievance.[5]
They next discussed the bribing of members of parliament, and
(on the strength of a rumour that Arlington had spent £20,000
on this object) a motion was made to administer a test, to be taken
publicly by all members, disavowing the receipt of money for their
votes. But this was not proceeded with; for many of the legislators
must have been aware of Ruvigny's two threats: first, that if such
a test were applied, he would publish the names of 'the devotees
of the rix-dollars of Holland'; and, second, that unless 'the
devotees of the crown pieces of France' spoke up more loudly
for the French alliance, he would publish their names also.[6]
These threats may have succeeded.

The historical parallel with the Long Parliament became more
obvious as this momentous session proceeded, and the Commons read and passed Bills involving the most far-reaching of
constitutional principles. Among these was a Bill for the better

---

[1] *Grey*, ii. 357.   [2] *L.J.* xii. 632.   [3] *Grey*, ii. 395.   [4] Ibid. ii. 398.
[5] *C.J.* ix. 305.   [6] *Ven. Trans.*, 14/40, Feb. 6/16, 1674.

election of members of parliament;[1] a habeas corpus Bill, intended
to facilitate the application of this remedy; a Bill to prevent
illegal exaction of money from the subject; a prisoners' transportation Bill; and a Bill for settling the fees and powers in the patents
of judges.[2] On February 21 they passed the first reading of a Bill
sent from the Lords, which would have had the effect of bringing
up the duke of York's children as Protestants;[3] they had already
before them a Bill to distinguish between Protestants and Papists,
and one of their committees was inspecting the laws in order to
see how far the king might commit a subject by his immediate
warrant.[4] Thus, in spite of the cessation of hostilities with Holland,
the Commons seemed resolved both to guarantee a Protestant
succession and to determine afresh the relations between executive and subject. But none of the measures proposed for these
objects was allowed to pass; for on February 24, 1674, the king
prorogued parliament until November 10, this being the third
successive prorogation without the passing of a single Bill.

Thus the two Dutch Wars had served to create a complete
change in the relations between crown and legislature. The war
of 1665-7 had stirred the Commons to set themselves up as critics
of war management and expenditure; that of 1672-4 incited
them to review the whole field of national policy, and to direct
attention to the most sacred element in the prerogative—the
succession to the throne. The duke of Newcastle's verdict[5] had
proved a true one, that a parliament which sits long will never
want work; indeed, the youthful loyalists of the Restoration
seemed to be entering on a middle age of republican pugnacity.
They were pitted against a king whose mental evolution had long
since been completed; a king possessed of one ambition—that he
might live in peace and comfort, secure from the scoldings of
Westminster. His dream was to be realized, but it was still in the
distant future.

The treaty which detached England from the last of the great
Dutch wars was signed in London on February 9, 1674, and is

---

[1] *C.J.* ix. 308, Feb. 12.
[2] Ibid. ix. 308-13; also *H.M.C. Rep.* ix, app., pt. ii. 42-6; and *Grey*, ii.
349-415.
[3] *H.M.C. Rep.* ix, app., pt. ii. 45.
[4] *C.J.* ix. 309.
[5] See *supra*, 146.

generally known as the treaty of Westminster.[1] The honour of the flag was ceded to England as 'a testimony of respect' in British waters, these being defined as stretching from Cape Finisterre to van Staten in Norway.[2] The Dutch agreed to allow English colonists to leave Surinam with their slaves and possessions; disputes in the East Indies were to be referred to arbitration. Each country undertook not to assist the enemies of the other. As the prince of Orange had been confirmed in the official stadholdership, he was not specially provided for in the treaty; nor was anything said about the right of herring-fishing in British waters. As indemnity, England received 800,000 écus.[3] This treaty was followed in December 1674 by a maritime treaty[4] which guaranteed for each nation free commerce everywhere, except in the East Indies, where the *status quo* was to be observed, both countries agreeing to prolong discussion of their differences there until an agreement was reached. 'Je voudrais bien vivre jusqu'à ce temps-là' was Ruvigny's comment on this clause.

Like the treaty of Breda, that of Westminster left undetermined the question of maritime supremacy, a question not to be settled by a few years of war, but by gradual changes in the relative resources of the two combatants. Ostensibly, the terms of the treaty seemed at least to 'save the face' of the English government; for the Dutch paid an indemnity, and they appeared to give way on the question of the flag. That our rivals and enemies consented to salute even a single British ship in the waters over which England claimed mythological supremacy appeared a recognition of British maritime achievement, and was so regarded in England; but in reality it was a triumph for the Dutch, because expressly conceded, not as an admission of our rule over certain seas, but as a mark of respect from a junior to a senior power. Moreover, the limits specified were 'too wide for dominion and too narrow for respect'.[5] In the East Indies the treaty marked the end of our attempts to gain a footing in the Spice Islands; thereafter, the Dutch were confirmed in possession. In these respects the treaty was unfavourable, or indeterminate for English interests. But the repercussions

---

[1] *Dumont*, vii, pt. ii. 253–4. [2] Possibly Stattland.
[3] Or nearly £200,000. [4] *Dumont*, vii, pt. ii. 282–5.
[5] T. W. Fulton, *The Sovereignty of the Seas*, 509.

of wars and treaties are often remote and indirect; for England obtained this unusual advantage that, while her chief enemies were left fighting each other, she was able to obtain a footing in some of their markets. In the west, New York had been restored after its capture by the Dutch in 1673; the Carolinas were steadily being peopled, and within a few years Pennsylvania was to be added to English possessions on the mainland.[1] In Canada the Hudson's Bay Company was persistently encroaching on French preserves, and preparing the way for English domination. Thus, in the four years of neutrality secured by the peace of 1674, England was able to make up for the handicaps with which she had entered the race for maritime supremacy, and in these years our French and Dutch rivals were weakened by prolonged war.

A striking contrast of motives was thereupon illustrated. The Dutch were left struggling for their national independence and security; Louis was fighting for glory and revenge, while the peaceable English were profiting by a policy of penetration and development. It was through no conscious principle on the part of Charles that England was able to reap these advantages; and so long as war is considered necessarily honourable and neutrality cowardly, this policy will be condemned. But the historians who applaud the progress of English commerce and colonial enterprise in these years must in fairness admit that these things were indirectly promoted by the foreign policy of Charles II.

[1] For these see Vol. II, Ch. XVIII.

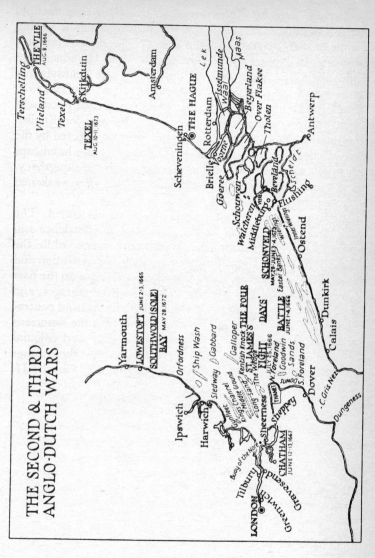

THE SECOND & THIRD ANGLO-DUTCH WARS

Compiled from the charts published by John Seller, Hydrographer to King Charles II

LONDON
Greenwich
Gravesend
Tilbury
Buoy of the Nore
Gunfleet
Ipswich
Harwich
CHATHAM JUNE 12–13, 1667
Sheerness
Sheppey
Queenborough
Maplin Sands
King's Channel
Middle Ground
Kentish Knock
Long Sand
Sledway
Ship Wash
Gabbard
Galloper
Orfordness
Yarmouth
LOWESTOFT JUNE 2–3, 1665
SOUTHWOLD (SOLE) BAY MAY 28 1672
THE FOUR DAYS' BATTLE JUNE 1–4, 1666
THE SWIN
ST. JAMES'S FIGHT JULY 25 1666
THANET
N. Foreland
Goodwin Sands
S. Foreland
DOWNS
Dover
Sheppey
C. Gris Nez
Dungeness
Calais
Dunkirk
Ostend
Inner Wielings
Willings
Easter Banks
SCHONVELD MAY 28–JUNE 3 & 4, 1673
Flushing
Middleburg
Walcheren
THE VEERE
Schouwen
Goëree
Brielle
Scheveningen
THE HAGUE
Rotterdam
Voorne
Beverland
Over Flakee
Tholen
Antwerp
Scheldt
Isselmunde
Beyerland
Maas
Waal
Lek
Amsterdam
Nijkduin
TEXEL AUG. 10–11, 1673
Texel
Vlieland
Terschelling
THE VLIE AUG. 8, 1666

XI

SCOTLAND AND IRELAND, 1661–79

B Y the conclusion of the Third Dutch War England had
achieved a standard of material well-being and an acuteness
of political consciousness such as could not be matched elsewhere
in Europe. In these achievements neither Scotland nor Ireland
had taken part. They were nominally sister-kingdoms, but really
alien dependencies, their religions, culture, and economic
interests being all considered foreign or even antagonistic to
those of Englishmen. In the years after 1674 there was this
change in the relationship, that English kinship with a majority
of the Scottish nation was coming to be realized, while racial
contrast with the native Irish was more sharply accentuated.
The Popish Plot and the reaction which followed helped ultimately to make possible the union of England with her northern
neighbour, for common danger brought about a realization of
common interest; equally the same crisis helped to confirm those
antipathies which have always separated the Saxon and Protestant Englishman from the Irish Celt.

There were two reasons why Ireland in this period was more
fortunate than Scotland, namely, Charles was in sympathy with
the Irish Roman Catholics, and the Irish had the good fortune to
possess a statesman of integrity and wisdom in the duke of Ormonde. James Butler, twelfth earl and first duke of Ormonde,
was one of the most notable of those Anglo-Irishmen who promoted the interests of their country by methods of conciliation and
compromise, and his services to the Stuart cause were comparable
with those of Clarendon, whom he equalled in prestige and
excelled in humanity and vision. He lost more than he gained
by his devotion to the Stuarts, and so great was his natural
dignity that, when out of office, it was difficult to say whether
the duke was out of favour with the king or the king out of favour
with the duke. 'Had he been dressed like a ploughman he would
still have appeared a man of quality';[1] 'a man of great expense,
decent even in his vices'[2]—these two tributes from different

---

[1] Carte, in *Ormonde*, iv. 692. [2] *Burnet*, i. 170.

quarters agree at least in attesting the gracefulness and nobility
of his deportment. Of the other Irish administrators appointed
by Charles none descended to the level of the Stuart agents
in Scotland. Robartes, who was lord lieutenant for two short
periods, at the Restoration and in 1669–70, was hard and grasping; he was also hated as a Presbyterian, but he was just. His successor John, first baron Berkeley of Stratton, was neither just nor
austere, but he was not vindictive, and as soldier and friend of
Roman Catholics he was popular with many Irishmen. After
two years of office he was succeeded (1672) by Arthur Capel, earl
of Essex. Though possessed of neither the finesse nor the personal
attractiveness requisite for Irish viceregal success, Essex applied
himself with zeal and diligence to the accomplishment of his
duties, and by mingling moderation with firmness succeeded in
conciliating both Papist and Ulsterman; he was also tolerant, in
spite of pressure from the zealots, and in his five years of office
(1672–7) proved himself one of the ablest and most conscientious
of Irish viceroys. On the whole, therefore, Ireland was fortunate
in her governors. Ormonde had already acted as lord lieutenant
in 1644–5; his second viceroyalty was from November 1661 to
March 1669; and his third was in the years 1677–84.

Ireland was a fruitful country, containing some of the best
pasture in Europe. Woods had diminished with the coming of
the English, but mines were being developed, notably the iron-
mines of lord Cork in Munster, and the lead-mines of Antrim and
Tipperary. Peat was abundant; freestone, marble, slate, and
coal were quarried.[1] The Navigation Acts did not seriously
affect Irish prosperity, since Irish provisions could be shipped to
the plantations,[2] and in these commodities there was an extensive
trade, notably to the West Indies; but a more serious restriction
was that of the import of Irish cattle into England,[3] one of many
measures intended to keep up English rents. As Irish cattle were
assessed at £2 10s. each in the Book of Rates, the crown had to
make a considerable sacrifice in its Customs receipts. In Ireland
there was complaint and dislocation[4] at first; but in the end, the em-

---

[1] G. Boate, *Ireland's Natural History* (1652), 85, 87, 125.
[2] *Supra*, i. 245.   [3] 18–19 Car. II, cap. ii.
[4] e.g. lord Orrery, who had extensive lands in Munster, complained that,
in consequence of the prohibition, his estate had fallen in value from £4,000

bargo led to the development of other enterprises, for cattle were thenceforth killed and exported as provisions, and as sheep were pastured in greater numbers, a new wool trade grew up. Hitherto the majority of Irish exports had been to England; thereafter, the majority was to foreign ports, a fact not without influence on the political sympathies of Irishmen. For a time there were restraints on the export of both wool and cloth, but special licences were frequently granted, except to Holland,[1] and there was also profit to be had by smuggling wool to France. That wool continued to be smuggled abroad may be inferred from the complaint of the English clothiers in 1676 that their continental trade was being ruined by the large quantities of Irish material exported to Europe.[2]

The public revenue was derived from two sources—the crown rents payable by prescription or custom, and the duties granted to the crown, including Customs, Hearth Money, and the Excise. During Charles's reign the average amount of the hereditary revenue was £250,000, made up of £70,000 from quit rents, £135,000 from Customs and Excise, £25,000 from Chimney Money, and the remainder from miscellaneous or casual sources.[3] In 1669 these dues were farmed for £219,000; but, after 1683, when the method of farming was abandoned, the revenue was collected by commissioners, and was supplemented by subsidies granted by the Irish legislature, some of them payable in wheat or oatmeal. These figures suggest that Ireland was heavily taxed in proportion to her wealth; but, on the other hand, this was a period of comparative prosperity, as evidenced by the fact that in 1670, 1680, and 1683 there was a surplus of yield over expenditure, the expenditure being accounted for by the Irish Civil List, the military expenses, and the pensions.[4] It became the practice of the later Stuarts to saddle the Irish revenues with claims having

---

to £500 per annum. (*Cal. S.P. Ire.*, *1666–9*, 282.) For Petty's estimate of the economic consequences of the prohibition see *Political Anatomy of Ireland*, ch. x.

[1] G. A. T. O'Brien, *Economic history of Ireland in the seventeenth century*, 176–7. For such wool licences see *H.M.C. Rep. Ormonde MSS.*, new series, iv.

[2] *Cal. S.P. Dom.*, *1676–7*, 219, quoted by O'Brien, op. cit. 181.

[3] For details see O'Brien, op. cit. 200 sqq.

[4] In 1676 the expenses on these three heads respectively were £45,906; £146,260; £10,400 (*P.C. Reg.* 65, March 10, 1675/6).

no connexion with either the administration or the interests of the sister kingdom.

Estimates of the population vary between the half million at which it was reckoned in 1659[1] and the conjecture of 1,100,000 made by Petty[2] in 1672. Petty thought that the population was made up of 800,000 Papists, 200,000 English, and 100,000 Scots. Among notes prepared for a parliamentary debate of February 1674[3] are these estimates: number of parishes, 2,278; of priests, 4,000; wealth of Ireland, a fifteenth part of that of England, and its revenue a sixth part. In a memorandum of 1679 the number of families was reckoned at 225,000, of which families only 15,000 lived in houses having more than one chimney; of these latter families, 8,000 were said to be Protestants.[4] Scarce a tenth of the 210,000 cottages were in Protestant possession. Roman Catholic man-power was placed at 150,000, mostly governed by priests; while the few rich Papist families were said to be influenced by their lawyers and by those of their number who had been in foreign parts. Irish shipping amounted to only 10,000 tons, and there were reported to be only about 1,000 seamen.

In accordance with the policy of saving the Irish from themselves, attempts were made to encourage the settlement of desirable foreigners in Ireland; and, as neither the Scots of Ulster nor the Cromwellian soldiers and adventurers were considered desirable, an invitation was extended in 1662 to foreign Protestants;[5] so also, during the Third Dutch War, it was thought that the Hollander might be induced to migrate to Ireland.[6] Sir William Petty, one of the few contemporary Englishmen who expressed a sympathetic view of Irish character,[7] favoured a state-aided scheme whereby Irishmen were to go to England, and Englishmen to Ireland;[8] while other proposals for dealing with the problem

---

[1] For the first of these estimates see *Transactions of the Royal Irish Academy*, XXIV. iii. 319, and O'Brien, op. cit. 122.

[2] Petty, *The Political Anatomy of Ireland*.

[3] *Cal. S.P. Dom.*, *1673–5*, 157–63. Some of the information was probably derived from Petty.   [4] Ibid., *1679–80*, 353.

[5] e.g. the printed proclamation in French in *Carte MS.* 32, f. 169, where foreign Protestant settlers are accorded the same privileges as Irishmen, and allowed to have six apprentices.   [6] *Supra*, i. 372.

[7] Fitzmaurice, *Life of sir William Petty*, 145–8. For Petty's scheme of union with Ireland see ibid. 277.   [8] Ibid. 148.

of the Celt were these: expelling from the country the small band of lawyers, clergy, and merchants who acted as advisers to the rich families; disarming the Roman Catholics and depriving them of horses; demolishing the thousands of wretched cabins standing in 'uncouth' places and rebuilding them in the way of tithings, that is close together; compelling Papists to attend the parish church; bringing 25,000 unmarried and marriageable Papist women to England and sending the like number of Protestant women to Ireland; and, lastly, by forming the 20,000–24,000 able Protestants into a militia.[1] That the native Irish were a menace to English security was more clearly realized as French power increased, especially as the threat of French intervention in Ireland was present throughout the Second Dutch War, and was repeated in later years when Louis XIV found that he was being fooled by Charles.[2] Had James II retained the military abilities of his earlier manhood he might have succeeded in setting up in Ireland a kingdom tributary to France.

More conciliatory was the proposal to secure Ireland by a legislative union. Such a scheme was put forward by a number of officers and other persons of English extraction residing in Ireland, who contended that, in the absence of union, English people in Ireland were considered foreigners; that descendants of English settlers became Irish and resisted improvements, and that many judges were not agreed whether laws made in England were binding in Ireland. A consequence of this ambiguity was that embezzling, erasure, and forgery of records were more often practised than elsewhere.[3] The truth of this last allegation is shown by the fact that, during the Popish Plot, boat-loads of perjurers were obtainable from Ireland, providing good material for the tuition of Shaftesbury and Oates.[4] It may be added that other legal reforms might have been expected to follow from a union of the parliaments. Thus, it was not so much poverty as

---

[1] *Cal. S.P. Dom., 1679–80*, 353 sqq.

[2] Thus, in August 1682 Louis was reported to have formed the intention of freeing himself altogether from Charles and possessing Ireland: (lord Preston to secretary Jenkins, Aug. 12, 1682, in *H.M.C. Rep. VII*, app. 334.) See also *Cal. S.P. Dom., 1683*, 62: information of Capt. Roger Tilly.

[3] *Miscellanea Aulica*, ed. T. Brown (1702), 203.

[4] See *infra*, 596. For an instance of 29 witnesses each perjuring himself in one case see *Cal. S.P. Ire., 1666–9*, 487–8.

insecure tenure that caused the prevalence of 'nasty, smoky cabins', occupied by men who held from May to May. Even the chieftains held their estates only for lives, and might be succeeded not by the eldest sons, but by tanists, who were elective; moreover the inferior tenancies were frequently divided among the males of the sept, in a manner not unlike that known in England as gavelkind. The result was that no incentive was provided for improvement; at times indeed human life seemed almost as precarious as in Turkey, and it was said to be not uncommon for restless Irishmen to convey their lands to feoffees in trust, reserving to themselves a life tenure, so that on judgement for treason their estates would not be forfeited.[1] These evils were intensified by the increasing number of absentee landlords, and so Ireland was dominated by three main classes who had nothing but hatred for each other—the native Celt, the Cromwellian soldier-farmer, and the courtier landlord living in London.

Until 1782 the relations between the crown and the Irish parliament were nominally controlled by the institution known as Poyning's Law, whereby the powers of the Irish legislature were limited to the acceptance or rejection of measures submitted by the lord lieutenant and the English privy council. But, long before 1782, the system had been considerably modified; for by 1692 the Irish House of Commons definitely acquired a part in the initiation of legislation, and this privilege appears to have been exercised at times in Charles's reign, through the initiative occasionally entrusted to drafting committees of the Irish Commons.[2] Generally, however, the parliaments of Ireland were as easily controlled as those of Scotland; indeed, except for their sessions in the first six years of the reign, when their aid was necessary for the granting of subsidies and the settlement of the land problem, there was little parliamentary activity in this period; but it may be doubted whether the country suffered much in consequence. From the point of view of the crown, the steady increase of Irish revenues made recourse to parliament less necessary.

Ormonde was appointed to succeed Robartes in November

---

[1] *The present state of Ireland* (1673).

[2] Porritt, *Unreformed House of Commons*, ii. 428 sqq. For the actual procedure see *P.C. Reg.* 59, June 6, 1666.

1661, but before he left England he made his personal conditions with the privy council. These were[1] (1) that no Irish suit for reward or pension should be considered until the ordinary Irish revenue was sufficient to sustain the charges of the crown; (2) that an express *caveat* be directed to the principal secretaries of state and the custodians of the Signet, the Great Seal, and the Privy Seal that no grant concerning Ireland be approved until the lord lieutenant was acquainted therewith; (3) that only fit persons be appointed bishops and judges; (4) that no complaint be received until the lord lieutenant had been informed; and (5) that no new offices be created in Ireland without the lord lieutenant's cognizance. These conditions illustrate the main difficulties confronting Irish administration, and give some colour to the contention that, for a conscientious viceroy, the English Court was a more serious problem than the Irish Celt. His conditions having been approved, Ormonde proceeded to Ireland, where he was soon occupied in the land settlement[2] and in securing the grant of a Hearth Tax by the Irish parliament. His rule was acquiesced in as much by Papist as by Presbyterian. It is true that the moderate Roman Catholics were inclined to expect overmuch from his commiseration, but at least they were encouraged to combine their religion with loyalty,[3] and in their Protestant lord lieutenant they had a statesman prepared to uphold Irish interests, as evidenced by his opposition to the Bill of 1666–7 prohibiting the import of Irish cattle into England. He also did much to develop a native linen industry, and promoted a Bill[4] which was passed by the Irish legislature in 1665–6 whereby it was provided that, after May 1, 1666, no one should let a cottage or cabin outside a corporate town to any one not possessing at least an acre of land, on one-eighth part of which the tenant was required to sow hemp or flax. This measure was supplemented by Ormonde's personal encouragement. Families of skilled workers were introduced from Flanders, the west of France, and Jersey; but the industry, centred at first in Charle-

---

[1] *P.C. Reg.* 55, June 9, 1662.   [2] See *supra*, i. 170–3.

[3] For the convocation of loyal Catholic clergy in Dublin in June 1666 see *Cal. S.P. Ire., 1666–9*, xx and xxx. Ormonde's scheme of separating the moderates from the zealots failed.

[4] *Statutes at large passed in the parliaments held in Ireland* (1786), ii. 157.

ville and Chapelizod, was afterwards developed mainly by Irish and Scots in Ulster.[1]

The only notable incident arising from the discontent occasioned by the land settlement was the plot of March 1663 for the seizure of Dublin Castle and the person of the lord lieutenant. As one of the confederates turned informer, the design was suppressed; but its leader, colonel Blood, after being concealed by the native Irish and Cromwellians, succeeded in escaping to Holland, afterwards to England, where he allied with the surviving Fifth-Monarchy Men, and in 1670 repeated his attempt (this time in St. James's Street) to kidnap Ormonde.[2] Otherwise the duke's administration was comparatively peaceful, and the country remained loyal during the Second Dutch War, when his son Ossory acted as deputy. There was a threat to this security when, in April 1666, a French man-of-war anchored in Kenmare Bay, and in July 1667 sir Jeremy Smith had to hold Kinsale against a possible attack from the Dutch; indeed English loss of prestige in this war might well have been followed by disastrous consequences in Ireland, because the links joining the two countries were as precarious as those uniting India to the British Empire to-day.[3]

The death of Southampton and the downfall of Clarendon in 1667 removed the only statesmen who could in any sense be considered his colleagues; and, as the most eminent of Clarendonians, Ormonde necessarily incurred the enmity of Buckingham and Arlington. His recall from Ireland in February 1668 was therefore not unexpected. He was succeeded in 1669 by lord Robartes, who had already enjoyed a short tenure of office as deputy *in absentia*,[4] and was now to administer Ireland for only a few months. Scrupulous but indiscreet, he encouraged private soldiers to present concerted demands on their officers for arrears of pay,[5] and he upbraided the officers in the presence of their men. A rebuke from the king on this score led to his resignation in May 1670. His successor, lord Berkeley of Stratton, was as dissolute

---

[1] O'Brien, op. cit. 187.

[2] For good accounts of Blood see *D.N.B.*, and W. C. Abbot, *Colonel Thomas Blood, Crown-Stealer*.

[3] For instances of disaffection see *Cal. S.P. Ire.*, *1666–9*, xxi.

[4] See *supra*, i. 169.　　　　　[5] Bagwell, *Ireland under the Stuarts*, iii. 94.

and dishonest as his predecessor was scrupulous and moral; in contrast also with Robartes, Berkeley favoured the Roman Catholics. Otherwise he had no special qualification for the post, and his rule was memorable chiefly for his altercations with the corporation of Dublin.[1] To his surprise, he was displaced in February 1672 by Arthur Capel, earl of Essex.

Though he had served little in public employment, Essex proved to be a most fortunate choice. He knew nothing of Irish affairs, but he made a study of them; and he remained friendly with Ormonde, from whom he obtained both advice and parliamentary support. The first question to be determined was whether the oaths of allegiance and supremacy should be applied to all persons seeking membership of corporations. Essex decided to enforce these oaths as a general rule, and to dispense with them as he thought fit. He was thus trying to carry out in Ireland the policy which Charles hoped to follow in England by the Declaration of Indulgence; but Charles's enforced withdrawal of the Declaration (March 1673) had its repercussion in Ireland, where the disabilities affecting Roman Catholics had again to be enforced. Like Ormonde, Essex mediated between extremes. He did not drive the Roman Catholics into hostility; nor did he yield to the demands of Orrery and the extreme Anglo-Irish party for the establishment of a strong Protestant militia.[2] His main difficulties arose from brigandage, caused by the dispossessions of the land settlement; to Presbyterian missionaries, who penetrated as far west as county Mayo, riding up and down the country 'like martial evangelists with sword and pistol';[3] to the corporation of the city of Dublin, its faction and turbulence a serious problem for most Irish lords lieutenant; and lastly to the veiled hostilities of lord Ranelagh, the notorious farmer of the revenues, and the irregularities of lord Orrery, who, in 1668, had been impeached by the Commons on the accusation of malversation in his office of lord president of Munster.[4] Behind Ranelagh and his uncle Orrery were Danby and the duchess of Portsmouth, who had a

[1] Ibid. 102.   [2] Ibid. 109–17.
[3] Bishop of Killala to Essex, Jan. 22, 1677, in *H.M.C. Rep.* vi, app., pt. i. 745.
[4] The impeachment had been quashed by the prorogation of parliament on Dec. 11, 1668.

scheme for making Monmouth lord lieutenant, with lord Conway as his deputy in Ireland.[1]

Nor were these the only problems. Essex wished to secure an elementary standard of honesty in the government of the country, and strove to resist the spoliation of Irish acres by English courtiers. Had the conditions insisted upon by Ormonde in 1662 been adhered to, it might have been possible for Essex to effect some reforms; but he soon found that the course of Irish administration was not allowed to run in its proper channels, and a refusal from one responsible authority might be followed by successful application to another.[2] Some officials, such as the Irish clerks of the crown and the clerks of the peace, increased their fees by instituting vexatious lawsuits; others made fortunes from extortion; all of them were 'quick in getting pardons out of England'.[3] In general, the details of appointments and revenue were so interlocked with the exigencies of the English Court that the powers of the lord lieutenant were to a large extent nullified, a condition of affairs particularly exasperating to a zealous viceroy. In truth, Essex was completely out of place in Stuart Ireland; moreover, Charles himself was at the mercy of Ranelagh, the corrupt tax-farmer, one of the foremost obstacles to efficient administration. The result was the recall of Essex in April 1677. On his return to England he joined the Country party and threw himself into the opposition against Danby; and thus a skilled and honest minister was forced into a fruitless opposition in which he eventually sacrificed his life. But Charles, like Henry VIII, could appreciate qualities which he himself did not possess, and so, instead of appointing Monmouth to the viceroyalty, as he was urged to do, he again selected Ormonde,[4] who was entrusted with the administration of Ireland for the rest of the reign.

When Ormonde returned to Ireland in 1677 he was confronted by a great network of corruption and influence controlled by

[1] Bagwell, op. cit. iii. 122.

[2] Essex to Conway, May 26, 1674, in *Essex Papers*, *1672–9*, i. 229.

[3] Essex to Arlington, May 23, 1674, ibid. i. 233.

[4] Charles may have been influenced by the opposition of the duke of York to the appointment of Monmouth, who was Danby's nominee. *Essex Papers*, *1675–7*, 125–7.

the tax-farmers. Before leaving England he had, for the second time, made his own terms with Charles,[1] and he came with the intention of summoning parliament in order to obtain a grant. To this, the tax-farmers objected that any additional levy might make more difficult the collection of the revenues for which they had contracted.[2] Nevertheless, he thought that a parliament was necessary in order to clear up the remaining anomalies and grievances of the land settlement; so he had a Bill drafted with the object of introducing greater security of tenure in Connaught and Clare, where many titles were in dispute. He also proposed to offer a Bill of Oblivion in order to end factious litigation, and he had in view also some modification of the Hearth Tax, to mitigate the evil practice whereby the collectors distrained on the bed and pot of defaulters. Once again there was a prospect that Ireland might benefit by sympathetic rule, and Ormonde's third administration might have been the most fruitful of all, but in the autumn of 1678 England was dragged into the whirlpool of the Popish Plot, and everything had to be sacrificed to the supreme object of keeping Ireland quiet. It was one of Ormonde's major achievements that he preserved his country for the Stuarts in these stormy years 1678–82. By a series of proclamations[3] the Roman Catholics were ordered to bring in their arms; Roman Catholic institutions were dissolved, and the Protestant militia was strengthened and armed. That complete order was maintained in Ireland served in a measure to discredit the Plot in England.

In the earlier versions of the Plot Ormonde had been included among those who were marked out for assassination; but soon his moderation made him suspect, and for this reason he incurred the implacable enmity of Shaftesbury, who was encouraged by correspondents in Ireland to hope that he might be lord lieutenant.[4] Ormonde's offence was not that his measures were too severe, but that they were not severe enough; for if the Irish had been goaded into rebellion, this fact would have provided conclusive proof that the Plot was a genuine one. How slender were the supports of English rule in Ireland during this crisis was

---

[1] *Ormonde*, iv. 532.   [2] Bagwell, op. cit. iii. 125.
[3] *Steele*, ii. 888, 889, 891, 895, 897, 898, Oct. 14–Dec. 12, 1678.
[4] *Shaftesbury*, L. no. 31, Nov. 30, 1680.

revealed by a report to the English Committee of Intelligence in August 1680,[1] when it was shown that there was danger of rebellion on the part of those who had lost or forfeited their estates, and that the Protestant militia was of negligible strength, because most of the soldiers were tenants and married persons concerned only with their farms, while others were old and unserviceable; and so not above 2,000 men were fit for active service. There was neither ammunition nor stores; all the forts, except that at Kinsale, were in ruins; the country was defenceless both against foreign invasion and internal tumult. That such an Ireland should have remained undisturbed[2] during the frenzy of the Popish Plot is one of the greatest tributes to the statesmanship of Ormonde; and when, in May 1682, he was at last able to leave Dublin for London, he could at least congratulate himself that he had not lost his ship.

It was Ireland's good fortune that she had comparatively little history[3] in the reign of Charles II. It was otherwise with Scotland. The Roman Catholic interest in Ireland was not destroyed until the Revolution; in Scotland, the Restoration witnessed the beginning of a strenuous attempt to impose prelacy on the national Protestant Church. Ireland benefited by the rule of Ormonde and Essex; Scotland was for long at the mercy of Lauderdale and Sharp. Neither country possessed those secular institutions which, in England, interposed between sovereign and subject, and accordingly in both of them could be discerned more clearly than elsewhere the real principles and implications of Stuart rule.

The northern kingdom received favourable notice from some travellers. Praise of a disinterested character was bestowed on it by an Italian Jesuit[4] who spent twelve years there, two of them in prison. He remarked on the variety of Scottish products —salmon, coal, linen, salt, and cattle, almost everything, in fact, *praeter vinum et aromata*. He was impressed by the existence in

---

[1] *Add. MS.* 15643. *Minutes of the committee of intelligence*, Aug. 8, 1680.

[2] This was one of Shaftesbury's greatest disappointments. *Ormonde*, iv. 580.

[3] In November 1670 the *Dublin Gazette* ceased to appear because there was no news. (*Cal. S.P. Ire.*, *1669–70*, viii.)

[4] *Introductio ad relationem missionis Scotiae 1660* in *Rome Transcripts* (*P.R.O.*), 98.

such a poor country of four universities; two of them, St. Andrews and Aberdeen, on the Paris model, and one, Glasgow, on that of Bologna; he admired also the architecture of Glasgow Cathedral. Of the fourteen Scottish bishoprics he noted with pride that no less than thirteen had been founded by popes. He marvelled at the great length of Scottish sermons, and at the custom, not abandoned until the nineteenth century, whereby beadles paraded the streets during the hours of divine service in order to arrest the 'stravagers' or wandering absentees. But this description is exceptional in two respects—it was written by one who had been in Scotland, and it is not abusive; for most of the contemporary 'characters' of Scotland were compiled by strangers who collected their epithets at home.

Scotland was poor, not in the sense that it was declining from prosperity, but in the sense that it had never been prosperous. Crown lands there were worth only £50,000 Scots, or about £5,500 sterling per annum; the total yearly exports, consisting mainly of fish, salt, and hides, did not, at the Restoration, amount to more than £200,000. The population was sparse, great tracts of land were uncultivable, inland communications were undeveloped, and there was a scarcity of capital. Holland was Scotland's best foreign customer, and through the staple at Dort or Campvere were conveyed regular shipments of salt, skins, stockings, and plaiding; but the two Anglo-Dutch wars made serious inroads on this trade, and Scotland was forced to look for other markets, an ambition not realized until, with the union of the parliaments, she was admitted to a full share in the English colonial trade. In spite, however, of these disabilities, Scottish enterprise, assisted to some extent by English capital and Huguenot co-operation, succeeded in establishing a number of capitalist ventures, including a bank, sugar refineries, paper, rope and soap works, and a linen company.[1] Exports of coal to England steadily increased, and in 1670 amounted to 50,000 tons;[2] Scotch linen was also in demand, and was hawked by pedlars whom English constable and justice tried in vain to expel. But for the religious difficulties and the absence of

[1] For this see W. R. Scott, *Joint Stock Companies*, and T. Keith, *Commercial relations of England and Scotland*. For Scotland and the English Navigation Acts see *supra*, i. 245.   [2] *Grey*, i. 232.

adequate 'vents' for her products and manufactures, Scottish prosperity might well have advanced in the reign of Charles.

This poverty necessitated a lower standard of life than that which prevailed in England, but there were other things which accentuated the contrast between the two countries. In the northern kingdom the nobility had never been tamed as in the south; in consequence the Scottish nobility were still almost medieval—numerous, powerful, turbulent, litigious, and oppressive.[1] Many of them despised their countrymen, and some looked to England for bribes; hence, few of them had the making of national leaders. Hence also, political life was practically non-existent, and the third estate was not merely powerless but despised, because composed almost entirely of tradesmen; nor was there a real middle class, since the lairds or small gentry were scarcely represented in the Estates at all. An example of the contempt in which the Scottish burgesses were held was provided in one of the agitations against Lauderdale (1673–4) when they sent a remonstrance to Charles, which induced Atholl to express indignation that 'vermine and mechanick fellows dare offer such things to His Majesty'.[2] No English peer could have spoken thus of the English House of Commons.

In this void there was only one great national institution—the Kirk, and the ministers were the only functionaries whose influence was unrivalled and uncontested. Nowhere else had the teachings of the Calvinist reformation been worked out to such extreme conclusions; no other race could have deduced so logically the consequences of the Fall and the imminence of the reign of Anti-Christ. Witness a 'tolerable Sunday' as passed by a Presbyterian diarist contemporary with Pepys:

1. May 1659. This morning being in Humbie, after familie duty done, I went to Church and heard Mr. James Calderwood lecture on Math. XXIII, 13. Observation 1: that Our Lord denounceth their woes rather to terrifie his Disciples than to curse the Pharisees. . . 3. That no sin is more odious to God than hypocrisie. 4. That

---

[1] Strongest in territorial influence was the family of Campbell (earl of Argyle) in Argyleshire and the Isles. Many of the boroughs were controlled by noble families, e.g. Cupar by Rothes, Dundee by Crawford, and many of the northern boroughs by Huntly.

[2] Quoted by O. Airy in *E.H.R.* i. 458.

the kingdom of God is shut upon us all by nature. . . . Thereafter he preached on Matthew V, 4. From the cohesion obs. 1. That such as are sensible of povertie of spirit are always great mourners. 2. That a mournfull spirit is verie agreeable to the Ghospell. 3. That the mourning which the Lord requires is ane inward serious bitter mourning. 4. That those who do thus mourne aright are blissed. Afternoon, he preached on Deut. X 4 and Exodus XX 2. Ane catecheticall question wherein the morall law is conteined. The morall law divided in two tables. 3 opinions concerning that morall law. . . .

After sermons I went home to Humbie and after retirement went about familie dutie.

This was a tollerable good day to me.

A verie filthy rain all day.[1]

Such a religious outlook could not be transformed into episcopalianism merely by the imposition of bishops. In the south and west, notably in Lanarkshire, Renfrewshire, Ayrshire, Dumfriesshire, and Kircudbrightshire, there was maintained an uncompromising hostility to the ecclesiastical system imposed by the Restoration settlement; but elsewhere, especially in Aberdeenshire and the east, episcopacy was quietly accepted, and only Papists[2] and Quakers remained outside the fold. Even in the conformist districts of Scotland, however, episcopalianism was generally little more than a thin disguise for Presbyterianism; for, in spite of bishops and surplices, much of the discipline and worship of the native church was retained. Kirk sessions met wherein laymen, presided over by their ministers, took cognizance of lesser scandals; for more serious matters there were presbyteries, meeting once a month, and provincial synods meeting twice a year, the latter presided over by the bishop. Lastly, appeal might be made to that supreme tribunal, the General Assembly, meeting once a year, at which the king was personally represented. Thus the old hierarchy of representative institutions was preserved almost intact, and into this the bishop

---

[1] *Hay of Craignethan's Diary, 1659–60* (ed. A. G. Reid, 1901).

[2] Then as now there were communities of Roman Catholics throughout the Highlands, but there is little information about them. For a general account of Catholicism in Scotland in this period see A. Bellesheim, *History of the Catholic Church in Scotland*, trans. D. O. Hunter Blair, iv ch. ii.

fitted as a 'perpetual moderator'.[1] But while room was found for the bishop, everything conspired to exclude the graceful ritual characteristic of Anglicanism, leaving Scottish episcopalianism too exotic for the native temper and insufficiently catholic to redeem it from provincialism. This is accounted for in part by the poverty of Scottish ecclesiastical architecture. The Reformation had led to the destruction of many ancient fabrics; only one cathedral on the mainland was left intact, and though Scotland retained her castles, she lost her parish churches. The new structures were unworthy of the old; for, in the country, they were sometimes little better than cottages, and in the towns they were bricked and tiled, and often fitted with galleries. The gallery provided increased accommodation; but its precipitous elevation was no substitute for the gradual ascent of nave, chancel, and altar.

That the enforcement of episcopacy did not destroy the old roots beneath the surface is shown by the continued importance of witchcraft in the national life. In no other country was the injunction *Thou shalt not suffer a witch to live* more faithfully observed than in Scotland, where the Old Testament was interpreted and applied with a literalism unmatched save in Holy Russia. Had the bishops been men of enlightenment, commissioned to wean the country from the judaic Calvinism of the preceding century, they might have set themselves against the cult; but their rule brought no diminution of this superstition, and the Devil retained his hold on the minds of the peasantry. The government did not at first countenance the parish witchhunters; indeed in 1662 arrests for witchcraft were prohibited, except on a warrant from the Council;[2] but this was not generally enforced; for, after a brief lull, there was a recrudescence, and in 1678 the superstition became an epidemic.[3] If it be proved that the instruments of Charles's government in Scotland were not themselves believers in witchcraft, then the conclusion might follow that they hoped to conciliate the populace by pandering to devil-worship; but even among educated Scotsmen of the

---

[1] For this see *A short account of Scotland* by Rev. T. Morer, from which extracts were printed in *Selections from the records of the Kirk Session, Presbytery and Synod of Aberdeen* (Spalding Club, 1846), lxv–lxix; also G. Grub, *An ecclesiastical history of Scotland*, iii. 215–19.

[2] *P.C. Reg. Scot. 1661–4*, xlii.   [3] Ibid., *1676–8*, xxxv.

time, few were sceptical. · Sir George Mackenzie, the cultured and 'bloody' lord advocate, may have had his doubts, but he kept them to himself.

In England, though the cult was by no means extinct,[1] yet the pursuit of possessed persons was not carried out with the system and thoroughness of the north. This is amply illustrated by Scottish literature. The reader of Wodrow,[2] Law,[3] and the Justiciary trials[4] cannot fail to be impressed by the absolute uniformity in the confessions of accused persons, so uniform that they might almost convince one of the existence of demoniac influence, as they certainly convinced contemporaries. But the methods employed to obtain confessions account for their uniformity. These methods were pricking by pins (in order to find the anaesthetized spots) and deprivation of sleep, producing delirium in which the victim might well give an affirmative answer to any question; and as these practices were applied to the very young and the very old, witch trials easily proved the ramifications of a satanic clientèle into every parish of Scotland. Moreover since there was no segregation of the insane, the lunatic had then opportunities for a public career now denied him, and one maniac might bring ruin or death to many sane persons. Incube and succube; devil dances and pulpit blasphemies in churches brightly illuminated at midnight; cattle-rot produced by the incantations of old women with hooves or without shadows; nightmares and premonitions; all the natural order of things converted into a wild phantasmagoria of magic, fairy tales and crude falsehood were united in the hysteria through which the nation passed before the native intelligence could assert itself.

This daily contact with the other world was maintained by those possessed of second-sight; by midwives, who sometimes secretly baptized their charges in the name of the Devil, and also

[1] See, for example, sir M. Hale, *A trial of witches at the assize held at Bury St. Edmunds, March 10, 1664* (1682).

[2] Robert Wodrow, *The history of the sufferings of the Church of Scotland from the Restoration to the Revolution*, 1721–2.

[3] Robert Law, *Memorialls, or the memorable things that fell out within this island of Britain from 1638 to 1684*, ed. C. K. Sharpe, 1818.

[4] *Records of the proceedings of the Justiciary Court of Edinburgh*, ed. W. G. Scott-Moncrieff.

by those who were deaf and dumb. Of the deaf-mutes there were two categories—those afflicted by God from birth, and those whose disability had been brought later in life by Satan. Both were 'mediums', their prototype being the damsel of the Acts of the Apostles who possessed a spirit of divination. Such a damsel was the servant-maid employed by sir George Maxwell of Pollock, whose affliction, dating from birth, enabled her to detect and reveal the secret assaults of the Evil One on her master. When, in 1677, sir George sickened and turned the colour of clay, she knew that some one was busily working at his image in clay, and made signs that she could discover the source of the malady. Accompanied by one of the laird's friends she went to the house of a witch's son, and there by candle-light she revealed, under a bolster, a clay image of sir George, not yet dry. The young man in whose premises the image lay was accused, with his sister, of sorcery. Both confessed, describing the extraordinary guise in which the Devil had appeared before them, accompanied by six women; how the Devil had formed the face of the image, and had stuck pins into its right side—a statement confirmed by the fact that sir George had experienced pain in his right side.[1]

From this successful discovery the servant-maid embarked on a career of witch-hunting, and in the following year a whole batch of her victims was burnt at Paisley. She then appears to have recovered her speech; whereupon she was pressed to declare how her powers of divination had been acquired. In answer, she denied correspondence with Satan, and accordingly her believers thought that she must have the gift of second-sight. Others, however, suspected the inspiration of the Evil One, so the maid was committed to the Canongate prison, where she still plied her trade, and revealed to an Edinburgh bailie how his wife was bewitched by two old women on the Castlehill. After being questioned by the privy council she was ordered to be transported as a cheat; but no ship-master could be found to give a passage to such a dangerous person.[2] So the Maid of Pollock survived, dividing Scottish opinion into two camps according as her exploits were fathered on God or the Devil; a pardonable division of opinion, since the distinction between those two powers was then a subtle one.

[1] Law, *Memorialls*, 119-27.   [2] Ibid. 128-31.

The judicial system of Scotland was an amalgam of medieval and Roman law elements. At the head of the structure was the hereditary justice general who exercised his office by deputies. A supreme court—the Court of Justiciary—was set up in 1672, consisting of five lords of session presided over by a lord justice clerk, all holding office during the royal pleasure. Local courts were held by the sheriff, whose office was then hereditary; his deputy did not necessarily have legal qualifications. Juries might be imprisoned for their verdicts. The Scottish privy council constantly interfered with the administration of justice, either by convening a case to be heard before it, or by granting special commissions to private and sometimes interested parties for the trial of offenders or crimes. Jurisdiction, civil and criminal, was also exercised by the lords of regality and barons within their regalities and baronies, who acted by deputies chosen by themselves. Procedure was quite unlike that of the English common law, the law of Scotland having been modelled on that of Rome during the 'Reception' of the preceding century. Thus, in addition to the king's advocate or public prosecutor, there might be private prosecutors, and it was possible for an aggrieved party or one of his relatives to initiate and conduct a prosecution. Written depositions of witnesses were admitted as evidence, and the testimony of women was excluded, except in cases of witchcraft; in political trials torture was frequently applied in order to obtain confessions, and there was no remedy such as the English habeas corpus. Owing to shortage of prison accommodation for recusants the Bass Rock had to be taken over in 1671 as a prison.[1]

The statute law of Scotland was not much more ferocious than that of England; but the judicial proceedings in the Scottish capital reveal a condition of things not unlike that associated with fifteenth-century England. Crimes of violence were specially numerous; 'hamesucken', or forcible entry into enclosed premises, was frequent; at least one peer of the realm stole title-deeds;[2] a sheriff court was reduced to confusion when the accused covered

---

[1] *P.C. Reg. Scot.*, *1669–72*, 392. For a full account of the Scottish judicial system see *Records of the Proceedings of the Justiciary Court of Edinburgh*, ed. W. G. Scott-Moncrieff, Introduction.

[2] Ibid., i. 88.

his accusers with a pistol;[1] a territorial magnate obtained a commission of fire and sword against a neighbour and (after executing justice) sent the heads of his victims to the privy council for public exhibition.[2] In many parts of the Highlands the king's writ did not run. An illustration of this may be cited from the indictment presented in 1674 against Macleod of Assynt, then a prisoner in the Tolbooth.[3] On his own initiative he had levied a tax on all ships entering Loch Inver; he had captured a neighbour and detained him for three days *tanquam in privato carcere* until he paid his ransom; he then garrisoned his house at Ardvreck (Loch Assynt) and defied the sheriff. The climax came in 1671 when a commission of fire and sword against him was granted to the earl of Seaforth and lord Lovat, a threat which caused Macleod to 'convocate' 400 armed men (presumably Macleods) and put up a stout defence against Seaforth and his 800 clansmen, who, with the help of a battering-ram, besieged Ardvreck for fourteen days. In the course of an address to the besiegers Macleod announced that he did not care a plack for the king. The trial was a lengthy one, but the accused's counsel appears to have served him well, for the verdict was Not Proven.

The Highlands remained a continual source of anxiety to Stuart administrators. Some degree of organization and control was ensured by the clan system, and if the chieftain could be won over, the clansmen would follow; so in 1664 council revived the old expedient of summoning the chieftains once a year to Edinburgh in order to give bonds for the behaviour of their dependants; but this was difficult to enforce, as so many chiefs feared to approach the capital lest they might be arrested for debt.[4] Even more troublesome were those who belonged to no clan and lived entirely by robbery, going about the country in the guise of cattle drovers. There were also lawless districts; for example, the whole of Lochaber was practically outside the sphere of civil jurisdiction, and Caithness was rent by the feuds of the Sinclairs and the earls of Sutherland.[5] Against this lawlessness the Scottish executive was impotent, but what arms could not enforce was accomplished to some extent by a book. In 1684 a Gaelic version of the Psalms

---

[1] *Records of the Proceedings of the Justiciary Court of Edinburgh*, i. xvii.

[2] Ibid. i. 127. [3] Ibid. ii. 226–8. [4] *P.C. Reg. Scot., 1669–72*, xxv–xxvi.

[5] For these feuds see *Records of the Proceedings of the Justiciary Court*, i. 264.

began to be circulated in the Highlands;[1] and if the clansman could not read, he might at least chant.

In contrast also with English institutions was the structure of the Scottish constitution. The three estates, clergy, tenants-in-chief, and burgesses, were represented. Of these, the bishops remained lords of parliament until 1689; the tenants-in-chief, as in England, were divided into the greater and lesser tenants, the former receiving a special summons as lords of parliament, but the latter never joined forces with the burgesses, so there was no coalition of those classes which, in England, served to create a powerful House of Commons. The burgesses were elected by the town councils of the royal boroughs, and were therefore representative of civic oligarchies, having little or nothing in common with the nobility and gentry or the bishops; for this reason the Scottish parliament conformed more to a feudal convention of estates than to an English parliament; and so, while in the south parliament was pressing its claim to be the 'grand inquest of the nation', that in the north was divided by rigid barriers into compartments, each concerned mainly with the affairs of one class. This exclusiveness was intensified by the practice of delegating important duties to commissions, of which the most important was the Lords of the Articles, a committee representative of each estate, in which was done much of the preliminary work for later confirmation by the whole assembly. By their personal influence the Stuarts were able to exercise great control over the choice of Lords of the Articles, and through them to exert pressure on parliament itself; moreover, with such a wily Commissioner as Lauderdale, it was possible for the king to direct that, when a Convention of Estates was summoned to grant a supply, care should be taken that nothing else was discussed. Such were Lauderdale's instructions in the summer of 1678, when Charles hoped to raise a large force in Scotland.[2]

Even thus, there were 'rivals'[3] to the Scottish parliament. In England the word 'Act' was generally confined to the legislative enactments of parliament; but in Scotland the word was constantly used of the decisions of bodies which in different degrees

---

[1] Ibid., *1673–6*, xxxiii–xxxiv.
[2] *Add. MS.* 23242 (*Lauderdale Papers*, vol. i), f. 64, June 13, 1678.
[3] R. S. Rait, *The Parliaments of Scotland*, 9.

shared the parliamentary prerogative. These were the Scottish privy council, the convention of Royal Boroughs, and the general assembly of the Church of Scotland. In the privy council the programme of parliamentary business was prepared; whatever was capable of enactment was then drafted into Acts by the Lords of the Articles. Of the other rivals, the convention of Royal Boroughs was a parliament devoted exclusively to the affairs of the boroughs, their rights and privileges, their commercial relations with the foreigner, the incidence of taxation in the towns, and the regulation of weights and measures. Here the burgesses formed decisions which they presented to parliament in their capacity of members of the third estate; to this extent, their interests were focused on one class of problem, and so were deflected from questions of national policy.[1] Lastly, the general assembly of the Church of Scotland, by its inclusion of laymen, both noble and commoner, was on a more national basis than the English Convocation, and served to give a voice to two classes practically excluded from parliament—the clergy and the lairds.[2] In consequence, the assembly might debate matters of wider import than the discipline and doctrine of the Church, and could even discuss the conduct of the executive; but its period of greatest power[3] was already past.

After the Restoration,[4] policy was at first directed not by the Scottish council sitting at Holyrood, but by a committee of council in London, in which were included Lauderdale, Monck, Ormonde, and Manchester.[5] That it was possible thus to control Scotland from a distance was soon demonstrated; for the activities of the first representative parliament of the reign (that of 1661) reflected not so much the subservience of the legislature as the expert management of the government; and the Act Rescissory[6] testified more to the zeal of Clarendon[7] than to the loyalty of Scotland. Indeed there could have been little opportunity for debate, so many measures were rushed through. In its second

---

[1] For its economic importance see Miss T. Keith, *Influence of the Convention of Royal Boroughs on the economic development of Scotland* in *S.H.R.* x, no. 39.

[2] Rait, op. cit. 15.   [3] i.e. 1639–51.

[4] For the Restoration in Scotland see *supra*, i, ch. iv.

[5] *P.C. Reg. Scot.*, *1661–4*, vi.   [6] See *supra*, i. 176.

[7] For Clarendon's share in the imposition of episcopacy on Scotland see the *Memoirs* of sir George Mackenzie of Rosehaugh (ed. 1821), 52–61.

session (May 8–Sept. 9, 1662) parliament ratified the re-establishment of episcopacy already decreed by king in council, and imposed a test on all office holders in the form of a declaration that both Solemn League and Covenant and National Covenant were illegal. Then followed a joint campaign of council and parliament against recalcitrant ministers; but this unanimity was impeded for a time by the rivalry of Lauderdale and Middleton, of whom the latter hoped to exclude the other by the clause in the Scottish Act of Indemnity[1] excepting twelve persons. When the twelve were balloted for, Middleton succeeded in procuring the inclusion of Lauderdale's name. But he was no match for Lauderdale in dexterity. Before the Act and the list of the twelve excepted persons reached him, Lauderdale gained the ear of the king; the ruse was therefore foiled, and in 1663 commissioner Middleton had to resign in favour of Rothes.

The session of 1663, the third of the Restoration parliament, was presided over by commissioner Rothes, acting as the instrument of Charles and Lauderdale. Four acts were passed which tightened still further the Stuart hold over Scotland—that conferring on the sovereign the right to tax imports at will;[2] that restoring the Lords of the Articles to their former privileges at the expense of parliament;[3] an Act for raising a force of 20,000 foot and 2,000 horse;[4] and finally a Bill imposing heavy fines on all absentees from the parish church.[5] The working of the constitution as now perfected was thus explained by Lauderdale: 'nothing can come to parliament but through the Articles, and nothing can pass in the Articles but what is warranted by His Majesty, so that the King is absolute master in parliament both of the negative and affirmative.'[6] Now that parliament was out of the way the council began its long campaign against dissent by the imposition of heavy fines and the quartering of troops on the peasantry; and, in the hope of obtaining some relief from the overwork involved in securing conformity, the council (in 1664) adopted Sharp's suggestion to revive the Court of High Commission. Its activities, however, did not last longer than two

---

[1] *Acts of the Parliaments of Scotland* (1820), vii. 415, Sept. 9, 1662.
[2] Ibid. vii. 503–4.   [3] Ibid. vii. 449.
[4] Ibid. vii. 480–1.   [5] Ibid. vii. 455–6.
[6] *Lauderdale Papers*, i. 172, quoted by R. S. Rait, op. cit. 78.

years.[1] These events showed how quickly constitutional progress could be made backwards.

That Scotland was known to be out of sympathy with the anti-Dutch policy of Charles II's government was used as a pretext for increased harshness to the Presbyterian dissentients of the south-west. Between eight and nine hundred persons had been placed by the Scottish Act of Indemnity in a special class, for whom there was to be pardon only on payment of a fine. It was thought in 1666 that the time had come for the exaction of this fine; accordingly soldiers were established in the houses of these delinquents until the money was paid, and a further use was found for the military in the harrying of the field conventicles conducted by the ejected ministry. The officers employed in this service had mostly served their apprenticeship in Muscovy, and their handling of unarmed peasants showed proficiency in semi-oriental methods. At last the inevitable rebellion took place. In November 1666 sir James Turner, the leader of a detachment of soldiers, was taken prisoner, and his captors formed the reckless resolve of marching on Edinburgh in the desperate hope that they would find sympathizers there. At Rullion Green, in the Pentlands, colonel Wallace with 900 men faced the government troops under sir Thomas Dalziel (Nov. 28). The rebels put up a brave fight, but having few arms they were overpowered; about fifty were captured, to whom were added thirty stragglers, and all were given up to justice.[2]

Justice was then in the hands of a privy council which was prepared to seize this opportunity of providing a sanguinary object-lesson. The contention that the insurgents had voluntarily surrendered to quarter was brushed aside; it was enough that they had been caught in the act of rebellion. For weeks the boot and the gallows ministered to Scotland's Bloody Assize. Dalziel was then sent to the south-west to replace the humanitarian Turner, and even Sharp and Rothes had reason to be satisfied with the reports of his doings.[3] But a temporary relief was provided by the fall of Clarendon in 1667; for with him went Sharp's main support, and for a moment Scottish episcopacy appeared

---

[1] P. Hume Brown, *History of Scotland*, ii. 393.   [2] Ibid., ii. 395–8.

[3] The persecutions were accompanied by a policy of disarming the shires of Lanark, Ayr, Wigtown, and Galloway. *Steele*, ii. 2306–7.

to be without friends in England. Another change was the removal of Rothes from office, and his appointment to the chancellorship, in spite of his protest that he knew neither Law nor Latin. A Militia of 20,000 men was raised in readiness to march wherever Charles ordered—'never was king so absolute as in poor old Scotland.'[1]

Scotland had a share in the experimental toleration which accompanied Charles's secret alliance with France. In June 1669 was issued the first Letter of Indulgence, which granted this moderate relief to ministers 'outed' by the proscription of Protestantism, that, provided their former cures were vacant, and if they accepted episcopacy and the royal supremacy in ecclesiasticals, they might be restored.[2] This attempt at reconciliation appears to have done more harm than good, since very few of the recusants took advantage of it, most of them preferring ostracism to episcopacy; while, on their side, the Scottish bishops resented even these concessions, and condemned the Indulgence because its acceptance implied a recognition of secular supremacy in the Church. For his remonstrance[3] against the Indulgence Burnet, archbishop of Glasgow, was cited before the council, removed from his see, and replaced by Leighton. Meanwhile, these years of vacillation coincided with suggestions for the union of the two countries. An Act of 1667[4] had appointed commissioners to treat concerning liberty of trade, and in 1669 a Scottish parliament was summoned to take part in discussions of the proposed union. But on neither side was there confidence or even friendliness. Lauderdale, who had been appointed lord high commissioner in October 1669, went to Scotland in order to enforce the policy which he had hitherto directed through Rothes, and he believed that his own and his master's interests would be better served by keeping the two kingdoms separate; for otherwise his powers would be reduced to those of a secretary of state, and Charles would, in emergency, have less opportunity of using Highland troops against rebellious Englishmen. So the project of union was abandoned.[5]

[1] Quoted by O. Airy in *E.H.R.* i. 446.
[2] *Reg. P.C. Scot.*, *1669–72*, 38–40.
[3] *Lauderdale Papers* (ed. Airy), ii, app. 1–2.   [4] 19–20 Car. II, cap. v.
[5] Scottish commissioners to treat of union were appointed in July 1670. On

These hints of conciliation only served to make differences more acute. Politics intruded more and more into sermons, and the Covenanters now began to appear armed at their meetings. In the often-quoted words of Leighton, it was 'a drunken scuffle in the dark',[1] a scuffle in which the advocates of compromise were invariably trampled upon. Dependent solely on Charles, Lauderdale now governed the country absolutely, managing the short sessions of parliament with such dexterity that there was no time for opposition to shape itself, while the bishops threw the weight of their influence against all suggestions of compromise. There was a faint glimmer of a nationalist movement when, in November 1673, the duke of Hamilton demanded that Scottish grievances should be taken into consideration, and some of his supporters even talked of impeaching the commissioner; but this movement was personal rather than constitutional, and Lauderdale parried the attack by successive adjournments of parliament. Hamilton and some of his party came to London in order to present their grievances; they were coldly received, however, as they were thought to be in league with Shaftesbury;[2] and they were unwilling to reduce their charges to writing, as that would have rendered them liable to the charge of leasing making. In June 1674 Lauderdale was made earl of Guildford in the peerage of England; in December of the same year Leighton resigned. To the Scottish privy council were now added Monmouth, Danby, Finch, and Ormonde, who, together with Lauderdale, were deputed to conduct Scottish affairs from London in such a manner as to strengthen Charles's power in both countries.[3] In September 1677 sir George Mackenzie of Rosehaugh, the 'Bluidy Mackenzie', was appointed lord advocate, and the Scottish officers of state were informed that they held office only during His Majesty's pleasure, and not for life.[4] These changes coincided with an increasingly vigorous campaign against the Covenanters.

In the conduct of this campaign there can be detected a certain

March 6, 1671, there was a council minute to the effect that Charles had adjourned the meetings of the commissioners until further notice. (*P.C. Reg. Scot.*, 1669–72, 306.)　　　　　[1] *Lauderdale Papers* (ed. Airy), iii. 76.

[2] O. Airy, *Lauderdale* in *E.H.R.* i. 452.

[3] *P.C. Reg. Scot.*, 1673–6, iv.　　　　　　　　[4] Ibid., 1676–8, 233.

harshness or deterioration in the character of Lauderdale, who now set himself to complete the work begun by Rothes; that is, to cause such discontent as to provide a pretext for the maintenance of a standing army.[1] The penal statutes already in force against Roman Catholics were accordingly directed against Covenanters; and many named malcontents were ostracized by the issue of 'letters of intercommuning' which forbade intercourse with them. A measure still more effective was the Act of the Council of 1674 imposing on all masters and landlords the obligation of signing a bond giving security for the behaviour of their employees and tenants. This was extended in 1677 to include all persons residing on their lands, and was enforced on the whig landlords of the south-west, including the duke of Hamilton. When it was objected that no security for the opinions and conduct of dependants could be given, Lauderdale completed a plan said to have been first suggested by the bishops,[2] namely, to utilize the military prowess of the Highlander not against the foreigner, but against the Scot. It was accordingly decided to quarter a Highland Host[3] on Ayrshire. Before the Celtic warriors were ready, the south-west had again relapsed into its uneasy quiet; but Lauderdale refused to see a deputation of Ayrshire gentlemen who came to protest that the shire was at peace; and in December 1677 Charles authorized the issue of commissions to the lords Atholl and Perth for the raising of Highlandmen, while the Scottish bishops prepared their strategical notes on 'what is fit to be done for suppressing disorders in the west'.[4] By thus pitting the Celtic cattle-dealer against the Saxon husbandman it was hoped by those responsible for the government to precipitate a racial quarrel in which the armed men would have the best of it. The two races were bitter enemies in Ireland; the one might now be used against the other in Scotland.

About 6,000 clansmen mustered at Stirling in January 1678, and were joined by 3,000 of the Militia. As they marched south they were quartered on the peasantry, special attention being shown to the duke of Hamilton's tenants in Lanarkshire.

[1] P. Hume Brown, *History of Scotland*, ii. 404–5.
[2] *Lauderdale Papers*, iii. 95.
[3] J. R. Elder, *The Highland Host of 1679*, 39, and *P.C. Reg. Scot.*, *1676–8*, xiv sqq. [4] Dec. 21, 1677, in J. R. Elder, op. cit., Appendix.

Renfrewshire and Ayrshire were occupied by this army of invasion, which made no distinction between those who had signed the Bond and those who had not. After six weeks of plunder the Highlanders were anxious to return home with their booty; and as they had not succeeded in causing a rebellion, it was resolved, late in February, that they should retreat; so their cart-loads of utensils, furniture, and money were conducted across the Forth, and the internal embellishments of several Highland mansions were improved in consequence. There had been little bloodshed, but much robbery with violence, and, as all the horses were seized, the land could not be ploughed; in consequence, many Scots migrated to northern Ireland.

'The patience of the Scots under their oppressions', wrote Andrew Marvell, 'is not to be paralleled in any history.'[1] But there were limits. In 1668 an attempt had been made on the life of archbishop Sharp by one James Mitchell. Six years later Sharp recognized Mitchell in the street, and had him arrested. The privy council, promising that his life would be spared, extracted some kind of confession from him, and for a time he was imprisoned on the Bass. In 1676 he was again brought to trial, this time on the accusation that he had taken part in the Pentland Rising. He was tortured on one leg with the boot (at the suggestion of the archbishop), and when it was proposed to apply the same treatment to the other leg, some of Mitchell's friends sent a letter to Sharp intimating that, if he persisted in ordering torture, 'he would have a shot from a steddier hand'.[2] The threat succeeded for the time; but two years later Mitchell was again tried, this time in the Justiciary Court on the original charge of the attempted murder of Sharp. The prisoner's advocate pleaded the pardon, but Lauderdale refused to have the original record of the privy council's pardon brought into court, and, as Sharp insisted on his victim, Mitchell was executed. Vengeance was not long delayed. On May 3, 1679, Sharp was pulled out of his coach as it was crossing Magus Muir and murdered. More than enough retribution was exacted for this crime. After assisting at the torture of prisoners, Mackenzie wrote thus to Lauderdale: 'remember [remind] the king that king Alexander II killed

[1] June 10, 1678. *Works of Andrew Marvell*, ed. Grosart, ii. 631.
[2] Law, *Memorialls*, 85–6.

4,000 for the death of one bishop of Caithness . . . and what law had he for that?'[1]

This incident coincided with another event which helped to strengthen the case for a standing army. Observance of the anniversary of the Restoration (May 29) was by Statute the duty of all Scotsmen. This date, a dolorous one for Scotland, was chosen in 1679 for a demonstration at Rutherglen, near Glasgow, when all the Acts of the government were burnt. A few days later the insurgents, a band of about 250 men, defeated Graham of Claverhouse and the royalist troops at Drumclog, near Strathaven. Charles's government acted promptly. Monmouth was appointed captain-general of all the royal forces raised or thereafter to be raised in Scotland;[2] Irish troops were ordered to be moved north for transhipment,[3] and the Militia of all the eastern Scottish counties was hastily assembled. Before the end of June 1679 Monmouth was assured of as many thousands of troops as the whigs had hundreds. Having been repulsed from Glasgow, the rebels mustered on the Clyde at Bothwell Bridge, where the dissensions of the ministers divided them into two hostile camps, one party declaring for the king's interest 'according to the Covenant', while the other was for repudiating that interest altogether.[4] Even more ominous was the fact that when they engaged the troops of Monmouth it was on the Sabbath Day (June 22, 1679). Monmouth's offer of peace on condition of laying down their arms was rejected by the advice of the ministers, with the result that soon one more Scottish defeat was attributable to interference by the clergy. Though holding a strong position on the south side of the river, the rebels were badly manœuvred by their inexperienced commander Robert Hamilton, and they were sharply divided even at the moment of battle. It needed only Monmouth's cannon to complete their defeat. Thereupon Monmouth showed a quality of mercy to which the north was unaccustomed; but the executions afterwards ordered by the council attested the severity, not of strength, but of weakness:[5] for while the rebels had been defeated, on the other hand

---

[1] *H.M.C. Rep.* v, app. 316. [2] *Add. MS.* 23244, f. 5.
[3] June 13, 1679. *P.C. Reg.* 68. [4] Law, *Memorialls*, 150.
[5] For the perturbation of the Scottish privy council at this period see *P.C. Reg. Scot., 1678–80*, 481–5, 495.

the musters of Militia had shown so many defections that this force could no longer be relied on to crush native discontent. The problem, therefore, was either to remodel the Militia or raise a paid army. Thus the government of Scotland in the summer of 1679 was in a position almost identical with that of James II after the 'victory' of Sedgemoor.

Contemporary Englishmen, however indifferent they might be to the fate of Scottish covenanters, might well have discerned in the melancholy history of the northern kingdom a foretaste of what was in store for them. English hatred of Presbyterianism was strong, but not so strong as hatred of slavery. Already in the summer of 1678 the Scottish Estates had made a liberal grant for the raising of regiments of foot, horse, and dragoons,[1] and Charles believed that there were great, untapped sources of military strength in the north.[2] To supplement the dragoons there were the law courts; and an illustration of how effectively these might be used was provided just after the battle of Bothwell Brig. An Edinburgh jury acquitted some men of the charge of having taken part in the rebellion; whereupon an assize of twenty-five noblemen and gentry was impanelled in order to try the jury. This assize gave their verdict that the jurymen had been guilty of an error of judgement, whereupon the offenders were committed to prison.[3] That Charles might attempt to enforce on England what was already accomplished in Scotland had for long been present in the minds of the English opposition, as witnessed by the reiterated attacks on Lauderdale. These attacks were renewed in May 1679, when the Commons petitioned for his removal, and in June the duke of Hamilton presented a petition from a section of the Scottish nobility attributing the Scottish unrest to the iniquities of the hated minister.[4] A year before (May 1678), when Hamilton protested in the king's presence against the imposition of the Bond, Charles remarked that the Koran might yet be imposed.[5] Thus, in 1678-9, the opposition in Scotland and that in England were united against Lauderdale,

---

[1] *Acts of the parliament of Scotland*, viii. 221-9.

[2] *P.C. Reg. Scot.*, *1676-8*, 402.

[3] *Cal. S.P. Dom.*, *1680-1*, 385, 388, July 1681.

[4] *H.M.C. Rep.*, *MSS. of the duke of Hamilton* (supplement), 99-100.

[5] Ibid. 97.

and the Exclusion party could depend on some support from Scotland,[1] where the extremists were in favour of disowning not only the duke of York but Charles himself. This was illustrated in June 1680 when there was affixed to the cross at Sanquhar (Dumfriesshire) a declaration repudiating Charles Stuart because of his perjury and breach of the Covenant.

At this moment therefore it seemed not impossible that a new Bishops' War would give a lead to English republicanism. But Charles was bending, not breaking, under the strain, and there was soon to be a recoil. The removal of Lauderdale helped to effect this. His health was failing, and in October 1680 he resigned his offices; two years later he died. A new and even darker period of Scottish history had commenced in November 1679 when the duke of York went to Edinburgh as commissioner to the Estates.

Scotland and England might long have remained divided because of their antipathies, had not the policy of the Stuarts brought them together in a common suspicion of the real intentions of that House. In a 'well-conditioned' country such as Scotland it was not difficult to enforce a system of government wherein every national institution was placed at the mercy of a capricious prerogative; but, in England, where these institutions had deeper roots, the process would be longer and more difficult. The Scottish covenanters may have been bigots as well as rebels; but at least they were monarchists, for whom Stuart rule had brought both disillusionment and persecution; the turn of the English moderates was yet to come. The Scots had given a lead,[2]

[1] It is likely that Shaftesbury communicated and corresponded with Hamilton and other Scotsmen, but the correspondence does not appear to have been preserved. It is referred to in *Shaftesbury*, vi a, 349.

[2] Cf. *A new year gift for the Whigs* (1684):

> The Scotch Covenanters, to rouse up our knaves,
> Have given us a signet, as they did before;
> When the bishop's brains against the coach-naves,
> They dashed out, to show what a God they adore.

This ballad was printed *in extenso* by sir Charles Firth in *S.H.R.* vi, no. 23. Cf. also the pamphlets regarding Scottish affairs published by the whigs just after the Revolution; notably, *An account of Scotland's grievances by reason of the duke of Lauderdale's Ministry. . . .* and *The Scotch mist cleared up* (in *State Tracts relating to the government of Charles II*, 1693).

but could not maintain it; Englishmen, on the other hand, were better equipped for the contest by their greater wealth, their ancient parliamentary traditions, and their guarantees for the liberty of the subject. Before describing the crisis of 1678–81, in which the two countries shared a common interest, it is necessary to return to England and consider each of these three subjects in turn.

XII

REVENUE AND TAXATION

THE increasing wealth of England in the reign of Charles II was due mainly to the steady development of overseas commerce, and was evidenced most obviously by the greater amount of taxation which the country was able to bear. This expansion was revealed also in a more scientific study of fiscal problems, and in the launching of experiments for facilitating the extension of credit. It is the purpose of this chapter to consider the financial expedients of Charles's governments, and the beginnings of a more adequate system of administering the national finances.

The Convention Parliament voted[1] to Charles for his life the subsidy of tonnage and poundage on wine imported and on woollen cloth exported, each at prescribed rates. Appended to this grant was a Book of Rates, containing a monetary valuation of hundreds of commodities of import and export, on which a poundage of one shilling in the pound was levied. Thus, of imports: oranges and lemons were valued at £1 per thousand; Irish cattle at £2 10s. each; anchovies at 7s. 6d. per small barrel; silk from the East Indies at 15s. per pound; Virginia tobacco at 1s. 8d. per pound; Brazilian tobacco at 10s.; cotton-wool from foreign countries at fourpence per pound, and that from English plantations free. Among the 'outward' rates were: apples, fourpence per bushel; butter, 'good or bad', £3 per barrel; rabbit skins, 15s. per hundred; and beer 2s. per tun. These rates were somewhat arbitrary; nor was any account taken of market fluctuations. The subsidies on wine and cloth together with these Customs duties on imports and exports provided the most important source of hereditary revenue at the Restoration, when their yield was estimated at £400,000 per annum. For the first four years of Charles's reign, the average return was barely £300,000; there was some falling off during the two Dutch wars, but after 1674 there began a steady increase until the Customs yielded between £500,000 and £600,000. This coincided with an increased revenue from Excise, and explains why Charles, in the

[1] 12 Car. II, cap. xix.

later years of his reign, and James II throughout his reign, were
not dependent on parliamentary grant.

Attempts were made to prevent frauds in the payment of these
dues. The Act[1] of 1660 empowered Customs officers to break
into suspected houses; that[2] of 1662 authorized them to search
ships inward and outward-bound, and provided that dutiable
goods should remain in store until the duties were paid. But
legislation was often evaded, nor was it easy to obtain a conviction, even where smuggling was proved; so the government
had to enlist the support of the judiciary and the officials of
corporate towns in its campaign for the enforcement of these
regulations. Thus, in a smuggling case tried before him, sir
Matthew Hale, chief baron of the Exchequer, was enjoined in
a communication from the lord high treasurer to see that the
officers were 'countenanced';[3] so also members of parliament
serving for maritime boroughs were asked to obtain information
of frauds on the Customs, and report to the Treasury.[4] Mayors,
aldermen, and justices were exhorted to assist the Customs
officials.[5] There was certainly need for these exhortations, for on
at least one occasion the soldiers who helped to effect seizures
were themselves sent to prison by the lord mayor of London.[6]
Other causes helped to impede the efficiency of this service. The
men who acted as tide and land waiters, searchers, and gaugers
were appointed by recommendation only; their salaries were
small (most of them received less than £50 a year), and they
might be dismissed without reason; consequently they were
recruited from those unfit for other employment. For many
years one of the normal duties of a member of parliament was
to obtain posts in this service for the more 'decayed' unemploy-
ables among his constituents. 'When anyone fails in business,' it
was said,[7] 'or a gentleman wants to part with an old servant,
interest is made to get them into the Customs as if into a hospital.'
That this was no exaggeration can be seen from such an instance
as that of the member of the Chiffinch family, aged 13, who had
to be removed from his post of searcher at Gravesend, because

[1] 12 Car. II, cap. xix.   [2] 14 Car. II, cap. x.
[3] *Cal. Tr. Bks.*, *1660–7*, 263.   [4] Ibid. 266.
[5] *Steele*, i. 3319.   [6] *Baschet*, 145, Apr. 29/May 9, 1680.
[7] *Shaftesbury*, iii. 105.

he paid no attention to his duties.[1] In spite, however, of its imperfect personnel there grew up in London and the outports a great preventive service, and soon the Customs became one of the most important branches of the civil administration.[2]

The Excise, first introduced by Pym in 1643 and exacted during the Commonwealth, was regulated by Acts of the Convention Parliament, the effect of which was to confer on Charles for life one moiety of a tax on ale, cider, beer, aqua vitae, coffee, chocolate, sherbet, and tea; the other moiety being granted in perpetuity to the crown as compensation for Charles's surrender of the Court of Wards.[3] By an Act[4] of 1663 brewers were required to give notice of setting up or enlarging their tuns or vats, and every one retailing excisable commodities was obliged both to obtain a licence, and to give security for the payment of the dues. Additional Excise duties were granted in 1671[5] and 1677[6] for six and three years respectively. The yield from these taxes amounted at first to an average of between £250,000 and £300,000; but, immediately after the English withdrawal from hostilities in 1674, there was a remarkable increase; for, in the year following the conclusion of the treaty of Westminster, the return from this source alone amounted to more than £700,000. Thereafter, the average was £400,000, and in the reign of James it rose to about £500,000.[7]

Whether from its supposed origin, or because it was the most obvious of the indirect taxes paid by the consumer, this was one of the most unpopular of taxes. In 1660 there were so many obstructions to its exaction that the king had to issue proclamations ordering his subjects to pay it;[8] in the same year, at several Quarter Sessions, men were sent to prison for assaulting Excise officers.[9] Justices going on circuit were asked to include in their charges to grand juries a reference to the obligation of the

---

[1] *Cal. Tr. Bks.*, *1681–5*, 226.

[2] For the cost of the Customs establishments in London and the outports see *supra*, i. 50–51. For the administration of Customs revenue between 1671 and 1814 see B. R. Leftwich, in *Trans. R. H. Soc.*, series iv, xiii.

[3] 12 Car. II, cap. xxiii and xxiv. See also *supra*, i. 159.

[4] 15 Car. II, cap. xi.   [5] 22–3 Car. II, cap. v.

[6] 29 Car. II, cap. ii.

[7] For the figures see Dr. Shaw's introductions to the *Cal. Tr. Bks.*

[8] *C.J.* viii. 157, and *Steele*, i. 3210, 3260.   [9] *Carte MS.* 222, f. 49.

subject to pay these dues;[1] and in all disputes between brewers and excisemen, the principle had to be observed that 'the law being in His Majesty's behalf, and his revenue the public concern, the interpretation ought to be in his favour, and no frivolous excuses admitted'.[2] Frequently the privy council summoned to its presence justices of the peace who had given a decision whereby the Excise revenue might suffer; in one case, where the justices of a city were suspected of favouring the brewers, council ordered that the magistrates and deputy-lieutenants of the county should be joined with the city magistrates for the administration of better justice in such disputes.[3] An additional complication was introduced by the fact that the collectors of Excise were not normally government officials, but paid employees of the Excise farmers, to whom they were personally responsible. The government was therefore intervening to protect one class of private person against another class, in its own interest and in that of the farmers. The result was constant confusion and irritation.

Serious loss to the revenue arose from the dependence of the government on the farmers; but, before the farming system is condemned, it should be recalled that, in the absence of a civil service, it was inevitable, and in some cases it worked equitably. Between the granting of a tax by parliament and the collection of the money there was a considerable interval; it was here that the farmer was useful, for his first business was to make an advance of money on the security of the tax. He was generally a capitalist, or speculator, or one of a syndicate able to lend a capital sum and pay a rent, in return for which he recouped himself from the proceeds of the tax assigned to him. Once having made his bargain with the Treasury, the farmer would not normally have to reveal the amount of his gains; but if he demanded 'defalcations', that is a rebate in his cash payments to the government on the ground that the yield of the tax was below expectations, then he might have to produce accounts, and content himself with a definitely assessed profit. An illustration

---

[1] *Cal. Tr. Bks.*, *1660–7*, 215.

[2] Ibid. 722–3. Lord treasurer Southampton to the justices of Middlesex on the acquittal of a brewer in an Excise case, March 1666.

[3] The city was Worcester. *P.C. Reg.* 61, Nov. 18, 1668.

of this was seen in Michaelmas 1667 when a lease of the Customs fell in. The out-going farmers contended that owing to war, plague, and fire they had incurred serious losses in the last two years (1665–7) of their five years' farm. When their case was heard at the Treasury, counsel on their behalf submitted that they had paid the full rent for the first three years, and that their expenses of collection had amounted to £120,000 per annum. To this the solicitor-general replied that £50,000 per annum was a reasonable amount for expenses. Eventually, the king ruled that the farmers were to keep their profit for the first three years, and render an account for the last two, in respect of which they were to be 'savers, but not losers', that is, to be allowed only expenses of management. Charles assessed their expenses at £70,000 per annum.[1]

Until 1671 the Customs were farmed,[2] and part of the proceeds was always pledged in advance for the loans of ready money made by the farmers; there was also a deduction in respect of interest on these loans. An example may be quoted from the arrangements made for the new farm commencing in Michaelmas 1667, when sir John Wolstenholme and others were granted a lease of the Customs for four years at a rent of £350,000 for the first three years, and £370,000 for the fourth.[3] From the monthly payments of about £30,000 advanced by the farmers, there had to be deducted a sum of £16,000, made up of £8,000 for the payment of tallies struck on the preceding farm to the amount of £214,213, and another £8,000 per month for repayment of an advance of £200,000 made by the new farmers. In effect, therefore, the lease started with a load of debt, from which it could not be cleared for at least two years, during which time about half the total yield was hypothecated.[4] Arrangements for managing the revenue were constantly bound up with such outstanding claims; and on at least one occasion these loans at 'devouring' interest had to be paid off by the sale of crown property.[5]

[1] *Cal. Tr. Bks.*, *1669–72*, 106–16, July 1669.

[2] For the appointment of the commissioners (Sept. 24, 1671) see ibid., *1669–72*, 935. For their instructions, ibid., *1672–5*, 35.

[3] *Cal. S.P. Dom.*, *1668–9*, 34.

[4] Report of the retrenchment commission, Oct. 1668, in *Add. MS.* 28078, f. 11 sqq.

[5] For example, when, after the death of lord treasurer Southampton,

Another consequence of the farming system was that great gains were reaped by men able to supply the one thing needed by all seventeenth-century governments, namely, ready money. Many London goldsmiths amassed wealth in this way; notable examples are sir Robert Viner and Edward Backwell, but on the other hand these men were hard hit by the Stop of the Exchequer in 1672. In the provinces small men built up great estates; in Ireland, lord Ranelagh appears to have accumulated a huge fortune from his profitable farm of the Irish revenues. Even more, the farmers were sometimes able to exercise some influence on policy, because, as they had a contract with the government, they could insist on measures necessary for securing strict observance of its terms; so also, in regulations for trade, the government had to bear in mind its obligations to the farmers. Thus, in April 1669, the farmers of the Customs protested against the Order in Council of March 13, 1668, whereby the king dispensed for a year with such parts of the Act of Navigation as restrained the import of timber, and gave liberty to his subjects to buy sixty foreign vessels to be naturalized for this trade. Against the proposed relaxation, it was urged by the farmers that, as double or aliens' duty would not be payable on the cargoes of these vessels, the Customs would be the losers. But, on the report from the Council of Trade, this objection appears to have been set aside.[1] So also when the Dover Composition Trade[2] was renewed in 1661 the Council of Trade reported that the farmers would not extend dispensation to the colonies, owing to the loss which they might incur; so this trade was limited to foreign ports.[3] When, in 1673, the lord lieutenant protested against the Act prohibiting all direct trade between Ireland and the plantations, it was urged by the Customs commissioners that, owing to the cheapness of Irish provisions, Ireland would be able to undersell England in the West Indies, and so Irish prosperity would be on the basis of

Clifford became a commissioner of the Treasury, he leased the Customs to a friend, alderman Bucknall, who was already one of the farmers of Excise. Knowing that the crown was anxious to raise money on the Customs, Bucknall and his partners made their own terms. This led to a quarrel between Bucknall and Clifford; whereupon Clifford 'broke' Bucknall's lease, and repaid him his loans from the sale of the king's fee farm rents. *Add. MS.* 28078, f. 392.

[1] *Cal. S.P. Dom., 1668–9,* 290.
[2] *Supra,* i. 234–5.
[3] *P.C. Reg.* 55, June 10, 1661.

English ruin.[1] The same reason had already been adduced in 1661 by the Customs farmers against the proposal to relax the Navigation Acts in favour of Scotland.[2]

Nevertheless, some of the worst abuses in the system were remedied; and it was due mainly to Danby that many debts were paid off, and the yield from the two main sources of hereditary revenue was increased. In the absence of facilities for credit, he could not dispense altogether with the farmers, but he secured a larger measure of control over them. Thus in 1678, in return for an advance made by Richard Kent, Receiver of the Customs, he undertook that the charges on this fund would not exceed £430,000 per annum, or £530,000 if the Wine Duty were restored. Out of his receipts Kent was to make certain regular payments, including a weekly payment of £2,500 to the treasurer of the Navy, and the salaries of judges and ambassadors; his recompense was to be 8 per cent. interest on his Customs receipts.[3] This arrangement recalls the fact that, in practice, the greater part of the Customs had come to be allocated to the Navy. A Bill[4] for making this allocation statutory was introduced in May 1675; later in the same year it was proposed to annex this provision to a Bill for raising a supply for twenty ships,[5] but this scheme was afterwards negatived,[6] possibly because a majority realized that it was superfluous to make statutory what was already the custom of the executive.

An increased measure of government control can also be traced in the history of the Excise, but here even more serious difficulties had to be faced. Until 1683 the Excise was farmed in three areas—London, the five counties round London, and the rest of the country;[7] throughout these districts were farmers and sub-farmers appointed by the lord treasurer or commissioners of the Treasury from persons nominated at Quarter Sessions. A special body of commissioners was deputed to administer the Excise; they appointed gaugers, having power to enter enclosed premises in order to search for unexcised liquors. Disputes with brewers

---

[1] *Essex Papers* (Camd. Soc.), i. 54, Feb. 10, 1672/3.
[2] *Cal. S.P. Dom., 1661–2*, 74, Aug. 30, 1661.
[3] *Cal. Tr. Bks., 1676–9*, 856, Oct. 1678.   [4] *Grey*, iii. 102.
[5] Ibid. iii. 459.   [6] Ibid. iv. 187, Mar. 5, 1676/7.
[7] *Cal. Tr. Bks.* vii, pt. i. Dr. Shaw's Introduction.

and inn-keepers were to be referred to Quarter Sessions, but if the justices failed, or neglected to adjudicate, then appeal was to be made to the sub-commissioners, and from them to the commissioners. Leases of farm were to be for three years.[1] This system does not appear to have worked as intended. Farms were leased to untrustworthy persons,[2] and sometimes even to brewers, who made considerable profit during the Plague and Great Fire from the excessive defalcations which they claimed and were allowed;[3] there was also mismanagement by the sub-commissioners, who sometimes kept large sums of money in their hands without account.[4] For long, the deficiencies in the returns from this source of revenue were a source of anxiety to the Treasury, deficiencies due to two main causes—the difficulty in securing reliable farmers and competent sub-commissioners, and the great number of illicit or 'crock' brewers. There were plenty of facilities for brewing one's own beer; it was done by cottagers, by keepers of prisons,[5] by Oxford and Cambridge colleges. Trinity College, Cambridge, opposed the exaction of Excise on its home-brewed beer,[6] so it is not surprising that, among the humble, evasions of the tax were regarded as a venial offence. The loss to the revenue from this source was said to be £30,000 per annum.[7]

Danby's object was to obtain greater control over the Excise farmers. In the lease commencing in 1674 they had to advance security of £65,000, to pay in their daily cash, and to account for the king's share of all fines. Comptrollers of Excise were to sit with the sub-commissioners as collectors of receipt, to inspect gaugers' returns, to sign acquittances, to demand accounts of the sub-farmers, and to inform the Comptroller in London of any impediment in the collection of the tax.[8] Thus government control was mingled with private enterprise, and stricter accountancy was insisted on; in this way the yield was improved. This fact, together with the expansion of trade, the increase of wealth, and the maintenance of a higher standard of living, accounts for the steadily increasing returns from Customs and Excise.

---

[1] 12 Car. II, cap. xxiii.　　[2] *Cal. S.P. Dom.*, *1661–2*, 420.
[3] Ibid., *1668–9*, 134.　　[4] *Cal. Tr. Bks.*, *1660–7*, 322.
[5] Ibid., *1672–5*, 805.　　[6] Ibid., *1660–7*, 444.
[7] Ibid., *1672–5*, 776.　　[8] Ibid., *1672–5*, 538, 571.

The third branch of the hereditary revenue—Hearth Money —was introduced by an Act[1] of 1662, which granted to the king, his heirs and successors, a tax of 2s. per annum on each fire-hearth or stove. All householders were required to deliver to the constables and head boroughs an account in writing of their hearths and stoves, and the justices were ordered to cause these accounts to be enrolled and sent to the Exchequer. The constables collected the money, deducting 2d. in the pound for expenses of collection; the high constables paid it to the sheriffs, deducting 1d. in the pound, and the sheriffs to the Exchequer, deducting 4d. in the pound. The Act exempted houses of less annual value than 20s. and stipulated that the revenue from this source should not be charged with pensions. By an Act[2] of 1663 provision was made for the better keeping of accounts; and in the following year the crown was empowered[3] to appoint officers for the collection of this tax who, together with the constables, were authorized to enter and search houses. All houses having more than two chimneys were now brought within the scope of this legislation.

The Hearth Tax was difficult to collect, and the revenue from it was liable to great fluctuations. In the first year of its levy only £34,000 was brought in, increased by 1667 to nearly £200,000. It was farmed in 1667, and thereafter produced an average of about £170,000. Like other branches of Charles's revenue, it was saddled with debt, the farmers having agreed to pay a certain proportion to the city of London in repayment of loans to the king.[4] Considering its comparatively small yield, it was probably the most unwise fiscal measure of the later Stuarts because of the inquisitorial system necessary for its enforcement, and also the great inequalities in its incidence. Some people walled up their chimneys, or gave false returns, or induced justices and constables to connive at exemption;[5] others divided up large houses into tenements, the occupants of which pleaded exemption on the ground of poverty.[6] Cottagers who had no vote at elections complained that they had to pay 2s. a year for a stone 'not worth twopence which the Chimney villains call a hearth'; men

---

[1] 14 Car. II, cap. x.
[2] 15 Car. II, cap. xiii.
[3] 16 Car. II, cap. iii.
[4] Cal. S.P. Dom., 1668–9, 138.
[5] Ibid., 1663–4, 371.
[6] Modern Reports, iii. 94.

having estates of 40s. a year had often to pay as much as those having estates of £50, or £100.[1] In spite of these complaints, the Treasury in 1665 gave rulings which made the tax even more harsh; ovens only were exempted; owners, if not paupers, had to pay in respect of empty houses; stopped-up chimneys were to pay; and the levy was to be enforced on free schools, mills, and garrisons. Smiths, braziers, and pewterers were liable unless they could prove that their hearths were used solely for the purposes of their trade.[2] In consequence of these strict regulations, there grew up a trade in the 'discovery' of untaxed hearths.[3]

There were also special abuses in the farming of this tax. In April 1668 the farmers demanded defalcations for Plague, Fire, and War; also for Exchequer charges and assaults on their employees.[4] The government did everything in its power to secure the co-operation of local magistrates in order to ensure easier collection of the tax, and similar pressure was brought to bear on the judges. When, in 1670, the chief baron of the Exchequer was asked why he did not give more assistance to the chimney sub-farmers against those who failed to pay, he answered that it would be vexatious to issue process against a man in Cornwall for twelvepence; whereupon Ashley reminded him that the revenue was made up of twelvepences.[5] To this the chief baron replied that the chimney farmers should be commissioned by the Treasury, for then they would be accountants on oath, and distress could be levied on defaulters—a sound suggestion, for the deficiency in this revenue was caused not so much by failure of the subject to pay as by misappropriation or withholding of funds by the private persons entrusted with its collection. These were so extensive that, in January 1668, a treasury warrant was issued to take all the farmers of the Chimney Money into custody, except sir Robert Viner.[6] So notorious was the mismanagement of this tax that, as early as 1666, the Commons offered to compound for it at eight years' purchase, on an estimated annual value of £200,000; but Charles refused.[7] Later in the reign Halifax demonstrated to the king how he was being cheated by

---

[1] Cal. S.P. Dom., 1675–6, ix.
[2] Cal. Tr. Bks., 1660–7, 689.
[3] For an example, ibid., 1667–8, 28.
[4] Ibid., 1667–8, 296.
[5] Ibid., 1669–72, 352.
[6] Ibid., 1667–8, 217.
[7] Diary of J. Millward, Add. MS. 33413, Oct. 15 and Nov. 8, 1666.

the farmers; and it was hoped by the whigs that the duke of York would be implicated in the revelations.[1] Thus, harshness in its incidence and abuses in its collection helped to make this tax the most unpopular of all Stuart expedients; moreover it was an intrusion not into an Englishman's castle, but into his kitchen, and so helped to destroy some of the glamour traditionally associated with Stuart rule. It was abolished immediately after the Revolution.

Customs, Excise, and Hearth Money were the main sources of hereditary revenue in the reigns of Charles and James. They were supplemented by receipts from a large number of miscellaneous sources, none of them producing a regular return comparable in amount with the sources above enumerated. An Act[2] of James I had given the crown power to seize two-thirds of recusants' estates. After his enforced withdrawal of the Declaration of Indulgence Charles was induced to consider this method of raising money, so in 1674–5 the Treasury issued commissions to certain persons in each county with power to seize the king's two-thirds.[3] But in July 1675 it was reported that little or nothing had been done in the matter—whose fault it was the Treasury did not know.[4] There were also the forfeited estates of persons convicted of treason; these were generally solicited by courtiers, sometimes before conviction had been secured—an abuse explicitly condemned by a clause in the Bill of Rights. Consequently the revenue from forfeitures like that from recusants was negligible in amount. Most important of these miscellaneous sources was the revenue from royal lands or territorial rights pertaining to the crown. Among these were the rents from lands in the duchies of Cornwall and Lancaster, and a mass of quitrents and other dues known as the Fee Farm rents, these latter being estimated at about £50,000 per annum. This does not mean that £50,000 in respect of these rents was paid into the Treasury, for a certain proportion was applied locally;[5] but this amount represented the gross annual sacrifice made by Charles when he consented to the Act[6] for their sale. The Act vested these

---

[1] *Cal. S.P. Dom.*, *1683*, 66, anon. to Jenkins, Feb. 20, 1683.

[2] 2 Jac. I, cap. iv.   [3] *Cal. Tr. Bks.*, *1672–5*, 694, Mar. 1674/5.

[4] Ibid., *1672–5*, 804.

[5] Ibid., *1672–5*, viii–ix.   [6] 22 Car. II, cap. vi.

rents in trustees for this purpose, and the proceeds[1] amounted to about £700,000. Most of these territorial rights and dues had accrued to the crown from Tudor confiscations, and from the enforcement of the Chantries Act of Edward VI; usually they consisted of small sums which must have been very expensive to collect. Some conception of their nature may be gleaned by reference to the contract[2] whereby the Trustees agreed with sir William Ellis for the sale of a parcel of such rents, totalling £826 per annum, for a sum of £12,800, this being equivalent to about sixteen years' purchase. Among the rents so purchased by sir William were £6 7s. 1d. in respect of a custom called 'the knowing every second year and a half' in lands at Windermere, within the manor of Cartmel; £2 8s. 4d. from Greenbank vaccary; £1 11s. 9d. from the chantry of the Blessed Virgin Mary in Spalding; and £1 3s. 4d. from a similar chantry in Batley. So these picturesque vestiges of medieval fancy and piety at last disappeared into the obscurity of private ownership.

Such was the hereditary revenue; the parliamentary revenue was more tentative and irregular. The simplest form of parliamentary grant was a statute authorizing private persons to subscribe to 'a free and voluntary present' to His Majesty, as by the Act[3] of 1661; this was declared to be a special grant and was not to be used as a precedent. The subscriptions of peers were limited to £400, of commoners to £200; the proceeds appear to have amounted to £26,500, of which the commoners contributed £13,100.[4] Resort was not again made to this method of raising money. Provision for extraordinary expenditure, such as that entailed in war-time, was most usually made by an Assessment, such as had been levied during the Commonwealth. The usual rate was £70,000 per month, granted for a specified number of months, from one to eighteen. In the statutes authorizing this levy, each county and city in England and Wales was assessed at a definite quota, and commissioners were appointed to raise this quota by a levy on all owners of real and personal property in each city or county. The general principles on which the various commissioners acted were similar to those enunciated

---

[1] *Cal. Tr. Bks.*, *1672–5*, xi.   [2] Ibid., *1672–5*, 735–7.
[3] 13 Car. II, stat. i, cap. iv.
[4] Certificate of J. Clutterbock, in *Shaftesbury*, xxxiv, no. 21.

in the Act[1] of Assessment passed by the Rump in January 1660; namely, they met within a specified time in order to agree who should act within each division of their respective areas; any two or more of those so delegated then proceeded to declare the proportion of the assessment in each parish of their division or hundred; and lastly, this sub-quota was raised by a pound rate levied in each parish by two or more assessors in that parish. The rate was imposed on lands, tenements, hereditaments, annuities, rents, and offices other than judicial, military or naval offices, or household and government offices. When an assessment was made out, it was signed and given to the sub-collector, with a warrant for its collection. For each hundred there was a head collector; for each county a receiver general; and one penny in the pound was paid to collectors and sub-collectors. Tenants who paid the tax were authorized to deduct the amount from their rent; appeals against over-assessment lay to the county commissioners, but in such controversies a commissioner was not allowed to vote in his own case.

Two general principles of assessment were recognized. First, the number of commissioners assigned to each county was large, and the Commons in 1666 objected to an increase in their number on the ground that the more commissioners the less the return, since they were likely to encumber each other and promote the interests of their friends.[2] Second, both the proportion between the total for the county and the total for the country, and that between the county assessment and that of the cities and boroughs within its limits became standardized. Objection on this score was answered by a characteristic argument. When the gentlemen of Cheshire complained that the city of Chester was under-assessed in relation to the charge imposed on the county, the solicitor general answered that 'for these hundred years' the city had been assessed at one-tenth of the county, and so it would remain.[3]

In theory, therefore, the yield from these assessments was definite and invariable, because fixed in advance. The taxpayer's fraction was estimated by 'the most able and sufficient' persons in the parish or township; and as these persons were

[1] *Acts and Ord.* ii. 1355 sqq. [2] *Parl. Hist.* iv. 354-5.
[3] *Cal. Tr. Bks., 1669-72,* 165.

usually substantial property-owners, they were not likely to over-estimate the share due from their class. From the smaller fry they received statements, not on oath, which they might accept or reject; or they might content themselves with a marginal comment, as in the Downton hundred (Wiltshire), when John Humby 'confessed to be neere £20', the assessors added the word 'double'.[1] Similar in its incidence and method of collection was the Land Tax[2] granted in 1677; also the Royal Aids, namely that[3] of 1664–5 for £2,477,500 and that[4] of 1666 for £1,256,347, both for the expenses of the Dutch War. It is noteworthy that the Act granting the second of these Aids definitely allocated the sum of £380,000 for the payment of seamen's wages, and enacted that if the treasurer of the Navy misapplied any part of this sum, he should forfeit treble the amount so diverted.

An older form of tax on land and property, the Subsidy, was revived in 1663, when parliament granted[5] four subsidies by the clergy and laity, a grant confirmed by the clergy in their Convocations and embodied in an Act of parliament.[6] This was the last occasion on which the clergy taxed themselves separately; for in 1664–5 Sheldon, in a verbal communication with Clarendon, agreed to surrender this ancient right of the clergy.[7] The rate was the standard one of 4s. in the £1 on the annual value of land and 2s. 8d. in the £1 on the capital value of personalty, aliens and convicted popish recusants to pay double. By the Act of 1663 the county commissioners were to direct precepts to not less than two nor more than eight of 'the most substantial, discreet and honest persons' within each hundred, parish, or other division; thereupon these select persons, under pain of a monetary penalty, were to appear in person before the commissioners and inquire into the value of the substance of all persons liable to be charged. Certificates of assessments were then to be made out and served. No oath was to be tendered, and peers were taxed by a special commission of peers. Personal property was taken to

---

[1] Rates paid by the tenants of Winchester College as contributions to the Royal Aid of 1666 (Winchester College muniments).

[2] 29 Car. II, cap. i.   [3] 16–17 Car. II, cap. i.

[4] 18–19 Car. II, cap. xiii.   [5] 15 Car. II, cap. ix.   [6] 15 Car. II, cap. x.

[7] The new form of grant appeared in the Speaker's address to the king on Feb. 9, 1665, when he announced the grant of a Royal Aid 'in the name of all the Commons of England'. *L.J.* xi. 654.

include sums owing from debtors, while sums due to others were deducted from the gross value of the estate.

This revival was not a success. England had grown unfamiliar with the old type of subsidy, and the experiment was not repeated. Charles complained[1] that men with £3,000 and £4,000 a year did not pay more than £16; this was because such men generally taxed themselves.[2] In the absence therefore of impartial methods of assessment, it was inevitable that these property taxes gave disappointing results. In some cases the local commissioners, in their interpretation of the phrase 'clear yearly value', deducted from the gross income all payments for hearth money, church rate, servants' wages, and cost of personal subsistence, and 'so the king's part would be little';[3] sometimes also exceptional personal expenditure, such as that for the funeral of a relative, would be adduced as a plea for a less stringent assessment.[4] There was similar elasticity in the rating of personal property in towns. Thus, in September 1663 the corporation of Bristol, consisting of the mayor, aldermen, sheriffs, and councillors, met to arrange for the collection of the subsidies granted in that year. They first considered a letter from the privy council informing them of the standard rates on land and movables, a letter containing this special request that the corporation would see to the due assessment of the subsidy, since, through long desuetude, it was unfamiliar to Englishmen. Having appointed assessors for the several wards, the corporation then proceeded to assess themselves. The mayor declared that in chattels he was worth £10; so he paid £2 13s. 4d. This was comparatively conscientious; for three of the wealthiest men in the city assessed themselves at £8, and it was publicly said that many men were being taxed at a hundredth part of their real wealth.[5]

This was the last use of the old Tudor subsidy, but the word 'subsidy' was still retained and used of assessments and other

---

[1] *L.J.* xi, 582. King's speech, Mar. 21, 1664.

[2] e.g. the letter of the lords commissioners for rating and assessing the peers to lord Rutland, asking him to assess himself. (May 18, 1671. *H.M.C. Rep.* xii, app. v. 23. *MSS. of the duke of Rutland.*)

[3] *Cal. S.P. Dom.*, *1671*, 452.

[4] Ibid. 320. Lord Conway to the commissioners for assessing a property tax, May 1671.

[5] J. Latimer, *Annals of Bristol in the seventeenth century*, 320 sqq.

taxes. An interesting example is the 'Subsidy' of 1670–1, which was intended to fall not on capital but on income and profits. Among the rates were: on lands and mines, 1s. in the £1 of annual value; on public offices, 2s. in the £1, with an allowance on one-third of income for necessary charges; on personal estates not otherwise charged, 6s. for each £6 of annual interest or revenue. There was also in this Act an entirely new tax—a levy of 15s. on every £100 of borrowed money kept on deposit by bankers, the banker being authorized to deduct 10s. on every £100 repaid to his customers. Loans were invited on the security of this Act, the lenders to have 7 per cent. interest. But this new departure was discredited to some extent by its poor yield;[1] and in practice income and profits were taxed in the Poll taxes.

To supplement these taxes, parliament on several occasions experimented with taxes having for their criterion the social or professional status of the subject, or his salary or profits of office, generally combining these things together in one Act, and so providing a primitive form of Income Tax. Thus the Poll Tax[2] of 1660 required dukes and archbishops to pay £100, earls £60, baronets £30, esquires £10, judges £20, the lord mayor of London £40, masters of city companies £10. The same Act imposed a levy of 40s. on every £100 worth of land, money, or stock; on every single person over 16, 1s.; on every one under 16, 6d.; and for every hackney coach, 10s. Social position, professional status, real and personal property, means of transport, and humanity itself were therefore the objects of taxation in this Poll. The Poll Bill[3] of 1666 imposed a similar scale, but at half these rates, money owing to the estate being taxed, but debts due therefrom being exempted, with the proviso that exemption could be claimed in respect of money lent to the government on the security of the Act of 1665 for raising £1,250,000 by an assessment.[4] Public officers taxed in the monthly assessments were, by this Act, to pay 1s. in the £1 on the profits of their offices; those not so taxed,

---

[1] 22–3 Car. II, cap. iii. The yield in 1670–1 was £59,000 and in 1671 £152,000. It had been thought that this tax would give £800,000. See *Cal. Tr. Bks., 1669–72*, x, and W. Kennedy, *English Taxation, 1640–1799*. This essay by the late W. Kennedy is a brilliant contribution to seventeenth-century economic history.

[2] 12 Car. II, cap. ix.   [3] 18–19 Car. II, cap. i.

[4] i.e. 17 Car. II, cap. i. For loans on security of the taxes see *infra*, 444–5.

3s.; on government pensions 3s. in the £1 was to be paid, and 1s. in respect of every 20s. of servants' board-wages. Some of these rates, with modifications, reappeared in the Poll Bill[1] of 1677-8, but income from administrative, professional, and judicial offices was then consolidated, and charged at 2s. in the £1. This Act derived additional importance from the fact that it appropriated the proceeds of the tax, with all loans thereon, to a war with France, and prohibited the importation of French wine, brandy, vinegar, linen, and silk for three years from March 20, 1678.

Other sources of revenue taxed in Charles's reign included (1) the profits of the Post Office;[2] (2) the wine licences;[3] (3) imported wine and vinegar;[4] (4) proceedings at law;[5] and (5) new buildings about London. The profits of the Post Office provided a perquisite for the duke of York; and rival schemes, such as that of Docwra, who proposed a penny post, were suppressed.[6] Licences for the retail of wine were issued by a body of commissioners, at such fees as they might appoint, and the revenue therefrom was not to be charged with any pension. On French and Spanish wine, and on strong waters, the Act of 1667-8 purported to raise the sum of £310,000; the later Acts (1670 and 1678) granted an imposition at definite rates, the first for eight years and the second for three; so the renewal of this levy was one of the inducements for keeping parliament in session.[7] The tax on proceedings at law, the earliest of our modern Stamp Duties, was accounted for by the various courts of justice in London and the provinces, and by town clerks and stewards of manors; in the first year of its levy, it appears to have yielded little more than £20,000.[8] In February 1677/8 the Commons resolved to tax the yearly value of buildings erected in London since 1656, some of the Commons having alleged that new

---

[1] 29-30 Car. II, cap. i.   [2] 12 Car. II, cap. xxxv.

[3] 12 Car. II, cap. xxv.

[4] 19-20 Car. II, cap. vi; 22 Car. II, cap. iii; 30 Car. II, cap. ii.

[5] 22-3 Car. II, cap. ix.

[6] For the Post Office see J. C. Hemmeon, *History of the Post Office*.

[7] Another inducement was the renewal of the Additional Excise of 1670-1 (22-3 Car. II, cap. v) which was granted for six years from June 1671 and renewed for three years in 1677.

[8] *P.R.O. Accounts*, bundle 528, no. xi.

buildings about London were a common nuisance; but no special levy for this purpose appears to have been made, except that in the assessment for 1678, the amount to be paid by Middlesex and Westminster was increased.[1] A tax on entertainments was proposed in 1670, at the rate of 1s. for each person occupying a box at the theatre, 6d. for places in the pit, and 3d. for other seats, but the proposal was opposed by the courtiers, who successfully urged that the actors were the king's servants,[2] and would be prejudiced by this levy.

Lastly, among the sources of Charles's revenue must be included the subsidy from France. At no time was this sufficient in amount to make Charles independent of parliamentary grant; it was the increase of his hereditary revenue, not French money, which eventually enabled Charles to dispense with parliament. The contributions from Louis were generally sufficient to provide comfort, where otherwise there would have been economy; and the total amount received in the course of the reign did not exceed £1,200,000, a sum which would have barely sufficed to defray the civil administration for one year. Nor was this supplementary income spent solely on pleasure; for of the £689,758 accounted for by Chiffinch[3] in 1681, over £330,000 had been paid for the Navy, £66,000 for Ordnance, and £18,000 for the repair and rebuilding of Windsor. Among the miscellaneous objects on which this money was spent were these: to the duke of Buckingham, expenses of mourning for the duchess of Orleans, £1,000; to Pepys, treasurer for Tangiers, £5,000; to the royal upholsterers, £2,700; for a George, set with diamonds for William, prince of Orange, £400. Nurseries for trees at Greenwich, repairing fences at Hampton Court, planting trees in St. James's Park, building and repairing walls in Hyde Park, providing hay for the deer in Windsor Park, and the renewal of the more shabby decorations of Windsor Castle—these were among the miscellaneous uses to which the French money was put.

Such were the main sources, hereditary, parliamentary, and exceptional of Charles II's revenue. It is difficult to estimate

---

[1] 30 Car. II, cap. i.   [2] *Parl. Hist.* iv. 456.

[3] *Cal. Tr. Bks., 1680–5*, 198. Chiffinch's account of French money, Feb. 1671–Dec. 1677.

what proportion of his income a tax-payer might have to sacrifice in taxation; since the methods of assessment differed so much, and so many taxes were non-recurrent, that the burden must have varied greatly in both place and time. Assuming the resources of a tax-payer as static, a portion of his sacrifice would vary with the enrichment or impoverishment of the county or city where he was domiciled; for the most usually recurrent of the property taxes was the assessment, in which the contribution of each administrative unit was fixed; accordingly, if one's neighbours became richer, they might have to pay a larger share of this fixed amount; and conversely, a decline in the prosperity of the administrative unit might necessitate a greater sacrifice on the part of those whose fortunes had not changed. An example of the latter class of county would be Suffolk; of the former, Kent. Local differences in rating and fluctuations in the value of land may also have helped to increase these inequalities. That there should be a regular survey of land, and a more uniform valuation of it were among the principles advocated by sir William Petty.

As the freeholder was the unit of society, so the taxes of the seventeenth century were levied mainly on the income derived from landed property. In a sense this was the price of the pre-eminence of land among articles of private possession. The yeomen and farmers paid, not on their gross agricultural income, but on the rental value of their holdings.[1] It was natural, therefore, that the landed classes generally should favour those taxes which appeared to spare the land. The Customs fell on the importer and so on the consumer; but there was a definite return for these charges, namely, the maintenance of a navy for the protection of commerce. The other great indirect tax was the Excise, and it was here that the landowners joined issue with the rest of the community. In 1660 this contest had been decided in favour of the landed classes, when the compensation for the abolished feudal tenures was saddled on the Excise, a settlement which accentuated a question of principle. On the one hand, from the point of view of the tax-payer, the Excise duties, by their incidence on common articles of consumption, might involve a

[1] Working landowners paid on the annual rental value of their land and also on their stock in the Monthly Assessments. In the Aids they did not pay on their stock. (W. Kennedy, *English Taxation, 1640–1799*, 47, n. 3).

comparative sacrifice by the poor greater than that imposed on
the rich; moreover, these duties were of comparatively recent
and foreign origin; they were being gradually extended, and
might well result in freeing the crown from dependence on parliamentary grants. From the point of view of the crown, on the
other hand, the Excise had these advantages; it was paid insensibly and continually, and its administration supplied the prerogative with an army of officials who, if they had votes, must use
them in the interests of the crown. Herein were the rudiments
of a party distinction, though they never quite fitted into the
compartments dividing whig from tory; but it is certain at least
that Excise came to be associated with absolutism, and the
popular prejudice against it survived late in English history. At
the same time, however, there was an increasing acquiescence
in the view, popularized by Petty,[1] that Excise is the best and
most just of expedients for revenue purposes, because it does not
fall on sheer necessities, and is adjusted to the tax-payer's consumption of excisable commodities. By the time of the Revolution no political party could have dispensed with it.[2]

The formulation of a general theory of taxation was attempted
by Petty in his *Treatise of Taxes*.[3] As a substitute for the precious
metals he sought a more scientific standard of value, and found
it in land and labour, the two ultimate sources of human wealth.
Between these two denominations, however, he failed to establish any definite correlation; he thought, nevertheless, that each
country possessed some 'easily gotten', or staple food, of which
the cost of production provided a constant. Increased rent he
considered was mainly due to increase of population. While it
is true that Petty did not fully develop these principles, they
provide some anticipation of the theories of the Physiocrats and
of Ricardo. The incidence of taxation was discussed in his
Verbum Sapienti.[4] He estimated that, towards raising the £70,000
per month assessment, men paid a tenth part of the annual value

[1] *Treatise of Taxes*, ch. xv.

[2] For a discussion of this subject see W. Kennedy, in op. cit. 60–2.

[3] In *Economic Writings of sir William Petty*, ed. C. H. Hull. For Petty's
theories generally see Dr. Hull's Introduction, and Lord E. Fitzmaurice,
Life of sir William Petty, 211–15.

[4] In *Economic Writings of sir William Petty*, vol. i.

of their estates, and he believed that, if the special taxation of
1665 for the Dutch War had continued for two more years, the
sacrifice would have been increased to a third part. In his view,
the public charge was laid very disproportionately; and, in a
justly distributed system of taxation, he thought that no man need
pay more than a tenth part of the annual value of his property.
In this connexion, it may be noted that taxation might have been
more equitably assessed had there been adopted a proposal
constantly advocated by both Puritan reformers and Caroline
publicists, namely, a Land Registry. Such an institution would
have safeguarded title to land; it would have greatly diminished
the legal cost of conveyancing, and would have provided a body
of statistics for a more scientifically adjusted scheme of taxation.
The Land Registry, one of the most constantly reiterated of
seventeenth-century reforms, has been adopted only in recent
times.

Similar improvements might have followed from the establishment of a national bank. This was frequently suggested, but
there was great difference of opinion regarding the true functions
of such an institution. In 1661 a Dutch writer, Gerbier d'Ouvilly,
proposed[1] the foundation in England of a Bank of Exchange as
'beneficial to sovereign and people'. His bank would have a
large stock, under 'fitting governors' ('to remove all jealousy of
its falling into the hands of those who control the Militia'), having
a coinage of its own called bank money, and empowered to lend
money on the security of real estate. The proposal appears to
have been not unlike that afterwards advocated, as a rival to
the Bank of England, by Chamberlayne. A scheme for a Corporation Bank of Credit in London was set on foot[2] in 1682,
towards which funds were invited, and for the administration
of which a committee of aldermen and councillors was appointed.
The scheme was that all persons having goods lying by them
should bring them in chests into the large store-house attached
to the bank. There they would be valued 'according to durable-
ness and market value', and made over to the Trustees by a bill,

[1] *Cal. S.P. Dom., 1661-2,* 78.

[2] For this see *England's interest, or the great benefit to trade by banks or offices
of credit in London,* 1682, in *Bodley* G.P. 1120, and *Corporation Credit, or a Bank
of Credit made current by common consent in London,* 1682, in *Bodley, Ashmole,* 1672.

a certificate being given to the depositor, who was then entitled to receive a credit for a proportion of the value so deposited. As the credit note was assignable, it was hoped that the scheme would enable men to embark on fruitful schemes, and 'engross the commodities of other countries', thereby beating the Dutch with their own weapons. But, except for its distinguished civic patronage and a complicated system of book-keeping, this institution was little better than a pawnshop, and therefore socially inferior to those schemes, such as land-banks, where the security did not have to be kept on the premises. That the civic bankers were conscious of this disability is shown in a literary effort to commend the 'good and painful undertaking' to the country customer. This was a *Dialogue*[1] *between a country gent and a London merchant.* The merchant disabused the countryman of the idea that the adventurers Chamberlayne and Murray were behind the scheme; he dwelt on the facilities of the bank, how credit could be created, goods deposited in safety, and taken away in proportion as the loan was paid off; he so convinced his inquirer that the dialogue ended with this tribute from the prospective client: 'if this be the constitution of the Bank, I must confess you have satisfied me that it is both Just, Safe, Useful, and Profitable.' Only the skill of the pictorial artist was wanting to depict the benevolence of the merchant and the complete satisfaction of the customer from the country.

In 1680 the English Treasury 'in its present hands' was recommended as a safe deposit,[2] on the ground that it gave 8 per cent. interest and its security was as good as that of any private person. This recalls the fact that existing government machinery very nearly provided the requisite organization for a government bank; indeed, it was only because an impossible task had to be performed by Charles's financial administrators that they did not succeed in grafting some kind of permanent bank on to the Exchequer.[3] This short-lived experiment origin-

---

[1] *Bank Credit . . .* 1683, in *Bodley, Ashmole,* 1672.

[2] Godolphin to the prince of Orange, May 4, 1680, in *Prinsterer,* v. 397.

[3] For this see W. A. Shaw, *The beginnings of the national debt,* in *Historical Essays of Owens College, Manchester* (ed. Tout and Tait); also Dr. Shaw's introductions to *Cal. Tr. Bks.* for the reign of Charles; also R. D. Richards, *Early history of banking in England.*

ated in the practice whereby the Exchequer began to administer loans as well as revenues. For example, there were the deposits made by the farmers when they negotiated their farm; next there were the private advances on such regular sources as the Customs, a security specially favoured by the bankers; then there were loans to which contributions from the nation were specifically invited, the security for which was placed on a definite tax. In 1662 Southampton and Ashley introduced an innovation[1] which helped to increase the confidence of the lender, namely the system of paying out 'in course'. At first, this appears to have been applied only to payment of tallies struck on the Customs receipts; it was intended to displace the older and more haphazard method whereby one man was served before another because of his importunity; or a little paid out to every one because there was not enough to pay in full. The innovation was intended to secure payment only according to strict, chronological sequence; and accordingly, the man who lent on the Customs might apply for repayment in a year or eighteen months, with a reasonable hope that his claim would not be sacrificed to that of some other lender.

Soon, the principle was extended, and Exchequer procedure was greatly developed by the reforms associated with the name of sir George Downing. It was by his initiative that certain innovations were embodied in the Act for the Additional Aid[2] granted by the Oxford parliament of November 1665, an Aid by which it was hoped to raise £1,250,000 as a further subsidy for the war. Against the strenuous opposition of Clarendon, Downing succeeded in carrying a clause whereby it was enacted that all money raised by this Bill should be applied only to a definite purpose, namely for carrying on the war. By this appropriation clause some limitation was imposed on the powers of lord treasurer Southampton, who had faithfully striven to make ends meet by supplementing one source from another; but nevertheless he set himself to carry out the revised procedure, though he complained of the difficulty of doing so, because payments had to be made 'in course' as registered; moreover, without his knowledge, this fund was soon saddled with com-

---

[1] *Cal. Tr. Bks., 1660–7*, 358, Feb. 3, 1662.
[2] 17 Car. II, cap. i.

mitments registered by the king and the duke of York.[1] But that
such an appropriation clause should have passed the Commons
was of importance, because it reflected the suspicion that funds
intended for the war were being diverted; and it was thus one
of the earliest suggestions of criticism of the executive by the
Cavalier Parliament. Once having secured a statutory appropriation of supplies, Charles's parliaments extended the principle; for in the following year they assigned £30,000 to the
Guards[2] (thereby giving some legal colour to the existence of
a standing army); in the Poll Bill[3] of 1677 they appropriated the
proceeds to a war with the French king, and in the Assessment[4]
of £619,388 voted in 1678 they allocated this sum to the disbandment of all the land-forces raised since September 29, 1677.
In 1677 an Assessment[5] of £584,978 had been granted for the
express purpose of building thirty ships-of-war. Thus the principle of appropriation of supplies had taken root long before the
end of Charles's reign.

Appropriation of a tax to a defined object, and payment 'in
course' of all expenditure defrayed therefrom were thus two
important innovations in English fiscal practice. Even more
important was the revival of a project first attempted in the
Poll Bill of 1660, namely, that of inducing the public to lend
money on the security of one of the national funds. In the Additional Aid of 1665 these three principles were for the first time
united—appropriation, payment 'in course', and an appeal to
the public for loans on the security of this more precisely regulated fund. There was a fourth innovation which may be
attributed definitely to Downing, namely, that the repayment
orders accompanying the Exchequer tallies were made assignable by endorsement. The effect of this last provision was that
a holder of tallies needing ready money before the assigned date
of repayment could now take his tallies and orders to a gold-
smith-banker and have them discounted. Between 1667 and
1671 many of these 'orders of loan' were issued by the Exchequer,

---

[1] *Cal. Tr. Bks.*, *1660–7*, 712, Jan. 5, 1666.

[2] 18–19 Car. II, cap. i, par. xxxi.

[3] 29–30 Car. II, cap. i. The appropriation is embodied in the title of
the Act.

[4] 30 Car. II, cap. i, par. i.   [5] 29 Car. II, cap. i.

and when the 'Stop' came in 1672 most of them were in possession of the bankers. It is possible, therefore, to discern in the
terms of this Additional Aid of 1665 the germ of three things—
a national debt, in the invitation to lend money on the security
of a portion of the national revenues; a national bank, in the
reorganization of the Exchequer system, whereby its repayments
of borrowed money became more automatic and less capricious,
thereby encouraging the lender and the investor; and lastly,
a paper currency, because these early Exchequer Bills were
negotiable instruments, and so might serve as a substitute for
currency. Had this scheme[1] succeeded, the monopoly of the
goldsmiths would have been destroyed, and England would
have had a national institution for the creation and circulation
of credit. Colbert tried to do the same thing for France when
in 1674 he established the *Caisse des Emprunts* for short-term
loans, redeemable in definite sequence; but the French experiment also failed.[2]

These facts have been cited to show that considerable progress
was made in fiscal administration in the reign of Charles, and
that some of the most notable financial achievements of the
Revolution whigs were not without their backing of earlier
experiment. But, as in so much else, this reign stands between
two worlds. On the one hand it was still thought by some that
the king should 'live of his own'. On the other hand, the enormously increased demands on the executive made this older ideal
no longer possible of fulfilment. So too with accountability; on
the one hand the king had his hereditary revenues for which he
had to render no account, while on the other he was obliged to
demand more and more money from parliament, for which a
rendering was required. The king was still a landed proprietor
and not yet an official; the Civil List was still mixed up with the
normal expenses of peace administration and the exceptional
expenditure necessitated by war. In these circumstances both
confusion and misunderstanding were inevitable, and these

---

[1] For this see R. D. Richards, op. cit., 59 sqq.; W. A. Shaw, *The beginnings
of the national debt* in *Owens College Historical Essays*, and J. Beresford, *Sir
George Downing*, ch. 12.

[2] Germain Martin, *L'histoire du crédit en France sous le règne de Louis XIV*,
i. 92–4.

things should be taken into account when the difficulty of
Charles's task is gauged. The scheme associated with the name
of Downing was an attempt to adjust the older financial system
to the newer needs of the state; but it was foredoomed to failure,
because the parliamentary provision for Charles's revenue was
so inadequate as to make bankruptcy (as then understood)
inevitable. That bankruptcy was merely being staved off is
seen from the steady increase of debt in the first twelve years of
the reign, until in 1672 it amounted to more than £2,000,000,
when a suspension of payments had to be resorted to. In addition, even had there been no debt, it is doubtful if a Stuart could
have acquiesced in a scheme, such as Downing's, which subjected
payments to strict routine.

One illustration in support of this last assertion may be cited;
it had its origin in the following way. As many of the farmers
and collectors were guilty of embezzlement or failure to account
for their receipts, parliament in 1667–8 passed an Act[1] requiring
the payment of 12 per cent. interest on such overdue accounts.
The enforcement of this penalty explains the motive of a petition
to the privy council in 1673 from one David Powell, Receiver
for an eighteen-months Assessment in the county of Mont-
gomery, who alleged that the money collected (£988) had mis-
carried on its way to London. These arrears were charged to
Powell; but interest in the debt was assigned to Killigrew (the
court jester) by the king, who may have thought that this was
not a very valuable gift. As security for the debt Killigrew
thereupon took over part of Powell's estate, and sold some of
the debtor's goods; he then demanded the full 12 per cent.
interest allowed by the Act. Powell petitioned[2] that the interest
should be reduced to 6 per cent. This example has been selected
because it shows how even from a debt an importunate courtier
might profit. On the royal assets, whether forfeitures, reclaimed
lands, or revenues, the demands were more continuous and
rapacious. The generosity of the king on these occasions con-
trasts with the niggardly attitude to humbler applicants; for
example, the widow of Charles I's shoemaker, to whom £1,100
was owing. Her claim was ordered to be paid out of the leather
forfeitures, from which highly speculative source she received

---

[1] 19–20 Car. II, cap. vii.   [2] P.C. Reg. 64, May 14, 1673.

only enough to support her in prison, where she was confined for debt.[1] Charles's private expenses were not excessive, nor were his women associates costly if one thinks in terms of millions, but the hangers-on and courtiers were an equally insidious source of profligacy, because their importunity was as secret and personal, and might be rewarded from any branch of national revenue. Many historians have emphasized the brilliance of Charles's Court, or his guiltlessness in the financial affairs of his reign; but behind these attractive things there is the background of dishonoured government bills, imprisoned creditors, and starving sailors.

The king's personal generosity crowned a wonderful edifice in which each compartment was kept completely separate. This meant that the different sources of revenue were reserved for separate commitments; thus, the assessment raised from one county would be allocated to the Wardrobe; or one month of Customs revenue would be assigned for a particular debt; or a pension might be placed on the Chimney Money, or on the Excise, with the result that if there was a shortage in one of these separate funds, the payments therefrom might fail.[2] Experience showed which were the more secure, which the less reliable funds. Customs and Excise were the soundest, the first being favoured by the goldsmiths for their loans, while the second was a good basis on which to assign the pension of a favourite. Chimney Money was highly speculative, owing to fluctuations in yield. The result was that there might sometimes be effected transfers of security from one fund to another—changes called *virements* in French finance; for example, Lord Mandeville, in 1668, asked that his pension of £1,000 per annum should be transferred from the Chimney Money to a better source.[3] Or the Exchequer officials might have to go round looking for a fund on which some payment could be placed; and in spite of the 'in course' system, it seems generally to have been possible for both the king and the duke of York to secure priority for a pension or payment, even though the fund allocated was already burdened with debt, and encumbered with registered claims. This is why the seamen suffered so much in the Second

---

[1] *Cal. Tr. Bks.*, *1669–72*, 1044.

[2] Ibid., *1669–72*, 7.

[3] Ibid., *1667–8*, 441.

Dutch War. Parliament had definitely allocated £380,000 for their wages, but who was to see that such a sum was applied for that purpose? Moreover, the seamen were far off, and obscure persons at best; while near at hand there were the Gentlemen of the Bedchamber, the Groom Porters, the Pages of the Backstairs, to name only some of the more reputable of those who frequented the Court.

Not dishonesty, but clumsiness and wastefulness were the characteristics of financial administration at this period. Only gradually was there being evolved the experience and public opinion requisite for the creation of a system more fitted to cope with the rapidly-expanding needs of the state. Not yet was the fiscal administration regarded as the prerogative duty of government departments, or civil service; for so long as there were tax farmers, there was an element of private enterprise and profit in the national finances; and indeed the levying of a tax might be committed almost entirely to an outside body, as for example when the Vintners advanced on loan the greater part of the proceeds expected from the Wine Act of 1667–8, and then made their own arrangements for its collection;[1] or when, at the Restoration, the proceeds of several taxes were administered by the Chamber of the city of London.[2] Perhaps the severest criticism of the executive in the whole of Stuart history was that implied by the proposal of October 1675 to lodge in the Chamber of the city the money to be raised for the building of ships. It was negatived by only 171 to 160.[3]

These things contributed to the rising flood of debt which, for a time, overwhelmed the structure. The issue of Exchequer Bills had facilitated the circulation of credit and was a perfectly sound scheme; but when these Bills were assigned on revenues already hypothecated for more than a year in advance they were really based on no security whatever.[4] Most of these 'orders of repayment' on the Exchequer had come into the hands of the

---

[1] For the irregularities to which this led see *Cal. Tr. Bks., 1681–5*, 118, where it is shown that those members of the Vintners' syndicate who had lost money by the first speculation of 1667–8 used their influence with parliament to have the Wine Act of 1670 passed, so that they could recoup their losses.

[2] Ibid., *1660–7*, Introduction.   [3] *Parl. Hist.* iv. 772–4.

[4] For this subject see Dr. Shaw's preface to *Cal. Tr. Bks., 1669–72*.

bankers and goldsmiths; a portion was held by government departments, and all these paper commitments came to be based on security already pledged up to the hilt. In January 1672 Charles issued letters patent suspending for one year all payments on asssignations in the Exchequer.[1] This measure did not involve the break-down of the finances of the nation, but it meant default in regard to a substantial portion of national debt. The Stop was renewed a year later, and its real effect was to make available for government needs the proceeds of the taxes as they came in, while leaving unsatisfied the claims due on the paper orders of loan issued in accordance with the scheme of 1665. The loss, amounting to just over a million pounds, fell mainly on the bankers, who in 1674 were given two years' interest on their capital; a more permanent provision was that made in 1677–9, when interest was paid to them by a scheme of annuities.

More than personal loss, the Stop of the Exchequer involved public discredit; for it appeared to confirm all the suspicions entertained of Charles's financial administration in the Second Dutch War, and it was partly responsible for England's withdrawal from the Third. Another consequence was that further financial experiment had to be postponed until after the Revolution.

[1] Ibid., *1669–72*, 1172, Jan. 20, 1671/2.

XIII

THE CROWN IN PARLIAMENT

THE central theme in the history of Charles II's reign is the attempt to establish a clearly defined relationship within the trinity which consisted of crown and both Houses, and was known as the crown in parliament. That the king was an essential part of the legislature; that he had supreme control over the Militia and all forces by land and sea; that his supremacy in ecclesiastical matters was not abridged by the abolition of the court of High Commission—such were among the principles enunciated by Statute in the first session of the Cavalier Parliament. To the restored monarch, more foreign than English in his education and sympathies, indifferent to the vague constitutionalism enshrined in the native common law, such a settlement must have seemed eminently just; for it appeared unreasonable that the polity of England should present an exception in the well-ordered ranks of European states. Herein was the true significance of Charles's somewhat fitful Catholicism—it suggested links with the oecumenic church and still more with the equally oecumenic and sacrosanct principles of government then being applied abroad, notably in France. Charles had been deprived of his birth-right for twelve years, and though much of his exile was passed in the Low Countries, where there were some local traditions of independence, he was yet taught to associate absolute kingship with order, and political experiment with anarchy. Of English patriotism, or respect for English tradition, there was no trace in his career.

Charles must have found some confirmation of his theory of kingship in the language of those who came into contact with him. Clarendon made no secret of his conviction that the roots of the late rebellion could not be destroyed 'until the King's regal and inherent power and prerogative should be fully avowed and vindicated, and till the usurpations in both Houses since the year 1640 were disclaimed and made odious'.[1] Men more learned in the law helped to confirm this doctrine of royal pre-eminence. Thus lord Guilford, citing Bracton, Britton,

[1] *Clar. Cont.* iii. 164.

and Fleta, contended that the king alone has supreme and ordinary jurisdiction in the state, all others having merely delegated jurisdiction; while from Tudor precedent he argued that the king is supreme governor in all ecclesiastical as well as temporal causes.[1] More generally, Guilford defended the prerogative on the ground that 'a King is above ambition, and it will be easy to obtain justice from one who hath almost all that he desires'.[2] The royal power was so extensive that its limits should not be inquired into—such was the expressed opinion of secretary Coventry in the House of Commons.[3] Its activities were also entitled to the protection of secrecy, for it was 'the law of the land' that no one might expose to public knowledge anything concerning the government without the king's licence.[4] According to Danby, peace and war, punishment and mercy, jurisdiction and its concomitants, all belonged to the king and to no one else; the phrase 'the body politic' was a trick of the lawyers.[5] It was generally agreed that the crown was not one of the three estates; to contend that it was an estate of the realm was a whig heresy.

The clergy provided even more strenuous advocates of the prerogative. At a meeting of Convocation of the University of Oxford in July 1683 a decree was passed condemning certain 'pernicious books and damnable doctrines'. Among the doctrines so condemned were these: that civil authority is derived from the people; that there is a contract between the ruler and his subjects; that a ruler who becomes a tyrant forfeits the obedience of his subjects; that the king is one of the estates of the realm; that covenants and associations are legal.[6] Unlike the lawyers, the churchmen had no reserves in their political theory, and they based their doctrines on something stronger than tradition—namely the Bible. It was a not inconsiderable part of Charles's achievement that he availed himself of the religious sanctions with which the Divine Right school

[1] Add. MS. 36086, f. 22.   [2] Add. MS. 32520, f. 221.

[3] Feb. 1673, in the debate on the Declaration of Indulgence. Parl. Hist. iv. 521.

[4] Jeffreys, at the trial of Henry Carr for printing and publishing The Weekly Packet of Advice from Rome. State Trials (1730 ed.), iii. 57.

[5] Add. MS. 28043, f. 102.

[6] H.M.C. Rep. Kenyon MSS., 163–6.

surrounded the throne; he confirmed these sanctions by the assiduity and success with which he touched for the King's Evil,
and no one could have worn more gracefully than did he the
halo with which Anglican devotion sanctified the royal head.

If it is impossible to define the limits of Charles's prerogative,
it is possible at least to describe some of the paths which con-
verged on it. Religion, sentiment, and expediency all found a
meeting point in the crown; even the much vaunted common
law tradition of England seemed to direct a finger in the same
direction; for had not Bracton declared: *parem non habet Rex in
regno suo*?[1] From this primordial dictum it had been argued in
the preceding century that the royal prerogative was above
human laws.[2] But unfortunately there was a disputed right of
way in this legal path towards absolutism; for elsewhere Bracton
had stated: *Rex habet superiorem, scilicet Deum; item curiam suam,
videlicet comites et barones, quia comites dicuntur quasi socii regis, et
qui habet socium habet magistrum.*[3] Here was an entirely different
conception of kingship, already well known to critics of the
prerogative. Lord President Bradshaw at the trial of Charles I
had quoted it to support his two contentions, that the function
of parliament was to redress the people's grievances, and that
in Saxon times parliaments had frequently called kings to
account.[4] Similar views were taught by Algernon Sidney on
the strength of the same authority.[5] This apparent inconsistency
in Bracton arose from the interpolation in a defective manuscript of a marginal gloss or comment—an explanation first suggested by a seventeenth-century Englishman, who contended
that the passage was an addition made to the text by someone
in sympathy with the ideals of Simon de Montfort.[6]

This has been quoted as one of the many instances where the
authority of secular tradition was invoked with somewhat
ambiguous results. Less ambiguous were the conclusions

[1] Bracton, *De Legibus Angliae*, f. 5 *b*.
[2] By Thomas Cromwell and Robert Cecil, *Parl. Hist.* (1751 ed.), iv. 191
and 465.   [3] *De Legibus*, f. 34 *b*.
[4] *Trial of king Charles I* (ed. J. G. Muddiman), 115–17.
[5] *Discourses concerning government* (2nd ed. 1705), 263–4.
[6] John Turner, in his reprint (1684) of *The Soldier's Catechism* (originally
printed 1644). In Prof. Woodbine's edition of Bracton (ii. 110) the passage
is classified as one of the 'addiciones'.

deduced from the maxim, the king can do no wrong. This was reiterated not by the churchmen, but by the lawyers, and connoted a legal rather than a moral irresponsibility. It related especially to the king's commands in writing under the Great Seal. As such commands were public and authenticated, it was possible for the subject to see for himself whether they were legal or not; if legal, he had to obey them; if illegal, it was his duty not to obey them. Consequently, any of the king's grants might be contested in one of his courts of justice. This, the more academic interpretation, imposed on the subject the requirement of finding out or testing the legality of the sovereign's commands, while absolving the crown from the duty of ascertaining whether these were legal before enunciating them; in a sense therefore this interpretation of the maxim amounted to no more than this, that everyone, except the king, is supposed to know the whole law of England. 'Every Englishman', it was said in the House of Commons, 'is born a common lawyer.'[1] But there was a more important deduction, destined to be brought into sharper prominence by the events of Charles's reign. This was that the king can do no wrong in the sense that his responsibility has to be apportioned among his ministers; accordingly, from a seemingly absolutist maxim, was deduced the doctrine of ministerial responsibility. Hence one of the most sacred rights of the Commons—the right to impeach: hence also their right to discuss and criticize the king's speeches, since these were put into his mouth by his ministers. But Charles strove to avert the attempt to attack him through his agents by exercising an undoubted right of his prerogative—the right to pardon, and it was Danby's plea of such a pardon which prompted the declaration in the Act of Settlement that no pardon under the Great Seal was pleadable in bar of an impeachment. Before a constitutional monarchy could be achieved, it was necessary to restrict not only what the king might do but what he might forgive.

From this fundamental maxim a third deduction was made, namely, that the king must not give reasons for his acts. His legal immunity was already so complete, that for him to explain or condone his conduct was to sacrifice that immunity, and to

[1] *Grey*, iv. 137.

descend from the throne to the tribunal. The Tudors had all avoided this trap; some of the Stuarts were always falling into it. James I wrote books and made speeches in the attempt to explain himself; Charles I was forced into the false position of having to protest his innocence and good faith; James II, convinced that he could bring even the most obstinate to his way of thinking, conducted an electioneering campaign, and made the worst mistake a king can commit, that of composing his own speeches. Alone of the male Stuarts, Charles II appreciated and respected this essential element of the prerogative, knowing as he did that a king who argues or excuses himself is lost; but so strong were the forces ranged against the unique but obsolescent system which he so skilfully directed, that even he was guilty of serious lapses, as when in October 1675 he gave his promise to parliament that, if a supply were granted, he would be more economical in future.[1] The worst lapse was in February 1673, after a prorogation during which he had caused his chancellor to issue writs for the filling of vacant seats. Having made his speech, he appears to have got up again with the extraordinary preamble 'One thing I forgot to tell you', and then proceeded to explain what he had done.[2] The Commons promptly unseated all the members so elected, and solemnly recorded the principle that it was for them to issue such writs.

When they granted to Charles the Customs and Excise for life, the legislators of 1660 may not have foreseen how this grant would ultimately absolve the crown from the necessity of recourse to parliament; later, they may have thought that some guarantee was provided by the Triennial Act[3] of 1664, which enacted that parliaments should be summoned and held 'once in three years at the least'. This Act contained no provision for its enforcement, and its violation by the crown commenced in April 1684, three years after the dissolution of the Oxford Parliament. But in a sense it was fortunate that such a life annuity was voted, because it spared Charles the necessity of raising money without parliamentary consent, and so helped to confirm the claim of the Commons to be the sole initiators of money grants. In this respect the aims of the Puritan Revolution were

---

[1] See *infra*, 534-5.　　　　　[2] *L.J.* xii. 526, Feb. 5, 1673.
[3] 16 Car. II, cap. i.

vindicated; here indeed was the most substantial link between the conduct of Charles Stuart and the principles formulated by the Long Parliament of 1640. One of the first acts of James II was to break this link, for he began his reign by levying Customs and Excise duties before the meeting of his parliament. But not only did Charles preserve inviolate this sacred right of parliament; he allowed also a parliamentary investigation of national expenditure in the Second Dutch War,[1] and in practice he devoted the greater part of the yield from the Customs to the needs of the Navy. He paid at least nominal respect to the privileges of the Commons, and he did not publicly resent criticism of his speeches. In these respects Charles acted as a constitutional monarch, and to that extent he made more easy the task accomplished by the statesmen of 1689. This process was further facilitated by an English institution not usually associated with constitutional progress—the Tower of London. Unlike the Bastille and other prerogative prisons, the Tower was not merely a place of confinement for personages arrested on a royal warrant, because it received into its custody persons committed on the warrant of either House of Parliament; and so, at least in the reign of Charles, the Tower served at times as a national repository for the safe custody of those whose temporary seclusion from public life was desirable.

Otherwise the relations between king and Commons showed a steadily increasing tension, ended by the personal triumph of Charles and the apparent discredit of parliamentary institutions. Though annihilated in the reaction of 1681-5 and reduced to impotence in the reign of James II, the whig opposition had nevertheless placed on record many of the fundamental principles on which sovereignty was afterwards to be based. These doctrines were formulated mainly in discussion or criticism of certain prerogative rights exercised by the crown, including (1) absolute control over the military forces of the kingdom, (2) the right to maintain ministers in office, (3) the right to summon, prorogue, and dissolve parliament, (4) the right to appoint judges during pleasure, (5) the right to veto legislation, and (6) the right to declare war and make peace, and, in general, to control the foreign policy of the country without recourse to parliament.

[1] See *supra*, i. 317.

The first was contested only to this extent, that a standing army was thought by the opposition to be illegal, in spite of the reference in the statute of 1661 to 'the Militia and all forces by land and sea'. Here parliament was trying to undo what the Restoration legislators had effected. The second, appointment to high offices of state,[1] and retention of unpopular ministers, was not opposed as a general principle, but only in particular cases where the Commons tried in vain to use their weapon of impeachment. Both Clarendon and Danby were, it is true, removed; but not directly at the suit of the Commons; Lauderdale on the other hand remained, impregnable in his master's support. The third right, that of summoning, proroguing, and dissolving parliaments, did not become a matter of concern until comparatively late in the reign. In 1668 sir Richard Temple brought in a Bill which conferred on the chancellor the power to issue writs in the event of parliament not having been summoned within three years, but he was ordered to withdraw it.[2] The Commons took a very different view during the Exclusion controversy; for in December 1680 a committee of the whole House resolved to introduce a Bill for the more effectual 'securing and sitting of frequent parliaments as one means to prevent arbitrary power'.[3] The fourth right was contested by the Commons in their demand, reiterated at the time of the Popish Plot, that judges should hold their offices not *durante beneplacito*, but *quamdiu se bene gesserint*.[4]

Of the fifth right, that to veto legislation, Charles made a very sparing use; nor would its exercise have been discussed had he not, in at least one instance, acted in a somewhat unusual manner. Only two public Bills were vetoed—one for confirmation of the office of Register of Sales[5] (1662) and a Militia Bill[6] (1678). In neither instance did the Commons show resentment, and in

---

[1] On appointment to all but the most important offices the duchess of Portsmouth exercised some influence. In 1671 Andrew Marvell wrote of her: 'all promotions, spiritual and temporal pass within her cognizance'. (Marvell, *Works*, ed. Grosart, ii. 394). These promotions included deaneries and even bishoprics.   [2] *Parl. Hist.* iv. 410.

[3] *C.J.* ix. 682.   [4] Ibid. ix. 682, and *infra*, 605.

[5] *L.J.* xi. 473. For the veto generally see C. E. Fryer, *The royal veto under Charles II* in *E.H.R.* xxxii.

[6] *L.J.* xiii. 394; also *infra*, 604–5.

the latter they tried to find out wherein their Bill had offended. But there were two occasions when a Bill ready for the royal assent was 'lost'; the first being a Bill for the stricter observance of the Sabbath[1] (1663), and the second a Bill for repealing the Elizabethan statute on which the penal legislation against the Dissenters was based.[2] Charles's complicity in the second 'loss' was suspected, and this unusual method of quashing legislation was keenly resented by the whigs of the Oxford Parliament (1681), one of whom lamented that the earlier loss (that of the Sabbath Observance Bill) had not been more strictly inquired into at the time, since the one mishap might have given some kind of precedent for the other. The result was a resolution for a conference with the Lords on the constitution of parliaments in the matter of passing Bills,[3] but Charles did not again have occasion to exercise ingenuity in the elimination of inconvenient legislation.

This moderate use of the veto helped to preserve the right intact, and in practice Charles quashed many bills by the expedient of proroguing or dissolving parliament. The result was the evolution of an almost stereotyped relationship between crown and Commons. On the one hand, the Commons held out the bait of a subsidy in return for some legislative concession; on the other hand, the crown strove, by its friends and agents in the House, to secure a grant without such concession, and when these expedients failed, the king prorogued parliament in the hope that delay would put the legislators in a better frame of mind; or else dissolved it, in the hope that the country would return a House of Commons more likely to repose faith in the executive. Charles skilfully utilized the English sentiment for royalty in his calls upon the confidence of the two Houses; he played assiduously on this harp until there was no string left; but his Commons showed more and more clearly that, while they regarded the king as a gentleman, they believed Charles to

[1] Ibid. xi. 577. It was 'taken from the table and is not now to be found'. Each peer gave his oath that he had not removed it.

[2] On Dec. 17, 1680, the Commons accepted the Lords' amendments to this Bill, L.J. xiii. 719. For the debates in the Oxford Parliament on its loss see Parl. Hist. iv. 1308.

[3] Parl. Hist. iv. 1311–13.

be a trickster.[1] The unfailing courtesy preserved throughout this relationship was a distinctively English achievement.

In regard to the sixth right, that to control foreign policy, the Commons knew that they could not dictate the crown's alliances, mainly because they were handicapped by a certain limitation implied in their writ of summons, the formula being: *ad consentiendum et deliberandum de quibusdam arduis regni negotiis*. The word *quibusdam*, contrasted with the Lords' *omnibus*, seemed to infer that certain exalted matters of state might be withheld from their cognizance, and the classical example was Elizabeth's refusal of the Commons' claim to discuss her marriage. But in the Third Dutch War the Commons made clear their disapproval of Charles's foreign policy, and in May 1677 they debated an address for a defensive and offensive alliance with Holland, a debate in which precedents were quoted to prove that, in the past, the crown had sometimes acted on the advice of parliament in making its treaties. This was objected to by secretary Coventry as a knocking at the prince's door, instead of the customary scraping, but the Commons were not to be deterred; and they coupled their address with an intimation declining a further supply until His Majesty's alliances were known.[2] Charles's reply was an uncompromising refusal to allow the slightest invasion of his fundamental power of making peace and war.[3] But the king himself was at the mercy of the very exceptional circumstances which controlled European policy in the crucial years 1677–8; and when parliament again met on January 28, 1678, he announced that he had formed an alliance with Holland. He appeared to yield still further; for in April he made known to the House the terms of his alliances.[4] These concessions were not changes of principle on the part of Charles, but were strategic moves in the negotiations with Louis XIV, whereby Charles was using the English demand for war with France as a means of extorting money from the French king. Herein was his most notable failure; he thought that he could

---

[1] e.g. in the debate of May 1677 Sacheverell was reported to have said: 'When peace was made with Holland, we desired it exclusive to France. It was said then: "trust the King"; and you were deceived then. Will you be deceived twice?' *Parl. Hist.* iv. 876.   [2] Ibid. iv. 870–9.

[3] *C.J.* ix. 426.   [4] See *infra*, 554.

yield to the Commons and also secure the foreign subsidy; but not even the wiliest of diplomats could have combined these two things in the crisis of 1678. Moreover, Charles's failure was an ungraceful one. His trickery was revealed to each of the two parties which he wished to dupe, and the shame of these proceedings helped ultimately to secure for the Commons an effective control over the foreign policy of the crown.

Charles yielded in the matter of the Dispensing Power, and his control over foreign policy broke down temporarily in 1678; but otherwise he preserved intact all the prerogatives with which his crown was endowed. Nor did he do anything to diminish the national veneration for the throne, however much his personal conduct may have aroused criticism. To the end he retained firm hold of a sceptre which at many moments seemed certain to slip from his hand, and he surmounted innumerable difficulties not by industry, but by inactivity; not by force, but by a histrionic gift and a supreme sense of tact. But, unknown to himself, his reign was steadily preparing the way for the constitutional government of modern times. From the core of the privy council there was evolving an administrative machinery controlled by experts; parliament became securely entrenched as an essential element in English life because of the gradual realization that its activities were the concern of the nation; still more, the events of the reign made Englishmen politicians, and there can be no real measure of parliamentary government until some standard of political education has been achieved. This political education was almost continuous between at least the years 1640 and 1688. The Long Parliament instituted rule by a single House; Protectorate and Commonwealth were little more than a series of experiments in adjusting the powers of the executive to the control of the Commons; at the reaction of the Restoration England seemed to be heading direct for absolutism, in the crisis of 1678–9 for revolution or republicanism, and throughout these years there was no lengthy intermission in the meetings of the House of Commons. Charles quickened the cause of constitutionalism by the suspicion which his conduct created, but he retained his throne by sheer political genius, and bequeathed to his brother the strongest prerogative in modern English history. The measure of James's failure is the measure of Charles's success—a success personal, solitary, and unique.

If there was doubt in regard to the extent of the powers enjoyed by the crown there was still more in regard to those of parliament. The theory still survived that parliament had first been instituted by king Alfred, but there was little agreement about the limits of its functions, advocates of contrary opinions finding support for their views in the heterogeneous mass of legend and tradition which had been readily devoured by lawyers and parliamentarians in the struggle against Charles I. An extreme view was that vouched for by the semi-spurious *Mirror of Justices*, and afterwards endorsed by Algernon Sidney— that parliaments were ordained to hear and determine 'all complaints of wrongful acts done by the king, queen or their children, and such others against whom common right cannot be had elsewhere'.[1] A more moderate definition was that given by the antiquary Petyt:[2] 'it is called parliamentum, because every member of the court should speak his mind, "parler le ment" '; in other words, a national council. It was at least certain that parliament was a court; that its origins were lost in the mists of antiquity; that the Lords, as perpetual legislators, were free from arrest in civil suits for their lives, and that this privilege extended to the Commons and their servants during a parliamentary session, and for a period of forty days before and after it. Either House might adjourn on its own initiative, and Charles sometimes adjourned parliament; but in both instances there was no session; on the other hand, by royal prorogation a session was constituted, and Bills which had passed either or both Houses but had not yet received the royal assent had to be commenced again at the next session.

A privilege shared by both Houses was the right to commit a member to custody when he infringed the rules or traditions of the House. From the point of view of a member of either House this might well prove a disability; for it was a sacred principle that in those cases the law courts had no jurisdiction. In 1677 Shaftesbury argued in the Lords that the length of the preceding prorogation had automatically dissolved parliament; a Court

---

[1] *A just and modest vindication* . . . in *State Tracts*, pt. i (1689), 181.
[2] *Lex Parliamentaria* (1689), cap. i.

majority thereupon ordered him and three other peers to acknowledge their error, and beg pardon of the king and House. On refusing, Shaftesbury and his fellows were committed to the Tower. He applied for a writ of habeas corpus, his counsel contending that to the courts of Westminster pertained the right of adjudging the validity of a commitment by either House, as well as the right of determining whether the Journals of Lords or Commons constituted records, or what was a session of parliament. In general, it was urged on Shaftesbury's behalf that, when the liberty of the subject is restrained, the proper place of appeal is the King's Bench; and, in particular, this committal by the Lords was tantamount to depriving the king of the advice of one of his peers. But these contentions proved of no avail against the general principle that offences in parliament cannot be adjudged elsewhere than in parliament, and to this extent therefore membership of either House involved a sacrifice of the protection afforded by the courts.[1]

Another important privilege common to Lords and Commons was that whereby each House had the right to determine its own composition. This was impugned by the Commons in their dispute with the Lords over the impeachment of Danby (1679), when the former challenged the right of the bishops to be present during the trial. Here the Commons failed to substantiate their claim. The Lords in this reign made at least one important decision regarding their membership; for in the Freschville peerage case (1677) they enunciated the principle that a parliamentary barony is not created by a mere writ of summons; nor is the blood of the recipient ennobled thereby; for there must be proof that the summons was obeyed.[2]

On the composition of their own House the Commons exercised an equal measure of control. They denied the crown's claim to limit or determine the franchise, as in the case of the borough of Newark, when the king granted a charter which confined the franchise to the corporation. The Commons in 1677 unseated the two members so returned, and thereafter the crown did not attempt to declare who should vote. They also determined when a writ should be issued for a by-election; they

[1] *English Reports*, lxxxvi. 792–800.
[2] Sir W. R. Anson, *Law and Custom of the Constitution* (4th ed.), i. 199–200.

decided all doubtful or double elections, and in at least one instance (that of the burgesses of Bristol) they subsequently admitted a candidate who had at first been rejected. This case had its origin in 1661, when lord Ossory (son of the duke of Ormonde) and sir Humphrey Poole were among the candidates for the suffrage of Bristol. Poole retired from the contest and 'resigned his interest' to Ossory; but a double return was made of these two, and the Commons chose Ossory. In 1666 Ossory, on his elevation to an English peerage, was called to the Lords; whereupon it was debated whether Poole should be admitted on the former double return, or whether there should be a writ for a new election; but, as Poole was a loyalist, he had the support of the Court, and the Commons decided to have him on the strength of his very dubious election of 1661.[1] This exclusive right to determine the legality of the returns made to their chamber was vindicated in the case of *Barnardiston* v. *Soame*. In the Suffolk by-election of 1672 sir Samuel Barnardiston was returned by a large majority of Dissenters and tradesmen; but the sheriff (Soame), whose sympathies were with the defeated candidate, made a double return, on the ground that Barnardiston's majority was due to the 'rabble', who presumably were not forty-shilling freeholders. Barnardiston (who was admitted by the Commons) obtained a verdict and damages in the King's Bench[2] against Soame; but, on a writ of error, this was reversed in the Exchequer, one judge stating that the misfeasance alleged was only 'pepper and salt and nothing'.[3] In 1689 the case was carried to the Lords, who affirmed the judgement of the Exchequer. In consequence, the sheriffs acquired this special protection that, as to declaring the majority, they were the judges, and no action could lie against them at common law for what they did judicially; more indirectly, but of even greater importance, the Commons were confirmed in their right to determine on the returns of elections and on the conduct of returning officers.

A still more valuable right was enjoyed by both Houses—that of freedom of debate. Outside the walls of parliament both peer

---

[1] *Diary of J. Millward* (*Add. MS.* 33413), Oct. 5, 1666.
[2] *State Trials*, vii (1730 ed.), 428 sqq.; also *English Reports*, lxxxvi. 615–17.
[3] *Grey*, iv. 141.

and commoner were at the mercy of the harsh treason laws, and their most casual words might be seized upon by spies and informers; but within these walls the only tribunal was that constituted by their fellow members, and to that extent debate was free from outside interference. There was much personal solicitation and, of course, there was bribery; but the independent peer or commoner suffered no punishment for either his speech or his vote. Here again Charles avoided the mistakes made by his father; and, however arbitrary his acts, he never violated those twin sanctuaries at Westminster, where the conduct of his executive was the theme of active debate.

If each House be considered separately, it may be noted that among the special privileges enjoyed by the Lords were these: (1) right of personal access to the sovereign; (2) right of voting by proxy; (3) right to trial by one's peers in cases of treason and felony; and (4) right of recording in the Journals a protest against a decision of the majority. The exercise of the first privilege called for circumspection, as Charles did not tolerate fools gladly; and his treatment of the earl of Bristol, who brought accusations of high treason against Clarendon in 1663, was a warning that the privilege must not be abused. It does not appear to have been practised by peers other than personal friends and ministers enjoying the confidence of the crown. The right of voting by proxy was still exercised and, save in moments of crisis, the attendance at the House was poor; but absentees without excuse or proxy were sometimes fined one shilling for the poor box. More important was the third right, that of trial by one's peers, a privilege liable to abuse, in so far as a peer might be tried not by neutral persons, but by a jury of friends and associates. There were attempts at reform. In 1675 the Lords passed a Bill amending the constitution of the court of the lord high steward, whereby thirty peers at least were to be present at the trial, of whom a minimum of twelve was necessary for a verdict of guilty;[1] in 1680 the Commons introduced a Bill intended to reform procedure and to abolish the Lords' privileges under the Statute of *Scandalum Magnatum*.[2] By the Trial of Treasons Acts (1696) the peers themselves benefited by the improved procedure intro-

---

[1] *H.M.C. Rep.* ix, app., pt. ii. 49–50. *MSS. of House of Lords.*
[2] See *infra*, 465.

duced into trials for high treason;[1] otherwise there was no change
in the principle by which peers were tried by themselves.

The fourth right, that of protest against a majority decision,
was really more a convention than a right, and its exercise over
a long period has proved of great value to the student of history.[2]
Two such protests may be noted. In 1663 a minority protested
against the restraint laid on the importation of Irish cattle, since
common right and the subject's liberty were thereby invaded,
and the impoverishment of Ireland was likely to follow.[3] Again,
in November 1675, when a proposal for an address to the crown
advocating the dissolution of parliament was rejected, a minority,
including Shaftesbury, Halifax, Buckingham, and Wharton, protested; alleging that, according to the ancient laws and statutes
of the realm, there should be frequent parliaments, and that it
was unreasonable for any body of men (such as the then House
of Commons) to engross so large a measure of the nation's confidence, 'since the mutual correspondence and interest of those
who choose and are chosen must admit of great variations in
course of time'.[4] On both these questions—restraint of the import of Irish cattle, and the continuance in power of the Cavalier
Parliament—the minority showed a wisdom that would be
applauded to-day, but the names of the dissenting peers in the
latter instance suggest that the protest was not absolutely disinterested, and that it was really a party move, intended to
popularize the demand for a new parliament in which, it was
hoped, the opposition would be more strongly represented.
Shaftesbury was the first to realize the value of these protests for
the purpose of propaganda.[5]

Other privileges enjoyed by the peers were the right of
personal exemption from the taking of oaths, and the right to
a special measure of protection against the slanders of others,
whether peers or commoners. The first was successfully vindicated by Shaftesbury and his followers in April 1675, when Danby

---

[1] See *infra*, 514.

[2] They were collected and published by Thorold Rogers in his *Protests
of the Lords*.

[3] *L.J.* xi. 571, July 24, 1663.

[4] *L.J.* xiii. 33, Nov. 20, 1675.

[5] Turberville, *House of Lords in the reign of Charles II*, in *E.H.R.* xliv.

attempted to secure the passage of his Non-Resistance Test.[1] Even when trying one of their fellows the Lords each gave his verdict not as a sworn juryman, but on his faith and allegiance to the king; and as a witness in the law courts he gave evidence not on his oath but on his honour. Thus while successive Houses of Commons saddled themselves with oaths and obligations, the Lords, as born legislators, maintained their freedom from commitments, a privilege saved for them in 1675 by a minority in the Lords and a majority in the Commons; nor, until 1678, were they required to take the oath against transubstantiation, a requirement which automatically disabled the Catholic peers from membership of the House. As regards the second privilege, the old statute *De scandalis magnatum* acquired a new lease of life in the passions aroused by the events of the reign. Every lord of parliament was, in law, a great officer of state, because he was required to support the king by his advice; and the statute *De scandalis magnatum*[2] gave them a special protection against critics and enemies. In 1676 this was suddenly revived from desuetude, though at first the lawyers were doubtful whether juries would respect such a medieval implement; experience, however, soon showed that juries were specially liberal in their assessment of damages sustained by maligned peers. It could be used even against a fellow peer, as in the case of *Shaftesbury* v. *Digby* (1676), when the former obtained £1,000 damages for this statement made to him by Digby: 'You are not for the king, but for sedition and a commonwealth, and by God we will have your head at the next sessions of parliament.'[3] It was a moderate price for such language. A few months later a Dr. Hughes had to pay £4,000 for these words spoken of lord Townshend: 'he is an unworthy man and acts against law and reason'. Hughes appealed, on the ground that the damages were excessive, and because one of the jury had admitted that they awarded lord Townshend such vast damages so that he would have the greater opportunity of showing himself noble by remitting them; but the court dismissed the appeal, on the ground that the judges always construed in favour of these actions, so as to ensure that the peers would not have to

[1] See *infra*, 532–3.
[2] 2 Ric. II, cap. v.
[3] This case was tried in the Common Pleas. *Modern Reports*, ii. 98.

exact vengeance themselves.[1] But the full potency of the action
of *Scandalum magnatum* was not revealed until 1684 when, in the
case of *Duke of York* v. *Titus Oates*,[2] the jury assessed the damages
at £100,000.

Protected against the criticisms of both equals and inferiors,
the Lords, who seldom numbered more than a hundred at their
sessions, permitted themselves a certain degree of informality in
their proceedings—an informality sometimes enlivened by the
remarks of the king, who began to attend the debates with some
regularity in 1670, when the Divorce Bill of lord Roos was discussed. From his station, not on the throne, but by the fire-place,
Charles did not scruple, by interjection and even solicitation, to
influence the course of debate; he never succeeded, however, in
breaking up the solid phalanx of the bishops. On at least one
occasion the House insisted that a certain minimum of public
decency should be maintained by its members; as when, in
February 1674, Buckingham was ordered to cease cohabitation
with the countess of Shrewsbury, an order to which Buckingham
promised obedience 'on his honour', each party giving security
to the amount of £10,000. But there were limits to this personal
interference by the Lords as a corporation. In 1678 lady Mohun,
a daughter of lord Rutland, was injured on the knee by a candle-
stick thrown at her during a quarrel with a lady friend. She drew
up a petition to the Lords on a breach of privilege, which her
father solemnly presented to the House. The Lords referred the
petition to the law courts, and did not accept the king's offer to
conduct a personal investigation of the extent of the injuries.[3]

By the readmission of the 26 spiritual peers in the summer of
1661 the total membership of the House of Lords was raised to
170; in 1685 the number was 181. Fresh honours were conferred,
most notably at the Restoration; and in 1681–2 for services
during the critical period of Plot and Exclusion, but the total
additions to the peerage in this period (64 in all) did little more
than make good the 53 extinctions.[4] The existing dukedoms
were increased by seven—those of Monmouth, Southampton,
Plymouth, Richmond, Grafton, St. Albans, and Northumber-

---

[1] *Modern Reports*, ii. 160; also *English Reports*, lxxxvi. 850–1.
[2] See *infra*, 651.   [3] *H.M.C. Rep.* xii, app. v. 49.
[4] A. S. Turberville, *House of Lords under Charles II*, in *E.H.R.* xliv. 403.

land, all conferred on the natural progeny of the king. Of the score of Catholic peers excluded in 1678, none had played a prominent part in politics, with the doubtful exception of lord Arundell of Wardour, a signatory to the secret treaty of Dover. In talent and integrity the Lords compared very favourably with the Commons, including as they did poets, statesmen, soldiers, admirals, and lawyers; while the bishops were ably represented by Sheldon, Morley, and Seth Ward. Moreover a society which included Buckingham, Ormonde, and Halifax was at least redeemed from mediocrity, and the fiery eloquence of Shaftesbury helped to raise the standard of debate.

In contrast with that of the Lords, the prerogative of the Commons was so ill defined that it seemed capable of almost limitless expansion. No one knew how far it might go.[1] That they were in the nature of a grand jury was the description which seemed best fitted to describe the functions of its members, a grand jury which found true Bills against many offenders, but succeeded in obtaining only one conviction—that of lord Stafford, a victim of the Popish Plot. But they succeeded in vindicating several important privileges. In 1667 they obtained the concurrence of the Lords in a ruling that the Act[2] concerning Richard Strode was a general law, indemnifying all members of parliament in respect of any proposal or declaration made in parliament.[3] They also established the right to choose their own Speaker. The occasion for this arose in March 1679, when Edward Seymour (with whom Charles had a quarrel) presented himself as the Commons' choice. Charles discharged him of his trust, claiming that it was an essential element of the prerogative to refuse as well as to approve the choice of Speaker.[4] Fierce debates, two addresses to the crown, and a prorogation were the immediate consequences of this challenge; the contest was ended only when Charles accepted another choice of the Commons—sergeant Gregory, and thereafter the privilege was left inviolate.

Attendance in the House was maintained by the threat of a fine, and at critical moments there was talk of committing

[1] Thus in 1678 Winnington confessed in the Commons that he was unwilling to declare what the House could not do. (*Parl. Hist.* iv. 937.)
[2] 4 Hen. VIII, cap. viii.   [3] *C.J.* ix. 19, Nov. 12, 1667.
[4] *Parl. Hist.* iv. 1092 sqq.

absentees to custody.[1] The observance of greater decorum appears to have been first proposed in October 1666, when certain reforms were suggested; as, that no member should be allowed to walk about with his hat on, or talk during speeches, and that the private door to the Speaker's chamber should be sealed up. The reason for this last precaution was that Buckingham was in the habit of coming up by the back door and listening to the speeches. Prynne's motion for a fine of 1s. on those absent from prayers does not appear to have found a seconder.[2] Expulsion was sometimes resorted to,[3] and in 1678 a convicted popish recusant (sir Solomon Swale) was expelled the House, and a writ issued for a new election.[4] Not only his religion, but in some respects his private conduct, might bring the member into clash with the House, and before its dissolution the Cavalier Parliament attempted to apply strict tests to its members. These tests related to popery, bribery, taking the sacraments, conversing with foreign ministers, public hospitality, and attendance at conventicles or mass.[5] Dissolution prevented these proposals being carried into effect; but it is significant that a parliament which began as an assembly of courtiers, and contained a high proportion of paid dependants of the crown, ended its sessions on a high note of personal responsibility.

Apart from the official records entered in the Journals, the expressed opinions of members in the House were, in theory, secret and informal—secret in the sense that the public was excluded, and there was no regular means for reporting speeches; informal in the sense that a speech must not be read from written notes. The surviving records of speeches in Charles's Houses of Commons are due mainly to the note-taking of Anchitell Grey.[6] An important step was taken in 1680, when it was ordered that the votes of the House should be published, in spite of secretary Jenkins's objection that the practice was unbecoming the gravity of the Commons, and was 'a sort of appeal to the people'.[7] But

---

[1] C.J. ix. 558, Dec. 18, 1678.
[2] Diary of J. Millward (Add. MS. 33413), Oct. 13, 1666.
[3] Parl. Hist. iv. 589.   [4] Ibid. iv. 1003.   [5] C.J. ix. 500, June 1678.
[6] His Debates of the House of Commons from the year 1667 to the year 1694 were published in ten volumes in 1769. An important record of debates by J. Millward (1666–8) will be found in Add. MS. 33413.
[7] Parl. Hist. iv. 1306.

the Commons were at first very sensitive to anything savouring of public criticism of these printed votes; for in November 1680 they attempted to find the culprit who, in a coffee-house, had appended the comments 'a damned lie' and 'voted like rogues' to their votes on the succession.[1] As parliamentary oratory acquired a great measure of publicity, an increasing use appears to have been made of written notes; indeed, speeches were sometimes read, a practice which dated back to the Long Parliament of 1640, when orators sometimes read their declamations 'out of a hat', or 'behind a friend'.[2] Soon, the printed oration rivalled the printed sermon.

Such were the powers and privileges specially distinctive of each of the two Houses. These were given sharper definition by their numerous conflicts with each other, in the course of which some principles of importance were enunciated. The rights to initiate money grants and to enforce ministerial responsibility were the two major rights on which the Commons insisted most strongly, leaving to the Lords the judicial functions of a supreme court, and the duty of trying those persons who might be impeached by the Commons. This division of powers was not always easy of application, as instanced by the case of *Skinner* v. *The East India Company* (1668). Skinner, an interloper, was aggrieved at the confiscation of his ships by the agents of the East India Company. Having made a direct appeal to the king in council, he was referred to the House of Lords, who, after hearing his case, awarded him £5,000 damages against the Company. The Commons immediately acted on a petition presented by sir Samuel Barnardiston, a deputy governor and a member of the House. They voted that Skinner's action in taking his common plea to the Lords originally was not agreeable to the laws of the land, and tended to deprive the subject of his rights under these laws; also, that the action of the Lords in taking cognizance of the suit, and giving damages against the Governor and Company was unwarranted. Meanwhile, Barnardiston was summoned to the Lords (May 8) for his contumacy in petitioning against their award, and sentenced to a fine of £300. The dispute between the two Houses was continued in the autumn session of 1669. On the one hand, the Lords contended that, as the case had arisen

[1] *Grey*, vii. 430. [2] *Letter from an ejected member to Sir J. Evelyn* (1648).

from acts committed overseas, it was not (except by a legal fiction) cognizable in the common law courts; on their side, the Commons challenged the Lords' entertainment of an action which had not come before them by way of appeal, and their punishment of Barnardiston for having petitioned against their judgement. The dispute was ended only by the erasure of the record in the Journals; but the Lower House by resolution affirmed the right of every commoner to present a petition to the House in case of grievance, and the right of the House to judge and determine of such petitions.[1] In effect, the victory lay with the Commons; for the Lords did not again act as a court of original jurisdiction in a matter cognizable by Westminster Hall.

In another dispute, however, the Commons proved to be in the wrong, and were encouraged to maintain an impossible position, so that the prorogation of parliament might be ensured. A plaintiff named Dr. Shirley, having lost his suit in Chancery, brought an appeal to the Lords, the defendant being sir John Fagg, burgess for Steyning. The Commons voted this a breach of their privilege, since thereby one of their members (Fagg) had to submit to the judgement of the Lords. They sent Fagg to the Tower for having presented himself in answer to the appeal, and they took into custody those serjeants, being members of the House, who had pleaded in this suit at the bar of the Lords. The Lords (May 17, 1675) insisted on their right, as Lords in Judicature, to receive and determine in time of parliament appeals from inferior courts even where a member of the Lower House was concerned; at the same time defining their status to be that of 'Lords in Parliament where His Majesty is highest in his royal state, and where the last resort of judging on writs of error and appeals in equity in all cases and over all persons is undoubtedly fixed and lodged'.[2] To this, the Commons replied that the definition implied a diminution of the dignity of the king 'who is highest in his royal estate in full parliament'[3]; moreover, they contended, the Lords were wrong in denying the House of Commons to be a court. But the Lords persisted in their attitude, in which they were encouraged by the eloquence of Shaftesbury, who warned his compeers that they would quickly grow burdensome if they grew useless: 'you have now', he said, 'the greatest

[1] *Parl. Hist.* iv. 422–6.   [2] *L.J.* xii. 694.   [3] *C.J.* ix. 354.

and most useful end of parliaments principally in you, which is not to make new laws, but to redress grievances and maintain the old landmarks. The House of Commons' business is to complain, Your Lordships' to redress not only the complaints from them that are the eye of the nation, but all the other particular persons that address themselves to you.'[1] The result was that the Commons did not again contest the right of the Upper House to hear appeals in which members of the Lower House were concerned, and so the supreme appellate jurisdiction of the Lords was tacitly recognized.

Of even greater importance were those disputes in which the right of the Commons to control taxation appeared to be infringed. In 1671 the Commons sent up to the Lords a Bill levying impositions on foreign commodities. The Lords, having received petitions from merchants who believed that their interests would suffer by the application of certain clauses in the Bill, proposed a conference thereon with the Commons. This was agreed to; but the representatives of the Lower House insisted on the resolution of their House 'that there is a fundamental right in the House of Commons alone in Bills of rates and impositions on merchandise, as to the matter, the measure and the time'.[2] In reply, the Lords argued that their writs of summons required them to treat and give counsel on the great and arduous affairs of the kingdom without exception; nor was there any record that they had ever divested themselves of any portion of this right. Moreover, when they sent a Bill down to the Commons they never challenged the right of the Lower House to make amendments; why should not the Commons reciprocate in the matter of a Bill sent up by them? Historical precedents were quoted on both sides,[3] and the Commons introduced this alternative argument, that if the Lower House had no precedent to justify its sole control over taxation, equally the Upper House had none to show how it had acquired supreme powers of judicature, to the exclusion of the Commons; to which the Lords properly replied that their judicature dated from a time before the existence of the House of Commons, when the peers constituted the

---

[1] Shaftesbury's speech in the Lords, Nov. 1675, in *Add. MS.* 32094, f. 389.
[2] *C.J.* ix. 239, April 20, 1671.
[3] Ibid. ix. 240–4; *L.J.* xi. 494–8.

grand council of the nation. This contest was ended by adjournment.

For the Commons the issue was a vital one, and they established their right. In 1678 they sent up a Bill of Supply for the disbandment of forces raised since September 1677. The Lords, in view of the situation abroad, introduced an amendment, extending the time for disbandment. The amendment was rejected by the Commons, and in July they placed on record their resolution 'that all aids and supplies to His Majesty are the sole gift of the Commons, and all bills for granting such aids ought to begin with the Commons; and that it is the undoubted and sole right of the Commons to direct, limit and appoint in such Bills the ends, purposes, considerations, conditions, limitations and qualifications for such grants, which ought not to be changed or altered by the House of Lords'.[1] The Commons, therefore, not only claimed the sole right to impose taxation, but denied to the Lords the right to amend any measure which directly or indirectly involved a charge on the subject. This principle has never since been surrendered, and thereafter the Lords retained only the right to reject such Bills—a right which they exercised with momentous consequences in 1909. Already the Commons had realized one use to which their privilege might be put, namely the device of 'tacking' a controversial measure to a money Bill in order that it might pass the Lords without amendment, and impose on the crown a choice between the alternatives of rejection or supply. A notable example was the measure prohibiting certain French imports for three years which was tacked to a Poll Bill[2] in the session of 1677–8. But it is to the honour of Charles that this practice was discouraged; for in May 1678 he announced that in future he would veto all Bills containing several matters tacked together, no matter how important they might be.[3]

In order that the vigorous political life of Charles II's England may be appreciated, it is now necessary to turn to the franchise, the elections, and the external influences that might be brought to bear on the elected representatives.

The House of Commons, as constituted in 1661, contained

[1] *C.J.* ix. 509, July 3, 1678. [2] 29–30 Car. II, cap. i. [3] *L.J.* xiii. 223.

509 members, made up of two burgesses from each of the 197 boroughs returning two members, one each from five boroughs[1] returning one member, two from each of the two universities, four from London, two from each of 39 counties, and 24 members from the Welsh counties and boroughs. These members were increased to 513 in Charles's third parliament (1679) by the addition of four members from the palatine county of Durham —two from the county and two from the city. The election of knights and burgesses was regulated by custom and statute. By a statute[2] of Henry VI's reign knights of the shire were required to be 'notable knights, or such esquires or gentlemen-born of the same county as are eligible to be knights'; and the franchise in the counties was, since the fifteenth century, the standard qualification of a freehold of at least 40s. annual value. There was greater latitude in the qualifications required of a burgess. By statute, a man was ineligible for a borough which he did not inhabit, but this disqualification was seldom insisted on; in effect any one was eligible, provided he was over 21, neither an alien nor a clergyman, not attainted of treason or felony, nor of unsound mind, and '*magis idoneus, discretus et sufficiens*'.[3]

In contrast with the county franchise, that in the boroughs was bewildering in its heterogeneity. Generally, it was widest in the scot-and-lot and pot-walloper boroughs; narrower in the freeman boroughs, and narrowest of all in the corporation and burgage boroughs. As an example of a very wide franchise Preston may be cited, where, by determination of the Commons in 1661, it was declared to reside in 'all the inhabitants'. The Commons may have established this very liberal franchise from their belief that the corporation of Preston was 'presbyterian'.[4] So, too, in those boroughs where the qualification was the payment of 'scot-and-lot', or the possession of one's own hearth, the franchise might be wide enough to include persons in receipt of poor relief. In the freeman boroughs, the freemen had originally

[1] The five boroughs which each returned one member were Abingdon, Banbury, Higham-Ferrars, Monmouth, and Bewdley.

[2] 23 Hen. VI, cap. xv.

[3] For the franchise before 1832 see E. Porritt, *The Unreformed House of Commons*. For elections to the parliaments of 1679–81 see E. Lipson in *E.H.R.* xxviii.

[4] Sacret, *The Restoration and municipal corporations* in *E.H.R.* xlv.

been those householders having the right to trade; but, by the seventeenth century, when votes were coming to be in demand, means were found for restricting the number of freemen, and the more coveted privilege was beginning to be conferred on non-residents by making them honorary freemen. The same process can be seen in corporation boroughs, where a landed gentleman might be appointed to the office of mayor or recorder. Equally amenable to manipulation were the burgage boroughs, where the franchise went with certain tenements or holdings, which might be houses, or (as at Droitwich) shares in salt-pits. In the corporation boroughs, as at Bath, the vote was exercised by a small corporation, kept in existence almost solely for the exercise of this right, and an election might represent little more than the opinion of an enterprising mayor or bailiff; for example, at Haslemere, the bailiff explained the principle thus: 'it lay in his little pate to return whom he would'.[1]

It was mainly in consequence of these anomalies that the greater territorial families were able to exert control over many boroughs. In the west the duke of Beaufort was supreme; for he united the lord lieutenancies of three English counties (Herefordshire, Gloucestershire, and Monmouthshire) with the lord lieutenancy of every Welsh county. In Cornwall and Devon the earl of Bath (Grenville) was building up his territorial influence; the Lancashire boroughs had to reckon with the earl of Derby, and many of the Wiltshire boroughs were controlled by the earl of Ailesbury. In the north the most notable borough-monger was the duke of Newcastle, whose influence extended through Northumberland, Nottinghamshire, Staffordshire, and Derbyshire. It was often through the Militia that this power was exercised. That it would be used in the service of the crown was generally assumed; indeed the captains of the Militia were considered the strongest bulwarks against the 'sedition' and dissent of the towns; and the monarch who had the support of the Militia was strong indeed.

But, as early as 1675, an instance was provided of how a determined and influential landlord could, with the help of the Militia, turn elections against the Court. In that year a knight of the shire had to be chosen for Norfolk, the two candidates being

[1] Porritt, op. cit. i. 53.

THE CROWN IN PARLIAMENT

sir R. Kempe and sir N. Catlyn, the former backed by the lord lieutenant (lord Townshend) and the deputy lieutenants; while the latter was put up by the loyal party and gentry against his will. Hitherto, Townshend had been distinguished for his loyalty, his influence, and his zeal in sending fanatics to prison. For whatever reason, he had now turned momentarily against the Court, and speedily demonstrated what he could do. He joined forces with sir John Hobart, an old Cromwellian; and the two made up their minds that Kempe and not Catlyn would be returned.

Having found out that many of Catlyn's friends were in the habit of dining at the *King's Head* in Norwich, the lord lieutenant commenced his campaign by an invasion of that hostelry, and so forced the enemy to transfer their head-quarters to the *White Swan*, 'a very inconvenient place'; the Militia had therefore won the first round. At the appointed day of election (the city being packed with voters) the writ was read by the sheriff, and the two rival knights stood on chairs before the assembled freeholders; but as the shouts for each seemed to be equal, the second round was considered indecisive. For a short period there was a truce, and the rival candidates rode about the market-place, while the sheriff retired to the grand jury chamber in order to settle 'such a method in the carriage of the business as might be equal and indifferent'—in other words the real contest was about to begin. After a speech on behalf of Kempe by sir John Hobart, it was resolved to draw up a written agreement, the essence of which was that the two sets of persons entrusted with the duty of recording the votes should be placed so close together that each could act as a check on the other, and so prevent electors from voting twice. Hobart, acting as electioneering agent on behalf of Kempe, penned the agreement, and the managers then set up two distinct polls, the lord lieutenant presiding over that for Kempe. Soon it was noticed by Catlyn's managers that some freeholders were voting twice at Kempe's booth; whereupon complaint was made, and the written agreement was invoked; but when this was produced, it was found that Hobart had omitted the vital clause which enabled each set of managers to keep an eye on the proceedings at the rival booth; moreover the lord lieutenant repudiated the agreement altogether, so there seemed no reason why the supporters of Kempe should not record their votes twice. It was now a race against time. Catlyn set up an extra booth, in order to get as many votes as possible, and proposed to continue the poll until late in the evening, as so many freeholders had not yet voted; but Kempe's party had the advantage of a good start, and accordingly the lord lieutenant sent to the grand jury chamber, and asked the sheriff to cast up the votes. The sheriff did so and pronounced that Kempe had a majority. When the result was announced, many of Kempe's voters said that they had voted not for the candidate, but for the lord lieutenant's sake, or on behalf of some colonel or captain in the Militia; the genuine supporters of Kempe appear to have been either 'fanatics' or Roman Catholics. 'You see how the Militia of Norfolk govern this county.'[1]

Not unnaturally, Townshend was removed from his lord lieutenancy, and thereafter he devoted himself to turning the Norfolk elections against the Court.[2] In this way was created a whig and a powerful whig. His career provided an anticipation of how the power usually exercised on behalf of the crown might be used with equal force against it; and when Charles completed the remodelling of the boroughs, he little realized that thereby he had strengthened that local influence of the nobility and landlords which was so soon to be directed against his own House. James II ruined his cause not by his constancy to Jeffreys or father Petre, but by alienating the country gentry.

The above account of a Norfolk election suggests that management rather than oratory was the deciding factor. This might be amply illustrated from the records of borough elections. In the year 1679 there were two general elections, both of which aroused intense national interest; and, at the first of these, many members of the preceding (the Cavalier) parliament were unseated, and their places taken by whigs. Abingdon had been represented since 1660 by sir John Stonehouse, who, whatever his views, appears to have maintained silence at Westminster for nineteen years; so at the general election of September 1679 a Mr. Dunch of Pewsey was put up against him. The franchise was popular, and as the corporation was in favour of the sitting member, all the tenants holding of the borough were informed that

[1] *H.M.C. Rep.* vi, app. 371–2. [2] *Cal. S.P. Dom.*, *1682*, 54 sqq.

if they did not vote for Stonehouse their fines would be raised, or they would not have their leases renewed. On the day of election (Sept. 6) crowds walked through the main street shouting 'A Dunch, a Dunch'. This cry was reiterated at the election, when the mayor granted a poll. The result showed 297 for Mr. Dunch, and 171 for sir John Stonehouse. The mayor and his brethren then retired to the council chamber to discuss the matter. Many queries were raised. What was the 'constant practice' of previous elections? What was the extent of their charter? Dunch then appeared in person to demand his return; but the mayor was playing for time, so he adjourned the proceedings until the following Monday. On Monday morning Dunch entered the town with 100 horse and 200 foot, all shouting 'A Dunch, a Dunch'; so the mayor again adjourned, and at 5 p.m. he told the corporation that he had examined the poll and found 171 was greater than 297, so he declared Stonehouse their burgess. After publicly announcing this return, he was hissed all the way to his house by the women and children, shouting 'A cheat, a cheat'; and next day the clamours for Dunch were so vociferous that the mayor was obliged to keep himself 'incognito' in the nettles behind the town hall until the dreaded Dunch had gone back to Pewsey. So sir John Stonehouse was again returned to Westminster, where he maintained his reticence throughout the remaining parliaments of Charles II and in the parliament of James.[1]

The tactics of the mayor of Abingdon were at least simple and straightforward; elsewhere more ingenuity had to be exercised. Witness sir John Reresby's account[2] of his election as burgess for Aldborough in 1673. At that time he noted the existence of two parties—the Country party, professing to protect the subject from over-taxation and to secure his privileges and liberties; and the Court party, committed in the abstract to these principles, but anxious that the king should have a sufficient revenue. Sir John noted also that an increasing number of men wished to enter parliament; for those in debt thereby obtained protection from their creditors, while others found in membership of the

---

[1] *Letter from a friend in Abingdon to a gentleman in London* (in Bodley G. Pamph., 1678).

[2] Reresby, *Memoirs* (ed. Browning), 91–2, 95–6.

House an avenue to Court favour. At the Aldborough by-election he had five rival candidates, of whom the most formidable was one Benson, who, beginning as clerk to a country attorney, had risen to be clerk of assize of the northern circuit, and now (through the favour of sir Thomas Osborne) was possessed of an estate worth £2,500 per annum. The traditional franchise at Aldborough was vested in nine electors, owners of nine burgage houses; but on the eve of the election the lord of the manor contended that formerly there had been 24 houses each conferring a vote. Hitherto he, as owner of these houses, had given only one vote in respect of them; but now he proposed to sell or alienate them so as to create as many votes. These 24 votes were acquired by the enterprising Benson. Reresby stood by the other burgage votes, of which he obtained a majority, while Benson was returned by his 24 houses; and, as the other candidates had retired from the contest, the field was cleared for Reresby and Benson. The result was a double return, in the traditional form—*executio istius brevis patet in quibusdam indenturis huic brevi annexis*, which Benson on his own initiative altered to *in quadam indentura*. But, because of this alteration, he lost his case when the double return was examined by the House of Commons, and so in this tortuous way Reresby became a burgess for Aldborough.

Sometimes an association of electors would undertake in writing to support the candidates selected by a majority of themselves, and also to induce as many electors as possible to join in the association, so that at the Polls there would be less opportunity for dissension, faction, or expense. Such an association was formed in Herefordshire, one of its declared objects being to propose and elect only persons well-affected to the government.[1] Or reference might be made to the wishes of some territorial magnate; in other cases, the election might be influenced by bribery, direct or indirect. An example of the latter was a written communication to the Mayor of Poole intimating that, if the writer were elected, he would oppose taxation.[2] A gift of money was sometimes made to a borough after election; or an offer might be made on condition of election, as when admiral Spragge

---

[1] The articles of association (undated) are in *Add. MS.* 11051, f. 227.
[2] *Grey*, i. 232.

offered £300 to the burgesses of Dover for this purpose.[1] Voters became accustomed to this association of their vote with some return, either in money, or privilege, or (at least) entertainment; and so the expenses of elections increased considerably. Danby's organized jobbery served to enhance the commercial value of a seat, and justified the dictum of Shaftesbury: 'men that buy dear cannot live by selling cheap'.[2] As there was a greatly increased demand for seats after the Restoration, successive elections were more keenly contested, and that for Bedfordshire in the spring of 1679 was said to have cost the candidates £6,000.[3] At other places there might have to be social enterprise, as at Buckingham, where the rival candidates (one of them a peer) danced all night with the wives of the burgesses, and the noble competitor assured his dance partners that his lady would welcome their acquaintance.[4] It was in 1679 that the word 'representation' first came into general use as a political term;[5] the word 'mob' had already been acclimatized.

Indeed, the old parliamentary boroughs provided the best training-ground for political strategy, because, as scarcely any two were alike, they each offered opportunities for individual treatment. Some might be taken by assault, others by a slow undermining, others by a ruse, most of them by money. The procedure of elections provided additional opportunities. Thus, there was often doubt where the poll was to be taken, and a candidate might lose the election by shepherding his supporters to the usual place, and find too late that it had been changed; or the election might be held at night (as at Bedford in 1685); or the voting might be adjourned so often that many electors went away in disgust.[6] Or the candidate who had lost his election on one franchise might demand his election on another, and win on it.[7] In cases of doubt (and these were numerous) the sheriff made a double return, leaving the House to decide the election. This right was after-

[1] Porritt, op. cit. i. 158. For this election see also A. F. W. Papillon, *Memoirs of T. Papillon*, 126.

[2] *Parl. Hist.* iv, app. vii.

[3] *H.M.C. Rep.* vii, app. 471, *Verney MSS.*

[4] Ibid. 478.

[5] *Hatton Correspondence* (Camd. Soc.), i. vii and 182.

[6] Luttrell, *Brief Historical Narration*, i. 341.

[7] e.g. the Tamworth by-election of 1670, *Grey*, i. 243-4.

wards used by the House to increase the strength of the party in power.

There were other and more insidious influences. By statute, the boroughs were obliged to pay wages to their burgesses. This had fallen into desuetude; and Andrew Marvell was probably the only person still in receipt of this allowance from his borough (Kingston-upon-Hull). When, in March 1677, the Commons ordered a Bill to be brought in for the repeal of this statute, it was mentioned in debate[1] that some burgesses had threatened to serve writs on their constituencies for arrears of wages in the event of their not being returned at the next general election. Another influence was that of the crown. This had long existed in the Cinque Ports and in ports and dockyard towns, where there was a tradition in favour of Court nominees, as instanced at the Liverpool by-election of 1670, when the king commanded a prospective candidate to desist, as he wished the seat for the Customs farmer sir William Bucknall.[2] Elsewhere this influence was more sparingly exercised; though it was felt as early as the election of April 1660, when the personal preference of Charles was cited in the favour of at least one candidate.[3]

These illustrations suggest not so much that the old franchise was corrupt, as that it had never been designed to withstand the invasion of the intruder armed with money, or influence, or ingenuity; for at first the boroughs had returned to parliament not politicians who valued the privilege, but burgesses whose travelling expenses had to be paid; and in this way the complicated franchises which at first returned the unwilling now became the battle-ground of the ambitious. The abuses of the system were so patent that there was a demand for parliamentary reform on the part of the more independent members within the Commons, and of more independent statesmen without, such as Shaftesbury. In January 1667 the House discussed certain regulations with a view to their embodiment in Bills. These included the requirements that voters should be such as had taken the sacrament; that only those having lawful votes should be allowed to attend elections, and that no soldiers should be present in the polling

---

[1] *Grey*, iv. 177, and Marvell, *Works* (ed. Grosart), ii. 525.
[2] *H.M.C. Rep.* x, app., pt. iv. 117.
[3] *Add. MS.* 11051, f. 229.

booths except those who had votes, and then only if unarmed.[1]
Complaint of the increasing expenses of elections was made in
January 1674, when members blamed the competition of non-
residents;[2] in November 1675 a residential qualification was
suggested by sir John Bramston, who pleaded also for a more
equal distribution of seats.[3] The result was the adoption of a
resolution[4] that if a candidate, after the issue of a writ and before
the day of election, should give to a voter or voters meat or drink
exceeding £5 in value in any place other than his dwelling-house,
his election should be void. This maximum of £5 was raised
to £10 in April 1677.[5] But 'dry' elections were regarded with
disfavour by the more conservative, and were thought by some
to be a device for 'introducing Presbytery by way of small beer',
as well as damaging the king, by reducing his revenue from
Excise.[6]

The whigs were the earliest advocates of parliamentary reform;
but after the Revolution of 1689, when they became strongly
entrenched, they lost heart for the cause, which was later taken
up by the tories. One of the first acts of the first whig parliament
(that of March 1679) was to draft a Bill[7] for regulating abuses
of elections. The main provisions of this Bill were these: (1)
limitation of the county franchise to persons having an estate in
fee of at least £200; (2) creation of a standard franchise in the
boroughs (except London, York, Norwich, Exeter, and Bristol)
consisting of all householders paying scot-and-lot who had
resided for at least one year in the borough for which they voted;
(3) a penalty of £500 and disability from sitting in parliament on
any one giving bribes or rewards for votes, and disfranchisement
of the borough where the bribery was committed; (4) no suit to
be prosecuted for wages by any burgess in respect of his service
in parliament, and all arrears of such wages to stand discharged;
(5) sheriffs, mayors, and bailiffs to complete the election at the
appointed time and place without adjournment; (6) persons
inducing a returning officer to make a false return, and returning

---

[1] *Diary of J. Millward* (*Add. MS.* 33413, Jan. 17, 1667).
[2] *Parl. Hist.* iv. 658. [3] *Grey*, iv. 2.
[4] *Parl. Hist.* iv. 784–5, Nov. 12, 1675. [5] *C.J.* ix. 411.
[6] *Savile Correspondence* (*Camd. Soc.*), 118.
[7] Printed *in extenso* in *Somers Tracts*, ed. 1748, pt. i, vol. i. 63–6.

officers making a false return for some valuable consideration, to incur a penalty, and the election to be void; and (7) in order to secure the benefits of successive parliaments, no future parliament to have continuance for more than two years.

This Bill may have attempted too much; for it combined a sweeping reform of the franchise with an effort to guarantee frequent parliaments. Unfortunately, there was no provision to secure that parliaments should even be summoned, an elementary safeguard not achieved until the Mutiny Act imposed on William III the necessity of annually renewing the legal status of his troops. Equally notable was the scheme of reform attributed to Shaftesbury.[1] There was an idealist object in this scheme—so to amend and strengthen the parliamentary constitution that it would be impervious to the attacks of fraud and corruption. He thought it of dangerous consequence that the crown should have the power to determine the franchise of a borough, as it had attempted to do with Newark.[2] More urgent, the anomalies and varieties of borough franchise should be brought to one head by 'a touch of the supreme authority', and there should be one uniform system in all these constituencies. Next, rotten boroughs should be disfranchised, and their members transferred to more populous centres; with this redistribution, it would not be possible to have a repetition of such a measure as the prohibition of Irish cattle, which, Shaftesbury contended, was passed by the votes of certain counties having an excessive proportion of borough votes to their share. Next, as the old 40s. freehold qualification was assessed on the value of money in the fifteenth century, it should be raised so as to correspond with its modern equivalent. So, too, as the electors ought to be men of substance, the person elected should have a good estate, in order to ensure his faith and honesty; for which purpose he should be worth at least £10,000, all debts paid, and should be of at least forty years of age. Lastly, there ought to be secrecy of voting; the electors coming in at one door, recording their votes at a table, and leaving by another.

Shaftesbury's House of Commons would thus have been an assembly of middle-aged plutocrats; men of gravity and circumspection, too old for folly or extravagance, and so rich that they

---

[1] *Somers Tracts*, pt. i, vol. i. 66–72.   [2] *Supra*, 461.

could be neither bribed nor bullied; primitive and pioneer whigs, with at least one Puritan in their ancestry, and a fortune acquired in a career of business rectitude. It was a type in the making; but the temper of Charles's reign did not favour its full development.

Such were the means by which men entered parliament, and the chief proposals for reform. On the members of the Commons Charles did not scruple to exercise his influence. This might take the form of a personal letter to members on whose support he could rely. Such letters were sent on April 1, 1675 to ten members, asking them to be present in their places 'for the King's interest', when 'His Majesty will communicate his good and pious resolutions of returning all things in Church and State to their legal state and condition'.[1] Before the opening of the autumn session of the same year Charles sent similar letters, expressing his alarm at the rumour that he did not intend to have a sitting of parliament, and asking his supporters to be present in good time, *preferably a day or two before the opening*.[2] This suggests that, like the Country party, the Court party was beginning to discuss the plan of campaign before the meeting of parliament. The Commons protested against this practice;[3] but it was resorted to again in March 1681, when the king commanded all his servants in the House to promote expedients in place of exclusion.[4] On an earlier occasion, when the Commons were pressing their right to appoint a committee to inspect war expenditure, Charles sent out the lord chamberlain to bring in the loyalists from the places where they were presumed to be engaged—namely the theatres and houses of ill fame.[5] More directly, the influence of the crown was exercised by the distribution of offices to members, on the implied condition that they would vote in the right way. Danby reduced this to a system. In May 1678, when the Commons renewed their attack on Lauderdale, the king ordered all his servants to attend the House, 'and such as

[1] These were sent to sir T. Peyton, sir F. Windham, sir Job Charleton, colonel Sandys, sir C. Fisher, sir Humphrey Winch, sergeant Jones, sir Henry Vernon, sir Francis Crompton, and sir T. Hanmer. *Coventry Papers (Longleat)*, 83, f. 78.　　　　[2] Sept. 21, 1675, ibid., f. 95.

[3] In their address that summons should be by proclamation only. *Parl. Hist.* iv. 780.

[4] *Prinsterer*, v. 490.　　　　[5] *Pepys*, Dec. 8, 1666.

either did not attend, or voted not according to their duty, he would turn out one after another'.[1] On this occasion sir William Lowther was dismissed from his post in the Customs for voting against the Court, which 'threw so great a terror into many members of the House' that the attack on the hated Scottish minister was 'minced'.[2]

This abuse was not allowed to pass unchallenged. Agitation against office-holders in the Commons had begun in 1675, when a Bill was introduced to make the holding of a public office in time of parliament incompatible with a seat in the House,[3] a proposal again discussed in 1679. On two occasions also[4] a test was proposed for administration to members, requiring them to declare whether they had received money for their votes, or whether they had been ejected from office because of their votes. The agitation culminated in May 1679, when sir Stephen Fox was forced by the Commons to reveal the names of those members of the late parliament to whom he had paid money from secret service funds.[5]

Public interest in this matter was stimulated by the appearance of a biographical compilation entitled *Flagellum Parliamentarium* (sometimes attributed to Marvell), containing the names of 178 members who in the period 1661–72 were alleged to have received 'snip', that is, a share of the spoils.[6] This parliamentary *Who's Who* was modelled on an earlier and equally candid publication, *The Mystery of the Good Old Cause* (1660), in which was contained a list of those members of the late Long Parliament who had held civil and military office contrary to the Self-Denying Ordinance. No feelings were spared in the *Flagellum*, and under the names of prominent politicians were to be found such summary descriptions as these: 'a poor Scot, therefore a knave'; 'a private forsworn cheat in the Prize Office'; 'a pimping groom of the bed-chamber'; 'king's jeweller, a great cheat at bowls and cards'; 'once a poor factor to buy malt, now a farmer

[1] *Lauderdale Papers* (*Camd. Soc.*), iii. 131.
[2] *Lauderdale Papers* (*Add. MS.* 23242), ff. 28–9.
[3] It was rejected by 145 to 113. *Grey*, iii. 53.
[4] 1675 and 1678.
[5] *Parl. Hist.* iv. 1137–42; see also *infra*, 589–90.
[6] See also E. S. De Beer, 'Members of the Court Party in the House of Commons', in *Bulletin of the Institute of Historical Research*, June 1933.

of the revenues'; 'a poor ale-house keeper's son, now has the Faculty Office and is one of the Masters of Requests'; 'a beggarly fellow that sold his vote to the Treasurer for £50'; 'Navy contractor'; 'son of Harbottle'; 'commissioner for Irish Claims'; 'the first mover for Chimney Money'; 'pays no debts, has a son in the Guards'. Such were the 'Court Cullies' of this libellous anthology. When it is recalled that French money was soon to supplement Court bribery, the wonder is that such an assembly contrived to maintain some degree of independence; but then the English House of Commons was a peculiar institution, and neither Charles II nor Louis XIV quite understood it.

The most notable failure of the Commons of Charles's reign was their inability to make full use of the weapon of impeachment. 'It is strange', complained a member, 'that all our addresses cannot remove a single obnoxious person',[1] a confession of impotence, it is true; for in this contest of wits the House was no match for the wiliest of monarchs. Nevertheless the Commons showed an uncouth strength before which even Charles yielded. He would not surrender Clarendon to their wrath, but he sent his minister into banishment; nor did he release Danby from the Tower until long after his last parliament had been dissolved. He resisted the attempt to dictate his foreign policy, but yielded in time to avert revolution; he disbelieved in the Popish Plot, but nevertheless he went the way of his Commons, even in their delirium. From Charles Stuart these were striking tributes. The Revolution settlement was peaceably effected because so many of its principles had already been enunciated in the parliaments of this reign, and because, in spite of the interludes of Cromwell and James II, these parliaments were the heirs of the Puritan revolution, and the ancestors of the Convention of 1689.

[1] Speech of Powle, May 1675, in *Grey*, iii. 214.

XIV

LIBERTY OF THE SUBJECT

Much is heard of the rights of seventeenth-century Englishmen, but less of the many duties that were silently enforced. The state was then thought of not as an instrument of social service, nor as an establishment for the political education of the masses; but as the armed force providing ultimate sanction for the enforcement of law and order. There was no abstract right to work, nor right to live; but there were innumerable obligations —the obligation to conduct one's trade in the manner prescribed by common and statute law; to serve one's turn in unpaid parochial office; to clear out one's ditches or mend the roads; to present one's neighbours for their sins; to eat fish on Fridays and in Lent; and, when destitute, either to live precariously on the dole meted out by churchwarden or overseer, or to retreat, under the blows of the constable, to the place of one's birth, there to die and be buried in woollen. 'Authority is the main point of government': this maxim, popular with the compilers of children's copy-books, adequately summarized the relationship between ruler and ruled. A more amplified version of the same principle may be seen in this report from the constable of a well-behaved village:

The poor are provided for; the stocks and whipping post are in good repair; hues and cries duly pursued; highways and bridges in repair; warrants executed; watch and ward duly kept, and all things belonging to my office are in good order to the best of my knowledge.[1]

A host of local functionaries and institutions co-operated in securing this state of affairs. Among these was the lord lieutenant, who combined executive with military functions. He was the king's vice-regent in the shire; he commanded the local militia; he was the custodian of the county archives, and, as head of the commission of the peace, he provided the link between the crown in council on the one side and a network of local officials on the other. His office was almost invariably conferred on one of the greater landlords or nobles, for whom it provided training in

[1] Quoted in S. and B. Webb, *English Local Government: the Parish and the County*, 471, n. 1.

administrative duties; in this way did the Howards, the Stanleys, the Cavendishes, the Herberts, and the Townshends acquire, within the bounds of their own counties, that practical experience in the handling of men which no other country could provide. His position was quite unlike that of the autocratic noble in provincial France;[1] for not only was his conduct under the close supervision of the privy council, but he had to act in conjunction with his deputy lieutenants, with whom he held regular meetings, at which petitions were heard and decisions made. There the disposition of the militia regiments was regulated; orders were issued for the levy of distraint on persons failing to provide their due quota for this territorial force, and the county share of the militia assessment was apportioned among the hundreds and corporations within their jurisdiction. Questions involving important principle had sometimes to be decided at these meetings, such as whether the clergy should be assessed and charged for the militia in respect of their spiritual estates;[2] and in moments of crisis, such as during the two Dutch Wars, the lieutenancies had to organize home and coastal defence.[3] These bodies often influenced the elections to parliament;[4] and in the scope of their deliberations they were themselves not unlike local parliaments. Together with the country gentry, the lord lieutenant and his deputies were the strongest support of the crown.

On the justices appointed by commissions of the peace devolved by far the greater part of the administrative and judicial work of the county. Hard-worked and unpaid, they have provided an endless source of surprised or admiring comment by foreign observers. Three qualifications were required of a justice: a competent estate, a good reputation, and a tolerable education.[5] By competent estate was meant a freehold of at least £20 per annum; good reputation was synonymous with receiving the sacrament according to the usage of the church of England at

[1] Thus, he could not dismiss an officer of militia, since these were appointed by His Majesty's commission. The marquis of Worcester had to be reminded of this fact in February 1676. (*Coventry Papers, Longleat,* vol. 83, f. 97.)

[2] Journal book of the lieutenancy of Norfolk, 1661–74, in *Add. MS.* 11061, f. 8. The Norfolk lieutenancy decided this question in the affirmative.

[3] See *supra,* i. 253. [4] See *supra,* 474–6.

[5] E. Bohun, *The justice of the peace, his calling* (1693), 13.

least once a year; and tolerable education meant an elementary knowledge of Latin. In practice, therefore, only the notorious among the landlords were debarred from office.

The duties of the justice may be enumerated according as he acted singly, or with another, or with all his colleagues of the county in general sessions. In his single capacity he could order the imprisonment of vagabonds and trespassers; he committed seditious persons, and he might declare a price at which an article should be sold. He could administer oaths, including that of allegiance; and by his warrant he authorized the churchwardens to levy a fine of one shilling on absentees from church. Two justices sitting together could license ale-houses, punish offenders against the numerous statutes regulating the cloth-manufacture, inflict fines on all persons using unlawful or unjust weights and measures, and enforce the greater part of the poor law regulations, including the levying of the poor rate, and the removal of paupers to their last place of settlement. In quarter sessions, the justices of the county took cognizance of all breaches of duty by parish officials; they received presentments on all matters concerning county structures, including gaols, roads, and bridges; they tried recusants, traders forestalling the market, persons breaking the gaming laws by keeping greyhounds or other sporting dogs; labourers who violated the statute of Apprentices, or erected cottages on the waste without licence. They made affiliation orders, and could punish by fine or imprisonment; they might also inflict a sentence of banishment to one of the plantations, the choice being generally left to the privy council.[1] For an increasing number of human activities the tacit or written approval of the justice or justices came to be necessary; and the statutes of Charles's reign imposed many additional duties on these country gentlemen, who depended for their legal knowledge on compilations written specially for their use, such as that of Dalton.[2]

[1] e.g. in 1682 the justices of Devon ordered four rogues to be banished, and asked the council to assign a suitable plantation. The Board thought either Jamaica or Barbados. (*P.C. Reg.* 69, Nov. 29, 1682.)

[2] M. Dalton, *The Countrey Justice*, first printed in 1622. For good accounts of the duties of the justices see S. and B. Webb, op. cit., *The Parish and the County*, and E. Trotter, *Seventeenth-century life in the country parish*, 211 sqq.

The variety of these functions may be illustrated by example. Thus, in 1664, the Hertfordshire sessions condemned a Quakeress to pay a fine of £20 or suffer six months' imprisonment; three Quakers who stood mute were ordered to be transported to Barbados; in 1668 a man was fined £22 for exercising the craft of brewer without having served an apprenticeship. The Hertfordshire justices received an indictment of a man for using false and scandalous words about a woman, namely, that she was a witch, and did bewitch his ale; in 1671 they heard a petition from a lame and diseased man who had been imprisoned for nearly three years because he did not frequent the parish church. There were also prosecutions for Sabbath-breaking and non-observance of Lent. More commonly, the work was administrative. Children chargeable on the parish were boarded out; fit persons for farming the Excise were recommended; persons impoverished by fire were given a licence to beg for alms; and orders were made for the mending of highways and bridges, and the scouring of ditches.[1] At the Shropshire sessions in January 1661 the business included the grant of an ale-house licence, and of a licence to build a cottage; a maimed soldier was assigned a pension; two 'settlements' of paupers were declared, and several Scotch pedlars were ordered to be punished and deported. In January 1685 they heard a complaint from prisoners in the county gaol alleging ill usage by the gaolers, and petitioning for relief from exorbitant charges; in answer, the justices ordered that the charges ordered by the statute[2] of 1670–1 should be enforced, and that, in accordance therewith, a list of the authorized fees should be hung up in gaol.[3] Urban areas had their special problems. Thus, at the Middlesex sessions of August 1686, the churchwardens of St. Clement Danes were ordered to attend, in order to show how many poor children they had put out to be apprenticed at the charge of the court; two years later, the justices visited the workhouse in Clerkenwell to see the condition of the poor children there. Much time was spent by the Middle-

---

[1] These examples have been taken from *Hertford County Records* (1581–1698), ed. W. J. Hardy, i. 166, 202, 217, 226.

[2] See *supra*, i. 119, 120.

[3] *Shropshire County Records*, ed. sir O. Wakeman and R. L. Kenyon, 71, 102, 108.

sex magistrates in hearing and determining the numerous petitions from scavengers and rakers for the money due to them. Disputes between apprentices and masters also provided much business for the court.[1]

The justice was the link between the county and the parish; indeed it was in the complete dovetailing of the functionaries of the one into the supervision and control of the other that the excellence of the old system was to be found. There were about 10,000 parishes in the England of Charles's reign. These were as heterogeneous in size and population as the 40 counties, but it was exceptional for a parish to have more than 500 inhabitants. Its affairs were regulated by four classes of unpaid officials—the churchwardens, the constable, the surveyor of highways, and the overseer of the poor. The churchwardens, generally two in number, were chosen in accordance with ecclesiastical rule; in dignity and responsibility they were its most important officers. The constable, as the corporal embodiment of 'law and executive authority', was the person with whom the wrong-doer came into earliest and closest contact. A surveyor of the highways was chosen by the constable and churchwardens; he inspected bridges and roads and saw that repairs were effected, for which purpose he was authorized, together with two or more substantial householders of the parish, to lay an assessment of not more than sixpence in the pound in any one year.[2] The overseers of the poor were, in theory, required to see that an adequate stock was provided on which the willing poor could be set to work; in practice they appear, at this time, to have done little more than supplement the churchwardens' doles by small payments to the impotent poor. Of the humbler officials the parish clerk, who held office for life, acted as caretaker of the parish church; the sexton and bell-ringer held office during satisfactory performance of their duties. In some parishes there was a beadle, who acted as assistant to the constable; and here and there was to be found the dog-whipper, who expelled dogs from church, and occasionally applied his ministrations to the more somnolent or disorderly of the congregation. Some parishes boasted an organist, a spare-

[1] Calendar of Middlesex sessions books (R.O.). See also E. G. Dowdell, *A hundred years of Quarter Sessions (1660–1760)*, 1932.

[2] 14 Car. II, cap. vi.

time occupation, usually rewarded with a salary of £2 10s. per annum. Thus in the parish was to be found not only an ecclesiastical unit, but a centre of administrative activity and disciplinary control.

It is because the churchwardens had to keep accounts that records of their activities have survived. In many parishes they assisted the farmer by paying money for the destruction of vermin, at such rates as 1d. for a fox's head; 4d. for a polecat; 2d. for a stoat, and 1d. for a dozen of sparrows. There is one recorded payment for 149 dozen sparrows. Not all their payments were in cash; for occasionally a sum might be spent in providing a draught of sack for the preacher; or a comparatively large sum might be spent on the conciliatory meal offered to the archdeacon when he made his visitation. More commonly money was spent on beer for workmen and ringers. There were many occasions on which the services of supplementary ringers were required; and 1688 was their golden year, because they officiated at four extraordinary occasions: Queen's being with child (6s.); birth of the prince of Wales (6s.); rejoicings for the prince of Wales (6s. 6d.); ringing for the prince of Orange (6s.). In addition to these national occasions, there were parish events commemorated by special expenditure, generally in beer; as 'when the organ came home'; 'when they had set up the organ'; 'when the bell was taken down'; 'when the plumber made a bargain for the lead at the top of the tower'; 'when we made the bargain with the bell founder'.[1] Money was also spent in giving alms to licensed beggars.[2] More exceptionally, the churchwardens bore the cost of removing undesirable persons, as witnessed in these successive entries:[3] 'given to a woman to remove out of the parish, 1s.; spent to remove her, 6d.'

[1] Most of the above examples have been taken from the accounts of the churchwardens of Abbotsbury and Puddle Hinton (Dorset), for access to which I am indebted to the kindness of Rev. Canon Moule and Rev. W. Newman respectively. Lists of such local records will be found in *Ecclesiastical records of the Diocese of Birmingham* (Birmingham, 1911), and *Shropshire Parish Documents* (Shrewsbury, 1903). Derbyshire has been done very thoroughly by J. C. Cox in *Churchwardens' accounts from the fourteenth to the seventeenth century*; for Durham see *Durham Parish Records* (Surtees Society, 1888). There is a good bibliography by Miss E. Philips in *E.H.R.* xv.

[2] See *supra*, i. 121–2.   [3] Chirbury accounts, in *Shropshire Parish Records*.

The unwanted were generally removed by the constable. His duties were numerous and exacting. He had to see that the king's peace was kept, for which purpose he arrested all that went offensively armed, or committed riot; he apprehended felons, and, when resisted, raised the hue and cry; he executed the statutes for punishing rogues and idle persons; he kept a watchful eye on sporting dogs and their furtive owners, on gaming-houses, and on all who sleep by day and walk by night. Among the rogues and vagabonds were included not only those who would now be classed as tramps, but many wayfarers of a superior degree, such as scholars and seafaring men that beg; persons using unlawful games or telling fortunes; counterfeit Egyptians; jugglers, tinkers, pedlars, and chapmen, if not provided with a sufficient testimonial; all proctors and patent-gatherers (except for fire); pretended collectors for gaols or hospitals; fencers, bear-wards, minstrels, players of interludes; released prisoners begging their fees; persons going to and from the baths and wandering out of their way; labourers leaving their parishes, or refusing to work for wages reasonably taxed; servants quitting service in one place to seek it in another; all wanderers infected with plague.[1] The sentence on these intruders into the parish was a simple one: they were stripped from the waist upwards, and 'whipped till their backs be bloody'. They were then sent from constable to constable until their place of birth was reached; or, if that were unknown, to the place where they had last spent a whole year; otherwise to the house of correction or gaol, there to be employed or put to some service. On completion of the statutory punishment, a testimonial, signed by the minister and constable, was handed to the rogue; this document was framed on the following model:

W. W. a sturdy vagrant beggar (aged about 40 years) tall of stature, red-haired and long, lean-visaged and squint-eyed, was this 24th day of A. in the 22nd year of the reign of our gracious sovereign lord king Charles the Second etc. openly whipped at T. in the county of G. according to the law for a wandering rogue; and is assigned to pass forthwith from parish to parish by the officers thereof the next streight way to W. in the county of B. where he confesses he was born; and he is limited to be at W. aforesaid within twelve days

[1] *The Compleat Constable* (1692).

next ensuing at his peril. Given under the hands and seals of C. W. minister of T. and J. G. constable there.[1]

Exceptions were allowed in favour of expectant mothers and persons desperately sick.

As the constable expelled strangers from the parish, so on its immobile inhabitants he exercised a vigilance whereby every exuberance or deviation was sternly repressed. He saw to it that all ale-keepers were licensed, and, on a warrant from the justice, he levied a fine of 3s. 4d. on all persons engaged in bear-baiting or common plays on Sundays. Sunday was his busiest day; for he had to apprehend all who violated it by attending wrestlings, shootings, bowlings, ringing of bells for pleasure, masques, wakes, church-ales, dancing, or any sport or pastime, the penalty on persons over 14 being 5s. He had to satisfy himself that no drover or carrier plied his trade on that day, that no meat was killed, and that no one travelled except by licence from a justice. In church, he had to apprehend any one disturbing a lawful minister by brawling, and he made a note of absentees from service in order that they might be committed to the justices. He could break open doors in search of conventicles; nor did he have to produce a warrant, 'I arrest you in the king's name' being sufficient introduction.

They [the constables] are bugbears to them that wander without a pass. Poor soldiers are now and then helped to a lodging by their means. They'll visit an alehouse under colour of search, but their desire is to get beer of the company. . . . It's a thousand to one if they give a soldier two pence, but they will send in their bills 'given sixpence'.[2]

Nor was this all. The constable had to assist the Excise officers in their pursuit of offenders; he was also a sanitary inspector, a billeting officer, a rate collector, a revenue official on the look-out for private tobacco-crops, a hunter of poachers, and an inspector of weights and measures. That he had so many duties, and that there was no material incentive to encourage competence, may account for his many mistakes; but that he should have functioned at all is a tribute to the sense of order and

[1] W. Brown, *The duty and office of high constables, petty constables and tithing men* (1677), 26–7.

[2] D. Lupton, *London and the country carbonadoed and quartered* (1632), 317.

discipline inherent in the humblest of Englishmen. Parliament was a wonderful institution; but the unpaid parish constable was much more remarkable.

Another administrative unit was the manor. The manorial organization, where it survived, was of importance mainly for the copyhold tenants holding in fee simple, in fee tail, or for life or lives 'at the will of the lord after the custom of the manor'. Uncertainty mingled with custom in the services of those who owed suit and service to a manorial court, and there was the greatest divergence of opinion regarding the status of the copyholder; some, with Fitzherbert, holding that he was really a villein, in possession of a base fee, while others considered him fully emancipated from every incident of villeinage, save his obligation to attend the lord's customary court. The manor itself was loosely defined as 'a thing compounded of demesnes and long services', in distinction from a lordship, in which a man might have services but not demesnes.[1] In consequence of Edward I's *Quia Emptores* the subject could create a new copyhold but not a freehold, a restriction partly responsible for the gradual decay of the manor.

The lord's jurisdiction was nominally exercised in three courts —the court of freehold tenants, where the steward was only *primus inter pares*, and the jurors gave judgement; the court of copyhold tenants, sometimes called court baron, sometimes customary court, where the steward was the sole judge, and the jurors were merely jurors of presentment; and lastly the court leet, generally a hundred court in private hands. The first of these courts was still summoned, but it was often difficult to obtain the attendance of freeholders. The distinction between the other two was sometimes ignored, and one court, generally called a court leet, served for the miscellaneous jurisdiction of those manors which were still active.

These court leets were disciplinary institutions of some importance. The presentments made by the homage covered a very wide range, such as the withholding of due services, pur-

---

[1] *The relation between the lord of a manor and the copyholder*, also *A manor and a court baron*, in Manorial Society Publications, nos. 17 and 3 respectively. See also S. and B. Webb, *English local government: the manor and the borough*, 13–21.

prestures on land or water, erection of walls or hedges to the annoyance of the people, diversions of roads or streams, encroachments on the highways, eavesdroppers standing under walls or windows to hear tales, breakers of hedges, keepers of brothels, common haunters of taverns, butchers selling bad meat, ostlers asking unreasonable prices for their hay, millers taking excessive toll, and artificers failing to produce good work. Stray cattle might be 'presented'; also diseased horses, poachers, persons taking away the spawn of fish, artificers conspiring to raise wages, unauthorized persons using such luxurious material as velvet, fur, damask, or chamlet. Many of these offences, now known as common nuisances, are regulated by sanitary and board of health authorities. The court leet could not imprison as it had no gaol; but it punished by fine, and as a court of first instance it referred serious cases to the general sessions or the assizes. Here also were appointed the constable who kept the king's peace within the manor; also, in some instances, the ale-conner and the pound-keeper; while in market towns within the leet jurisdiction there might be inspectors of weights and measures, scavengers, dog-muzzlers, clerks of the wheat, fish, or butchery market. To some extent this jurisdiction overlapped that of the parish, but throughout England the latter was gaining at the expense of the former.

Side by side with the jurisdictions of county, parish, and manor was that of the church. This was exercised in the courts of the archdeacon and bishop, and in such archiepiscopal courts as the court of Arches; the Prerogative or Testamentary court, and the court of Peculiars (Canterbury); and in the Consistory, the Prerogative, and the Chancery courts of the archbishop (York). In the reign of Charles there was much ambiguity in regard to the spheres of the lay and clerical courts; but it was generally agreed that to the church pertained the probate of wills, in so far as personalty was concerned; the administration of intestates' estates; all cases loosely defined as matrimonial; suits for tithes and church rates; moral offences, whether committed by clergy or laity. They might determine at what age a person is capable of making a will, and when they granted probate to the executors of a boy of 15, the King's Bench refused to interfere.[1] The fre-

[1] *Modern Reports*, ii. 315.

quency with which the lay tribunals issued prohibitions to clerical courts, inhibiting them from proceeding further in cases brought before them, is sufficient to attest the dubiety surrounding the jurisdiction[1] of the church; and that so much of this jurisdiction should have remained is evidence not only of the lack of clarity in our judicial system, but of the strength of survivals.[2]

The recusant of Elizabethan and early Stuart times had felt the heavy hand of the court of High Commission; but this court was abolished in 1640, and, thereafter, dissent was dealt with by the justices in secular courts, in accordance with the statutes which handed the recusant over to the lay power. In consequence, a great field of activity was removed from the church courts (which nevertheless did not surrender their jurisdiction in matters of heresy and recusancy); in practice, therefore, the ecclesiastical tribunals were concerned not with bringing dissenters back to the fold, but with testamentary cases, and with the duty of imposing on the communicant strict standards of conduct and morality. For the smaller fry there was the court held by the archdeacon or his deputy, who at regular intervals conducted a visitation so exacting in character that at times it must have seemed an inquisition; for, on these occasions, he commenced with the minister. Was he a man of orderly life? Did he observe all the canonical requirements? Did he neglect his duties of preaching and catechizing? Then came the turn of the churchwardens. Did they keep the church fabric in good repair? Were the pulpit and ornaments clean? Were their accounts in order? Through a descending scale of parish clerks and sextons the ordinary laity were at last reached; and here there was plenty of scope for a conscientious archdeacon. He inquired into absentees from church, including those who left their pews after the first lesson, or neglected to receive communion; sabbath-breakers, brawlers, swearers, ne'er-do-wells, and unbaptized children were all good game for him; he was inquisitive about married couples living apart and unmarried ones living together; he saw to it that legacies left to the church were paid thereto;

[1] In practice the ecclesiastical law consisted mainly of all the old canon law which had not been repealed by statute.

[2] For this see *Report of the ecclesiastical commissioners of 1832*; also Claude Jenkins, *Ecclesiastical Records*.

that unlicensed persons did not keep school; that wills were proved, or letters of administration taken out. Accused persons protesting their innocence had to do canonical purgation, either by personal oath or, more often, by the oath of their neighbours; convicted persons might be required to do penance, as by standing up in church and confessing the fault. Such a penance might be preceded by forty days' excommunication. The archdeacon could also punish by fine, as 2s. for not paying marriage dues, or for not producing a marriage certificate. Whatever escaped through the sluices controlled by constable and justice was captured in the finer mesh of the archdeacon's net. The one set of authorities dealt with positive wrong-doing, the other with acts of omission and frailty. It was chiefly the unmarried mothers of England who provided this medieval functionary with an excuse for his continued existence.[1]

Similar in their scope were the presentments made to the commissary and consistory courts of the diocese, when the churchwardens were required to pass in review the condition of churches and churchyards; the state of repair of rectories and glebes; the absences of the rector or vicar; whether holy and fast-days were observed; if any refused infant baptism; or if any were unlawfully married or divorced, or remained in a state of excommunication; if any schoolmasters, physicians, surgeons, or midwives were pursuing their calling without licence; whether any one was under suspicion of immorality.[2] Diocesan courts decided matters also of purely spiritual discipline; they had power to suspend or deprive clergymen; they might declare a marriage void, or separate a married person *a mensa et thoro*. Much of their business related to the disposition of personal property by will. Superior to these were the courts of the two archiepiscopal provinces. The prerogative courts of Canterbury and York granted probate to executors and administrators within the jurisdiction of the province, wherever the deceased had had personal

---

[1] For the archdeacon see examples of churchwardens' presentments, such as those for Berkshire, in Bodley. Also S. A. Peyton, *Oxfordshire Peculiars* (*Oxford Records Society*), and *Act book of the archdeacon of Taunton* (*Somerset Records Society*, xlii, ed. C. Jenkins).

[2] These are taken from the *Articles to be enquired of within the commissarship of Westminster* (*Bodley*, B. 7, 9. Linc.).

property exceeding a certain amount in more than one diocese; the court of Peculiars had jurisdiction over those deaneries and peculiars which were outside episcopal control; the court of Arches had appellate jurisdiction over all the diocesan and most of the peculiar courts of the province of Canterbury. Crowning the whole edifice was the court of Delegates, originally established by Henry VIII, a tribunal composed of clergy and laity, to which appeal might be made from any of the lower courts.

By a reference to some of the appeals taken to the Delegates[1] in this period it is possible to form some conception of the jurisdiction of the church. Thus, in February 1664 they heard a case of some general interest. Shortly after the Restoration a person named Josiah Slader intruded himself into the rectory of Birmingham. His conduct was displeasing to the parishioners; for he was disaffected; he preached among Quakers; he was guilty of swearing, gaming, and perjury; he performed juggling feats in public, in which he purported to cut off his son's head and put it back again. Such were the allegations made by thirty-seven inhabitants of Birmingham in their petition to the bishop of Lichfield and Coventry. On account of doubt regarding his ordination, the bishop suspended him (Oct. 1662). Meanwhile, there were rumours that Slader's ordination papers were forged; whereupon the court of Arches inhibited him, until it should be determined whether or not he was lawfully ordained. The case then appears to have been considered by the Arches, which annulled the bishop's suspension, and gave costs against the Birmingham plaintiffs, reserving the question of Slader's orders (July 1663); but a few months later, the same court found that Slader was an intruder; that he was guilty of the offences charged against him, and that he was 'a mere layman'. Slader appealed to the Delegates (Feb. 1664), who upheld the decision of the Arches, decreed that Slader be sequestered from his living, and ordered the mesne profits to be paid to the churchwardens. It is of interest that in the course of the proceedings the appellant moved for a prohibition on the ground that forgery was triable by common law; but the prohibition was denied, because the forgery was 'touching an ecclesiastical matter'.

[1] For these see H. C. Rothery, *Return of all appeals in causes of doctrine and discipline made to the high court of Delegates* (1868).

A case where the verdict of the Delegates is not on record was that of a parishioner in a village of the Salisbury diocese named Robson who, in the consistory court, charged White and Harris with committing adultery. The charge appears to have been proved to the satisfaction of the court, which sentenced both parties to be canonically corrected, and cited the two for the imposition of penance. The female defendant Harris did not appear; but shortly afterwards she was allowed to come into the consistory court with three neighbours as compurgators, who swore on oath that she had not committed adultery with White. The situation was now somewhat complicated; but the bishop's deputy adopted a middle course: he pronounced that she had purged herself sufficiently; and he restored her, so far as he could, to her former good name; but at the same time he warned her not to be seen in the company of White except in church or market-place. He gave her a testimonial to this effect. Thereupon the unsatiated Robson appealed to the Arches against the admission of Harris to purgation, and her absolution from the sentence of penance originally imposed upon her; but the Arches upheld the proceedings of the consistory court, and gave costs against Robson. Whether he eventually recovered these from the Delegates is not known.

Altogether thirty-seven cases were taken to the Delegates, including one from the consistory court of Dublin; some of these were carried the whole way from the archdeacon's court by way of consistory court and Arches. Two appeals were lost by persons who were alleged to have secured their livings by means of forged credentials; another offence penalized was that of teaching boys without a licence; in another case it was ruled that the archdeacon's court could punish any one not attending church, in spite of the plea that the matter pertained to lay jurisdiction. A study of these cases tempts one to conclude that, apart from their probate administration, much of the work of these spiritual courts was made by the busy-body and informer. These are to be found in every society, but there was unlimited scope for them in the times of the later Stuarts. It may be added, however, that, with the foundation of societies for the reformation of manners, such as those instituted after 1689, a somewhat different attitude to moral offences was gradually introduced.

Such were the jurisdictions, lay and clerical, with which the average offender was most likely to come into contact. Of the tribunals at Westminster the court of Common Pleas was that nominally reserved for pleas of subject against subject and for cases where the crown was not plaintiff; in practice, however, much of its work was being 'poached' by the King's Bench and Exchequer, of which the first had originally been instituted for pleas of the crown, and the second for cases arising from the administration of the revenue. In effect, therefore, by the seventeenth century these three central tribunals were common law courts, their respective provinces not very clearly defined, save that the King's Bench was the superior, and was that wherein the crown instituted proceedings against the more serious political offenders. Moreover, many cases between subject and subject were disposed of in circuit under the *Nisi Prius* procedure, and the judgement of the central court was generally based on the finding of the local jury. Of the political trials there are few absolutely authentic records; for some of the State Trials, notably after 1678, appear to have been edited with party bias, and this is one of the most serious impediments in the way of an impartial account of the events of this period.[1]

There was more dubiety and debate about the functions of the fourth of the central courts—that of Chancery. Its functions were thus described in the earl of Oxford's case (1615):

The cause why there is a Chancery is for that men's actions are so diverse and infinite that it is impossible to make any general law which may apply with every particular act, and not fail in some circumstances. The office of the chancellor is to correct men's consciences for frauds, breach of trust, wrongs and oppressions of what nature soever they be, and to soften and modify the extremity of the law which is called Summum Jus.[2]

To illustrate from example. Chancery reviewed decrees of tithe;

---

[1] The first edition of the *State Trials* appeared in 1719, an edition very rarely met with; the second appeared in 1730. The reporting and editing of the trials of 1679–83 were done mainly by Robert Blaney, who may have tampered with some of the evidence. For this see J. G. Muddiman, *State Trials, the need for a new and revised edition* (1930). The opinion of the present writer is that the contemporary material does not make possible the completion of an absolutely dependable edition of the *State Trials*.

[2] *English Reports* (Chancery), xxi. 486.

enforced the customs of such cities as London and York, wherever the orphans of freemen were concerned; gave relief where conveyances were defective; adjudicated in breaches of trust and in construction of wills; and in general entertained all cases where the subject was aggrieved either by the enforcement of the letter of the law, or by unjust practices under cover of the law. By the issue of an injunction it could restrain any one from doing an act otherwise lawful. Chancery could determine what were or were not superstitious uses; and wherever a charitable use was intermixed, it decreed what was charitable and what superstitious, the latter being given to the crown. It was also a court of appeal from customary courts, from the vice-chancellor's courts of the two universities, and from the palatine courts of Chester and Durham. It had incurred the enmity of great common lawyers, such as Coke, because it was supposed to administer laws alien to the native jurisprudence, and because it frequently issued injunctions to the prejudice of common-law courts. Its abolition had been advocated by many Puritan reformers, because of its expense and delay, and since it seemed to be a jurisdiction outside the common law, and hostile to it; but, after 1660, its prerogative was seldom impugned, and its prestige was enhanced by such a lord keeper as Bridgeman, one of the greatest conveyancers of the century, and by lord chancellors such as Shaftesbury and Nottingham, of whom the one acted with such fairness and justice as to win the praise even of his enemies, while the other prepared the way for Eldon by the measure of system and uniformity which he introduced into the administration of equity. Nottingham is remembered by lawyers to-day as the 'Father of Equity'.

The historian is familiar with those suits where constitutional principle was involved; but something may also be gleaned from cases which, though of primary interest to the lawyer, provide evidence of social conditions. Among such are the cases relating to personal status, as illustrated mainly from questions of professional privilege or personal disability.

For example, a practising physician was chosen constable by the officers of his parish. A writ of privilege was thereupon moved for him in the King's Bench on the ground that his profession exempted him from parochial office. The privilege was refused, on the ground that a physician is in a different status from an attorney or barrister-at-law; for while these attend public courts, he is exercising a private calling.[1] A similar motion was made on behalf of the archdeacon of Rochester, praying that he might be discharged from an office to which he had been appointed by commissioners of Sewers in respect of lands which he held in Kent. On his behalf it was argued that the office was a mean one, and that the lands were let to a tenant. The privilege was granted, because he was a clergyman, and the land let in lease.[2]

Cases of interest for the history of the legal profession were those of maintenance and barratry. The statute legislation of the later middle ages abounded in prohibition of those two offences, prohibitions based on the principle that it is immoral to profit by the financial encouragement of other men's suits, or to defend a suit where there is reason to believe that it is an unjust one. Insistence on the second of these principles might have seriously hampered the growth of at least one branch of legal practice. To quote from an example. A was arrested at the suit of B in an action for debt. When the case came for trial, C, a barrister-at-law present in court, solicited the suit, 'when in truth at the same time B was indebted to A in £200', and A did not owe B anything. When it was shown that C had several times entertained B in his house, it was thought at first that his offence was maintenance; but when it also transpired that C had several times brought actions on behalf of B where nothing was owing, the court found C guilty of barratry. This distinction was embodied in the judgement that a man may lend money to another in order to help him to recover a just right at law; but if he lend money to promote and stir up suits, that is barratry.[3] Litigation as an object of speculation was therefore discouraged.

The courts insisted on a difference between the status of a lunatic and that of an idiot, a difference clearly illustrated in the case of *Prodgers* v. *Frazier*.[4] Here both sides recognized the right of the king to grant the custody of an idiot to whomsoever he pleased, without account; but it proved to be otherwise with a lunatic. An idiot was afflicted *a nativitate*, and could at no time

[1] *Modern Reports*, i. 22. Case of Dr. Pordage.
[2] Ibid. i. 282. Case of Dr. Lees.
[3] Ibid. iii. 97.   [4] Ibid. iii. 43.

have views on the administration of his property; he was therefore at the mercy of the person to whom his custody was allotted;
but a lunatic might have lucid intervals, in which he could call
his administrator to account. So the custodian of a person of
unsound mind kept accounts of his stewardship only if the misfortune of his charge did not date from birth; but with a 'natural
fool' he took the profits without waste or destruction and found
his charge in necessaries.[1]

Another question affecting status was the relationship between
master and apprentice. The law was clear that a master could
punish and correct the apprentice; but some justices were not
certain whether an apprentice who beat his master could be
discharged of his apprenticeship, until this was affirmed by the
King's Bench on appeal from the general sessions of Bristol.[2] A
freeman of London might turn away his apprentice for gaming.[3]
Wherever a capital sum had been paid by the apprentice at the
signing of his indentures, a portion of this was to be repaid on
his dismissal for negligence. It was held also by the courts that
a master might summon his servant from a conventicle or an
ale-house, and might use a moderate amount of force in so doing,
because the lord had the right to beat his villein without cause;
but if he commanded another to do it, then an action for battery
would lie.[4] Occasionally also there filtered through from the
church courts a case affecting the relations of husband and wife.
Thus, for a box on the ear and bad language, a spiritual court
awarded a woman £4 a week alimony against her husband, who
thereupon moved for a prohibition, on the ground that he had
chastised his wife for a reasonable cause, as he was allowed to do
by common law. The church court replied that it had jurisdiction *de saevitiis*; to which the husband rejoined that subsequent
reconciliation had taken away that *saevitia*.[5] In practice, however, the right of the spiritual tribunals to try such cases was
rarely contested.

Another sphere of litigation not without interest to the student
of social history is that of slander. The great number of such cases
in the later seventeenth century suggests that public fame and

---

[1] *English Reports* (Chancery), xxii. 488.   [2] *Modern Reports*, i. 286.
[3] *English Reports* (Chancery), xxi. 1065.   [4] *Modern Reports*, ii. 167.
[5] *English Reports* (Common Pleas), cxxiv. 414.

reputation were coming to be more highly prized, and that the remedies provided by the courts were more frequently invoked. When a shoemaker brings an action against a man for calling him a cobbler,[1] it is clear that social differentiation has proceeded far; indeed, modern society reposes on these subtle distinctions. Generally, for success in these actions, it had to be shown that material loss had ensued, or was likely to ensue; thus a man might with impunity be called a bungler, but if the words were spoken with reference to his trade, then the word was actionable. But it was not so with a peer; for any slander about him was actionable under the statute *De scandalis magnatum*, even if it did not expressly imply inaptitude for his hereditary office of adviser of the king.[2] There was considerable doubt whether the epithet 'papist' was libellous; some thinking that, like the word 'heretic', it related to something spiritual, and was therefore cognizable in the church courts; others held that at one time it would be actionable to use such an epithet, though not so at another time; for the meaning of a word may change, as shown by the term 'knave', formerly meaning a servant, and now libellous if used of an attorney. In 1683 the King's Bench gave a verdict in favour of sir T. Clarges against a defendant who had called him 'papist' at a parliamentary election.[3] So, too, there were epithets which, when applied to one person were libellous, but not necessarily so when used of others. Thus, it was libellous to say of a farmer that 'he owes more than he is worth', or of a tradesman, 'he is broke, and run away'. On the principle perhaps that there is no libel like the truth, each occupation acquired a special susceptibility, and had to be accorded protection against imputations touching on that susceptibility.

One of the most important questions of status was that of the soldier. The professional soldiers of the later Stuarts were not distinguished for stature or personal appearance; indeed, some of the garrison which came back from Tangier were decrepit men of 60 and 70; in consequence, the army was not a caste. Nor, at first, did they have buildings permanently allotted for their use, and it was not until 1684 that a beginning was made in the establishment of Chelsea Hospital, for the accommodation of

---

[1] *Modern Reports*, i. 19, where a judge stated that such an action had been brought. [2] Ibid. ii. 165. [3] Ibid. iii. 26.

400 aged or disabled soldiers. The standing army was not illegal, but it was extra-parliamentary, in the sense that while several statutes recognized its existence, either directly or by implication, no parliamentary provision[1] was made for its maintenance, as was made for Militia and Navy; even more, a red coat was anathema to every English patriot, because the recollection of army rule was still fresh.

In theory, the soldier did not sacrifice any of his civilian rights when he entered the army; and in practice he shared with the civilian a strong objection to anything with 'martial law in it'. In the summer of 1673 there was assembled on Blackheath an army for transport to the Continent; the men composing it were to be disciplined by the Articles of War promulgated in the preceding year. Their attitude to such restraints may be inferred from the following letter:

The soldiers at Blackheath are almost ready to mutiny on the rumour that they are to fight alongside the French. Men are wondering who dared to print the Articles of War . . . they scruple the oath in it, and say that to swear at large to obey the King's commands is strange; for then he may command things for which the persons that do them shall afterwards be hanged. The words of this horrid oath are:—'I, A.B. swear to be true and faithful to my sovereign lord king Charles . . . and to be obedient in all things to his General or Lieutenant General for the time being, and will behave myself obediently towards my superior officers in all that they shall command me for His Majesty's service, and I do further swear that I shall be a true, faithful and obedient soldier, every way performing my best endeavours for His Majesty's service, obeying all orders, and submitting to such rules and articles of war as shall be established by His Majesty.'[2]

That English paid soldiers should have objected to this 'horrid' oath is one of the most striking tributes to the pre-eminence of common-law traditions; for in some general way, these men on Blackheath believed that, unlike foreigners, they had over them the protection of Magna Carta and the Petition of Right; more-

[1] For an exception see *supra*, 444.
[2] Henry Ball to Williamson, July 18, 1673, in *Letters to Williamson*, ed. Christie (*Camd. Soc.*), 117. At the trial of lord Russell in 1682 it was argued that the King's Guards are not his Guards in law, but are merely a company of men in the king's pay. (*Burnet*, ii. 375).

over, soldiers, like sailors, were still tried by civil courts for offences not cognizable by courts martial, and the sphere of military jurisdiction was much narrower than it is to-day. It was also more vague; for there was considerable doubt whether, in law, desertion was punishable as a felony;[1] and there existed a court—the court of Chivalry or Marshal's court—which could deal with matters not pertaining to common law. But this court was in abeyance, and its reputation was bad. Nevertheless, as the crown imposed, by proclamation and articles of war, a more comprehensive and definite system of discipline,[2] there grew up a clearer distinction between soldier and civilian, and so was created the nucleus of military law. The Stuarts had no difficulty in obtaining from their judges a ruling that by statute law desertion was a felony. This evolution may be summarized thus: at the Restoration, a deserter might be punished by fine or imprisonment in the court of a justice; in the last years of the reign he might be hanged as a felon, in one of the places of execution under the jurisdiction of the tribunal which sentenced him; in the reign of James II he might be hanged as a felon, by sentence of a civil court, but in a special place, selected by the crown—in the view of his regiment.[3]

This confusion was increased by the distinction between discipline in time of peace and in time of war, between service at home and abroad, and by the fact that two different terms, martial law and military law, were often used for the same thing. Martial law was properly the suspension of common law in time of emergency, and so might concern any one; in 1678 it was defined as 'the law which dependeth on the King's will and pleasure, or his lieutenant's in time of war'.[4] Military law, on the other hand, was a set of rules, regulating the discipline of the soldier in his pro-

---

[1] For this see Holdsworth, *History of English Law*, vi. 225–30.

[2] C. Walton, *History of the British Standing Army*, 531. For the subject generally see Clode, *Military Forces of the Crown*.

[3] Herbert C.J. objected to this on the ground that the execution could legally take place only in Middlesex. The court was informed of the king's will—that the execution should take place in Plymouth, before his regiment; and soon afterwards Herbert was removed from the King's Bench, and replaced by Wright. (*Modern Reports*, ii. 124, *Rex* v. *W. Beal*.) For an execution in Covent Garden before a regiment see Luttrell, *Brief Historical Relation*, i. 400.

[4] Chamberlayne, *Angliae Notitia*, quoted in C. Walton, op. cit. 533.

fessional capacity; a code not yet clearly defined, but in process of formulation by edicts. Within the limits of these edicts, commanding officers enforced their jurisdiction in courts of inquiry and in courts martial; but punishments amounting to loss of life were not inflicted by these in peace time; so in this respect at least the scope of such tribunals was substantially limited, a restriction for which the old respect for Magna Carta and the Petition of Right was mainly responsible. Had Stuart relations with the legislature been harmonious, it would have been possible to end this anomalous state of things by legislation; but parliament could not take this work in hand till after the Revolution. The Mutiny Act, by its subjection of the soldier to a definite military code, ended the old confusion; and it had this important corollary, that an army not definitely and annually authorized by parliament is illegal.

The scope of military law in this period may be illustrated from surviving records of courts martial. In Tangier,[1] the discipline appears to have been that of an army in time of war, and was dispensed by courts consisting of four captains, four lieutenants, and four ensigns, presided over by a senior captain; its commission was derived from the warrant of the Governor and Commander of the Garrison. Here the most usual penalty was corporal punishment, varying from 31 to 39 lashes for such diverse offences as wounding another soldier, selling provisions, pawning uniform, and assaulting a Frenchman. To ride the wooden horse with muskets attached to each heel appears to have been a favourite punishment; this was inflicted on a private who, when in drink, disobeyed a sergeant. Refusal to obey an officer was punished by dismissal from the service, and a drummer who refused to beat his drum when ordered to do so had to stand at the gibbet with a rope round his neck, and a placard on his chest, on which the offence was inscribed. The most serious case heard by the Tangier courts was that arising from a mutiny in October 1677, when two soldiers went to the Governor's house and demanded the release of one of their companions who was imprisoned for disobedience. The ringleader was shot on the spot by the Governor, and the other was shot by order of a court

[1] 'Tangier Courts Martial', 1676–83, in Worcester College, Oxford, MS. no. 121.

martial. These records suggest that the Tangier garrison was more than usually turbulent, and that the discipline, though more severe than that prevailing in the army at home, was much less severe than that afterwards exercised.

The gradual imposition of a distinctive code on the soldier helped to disabuse men of the notion that in some way Magna Carta had provided one uniform law for all Englishmen. In other respects also the reign of Charles II is of great importance in the history of English law. To the Puritans we owe the earliest experiments in legal reform; and though it was long before the more far-reaching proposals of Commonwealth visionaries could be adopted, the legislation of Charles II owes a substantial debt to that of the preceding age. Outside of parliament there were public-spirited men like Petty who believed that the energy thrown by the Commons into penal legislation against dissent might be better employed in the promotion of measures for the advance of trade and national well-being; others would have had the law itself simplified, and in 1666 a Bill was introduced into the Commons for reviewing all the statutes and bringing them to one head,[1] but it appears to have been dropped. Another reform was that of trying to reduce the excessive number of attorneys. Both puritan and cavalier legislators tried their hand at this, but with the same result. Thus, a committee of the Commons, after hearing the evidence of the judges, proposed to limit the number of attorneys to a certain quota in each county; but it never reported.[2] More serious defects in legal administration were the numerous harsh punishments for minor offences, and the comparative impunity with which perjury and forgery might be committed. Sir William Temple protested against the sanguinary laws for common thefts, because these deprive us of so many subjects and do not cure the disease;[3] other writers echoed these views.[4] Had perjury and forgery been felonies in law, the Popish Plot might never have been concocted; that they should be felonies was advocated by at least one writer.[5]

---

[1] Oct. 5, 1666. *Millward's Diary.*

[2] *H.M.C. Rep.* ix, app., pt. ii. 20, Feb. 14, 1673; see also *supra*, i. 132–3.

[3] Sir W. Temple, *Works* (1770), iii. 55.

[4] e.g. *England's Wants . . . by a true lover of his country* (1668), in *Bodley, Godwin Pamph.* 1125.   [5] *Brief reflections upon . . . forgery and perjury* (1685).

Nevertheless, some important legal reforms were effected by statute. An Act of 1665 provided that in all actions, real, personal, or mixed, the death of either party before verdict and judgement should not be allowed for error, provided the judgement was entered within two terms after the verdict.[1] A measure which helped to lessen delays in the execution of justice was the statute of 1664–5 which decreed that judgement on a verdict of twelve men in any action or suit should not be stayed for a technical error, such as a mistake in the Christian name or surname of plaintiff or defendant.[2] So, too, vexatious lawsuits were discouraged by the provision that in personal actions where the jury awarded damages of less than 40s. the plaintiff should not have greater costs than the amount of the damages awarded him.[3] A ruling was given on the period of time after which the death of an absentee might be presumed; seven years of such absence abroad, without evidence of existence, was the period made statutory in 1666.[4] Another limit recognized by the law was that prescribed in the Gaming Act of 1664, whereby any one losing more than £100 in a game of chance was not bound to pay.[5]

Of greater importance were the Statute of Frauds[6] (1677) and the Act for better securing the liberty of the subject[7] (1679), usually known as the Habeas Corpus Act. The first of these, with the intention of diminishing opportunities for fraud and perjury, enacted that, in future, all parole leases of lands and interests of freehold should have the force of estates at will only, and also that devises of freehold lands or tenements must be in writing, and signed by three or four witnesses. Declarations or creations of trusts in lands or tenements were also to be in writing and signed, and the validity of contracts for the sale of goods above £10 in value was subject to certain alternative stipulations, including the requirement that a note or memorandum of agreement should be signed by both parties. So too with wills. A nuncupative will (that is, by word of mouth), where the estate

---

[1] 17 Car. II, cap. viii.
[2] 16–17 Car. II, cap. viii.
[3] 22–3 Car. II, cap. ix.
[4] 18–19 Car. II, cap. xi.
[5] 16 Car. II, cap. vii.
[6] 29 Car. II, cap. ii. See also Holdsworth, *History of English Law*, vi. 384–97.
[7] 31 Car. II, cap. ii.

exceeded £30, was invalid unless proved by three witnesses on oath, and made during the last sickness of the testator, an exception being allowed in favour of soldiers and sailors in actual service.

The legal importance of the Statute of Frauds has sometimes been exaggerated by historians, who have been tempted to think that it effected a revolution in conveyancing. Already, before the passing of the Act, transactions relating to land were generally in writing; for estates of importance this was almost invariable. Moreover, the statute gave rise to several technical abuses in conveyancing; and, in general, it was possible for Chancery to drive a coach-and-four through it. In reality, it provides a good instance of the piece-meal character of English legislation; how an abuse may be remedied not by a sweeping reform, but by a limitation of the abuse. Until 1863 there was a common-law rule whereby neither party to a civil suit could give sworn evidence at the trial, a rule which at times provided considerable scope for the suborned witness who, in return for money, would give false evidence on oath; consequently, the framers of the Statute of Frauds, instead of allowing the principal parties to give evidence, merely insisted that in certain contracts, something more than parole evidence should be forthcoming. For the sale or purchase of goods over £10 in value, a safeguard was provided by the requirements as to written contract, acceptance, or delivery; but for goods under £10, the subject had still to take the risk of losing his case on the sworn evidence of the perjurer. Hence the Statute of Frauds is of profound importance to the student of history; for it reveals how widespread was the menace of perjury, and only with this knowledge can the Popish Plot be understood.

There was also a moral as distinct from a legal significance in Shaftesbury's Act for better securing the liberty of the subject and for prevention of imprisonment beyond seas.[1] Part of this moral significance lies in its date—1679, one of the really critical years in the history of England, when the Commons were fighting a fierce battle against the king, and when additional security for the liberty of the subject, no matter how slight, was a

[1] For a good account see Holdsworth in op. cit. ix. 112–25; also J. Patterson, *Commentaries on the liberty of the subject*, ii. 205–18.

tremendous achievement. This Act, commonly known as the Habeas Corpus Act, was the culmination of a series of efforts to make statutory what had long been a common-law right, and to facilitate the exercise of that right by providing that no one should be imprisoned in a place where the writ could not easily be served. In this respect it was the most notable statute of the century, and it appears to have passed the Lords by a mistake in the count.

The writ of habeas corpus could be demanded from the King's Bench by or on behalf of a prisoner; by its terms, the gaoler or detainer was required to produce the body of the prisoner, with the date and cause of his detention, to the judgement of the court issuing the writ. In practice there were many difficulties in applying this remedy. For example, the writ was sometimes refused by courts other than King's Bench, and as a rule was issued only in term-time; again, a second and even a third writ might have to be applied for; still more, the prisoner might have been transported to one of the Channel Islands (as was Prynne), and a whole winter might pass before the writ could be served. In effect, therefore, a political prisoner might be placed in custody and kept there for a long period before trial, and it was in the interests of the Stuarts to restrict, as far as possible, the application of the remedy, because it was often deemed inadvisable that the cause of commitment should be investigated by the courts. In 1676 a London alderman named Jenkes was committed for a speech at the Guildhall in which he urged the common council to petition for a new parliament. As he was arrested in vacation the writ was refused by Chancery; and his release was due to the initiative of Rainsford L.C.J., who told the chancellor (Finch) that the writ was of right.

Repeated efforts had been made to remedy these defects by statute, and it is notable that some of these date from the period immediately following the banishment of Clarendon. A prisoners' transportation Bill[1] was introduced in 1669–70, and again[2] in 1673–4, together with a habeas corpus Bill, the object of which was to amend the working of the writ, and to make illegal the imprisonment of English subjects beyond seas or in Scotland. These provisions were embodied in Shaftesbury's Act,[3] which-

---

[1] *H.M.C. Rep.* viii, app., pt. i. 142.
[2] Ibid. ix, app., pt. ii. 42.   [3] 31 Car. II, cap. ii.

required sheriffs, gaolers, or other detainers, within three days of the service of the writ (except in cases of treason and felony), to produce the prisoner before the court to which the writ was returnable, and at the same time to certify the cause of commitment. In vacation, a petition for the writ might be directed to the lord chancellor, or to any of His Majesty's judges. Persons committed for criminal matters were not to be moved from one prison to another, but by writ of habeas corpus or other legal writ.

It was characteristic that the Act did not introduce any new principle, and that it achieved only a partial remedy. Its limitations were clear; for it did not regulate the amount of bail that might be demanded; nor did it apply to treason or felony; nor was there any provision whereby the court might investigate the truth of the facts alleged by the gaoler. These deficiencies were chiefly evidenced in the later administration of the bankruptcy legislation and the laws enforcing military service; but in practice the judges of the eighteenth century extended its scope, and what had hitherto been informal was made statutory in 1816, when the remedy acquired its present form. Before that date, it had been invoked in many cases not only of imprisonment but of wrongful detention, whether of wives or children, or of persons reputed to be insane; and herein is its true significance, that it provides the right to public investigation in all cases where the liberty of the subject is unwarrantably restrained.

Of the laws which limited the liberty of the subject, the most notable were those relating to treason and the press. The law of treason was based on the statute of 1353, which had reduced the crime to seven definite heads, with a proviso that parliament might in future adjudge any political offence as treason. But while this Act protected the king against war and violence, it did not deal with conspiracy, until the conspiracy had become open war. Parliament and judicial bench combined to remedy this defect, with the result that many things, including riots, came to be construed as overt acts tending to expose the king to danger, or to deprive him forcibly of some part of his authority. Hence the so-called law of constructive treason; hence also the potency of this weapon in the hands of a determined executive; for a servile bench might be trusted so to interpret the law as to secure the removal of a political opponent, on the ground that his words or acts were likely to prejudice the powers or safety of the sovereign. This was the weapon with which the later Stuarts removed many of their critics.

The first statute of the Cavalier Parliament was a treason Act.[1] This defined treason within the terms of the Statute of 1353, and included in the category of overt acts all printing, writing, preaching, or malicious and advised speaking calculated to compass or devise the death, destruction, injury, or restraint of the sovereign, or to deprive him of his style, honour, or kingly name. Overt acts had to be proved by two witnesses; but at the trial of the Regicides in 1660 it was ruled by Bridgeman that two witnesses were not required for each overt act; one witness proving one such act, and another witness proving another being sufficient.[2] In 1668 there was provided a good illustration of how far the law of treason could extend. Early in that year Peter Messenger and fourteen other apprentices tumultuously assembled themselves in Moorfields under colour of pulling down houses of ill fame—such was the allegation in the indictment of high treason preferred against them; though it was well known to the court that the affair was merely an apprentices' riot. Kelyng L.C.J., who was not devoid of sympathy for the accused, defined treason in these terms:

By levying of war is meant not only when a body is gathered together as when an army is, but if a company of people will go about any public reformation, that is High Treason . . . for they take upon them the royal authority; the way is worse than the thing. These men do pretend that their design was against bawdy houses; now for men to go about to pull down houses with a captain and an ensign and weapons; if this thing be endured, who is safe? It is High Treason because it doth betray the peace of the nation . . . for if every man may reform what he will, no man is safe.[3]

These words admirably describe two things—a judicial construction of the law of treason, and the panic fear with which, for long after the Restoration, the government regarded everything that seemed likely to result in a mass movement. The jury gave a verdict that Messenger and three others had met in a riotous

[1] 13 Car. II, stat. i, cap. i.   [2] See *supra*, i. 197–8.
[3] *State Trials* (1730 ed.), ii. 583.

manner; the judges then deliberated whether this was treason or not. They decided that it was, Hale only dissenting; accordingly these four men suffered death in the barbarous manner then prescribed for those convicted of this offence. It is not surprising, therefore, that when, after 1681, the attack on the whigs was launched, the judges were able to prove that almost anything was treason. Thus in 1681, when Shaftesbury was indicted at the Old Bailey, Pemberton L.C.J. stated that, according to the Act of 1661, the intention to levy war on the king was now treason; and so also were words, if they imported any malicious design against the king or government.[1] Two years later Algernon Sidney was convicted on the opinions expressed in his unpublished writings. Perhaps the most extraordinary case of all was that of Rosewell, a nonconformist preacher, who in 1684 was found guilty of high treason on the evidence of two women, who swore that, in a sermon, he had compared Charles to Jeroboam, and asked why people flocked to the king on the pretence of being healed. In this case, the attorney-general had pressed for a verdict on the ground 'that the government is greatly concerned in the matter'. This is noteworthy as one of the few trials at which Jeffreys acted with fairness; for in face of the jury's verdict he suspended judgement, and shortly afterwards Rosewell obtained the king's pardon and was discharged.[2]

A man accused of high treason was therefore at the mercy not so much of the law as of the judge and jury which tried him; but even if these were impartial he was handicapped by the method of procedure. He did not receive a copy of the indictment until the day of the trial; nor was counsel allowed him; he had therefore to conduct his own defence, and without preparation of any kind. It was here that Jeffreys showed himself at his worst; for he railed and jeered at men struggling to exculpate themselves from all sorts of hearsay evidence levelled against them by enemies and perjurers. These and other defects were not remedied until 1696, when the Trial of Treasons Act[3] allowed counsel to the accused, and required two witnesses for each overt act.

Censorship of the press, originally exercised by the Church,

---

[1] See *infra*, 629.   [2] *State Trials*, iii. 982–3.
[3] Holdsworth, op. cit. vi. 232–4.

had long been controlled by the crown, and was placed on a statutory basis by the Licensing Act of 1662.[1] This Act prohibited the printing or importing of any books or pamphlets containing doctrines contrary to the principles of the Christian faith, or to the doctrine and discipline of the Church of England, or tending to the scandal of government or governors in church or state. For purposes of inspection, all books had first to be entered at Stationers' Hall, and were licensed according to their subject— law books by the lord chancellor; books of history or affairs of state by one of the principal secretaries of state; books of heraldry by the earl marshal, and all others by the archbishop of Canterbury and the bishop of London. This Act remained in force until 1679, when its place was taken by a proclamation[2] ordering the seizure of all libels against the government, and the apprehension of their authors and printers; with a reward of £40 for informers. In 1685 the Act was renewed, and eventually expired in 1695. The noted Roger L'Estrange was appointed in 1663 to enforce these licensing regulations, after he had distinguished himself by his devotion to the royalist cause and by his extreme views on the functions of the censorship. Before he was appointed 'surveyor of imprimery' he had enumerated[3] most of the seditious opinions which he thought an efficient censorship should suppress; among these were the following: (1) that the execution of Charles I was justified; (2) that the king is one of three estates; (3) that in cases of necessity sovereignty resides in the two Houses; (4) that the power of the crown is fiduciary; (5) that the king's person, as distinct from his authority, may be resisted; and (6) that the king has no supreme power in ecclesiastical matters. L'Estrange became the greatest of the tory pamphleteers; prolific, unscrupulous, and completely deaf to ridicule.

The rights of the subject in regard to printing and publishing were properly summed up by Scroggs when he declared that there was no such thing as liberty of the press.[4] This was made

---

[1] 14 Car. II, cap. xxxiii.　　　[2] Oct. 31, 1679, *Steele*, i. 3699.

[3] In his *Considerations and proposals in order to the regulation of the Press*. This was issued in June 1663; in August he was appointed 'surveyor of the imprimery'.

[4] *State Trials* (1730), iii. 57. Trial of Henry Carr for printing and publishing a libel, July 2, 1680.

more explicit by Jeffreys in his pronouncement that the law forbade the publication of anything concerning the government without the king's licence.[1] Already the courts had illustrated how the doctrine was applied. In 1664 L'Estrange forced his way into the premises of a printer named Twyn, where he seized the sheets of a book *A Treatise of the execution of Justice*, probably an apologia for the execution of Charles I. Twyn was indicted for high treason, convicted, and executed.[2] As the state was protected, so was the church. In the same year as Twyn was executed Benjamin Keach was indicted for libel at the Aylesbury Assizes, the libel relating to his book *The Child's Instructor*, wherein were these statements: that infants ought not to be baptized; that laymen might preach the Gospel, and that Christ would reign personally on earth in the latter day.[3] His sentence was fourteen days' imprisonment, a fine of £20, and the pillory. His book was burnt in front of him by the common hangman.

Expression of personal opinion was therefore strictly limited by the law of treason and the law of the press. In 1678 a statute[4] was passed taking away the old writ *De haeretico comburendo*; but this left intact the rights of the spiritual courts to punish heresy, and of the common law courts to punish blasphemy.[5] In theory the church courts still had the right to punish recusancy;[6] but in practice the civil courts now administered all the penal legislation against Dissenters and Catholics. In effect, therefore, the control of opinion was almost altogether removed from the church and vested in the state. This was not without importance in the history of toleration since, in its imposition of particular doctrines, the state had at least the argument of expediency in its favour; on his side, the subject might, in the interests of public security, subscribe to doctrines which he would have repudiated if tendered to him by a priest. In this way did theological opinion merge with social safeguard; and the process was further assisted by the fact that, unlike the theologian, the statesman insisted on doctrines few in number and straightforward in expression. Three doctrines came to be enforced on all who desired the full

---

[1] *State Trials* (1730), iii. 57.
[2] Ibid. ii. 524–9.
[3] Ibid. ii. 546.
[4] 29 Car. II, cap. xxix.
[5] For an instance see *English Reports*, lxxxvi (King's Bench), 189, Taylor's case.
[6] See *supra*, 496, 499.

privileges of English citizenship, namely: (1) that there is no transubstantiation of the elements in the sacrament, (2) that the invocation of the Virgin Mary or of any other saint, and the sacrifice of the mass as practised by the church of Rome are idolatrous, and (3) that these affirmations are to be understood 'in the plain and ordinary sense of the words'. The first of these doctrines was imposed by the Test Act[1] of 1673 on all office-holders; all three were imposed by the Act of 1678[2] on members of both Houses, and on sworn servants of the king and queen. Together with the oaths of allegiance and supremacy, and the taking of the sacrament at least once a year according to Anglican practice, these doctrines constituted the state religion of England until 1828-9. They were enforced for a political, not a religious object, and by penalties not spiritual but civil. Protestantism and patriotism were therefore wedded by indissoluble bonds, and if Anglicans themselves had no very clear-cut theology, they were committed to emphatic opinions about the essentials of the rival system. English independence was therefore preserved not by forging new weapons, but by selecting the strongest weapons of the enemy and throwing them in his face. To this extent also were the opinions of Hobbes[3] put into practice, and the cause of toleration was hastened not by the laxity of the state, but by its strictness in the enforcement of those few doctrines which seemed requisite for national security.

There was another respect in which the views of Hobbes found illustration and vindication in the legislation of the Stuarts, namely, in the policy adopted towards corporations. Hobbes[4] had compared the municipal franchises to the worms which eat into the intestines of the body politic; the Corporation[5] Act of 1661 and the writs of *quo warranto* make the words of Hobbes seem like prophecy. By this Act five obligations were imposed on all holders of municipal offices,[6] and the commissioners appointed to administer the Act were authorized not only to impose these obligations, but to remove officials at their discretion, even where they had complied with the statutory requirements. One of

---

[1] For the Test Act see *supra*, i. 368-9.
[2] 30 Car. II, stat. ii, cap. i. For this see *supra*, 467, and *infra*, 574.
[3] For Hobbes see *infra*, 741-6. [4] *Leviathan*, ch. xxix.
[5] 13 Car. II, stat. ii, cap. i. [6] For these see *supra*, i. 198.

Prynne's last services was to oppose this Bill.[1] Within the period of three years allotted to the commissioners, the crown succeeded in 'purging' several boroughs, generally with the help of local commissions composed of country gentry, presided over by the lords lieutenant; and in this way a threat was directed against the whole principle of parliamentary representation. After the lapse of the commissioners' powers, the executive continued to make use of the statute; but difficulty was experienced in obtaining suitable persons as substitutes for those ejected, and the increasing practice of occasional conformity permitted the entry of men whose loyalty was nominal. But by the issue of a *quo warranto* for alleged misfeasance, the crown was enabled to remodel several charters; moreover, it was possible to levy blackmail on a borough, by threatening forfeiture unless some technical defect was compounded for in money.[2] That Clarendon had done so was one of the accusations against him.[3] The crown soon saw how far it might go, and how it might depend on the support of the country gentry. Thus, the charter of Gloucester was forfeited in 1671;[4] in the following year a *quo warranto* was directed against Northampton, because of its disrespect to the earl of Peterborough 'who had honoured them by accepting' the office of Recorder;[5] and the franchises of Nottingham tottered in the balance because the duke of Newcastle did not find the corporation sufficiently obsequious.[6] In its progress towards constitutionalism, England had to go through a long process of 'purging' —first of parliaments; then boroughs; next, justices, lords lieutenant, and universities; the purging stopped short only at the church and the army. It was James II who carried out this process most conscientiously; even the man who showed visitors round the tombs in Westminster Abbey was removed from office.[7]

The process of remodelling the boroughs enabled and encouraged the landed gentry to impose their yoke on the municipal

---

[1] He wrote a pamphlet against it and was censured by the Speaker, *Steele*, i. 3313, July 15, 1661.

[2] For a good account of this subject see R. H. Sacret, *The Restoration government and municipal corporations* in *E.H.R.* xlv.

[3] See *supra*, i. 315.   [4] *P.C. Reg.* 63, Nov. 3, 1671.

[5] *H.M.C. Rep.* xii, app., pt. vii. 98.

[6] *Coventry Papers* (Longleat), 83, f. 106.

[7] N. Luttrell, *Brief historical relation*, i. 368.

corporations; for they were frequently intruded as mayors or recorders. Hitherto, the recorder was presumed to have legal qualifications; but under the new and more aristocratic dispensation these might be done without. Such was the conclusion to be deduced from the case of lord Hawley (1671). He had been 'put in' as recorder of Bath by the Corporation Act commissioners in 1663; but the corporation removed him in 1669 because he had been absent for five years without reasonable excuse, and was *nullo modo peritus in lege*. The court of King's Bench issued a *mandamus* restoring him to his office; and some curious arguments were adduced for this course. The phrase *nullo modo peritus in lege* was too general; there were precedents where recorders, ignorant of the law, had given erroneous judgements; and were they ineligible because of that? As for the five years' absence, this was no disqualification; by analogy, a park keeper does not forfeit his office for non-attendance, unless a deer is killed in his absence.[1] The analogy was an apt one. The Stuarts imposed 'park keepers' on the boroughs; thereby strengthening that class which was to prove most inimical to themselves, and laying the foundations of the political power exercised by the landed families of the eighteenth century.

Liberty of the subject was controlled and determined by these courts and laws; it was influenced also by the character of the men who served on juries, or sat on the bench. That jurors should be substantial freeholders was a generally accepted principle, because poor men might be more easily influenced, or might fail to discern the matters in question; accordingly, an Act[2] of 1664-5 required that in trials of issues they should be worth at least £20 per annum in freehold lands. But this was often difficult to enforce, especially in London, as the estates of the city belonged mainly to great nobles and corporations;[3] in consequence, for the political trials of Charles's reign, Middlesex juries were sometimes empanelled from persons not all of whom were freeholders. Most of the Stuart judges had clear notions

---

[1] *English Reports*, lxxxvi (King's Bench), 98-9.

[2] 16-17 Car. II, cap. v.

[3] At the trial of lord Russell the court refused to uphold the objection that some of the jury were not freeholders of London: *The Tryals of W. Walcot, W. Hone, lord Russell . . .* (1683), 32-5.

of the qualifications of the ideal juryman; and, had Jeffreys had his way, he would have enlisted the help of personal servants of the king in cases where the crown was prosecutor, in spite of an opinion to the contrary in that 'straggling'[1] book, Coke's *Institutes*. When a jury gave substantial damages to the tory lord mayor sir W. Pritchard against the whig sheriff Papillon, the lord chief justice made a significant remark: 'You seem to be persons that have some sense upon you and consideration for the government';[2] still more, when juries which had convicted papists were called upon to convict whigs, it was clear that the weapon which had served indirectly against the Court might be used with equal efficacy against its enemies. By their remodelling of the corporations after 1681 the Stuarts could be nearly as sure of their juries as they were of their judges; such was the moral to be deduced from the following interchange of courtesies between Jeffreys and Oates, when the latter was on trial for perjury (1685):

> *Oates.* We know how juries have gone a'late.
> *Jeffreys.* Ay, very strangely indeed, *Mr.* Oates, and I hope so as we shall never see them go again.[3]

The epidermis of Oates was soon to bear eloquent testimony to the significance of Jeffreys' remark.

But it was characteristic of the reign that, in the midst of legal abuses, there was secured one of the most important judicial reforms of modern times. This was the principle of the inviolability of the jury for its verdict. In 1670 two Quakers, Penn and Mead, were indicted at the Old Bailey for preaching in the streets. Despite the directions of the recorder, the jury (whose foreman was Bushell) gave a verdict for acquittal. For this they were fined; and their foreman, in default of payment, was committed to prison with some other members of the jury. A writ of habeas corpus was applied for and obtained from the court of Common Pleas, the judges of which court discharged Bushell on the ground that to find against the evidence or direction of the court was not sufficient cause to punish a jury.[4] One of the

---

[1] *The Tryal and Conviction of John Hampden Esq.* (1684), 2–4.

[2] *An exact account of the trial between sir W. Pritchard and T. Papillon* (1689), 32.

[3] *The Tryals, Convictions and Sentence of Titus Otes upon two indictments for Perjury* (1685), 10.   [4] *English Reports*, cxxiv (Common Pleas), 1006–18.

jurymen then brought an action against the recorder for false imprisonment; but it was ruled that an action does not lie against a judge for what he does judicially, though erroneously.[1]

Under the Commonwealth, judges had held office during good behaviour; but, at the Restoration, they again became wholly dependent on the crown. With the development of a concerted opposition in the Commons, it was inevitable that attention should have been directed to the relations between crown and bench, and as early as 1674–5 a Bill was introduced for making the tenure of judges *quamdiu se bene gesserint*, instead of *durante bene placito*.[2] The matter became of increasing moment during the Popish Plot, when it was not their severity but their occasional moderation which brought on the judges the condemnation of the House. On December 23, 1680, a report was received from a committee appointed to review the proceedings of the judicial bench; the result was a series of resolutions condemning certain recent proceedings, including these:[3] (1) the conduct of Scroggs and Jones in discharging the Middlesex grand jury when a Bill had been presented indicting the duke of York as a popish recusant; (2) the infliction of a fine of £1,000 on one who expressed the opinion that the English constitution consisted of three estates; and (3) the extraordinary charge given at the last Assizes of Kingston by baron Weston, who was alleged to have stated: 'Zwingli set up his fanaticism, and his disciples are seasoned with such a sharpness of spirit that it concerns magistrates to keep a sharp eye on them.' These words, resolved the Commons, were 'a scandal to the Reformation'. As a result of these and other revelations the Commons resolved that Scroggs and Weston should be impeached, and that judges should hold office only during good behaviour. A lead to the movement had already been given by Sacheverel in February 1678, when he objected that the judges did as the Court directed, and cited facts to prove his contention.[4] Moreover, England had old and memorable traditions about her judges. Edward I had conducted a great inquiry into their conduct in 1288, with drastic and salutary results; and his predecessor king Alfred was said to have kept his judicial bench

[1] *Modern Reports*, ii. 218.
[2] *Grey*, ii. 415.
[3] *C.J.* ix. 688 sqq.
[4] *Grey*, iv. 140–1.

spotless by periodical hangings of whole batches of unjust judges.[1]

The Stuarts frequently consulted with their judges; for example, before the trial of the Regicides in 1660, they had to confer with the solicitor-general and attorney-general, so that there might be no hitch in the proceedings.[2] In revenue cases this was a frequent procedure.[3] More serious, and more customary in the reign of James, was the practice of removing judges whose conduct was not in accordance with the wishes of the executive, and substituting for them others on whom reliance could be placed. For this purpose there was good material to hand. In private litigation the judges might have to decide against the validity of one of the king's grants, or they might quash an indictment by the crown; but, where the interests or the supposed interests of the Court were concerned, the judges, almost without exception, were tools. Sir Matthew Hale was a notable exception, but his puritanism and punctiliousness savoured of an earlier age; lord keeper Guilford proved himself a man of humanity and judgement, until he was called upon to try whigs, such as Stephen College. Scroggs hounded many innocent victims of the Popish Plot to their death; until, in the trial of sir George Wakeman, when the queen's honour was concerned, he suddenly changed round, and impugned the evidence of Oates and Bedloe. It was the need for the right kind of judge which caused the elevation of sir Francis Wythens to the Bench in April 1683, after distinguished service for the crown against Fitzharris and Shaftesbury. Sir Francis Pemberton, who succeeded Scroggs as lord chief justice of the King's Bench, had already imperilled his career by a reputation for impartiality; but he succeeded in living this down, for at the trial of archbishop Plunket he refused the prisoner time to collect his evidence; and at the indictment against Shaftesbury he prohibited the grand jury from inquiring into the credibility of witnesses. All of these were men of legal acumen and judicial fairness, except wherever the government was concerned. The same is true of Jeffreys, whose most famous exploits belong to a

---

[1] *The triumph of justice over unjust judges* (1681). This is based on Horn's. *Mirror.*

[2] Pollock, *The Popish Plot*, 279.   [3] See *supra*, 423-4.

later reign. With the general rehabilitation of the Stuarts he has come to be regarded as a misunderstood and maligned man; he has even been credited with a sense of humour,[1] and other virtues may yet come to light. But the Stuart taste in judges as in personal friends was peculiar, and the apologist of Jeffreys needs consummate literary skill.

Such were the main institutions and laws for preserving or restricting the liberty of the subject in the reign of Charles. They attest the great strength of survivals in English national life, and provide evidence of a degree of corporate intelligence and responsibility such as no other race had attained. Many of them were to be strained to breaking-point in the years 1675 to 1688, and so the narrative of events must now be resumed.

[1] H. B. Irving, *Judge Jeffreys*, 43.

XV

DANBY AND THE PARLIAMENTARY OPPOSITION,
1674–8

IT has been seen that in three respects England was better qualified than the sister kingdoms for a contest with the Stuart prerogative—in her comparative wealth, her unique parliamentary institutions, dominated mostly by landowners, and her great common-law traditions, which habituated Englishmen both to acquiescence in order and discipline, and to resentment of encroachment from without. These exceptional advantages gave weight to the claims of the Commons, claims which had steadily become more insistent after the first symptoms of suspicion had entered into the minds of the legislature; and, by the end of the year 1674, the Lower House could look back on a considerable measure of achievement. The Second Dutch War, which was embarked on at the solicitation of the Commons, had ended the domination of Clarendon, and with it the conception of the rigid state; the Third Dutch War had been concluded by pressure from the Commons, and had resulted in a fierce but unorganized attack on the men who shared Clarendon's power among them. Of these men Clifford had died in less than a month after his resignation from office (Aug. 18, 1673); Arlington, his rival, resigned his secretaryship to Joseph Williamson in September 1674 and, as lord chamberlain, tried thereafter to gain the favour of the Commons, and to supplant those who had superseded him; Buckingham, no longer bound to the Court by the ties of office, was now setting up as the apostle of Protestantism and Patriotism, while retaining his close personal attachment to Louis XIV. Shaftesbury, fooled in the secret negotiations with France, but resolved not to be fooled further, was now the most vehement denouncer of the Popish interest, talking publicly of exclusion, of the menace of a French invasion of Ireland, and the necessity of a royal divorce and marriage with a Protestant. Lauderdale, still secure in his master's favour, was the solitary survivor from the wreckage.

Of the other great personages the duke of York was the most

consistent but the most undecided. Had he been gifted with political acumen, had he even possessed any real knowledge of the country over which he was one day to rule, he might easily have created a powerful following of his own, as there were always Dissenters ready to welcome his alliance against Anglicans; but he had neither resilience nor flexibility, the two essential qualities for political success in this reign; and even his virtues, namely industry and intense seriousness of purpose, were being exercised at the one period of English history when these things had their dangers. In contrast with him was the duke of Monmouth, who 'seemed born as if only for love', and was then combining his escapades and gallantries with the chancellorship of the university of Cambridge, everywhere showing promise that he would perpetuate the unconventionalities and personal charm of his father. He had already distinguished himself in arms; within a few years he was to become a serious element in politics, because of two things, his Protestantism and his illegitimacy. The events of the Popish Plot placed a substantial premium on the first, while the second commended him to those who thought that a weak claim to the throne was the best guarantee of constitutional rule.[1]

The third personality of importance at this time was William, prince of Orange. He did not inspire love, nor had his career in arms shown higher qualities than determination; but he had this asset, that by some Englishmen he was accepted as the only man able to save Europe from the domination of France and Popery. Now that England had deserted the ranks of his enemies William was determined that she should become one of his active allies; and after his defeat at Seneff in August 1674 he devoted himself to this object. In September, in response to Charles's friendly overtures, he sent to England an agent named Sylvius, nominally to secure the renewal of his uncle's good graces as a preliminary to a separate Dutch peace with France, but really in order to guide the anti-French feeling of the Commons into

---

[1] And nobler is a limited command
    Given by the love of all your native land,
    Than a successive title, long and dark,
    Drawn from the mouldy rolls of Noah's Ark.
                                    Absalom and Achitophel.

active co-operation against Louis XIV. Though fully aware of the prince's correspondence with the opposition, Charles showed unfailing indulgence; and in November of the same year he sent Arlington and Ossory on a conciliatory mission, with an offer of the hand of the twelve-years-old princess Mary. The prince refused the proposal, nominally on the ground of the princess's youth, and the possibility that the duke of York might yet have an heir; but really because the offer was represented to him by his English correspondents as a trap.[1] From this point dates that Dutch pressure on English politics which, coupled with the whig opposition, was to result in the Revolution.

Increasing solicitude for an undiminished prerogative caused William to sacrifice a certain amount of popular support; but his agents had not found it difficult to stir up anti-French feeling in this country. During the Third Anglo-Dutch War the prince had helped to discredit Stuart policy by aiding the circulation of a pamphlet[2] attacking the Anglo-French alliance; and the successful result of these activities was evidenced by the fact that in February 1674 the Venetian envoy noted the existence of a Dutch party,[3] distinguished by hostility to the duke of York, and committed to the cause of a legitimate and Protestant succession. There were other groups, not unconnected; all of them supplying rallying points for a concerted opposition. Thus, lord Holles was an almost traditional nucleus for associations of Presbyterians and old Commonwealth's men, none of them very enduring; Buckingham also tried to create a following out of similar material, but without much success; Shaftesbury led the party which advocated the king's divorce and marriage with a Protestant; when this failed, he pressed for a dissolution of parliament, led the exclusionists and backed Monmouth. More moderate men favoured severance of the French connexion and maintenance of good relations between crown and legislature. From such shifting groups the Country party had begun to take shape in the autumn session of 1673, when a determined opposition was

---

[1] *Mignet*, iv. 325.

[2] *England's appeal from the private cabal at Whitehall to the grand council of the nation.* The original was composed by the imperialist envoy Lisola; the translation was by Pierre du Moulin, who was in the pay of William.

[3] *Ven. Trans.* 14/40. Feb. 20/March 2, 1674.

led in the Commons by lord Cavendish, William Russell (afterwards lord Russell), William Sacheverell, sir William Coventry,
sir T. Lee, and sir T. Meres, and in the Lords by Shaftesbury
and Halifax. Opposition to Arlington, Buckingham, Lauderdale, and the French alliance was in effect opposition to the
Court, a fact which accounts in part for the term Country party;
but the name at first denoted not so much the aims of a nationalist movement, as of men who, untied by office or personal favour,
demanded a more disinterested and economical management
of the affairs of state.

Hitherto Charles's policy, if such a phrase may be used, had
been influenced mainly by the duke of York and by Arlington.
The zeal of the one and the pliability of the other had resulted
in the Declaration of Indulgence, the enforced withdrawal of
which was the only public rebuff ever suffered by the king. In
consequence, the pathway to Rome *via* toleration was now
barred, and the Test Act was as sacrosanct as Magna Carta, a
lesson not lost on Charles, for whom this meant the termination
of a period of experiment. But at the very moment when the
complete failure of this experiment left the crown exposed to an
opposition steadily becoming more formidable, fortune placed
in his hands a minister whose services are commensurate with
those of Clarendon. This was sir Thomas Osborne, who was
born in Buckingham's county (Yorkshire) in 1632. He had
combined hostility to Clarendon with the foundation of a personal interest at Court, based on Anglicanism and Cavalier
loyalism; more distinctive was his financial aptitude, his competence in all matters of accountancy. Appointed joint treasurer
of the Navy in 1668 and sole treasurer of the Navy in 1671, he
resolutely set himself to the task of paying off debt, and diminishing the opportunities for fraud. 'A pay was made of old
tickets' is a frequent entry in the journal[1] which he commenced
in September 1671; he also introduced a more regular routine
by accounting weekly to the Navy Board. In June 1673 he
succeeded Clifford as lord high treasurer, and by strict order
and retrenchment he succeeded in diminishing the rate of interest on government loans. He restored a measure of national
credit by providing for the payment of interest, amounting to

[1] *Add. MS.* 28040. These entries occur frequently after f. 12.

£77,000 per annum to the bankers after the Stop of the Exchequer; he obtained better terms from the farmers of Excise, securing from this source alone an increase of £20,000 per annum; and, by good management, he improved the yields from the Hearth Tax and the Irish revenues, measures which resulted in clearing off old debts and enriching the hereditary revenues by more than £100,000 per annum.[1] In this work of reconstruction he was at first helped by the rapid expansion of English trade immediately after England's withdrawal from the Third Anglo-Dutch War; but this was not steadily maintained, and so he was obliged to insist on a policy of retrenchment. He was created a privy councillor and viscount Osborne in 1673, and a year later he became earl of Danby.

During his tenure of office Danby's activities helped to strengthen the association between the White Staff and responsibility for government policy, thus illustrating the change whereby the purse-bearer displaced confessor, favourite, and lawyer. Southampton was the last of the old lord treasurers, for whom the post was the crowning reward of devoted service; the personal opportunities of the office had been snatched from Clifford by the Test Act, and were now to be utilized to their fullest extent by his successor. Successful accountancy and an accommodating manner established Danby in Charles's confidence, and by March 1675 he was chief minister. Considering his impregnable Anglicanism he had unusual supporters, these at first including York and Buckingham; and so far as he had any political mentor, it was Lauderdale, whose alliance he secured, and whose silent methods of governing Scotland he admired.

Danby had a definite policy. He was for alliance with the prince of Orange and a commercial understanding with Spain; he knew of no advantages from a French alliance,[2] and he believed that Louis should be kept strictly to the Triple Alliance. That the English and Irish revenues ought to be maintained, and embezzlement stamped out, were for him matters of principle.[3] He recognized the two alternatives: that Charles must either 'fall into the humours of the people' and accept the con-

---

[1] For his financial reforms see *supra*, 427–8; also A. Browning, *Life and letters of sir T. Osborne, earl of Danby*, i, cap. v, vii and viii.

[2] *Add. MS.* 28042, f. 13, 'Memo in year '77 for the King'.   [3] *Ibid.*, f. 15.

trol of parliament; or he must have sufficient revenue to dispense with parliament. By conserving the national finances he hoped to establish royal independence; by bribing the lesser members of the Commons he obtained the votes of the obscure, even though they cost him the diatribes of the eminent; for he rejoiced more in the votes of ninety-nine silent legislators than in the conversion of one notable opponent. He was not the first English statesman to use bribery or influence, but he was the first to realize the value of organized system and personal mediocrity in the methods and material of politics, with which aids he contrived to establish Charles's absolutism on a basis, if not of consent, at least of negotiation and influence. Nor was this all. Knowing that the fitful breezes of toleration were dreaded as the likely forerunners of a popish hurricane, he proposed to steer the ship-of-state on the never-failing current of uncompromising Anglicanism; the absolutist edifice which Charles and Louis had thought to balance on the slim shoulders of soliciting priests and metropolitan *demimondes*, he would rest securely on the broad backs of the English bishops. Herein he showed common sense, his most characteristic quality.

Charles had enough personal honour to cause him feelings of regret that he had been obliged to abandon the French alliance; accordingly in July 1674 he informed the French ambassador that he would prorogue parliament until April 1675. He thus obtained a respite of a few months; but his difficulties had to be faced in more intensified form in the spring of 1675, when Ruvigny pressed for a dissolution. It was Danby who opposed this suggestion most strenuously; for he knew that both the urgent needs of the fleet and the clamours of the opposition made a session absolutely essential. Through the duke of York a hint was conveyed to Ruvigny that a renewal of the French subsidy was the only possible alternative.[1] But the ambassador's offer of £100,000 for a prorogation of at least one year was not acceptable to Charles, because Danby's preparations now made it permissible to hope that parliament would be more compliant. These preparations consisted of proclamations, issued early in 1675, reinforcing the laws against conventicles, and imposing

[1] *Mignet*, iv. 330–1.

severe penalties on Englishmen attending mass, even in privileged places, or receiving Catholic orders.[1] With these concessions to intolerant Anglicanism Danby won over the Court
and Lauderdale to his design of parliamentary reunion, a
design in which Charles at last acquiesced; so the Commons
were carefully 'nursed' before their reassembly in April 1675.
The lord treasurer had already bribed them with edicts against
popery and dissent; Spanish money was ready for distribution
in order to induce them to press for war; Dutch money was
available for the policy of mediating peace terms which, if not
accepted by Louis, might furnish a pretext for compelling England to enter the fray. The arrival of the Spanish ambassador
Ronquillo had been preceded by that of a Jewish paymaster;
and van Beuning took a house in Westminster, where he entertained on a lavish scale. Louis sent over £100,000; not for
Charles, but for the reconciliation of the enemies of France in
the Commons and the encouragement of her friends; while
Danby began to dole out bribes and offices in a system which
combined judgement with economy. On the Continent the
summer campaign had already begun, when Louis, first in the
field, appeared in Flanders with an army of 70,000 men, backed
by the most highly equipped organization ever known in Europe.

The stage having been set, parliament reassembled for its
thirteenth session on April 13, 1675, after a prorogation of nearly
fourteen months. In his speech Charles asked the legislators
what they thought was still wanting for securing religion and
property, and restoring that right understanding which had been
disturbed by the pernicious designs of ill-intentioned men. As
he had demonstrated his zeal for the Church of England, he
commended for consideration the condition of his Fleet. Finch
followed suit by assuring both Houses that the king's solicitude
for the Church arose from his conviction that it best suited
with monarchy; the revived laws against Dissenters had lost
none of their strength, while those against Papists were now
edged with new rewards for informers. What more would they
have? A strong fleet and the compulsory limitation of new
buildings about London were the measures in which the crown
hoped to secure the concurrence of the legislature.[2] The response

---

[1] *Steele*, i. 3608 and 3609.   [2] *L.J.* xii. 653-5.

of the Commons was not conciliatory; for they began with addresses praying for the recall of British subjects in French service (April 19) and for the removal of the duke of Lauderdale (April 23).[1] Against Lauderdale the chief accusations were: (1) the opinion attributed to him that royal edicts have the force of laws, an opinion implying a justification of the Declaration of Indulgence, and (2) his part in procuring the settlement in Scotland of a militia of 20,000 foot and 2,000 horse, obliged to be in readiness to march into any part of His Majesty's dominions.[2] Burnet was called in to give evidence of Lauderdale's assertion that Scottish troops might be used to enforce the Declaration of Indulgence, and Irish Papists to suppress the Scottish Covenanters.[3] In reply, Charles refused either to part with his Scottish minister or to recall his troops still serving with the French flag; but he undertook not to send any more men to Flanders.

The Commons had lost the first round; the second began on April 27 when sir Samuel Barnardiston, supported by Arlington and the leaders of the Country party, brought in articles of impeachment against Danby on accusations as vague as those already cited against Lauderdale. He had, it was alleged, violated the ancient course of the Exchequer by perverting the method of receipts and payments; he had engrossed the sole power of disposing revenue into his own hands; moreover, he had declared that a new proclamation was better than an old law.[4] In regard to those charges relating to Danby's conduct as treasurer, the Commons became involved in a mass of technical detail, and had eventually to accept the assurance of sir William Coventry: ''Tis a hard thing that all the king's ministers of state must answer all circumstances of law; if so, then 'twill follow that no great officer of state but must be a studied lawyer.'[5] The opposition was evidently not agreed that the charges could be pressed home, and after further investigation they had to be dropped.[6] Another success was scored for the lord treasurer when the Bill to incapacitate parliament men from holding office of benefit was rejected by 145 to 113.[7]

How evenly parties were divided and how strongly personal

[1] *Parl. Hist.* iv. 678, 684.   [2] *Grey*, iii. 28–9. See *supra*, 411, 413.
[3] Ibid. iii. 30 sqq.   [4] *C.J.* ix. 324.   [5] *Grey*, iii. 62.
[6] *Parl. Hist.* iv. 695.   [7] Ibid. iv. 698, April 29.

feelings had been aroused was shown when the question of a further address for the recall of British soldiers abroad was first put to the House in grand committee (May 10); for 135 were counted on each side, and when the numbers were disputed, there was a scene in which periwigs were torn off, swords were drawn, some honourable members spat in the faces of their opponents, while others put their feet on the mace, which lay under the table (its usual place when the House was in grand committee). When the tumult seemed likely to result in casualties, the Speaker restored quiet by wrenching the mace from under the feet of the disorderly and placing it on the table, thereby terminating a riotous committee meeting and restoring a House of Commons.[1] Order being restored, sir T. Lee moved an engagement on the honour of each member that he would proceed no further in the matter after the House had risen; and when this motion was passed each member, standing in his place, gave his promise.[2] On the original question being again put on May 11, it was negatived by only one vote.

These events did not augur well for the measure which the Court hoped to make law in this session, a measure whereby a non-resisting test was to be imposed on all office-holders, including members of parliament, who, in the terms ultimately approved by the Lords, were to be required to take this oath:

I do declare that it is not lawful on any pretence whatsoever to take up arms against the King; and I do abhor the traitrous position of taking up arms by his authority against his person, or against those that are commissioned by him, according to law, in time of rebellion, and acting in pursuance of such commission. I do swear that I will not endeavour any alteration of the Protestant religion, now established in the church of England, nor will I endeavour any alteration in the government in church or state as it is by law established.

The Bill[3] imposing this oath passed the Lords, in spite of strenuous opposition from Shaftesbury; indeed its passage elicited a protest from fifteen peers who objected that the measure was an invasion of their privilege acquired by birth, and therefore

---

[1] *Essex Papers* (ed. C. E. Pike), ii. 9.

[2] *Grey*, iii. 128–9.

[3] For its terms see *Rawl. MS.* A. 162, f. 54. See also *H.M.C. Rep.* ix, app., pt. ii. 51–2.

inherent in and inseparable from their status.[1] What would be the fate of the Bill in the Commons was a question of equal moment for Court and Opposition. Its intention was obviously to confine office-holding and even membership of the two Houses to high episcopalians and the old Cavalier party, 'and to fight the old quarrel over again now that they have the arms and forts of the nation'.[2] If it passed, the constitution would have become static; for political criticism or opposition might thereby have been construed as violation of an oath, and with this weapon England could have been reduced to the uneasy quiet of Scotland. Accordingly, for Shaftesbury and the opposition a prorogation was more than ever imperative, and an opportunity for this soon presented itself, because the case of *Shirley* v. *Fagg* suddenly diverted the two Houses into a hot contest over their privileges.[3] The Houses were still contesting this point when, on June 9, they were prorogued until the following October.

Thus, Danby's first political experiment had met with only qualified success. He had, it is true, escaped impeachment, but he had failed to obtain a supply, and his abortive non-resistance test had served to make public the real designs of his ministry. He had created the nucleus of a tory party by his alliance of crown and church; but indirectly he had also given cohesion to an opposition, determined to subordinate the crown to parliament. By his audacity he had limited and clarified the issues; but his supporters would have to be held together by rewards, while his opponents would become more united in their insistence on constitutional principle. In this way did Danby help to create the distinction of whig and tory. He might have been sacrificed at this point but for two things—his skilful administration of the finances, and the exceptional yield from the Excise in the years 1674 and 1675 whereby Charles's hereditary revenue for 1674–5 rose to £1,400,000.[4] For the first time in his reign Charles was solvent and could therefore afford to take a risk.

But this state of affairs was transitory, and Charles was soon

[1] *L.J.* xii. 677. Among the protesters were Buckingham, Shaftesbury, Salisbury, Delamere, and Wharton.

[2] *Letter from a person of quality* in *Parl. Hist.* iv, app. v.

[3] For this see *supra*, 470.

[4] *Cal. Tr. Bks.*, *1672–5*, Introduction, xviii–xix.

restored to his position of perilous oscillation. With the death of
Turenne, and increasing French exhaustion in the summer of
1675, the menace from Louis XIV became perceptibly less, and
the continuation of the war by Orange and his allies grew more
desperate. In these circumstances the English parliament became a factor of international importance. If it remained long
enough in session, Dutch and Spanish bribery might prevail on
a majority of its members to force Charles into hostilities against
France; but a long prorogation would remove this possibility,
and so facilitate the peace for which Louis was now so anxious.
Charles's negotiations with Louis were therefore renewed; and
it was eventually (Aug. 17, 1675) agreed that parliament should
meet in October and be given an opportunity to vote money,
unconditioned by clauses directed against France. If it failed
to do so, Charles was to dissolve parliament, and during the
cessation of its activity to receive an annual subsidy of £100,000,
which sum, together with the enhanced yield from the hereditary
revenues, might serve to make him independent of parliamentary
grant, and so free to choose his own policy. A condition attached
to this agreement was that William of Orange should be discouraged from undertaking his proposed visit to England.[1]

Accordingly, the Commons were given one more chance.
Their session, which opened on October 13, 1675, was preluded
by the customary duet of king and lord keeper,[2] when Charles
asked for supplies to take off the anticipations of his revenue—
these having been caused mainly by the war and the building of
ships; this demand he coupled with the extraordinary admission
that, while he had not husbanded his financial resources in the
past so well as he might, he was resolved that there should be
improvement in future. Equally conciliatory was Finch, who
reported the King's resolve to enter on terms of strictest endear-
ment with his parliament, to take its counsel in weighty affairs
and acquaint it with all the royal wants and necessities. He
adjured all the members of parliament to behave like those who
deserve to be called king's friends; and, now that the faith was
absolutely secure, they were invited to concern themselves with

---

[1] Charles at first demanded 500,000 écus, but eventually agreed to accept
400,000 écus, the equivalent of £100,000. *Instructions Données*, ii. 183, 238.

[2] *Mignet*, iv. 366–70.

[3] *L.J.* xiii. 4–5.

matters of commercial and domestic importance—'a little time will serve to make many excellent laws, and to give you the honour to be the repairer of all our breaches'. On returning to their House, the Commons looked at each other for some time, until sir T. Meres asked the Speaker to recapitulate the substance of the king's speech, a request which was properly declined.[1] Waller then hinted at the inconsistency between the king's admission of ill-husbandry and the doctrine that the king cannot err. This personal admission of wrongdoing was an innovation for which the Commons were unprepared.

Their subsequent proceedings show how evenly divided and efficiently organized were the Court and Country parties, the former controlled by Danby with the two secretaries of state (Henry Coventry and sir Joseph Williamson), while the latter looked for leadership to Shaftesbury, who included Buckingham among his lieutenants. In committee the Commons refused by 172 to 165 to grant a supply for taking off the anticipations on the revenue (these were estimated at £800,000) on the ground that the anticipations were directly due to a war (the Third Dutch War) and that war was not theirs.[2] On October 21 a Bill for appropriating £400,000 from the Customs to the use of the Navy was read a second time and committed; it was resolved also that twenty ships, at a cost of £300,000, should be built, and only by a narrow majority was it decided that this sum should be deposited in the Exchequer, and not in the Chamber of the city of London. Otherwise, the Commons did little but discuss grievances; including the falling of rents and the increase of atheism (not unconnected); the bribing of members (against which a test was proposed), and even their own continued existence. 'A standing parliament', said the septuagenarian sir Harbottle Grimstone, 'is as grievous as a standing army.'[3] 'I am afraid of a dissolution,' said sir John Birkenhead, another venerable legislator, 'because God is my witness, I am afraid the next will be worse'[4] (*laughed at*). Dissolution of parliament now seemed the only means of eliminating Danby's influence, and in the Lords a motion for an address to the king to dissolve parliament was supported by the duke of York, together with

[1] *Grey*, iii. 290.   [2] *C.J.* ix. 359.
[3] *Grey*, iii. 341.   [4] Ibid. iii. 342.

Buckingham, Shaftesbury, Essex, Holles, and Townshend[1]—a conjunction which suggests that Papists and Dissenters were once more bedfellows. Charles was tempted to adopt this policy; but, on the other hand, he knew that many members of the Commons were of noble family, and therefore attached to the monarchy; whereas a new parliament might be composed of 'Presbyterians'.[2] It was therefore deemed inadvisable to dissolve; but a revival of the dispute of *Shirley* v. *Fagg* provided once more a pretext for prorogation. On November 22, 1675, parliament was prorogued for the unprecedented period of fifteen months.

The conditions attached to the payment of the French subsidy had not been completely fulfilled, but Louis grudgingly agreed to perform his part of the bargain, and the first quarterly instalment was promised for March 1676. This concession may have been owing to Ruvigny's knowledge that, just before the prorogation of November, Charles was being pressed by Danby to conclude an engagement with the Dutch.[3] Relations between Charles and Louis were now regularized by a secret treaty (Feb. 16/26, 1676) in which both kings bound themselves to give no aid to the enemies of the other, nor make any treaty without the participation of the other. Danby was unwilling to countersign this treaty,[4] though he had made a feint of entering into negotiations; even Lauderdale at first refused to be a party to it, but he eventually witnessed Ruvigny's signature to the treaty as copied by Charles and sealed by him on February 16, 1676. This secret engagement renewed all previous treaties between the two monarchs, and expressly named the States General as the power with which neither king would treat, except conjointly. Thus, having failed to secure peace by mediation, and having successfully resisted efforts to drag him into war on behalf of the Dutch, Charles now renewed the old intimacy with Louis, so enabling the French king to achieve by diplomacy what he appeared unable to obtain by arms. Having divided Charles from Protestant England, Louis now strove to detach the Dutch from Spain, the prince of Orange from the States General, and the princes of

---

[1] *L.J.* xiii. 33, Nov. 20, 1675.
[2] *Baschet*, 132, June 12/22, 1676.
[3] Ruvigny to Louis XIV, Dec. 30, 1675/Jan. 9, 1676 in *Mignet*, iv. 377.
[4] *Mignet*, iv. 381–6; *Instructions Données*, ii. 163, and 197–200.

Germany from the Emperor, and thus secured his immediate ends by fomenting discord among his numerous enemies.

The conclusion of the treaty was followed by the recall of the aged Ruvigny, who was glad to quit a post possibly the most difficult of any in the service of France. He was succeeded by Honoré Courtin, whose earlier experience of England led him to avoid the ceremonial 'entrée'. His instructions[1] provide an apt comment on the relations between the two monarchs, and contain a glimpse of English history as seen by the interested foreigner. 'England', he was told, 'may, properly considered, be reduced to the king, the duke of York, the royal ministers, and "l'ésprit de la nation en général".' Charles's withdrawal from the Dutch War proved (according to these instructions) that he is not master in his own house. Lauderdale is most in the royal confidence; Arlington has unfortunately drifted away from the French alliance; Buckingham, though out of office, is important and has a special affection for the French king. Danby's appointment was due solely to his favour with the duke of York and to his ability in restoring the finances; he considers himself strong enough to be independent, and has been joined by the duchess of Portsmouth,[2] in spite of the presents she has had—diamonds, and (at Charles's request) the territory of Aubigné. Another lady worth watching is Hortense Mancini, duchesse Mazarin, who, having run away from her husband and established herself at the English Court, has induced Charles to intercede on her behalf for an increase in her alimony and the return of the jewels she left behind. She may succeed in casting her spell over Charles and, unless carefully handled, will use her influence against France; so, although her demands are grossly unjust, Courtin is to assure her *en termes généraux* of Louis's solicitude on her behalf. Thus one of the major problems of French diplomacy was the French women at Charles's Court.[3]

English dislike of France, Louis said, was owing to France's

[1] *Instructions Données*, ii. 169–97, April 5/15, 1676.

[2] Possibly because Danby gave her money with which to buy jewels. *Essex Papers*, i. xi.

[3] In June 1676 Courtin reported that the duchess of Portsmouth was losing favour at Court and was likely to be displaced by duchesse Mazarin. He suggested that the latter should be sent back to France. (*Baschet*, 132, May 29/June 8, 1676.)

greatness, especially at sea, and to a fear that, on the basis of the French alliance, Charles might become absolute. Courtin was therefore to persuade the king to manage his revenues with such economy that he might dispense with parliament. The ambassador was to discourage the projected marriage between William of Orange and Mary Stuart; but he was to promote the interests of that prince; for it was desirable that he should acquire sovereign power in order that the States General might be detached from their alliances, and thus there would be one republic less in the world. Courtin was also to quieten English qualms about British troops in French service, and to see that Charles rendered good service as a 'benevolent mediator'.

The French ambassador, who was endowed with a sense of humour, did his best to carry out these difficult tasks. His first concern was with the maritime advantages which England was deriving from her neutrality. He protested against English ships supplying Spanish and Dutch ships with stores in the Mediterranean; in reply, he was assured by Charles that merchants would do anything for gain. Courtin was then asked to induce his master to remit, in favour of English ships, the tax on English merchandise imported into France, a demand supported by Lauderdale (a proprietor of Scottish coal-pits) on the strength of the old Franco-Scottish alliance. But this failed. If Lauderdale's demand were granted, wrote the French secretary for foreign affairs, 'every Englishman would call himself a Scotsman'. Courtin's main achievement was his part in the completion of an Anglo-French maritime treaty,[1] signed in Paris on February 14, 1677. The occasion for the treaty was this. Many English ships were doing a profitable trade with Dutch cargoes, protected by the flag; in some cases Dutch ships were manned by English crews in order to escape confiscation; both classes of ship were being seized by the French,[2] on the excuse that they were really Dutch, whereas Scottish and Irish ships with Dutch cargoes were

---

[1] *Dumont*, vi, pt. ii. 327–9; *Instructions Données*, ii. 205–10. It was followed by a proclamation (May 26) enforcing neutrality in English waters. Contraband, that is munitions of war, was to be searched for in outgoing English ships. *Steele*, i. 3631.

[2] For lists of ships captured by the French see *A list of several ships belonging to English merchants . . . in Bodley, G.P.* 1120.

usually spared. As a sop to English interests Louis made some important concessions in this treaty. Contraband was clearly defined; English ships were allowed to trade between neutral ports and enemy ports, or between enemy ports; and it was expressly declared that the goods of enemies of France (except contraband) found on English ships should not be confiscated, even though they formed the main part of the cargo.[1] In other words English ships might carry Dutch cargoes without molestation from the French, a concession of more value to our carrying trade than the winning of several naval battles, particularly as it was granted at a time when the two commercial rivals of England were engaged in a fiercely contested war with each other. In this way French dependence on English neutrality proved of direct value to English trade; and it was partly due to Louis XIV that this country was able to make serious inroads on the Dutch monopoly of the carrying trade.

Other concessions were demanded of Louis. In February 1677, when peace terms were first outlined by the assembled representatives at Nimeguen, it was seen that the Dutch wanted Maestricht and the principality of Orange; Spain and the Emperor demanded restoration of all their lost territories; the duke of Lorraine sought for restitution; while Denmark and Brandenburg asked for an indemnity. The exorbitance of these demands showed that the allies were hoping for action on the part of the English parliament, then due to meet after the fifteen months' prorogation; and so pressure on Charles was increased at the moment when his financial difficulties were at their most serious point. In the previous November he had failed to obtain a loan from the city of London; and he confessed to Courtin that he was over a million pounds in debt, £200,000 of this being attributed to the cost of suppressing Bacon's rebellion in Virginia and the loss in Customs revenue directly due to that rebellion.[2] These figures may have been exaggerated; but they induced Louis to offer him, for the year 1677, the same sum as had already been paid for the cessation of parliamentary activity in 1676, namely, £100,000; together with an additional sum if he would prorogue parliament until 1678.[3] On the other hand, Danby urged the

[1] Cl. viii of the treaty.   [2] For this see *infra*, 670–1.
[3] *Mignet*, iv. 430; *Instructions Données*, ii. 215.

necessity for a session, because the additional excise granted in
1670–1 was due to expire in June 1677, and there was still just
a chance that the Court party in the Commons would be strong
enough to obtain a supply. Between these two alternatives
Charles vacillated. No sooner was it known that he intended to
summon parliament than Louis sent 200,000 livres to Courtin
for 'his service in parliament'; that is, for countering the propaganda of van Beuning, and (in conjunction with the duke of York,
Shaftesbury, and the Country party) for subsidizing opposition
to Danby, if the latter showed anti-French tendencies. Alternatively, Courtin was to direct his efforts at embroiling the two
Houses so that nothing definite would result from the session.[1]
The solution of the European conflict was therefore to be sought,
not at Nimeguen, but at Westminster; French money was to
assist the early training of English party politicians, and the
greatest monarch in Christendom eagerly waited for a revival
of *Shirley* v. *Fagg*.

The long recess (Nov. 1675–Feb. 1677) provided a breathing
space. Charles, in the summer of 1676, set the fashions of evening
rowing and bathing in the Thames, diversions in which the
women do not appear to have taken a part; indoors, the monarch
whiled away the hours after dinner by beating time to his favourite song, the 'Récit du Sommeil', sung by French voices to the
accompaniment of clavichord and flute;[2] or dallied with the
duchesse Mazarin, to the disparagement of the more feminine
charms of the duchess of Portsmouth. The duke of York could
not conceal his hopes that the parliament would be dissolved; if
it must meet, he thought that the 'Presbyterians' should be made
use of in order to divide the two Houses;[3] nor was he alone in
thinking that dissolution was overdue, for this view was shared
by Arlington, Ormonde, and prince Rupert. Lord Holles suggested an alliance between himself, the duke, and the French
ambassador as a rival opposition to that of Shaftesbury; but the
duke refused to be a member of a cabal.[4] Danby talked of joining

---

[1] *Mignet*, iv. 434, letters of Louis XIV to Courtin, Jan. 17/27 and Jan. 23/
Feb. 2, 1677.

[2] *Baschet*, 133, June 22/July 2, 1676.

[3] Ibid. 133, Aug. 1/11. Courtin's conversation with the duke.

[4] Ibid. 134, Jan. 11/21, 1677.

forces with Lauderdale in the headship of a Protestant and anti-French interest.[1] Shaftesbury, who had been repeatedly advised to leave London, moved from Exeter House in the Strand to a house in Aldersgate Street, where he so busied himself with the affairs of the Green Ribbon Club that its votaries began to be noted in the streets of London from the distinctive badge which they wore.[2] Courtin, who complained that one can never depend on anything in England, urged Louis to send money in good time —at least three weeks before the opening of parliament, 'the time when the cabals form'.[3] Every one was busy, except the king.

Nor was interest in public affairs confined to the grandees. An alderman named Jenkes was committed for what was considered an inflammatory speech;[4] and there were fears that the election of a new lord mayor in November would be the occasion for attacks on the duke of York, now the most unpopular man in England.[5] Throughout the country there was apprehension lest the unusually long intermission of parliament might forebode some change of consequence; hence the tide of anti-French and anti-papist feeling steadily rose. Its height may be gauged from the popularity of Andrew Marvell's *Account of the growth of popery and arbitrary government in England*, a book first published in 1677, the contents of which were so outspoken that the government offered a reward of £100 for the discovery of its author. This book gave emphatic expression to the dominating feeling entertained by humbler Englishmen at that time—the feeling of suspicion. It was Marvell's thesis that for some years there had been a design to change the lawful government into an absolute tyranny, and convert the established religion into 'down-right Popery'. 'Were it either open Judaism, or plain Turkery, or honest Paganism, there is yet a certain bona fides in the most extravagant belief . . . but this [Popery] is a compound of all the three, incorporated with more peculiar absurdities of its own, and all this deliberately continued by the bold imposture of priests under the name of Christianity.' Added to this was the French slavery, which men had been trying to introduce since

---

[1] *Baschet*, 133, Nov. 23/Dec. 3, 1676.
[2] Ibid. 133, Oct. 23/Nov. 2, 1676. For the Green Ribbon Club see sir G. Sitwell, *The First Whig*.
[3] Ibid. 133, Nov. 23/Dec. 3, 1676.
[4] See *supra*, 511.
[5] *Baschet*, 133, Oct. 23/Nov. 2.

that day in May 1670 when the king went to meet his sister at Dover. These words were potent because they confirmed a vague dread.

When, on February 15, 1677, the fifteenth session of the Cavalier parliament was opened, Charles offered further securities for liberty and property, at the same time reminding his listeners of the need for providing an adequate supply. Lord chancellor Finch followed with a speech containing a hint that foreign policy was outside the sphere of parliament, the proper concern of which was the peace of church and state; he appealed also to their patriotism by deprecating those 'ill meant distinctions' between Court and Country.[1] On this, as on other occasions, the verbosity and innuendoes of the chancellor helped to destroy the good impression created by the tact and reticence of the king's speech. The campaign commenced in the Lords, where Buckingham, supported by Shaftesbury, Salisbury, and Wharton, spoke for a dissolution, on the ground that by the fifteen months' prorogation parliament was automatically dissolved, since the statute[2] of Edward III required that parliaments should be holden every year once, and more often if need be; but their motion for dissolution was rejected; and the four peers, having refused to ask pardon for their contempt of the House, were committed to the Tower. In the Commons the majority of the Opposition maintained that, while the prorogation was illegal, the parliament was a legal one nevertheless.[3] Thus unexpectedly the leaders of the Country party in the Lords had played into the hands of Danby and the Court, an initial success followed on February 21 by a vote of supply of £600,000 for building ships, and on March 12 a renewal of the additional Excise. This last measure had passed the Commons in spite of strenuous opposition from Meres, sir William Coventry, and Powle.

Danby now succeeded in passing through the Lords one of the most curious Bills ever considered by the legislature. This was a Bill for securing the Protestant religion by educating the royal children in the Protestant faith. Together with safeguards for the election of bishops, there was a test for the next successor to the throne, in the form of an oath against transubstantiation, an oath which was to be tendered within fourteen days of the death

[1] *L.J.* xiii. 36–7.   [2] 4 Ed. III, cap. xiv.   [3] *Parl. Hist.* iv. 825–34.

of the then king by a deputation of nine bishops who, for this purpose, were to remain about the Court until commanded by the sovereign to administer the oath. As their vigil was limited to fourteen days, no great strain was imposed on the patience of the episcopal quorum.[1] To this Bill the Commons gave two readings, in the course of which its potential dangers were brought to light. It was objected first of all that it was based on two hypotheses: that the king would die or forsake the Church of England. This was tantamount to imagining both the death and the wrongdoing of the king, thereby committing treason and violating the constitution at one stroke; for 'if once an offence be sheltered under error of the King, you may seek impeachments elsewhere than in the House of Commons'.[2] It was objected also that the measure would subordinate the crown to the mitre, and it was now a thesis among churchmen that the king was not king but by their magical unction. The Bill was therefore 'a great invasion of the prerogative'; it strove to promote a good end, but by entirely unconstitutional means, and although it was committed, 'it died away' (Marvell). An even worse fate befell another Bill for preserving the Protestant religion, sent down from the Lords on April 4. Under the mask of sharper penalties on Dissenters, this measure, while retaining the Test, discriminated in favour of Papists, and so it was unanimously rejected at the first reading, on the ground that its title was entirely different from its contents.[3]

But the attention of the Commons was soon directed to an even more serious quarter. A great French offensive was launched in Flanders in March 1677; and by the end of April Louis had scored a series of successes which provided an effective reply to the peace proposals of the allies, whose representatives were then negotiating at Nimeguen. Valenciennes and Cambrai were taken, and the prince of Orange was defeated at Cassel.

[1] For the terms of the Bill see *Rawl. MS.* A. 162, f. 23. See also *H.M.C. Rep.* ix, app., pt. ii. 81–2, March 1, 1677.

[2] Vaughan's speech, March 27, 1677, *Grey*, iv. 321.

[3] This Bill appears to have provided for the registration of Roman Catholics and their exemption from the penal laws on their paying 52s. each, together with 5 per cent. of their revenues and submitting to a new oath of fidelity. (*Baschet*, 135, April 4/14, 1677.) See also *H.M.C. Rep.* ix, app., pt. ii. 82–3.

This threat to the Netherlands caused the Commons to draw up an address[1] to the king (March 10) requesting him to strengthen himself with such stricter alliances as might secure his kingdoms and preserve the Netherlands; and, in quick succession, they voted three addresses (March 29, April 13, April 16) urging active measures against France; for which purpose the king was authorized to borrow £200,000 on the additional Excise, with an assurance of further supplies if he conformed to the spirit of the addresses.[2] Charles continued to ask for money; but would not commit himself to the policy pressed upon him,[3] and in the midst of this deadlock both Houses were adjourned on April 16 to May 21.

By a mixture of evasion and inflexibility Charles had succeeded in preserving the French interest, not only against Danby and a section of the Court, but against the demands of an opposition now national in character. But it was no easy task. With some truth he confessed to Courtin that he was sacrificing the love of his subjects in the interests of Louis;[4] and he begged the French ambassador to urge his master to secure peace before the winter. Throughout the summer of 1677 there was no respite; for the campaign against his neutrality was directed from a triple front. In June the Imperial envoy Waldstein arrived in London in order to supplement the efforts of van Beuning and of Borgomaniero, the newly arrived Spanish ambassador; and it was the avowed object of these three emissaries to induce Charles to enter into an offensive alliance against France. But Charles refused to exchange his mediation for war. Meanwhile French successes and Orange defeats served to prolong hostilities, which could be terminated neither by Louis's attempts to obtain a separate peace with the Dutch, nor by increasing disagreement among the allies. Charles's determination to control his own foreign policy was to undergo still further test.

When the session was resumed on May 21 Sacheverell led the debate on alliances, calling for a statement of what leagues had been made since their last meeting.[5] Secretary Coventry's reply

---

[1] *C.J.* ix. 396.
[2] Ibid. ix. 408, 419–20, 423.
[3] Ibid. ix. 418, 422.
[4] *Mignet*, iv. 445.
[5] *Grey*, iv. 355.

that alliances were not to be talked of in public incited the Commons to go into full committee for the purpose of more free debate, which resulted (May 25) in an address[1] declining a further supply until His Majesty's alliances were made known, and again urging the king to form a defensive and offensive alliance with Holland. Charles's reply was a direct refusal to allow any invasion of his fundamental power of making peace and war; nor would he have the manner or circumstances of leagues prescribed to him.[2] With this definitive pronouncement he adjourned parliament (to July 16). There was a scene in the Commons when the Speaker, on rising to announce the adjournment, was called back to his place by several members in a manner which recalled famous episodes earlier in the century; and only by securing and removing the mace could he bring the meeting to an end.[3] When it reassembled on July 16 parliament was again adjourned until December 3, and did not resume proceedings until January 28, 1678.

Charles knew that he was risking the gravest discredit that a statesman can incur—that of refusing to embark on a war for which there is a popular demand—but he had his reasons for avoiding concession to war fever, as he had some experience of the amount of financial support he might expect once the fever was past. At a secret interview with Courtin in June 1677 he drew up a memoir[4] advocating a separate peace between Louis and the Dutch, on the basis of the retention of Franche Comté by Louis, and the creation of a strong Flemish barrier, guaranteed by England. His debts, he confessed, amounted to £2,200,000; without French aid he would be forced back on parliament, and so the war would be prolonged. After some negotiation, Courtin at last induced Charles, in return for the promise of two million French livres, to delay the meeting of parliament until April 1678. Danby was privy to these negotiations, and had delayed the settlement by insisting on a larger sum.[5] This was Courtin's last negotiation in England, for in August he was succeeded by Barrillon, whose embassy was to last until 1688.

Another event decisively influenced the peace negotiations.

[1] *C.J.* ix. 425. [2] Ibid. ix. 426, May 28, 1677.
[3] *Grey*, iv. 390. [4] *Baschet*, 136, June 11/21, 1677.
[5] *Mignet*, iv. 498–500; *Instructions Données*, ii. 215.

This was the marriage of the prince of Orange. Three years before he had been the most popular man in Holland; now, by his repeated failures, he was risking the allegiance of his compatriots,[1] and there seemed a chance that the States General might even conclude peace without his participation. The help which he had not hitherto obtained by threat and bribery, he might now secure less directly but more effectively by marriage alliance with the dynasty which held the casting vote in the European deadlock. On consulting Temple regarding the good policy of such an alliance and the personal character of the princess Mary, William was warmly reassured on both points by the English ambassador, ever intent on securing good relations between English and Dutch. Both Danby and Arlington eagerly seconded the proposal as the measure best fitted to restore Protestant confidence, and impede the progress of French influence; but the final decision lay with Charles, who confided to Barrillon his reasons for approving the match.[2] The alliance, he said, would remove the suspicions in England that his friendship with France was intended to bring about a change of religion, suspicions mainly due to the rash conduct of the duke of York, who alone was responsible for English jealousy and dislike of France. By bringing William into the family these suspicions would be allayed, and the ground would be removed from anti-Court cabals. It was true, remarked Charles, that the prince ought to have asked the consent of Louis before addressing himself to the princess;[3] but on the other hand, by the measure of public confidence thereby created, the marriage was as much in the interests of Louis as of Charles. Both the French ambassador and his master experienced some difficulty in following this explanation; which amounted in effect to this, that as Charles now had a closer personal association with Protestantism and respectability, he might enjoy a larger measure of the nation's confidence, and was therefore all the

[1] The revival of the Republican party in the United Provinces was noted as early as 1675 in a memoir entitled *Relation of the present state of affairs in the United Provinces* [*S.P. For.* (*Holland*), 198]; see Miss M. Lane's account of this document in *E.H.R.* xxx. 304 sqq.

[2] *Mignet*, iv. 509–10.

[3] *Baschet*, 137, Oct. 18/28.

more worthy of a French subsidy. As the reasoning seemed specious, Barrillon tried to induce both the duke of York and the duchess of Portsmouth to use their influence against the match.[1]

The betrothal of William and the princess Mary was announced on October 22, 1677, and was speedily followed by the wedding. In this way did the zealous convert of the treaty of Dover link the destinies of his House with the leader of European Protestantism and the most formidable of Louis's enemies. What were Charles's real motives in consenting? There may have been secret reasons; but it was obvious that this alliance with Dutch Calvinism provided some kind of rampart against the anti-popish opposition. It also imposed a brusque and ambitious son-in-law on the duke of York; to that extent it was Charles's revenge on a brother whom he disliked. With greater certainty the immediate effect of the union can be stated. Louis insisted on having Condé, Valenciennes, and Tournai, which he considered necessary for the defence of Artois and Lille; the Dutch, now more confident, refused to assent to the acquisition of these three towns by France.[2]

Curiously enough, this alliance did not appear to imperil the French subsidy; and if, by its means, the prince of Orange could be induced to turn his thoughts to peace, then both the senior rulers would benefit. Its effect, on the contrary, was to harden the prince's determination. There was another miscalculation. Just as Charles and Louis thought that Orange would yield because of his defeats, so Charles and Orange thought that Louis would yield in spite of his successes. Disillusionment came when Louis rejected the joint proposals sent to him by Charles and his nephew, these being based on the cession to France of Franche Comté, Cambrai, Aire, and St. Omer, in return for the surrender, by France, of Maestricht (to the Dutch), Charleroi, Oudenarde, Ath, Tournai, Condé, and Valenciennes (to Spain), and the restoration of his duchy to the duke of Lorraine. Louvois told the English ambassador Montagu that Louis would rather make war for a hundred years than sacrifice Valenciennes, Condé, and Tournai; and that if necessary he would rather

[1] Ibid. 137, Oct. 22/Nov. 1, 1677.
[2] *Instructions Données (Hollande)*, i. 354–5.

pawn his jewels than suffer the English parliament to meet.[1] The marriage therefore did not appear to bring the end of the war any nearer; and so Charles was restored to his position of unstable equilibrium between Danby and Barrillon, forced to choose between the alternatives of an uncompromising legislature and a foreign subsidy. As the time for the reassembling of parliament approached, the trepidation of Charles increased. He seemed to lose some of his buoyancy; he talked to Barrillon of the time when he would retire from active politics, and (most ominous of all) he even lost some of his healing power, so that those who came for his ministrations had to take their chance.[2] The French subsidy seemed farther off than ever; while close at hand were the coffee-houses, the clubs, and the town dinners, where, from cup, pot, or bottle, the legislators were fortifying themselves for the rigours of the coming campaign.

Faced with the prospect of another period of continental travel, Charles yielded to the counsels of Danby; and on December 31, 1677, the English plenipotentiary, Lawrence Hyde, signed a treaty with the States General (in agreement with the prince of Orange) whereby the two contracting powers undertook to restore a general peace on the principle of French retention of Franche Comté, Cambrai, Aire, and St. Omer, and her surrender to Spain of Sicily, with Charleroi, Courtrai, Ath, Oudenarde, Condé, Tournai, and Valenciennes.[3] The kings of France and Spain were to be induced, by force if necessary, to accept these terms, for which purpose Ostend was assigned to England as the base of an expeditionary force of 11,000 infantry and 1,000 cavalry; and thirty English ships of war were to be fitted out, part for the Mediterranean, part for the Channel. British troops in French service were to be recalled. This instrument was ratified by the Dutch on February 20, 1678. Differences on both sides, however, prevented the fulfilment of the conditions of this treaty, which was intended to be the preliminary to a more general offensive and defensive alliance of England

---

[1] Montagu to Charles II, Dec. 19/29, 1677, in *H.M.C. Rep.* ix, app., pt. ii. 453.   [2] *H.M.C. Rep.* vii, app. 494 (Verney Papers).

[3] *Dumont*, vii, pt. i. 341. For a full account of these negotiations see C. L. Grose, *The Anglo-Dutch Alliance of 1678* in *E.H.R.* xxxix; also C. Brinkmann, *Relations between England and Germany* in ibid. xxiv.

and Holland in European waters. Such a general alliance was signed at Westminster on March 2, 1678, and was ratified by the States on March 28. But it was never ratified by England, because the real executive (i.e. Charles) had no desire for an alliance with the Dutch, and was merely playing for time. There were, therefore, two treaties between England and the States: one intended to force peace on France and Spain in certain terms; the other designed to safeguard the interests of the two Protestant powers in Europe against aggressors. To both, the Dutch had committed themselves; but the English government gave its full sanction to neither.

Ostensibly, therefore, Charles had yielded to the popular demand; and the treaty of December 31, 1677, appeared to detach him from France. To Barrillon he explained that he consented to these measures in order that he might have the credit for them;[1] otherwise, he would be forced by parliament to adopt them; at the same time he pressed Louis to concede a two months' truce in the Netherlands, not for the advantage of the Allies, but for the benefit of the English king's domestic affairs.[2] Diplomacy had indeed reached a high point of subtlety. On the one hand Charles had entered into an offensive alliance with the Dutch; he had summoned parliament for December 1677 instead of April 1678; he had married his niece to the prince of Orange—such was his public policy. On the other hand he continued the secret negotiations with Versailles, whereby he proposed to leave Louis a free hand in return for a subsidy. In other words, Charles was proving an apt pupil at the game of saying one thing and meaning another; but in this instance he played the game too long, even for his patient instructor and paymaster.

In the midst of these negotiations parliament was adjourned from December 3, 1677, to January 15, 1678, and finally to January 28. This gave Danby time to make preparations for securing a working majority in the House. When parliament met, the speech from the throne enumerated the efforts that had been made to secure an honourable peace by mediation; the benefits derived by England through her abstention from

[1] *Mignet*, iv. 529.
[2] Montagu to Charles, Dec. 31, 1677, in *H.M.C. Rep.* ix, app., pt. ii. 454.

hostilities; the recent alliance with Holland; the recall of British troops from France, and the necessity of fitting out a large fleet. In the pursuit of this policy Charles had spent more than the sums received from the two special parliamentary concessions, namely, the grant for building ships and the authority to borrow £200,000 on the Excise. The rebellion in Virginia,[1] a war with Algiers,[2] and the cost of a dowry for his niece had added to his expenses. Having done these things, he looked for a plentiful supply and the renewal of the impost on wine.[3]

The Commons, irritated by the successive adjournments of the House, opened with an acrimonious debate[4] on the Speaker's refusal to submit these adjournments to the approval of the House. Thanks were then voted to the king for his speech, with an address (Jan. 31) that no treaty of peace be considered until France was reduced to her frontiers of the Pyrenean treaty; that, until then, commercial intercourse with her should cease, and that meanwhile the king should communicate his alliances to the House. Charles replied that to reduce France to the Pyrenean treaty was a determination not for him but for Providence.[5] 'In sum, Gentlemen, the right of making and managing war and peace is in His Majesty; and if you think he will depart from any part of that right, you are mistaken.' Having heard this clear-cut pronouncement, the Commons then proceeded to debate a supply for a war against France; but in the course of the debate there emerged a new and more insidious fear. They were proposing to raise money for red-coats; but to what use might not these red-coats be put? They were enabling the king to take some one by the beard, but whose beard?[6] The Cavalier Parliament had become as suspicious of Charles II as the Long Parliament of his father. The Commons tried at first to compromise by voting only £600,000 for the setting out of 90 ships and 30,000 troops, though the Speaker assured them that three millions would be required;[7] they eventually agreed (Feb. 18) to raise a million for 'an actual war' with the French king, £600,000 of which was to be raised by a Poll Tax, and the remainder by a levy on new buildings erected about London since 1656. Thus

---

[1] See *infra*, 670–1.   [2] See *supra*, i. 279–80.   [3] *L.J.* xiii. 130–1.

[4] *Grey*, v. 7–17.   [5] *C.J.* ix. 431–2, Feb. 4, 1678.

[6] *Grey*, v. 89.   [7] Ibid., v. 177.

the king received a grant; but it was coupled with a strict appropriation clause, and with a prohibition of the import of French wine, linen, and brandy for three years.[1]

The inadequacy of this supply, the stringency of its appropriation, and the frank avowal of suspicion by members of the opposition such as Sacheverell, so disturbed Charles as to cause him to express the opinion that the opposition had been bribed. His conjecture was right. Louis had now set in motion a vast organization for sowing dissension among his enemies, and now that his former ally was a potential opponent he resolved that he would be disappointed in his hopes of parliament. In January Barrillon had been joined by the younger Ruvigny, so that French influence was now directed from a double front—the former to control the Court, the latter to control the Commons. For the expenditure of the large sums entrusted to him Ruvigny had no difficulty in obtaining coadjutors in such members of the Country party as Buckingham, Holles, Russell, and (after his release in February) Shaftesbury. Meanwhile, Danby borrowed £60,000 from the London bankers in January for a campaign of counter-bribery; there were also Dutch and Spanish paymasters, and in consequence only the ultra-scrupulous remained unbribed. The position was therefore one of unusual complication. Charles was anxious mainly to keep England out of the war with France, and thereby qualify for the promised French subsidy; Louis, engaged in sterilizing all political activity against himself, knew that parliament might well prove too strong for the English king; so he turned his attention to the Country party with presents of money[2] and assurances that if they helped him in parliament he would not attack their liberties or religion. Danby on behalf of the Court was anxious to obtain a large parliamentary grant for the war, unfettered by conditions. The opposition, hitherto clamorous for war against Louis, now began to fear that the troops for which they voted might be turned against themselves, and accordingly some of them found it in their interest to act in accordance with French dictates. Behind it all was this dominating uncertainty: Charles had ostensibly yielded to the Commons; but did not this yielding conceal some subtle design?

[1] See *supra*, 437.　　　[2] *Instructions Données*, ii. 259, 265, 268–72.

The game continued to be played for some months. Charles urged Louis to surrender his claim to places on the Scheldt; but instead of listening to proposals for compromise Louis with 70,000 men captured Ghent and Ypres in the early spring of 1678, thus completing his north-eastern frontier, and placing the Spanish Netherlands at his mercy. Accordingly, the terms of the Anglo-Dutch treaty had to be carried out, and Charles was obliged to send several battalions to Ostend under the command of the duke of Monmouth, a measure which he explained to Barrillon as merely a popular demonstration, intended to appease the English thirst for war, and not an indication that he desired war. To the same confidant he expressed also his disgust at the bellicose attitude of his brother, when neither of them had a *sou* to spare for the raising of troops; moreover, he knew that nothing good could come from Anglo-Spanish military co-operation in Flanders, as Spanish military personnel was notoriously defective.[1] Thus by the end of February 1678 Charles had sent to the Continent an expeditionary force intended to co-operate with Spanish troops, in whom he had no confidence, against a power on which he had no intention of declaring war, and with which he desired to continue his secret alliance in return for a subsidy. He would remain master of his foreign policy as long as possible.

When on March 14, 1678, the Commons debated the state of the nation and the removal of evil counsellors, seriousness was mingled with platitude as never before in the history of the House. Colonel Birch produced for the third time his comparison of Louis XIV with a glass bottle which might easily be broken with an English crab-tree cudgel; sir John Ernly, after remarking that every tub must stand on its own bottom, asked his listeners: 'An house is on fire; will you not quench it?' Russell, after insisting that the saddle must be set on the right horse, asked for a committee to consider their deplorable condition and their apprehensions of popery and a standing army; sir Charles Wheeler reminded them that inquiry into evil counsellors began the former civil troubles. Some members thought that 'we were in jest', others that 'we are in the dark'.[2]

---

[1] *Mignet*, iv. 541, and *Baschet*, 139, March 25/April 4.

[2] *Grey*, v. 223–30.

More clear expression of the national temper was revealed in the words of the aged sir Philip Warwick: 'I have feared the greatness of the French king these forty years. . . . I am willing (like Balaam's ass) to crush my master's foot when an angel stands in the way.'[1] The impotence or paralysis of which the Commons gave evidence was really due to this, that their war-like temper was almost completely neutralized by the interplay of powerful forces, including bribery by Danby and Ruvigny; the fear that a Stuart alliance with Orange might result in joint action against dissentients in both countries; the dread of a standing army; and, above all, intense suspicion of both Charles and Danby, even when they seemed most conciliatory. Behind the scenes were double sets of diplomatic negotiation, each of unparalleled complexity;[2] the one set intended to group England in a triple or even quadruple alliance against France, so that English opinion might be conciliated, and the other to secure French money for English neutrality. These two objects did not seem inconsistent; since by ranging himself with the allies and obtaining a war vote from his parliament, Charles's bargaining power with Louis appeared to be increased. Both sets of negotiations failed. The failure of the negotiations with the States General and Spain was probably intentional, but at least time was gained; the failure of those with France was unintentional, and proved to be of disastrous consequence, because they came to light.

These proceedings, together with the short recess of March 26–April 11, enabled Charles to dally still longer with his apprehensive Commons. On April 29 a long speech by lord chancellor Finch[3] reciting Charles's peace efforts as mediator, and inviting the advice of both Houses on the defensive and offensive alliances then being negotiated with the Dutch, evoked a request from the Commons that the king would communicate, for the benefit of the House, all the leagues and treaties mentioned in this speech. While awaiting this information the Commons discussed evil counsellors, the growth of popery, and the breaking

[1] *Grey*, v. 230.

[2] For a full account of these see C. L. Grose, *The Anglo-Dutch Alliance of 1678* in *E.H.R.* xxxix. 349 and 526; also A. Browning, *Life and Letters of sir T. Osborne, earl of Danby*, i, ch. xii.　　　　[3] *L.J.* xiii. 206–7.

of civilian heads by red-coats, who 'might fight against Magna Carta',[1] and devoted the greater part of a day to hearing evidence about concealed priests and chapels in the county of Monmouth.[2] On May 2 the offensive and defensive league of December 31, 1677, and the proposed league of perpetual defence with Holland were read in the House, which, after considering them, voted that they were not pursuant to their addresses.[3] At the same time the king was urged to enter into a quadruple alliance with the Emperor, Spain, and the States General[4] for the vigorous conduct of war against France. This was followed on May 7 by another address for the removal of Lauderdale; but Charles kept his Commons to the main point— supplies; in spite of their expressed opinion that the whole affair was 'a work of darkness'.[5] Charles would neither declare war on France nor disband his troops; the Commons were unwilling to grant money either for their maintenance or disbandment. After two short adjournments the Commons found a loophole through which they hoped to escape from the dreaded redcoats; for on June 4 they voted £200,000 for the disbandment of the army (provided this was completed by the end of June), and an additional £200,000 for the expenses of the fleet. This time-limit was subsequently extended to July 27. The additional sums granted for paying off the extraordinary charges of Navy and Ordnance and for the dowry of the princess of Orange were merged into a consolidated act[6] for raising £619,368 by a land-tax, which passed the Commons on July 8, and received the royal assent on July 15.

Having secured the impotence of England by setting parliament against the king, Louis next succeeded in setting the States General against the prince of Orange. This was not a difficult task, especially as, in the projected permanent alliance between England and the States, there was said to be a secret clause providing for reciprocal assistance in dealing with rebel-

---

[1] *Grey*, v. 287.   [2] *C.J.* ix. 466–70.   [3] Ibid. ix. 475, May 4, 1678.

[4] On March 26 a conference on this subject was held by Danby with the Imperial, Spanish, and Dutch envoys; Charles later gave it to be understood that he would declare against France if parliament granted him the money. But because of Charles's ambiguous attitude the alliance never ripened.

[5] Col. Birch's description (*Grey*, v. 385).   [6] 30 Car. II, cap. i.

lious subjects in exile. D'Estrades, one of the French agents, made good capital out of this rumour, and thereby helped to widen the cleavage in Dutch sentiment, so that the prince of Orange found himself pitted against a strong peace party in his own country. When Louis offered to surrender Maestricht, to renew the commercial treaty of 1662, and to sacrifice the severe tariffs of 1667 in favour of the moderate ones of 1664, Amsterdam took the lead in the demand for peace, since this would now bring the restoration of commercial relations with France on exceptionally favourable terms. In effect, therefore, French diplomacy was willing to surrender her exceptional weapon against Dutch prosperity in return for peace and frontier possessions. On May 15, in spite of opposition from the prince of Orange, the States General announced its intention of sending an extraordinary ambassador to the French king.

At this point a patriotic king would either have declared war on France, or would have used his mediation to secure what is called 'the balance of power'; but Charles, it must be repeated, had only one object—money. Through no fault of his, he had failed to arrive at a satisfactory arrangement with the Dutch, whose polity was complicated and difficult of comprehension; so he fell back on France, where conditions were at least more easily understood.

For some time there had been secret negotiations with France. On January 9, 1678, Danby had written to Montagu complaining of the difficulties into which Charles was forced by the cessation of the subsidy, and concluding with these significant words: 'Unless some balm from heaven be applied to the wound I do not see but that it must bleed very suddenly.' Danby later erased the words 'from heaven'.[1] The balm consisted of six million livres a year for three years, in return for which Charles was to use his influence with Spain and the Dutch to procure peace. This audacious proposal was made in a letter sent by Danby to Montagu on March 25, to a draft of which Charles, in his own hand, added the postscript: 'I aprove of this letter.' The negotiation lapsed; but when in May there were clear

---

[1] A copy (with alterations in Danby's later handwriting) will be found in *Add. MS.* 38849, f. 118. For a full account of a complicated subject see A. Browning, *Life and letters of sir T. Osborne, earl of Danby*, i, chs. xi and xii.

indications of Dutch willingness to accept a separate peace, Charles decided again to make what capital he could out of his now threadbare mediation, and at the same time to fortify himself against a malignant opposition. After a week's negotiation, a secret treaty was signed on May 17, 1678, by Charles and Barrillon, whereby the English king undertook to maintain absolute neutrality during the continuance of the war, and to withdraw his troops from the Continent in the event of the allies not accepting the French terms within two months. The 3,000 troops raised for Scotland were to be retained,[1] and parliament was to be prorogued for at least four months from the date of the expiration of the two months. In return, Barrillon undertook to pay six million livres, the first half payable two months after signature of the secret treaty, the remainder by quarterly instalments thereafter. The preamble to this secret engagement recited that Charles had been urgently solicited by the States General to use his good offices with Louis to induce him to keep open the terms offered in April 1678, in spite of any subsequent successes of French arms; ostensibly therefore this bargain was in the interests of the Dutch, a presumption which would prove useful if by chance its terms had to be made public. Neither Danby nor Lauderdale signed the treaty.

Within a few days Louis realized that it would not be necessary to spend this money; for on May 22 he received from the States General a letter announcing willingness to negotiate terms on the basis of those proposed in April at Nimeguen. Louis thereupon granted the Dutch a truce of six months to date from July 1. Peace seemed assured; but Louis renewed his demands that to his ally Sweden should be restored those of her possessions which had been captured by the elector of Brandenburg. To enforce this demand, Louis would have had to invade Germany and occupy Cleve and Mark, territories in close proximity to the Dutch frontier; a prospect which revived the war spirit among the allies, and with it the hopes of Orange that the proposed separate peace would be abandoned. Even the States General were unwilling to accept peace on such terms, and so the war trumpets of Europe were once more in full blast. The project of a permanent Anglo-Dutch alliance

[1] *Baschet*, 139, May 18/28, 1678.

against France was therefore resumed, and Temple was sent to The Hague, where, on July 16–26, 1678, he secured the adhesion of the States to a joint ultimatum in which France was given a fortnight to yield her demand on behalf of Sweden, and come to terms[1] on the conditions already laid down in the Anglo-Dutch treaty of December 31, 1677. Temple was surprised when the document was repudiated in London; he knew only one of the two sets of negotiations.

It might seem that these events were sufficient to destroy the secret Anglo-French treaty; but this compact was still in being, and Charles was reminded of his undertaking to disband his troops by the middle of June. To this he replied that if he dismissed his troops then, and France meanwhile made any important conquest in Flanders, he would be in danger of expulsion from England as a traitor. Additional English regiments were accordingly sent to the coast for transport to Flanders; and Danby continued to quibble over the interpretation of the stipulation that the troops should be dismissed at the end of two months from the signature of the secret treaty. Publicly therefore Charles was maintaining a free hand in the European impasse; but secretly he was on the alert for every chance of grasping the French subsidy which for so long had dangled before him. Even the demand for Swedish restitution seemed to offer such an opportunity. England had the troops; she had also an available princess (Anne) for a Swedish matrimonial alliance; so Sunderland was sent over to Paris in order to realize these assets. But it may be doubted whether Louis really intended to hold out on behalf of Sweden; it is certain that he was relieved when the Swedish agents announced that they would not insist on such restitution. Freed from a troublesome allegiance to his ally, Louis was therefore able to sign peace with the Dutch on July 31, 1678, followed later by treaties with Spain (Sept. 1678), the Emperor, Brandenburg, and Denmark (Feb. and June 1679).

Even thus, Charles did not give up hope. In October Sunderland returned after a fruitless mission, and Charles reduced his demand from six million livres to three;[2] but, once more, he had over-estimated the generosity of Louis. In the midst of a great

---

[1] *Dumont*, vii, pt. i. 348.   [2] *Mignet*, iv. 704.

European pacification, the position of England now seemed one of innumerable possibilities. When other nations were in the last throes of resistance to the all-conquering arms of France, England, hitherto a naval power, had suddenly raised an army. To what use could it be put? For a joint campaign with the Emperor and the northern powers on behalf of Sweden? Or, in conjunction with France, for a war against the Emperor and the northern powers? Or for a war against France and Holland?[1] If these seemed too speculative, the army might be used at home to secure the king in a non-parliamentary absolutism. Charles, it is true, had not succeeded in obtaining the French money, but he kept his army, the gift of a House of Commons which was now in terror of the weapon it had placed in his hands. All the fears and hatreds steadily accumulating for more than a decade were now to be unloosed in wild panic, and a fierce storm preceded the calm for which Charles yearned.

[1] *Baschet*, 141, Sept. 23/Oct. 3.

XVI

THE POPISH PLOT, 1678–81

1. THE EARLY STAGES OF THE PLOT, AUGUST 1678—FEBRUARY 1679

THE summer of 1678 abounded in omens that great events were impending. 'There seems a more than usual concernment among all men,' wrote Andrew Marvell, 'as if some great, and I hope good thing were to be expected.'[1] The fourth of the five acts in the second Caroline drama was about to be staged; and men looked eagerly for the raising of the curtain which would reveal whether the scene was laid in Rome or Paris. In the heavens something uncommon was afoot; for in that year there were three eclipses of the sun and two of the moon,[2] and in April of the preceding year there had appeared a blazing comet, the effects of which were still awaited with apprehension.[3] Astrologers prophesied 'frenzies, inflammations and new infirmities proceeding from cholerick humours',[4] as well as 'troubles from great men and nobles';[5] while readers of literature less ephemeral than the Almanacs were assured that a great trial would be brought on England by the Papists, those worshippers in the outer court; indeed it was alleged that the late archbishop Ussher, when predicting these trials, had swooned at the thought of what was in store for the nation.[6] Even in the occult world there was more than usual activity, for a great revival of witchcraft occurred in Scotland, and in August the Devil himself presided at a general convocation of witches, attended by a warlock who, originally a presbyterian minister, had conformed when the bishops came in.[7] Charles would need that gift of second-sight, with the possession of which his clan was sometimes credited, and with which he appeared at times to be endowed.

Plotting was one of the spare-time occupations of the seven-

---

[1] May 23, 1678, in *Poems and Letters*, ed. Margoliouth, ii. 226.

[2] Dove, *Speculum Anni*, 1678.   [3] W. Andrews, *News from the stars*, 1678.

[4] Dade, *A prognostication* . . . , 1678.

[5] J. Partridge, *Calendarium Judaicum*, 1678.

[6] *Strange and remarkable prophecies and predictions of the holy, learned and excellent James Ussher*, 1678.   [7] Law, *Memorialls*, 145.

teenth century, one of the undesirable things that have disappeared with washed faces and outdoor games. Messages were often composed in cypher that might quite well have been written in plain script, considering the jejune character of their information and the ease with which the cypher could be unravelled; but the disguise helped to create the atmosphere of consequence and secrecy, so stimulating when men combine for the achievement of some undisclosed object. Another factor helped to foster the plot mentality; namely, that few men applied reasonable tests for determining the truth of a statement. Rumour and hearsay were often taken for proofs; in the courts, a prisoner was generally assumed to be guilty before he was tried, and personal animus did not debar one from giving evidence. It was an age of oaths, perjurers, and informers; when every one was scrupulously religious, and personal honour still undeveloped. A third contrast has to be noted. We live in an economic age, and seek to interpret the past in terms of that age. But in the England of Charles II the Scarlet Woman was more prominent than the Economic Man.

Venner's Rising, the Derwentdale Plot, the Plague and Fire of London, the disgrace of Chatham; all these in succession helped to put the nation into a state of mind in which anything might be believed. In both England and Ireland plots were of almost regular recurrence. Hidden in garden or thatch, Irishmen sometimes found bundles of mysterious documents containing evidence of gigantic conspiracy; one such bundle found in 1673 was found to be written 'in perfect Irish-English and some parts have no sense'. 'Had I troubled you with a narrative of every little plot I have been informed of,' wrote the bishop of Ferns on this occasion, 'it would have been endless; for as those of the Roman persuasion have been perpetually forward to invent plots and conspiracies which they pretend those of the fanatic party are engaged in, so those others have not been unfruitful of the like inventions against the Romanists.'[1] This was almost equally true of England. Sir John Bramston, a knight of the shire for Essex, was the victim of a plot engineered by a hostile neighbour named Mildmay, who employed a Portuguese adventurer to swear that a papal visitation was held at Bramston's

[1] *Cal. S.P. Dom., 1673*, xlv.

house, attended by the knight, who (according to the sworn evidence) received both dispensation and a pension.[1] In January 1674 Shaftesbury made a violent speech in which he said that there were about 16,000 papists round London ready to execute a desperate stroke, and that no one was sure of his life; at the same time a boy of 13 was examined by the Lords with regard to his discovery in the streets of a letter from a Roman Catholic containing plans for the destruction of both Houses by gunpowder. This juvenile witness had *un résolution qui n'est pas de son age*; and, when the Commons were informed of these revelations, they proposed to ask the king to put the Militia into readiness, and to arm the Protestants of London.[2] Two years later the queen was informed of the accusation that popish books were being stored over the stables at Somerset House, and a search was ordered to be made;[3] this building was soon to come into more lurid publicity. In April 1678 the Commons investigated the secret ramifications of popery in the county of Monmouth,[4] a county which was afterwards to produce the informer Bedloe. England was ripe for a plot.

Among the plotmongers was Ezerel Tonge, born in 1621; the rector of St. Michael's, Wood Street, a doctor of divinity of Oxford, and an enthusiast for botany, alchemy, and the revelation of Jesuit designs. He acquired a certain amount of reputation as educator and researcher; for he taught children to write by a new method of inking over copper-plate copies;[5] he also communicated to the Royal Society his papers on the flow of sap in plants. Diffusion of interests and a certain clownishness of manner had hitherto interfered with personal success; but in the winter of 1676–7 he chanced to meet, at a house in the Barbican, one possessed in full measure of the personality and self-confidence requisite for success in a heavily overstocked market. This was Titus Oates, who, although Tonge's junior by 28 years, could, at the age of 27, look back on an extremely varied life; for this ecclesiastic was already distinguished in three distinct spheres— sanctimoniousness, indecency, and perjury. Though no scholar, he had a fund of native cleverness, and was gifted with a large,

---

[1] Bramston, *Autobiography* (*Camd. Soc.*), 146 sqq.
[2] *Baschet*, 130, Jan. 11/21, 1674.   [3] *Cal. S.P. Dom.*, 1676–7, xviii.
[4] *Supra*, 554.   [5] *Aubrey*, ii. 261.

imposing figure, impressive at a distance, and needing only a doctor's gown and bands to create what in some circles is called 'presence'. Another asset was his chin, the longest in England, supporting his mouth as by a pedestal, and helping to confer on his utterances a gravity and portentousness not confirmed by his small, shifty eyes. Having been expelled from a naval chaplaincy and from a living in Kent, Titus was in one of the penurious 'vacations' of his career, when he chanced on this meeting with Tonge, still contriving to supplement his stipend from the vapourings of his pens and his alembics. According to his own account Oates called on Tonge in order to have the counsel of that experienced theologian on 'a case of conscience'.[1]

The two combined forces and for a time appear to have tried hard to discover a real plot. Oates had already seen something of Roman Catholic society as chaplain to the Protestants in the duke of Norfolk's household, and in 1676 he became a member of a mixed Roman Catholic and Protestant club, which met at the *Pheasant* in Fuller's Rents. At this club, in spite of the rule forbidding talk of religion or politics on pain of a fine of sixpence, Oates railed against the Church of England and proclaimed that the king was only one of three estates;[2] it was also noted that he generally wore full canonicals. There he met several Jesuits; but in order to 'dive into their secrets' more deeply, he decided to become converted, and according to his version he was received into the Society of Jesus on Ash Wednesday, 1677.[3] For the purposes of his novitiate he was sent to Spain in order to bring back the body of lord Cottington from Valladolid. He was given to understand that his sole mission was to bring back the body, but a sealed packet entrusted to him for delivery in Madrid led him to assume that there was something else on hand; so at Burgos he opened the packet, and 'made himself master of all the secrets thereof'. After trying to stick down the wafer, he explained that it had come undone through being rubbed in his pocket. Armed with this knowledge, he was able to worm out still more secrets from the fathers in Madrid. Nor did he obtain only information in this mission; for he brought back to England, not the body,

[1] *Grey*, vi. 327.

[2] W. Smith, *Contrivances of the fanatical conspirators* (1685).

[3] *Add. MS.* 38847 (*Southwell Papers*), f. 201.

but a doctorate of divinity of the university of Salamanca, a 'rabbinical degree' which proved the best accessory in his outfit.

Another mission enabled him to perfect his knowledge of Jesuit designs. In December 1677 he was sent to the College at St. Omer, where he was known sometimes as Sampson Lucy, and sometimes as Titus Ambrosius.[1] His unusual deportment occasioned considerable mirth among the junior members of this sodality; and in a game known as 'sawing the witch' he had a pan broken over his head 'for recreation'. Owing to his seniority, he sat at a small table in Hall by himself, near the High Table; for he could not diet with the young students; there he specially distinguished himself by canting stories after dinner. At St. Omer he found plenty of evidence, and when he learned the indignation of his hosts at Tonge's translation of a book named *Jesuits' Morals*, he offered to return to England and poison Tonge. This offer, according to his own account,[2] was accepted, with the promise of a modest £50 if he succeeded; and so, when he returned to England in June 1678 he was a pseudo-Jesuit, commissioned to murder the man with whom he was co-operating in the discovery of a great plot.

With all this miscellaneous information, the allies set to work; and an indictment of 43 articles was speedily drawn up. How to bring this to the notice of the king was the next point; but they succeeded in getting into touch with Christopher Kirkby, who appears to have had some employment at Court as a chemist, and in this way they obtained some knowledge of the king's movements. On August 13 Kirkby intercepted the king as he was walking in St. James's Park; but Charles referred him to Chiffinch and passed on; the same evening Kirkby brought Tonge to the king at Whitehall, and the matter was now referred to the lord treasurer. Tonge communicated a copy of the indictment to Danby, who questioned his informant personally about the revelations.[3] Briefly, the substance of the 43 articles was that pope Innocent XI had deputed to the Jesuits supreme control

---

[1] Evidence of the Jesuits at Oates's trial for perjury, May 8, 1685, in *The tryals, convictions and sentence of Titus Otes upon two indictments for perjury* (1685), 10, 19, 25.   [2] *Add. MS.* 38847, f. 204.

[3] C. Kirkby, *Discovery of the Popish Plot*, 1679; *P.C. Reg.* 66, Sept. 28, 1678; J. Pollock, *The Popish Plot*, 13, 70–1.

of the Roman Catholic interest in England for the purpose of overthrowing king and government; money was to be provided by the Spanish Jesuits and by the French king's confessor, père la Chaise; two Jesuits had been paid to shoot the king, four Irish ruffians to stab him, and sir George Wakeman, the queen's physician, to poison him. In addition to all this, there was to be a massacre of Protestants and a French invasion of Ireland; the duke of York was to become king, and rule under the direction of the Jesuits. This was the original version of the Plot; other details were afterwards added;[1] such as that lord Arundell was to be lord chancellor; lord Powis, lord treasurer, and Coleman secretary of state. This design had been finally agreed upon by the Jesuits at the *White Horse* tavern in the Strand on April 24, 1678, when Oates, as one of their trusted members, carried the documents from room to room for the signatures. Oates was at St. Omer, not in London, in April 1678, but that was a minor discrepancy; for no one at that time knew his movements.

At this point a new and tragic figure entered the scene. One of the best known of the London magistrates at that time was sir Edmund Berry Godfrey, then in his fifty-seventh year. Of good family, he had been educated at Westminster and Christ Church, and had prospered in the trade of wood and coal merchant. He had distinguished himself during the Plague by remaining at his post, and pursuing robbers of the dead even into the pest-houses; for these services he was presented with a piece of plate. In 1669 he was placed in custody for a few days because he had procured the arrest of the king's physician for debt, an occasion when his resolute behaviour still further confirmed his reputation for staunchness of character. He was known as a strict but tolerant Protestant; his generosity and courtliness brought him into contact with men of different faiths, including Papists; and he was received in good society. He appears to have had some kind of friendship or association with Coleman, the duchess of York's secretary; and was thus an exceptional, but in some ways mysterious man; for while he was liked and respected, his circle of acquaintance was wider than comported with the standards of safety. His short imprisonment of 1669 may have saddened

[1] For these see T. Oates, *A true narrative of the horrid plot* (1679). This pamphlet contains 81 counts and was dedicated to Charles.

him; certainly the engraving from the only existing portrait shows a man of somewhat melancholy features. In the spring of 1678 he went to the south of France for the benefit of his health, returning in the summer of that year.

Early in September Oates and Tonge called on Godfrey with the request that he would take their depositions on oath as to the truth of the accusations contained in the papers which they brought with them. The magistrate declined to do so unless he was informed of the contents of the papers; some days later (Sept. 28) he was provided with a copy, and the depositions were then taken on oath. It appears that Godfrey, who was visibly distressed by the serious nature of the depositions, at once revealed them to Coleman (possibly as a warning), but Coleman did not profit by the hint to destroy all the incriminating letters in his possession. Meanwhile the government, possibly at the instigation of the duke of York, had decided to investigate the matter, and on September 28, at a Council meeting presided over by the king,[1] Williamson produced a bundle of papers received from Tonge, the king remarking that on August 13 he had been told about a conspiracy by Tonge, and had referred him to the lord treasurer. Danby reported that, when he sought for further information, he was informed by Tonge, in a letter of September 3, that evidence would be forthcoming if letters directed to father Bedingfield (the duke's Jesuit confessor) were intercepted at Windsor post office. Danby had tried to intercept them, but was too late;[2] for Bedingfield had himself collected the packet, and as the letters contained some 'mysterious expressions' apparently tending to an unlawful design, he had taken these to the duke of York, who brought them to the king, and in this way they were communicated to the council board. On examining them, several councillors pronounced the letters counterfeit because of the bad spelling, and because, in spite of the forced hand, they appeared to have been written by the same person. Indeed they were such clumsy forgeries that no use could afterwards be made of them.

Tonge was then called in. His manner showed nervousness, but he was assured that he need have no apprehension. He said that of his own knowledge he knew nothing, as all his information

[1] *P.C. Reg.* 66, Sept. 28, 1678.   [2] Pollock, op. cit. 73–4.

was from Oates. He was asked to fetch his friend, and at the afternoon session Titus was ushered in. It was not his first appearance before the council; for in April 1675 he had been summoned thereto with his father to substantiate his allegation against one of the jurats of Hastings of having spoken scandalous words of the council,[1] an occasion when he had failed to prove his accusations. On this, his second appearance, he shared none of his friend's hesitation, his first request being that he should be put on oath. This having been complied with, he was shown the Bedingfield letters, and at the mere sight of a few lines he swore to the authorship of each—this was written by Nicholas Blundell, that by Dr. Fogarty, another by Thomas White, another by William Ireland. The confidence of Oates, his unhesitating answers, his wealth of detail, all these carried the council before them; and as a result the arrest was ordered of the men whom he named. It was not unimportant that Charles was absent from this afternoon session (having gone to Newmarket), for the fate of the Plot might have been very different had the king exposed the falsehoods of the informer at this early stage. Having gained the confidence of his audience, Oates then retailed a picturesque anthology from the more recent incidents of his career. The matter was now deemed so serious that a special meeting of Council was held on the afternoon of the next day (Sunday, Sept. 29) at which the king was present, when Charles tested Oates on his reference to Don John of Austria, and convicted him of falsehood; but this did not shake the confidence of the councillors, who ordered the arrest of Coleman and the attendance of sir George Wakeman.

At the council meeting on the following day, Oates repeated his statements, and charged the Jesuits Ireland, Grove, and Pickering with having been of the Jesuit consult at the *White Horse* tavern. He also cited a letter from Thomas White, Provincial of the Jesuits, as proof that sir George Wakeman had agreed to poison the king for £15,000, £5,000 of which had already been paid to an agent by Coleman. By this time the dimensions of the Plot had swollen to a capacity as great as the credulity of the informer's listeners. Twenty-four English Jesuits, nineteen foreign Jesuits, twelve Scottish Jesuits, nine Benedictines, three

[1] *P.C. Reg.* 64, April 14, 1675.

Carmelites, two Franciscans, nine Dominicans, fourteen secular priests, four secular persons (Fogarty, Wakeman, Coleman, and Groves), four Irish ruffians, and two archbishops, all jumbled up mostly in multiples of three and four, appear to have been kept clear and distinct only in the ever-resourceful mind of Oates.[1]

There then elapsed a period of seventeen days (Oct. 1–17, 1678), perhaps the most mysterious in the history of England. Oates's revelations were now public property, and what the council had swallowed was not likely to be rejected by the populace. The mine was laid; it needed only a spark to fire it; but who fired the spark may remain one of the unsolved problems of history. Godfrey, who is said to have shown signs of apprehension, and to have expressed a premonition of personal danger to himself,[2] left his house in Green's Lane near the Strand on the morning of Saturday, October 12. He was seen to go up St. Martin's Lane, and was said to have asked an acquaintance the way to Primrose Hill (near Hampstead); he was also reported to have been seen at Marylebone; though there was another story that at noon he was in the company of one of the churchwardens of St. Martin's-in-the-Fields. There is no contemporary reference to his movements after one o'clock. He did not return to his house that night, and sinister rumours were soon afloat. On the following Thursday, the 17th, about 6 p.m., two men, a baker and a farmer, were passing some waste ground on the south side of Primrose Hill, when they noticed a stick and a pair of gloves lying by the hedge. On reaching the *White House* tavern, they told the landlord, who accompanied them back to the spot; where, behind the bushes, they found the body of Godfrey, fully dressed, head and face downward, transfixed with a sword, the point of which projected about six inches out of his back. His hat and periwig were in the bushes over his head, but neither his laced band nor cravat could be found. His money was intact, but his pocket-book had been removed.[3]

---

[1] *Harleian MS.* 3790, f. 46; see also *L.J.* xiii. 313–30.

[2] L'Estrange, *Brief History*, iii. 172. Elsewhere (iii. 293) the same writer says that Godfrey inquired the way to Paddington woods. L'Estrange's evidence is to be received with caution.

[3] *True and perfect narrative of the late terrible and bloody murder of sir Edmund Berry Godfrey* (1678).

The inquest was conducted next day at the *White House* tavern by the coroner for Middlesex.[1] Two surgeons described the wounds—one, superficial, on the chest; the other on the left breast, going right through the body. There was a livid circle round the neck, which appeared to show that he had been strangled; and to this cause the medical witnesses attributed his death. The murder did not appear to have been committed on the spot, for there was no evidence of a struggle; nor, although the ground was muddy, were there marks of soil on the soles of the shoes; it seemed likely, therefore, that the body had been carried there and pierced with his own sword. One of the jury stated that, on the previous Monday and Tuesday, two boys, searching the spot for a missing calf, had noticed neither body, nor stick, nor gloves. The verdict was wilful murder. After lying in state, the body was accompanied by a long procession to St. Martin's-in-the-Fields, where it was buried (Oct. 31). A commemorative medal was struck, inflammatory sermons and pamphlets poured forth, and a reward of £500 was offered for the discovery of the murderers.

This reward speedily brought forward a claimant, William Bedloe, who had already achieved an eminence in a military career nearly as high as that of Oates in an ecclesiastical; like Oates also he knew the value of a title, and boasted a captaincy of dubious origin. Moreover, he had been to Spain; he had delved into the secrets of the Catholics by pretending to be one of them, and he had been commissioned to set fire to London.[2] Writing from Bristol, he offered to give information; and when his offer was coldly received he came in person to make his revelations. On November 8, before the committee of the Lords appointed to investigate the murder of Godfrey, he related how Chepstow Castle was to be seized by lord Powis, who, with a large army, was to join with lord Belasyse and restore popery by force. He himself, according to his story, was to have been one of Godfrey's murderers; and on Monday night, October 14, he had been taken to Somerset House to see the body of the magistrate, where he noticed two men, one a servant of lord Belasyse, and the other

---

[1] The evidence taken at the inquest will be found in the above pamphlet, and also in L'Estrange, op. cit. iii. 236 sqq.

[2] Bedloe, *Impartial discovery of the horrid popish plot* (1679).

Mr. Atkins, a servant of Pepys.[1] Atkins was arrested, but was afterwards able to prove an alibi. Another arrest now helped Bedloe to make out a more substantial story. On December 21 a Roman Catholic silversmith named Prance was taken into custody on the information of a lodger in his house, the information alleging that Prance had been absent from his house for the four nights preceding the discovery of Godfrey's body.[2] This was poor evidence, especially as the lodger was in arrears with his rent; but it led to extraordinary consequences. On being confronted with Prance at a meeting of one of the Commons' committees, Bedloe claimed to recognize in him one of those who had been present at Somerset House. Prance was then lodged for two nights in an icy-cold cell at Newgate, where he was visited by an unknown person (said by L'Estrange to be Shaftesbury) who told him what to say if he would save his life.[3] Thereupon he made a confession to the effect that an Irish priest named Fitzgerald had commissioned him to murder Godfrey, as one of the queen's enemies. Three other men (according to his statement) acted with him—Hill, Berry, and Green, of whom the first two were servants at Somerset House.

Prance's story amounted to this: Godfrey was followed along the Strand on the fatal Saturday, lured into Somerset House and strangled by Green. The body was then removed to a small room in the building, and on Wednesday was taken in a sedan chair to Soho, where it was placed on a horse and conveyed to Primrose Hill. Two days later Prance recanted the whole story; but a second immersion in the condemned hole at Newgate made him reaffirm his original version. Prance, as the price of his life, then swore that he himself was one of the murderers, now turning king's evidence; in this way (possibly with the help of Shaftesbury) Oates and Bedloe used Prance to strengthen their stories, and establish the vital connexion between Godfrey's death and the Plot. It was on this evidence that Green, Berry, and Hill were afterwards (Feb. 1679) hanged for the murder.[4]

But long before these innocent men were executed, the Plot

---

[1] J. Pollock, *The Popish Plot*, 108 sqq.
[2] L'Estrange, op. cit. iii. 51.   [3] L'Estrange, op. cit. iii. 25.
[4] For a comparison between the evidence of Prance and Bedloe see J. Pollock, op. cit., ch. iv.

had grown to uncontrollable dimensions. Parliament re-assembled on October 21, when the king announced that he would forbear any opinion on the subject of the design attributed to the Jesuits. Thereupon both Houses set to work and appointed committees for the examination of witnesses; one was deputed to search the vaults under the Houses, another was to inspect the fireworks on sale at M. Choqueux's in the Savoy, and a third was to examine the letters seized in Coleman's lodging when he was arrested. The first of these committees ordered a search under all rooms for gunpowder; and, as the fifth of November approached, the underground inspections became more rigorous. Householders in the neighbourhood of Old Palace Yard reported having heard great knocking at night; so a committee was appointed to inquire into this;[1] and to make the Houses of Parliament quite secure, sir John Cotton was required to remove his coal and faggots from beneath the Painted Chamber;[2] Monmouth was set in command of sentinels at the doors, while sir Christopher Wren helped the committee to search all the walls, inside and outside, of the vaults stretching from under the Thames to beneath Westminster Hall. Houses in the vicinity were searched for arms; and in Chelsea the lodging of the bishop of Winchester was visited in order to investigate the stories of a bricklayer who had worked there eighteen months before.[3] Nor was this the end of the digging; for on a rumour that the 'plot money' (amounting to hundreds of thousands of pounds) was buried in the Savoy, the excavators busied themselves in that neighbourhood,[4] already suspect because of the firework store of M. Choqueux. No line of inquiry was left unexplored. Shaftesbury, one of the most assiduous coadjutors of Oates, solemnly recorded on paper statements made by boys of 15 and 17 of what had been said to them by a child of 6.[5] Even Pepys's nag came on the scene; for a man was sent to Gravesend to apprehend a suspicious character inquiring after it.[6]

[1] C.J. ix. 530, Nov. 1, 1678.

[2] The Cotton family had a house in Westminster, and the reference here is to the cellars of that house. [3] H.M.C. Rep. xi, app., pt. ii. 16–17.

[4] Hatton Correspondence (Camd. Soc.), i. 182.

[5] Shaftesbury Papers, vii, no. 496, Nov. 6, 1678.

[6] H.M.C. Rep. xi, app., pt. ii. 16. See also J. R. Tanner, Pepys and the Popish Plot in E.H.R. vii.

The firework committee examined M. Choqueux, a surgeon in the Savoy. There was an old association between the Jesuits and pyrotechnics. The name Ignatius obviously denoted something incendiary; the saint himself was known for his hot temper, and either the Jesuits or the Pope must have set fire to London in 1666, indeed a woodcut of 1667 depicted the Pope plying a pair of bellows, while London burned.[1] So great things were expected from an examination of M. Choqueux's stock-in-trade, which was found to consist of 6,914 empty serpents, 10,400 water balloons, and many empty rocket cases. From his information, it appeared that he had sold fireworks for eighteen years, and the empty cases in his possession were kept for filling whenever the king wanted a display. The 'manacles' found on his premises seemed intended for some sinister object, until he explained that they were used for screwing down candlesticks. Having noted this information, the committee ordered a guard to be set over the surgeon's house. His explosives were then carefully examined by two Ordnance officers, who reported that they were quite harmless. The committee thereupon ordered M. Choqueux to be publicly rebuked.[2]

More serious business was stirring at the committee for examining Coleman's letters. Edward Coleman, a convert to Roman Catholicism, had served as secretary first to the duke and then to the duchess of York. An enthusiast for the cause of his adopted religion, he was so indiscreet and communicative that the duke was several times advised to dispense with him altogether; but this course was never adopted. Beginning in June 1674 he wrote numerous letters to persons abroad, not about any definite plot, such as Oates was purveying, but about the general design of restoring the Roman Catholic faith in England.[3] He foolishly kept his correspondence, the veiled allusions of which might seem to imply something more serious than he intended. He may have been overcome by the high rank of the persons with whom he was in communication, or the momentous cause for which he corresponded; moreover he gave his letters a special consequence

---

[1] See *supra*, i. 307.   [2] *H.M.C. Rep.* xi, app., pt. ii. 18.
[3] These letters were published in 1681 by order of the Commons under the title of *Collection of letters . . . from the originals in the hands of sir G. Treby*, 2 pts. (1681).

by using a cypher, and ensured some publicity for their contents
by his vanity and garrulity. They were mostly requests for
money. Thus, in September 1674 he wrote to père la Chaise
asking for funds in order to increase the credit of Charles and
his brother, in return for which the duke 'would afterwards perform all that His Most Christian Majesty can ask of him'.
Another letter of that month referred to 'the great design', which
was 'to undermine the intrigues of that company of merchants
who trade for the parliament and the religion, and to establish
that of the associated Catholics in every place'. This, he thought
might be done with the assistance of Pope and Emperor. Written
on the back of one of the letters was this memorandum: 'King's
power to command his subjects' service against all acts of parliament.' A continually recurring theme in these letters was
Charles's debauchery and James's merit; how money intended
for the one might be put to far better use by the other. It is noteworthy, also, that his correspondents confirmed the view that
money given to Charles would be wasted. Coleman was trying
to obtain for James what Charles had already procured for himself by the secret treaty of Dover; but the secretary was no
diplomatist, and what in the letters of royal personages was high
policy, appeared an infamous plot when propounded by an
ordinary person. Hence the Commons seized on statements like
these: '£300,000 certain is better than the bare possibility of
getting money from parliament',[1] and 'we have here a mighty
work on our hands, no less than the conversion of three kingdoms,
and by that perhaps the subduing a pestilent heresy which has
domineered over part of this northern world a long time'.[2]

In a sense, therefore, Coleman's plot consisted in a development of the scheme concocted in 1670 between Louis XIV and
Charles, with the substitution of the duke for the king. His letters
supplied the proof for which the Commons were looking. Their
committee spent weeks in translating and deciphering the correspondence; and the men who had suspected the existence of gunpowder in the vaults, and of high explosive in M. Choqueux's
fireworks, had no difficulty in elucidating hidden works of darkness from the somewhat vague but always compromising corre-

[1] Letter to la Chaise, Sept. 29, 1675, ibid., pt. i. 111.
[2] To la Chaise, undated, but probably late in 1675, ibid., pt. i. 117.

spondence of the secretary. For example, there was a letter from cardinal Norfolk referring to the appointment of a Roman Catholic bishop for England; on the margin, one of the committee wrote: 'this confirms Mr. Oates'. Similarly, a letter from the earl of Berkshire referred to trees and gardeners; these, noted the transcriber might well be kings and governments. Southwell, who wrote a précis of the papers, declared that 'the general scope of all these letters tends to bring the Roman Catholic religion into England'.[1] In the House, sergeant Maynard declared that the letters tallied with Oates's discoveries 'as a counter tally in the Exchequer'.[2] When a shrewd government official and a trained lawyer were convinced, it is not surprising that belief in Oates became an article almost of religious belief;[3] and to doubt that Godfrey was murdered by the Jesuits was a heinous offence, punishable in the courts.[4]

From the day of their reassembly (Oct. 21, 1678), Lords and Commons exercised the functions of grand jury of the nation. Five popish lords—Arundell, Belasyse, Powis, Petre, and Stafford —were sent to the Tower; and the Commons resolved 'that there has been and still is a damnable and hellish plot, contrived and carried on by popish recusants for the assassinating and murdering the king, and for subverting the government and rooting out and destroying the Protestant religion'.[5] This was followed by debates for an address to the king that the duke of York might be required to withdraw from the king's person and counsels, many members supporting this proposal because Coleman's letters seemed to confirm the duke's guilt; but the House was mollified to some extent by the king's verbal assurance[6] that he would consent to reasonable Bills for safeguarding their rights in the

---

[1] *Add. MS.* 38142, f. 3. Southwell's report on Coleman's letters.

[2] *Grey*, vi. 295.

[3] See, for example, the *Narrative of the horrid conspiracy of T. Knox, W. Osborne and John Lane to invalidate the testimonies of Dr. Oates and Wm. Bedloe. Published by the appointment of me*, Titus Oates (1680). In this book (dedicated to the king) Oates attempted to refute the charge of sodomy brought against him.

[4] In June 1682 two men were fined and pilloried for printing and publishing letters which implied that Godfrey had committed suicide. *State Trials* (1730), iii. 501.

[5] *C.J.* ix. 530, Oct. 31.

[6] *Grey*, vi. 172.

reign of his successor, provided the principle of the succession was
not violated. The Lords then proceeded with their Bill for disabling the Papists from sitting in either House; on November 20
this was sent back to the Commons with an amendment exempting the duke of York.[1] Here was a severe test for the loyalty of the
Commons. 'If the prince should go into another place', declared
secretary Coventry, 'it would cost you a standing army to bring
him home again'; sir Jonathan Trelawney urged that, by rejecting
the proviso, they would drive the duke into popish hands; sir
William Killigrew wept after declaring, 'I dread taking the duke
from the king'.[2] Those against the proviso sat silent; it was
accepted by 158 to 156. By the passing of this Bill[3] about a score
of Roman Catholic peers were deprived of their seats in the Lords,
including the duke of Norfolk, the earls of Shrewsbury, Berkshire, and Powis; lords Stafford, Petre, Arundell, and Belasyse.

For a moment the Commons turned from the Papists to the
Army. About 25,000 troops were still under arms, and some
members regarded the Plot as a trap to make them acquiesce in
the existence of this standing army;[4] while others thought the
soldiers little better than rioters, and there was a feeling in the
House that they should be voted a grievance to the nation.[5] A
Militia Bill which provided for their disbandment was rejected
by the king on November 30, on the ground that by its terms the
control of the Militia would be out of his power for a time, and he
would not part with that control, even for half an hour; whereupon the Commons read their Bill again in the hope of finding
a valid reason for its rejection, but could not discover wherein
they had encroached on the prerogative. Having failed to remove the menace of the Army, they turned with fresh zeal to the
Plot. On November 28 Bedloe was called in and the door of the
House locked.[6] Having been given a full pardon in advance,
Bedloe proceeded to relate how a Jesuit consultation was held at
Somerset House on May 11 in a room near the chapel, attended
by lord Belasyse, lord Powis, two French abbots, Mr. Coleman,
and two others who, by the respect shown them, were persons of

---

[1] *L.J.* xiii. 365.   [2] *Grey*, vi. 243.
[3] 30 Car. II, stat. ii, cap. i. See *supra*, i. 368–9; ii. 467.
[4] *Baschet*, 141, Oct. 28/Nov. 7, 1678.   [5] *Grey*, vi. 266–9.
[6] Ibid. vi. 287.

quality. The queen joined them, while 'Father Walsh' and Bedloe remained in the chapel. The result of the conclave was that the queen, though with tears, at last consented to 'taking off' the king. Bedloe thought that the persons of quality who stood with their backs to him might be the dukes of York and Norfolk. Then came the turn of Oates. He had already made known to the king his accusation against the queen, but from Charles's reception of the insult, he knew that he had overstepped the mark, and must thenceforth depend on his reputation with a credulous nation. So when he followed Bedloe at the bar of the House he was a lugubrious martyr, encircled by the forces of evil which he had exposed at the risk of his life. He complained that after revealing the queen's designs, he had been refused pen, ink, and paper; his father and friends had been denied access to him; the Yeomen of the Guard had smoked in his chamber. He was in danger of being poisoned. It would be in his interest to make no further discoveries.

Oates was a profound psychologist. Just as he asked the readers of one of his printed sermons to 'drop a tear in private' because he was in danger of persecution,[1] so he stood before the Commons, a prospective candidate for the martyr's crown. Without a single dissentient, his audience expressed complete confidence in him.[2] He then confirmed Bedloe's accusations against the queen. The result was an address to the king asking him to remove his consort and all her household from Whitehall, a request which Charles ignored.[3] But though the king knew that the Plot was an imposture, he was almost completely solitary in that knowledge; and he realized that, if he resisted the tide, he would be swept under by it. Already the heads of the victims were beginning to fall. On November 27 Oates gave evidence against Coleman at the King's Bench, and on December 3 he was executed, perhaps the only victim who in any sense deserved his fate. Three Jesuits, Ireland, Grove, and Pickering, who, on Oates's testimony, had been present at the *White Horse* tavern on April 24, were next tried and sentenced to death. On December 5 it was resolved to impeach the five popish lords in the

---

[1] Preface to a sermon preached at St. Michael's, Wood Street (*Bodley Pamph.* 146). This was Tonge's church.　　[2] *Grey*, vi. 295–6.
[3] *C.J.* ix. 549–50, Nov. 28, 1678.

Tower. Meanwhile the Doctor, comfortably housed and in receipt of a handsome weekly allowance, was entering on the zenith of his career, and was setting up for a representative of the older English aristocracy by having engraved on his plate the arms of sir Otes Swinford, husband of the lady who afterwards married John of Gaunt.[1] He dined with the king, to the disgust of the duke of York. Even captain Bedloe could not rival this metropolitan of perjurers, and the innumerable small fry of informers filled in the few gaps left in the gigantic edifice.

Such was the national aspect of the Plot. Its reaction on each of the leading characters on the stage differed considerably. Charles was firmly keeping his legislature to a choice of alternatives—a standing army or a subsidy for their disbandment. The duke of York's position was more ambiguous. His religion and his unpopularity had been taken advantage of by the plot-mongers; but, had he been gifted with agility or imagination, he might have profited by the occasion to find allies in the chaos to which parties were reduced. But he had no gift for these things; and when he made public his opinion that his safety depended on the retention of a standing army, he was deserted by men who might have rallied round him[2] in opposition to Danby and Anglican intolerance. So too, if he had kept his alliance with Danby, the two together might have weathered the storm; but Barrillon was now directing all his efforts to their separation, in order that the impending attack on the lord treasurer might be assured of success.[3] Danby was thought by some to have encouraged the Plot as a means of ridding himself of the duke and strengthening himself in anti-Catholic hatred;[4] but, on the other hand, Oates had not hesitated to use his name, and there was a chance that he might be accused of misprision of treason if only because he had not acted immediately on the revelations made to him in August.[5] He had even more adroit enemies. Louis XIV, who had never forgiven him his conduct in the subsidy negotia-

[1] W. Smith, *Contrivances of the fanatical conspirators*, 15.

[2] *Baschet*, 141, Nov. 4/14 and Nov. 7/17.

[3] Ibid. 141, Nov. 14/24.

[4] Ibid. 141, Oct. 28/Nov. 7.

[5] A contemporary hinted that, for this reason, Danby had been instrumental in the murder of Godfrey (*Some Reflections upon the case of Danby in relations to the murther of sir Edmundbury Godfrey*, in *Bodley Ashmole*, F. 51).

tions, willingly lent himself to a scheme for the lord treasurer's downfall. The tool employed was Ralph Montagu, who had just been dismissed from the post of ambassador in Paris.

Montagu, a follower of Arlington and an enemy of Danby, had already (in 1676) been instrumental in bringing over to England the duchesse Mazarin in order that she might help to reinstate Arlington and displace Danby.[1] Thereafter, he strove to ingratiate himself with Charles by obtaining better terms from Louis. But meanwhile he had several grievances. Early in 1678 he had agreed with Henry Coventry for the reversion of a principal secretaryship; but Danby, in the interests of sir William Temple, refused to ratify the bargain, and so made an enemy of the man to whom he had written compromising letters. Montagu soon experienced a more serious rebuff. In a spiteful letter[2] written from Paris the duchess of Cleveland reported disparaging remarks made by him about the king; and when the ambassador left his post without leave in order to exculpate himself, he found himself dismissed from his embassy and from the privy council. He therefore joined forces with Barrillon, and obtained the promise of a large pension for his assistance in the attack on Danby; he would make public the letters, while Louis was to reveal the real intentions of the English Court, and the purpose of the standing army.[3] Having been elected a burgess for Northampton, the ex-ambassador then awaited his opportunity to produce the letters. Knowing his intention, Charles ordered the seizure of his papers, on the allegation that he had been in communication with the papal nuncio in Paris; whereupon the House took up his cause, and ordered his papers to be fetched and examined. Here was a fresh set of treasonable materials for the unsatiated Commons; Montagu for a time displaced Oates, and fears were expressed that he might share the fate of Godfrey.[4] When his box was delivered up and broken open he selected the two fateful letters sent to him by Danby on January 17 and March 25, 1678. Both letters were read to the Commons, including these incriminating words: 'in case the condition of peace shall be accepted, the King expects to have six millions

---

[1] A. Browning, *Life and letters of sir T. Osborne, earl of Danby*, i, ch. xi.
[2] *Harleian MS.* (B.M.), 7006, f. 171.
[3] *Baschet*, 141, Oct. 14/24.
[4] *Grey*, vi. 346.

of livres yearly for three years, from the time that this agreement shall be signed between His Majesty and the King of France, because it will be two or three years before he can hope to find his parliament in humour to give him supplies, after your having made any peace with France'. Charles's postscript, 'I aprove of this letter', appended to the original draft of the letter, was afterwards altered by Danby to 'this letter is writ by my order'. On the question being put that there was matter sufficient to impeach the earl of Danby, it was carried by 179 to 116.[1]

On December 21 the articles of impeachment were read. These included: the traitorous encroachment of royal power by treating of peace and war with foreign princes without communicating with the secretaries of state; his attempted subversion of the ancient form of the constitution by the introduction of an arbitrary and tyrannical form of government, with which object he had designed the raising of a standing army on pretence of war against France; he had continued the army contrary to the statute disbanding it; he had negotiated a peace with the French king disadvantageous to His Majesty, and tending to hinder the meeting of parliament, and had endeavoured to obtain a large sum from the French king; he was popishly affected, and had lately concealed the horrid plot and had suppressed the evidence; he had paid for unnecessary pensions and secret service the sum of £231,602 within two years; and, lastly, he had procured for himself considerable grants of inheritance of the ancient revenue of the crown.[2]

The Lords refused to commit Danby, and it seemed likely that this would provoke an interminable duel between the two Houses. Accordingly on December 30 the king, having declared: 'I think you are all witnesses that I have not been well used',[3] prorogued parliament to February 4, 1679. On January 24 the parliament was dissolved by proclamation,[4] a new one being summoned for March 6. So ended that Cavalier Parliament which, having begun its career by removing every shackle from kingship, was now, in the terrors of a nightmare plot, attacking everything sacred in the prerogative—the king's minister, the

---

[1] *C.J.* ix. 559–60, Dec. 19. See *supra*, 555–6.   [2] Ibid. ix. 561–2.
[3] *L.J.* xiii. 447.
[4] *Steele*, i. 3679, Jan. 24, 1679.

king's control of the army, the morality of his consort and the
loyalty of the heir presumptive.

At this point it might well be asked whether there was any
meaning in the madness through which the nation passed in these
months. Who murdered Godfrey, and why? What was the connexion between his death and the plot? Or did he die by suicide?
Was there anything serious behind Coleman's letters? Was the
Court using the plot for some sinister purpose? The problem is
not that of finding a key to fit a lock, but rather that of finding a
key-hole; for, on the evidence which was then considered good
enough to hang a man, it is possible to construct almost any theory.
It must remain a theme for conjecture rather than proof.[1]

The mystery of the plot is bound up in the mystery of Godfrey's
death. Before the cause of that death can be conjectured, it
should be recalled that medical jurisprudence was then in its
infancy; nor is there sufficient medical evidence to justify a
resumed inquest by modern experts. The inquest verdict was
murder by strangulation; but medical opinion has recently been
invoked to substantiate the view that the livid mark round the
neck was owing to post-mortem hypostasis; hence the theory of
suicide, presumably by his own sword. This latter theory may
be dismissed at once as improbable, owing to the great difficulty
which a fully dressed man would experience if he sought his
death by throwing himself on an upright sword of average length;
but there is still left the possibility of suicide by hanging. This
amended conjecture of suicide has still to face the problem of the
sword-thrust, an objection to which the murder theory is not so
liable; since the murderers might quite well have completed their
work by impaling the magistrate with his own sword.

At the outset, therefore, it is by no means certain how Godfrey
met his end, and this leads to a dual series of suggested solutions
of the mystery. A second question or rather set of questions

[1] Among the best-known contributions to the problem are J. Pollock,
The Popish Plot; A. Marks, *Who killed sir Edmund Berry Godfrey?*; J. Gerard,
The Popish Plot and its newest historian (containing criticisms of theories
advanced by Mr. Pollock), and sir John Hall, *Four Famous Mysteries*. See
also Andrew Lang, *The Valet's Tragedy*. Of contemporary sources the third
volume of L'Estrange's *Brief History of the Times* is important but not always
reliable; it favours the suicide theory.

centres in the career of Godfrey. He was one of the commissioners
for recusants in the county of Middlesex,[1] appointed in accordance with the scheme of 1675, whereby the crown hoped to confiscate a portion of recusants' estates;[2] he appears also to have
been entrusted by Danby with a sum of £300 for the making of a
sewer by St. James's Park;[3] but neither of these facts attests more
than the Protestantism and the integrity of the magistrate. Nor
is there any suspicion that Godfrey was in financial embarrass-
ments such as might account for suicide. There are two great
questions about him which have never been satisfactorily
answered; what were the nature of his relations with Coleman;
and why did Oates choose him for his depositions? To the first
query it might be answered that the relations between the two
men amounted to no more than friendly intercourse; or it might
be suggested that Godfrey was really a man of double life, who,
behind the mask of Protestantism, was planning vast designs
with his confederate. The difficulty confronting the first answer
is that friendly intercourse would not usually be maintained by
two such men, living as they did in very different spheres, and
divided in both religion and temperament; to the second answer
it might be rejoined that, if Godfrey was secretly a Catholic, he
was not in a position to perform services of much value to
an international schemer such as Coleman. Then, as regards
Oates's choice of Godfrey. This may have been pure accident
or from deliberate design. If from design, the selection may have
been made because Godfrey was noted for his character and his
Protestantism; or from some more subtle reason, such as that
Oates had contrived to learn a little about Coleman's correspondence and his friendship with sir Edmund, knowledge which
Oates might have put to several purposes, including attempted
blackmail.

Already it will be seen what a large number of possible suggestions are opened up. Oates noted the extreme trepidation of
the magistrate when he swore his depositions before him;[4] why
Godfrey should have been so disturbed it is hard to explain; still
more, why he should have communicated these depositions to

[1] *Cal. Tr. Bks., 1672–5*, 790, July 1675.
[2] For this see *supra*, 431.   [3] *Cal. Tr. Bks., 1676–9*, 1196.
[4] W. Smith, *Contrivances of the fanatical conspirators* (1685), 8.

Coleman on September 28. Again, why did not Coleman take advantage of the warning to destroy *all* his papers, since those up to October 1676 were left intact? Were there any after that date; and did these (if they existed) contain the secret? Were the papers prior to 1676 left intact because thought to be less incriminating, and so likely to divert attention from questions about the presumably more serious letters that may have been destroyed? Godfrey is alleged to have written a series of more than one hundred letters (to whom is not known) which, if discovered, would (it is held) give the secret history of the reign.[1] It will be seen, therefore, that at the very threshold of the problem there is a host of unanswered questions.

Contemporaries had a simple theory to account for the murder, namely, that the Jesuits procured it because of the damning revelations in the papers entrusted to him by Oates. This explanation is not impossible; but it is based on the assumption that the murderers were foolish, since obviously the one way of giving verisimilitude to Oates's stories was to destroy the Protestant magistrate to whom they were confided. The same criticism, though in a less degree, might be urged against the contention of a modern writer of distinction who has demonstrated that, among the nonsense sworn to by Oates, there was a germ of truth; namely, that on April 24, 1678, a consult of the Jesuits did actually take place, not at the *White Horse* tavern in the Strand, but at St. James's Palace; and as this was a profound secret, revelation of which would have implicated the duke of York, there was good reason for destroying Godfrey, whose murder was therefore 'a cruel necessity'.[2] On this theory some kind of plot was being engineered; Oates knew just enough about it to make his communications dangerous, and so the man who received the sworn information was removed, as otherwise he would have had to divulge it. But Oates copied out his depositions in duplicate, leaving one with the magistrate and taking the other to the council; and so the depositions, with their truth or falsity, were already, in a sense, public property. Nor do we know what Coleman may have revealed to Godfrey.

---

[1] Andrew Lang, *The Valet's Tragedy*, preface, viii–ix.

[2] J. Pollock, *The Popish Plot*, 149–54. Mr. Pollock suggests that Coleman revealed this secret to Godfrey.

The theories which attribute the guilt to the Jesuits do not satisfactorily explain the motive; though, on the other hand, it is not
impossible that some rash but ardent Catholic may have thought
(wrongly) that by killing Godfrey he was hushing up a great secret.

Another theory is that Oates murdered Godfrey as a means
of securing for the Plot both publicity and confirmation.[1] Here
the motive is more clear, for Oates himself afterwards admitted
that the murder made the fortune of the Plot; but Oates does
not seem the type of man who would resort to violence, and
assassination would have been a clumsy weapon for a man
capable of his supreme craftsmanship. A third theory is
that the murder may have been quite unconnected with the
Plot. As a magistrate, Godfrey had come into contact with
many dangerous characters, and it is not absurd to suppose that
the crime was a work of revenge on the part of one who had
fallen foul of him. This theory, first suggested by Hume, has at
least the merit of simplicity, and so is free from the strong objections that can be urged against almost every other hypothesis.
There was at least one man who may have had a grudge against
Godfrey. This was the earl of Pembroke, who, in April 1678, was
indicted of the murder of one Coney, by a grand jury of which
Godfrey was foreman. Pembroke was the most violent homicide
of his age and Godfrey may have been one of his victims.[2]

A fourth theory may be suggested; it is based on the
assumption of suicide by hanging. There is evidence that
Godfrey was of a melancholy disposition, and the one common
element in all the conflicting evidence about his movements
before death is that he was exceedingly depressed. This may
have been caused by threats of violence; it might also be attributable not to any definite threat, but to a feeling of disquiet,
due as much to bad health as to the import of the depositions
sworn before him; and, if the magistrate was verging on a break-
down, the affair may have been too much for him. He may
have been threatened in some way by Coleman, and called
upon 'to fulfil some promise or to redeem some pledge';[3] his

---

[1] This has been suggested by sir J. Stephen, *History of the Criminal Law*,
i. 393.   [2] This has been suggested by Mr. J. G. Muddiman.
[3] Sir John Hall, *Four Famous Mysteries*, 135. Sir John Hall, in his very
interesting discussion, inclines to the murder theory.

failure to do so may account for his assassination, but it might equally well account for his suicide. More generally, a sensitive man might well have felt apprehension that he was dragged into an affair involving such great matters and such high personages, and he had already experienced how the displeasure of the mighty was not lightly to be incurred; moreover, he had been informed of treasonable designs, and he had communicated the information to Coleman, but he had not himself revealed it to the government. This was misprision of treason, and the longer he delayed action, the more perilous his position must have appeared. Still another reason for suicide may be suggested. Oates was an absolutely unscrupulous man who probably knew just a little of Coleman's activities and of his relations with Godfrey. This would be sufficient for a blackmailer, and so Oates may have chosen Godfrey for this purpose. On a broad view of the case, suicide is the most likely theory; such was the king's opinion,[1] and a slight element of confirmation is provided by the fact that Godfrey appears to have taken no food within two days of death.[2]

This conjecture of suicide by hanging is consistent with the contemporary evidence that, at the inquest, the neck was found to be dislocated.[3] But there is still left unexplained the extraordinary position in which the body was found. Why the spectacular sword-thrust? There is fairly general agreement that the sword pierced a corpse; the corpse may as well have been that of a suicide as of a murdered man. The theory of blackmail is compatible with the hypothesis that, at least after the fatal 28th of September, the magistrate was being shadowed, whether by Oates or by some one interested in his movements; hence, the man or men on his trail may have been the first to come upon him while he was still hanging. If Oates or an accomplice made this discovery, he may suddenly have realized that, for the purposes of the Plot, more could be made of sir Edmund dead than alive; and as it is likely that the discovery was made

---

[1] *Baschet*, 141, Oct. 21/31, 1678.　　　[2] *Cal. S.P. Dom.*, *1678*, 472.

[3] See *supra*, 567, for the contemporary sources for the evidence at the inquest, where the doctors pronounced that the neck was broken. This is repeated in *Burnet*, ii. 164. But even thus, the fact cannot be regarded as absolutely certain.

in a solitary place, it would not be difficult to pierce the body with the sword, and leave it in a position which would suggest a death as spectacular as the other incidents retailed in the depositions. This hypothesis attributes to Oates a genius for propaganda, a not unreasonable attribution; nor is it inconsistent with the little we know of Godfrey's life and temperament; and it accepts consistency of motive as the principle inspiring the actors in the drama. But endless theories might be suggested; some just possible, others having serious objections; and so the death of sir Edmund Berry Godfrey is likely to remain one of the unsolved mysteries of history.

2. PARLIAMENT AND EXCLUSION, FEBRUARY 1679–FEBRUARY 1681

In order that the complicated events of these two years may be more easily followed, it should be noted that within this short period Charles summoned and dissolved two parliaments—the third and fourth of his reign; that in each of these the Commons passed an Exclusion Bill, and that in the interval between the two parliaments (Oct. 1679–Oct. 1680) the excitement of the Plot reached its zenith. Thereafter a surfeited nation gradually quietened down, and a harassed king finally cut the knot tying him to parliament, and obtained a renewal of the subsidy from France.

Shortly after the dissolution of the Cavalier Parliament Charles tried to strengthen himself by compromise; and as he had failed to obtain money from Louis, he was obliged to be conciliatory. The most serious problem was his brother, who adopted a hint that he should leave the country, on condition that the hint was conveyed in a written command, and provided also that the illegitimacy of the duke of Monmouth was definitely declared. With these conditions Charles complied; the order was written out, and at a council meeting of March 3, 1679, Charles produced a signed declaration to the effect that he had never married any one but his consort. This declaration, having been attested by the sixteen councillors present, was deposited in the council chest.[1] The duke then went to Brussels. Charles now furnished himself with a new adviser. Robert Spencer, second earl of Sunderland, returned to England in February

[1] *P.C. Reg.* 67, March 3, 1678/9.

1679 from his fruitless embassy to France, and on the retirement of sir Joseph Williamson from the secretaryship of the northern department, Sunderland paid him £6,000 for the post (Feb. 10). On the 26th of March Danby resigned his treasurership, which was put in commission; and so against a formidable opposition Charles had at his side only the two secretaries, sir Leoline Jenkins and lord Sunderland.

This appearance of conciliation was strengthened by an adroit use of sir William Temple's reputation. With the conclusion of the peace at Nimeguen his diplomatic labours were for the moment at an end, and in February 1679 he was pressed to take a secretaryship of state, but he declined on the ground of ill health. His name was invoked, however, for the scheme whereby the privy council was remodelled, as the result apparently of his advice. By this scheme the council was to be reduced to thirty members, representative of the executive, the opposition and the landed interests, and the councillors were individually to be of sufficient prestige and influence for mediation between crown and opposition.[1] Twenty-seven members of the old council were retained in the new, which included a majority of the opposition, notably Shaftesbury, Essex, and Halifax.[2] Charles announced that he would be guided in weighty affairs by his remodelled council, whose advice would have second place only to that of parliament.[3] Such were the preliminaries with which the king prepared himself for the ordeal of his third House of Commons, the first to be returned by the nation since the loyalist enthusiasm of eighteen years before.

The general election of February 1679 was the first to be fought on distinctively party lines. On both sides there was propaganda and an unsparing use of influence. Monmouth, on the strength of his governorship of Hull and his chancellorship of Cambridge, wrote to the port and the university recommending his candidates; the secretaries wrote to the lords lieutenant on behalf of government nominees,[4] and Barrillon asked Louis to send money for beer.[5] In some constituencies electors were

---

[1] *P.C. Reg.* 68, April 21, 1679. [2] *Halifax*, i. 149.
[3] *L.J.* xiii. 530, April 21, 1679.
[4] *Cal. S.P. Dom.*, 1679–80, 78. [5] *Baschet*, 142, March 30/April 9.

warned not to return bribe-takers or pensioners, and even in loyalist Devon it was conjectured that scarcely one of the old burgesses would be returned.[1] In a pamphlet attributed to William Penn the main objects of the opposition were defined as follows: (1) the further discovery of the Plot; (2) evil counsellors to be brought to justice; (3) pensioners of the previous parliament to be punished; (4) measures to be adopted for securing frequent parliaments, for the ease of Protestant Dissenters, and for safeguarding the nation from popery and slavery. The electors were advised not to give or receive bribes at elections; not to choose a pensioner, or a court official, or any one who held *durante bene placito*; also to be avoided were indigent or voluptuous persons, ambitious men, non-residents. The votes and inclinations of former members were to be reviewed if they stood for election. Choose sincere Protestants, men with an eye to the improvement of industry, men of 'large principles' who will maintain civil rights; prefer a good stranger to an ill-affected neighbour—such was the advice in this, one of the first clear statements of party doctrine ever put before the English electorate.[2] That such appeals met with some response was shown in the composition of the new House of Commons; for it was said to contain not more than thirty or forty on whom the Court could rely, and it differed from its predecessor mainly in the fact that it was now possible to speak plainly of political miscarriages without being dubbed a 'Presbyterian'.[3] The shorter word 'whig' was now displacing that ancient term of abuse. Barrillon noted that the new House contained a large proportion of men having no parliamentary experience, who swamped the old cabals.[4]

The first session of the new parliament opened on March 6, 1679. 'I meet you', said Charles to the assembled legislators, 'with the utmost desire that man could have to unite the minds of all my subjects, both to me and to one another.' He recalled how he had sequestered the popish lords; he cited the executions

[1] *Cal. S.P. Dom., 1679-80*, 78.

[2] *England's great interest in the choice of this new parliament* (1679). By 'Philanglus'. Shaftesbury may have had something to do with its composition. For a copy see *Bodley*, 22858, c. 6.

[3] *Grey*, vii. 374.   [4] *Baschet*, 142, March 27/April 6.

for participation in the Plot and for the murder of Godfrey; how
he had disbanded as much of the army as he could with the
money supplied to him; and, above all, that he had commanded
his brother to absent himself. Money for disbanding the army,
for paying the fleet (which parliament had provided for only
until the previous July), and for discharging the anticipations
on his revenue was earnestly solicited; and he concluded by
drawing attention to the loss in his Customs revenue through
the embargo on French wines and brandy.[1] Finch having
followed suit at intolerable length, the Commons appointed a
committee of secrecy to prepare evidence against the five noble
prisoners in the Tower, and reminded the Lords of the impeachment of Danby.[2] As the Upper House decided by resolution
that impeachments from the preceding parliament still stood,[3]
there seemed a likelihood that the lord treasurer would be
brought to trial. From these matters the Commons turned
for a moment to Oates and Bedloe, from whom further revelations were recorded. Bedloe was voted the £500 reward for the
discovery of the murderers of Godfrey;[4] a large bill of expenses
presented by Oates was honoured, and a resolution reaffirming
belief in the Plot was passed.[5]

There occurred a dramatic moment in the proceedings against
Danby, when the king announced to both Houses (March 22)
that he had granted the earl a pardon under the great seal, with
a reminder that on a former occasion he had done the same
thing for Buckingham and Shaftesbury.[6] The manner in which
the pardon had been granted was explained to a committee of
investigation thus: the king commanded the seal to be taken out
of the bag, and directed the pardon to be sealed; whereupon
the person who usually carried the bag affixed the seal, and
during this process the lord chancellor (Finch) did not regard
himself as having custody of the seal.[7] The Commons voted the
pardon illegal, and remonstrated against the dangerous consequences of granting pardons to persons under an impeachment;[8]
in this way was raised a question, not to be answered until the

---

[1] *L.J.* xiii. 449.   [2] *C.J.* ix. 572, March 20.
[3] *L.J.* xiii. 466, March 19.   [4] *C.J.* ix. 573.
[5] Ibid. ix. 572, March 21.   [6] *Grey*, vii. 19, and *L.J.* xiii. 471.
[7] *C.J.* ix. 574–5.   [8] Ibid. 575.

Act of Settlement: can a royal pardon be pleaded to an impeachment? Meanwhile the Lords ordered Danby to be taken into custody,[1] while the Commons then proposed to proceed against the ex-treasurer by Bill of attainder,[2] and objected to the amendments of the Lords which turned the Bill into one of banishment;[3] but Danby himself settled the difficulty by surrendering to the usher of the black rod (April 15), by whom he was removed to the Tower, where he was to remain for five years. There he was safe from the fury of the Commons; indeed he threatened that if he were abandoned to them he would reveal things dangerous to the Court.[4] Like Lauderdale, he had only one friend—the king.[5] A few days after Danby surrendered himself, the Commons voted a supply of £206,462 for disbanding the forces.[6]

Having failed to bring Danby to account, the Commons next turned to the duke of York; and on April 27 voted an address to the effect that the likelihood of his succession to the throne was one of the chief encouragements of the Plot.[7] Three days later Charles announced through his chancellor that he was willing to consent to laws guaranteeing religion and property in the reign of his successor, provided the succession itself was left intact.[8] Reasonable as this concession appeared, those who doubted whether there could be any security under James proved ultimately to be right. 'What is offered', said Sacheverell, 'will not do your work'; for he had seen a computation by Coleman how the king might live without parliament, and another 'how the king might have a standing army in masquerade in the fleet'.[9] With each week of the session personal bitterness against the duke increased, until on May 11 one of the members of the city of London, Thomas Pilkington, proposed that he should be impeached of high treason;[10] and a

---

[1] *L.J.* xiii. 475, March 24.　　[2] *C.J.* ix. 576, March 25.
[3] Ibid. 589, April 8.　　[4] *Baschet*, 145, May 10/20, 1680.
[5] He was given a warrant for the marquisate of Danby.
[6] *C.J.* ix. 597, April 16.　　[7] Ibid. ix. 605.
[8] Ibid. ix. 606, April 30.　　[9] *Grey*, vii. 159–60.
[10] Ibid. vii. 238. In *Sloane MS.* (*B.M.*) 2496, f. 55, there is a list of the accusations on which the charge was based. These were (1) that he had confederated with foreign powers to alter and subvert the government in church and state; (2) he was a party to the Popish Plot; (3) he made use of

debate ensued in which it was declared that the Protestant religion and a popish successor were as incompatible as light and darkness. Richard Hampden, son of the great Hampden, thereupon moved for the introduction of an Exclusion Bill, and on May 15 was read the first of the Bills for disabling the duke of York from inheriting the crown, a Bill which included the crowns of Scotland and Ireland within its scope, in spite of the fact that these kingdoms possessed legislatures. Those against the Bill on its first reading would not be counted, and so 'yielded the question';[1] on its second reading it passed by 207 to 128.[2]

The first Exclusion Bill contained a preamble to the effect that the duke of York had been seduced by the Pope's agents to enter the Church of Rome, and had advanced the power of the French king to the hazard of these kingdoms. The measure disabled him from the succession, and enacted that all acts of sovereignty committed by him should be high treason and punishable by death. On the demise of the crown, the crown should devolve on the next in succession, as if the duke were dead.

From this, the House turned to the investigation of moneys paid to members of the previous parliament by Sir Stephen Fox from secret-service funds. Forced to name the pensioners, Fox gave a long list of grants of between £200 and £500 per annum, mostly out of the Excise;[3] and the committee of investigation found that £20,000 per annum had been paid by the commissioners of Excise to members of the last parliament. Here was another plot. Sir Francis Winnington declared that several witnesses willing to make discoveries had been threatened; he was personally afraid to have any of his papers about him, lest he might be served as Godfrey was. Then came the explanations. One of the members on Fox's list (sir John Talbot) showed how he had come by the money—he had taken an Excise farm and paid the rent, when Clifford made a bargain over his head with other farmers before his lease was out; so

his control of the Post Office to prevent the examination of suspicious letters; (4) he had advised the breach of the Triple Alliance; (5) he had maintained friendship with the French king for promoting popish designs; (6) he had procured commissions in the Navy for Papists; and (7) he had tried to discredit Oates's testimony.

[1] *Grey*, vii. 260, Sunday, May 11, 1679.
[2] Ibid. vii. 314.
[3] Ibid. vii. 323–4.

the pension was compensation for his surrender of the lease. Other members followed with equally unspectacular explanations of the payments which they had received; and the sum of it all was a demonstration that the moneys were not really for 'secret service' at all, but were payments consequent on an extremely clumsy and wasteful fiscal system. These actuarial investigations were suddenly interrupted (May 27) when Black Rod knocked at the door and summoned the Commons to the Lords, where the king, having passed the Habeas Corpus Amendment Act, prorogued parliament to August 14, 1679. But before that date it was dissolved by proclamation.[1]

The balance of success as between Charles and his third parliament had on the whole been with the king. By a pretext of conciliation he had united his enemies with his friends in a harmless council, and he had neutralized some of the activity of Shaftesbury by the fiction of confidence. He had thrown over Danby; but, as the Commons never succeeded in bringing him to trial, there had been no damaging disclosures; moreover, the prerogative of pardon, contested by the Commons, had not been disallowed by the Lords; and, as most of the energies of the opposition had been concentrated on the Papists, they had been diverted to that extent from the crown. The Exclusion Bill had been shelved by prorogation, and so Charles might hope to gain something from time, the most valuable asset for a man facing a host of enemies. Never had Charles been more solitary; and he was also handicapped by relatives who had none of his tact: by York in Brussels, fuming at the royal offer to restrict some of the powers of the successor to the throne; by Monmouth, fresh from his triumph at Bothwell Brig (June 22, 1679), a ready tool for cleverer men; and lastly by William of Orange, now being cultivated by Henry Sydney, envoy at The Hague, who was acting in co-operation with Halifax and Essex.[2] Finally, Charles was forced to acquiesce in the judicial murders which throughout the year 1679 were removing men whom he knew to be innocent.

These executions followed quickly on each other throughout

---

[1] *Steele*, i. 3691, July 12, 1679.

[2] For their correspondence see *Diary of the times of Charles II . . . by Henry Sidney, earl of Romney* (ed. R. W. Blencowe, 2 vols.).

the greater part of 1679. Coleman had been executed in December 1678; then followed the Jesuits Ireland, Pickering, and Grove, together with Green, Berry, and Hill, the supposed murderers of Godfrey. In June 1679 came the turn of Whitbread, provincial of the Jesuits, with his colleagues Fenwick, Harcourt, Turner, Gavan, and the barrister Richard Langhorne, all convicted on the testimony of Oates and Bedloe. There was more game in reserve, for the popish lords were in the Tower awaiting trial. In July occurred the first misfire, when at the trial of sir George Wakeman (accused of attempting to poison the king) Scroggs, in his summing up, went so far as to question the evidence of Oates, who had not hesitated to hint at the co-operation of the queen. It was like questioning the truth of the Bible, but it had sufficient weight with the jury to induce them to return a verdict of Not Guilty. Contemporaries believed that the judge had been bribed by the Portuguese; but, on the other hand, the introduction of the queen's name may have caused the Court to give a hint to the judge. That he took a grave risk was shown by the fact that Oates and Bedloe exhibited articles against him before the privy council on the counts that he had disparaged their evidence, and had misdirected the jury; moreover popular indignation against Scroggs, because of his conduct in this case, helped to reinforce the demand that judges should hold office not *durante bene placito*, but *quamdiu se bene gesserint*. So the establishment of judicial responsibility and impartiality was due as much to indignation at the inspired fairness of Scroggs as to satisfaction with the anti-Catholic bias of his brethren.

Throughout these events the one element of continuity was the crown. Had Charles died at any time in 1679 there would probably have been a revolution; this was brought within measurable distance by the sudden and serious illness of the king in August of that year, when the duke of York had to be sent for from his exile; and for a moment it seemed that the monarchy itself would disappear in the whirlpool by which it was surrounded. But Charles quickly recovered, and it was now as necessary to get rid of the royal brother as it had been to secure his attendance; for it was known that his stay in England would do more harm than good to the Catholic cause; indeed

pope Innocent XI pressed upon him the necessity of moderation, and the desirability of postponing, in the interests of the
faith, all active measures.[1] The duke would have preferred to
stay, and would have used French support and the army in
order to establish himself securely; but at last he was induced
to depart by a bribe—the sacrifice of Monmouth, whose popularity in the summer of 1679 was, next to the Plot itself, the most
serious asset in Shaftesbury's propaganda. Having been deprived of his post of commander-in-chief, Monmouth was exiled
to Holland (Sept. 24); and a few days later the duke of York
returned to Brussels, ostensibly in order to continue his exile, but
really in order to fetch his wife and take her with him to Scotland,
where (despite the vehement protests of Shaftesbury) he was to
serve as High Commissioner to the Scottish estates. Thus early
had the balance in favour of the crown been redressed. Monmouth was removed from his adherents in England, and the
duke of York now succeeded to the prerogatives of Lauderdale.
Even the moderates were divided; for while Essex was for exclusion, Halifax was still in favour of the duke's succession, with
restrictions. Thus Charles's illness and recovery prepared the
way for the break-up of the opposition, and rallied the waverers
to the cause of monarchy and legitimacy. Before the end of 1679
it was being demonstrated also that the weapons of the plot-
mongers could be turned against themselves, as was shown by
one Thomas Dangerfield, who claimed to have discovered a
great 'presbyterian' or whig plot, the evidence having been concealed under the meal tub of his female associate Mrs. Cellier.
His disclosures, which implicated Halifax and Essex, had all
the appearance of a popish counter-move; but it proved to be a
plot within a plot, and Dangerfield then accused prominent
Catholics of having planned it.

The new or fourth parliament had been summoned for
October 7, 1679; but when it met, both Houses were immediately prorogued and then adjourned by successive stages for
a year. One reason for this was that throughout the autumn
months of 1679 Charles was trying hard to secure a subsidy
from Louis that would help him to dispense with parliament,

---

[1] Innocent XI to the duke of York, Sept. 1679, in *Add. MS.* 15395, f. 188,
quoted in Campana de Cavelli, *Les derniers Stuarts*, i. 302.

but, as the sum could not be agreed upon, these negotiations lapsed.[1] Charles's immediate object at this time was to save the succession; so he decided to rule by councillors of his own choice. Shaftesbury was therefore dismissed from the Council (Oct. 1679); and the stage was cleared when Halifax and Essex, disgusted by the long prorogation, went into temporary retirement. Having divested himself of parliamentarians, Charles now formed a ministry of courtiers to which the name The Chits has been given; this consisted of Sunderland (a secretary of state), and two young commissioners of the Treasury—Sidney Godolphin and Lawrence Hyde, of whom the latter was appointed first lord of the Treasury on November 19. These men were in office primarily as royalists and opponents of exclusion; they were nominally committed to the cause of the duke of York and the projected French alliance, and all three were in correspondence with the prince of Orange.

This, the earliest tory 'cabinet', was therefore an accommodating ministry, anxious above all to protect itself against sudden changes in the political barometer, primarily responsible to the king, on good terms with both York and Orange, and anxious to have something to show when parliament met. Individually, each was not without personal distinctiveness. Lawrence Hyde, afterwards earl of Rochester, inherited the great Anglican traditions of his father, and was useful as a secular representative of the Church of England; he had some ability in finance, but in character he was haughty and arrogant. Sidney Godolphin, afterwards first earl of Godolphin and minister of queen Anne, had also a good head for figures, but he had greater agility, and a certain permanent manner of unobtrusiveness. As occasion required he shed his toryism for whiggery, and the extreme caution of his political speculations ensured

[1] In July 1679 Charles made it known to Louis XIV that he was determined to prorogue parliament in order to give Louis time to make up his mind regarding his English policy and his interest in preserving the Stuart monarchy. *Aff. Étr. (Angleterre)*, 135, f. 70, July 24. Charles at first demanded a subsidy of six million livres, but reduced his price; the duke of York guaranteed the entire dependence of England on Versailles for two million livres a year. *Baschet*, 143, Sept. 25/Oct. 5, 1679. On Sept. 4 the duke of York wrote to Louis begging the renewal of the subsidy as his (the duke's) affairs were desperate. *Aff. Étr. (Angleterre)*, 135, f. 169.

him a considerable measure of success. More enigmatic was Sunderland. He was probably the ablest of the three; though he made some wild plunges, as when he supported the cause of exclusion, lost his post and then had to work hard for several years in order to restore himself. Endowed with a 'managing' disposition, he co-operated with the duchess of Portsmouth in the enterprise of 'mothering' Charles, so that the monarch should as far as possible be spared trouble. This tutelage he afterwards exercised with greater success on James. He was the most ingratiating and subtle of the three; a representative of that type of minister which could have retained high office only under a Stuart dynasty. The real function of this ministry was to serve Charles's object of gaining time by the fiction of concession; and even Shaftesbury was included in this policy; for in January 1680 he had nightly interviews with the king, in which a compromise was discussed, on the basis of a Protestant marriage for Charles in return for a life revenue.[1] Halifax was urged by his brother-in-law Sunderland to emerge from his retirement at Rufford in order to give some much-needed prestige to the administration;[2] there was some talk of an alliance with Holland, and there was actually signed (June 10, 1680) a treaty of union and defence with Spain,[3] limited to Europe, by which it was agreed that, if the one were attacked, the other would come to his aid within three months of being asked to do so. The Chits made no secret of their belief that this treaty would be very useful for parliamentary purposes.[4] Once more, the French ambassador found himself unable to follow the gyrations of English politics; so he decided to wait for the return of James before renewing the treaty negotiations,[5] and sent this message to Louis: 'it would be very difficult to explain to Your Majesty what is the real design of the king of England and his ministers';[6] and a few days later he had to confess that England was more concerned with horse-races and cock-fights than with anything else.[7]

During this year of parliamentary recess (Oct. 1679–Oct.

---

[1] *Baschet*, 144, Jan. 8/18, 1680.   [2] *Halifax*, i. 208.
[3] *Dumont*, vii, pt. ii. 2–4, Windsor, June 10, 1680.
[4] *Baschet*, 145, June 17/27, 1680.   [5] Ibid. 144, Feb. 12/22.
[6] Ibid. 144, March 11/21, 1680.   [7] Ibid. 145, March 29/April 8.

1680) there seemed no limit to the insanity through which the nation was passing; for no class was spared by the infection, whether the London mob, inflamed by their pope-burnings, or the landed nobility, encouraged to fear that, under a papist king, they would have to restore their church lands. 'Any who have estates in abbey lands,' declared a pamphleteer,[1] 'who desire to beg their bread, and relinquish their habitations and fortunes to some old, greasy, bald-pated abbot, monk, or friar, then let him vote for a Popish successor.' Never before were the printing-presses so busy; for men who hitherto had been content to leave politics to the gossips now turned to the printed reports of trials, and the narratives of gunpowder and incendiary plots, all of them providing crude material from which was to be created a vivid political consciousness. 'Since this damnable Popish Plot has been discovered', declared countryman Hodge in a printed dialogue, 'there have come out so many notable good and bad books on all sides that I vow to thee I am become sublime like a philosopher, and can hold out *pro* and *con* with the best of them.'[2] The autumn of 1679, with its national anniversaries and civic processions, brought the climax, and on the annual commemoration of Elizabeth's accession (Nov. 17) there was a pope-burning attended (it was said) by 200,000 persons,[3] the ritual culminating in a conflagration under the statue of queen Elizabeth. The order of the procession was thus:

Six whistlers to clear the way.

A bell-man ringing and shouting, 'Remember Justice Godfrey'.

A dead body, representing Sir Edmund Berry Godfrey, in the habit he usually wore, the cravat wherewith he was murdered about his neck, with spots of blood on his wrists, shirt and white gloves, riding on a white horse, one of his murderers behind him to keep him from falling, representing the manner he was carried from Somerset House to Primrose Hill.

A Jesuit giving pardons very freely to those who would murder Protestants.

Six Jesuits with bloody daggers.

A consort of wind music called The Waits.

Four Popish bishops in purple and lawn sleeves.

[1] *Appeal from the country to the city* (1679).
[2] *Humble Hodge and Ralph holding a Discourse* . . . 1680 in *Bodley, Ashmole*, 737.
[3] *Diary of Henry Sidney* (ed. Blencowe), i. 190.

> The Pope's chief physician with Jesuit's powder[1] in one hand and an urinal in the other.
>
> Lastly, the Pope, preceded by silk banners with bloody daggers painted on them for murdering heretical kings, and behind him his counsellor the Devil.[2]

Nor was the excitement confined to London; for the Plot spread to Yorkshire,[3] where there was a conspiracy of informers (headed by one Robert Bolron, the Oates of the north) to take away the lives of prominent Catholics, including sir T. Gascoigne, who was accused, among other things, of plotting to murder the king and set fire to both London and York. Gascoigne, a man of 85, was tried in London and acquitted (Feb. 1680). Shaftesbury made frantic efforts to extend the Plot to Ireland, and urged that the English penal laws should be enforced there. When he failed to procure the passage of such measures as would goad the Irish Papists into rebellion he organized a campaign to obtain Irish informers, who for comparatively small sums could be induced to swear anything.[4] These men came out of Ireland 'with bad English and worse clothes, and returned well-bred gentlemen, well-caronated, periwigged and clothed', their brogues and leather straps changed to fashionable shoes and glittering buckles.[5] But soon these informers were being paid by the Court to give evidence against the opposition, including Shaftesbury himself.[6] Nor was the Plot confined to land. In the last days of the Third Parliament there had been talk in the Commons of a 'sea plot' in which Pepys, from his connexion with the duke of York, was said to be implicated, and in May 1679 the diarist's domestic affairs were carefully scrutinized by the House on the accusations of a

---

[1] i.e. quinine, then just coming into use.

[2] This description, with an engraving, will be found in *Bodley, Wood*, 417.

[3] For this see T. B. Parkinson, *The Yorkshire branch of the Popish Plot*, in *The Month*, xviii (1873). An account of the trial of Gascoigne will be found in *Bodley, Wood*, 426, no. 2.

[4] *Ormonde*, iv. 582 sqq. These men were drilled by Oates and by one of Shaftesbury's agents named Hetherington. The disclosures of one of them, Carey Murphy, will be found in *Cal. S.P. Dom., 1682*, 603.

[5] Ormonde to the earl of Arran, Nov. 17, 1681, in *Ormonde*, v. 164.

[6] For the crown's use of spies and informers see J. Walker, *Secret service under Charles II and James II* in *Trans. R.H. Soc.*, series iv, xv.

dismissed butler, who alleged that Pepys was scheming something with an alien named Morello, who had been seen at mass
in Somerset House. The sum of the butler's evidence was that
Pepys remained with Morello until three in the morning singing
psalms; but this testimony was discounted to some extent when
Pepys showed that his accuser had a grievance against him,
having been dismissed for an affair with a housemaid.[1]

In truth, the history of England at this time was providing
apt comment on the old proverb, 'the Devil is as bad as the
broth he is boiled in'. Round Oates there surged a broth, all
the ingredients of which had the same characteristic flavour.
Incriminating letters were found behind wainscots or at the
bottom of tubs; concocted papers were 'planted' on victims and
then searched for; accused persons turned informers, and vic-
timized others; the families of the arch-informers took up the
prosperous trade of papist-hunting, or made money by informing against their own relatives; confessions were recanted and
again sworn-to; both truth and honour were completely dissolved in this boiling mass. As every age has its favourite malady,
so it has its special sin; whether it be corrupt litigation, as in the
later middle ages, or blackmail and certain kinds of company-
promoting in modern times. During the Popish Plot an outlet
for pent-up evil was provided by informing. The imitators were
not built on the grand lines of their original; but they kept the
trade going nevertheless. Tonge's son, Simson Tonge, dabbled
in the profession, and obtained small sums from patrons who
induced him to swear that the original plot had been invented
by his father and Oates; but this enterprise became extremely
complicated when one of the parties turned traitor, and
stole important papers while his confederates were being
entertained to a fish dinner in the Savoy by M. Choqueux, who
appears to have exchanged pyrotechnics for plots;[2] so, too, the
family of Oates were proving that aptitude can be trained as
well as inherited, and soon they hoped to emulate the master
himself.[3] As Titus had his followers in Bedloe, Prance, Bolron,
and Dangerfield, so even the unfortunate Godfrey had an

[1] *Grey*, vii. 304–10.
[2] For Simson Tonge see his affidavit in *H.M.C. Rep.* xi, app., pt. ii. 246–50.
[3] For the Oates family see *infra*, 640.

imitator in a Protestant magistrate named John Arnold, who claimed to have been savagely attacked by Papists in Bell Yard, Fleet Street, on April 15, 1680.[1] When originality was at an end, the past was raked for supplies, which were heated up for immediate consumption; from the ashes there glowed again the Fire of London, the Gunpowder Plot, and the infamies of Mary, queen of Scots; while above the smoke of the pope-burnings towered the statue of queen Elizabeth, the sardonic emblem of outraged Protestantism.

But as the Plot worked itself out the squibs failed to explode. The assault on Arnold was construed as one more Jesuit attempt at murder, but a surfeited populace refused to be excited by it; Dangerfield was busy laying informations against prominent Catholics, but his inconsistencies were too great, even for that age; Shaftesbury, still working at his Irish Plot, announced that he was in danger of being assassinated, but even this possibility did not arouse the apprehension which he had expected. Oates was not yet a bishop, nor even a doctor of divinity of Oxford; worse still, his salary was reduced in July 1680 from £12 to £2 per week, and so he was obliged to combine his coaching of perjurers with the ferreting out of concealed Catholic estates. His decline had begun, a decline accentuated by acrimonious disputes with Tonge about the proprietorship of the original Plot. Most signal failure of all, when Shaftesbury procured the indictment of the duke of York and the duchess of Portsmouth as popish recusants, the judges in Westminster Hall, by collusion with the Court,[2] discharged the juries summoned to adjudicate on the Bills. Thus Charles had acted wisely in giving England one year of respite from parliamentary government in order that the excitement of the Plot might subside; but the embers were still red, and his fourth parliament was to prove as unfriendly as the third.

The meeting of parliament in October 1680 was preceded by complicated negotiations, due to the unique possibilities then confronting English diplomacy; for in the summer of 1680 England was in a position analogous to that of the earlier months of 1678, when there had been a chance of the formation of a

---

[1] For Arnold see J. Pollock, op. cit., Appendix D.
[2] *Baschet*, 146, July 1/11, 1680.

general European confederation, consisting of England, the Emperor, Spain, and the States General; and already the English alliance with Spain (June 1680), coupled with the feint of overtures to the other two powers, had served to give Charles's policy an anti-French complexion. But men were now distrustful of these appearances, and so there was a chance that, whether by bribery or persuasion, the Spanish envoy Ronquillo and his Dutch colleague van Beuning might induce the Commons to insist on Charles going the whole way, and entering into active measures with the continental allies prescribed for him. Of the foreign envoys who were deputed to guide the House of Commons into the right path Barrillon was faced with the greatest number of difficulties. Hitherto French money had been directed to securing the elimination of England from decisive influence in European politics. With much difficulty, and at great cost, this object had, to a large extent, been achieved; but Louis was now at peace; so Charles's neutrality had for the moment lost its value. Money might still be spent in setting every party in England by the ears; but what did that lead to? Louis had begun by bribing the king; he was now spending money in bribing parliament; the duke of York wanted money, so also did Monmouth; and as each party was subsidized against the other, everybody's terms went up. The money was there, but not even Barrillon was sure how it should be spent.

To what useful object could French money be put? In May 1680 the French representative suggested bribing the 'Presbyterians'; but this might benefit only the prince of Orange. Money spent in defeating the objects of Charles and James might in the end benefit them more; nevertheless, money could always be usefully employed in bribing Montagu, and some clerks of the secretaries of state.[1] In July Barrillon reported that, acting on instructions, he was supporting Monmouth's cabal;[2] but a month later he noted the order that he was not to maintain close connexion with the Protestant duke.[3] A few days before he had informed Louis that as the duke of York's party was the feeblest, it might be well to support it,[4] apparently on the principle of preserving the balance of power in the internal affairs

[1] *Baschet*, 145, May 24/June 3. [2] Ibid. 146, July 8/18.
[3] Ibid. 146, Sept. 27/Oct. 7. [4] Ibid. 146, Sept. 9/19.

of England;[1] in November, he thought it expedient that Monmouth should imagine that France was supporting him, so that he might not suspect Louis's real design of supporting the duke of York;[2] but this piece of deception would cost more money, as Montagu (who was already being paid as a spy) was acting in the interests of Monmouth, and would demand an extra subsidy when he knew that his principal was being cheated. Late in November 1680 Barrillon announced that his main object was to prevent the union of Charles with his country;[3] but in February of the following year he urged that it was Louis's interest to preserve the monarchy in England, and that the interests of Catholicism in England were bound up with the succession of the duke of York.[4] Such is a small selection from the voluminous correspondence with the help of which Louis formulated his schemes for England.

What really were Louis's intentions? It has been contended by historians that the neutrality which Louis enforced on England was the most brilliant of his many diplomatic achievements, and that throughout his relations with England the French king was directed by motives of foreign policy. There are difficulties in the way of both views. That Louis secured English neutrality is certain; but it is not so clear that he obtained substantial benefit therefrom, since his gains by the treaty of Nimeguen were ludicrously incommensurate with the objects which had induced him in 1672 to declare war, and most of his conquests after 1678 had to be surrendered at the peace of Ryswick. Moreover, by 1678 the English Navy was in a state of temporary decay, and certainly could not have interfered with the territorial *réunions* on which Louis embarked after 1681. Nor could Louis have feared the English Army, because in numbers it was but a small fraction of his own; nor could he have valued it as an ally, because English personal dislike of France was notorious. Louis made no secret of his belief in two things: that, so far as military strength was concerned, England might be ignored,[5] and that in

---

[1] *Baschet*, 146, Sept. 20/30.   [2] Ibid. 147, Nov. 18/28.
[3] Ibid. 147, Nov. 25/Dec. 5.   [4] Ibid. 148, Feb. 3/13, 1681.
[5] 'Quoiqu'il n'y ait plus rien à espérer de son [of Charles II] alliance, ni à craindre de son inimitié, néanmoins l'intérêt que j'ai à maintenir la royauté en Angleterre ne me permet pas d'abandonner ce prince [duke of York]

his engagements with him Charles II had played him false.[1] So far, therefore, as foreign policy was concerned, the considered opinion of Louis XIV was that, after 1678, English neutrality was not worth purchasing; and it is probable that he was right.

It has already been seen that, in negotiating the treaty of Dover, Louis was inspired not by economic interests, nor even by consistent motives of continental policy, but by righteous indignation and a desire to assist in the restoration of Catholicism in England.[2] There was a certain profuse sentimentality and hazy idealism in the character of Louis XIV, to which even high policy was sometimes subordinated; and though, by 1680, he had to admit that the enforcement of Catholicism would have to be abandoned, he was nevertheless very anxious that the persecution of Catholics should cease, that the Catholic Church in England should be preserved, and that the interests of the faith should be maintained by a strong Catholic monarchy.[3] He had lost his faith in Charles, but he had great faith in James, and consequently he was anxious that the duke should remain by his brother's side in order to counteract the vacillation of the monarch, and to provide a bulwark for monarchy and the Catholic religion. It was for these reasons, not in order to secure English neutrality, that the subsidy was renewed in March 1681.[4] Louis XIV's calculations were based on the assumptions that Charles was politically negligible as well as unreliable, and that James was the man from whom

dans l'extrémité où il se trouve.' Louis XIV to Barrillon, Jan. 26/Feb. 5, 1681, *Aff. Étr. (Angleterre)*, 142.

[1] 'Vous le savez que je dois être persuadé par une longue expérience que —je ne puis faire aucune fondement sur les traités que le roi d'Angleterre pourrait faire avec moi.' Louis XIV to Barrillon, Jan. 14/24, 1681, in *Aff. Étr. (Angleterre)*, 142.   [2] *Supra*, i. 336-7.

[3] In July 1679 Louis declared that his chief desire in regard to England was 'd'empêcher la ruine de la religion Catholique', *Aff. Étr. (Angleterre)*, 135, f. 40. In September of the same year he defined his object as 'la confirmation de la royauté et de la religion Catholique en Angleterre', ibid., f. 177.

[4] 'Je ne lui demande point d'autre reconnaissance des 500,000 écus que j'offre de lui faire payer chaque année que celle de se rétablir par la prorogation de son parlement dans la juste possession de l'autorité royale . . . de rappeler ensuite auprès de sa personne le duc de York, et j'aurais à lui demander pour mon intérêt, mais encore plus pour le sien propre et celui de sa couronne, de ne plus attirer la colère de Dieu par d'injustes persécutions des Catholiques.' Louis XIV to Barrillon, Jan. 14/24, 1681 in *Aff. Étr. (Angleterre)*, 142, f. 67.

salvation might yet come to England, assumptions which were
not challenged by Charles so long as he got the money.

Charles's fourth parliament commenced its first session on
October 21, 1680, when the king announced that the prorogations had been very useful to him as he had been enabled to form
an alliance with Spain. He pointed to the danger threatening
Tangier from the assaults of the Moors and the need of money
for its defence. A further examination of the Plot having been
recommended, Charles made a plea for unity among his subjects,
because 'all Europe have their eyes on this assembly'.[1] The first
act of the Commons was to bring Dangerfield to the bar in order
to hear his revelations; they then debated the proclamation[2]
forbidding petitions against the prorogation or dissolution of
parliament; they resolved also (Oct. 27) that it is, and ever has
been, the right of English subjects to petition the king for the
calling and sitting of parliaments, and that to represent such
petitioning as seditious was to betray the liberty of the subject.[3]
Francis Wythens (later known as knight and judge) was then
expelled the House for having promoted, during the recess, an
address to the king expressing abhorrence of the petitions. Two
names were thus introduced into political terminology—Petitioners and Abhorrers. After ordering their votes to be printed,
the Commons brought in a second Exclusion Bill,[4] which not
only debarred James from the succession, but declared him guilty
of high treason if he should exercise authority or return to England after November 5, 1680. This measure was read for the first
time on November 4, when Jenkins opposed it in a speech which
hinted at the nature of the support being invoked by the prerogative.[5] The Bill, he claimed, was contrary to natural justice, because it condemned without conviction and without calling the
injured party to his defence; it was contrary to the principles of
their religion, since it dispossessed a man of his right for no other
reason than that he differed in point of faith; still more, the
kings of England held their right from God alone, and no power
on earth could deprive them of it. To pass the Bill would be to
make the monarchy elective. Lastly, it was against their oath of

[1] *L.J.* xiii. 610–11.   [2] *Steele*, i. 3703, Dec. 12, 1679.   [3] *C.J.* ix. 640.
[4] For its terms see *H.M.C. Rep.* xi, app., pt. ii. 195–7.
[5] *Grey*, vii. 418–20.

allegiance; for by binding all persons to the king, his heirs, and successors, the oath included the duke as heir presumptive. Nor could there be a dispensation of such allegiance. The astute Jenkins did not scruple to insist on the dilemma which confronted the advocates of exclusion.

The second Exclusion Bill passed the Commons on November 11 and was taken to the Lords by lord Russell, accompanied by a procession composed of members of parliament, with the lord mayor and aldermen of the city of London. Barrillon noted how dangerous for the monarchy was this union of the Commons with the City.[1] The House next turned to the question of Tangier. That it might fall into French hands was admitted; but there were two difficulties confronting the allocation of a vote for its defence—the money might be embezzled; and, even more, Tangier garrison was a nest of papists. Sir William Jones summed up the general feeling when he said: 'Tangier is a place of great moment, but I take the preservation of religion to be far greater.'[2] So the upshot of this debate was a resolution to present an address to the king representing the dangerous state of the kingdom. Meanwhile, the real struggle had been transferred to the Lords, where Essex and Shaftesbury (Nov. 15) spoke vehemently for the Exclusion Bill; and the debate was prolonged late into the night, the king and members of the Commons attending as spectators. For seven hours a forensic duel was maintained between Shaftesbury and Halifax, the latter answering his opponents sixteen times, and eventually winning the day by his persistence and eloquence. In these speeches he cited the duke of York's credit in Ireland and with the Fleet; he emphasized the danger of civil war and the efficacy of limitations; nor did he hesitate to condemn the conduct of Monmouth, who was present with his supporters.[3] As the night wore on, the tension became more extreme; when at last it was clear that Halifax had won over the waverers, several peers drew their swords, while others clustered round the orator to preserve him from violence. The Lords rejected the Bill by 63 to 30.[4]

---

[1] *Baschet*, 147, Nov. 15/25.   [2] *Grey*, viii. 5, Nov. 17, 1680.
[3] *Halifax*, i. 246–8.
[4] *Parl. Hist.* iv. 1215. The protest against its rejection was signed by 25 peers, including Monmouth, Shaftesbury, Sunderland, and Essex.

This was followed by an anti-climax in the Commons, when Hotham suggested that, since their Bill was rejected, they had no means of justifying themselves but by printing Coleman's letters.[1] This they agreed to do; they also adopted Montagu's motion for an address to the king advising the removal of Halifax from the royal counsels, and that he be declared an enemy of the king and kingdom.[2] Articles of impeachment were then read against Edward Seymour, treasurer of the Navy, which alleged that, of the £584,978 appropriated for the building of thirty ships, he had lent £90,000 for the continuance of the Army, after the forces ought by law to have been disbanded.[3] The conduct of Scroggs next engaged their attention. His sins were many; he had disparaged the evidence of Oates in the trial of sir George Wakeman; he had discharged the Middlesex grand jury when the duke of York was presented as a papist; against such misdeeds there could be no remedy, said Sacheverell, so long as judges were *durante bene placito*. The impeachment of lord chief justice North was next voted on the ground that he had advised the proclamation against tumultuous petitioning.[4] Having failed in their main object, the Commons were eagerly looking about for a victim; this they found in the aged lord Stafford, one of the five popish lords in the Tower; so on November 10 they resolved to commence with him. At the trial, which began in Westminster Hall on November 30, Oates, Dugdale, and Turberville swore that he had procured a commission from the pope, and had tried to arrange the murder of the king. On this evidence the Commons secured a conviction, and their helpless victim was executed. This was the only successful impeachment by the Commons in the reign of Charles.

In the few remaining weeks of its existence this parliament succeeded in passing resolutions which in many respects anticipated the settlement achieved after the Revolution. Late in November the Lords discussed 'heads' of Bills for securing the Protestant religion, including the proposals that, if the duke came to the throne, he should have no veto, and that he should have the legal capacity only of a minor; another proposal was that the king's marriage should be dissolved, and that he should be married

---

[1] *Grey*, viii. 21, Nov. 17, 1680.   [2] *C.J.* ix. 655, Nov. 17, 1680.
[3] Ibid. ix, 658–9, Nov. 20.   [4] Ibid. ix, 662, Nov. 24.

to a Protestant.[1] They considered also a Protestant Association
Bill, whereby all bishops, judges, officials and members of parliament were to be formed into an association which was to take
up arms on the death of the king, and remain armed until parliament met.[2] On November 23 they resolved on these general
axioms: (1) no forces to be raised without parliamentary consent;
(2) the proviso exempting the duke from the Disabling Act of
1678 to be repealed; and (3) the royal veto and the principles of
appointment to spiritual and civil offices to be regulated for the
contingency of a Catholic succession. Herein were the rough
materials from which the Lords, under the guidance of Halifax,
hoped to enforce limitations as the alternative to exclusion.[3]

The Commons went farther. They discussed legislation for
these objects: to secure frequent parliaments; that judges should
hold office only *quamdiu se bene gesserint*, and that the illegal exaction of money from the subject should be high treason.[4] They
proposed to include in the Bill for regulating the trial of peers[5]
a clause abolishing the lords' privileges under the statute *De
scandalis magnatum*, and another clause whereby impeachments
should have statutory continuance after the prorogation or
dissolution of parliament;[6] and they resolved that no member
should accept any office or place of profit under the crown without the consent of the House.[7] On November 27 the Commons
presented a long address hinting at supplies for Tangier as the
price of royal consent to exclusion;[8] this the king rejected.[9] On
January 7, 1681, they resolved that no further supply should be
granted until the Exclusion Bill was passed; that Halifax had given
pernicious counsels, and was a promoter of popery; and that
whoever should lend money on the security of the king's hereditary revenue would have to answer for it to parliament.[10] Realizing that their time was short, the Lower House hurriedly passed
resolutions (Jan. 10, 1681) that whoever should advise His

---

[1] *H.M.C. Rep.* xi, pt. ii. 209–10.   [2] Ibid. 210–11.
[3] *L.J.* xiii. 684. Repeal of the proviso exempting James and provision
for the meeting of parliament on the king's death were embodied in the
Protestant Security Bill. *H.M.C. Rep.* xi, pt. ii. 220–2.
[4] *C.J.* ix. 682, Dec. 17.   [5] *H.M.C. Rep.* xi, app., pt. ii. 127 and 157.
[6] *Baschet*, 147, Dec. 20/30.   [7] *C.J.* ix, 695, Dec. 30.
[8] Ibid. ix. 665–6.   [9] Ibid. ix. 676, Dec. 15.
[10] Ibid. ix. 702.

Majesty to prorogue the existing parliament in order to prevent the passage of an Exclusion Bill was a betrayer of the king, a promoter of the French interest, and a pensioner of France; that Monmouth had been removed from office by the influence of the duke of York, and that the presentation of the Protestant Dissenters on the penal laws was grievous to the subject and an encouragement of popery. There was an anti-climax in the final resolution—that the Great Fire of London was the work of Papists.[1] In the midst of these momentous proceedings, the ominous tap was heard at the door and parliament was prorogued to January 20, but dissolved[2] on January 18, leaving 22 Bills depending and 8 ordered to be brought in.

3. EXCLUSION AND PARTY POLITICS: THE OXFORD PARLIAMENT, FEBRUARY–MARCH 1681

By dissolving parliament Charles was taking a grave risk, but at least the air was cleared. Halifax, who had again won the favour of the Court by his victory over exclusion, was alienated by the dissolution, mainly because it shelved the Lords' schemes for limitations as the only feasible alternative to exclusion; this caused him again to retire to Rufford. At the same time the 'exclusionist juncto', Sunderland, Essex, and Temple, were dismissed from the privy council, and Sunderland's secretaryship was given to lord Conway. Of these men, Temple went into final retirement at Sheen; Essex, whose political evolution had been unusually rapid, changed from a trusted minister of Charles and friend of the Orange interest to a keen opponent of the Court and a supporter of Monmouth; Sunderland, whose disgrace was caused as much by his tactless overtures to the prince of Orange as by his support of exclusion, devoted himself, with the help of Barrillon and the duchess of Portsmouth, to the recovery of office and influence. After this shaking out, there remained among the king's advisers only the duke of York (then in Scotland, talking of civil war); sir Leoline Jenkins, secretary of state, a firm believer in divine hereditary right; and Lawrence Hyde, second son of the chancellor, the chief ministerial supporter of legitimacy.

Meanwhile a birth has to be recorded—that of the modern party system. Its gestation was a long one, and the travail that

[1] *C.J.* ix. 703–4. [2] *Steele*, i. 3724.

ensued almost rent the nation in sunder. Many ancestors contributed to the lusty vigour of this new arrival in national life. There were men who, by family tradition or sentiment, had long been accustomed to range themselves with the Court; temperamental loyalists they might be called, such as Hyde, Seymour, Ormonde, Jenkins, lords Nottingham and North.[1] In different degrees these men preferred a bad king to a good opposition; they were churchmen to whom kingship was an essential part of religion; but only two of them, Ormonde and Seymour, can be considered absolutely disinterested in their devotion to the prerogative. Opposed to them were those who, while divided in allegiance between prince of Orange and duke of Monmouth, were united in one central doctrine, namely, the sovereignty of parliament, to be guaranteed by its frequent and regular summons, by its complete control of taxation, and by its freedom from the influence of the Court. This party believed (rightly) that James Stuart would not rule as a parliamentary sovereign; that, in alliance with France, he would try to introduce popery and absolutism. Rather than have such a bad king, they would change the succession altogether, and choose either the prince of Orange, the enemy of popery and France and therefore (by implication) likely to rule constitutionally, or the duke of Monmouth, whose illegitimacy was still more likely to ensure his subservience to parliament. Intermediate between these extremes were the Trimmers, represented by Halifax, Temple, and sir Thomas Littleton, who, while devoted to liberty and constitutionalism in the abstract, were prepared to tolerate a certain amount of imperfection in kings as in everything else:

Our government is like our climate. There are winds which are sometimes loud and unquiet, and yet, with all the troubles they give us, we owe a great part of our health to them; they clear the air, which else would be like a standing pool. There may be fresh gales of asserted liberty without turning into such storms or hurricanes as that the State should run any hazard of being cast away by them. . . . The cases themselves will bring the remedies along with them, and he is not afraid to allow that, in order to its preservation, there is a hidden power in government which would be lost if it was defined,

---

[1] For a good analysis of parties at this time see K. Feiling, *History of the Tory Party*, 187 sqq.

a certain mystery by virtue of which a nation may at some critical times be secured from ruin.[1]

The views of Halifax did not find their fullest expression until they were given volume and force in the torrential prose of Burke; moreover, the term Trimmer savoured of compromise and so was not a good label. Baptism ensured a more assertive individuality for each of the two extremes. Both 'loyalist' and 'yorkist' seemed too generous for use by opponents of the Court party; 'tantivy' served for a time to suggest riding post-haste to Rome; but eventually 'tory' met the case, because, as it meant Irish robber and outlaw, it emphasized the duke of York's alleged association with the wild Irish. As Ireland provided the name for one party, so Scotland supplied that of the other, for the reason perhaps that English civilization did not appear to provide anything suggestive of that degree of contumely which each party stigmatized in the other. At first, the opponents of the Court may have adopted for themselves the name 'Country Party' in a mood of deliberate self-depreciation, in the same way as the 'Sea Beggars' and the 'Old Contemptibles' took pride in epithets applied to them; for the term 'Country', as contrasted with 'Court', implied a certain ostracism or social disability, similar to that which prompted the contemporary use, in France, of the word *hobereaux* for those nobles who were not received at Versailles. But this may have been too subtle; 'fanatic' was a useful substitute; then 'petitioner', and finally 'whig', or Scottish outlaw and Covenanter, a type supposed in England to be as infamous as the Irish tory, and presumed to be as uniformly sanctimonious and cantankerous as his Celtic opponent was said to be irresponsible and treacherous. So the field was left clear for the two short terms of abuse, whig and tory; and into these moulds were poured the lava-like prejudices and passions which proceeded from the Exclusion controversy and the Popish Plot. It was not in the tepid amenities of academic debate, but in the vituperation of the street, the coffee-house, and the scaffold that the distinction of whig and tory took hold on the minds of Englishmen.

The distinction, as it emerged, pervaded almost the whole field of national life, and was as potent an inspiration for the frivolous

[1] *Character of a Trimmer* in *Halifax*, ii. 297.

as for the serious. It can be traced in oaths—that of the tories being 'God Dammee',[1] while that of the whigs (following Oates) was 'So help me *Goad*';[2] in colours, red ribbons for the duke of York and blue for Monmouth;[3] in drinks, coffee for many whigs, and beer for all tories, a preference which explains the antithesis between 'sotting' and 'plotting'.[4] Each party had its favourite English sovereign; for the tories were devoted to the cult of Charles I, while the whigs found their ideal in queen Elizabeth.[5] Each attributed to the other a definite origin. The tories, from their red ribbons, were mothered on the Scarlet Woman;[6] while the whigs must obviously be descended from the first of critics, the Devil; or directly from his descendant, Titus Oates; or they had been engendered from the spread of debauchery; or the increase of luxury, as evidenced from the fact that merchants' wives now dressed like noble-women, and every servant-maid had her silk gown and holland sleeves; or from the practice of travelling to such republican places as Amsterdam and Venice; or even from the increase of free schools, where boys remained until they were 16 or 17, and were then fit only for some idle trade or the university, where they were taught to preach and wrangle.[7] These distinctions were at least such as the most unlettered could understand.

There was the same uncouth vigour in descriptions of each other. The tory was thus described:

A Tory is a monster with an English face, a French heart and an Irish conscience. A creature of a large forehead, prodigious mouth, supple hams and no brains. They are a sort of wild boars, that would

---

[1] In Oct. 1680 sir Robert Carr, in the course of remarks to the effect that there was no Popish Plot but a Presbyterian Plot, was heard to use the words 'God Dammee'. He was sent to the Tower. *Grey*, vii. 385. 'Fannees' and 'God Dammees' were respectively Fanatics (whigs) and tories.

[2] *Character of an Ignoramus Doctor* in *Bodley, Wood*, 417.

[3] Luttrell, *Brief Historical Relation* (ed. 1857), i. 111, July 1681.

[4]   And better it is to be honestly sotting
       Than live to be hanged for caballing and plotting.
                          The Pot Companions in *Bodley, Wood*, 417.

[5] e.g. *Honour and carriage of our English parliaments in the reign of Queen Elizabeth* (1681) in *Bodley, Ashmole*, 730.

[6] *Character of a Tory* in *Somers Tracts* (1750), pt. ii, vol. iii. 282.

[7] *Dialogue of a statesman and a countryman* (1681), in *Bodley, Ashmole*, 730.

root out the constitution . . . that with dark lanthorn policies would at once blow up the two bulwarks of our freedom, Parliaments and Juries; making the first only a Parliament of Paris, and the latter but mere tools to echo back the pleasure of the judge. They are so certain that monarchy is *jure divino*, that they look upon all people living under Aristocracys or Democracys to be in a state of damnation; and fancy that the Grand Seignor, the Czar of Muscovy and the French King dropt down from Heaven with crowns on their heads, and that all their subjects were born with saddles on their backs.[1]

Brainlessness and effusiveness were the two accusations most commonly made against the tories; but the whigs were as easily caricatured, because of their associates; whether these were Geneva or Salamanca Doctors, *ignoramus* juries, lay preachers, or Scottish Covenanters. They were all, of course, 'Presbyterians'; the most common accusation against them was that they reincarnated the men of 1641,[2] and their insistence on abstract principle brought upon them the accusation of hypocrisy. 'These Geneva Whigs', noted a pamphleteer,[3] 'are demure, conscientious, prick-eared vermin.' Chief justice Jeffreys was voicing the same opinion when he referred in court to 'snivelling saints', with their cropped hair and demure looks.[4] They were really Jesuits disguised in Scotch bonnets.[5] Under the mask of scruple the whig was changing 1681 to 1649:

His principles are like chaos, a gallimofry[6] of negatives. He talks of nothing but new light and prophecy, spiritual incomes, indwellings, emanations, manifestations, sealings . . . to which also the zealous twang of his nose adds no small efficacy. He treads the antipodes to everything commanded, and for no other reason but because commanded. . . . This little horn takes a mouth to himself, and his language is Overturn, Overturn. His prayer is a rhapsody of holy hickops, sanctified barkings, illuminated goggles, sighs, sobs, yexes, gasps and groans. He prays for the King, but with more

---

[1] *Character of a Tory* in *Somers Tracts*, pt. ii, vol. iii. 282.

[2] Cf. the reprint in 1681 of John Birkenhead's sarcastic *Assembly Man* (first published in 1647).

[3] *Letter from a friend in London to another at Salamanca*, in *Bodley*, G. Pamph., 1678.

[4] *An exact account of the trial between sir W. Pritchard and T. Papillon* (1689), 29.

[5] *The Loyal Litany* (1681) in *Bodley, Wood*, 417.

[6] i.e. hotch-potch.

distinctions and mental reservations than an honest man would have in taking the covenant.[1]

There was one respect, however, in which the pre-eminence of the whigs could not be challenged—they had the best horses, and they inaugurated the close connexion between English politics and the turf. The tories, it is true, could boast the university of Oxford as their stronghold; but the whigs held an even more important national fortress—Newmarket; and even Charles failed to establish a tory racecourse at Winchester.

This last fact helps to support the view that the whigs were not the socially-ineligible fanatics caricatured by their opponents, since they included a considerable proportion of both the landed nobility and the landed gentry, as well as many city merchants and rich Dissenters. From these constituent elements can be deduced two of their fundamental principles—sanctity of private property and religious toleration. They were by no means a democratic body, and it is significant that, in his second *Treatise of Civil Government*, Locke insisted on his axiom that men enter into society in order to preserve their property, and that the main object of legislation is to provide 'guards and fences' to that property.[2] What gave real direction to whig doctrine was its concerted effort to adjust a fact to a maxim; the maxim was, 'The king can do no wrong'; and the fact, king Charles II was doing a great deal of wrong. The first was an abstraction; the second a certainty; they were to be harmonized by depriving the king of the opportunity of wrongdoing, and making his legislative innocence the standard in reference to which the guilt of his servants might be judged. From this flowed most of their distinctive doctrines; such as that the judicial bench should be independent of the Court; that the military forces should be parliamentary; that ministerial responsibility should be enforced by an unrestrained right to use the weapon of impeachment; that parliament should have the right to debate and criticize the king's speeches; and that placemen should be excluded from the House of Commons. They insisted on the sanctity of parliamentary privilege and tradition; and they were among the earliest exponents of a reformed franchise; but, after the

[1] *Character of a Protestant Jesuit* in Bodley, *Ashmole*, G. 12.
[2] Locke, *Of Civil Government*, ii, ch. xix.

Revolution, when they became strongly entrenched, this last ceased to be one of their distinctive doctrines. Consistently with the fiction of the king's absolute innocence, they would have taken from him two of his personal responsibilities—the right to choose his consort and the right to direct his foreign policy. Lastly, the contract theory as enunciated in the Bill of Rights and expounded by Locke gave a semi-philosophic element to whiggery; and so, by the time of the Revolution, this party might make some claim to both enlightenment and political morality.

It is easy, however, to read too much into the distinction of whig and tory as it was known during the Exclusion controversy. Provincialism still counted for much in English life;[1] parties were less clearly defined than personalities; politics were local rather than national, and a man might vote at the dictation of his landlord or militia officer; or the politics of a borough might reflect not a conflict of principle, but a contest among the neighbouring gentry, or even a feud between different trades. The strategy of the polling-booth was subtle, but it was not always the strategy of men fighting for a great cause.[2] Nevertheless, in the years 1678–81, there was one dominant influence which, for the time, made politics national. This was fear. It was the panic fear engendered by the Popish Plot which compelled Englishmen to take sides, and to concern themselves actively with matters of state hitherto beyond their ken; hence it was the simple choice of exclusion or a popish successor that crystallized amorphous masses of prejudice, instinct, and misgiving into the clear-cut forms of political party. The audacity of Titus Oates and the driving force of Shaftesbury set a pace which opponents could not follow; nor for many years afterwards could the tories boast a set of political doctrines comparable with those professed by the whigs.

To this extent the whigs might claim to be the party of progress, but this word was rarely used in the seventeenth century, and its connotation is distinctively modern. Both parties appealed to the past. The whigs were the heirs not only of the Puritan revolution, but of the accumulated labours of those scholars, jurists, and antiquaries who, earlier in the century, had

[1] For a good account of this see K. Feiling, *History of the Tory Party*, 14–18.
[2] For this see *supra*, 474–8.

discerned in the mists of remotest medievalism the majestic lines of a constitution wherein common law and civil right were supreme. It is true that these researchers committed (in perfect good faith) many mistakes of interpretation, and that the monument which they dedicated to the achievements of the past was little more than a record of their own aspirations; but nevertheless, since no tory was learned enough to expose misconceptions about the *Mirror of Justices*, or the *Statutum de tallagio non concedendo*, or Alfred's common-law judges, the whigs were left in undisturbed possession of their magnificent pedigree. On their side the tories could point to precedent even more hoary, because from the Old Testament they deduced a doctrine of divine and indefeasible hereditary right, whereby disobedience was counted for sin, and criticism for blasphemy. To the tory, therefore, government was both absolute and paternal, its unvarying principles expounded in the careers of biblical potentates and in the pages of Filmer's *Patriarcha*.[1] The unqualified submission entailed by these principles was not only a Christian duty, but was something which satisfied that natural instinct whereby men subordinate their wills to some great external force or personality, and at least this instinct is less artificial than the hypothesis of the social contract on which whig philosophy came to be based. But here, for a time, religion had to give way to philosophy; for it was an age of research into the forces of nature, and inevitably therefore the Old Testament lost some of its authority as a guide to statecraft; nor could divine right be satisfactorily adjusted to the newer creeds which rejected revelation for reason. In consequence, the title-deeds of toryism were called in question. That the creed survived at all may have been due to the warm blood of human sentiment with which it was permeated; it was with this that Bolingbroke, Burke, and Disraeli afterwards restored and recreated the party.

Such was the state of parties in January 1681 when the danger threatening the monarchy and the succession by the dissolution of parliament may have roused Charles from the lethargy

---

[1] Sir Robert Filmer died in 1653 and his manuscript of the *Patriarcha* was printed by the tories in 1680, and a second edition in 1685. It was considered by many as the classic English exposition of the theory of divine hereditary right. For this see J. N. Figgis, *The theory of the divine right of kings*.

into which he had fallen a few months before.[1] Now that he was rid of both Halifax and Sunderland, he was less likely to be deterred by the one or cheated by the other; and in Hyde and Jenkins he had subordinates who, if not eminent, were at least faithful and serviceable. He had survived a plot in which his consort and brother were accused of the design of murdering him; his natural son, Monmouth, was a tool in the hands of experienced rebels; his nephew, the prince of Orange, was displaying a public and occasionally tactless interest in English affairs;[2] his House of Commons was demanding exclusion, and his Lords rigid limitations of the power of his successor; everywhere there were rumours of the appeal to force and civil war. It was not surprising, therefore, that Charles turned again to France, as he was pressed to do by the duke of York, who sent John Churchill from Edinburgh with the advice that Charles should enter into such an engagement with Louis as would enable him to dispense with parliament, and thereafter engage in 'resolute counsels'. Only Hyde and the duke were in the secret of the verbal treaty of March 1681, whereby Charles undertook to free himself from the slender shackles of the Anglo-Spanish treaty of June 1680, and take measures to counter-act commitments to parliament that might be inconsistent with the obligations which he was assuming by the treaty. Louis, in return, promised to preserve European peace, and to pay Charles two million crowns for the first year, and 500,000 crowns for each of the succeeding years.[3] These were generous terms; as in the secret treaty of Dover, the conditions imposed on Charles were vague, and Louis appears to have desired not so much English neutrality,[4] as the maintenance of friendly rela-

---

[1] *Baschet*, 147, Nov. 1/11, 1680.

[2] The evidence for this is in the *Diary of Henry Sidney* (ed. R. W. Blencowe), *passim*. There is reason to believe that William, in spite of his friendly correspondence with James, approved of the exclusion project. This is asserted for a fact by lord Guilford, *Add. MS.* 32520, ff. 204–6. The Italian envoy Rizzini states that, during his visit to England in the autumn of 1681, William was reproved by Charles for encouraging the efforts to supplant James. (Campana de Cavalli, *Les derniers Stuarts*, i. 378.)

[3] *Baschet*, 148, Feb. 3/13, 1681; March 4/14, March 7/17, and March 24/April 3.

[4] *Supra*, 600–1. 'Quant aux stipulations réciproques je vous ai déjà dit qu'il

tions with the Stuarts and the eventual succession of James. It is significant that Hyde referred to the subsidy as a gratuitous payment.[1]

According to Barrillon, Hyde had advised the dissolution of the fourth parliament, and now recommended that the fifth should be summoned to Oxford,[2] where the Commons, free from the influence of the London mob, might prove more conciliatory than their predecessors. From the point of view of the Court, therefore, the Oxford Parliament was a gamble, and from the point of view of Charles (already practically assured of the subsidy) it was little more than a comedy. But it was taken very seriously by the whigs, and a whole party organization was exercised at the elections by Shaftesbury,[3] whose efforts nevertheless failed to maintain the whig majority of the previous parliament.[4] The alternatives were exclusion or limitations. The latter, known as 'the expedient', had been formulated by Halifax, possibly at the suggestion of Littleton;[5] it had the approval of the king,[6] and contained these provisions: (1) banishment of the duke during his lifetime; (2) on the death of Charles, the princess of Orange was to be regent, and, failing her or her issue, the princess Anne; (3) if the duke of York had a son educated a Protestant, then the princess should have the regency only during the child's minority; (4) the regent was to nominate members of the privy council with parliamentary approval; and (5) the regent was to govern in the name of James, but it was to be a capital offence for any one to take up arms on behalf of James.[7] These conditions were less stringent than the limitations previously proposed, and their acceptance would have destroyed the party of Shaftesbury and Monmouth; they show how far Charles was prepared to go in order to secure peace.

n'était pas nécessaire de rien signer et je suis bien persuadé que le roi d'Angleterre étant dans une alliance secrète avec moi, il ne fera rien contre mon intérêt.' Louis XIV to Barrillon, March 4/14 in *Aff. Étr.* (*Angleterre*), f. 227. This statement should be compared with Louis's earlier statement that he could not rely on Charles's promises, *supra*, 601.

[1] *Baschet*, 148, March 24/April 3.   [2] Ibid. 148, Jan. 27/Feb. 6.
[3] For this see E. Lipson, *Elections to the Exclusion Parliament* in *E.H.R.* xxviii.
[4] *Baschet*, 148, Feb. 10/20.   [5] *Halifax*, i. 286.
[6] Hyde to the prince of Orange, March 29, 1681, in *Prinsterer*, v. 490.
[7] *Add. MS.* 38847, f. 83.

The alternative to this was Shaftesbury's plan, that is, exclusion, together with (1) a recognition of the right of the people to have annual parliaments 'for the despatch of their important affairs', and (2) restoration of the liberty enjoyed until the last forty years of being free from guards and mercenary soldiers.[1]

The arrangements testified to the great things expected of this, Charles's last parliament. Lord Oxford's regiment was placed on the road from London to be ready for emergencies, and many members came armed. Elaborate provisions were made by the vice-chancellor of the university. All the younger students were required to go down, but their time of absence was to be counted for degrees; accommodation was procured for the court in Christ Church, Merton, and Corpus Christi; and all other available places were to be at the disposal of parliament. Each college housed those legislators who were old members, as had been done when parliament met at Oxford during the Great Plague. Convocation House was assigned for the deliberations of the Commons; the Geometry School (now occupied by the Bodleian) for the Lords. The king's arrival on Monday, March 14, was marked by a demonstration, people in the streets shouting into the royal coach: 'Let the King live and the Devil hang the roundheads'; there was such 'flinging about' and throwing of hats that several limbs were broken, and tables of reception were set out in the streets at which all who passed were forced to drink a health to Charles on their knees.[2] On Tuesday Charles was hailed in a speech by the Public Orator, and from the vice-chancellor he received one more bible for his collection.

Proceedings commenced on Monday, March 21, when the king in a speech, probably penned by Halifax, adjured the Commons not to lay such weight on any one expedient against popery as to determine that all others were ineffectual; without the safety and dignity of monarchy, he said, neither religion nor property was safe; he would therefore be willing to receive favourably any expedient for preserving the administration in Protestant hands, in the event of a popish successor coming to

---

[1] These were drawn up as instructions by the electorates for their representatives. B. Martyn and Dr. Kipps, *Life of the first earl of Shaftesbury*, ed. E. Wingrave Cooke, ii. 268.   [2] *Wood*, ii. 525 sqq.

the throne.[1] But this, the last formal exposition of the older prerogative, was made to an assembly the majority of which had already made up its mind. The Commons began by resolving to print their votes and proceedings; they then debated the miscarriage of the Bill to repeal the Elizabethan statute[2] which had passed both Houses in the preceding parliament. It was next resolved to impeach Fitzharris of high treason. Edward Fitzharris was one of the Irish informers employed by the Court against the whigs; and the Commons were convinced that, in an impeachment managed by themselves, some damaging disclosures would be made. Secretary Jenkins refused to carry this impeachment to the Lords, but after an angry debate he was obliged to comply.[3]

Not till Saturday, March 26, did the Commons debate the vital point—exclusion or a regency. Historical precedents were quoted in favour of the latter; but against these it was argued that the person of the king could not be divided from his power, and that, moreover, regency was never heard of except where the prince was a minor or a lunatic, when it had generally proved to be an unfortunate device. Sir Francis Winnington pointed out the inconsistency of making a man king and denying him the exercise of sovereignty; sir T. Meres reminded the House that their business was religion, and that something must be done for the people, to quieten their fears of popery.[4] The sense of the House was definitely against a regency, and it was then resolved to bring in the Bill excluding James and all popish successors from inheriting the imperial crowns of England and Ireland.[5] At this point a message was received from the Lords that they refused to accept the impeachment of Fitzharris, on the ground that they were not required to proceed on any one not a member of their own body. A minority in the Lords, led by Shaftesbury, had protested against this refusal, for the reason that an impeachment is at the suit of the people, and that there-

[1] L.J. xiii. 745-6.
[2] For this see supra, 457. The Elizabethan statute was 35 Eliz., cap. i; the Bill of repeal was sent up to the Lords on Nov. 26, 1680. C.J. ix. 664. It passed the Lords, but was not tendered to His Majesty for his assent. C.J. ix. 708.
[3] Parl. Hist. iv. 1314.
[4] Ibid. iv. 1326-8.
[5] C.J. ix. 711, March 26.

fore the Lords ought to entertain it;[1] but meanwhile, intimation of the Lords' decision produced consternation in the Lower House, which contrasted this denial with the Lords' willingness to take up the cause of Skinner in his original plea against the East India Company. Once more the Commons had to admit that they were in the dark. 'There is something in this more than ordinary,' said sir Robert Howard; to Maynard, it seemed that the action of the Lords had made them no parliament; sir T. Player interpreted the Lords' conduct as confirmation of the plot to murder the king. The Commons at last brought a momentous day to a close by resolving that it is the undoubted right of the Commons to impeach before the Lords any peer or commoner for treason, or any other crime; and that the Lords' denial of this principle in the case of Fitzharris was a violation of the constitution of parliaments and an obstruction to the further discovery of the Plot. They resolved also that for any inferior court to proceed against Fitzharris was a breach of the privilege of parliament.[2]

On the same day as these resolutions were passed in the Convocation House a remarkable scene occurred in the Geometry School, where the king was present while the Lords were taking their places. By the aid of the marquis of Worcester, Shaftesbury passed to Charles a paper whereon was the proposal that, in order to guarantee the Protestant succession, the duke of Monmouth should at once be declared successor. There then followed a conversation between the two men, overheard by some of the peers, including Monmouth. Charles objected that the proposal was contrary to law and justice; Shaftesbury replied: 'If you are restrained only by law and justice, rely on us and leave us to act. We will make laws which will give legality to a measure so necessary for the quiet of the nation.' It was a tempting offer, and was made on behalf of a son whom Charles loved against the interests of a brother whom he disliked. But the bait was refused:

'Let there be no delusion,' said the king; 'I will not yield, nor will I be bullied. Men usually become more timid as they become older; it is the opposite with me, and for what may remain of my life I am determined that nothing will tarnish my reputation. I have law

---

[1] *L.J.* xiii. 755, March 26, 1678.　　　　[2] *C.J.* ix. 711.

and reason and all right-thinking men on my side; I have the Church'—(here Charles pointed to the bishops)—'and nothing will ever separate us.'

In these words was the doom of Shaftesbury's cause.[1]

Charles may have derived a certain amount of amusement from the proceedings of his last parliament. On March 22, the day after its session commenced, he had definitely concluded his verbal treaty with Barrillon; and as the Commons were resolved on exclusion, it remained only to dissolve parliament. On Monday, March 28, the Commons read their Exclusion Bill, against which Jenkins repeated his old arguments, with the explicit addition: 'We ought to pay obedience to our governors, whether good or bad, be they ever so faulty or criminal.'[2] His speech passed without notice; his motion for rejection of the Bill did not even find a seconder, and his doctrines sounded out of place in the midst of allusions to *lex terrae* and *judicium parium suorum*. It was while Magna Carta was being cited in support of their impeachment of Fitzharris that the Commons were startled to hear the knocking of Black Rod on the door; this time they were not prorogued, but dissolved. 'It is His Majesty's royal pleasure and will that this parliament be dissolved; and this parliament is dissolved,' such was the formula in which the chancellor announced the sequence of cause and effect. Round them were tennis courts and college gardens on which the Commons might have reunited themselves by an oath more solemn than any which they had yet sworn; but they dispersed: some to London, others to the country, and many to the horse-races at Burford.

---

[1] *Baschet*, 148, March 28/April 7. The dispatch in full is printed in Christie's *Shaftesbury*, ii. cxvi–cxvii.

[2] *Parl. Hist.* iv. 1338.

CHARLES, who had so long parried checkmate, could now deal
leisurely with his pieces, and could select from a variety of
alternatives the best method of attack on the disordered forces
of Shaftesbury and the whigs. He could secure the support of
the church by harrying Dissenters; he could win over the nation
by persecuting Papists; he might release Danby from the Tower
and restore the policy of Anglicanism and economy, or leave his
ex-minister in custody and practise these virtues with the help
of Hyde, Seymour, and Jenkins. Or he might choose to be guided
by Halifax, and complete the discomfiture of the exclusionists
by conciliating the Dissenters and the moderate whigs. A more
daring plan was to be guided by the Duke of York and secure
obedience and uniformity by exile and the gibbet. Of two things
Charles was assured—the subservience of the judicial bench and
a popular reaction in favour of the crown.[1]

Foreign affairs demanded immediate attention; for Louis was
now provoking European opinion by his enforcement of pre-
tensions on neighbours unable to retaliate. In the midst of
Louis's *réunions* Charles had to maintain some degree of consistency between his public alliance with Spain and his secret
agreement with France; for his subsidized 'neutrality' had now to
withstand the scrutiny not of his parliament, but of his nephew.
William realized that he had shown his hand too clearly in his
dealings with the exclusionists; but he had sufficient confidence
in his influence to think that he might yet obtain active English
support against France. Accordingly, the old expedient of a
personal visit was revived and, with the consent of Charles, he
came to England late in July 1681, and at Windsor had a long
interview with the king in the presence of Halifax (again restored
to favour), with Hyde and the two secretaries, Jenkins and Conway. At this conclave the prince urged the intervention of
England in order to save Flanders; he talked of the advisability

---

[1] For example, a large number of London apprentices offered to serve
the king wherever he pleased and at their own expense. *Baschet*, 149,
Aug. 11/21, 1681.

of summoning parliament, and hinted that if Charles preserved an ambiguous attitude, the States General might send their ships into the Thames in order to unite with the English people in the demand that Charles should come into line with the Dutch. The allusion was not a tactful one; but the king, who preserved his patience, contented himself with reminding the prince that the recall of parliament involved the revival of exclusion or limitation projects. Of these things William expressed his disapproval; and when asked to suggest an alternative, he requested permission to confer with his friends in London. There he consulted with lord Russell and other exclusionists, and his acceptance of an invitation to attend a public dinner given by the lord mayor and aldermen caused Charles to recall him to Windsor.[1]

But William did not go away empty-handed, for he added to the number of his English correspondents, and restored his amicable relations with Halifax; moreover, he had obtained some promises from a king for whom it was now second nature to make apparent concessions in order to gain time. Charles, it is true, would not actively assist his Spanish ally until France declared war; but he had promised William that, in the event of Flanders being invaded, he would summon a parliament and break with France; he promised also to join with the Dutch in a remonstrance against the aggressions of Louis.[2] In the verbal treaty the French king had undertaken in a general way that he would not disturb European peace; but when, in September, he took over Strasburg and Casale, it was apparent that he did not interpret this condition strictly, and it seemed inevitable that the English king would have to implement his public promises. So one more anti-French alliance was formed; this was the compact between William and Charles XI of Sweden, whereby both united to maintain the terms of the treaty of Nimeguen. If his promises meant anything, Charles must join this league and summon parliament; he would thereby have the honour of heading a great 'peace' confederation, with the additional advantage that his foreign policy would provide a remedy for internal troubles. To this demand Charles replied that English interests did not extend so far as those included in the treaty of Nimeguen; that the

[1] *Baschet*, 149, July 25/Aug. 4, 1681, and *Halifax*, i. 307–8.
[2] *Halifax*, i. 309.

German princes, far more than England, were concerned in that treaty, and that only when they, with the Emperor and Denmark, were included in the league would he join it. But, that this might not sound too uncompromising, it was coupled with a renewal of the promise to summon parliament if French troops invaded Flanders. This was the reply handed to the Dutch ambassador on November 8; it had previously been submitted to Barrillon, who received a verbal assurance that the promises contained therein would not be fulfilled. As the existence of the secret treaty was unknown to Halifax, the prince of Orange, the Dutch agents, and even the duchess of Portsmouth, all of these were deceived by Charles's response.[1]

Within a few weeks Charles's 'neutrality' was subjected to an even greater strain. In November Louis proceeded to invest Luxemburg, which he claimed as compensation for his cessions in Flanders; once more, therefore, it seemed inevitable that England must be dragged into continental politics. At Court there was talk of another parliament, and Halifax schemed measures for the conciliation of the extremists; below the surface was Ralph Montagu, soliciting more French money on the pretext that he could bribe the parliamentary leaders to acquiesce in neutrality.[2] Always polite and secretive, Barrillon listened to every one and assured them how innocuous were his master's designs. 'I am explaining how unimportant Luxemburg is,' wrote the French ambassador to Louis; 'it is not on a river, and cannot be used for the defence of the Low Countries. They will talk for a few days of Luxemburg as they did of Strasburg, and then, like the rest of Europe, they will be glad to have peace.'[3] But this proved true only in part. The French king was obviously threatening European peace, and if Charles was to hold his hand any longer, he must have an extra payment. So on November 21 Charles agreed with Barrillon to accept a supplementary sum of one million livres, in return for the promise that he would not hinder Louis's designs on Luxemburg. When, in December, the investment became a siege, Charles was so harassed by the difficulty of honouring his private promises and his public commitments that

[1] *Baschet*, 150, Sept. 29/Oct. 9, Oct. 13/23, Nov. 5/15, 1681, and *Halifax*, i. 322–3.

[2] *Baschet*, 150, Nov. 14/24.

[3] Ibid. 150, Nov. 7/17.

he begged Barrillon to extricate him: 'You know what devils my members of parliament are,' said the king; 'for God's sake get me out of this fix, or I shall have to summon parliament.'[1] The appeal was not in vain; if Charles could not get money from parliament, he could get money from the threat to summon parliament, and on this occasion he preserved reputation as well; for when, early in 1682, Louis announced that he had decided to raise the siege, this step was rightly attributed to the intervention of Charles.[2] Not until 1684, when there seemed little likelihood of parliament being summoned, did Louis eventually make himself master of Luxemburg. Meanwhile Charles, ostensibly shaping his policy under the sagacious direction of Halifax, had preserved money with honour, and his envoy in Paris could write: 'It is a most glorious figure which His Majesty makes abroad.'[3]

The king's choice of diplomatic personnel provided a further proof that he intended to retain his friendship with France and withstand the solicitation of the Dutch. In 1682 Henry Savile was succeeded in the Paris embassy by Richard Graham, lord Preston, a high tory, and a close friend of the duke of York; Henry Sydney (devoted to the interests of the prince of Orange) was recalled from The Hague and replaced by Bevil Skelton, whose French sympathies were so patent as to justify a protest from William; at the same time Bodmin was recalled from Copenhagen, Middleton from Vienna, and Charles Bertie from Germany.[4] At home, an early start had been made in the preparations for an era of non-parliamentary rule. In December 1679 the privy council had ordered retrenchments to be made in the pay of naval officers and seamen—one of the many indications that the English Navy would not be used for active intervention in European affairs; at the same time a committee was appointed to inspect the lists of justices of the peace in order to remove

[1] Ibid. 150, Dec. 12/22.

[2] *Add. MS.* 37980, f. 101, Chudleigh to Conway, May 2/12, 1682, and *Add. MS.* 34339, f. 86, van Beuning to Fagel, Oct. 12/22, 1682.

[3] Lord Preston to the bishop of Oxford, Dec. 31, 1681/Jan. 10, 1682, in *H.M.C. Rep.* vii, app. 278.

[4] For this see the introduction by F. A. Middlebush to *Despatches of T. Plott and T. Chudleigh, English envoys at The Hague* (in Ryks Geschiedkundige Publicatien).

unsuitable persons;[1] and three months later a circular letter was ordered to be sent to all corporations requiring them to put into force the Act of 1661 for their better regulation, and to report on how far they had achieved this object.[2] These steps were followed in December 1681 by an order-in-council requiring the justices to put into execution the laws against Papists, Dissenters, and conventicles. In this way Danby's principles of government were to be reproduced in a harsher form, with one important addition—the whole structure of local government was to be revolutionized, in order that the crown might be assured of the loyalty of justices, mayors, sheriffs, and council men. By these means the return of tory juries would be secured; and, if a parliament did have to be summoned, the reformed boroughs would be likely to return only tory burgesses. As this policy was developed, numerous loyal addresses from grand juries throughout the country confirmed Charles in the belief that he might depend on a large measure of popular support.

Against the whigs, the campaign commenced in the law courts. On April 11, 1681, Scroggs was removed from the office of lord chief justice and his post was conferred on sir Francis Pemberton, on whom the Court could rely. Two weeks later commenced the trial at the King's Bench of Fitzharris, when the grand jury returned a true Bill, after having been assured that it was fit for them to proceed in a matter which had already been the subject of impeachment by the Commons. What precisely was Fitzharris's crime may never be determined. By impeaching him, the Commons had hoped to prove the complicity of Danby and the duke of York in the Popish Plot; it is possible that he was in possession of important secrets, and the king was anxious that he should be hanged,[3] because he had been won over by the whigs with an assurance of pardon if he would reveal these secrets when impeached. His counsel included Winnington, Pollexfen, and Treby, then considered the ablest of the parliamentary advocates, who made a strenuous effort to induce the court to accept the plea that the accused could not be indicted before an inferior tribunal

---

[1] P.C. Reg. 68, Dec. 3, 1679. For the removals of justices see H.M.C. Rep. xi, app., pt. ii. 172–93. For the decline of the English Navy at this period see supra, i. 276, 280.

[2] P.C. Reg. 68, March 12, 1680.　　　　[3] Baschet, 148, April 4/14, 1681.

after indictment in a superior; but this plea was overruled by Pemberton, with the concurrence of Jeffreys. Not till June 9 did Fitzharris answer to the indictment, which set forth that he was the author of a libel *The True Englishman*, a pamphlet which charged Charles I with the authorship of the Irish rebellion, and Charles II with the exercise of arbitrary power; of special significance was the fact that the pamphlet cited the depositions of two kings, Richard II and Henry VI.[1] Everard, the chief witness against the prisoner, swore that Fitzharris had represented to him the advantages of adhering to the French and popish interests, and had suggested the plan of writing a seditious pamphlet in order 'to set England by the ears'. This pamphlet was then (according to Everard) to be delivered to père la Chaise in the name of the English Dissenters, and its authorship fathered on them.[2] Oates next gave evidence. He had been told by Everard that the pamphlet was to be printed and sent by the post to the most notable of the whig Lords and Commons, who were then to be 'taken up' for having it in their possession.[3] Oates had heard from Everard that the Court had a hand in the business. Other witnesses, including sheriff Cornish, sir William Waller, and lord Howard of Escrick, gave evidence pointing to Fitzharris's connexion with the Court.

Few of the witnesses called on his behalf could recollect the events alleged by Fitzharris. Secretary Conway attested that, to his knowledge, the king had employed the accused on some trifling business; the duchess of Portsmouth denied that she had received papers from him,[4] or that she had obtained by his means information of the intended impeachment against her; the money which she had given him was, she said, for charity. His witnesses having failed him, Fitzharris defended himself with the plea that his acts had been commissioned by the Court; that he had been doing paid, secret service. 'I hope what I did was with a design to serve the King in discovering what was designed against him. . . . I hope you will consider these are great persons that I have to do with; and where great state matters are at the bottom, it is hard to make them tell anything but what is for their advantage.'[5] He accused Everard of being the author of the libel.

---

[1] *The tryal and condemnation of Edw. Fitz-harris Esq.* (1681), 7–9.
[2] Ibid. 12–26.   [3] Ibid. 28.   [4] Ibid. 40.   [5] Ibid. 41.

The solicitor-general (Heneage Finch) and serjeant Jeffreys made short work of the defence. Finch reduced Fitzharris's argument to two heads: he was not the author of the libel, and what he did was for secret service. 'He would fain have it that you should believe the king should hire him to raise a rebellion against himself.'[1] That was precisely what the whigs suspected the Court of doing; it seemed incredible, but all the events of the last three years had been incredible, and now the jury was asked to believe that, because an incredible thing was imputed to the Court, it was therefore false. Serjeant Jeffreys followed with the conclusive argument that the prisoner was a Roman Catholic;[2] he had libelled the crown as well as Protestant witnesses; here was an Irish Papist who intended to set England by the ears and bring in the French. Then followed Pemberton's summing up. The libel was 'a piece of the art of the Jesuits'.[3] The king, it is true, had given Fitzharris money, but only for charity. It could not be believed that the king would do such things as had been laid at his door. The jury found him guilty, and he was executed at Tyburn on July 1. On the same day, and at the same place, was executed Oliver Plunket, Roman Catholic archbishop of Armagh, on charges originally brought by Oates in September 1678 to the effect that he had conspired to bring a French army to Ireland. He was the last victim of the Popish Plot, and died in the company of the first victim of the counter-attack.

The judicial campaign against the scattered forces of the whigs was soon in full swing. A joiner named Stephen College was put on his trial at the Old Bailey for seditious words and actions at Oxford during the meeting of the parliament there.[4] The Middlesex grand jury, selected by the whig sheriffs Slingsby Bethell and Henry Cornish, threw out the Bill with an *Ignoramus*. A mean device was then adopted to secure the conviction of a rash but harmless man who, with some native wit, spiced with obscenity, had made himself prominent during the Oxford parliament. It was contended that, as the acts complained of had taken place at Oxford, he should be tried there; and accordingly he was indicted at Oxford court-house on August 17, 1681, before

[1] *The tryal and condemnation of Edw. Fitz-harris Esq.* (1681), 44.
[2] Ibid. 46.   [3] Ibid. 48.
[4] *The arraignment, tryal and condemnation of Stephen College* (1681).

lord Norris, Francis North (lord chief justice of the common pleas), with justices Jones, Raymond, and Levinz. He was charged with having prepared arms at Oxford to wage war against the king, and with having intended to seize the king. The Oxfordshire grand jury returned a true Bill, and the trial that ensued was one of the most unfair in a period abounding in judicial murders; for College was refused both a copy of the indictment and a list of jury and counsel; he was not allowed access to his papers; and his plea that, as a freeman of the city of London, he was not impleadable outside the liberties of the city was overruled. The case against him was this: he had collected arms worth about twice the value of his estate, with the intention of seizing the king; he had armed himself with a horse, pistols, a coat of mail, a carbine, and a head-piece; 'and so, being armed cap-a-pee with that design he came hither to Oxford, and you will judge whether these be fit tools for a joiner'. Still more, he had induced others to join him, and had boasted that he would soon be a colonel; he had defamed the king in taverns and coffee-houses, and he was one of the accomplices of Fitzharris. If the matter were thoroughly inquired into, it would probably be found that he was really a papist in disguise.[1]

Dugdale, the first witness for the prosecution, deposed that College had referred to the king as one from whom nothing but arbitrary government could be expected; he had also received from the accused, for distribution, a supply of blue ribbon, on every quarter yard of which was inscribed the legend: 'no popery: no slavery'; he had also seen College carrying pistols, and he had heard him sing a song at lord Lovelace's house in which was the refrain, 'when all the bishops were changing their hats for cardinals' caps'. Dugdale admitted that the crown was paying his travelling expenses, but would not confess to any larger subsidy.[2] The informers Turberville and Haynes thereupon supported the evidence about seditious words and the hawking of blue ribbons. Oates then appeared in a role still unusual to him, namely as a witness for the defence; but unfortunately for College, the witness whose word was good enough to send nearly a score of innocent men to the scaffold did not now have sufficient credibility to save one innocent man. The Doctor

[1] Ibid. 16–17, speeches by the attorney-general.   [2] Ibid. 23.

swore (and here he may have been telling the truth) that, in talk about the College case, Turberville had said to him: 'The Protestants have deserted us, and God damn him, he would not starve.'[1] This was a damaging innuendo against one of the witnesses for the crown; but from Oates it was valueless, and the attorney-general (sir Cresswell Levinz) sneeringly reminded Oates that he had changed sides, whereas Turberville had not. There then followed a duel between Oates and the witnesses for the prosecution; and, though College drew the attention of the court to statements made on his behalf by Oates, lord chief justice North suppressed him with the very unjudicial remark that there were three to one witnesses against him,[2] and brushed aside his defence with the significant words: 'Truth! Why, if yours or any man's word in your case should go for truth, no man that stands at the Bar could be convicted.'[3] These words aptly describe the attitude of Stuart judges in the majority of the political trials. College's ordeal had now been prolonged long beyond midnight, and feeling in the crowded court-room was tense; in vain did the accused protest that nothing of fact had been proved against him but a pair of pistols, a sword, and a horse. At three o'clock in the morning, amid a great shout, the jury announced a verdict of Guilty. He was executed on August 31, the first martyr of the whig cause.

But the Court was aiming at bigger game than the 'Protestant Joiner'; and already on July 2 Shaftesbury had been sent to the Tower on a charge of high treason. His papers were impounded; his application for bail or trial in terms of his own Habeas Corpus Act was refused on the ground that the Tower was outside the jurisdiction of the judges; likewise his offer to retire to Carolina, if released. Meanwhile 'evidence' against him was easily extracted from the Irish informers whom he had himself at one time suborned. On November 24 a special commission was issued for his trial, and he was indicted at the Old Bailey[4] of the *intention* of levying war against the king, which, in terms of the Act of 1661, constituted high treason. The grand jury of Middle-

---

[1] *The arraignment, tryall and condemnation of Stephen College* (1681), 48.
[2] Ibid. 50.
[3] Ibid. 82.
[4] *The proceedings at the Sessions House in the Old Bayly . . . against Anthony, earl of Shaftesbury* (1681).

sex (selected by the whig sheriffs) included sir Samuel Barnardiston (foreman), T. Papillon the merchant, and Michael Godfrey
(brother of sir Edmund and father of one of the first governors
of the bank of England). In his charge, Pemberton explained
how, by the Act of 1661, the treason law of Edward III had been
modified to include intention, even if no overt act followed; in
effect, therefore, words, if importing any malicious design against
the king's life or government, or any traitorous intention, were
now sufficient; and two witnesses each testifying to different or
the same words were enough. With a suggestion of menace in
his voice, Pemberton reminded the grand jury that compassion
was not their province,[1] and they must find a true Bill if there
was probable evidence for the accusation.

A hint of the careful preparation which had preceded the trial
was conveyed in the reason given by the judge in refusing the
jury's request for permission to examine the witnesses in private
—they need have no fear, he said, of betraying the king's secrets,
for the crown had carefully investigated its case, and so its witnesses were not likely to be 'raw'.[2] The indictment was then read.
It rehearsed, among other things, that, in discourse with one
Booth, Shaftesbury had intimated that, if the king refused to pass
an exclusion Bill at the Oxford parliament, he and his supporters
would use force. He had also said that the king was a man of no
faith; that he ought to be deposed like Richard II, and that he
(Shaftesbury) would not desist until he had established a commonwealth. Evidence was then given by the informers Mac-
namara, Dennis, and Haynes to the effect that the accused had
discussed the duke of Buckingham's claim to the throne, derived
from Plantagenet ancestors; he had spoken irreverently of the
king, and had talked of rebellion. Of actual rebellion the only
hint was that contained in a paper found in Shaftesbury's lodging
whereon were outlined the principles of a Protestant association,
bound by an oath against popery, mercenary armies, and the
succession of the duke of York.

Having heard these attestations, the grand jury asked if any
of the witnesses stood indicted, only to be told that this was no
concern of theirs and must be left to the petty jury, an answer
which evoked from Papillon the rejoinder that, if they could not

[1] *The proceedings . . . against Shaftesbury*, 5.   [2] Ibid. 7.

consider the credibility of the witnesses, they could not satisfy their consciences.[1] In the hope of satisfying these qualms, the witnesses swore that they gave their evidence voluntarily; and Pemberton did his best to reconcile the inconsistencies in the statements which they made; but he would not allow the jury to ask them whether they had been bribed.[2] As the case proceeded it became more clear that the Middlesex whigs would not be brow-beaten; so Pemberton was reduced to the argument that the treason laws now included a very wide range of things, while North informed them that the Protestant association imputed to Shaftesbury's authorship was not recognized by the statutes. After retiring to consider their verdict, the jurymen returned with the Bill marked *Ignoramus*, whereupon the spectators in court (many from Wapping) fell 'a hollowing and shouting', a fact which the attorney-general asked the judge to place on record.[3]

But the victory was more than discounted by an event contemporaneous with the trial of Shaftesbury—the publication of Dryden's *Absalom and Achitophel*. It was with this great political satire that the poet laureate won a national public; for, by the autumn of 1681, the Popish Plot could at last be seen in its gaunt perspective, and the nation was now rallying to the throne after the assaults of the exclusionists. The biblical background of the poem was a happy thought, since, in the turbulent history of early Israel, it was easy to find many close parallels; its personal names provided a transparent disguise, and enabled the poet to work in a medium then the best known to Englishmen. Everything conspired to draw from him his best—desire to please the king; to wipe off old scores against Buckingham; to give full expression to a mordant wit. So there were no superfluous strokes, and with a minimum of effort every thrust went home; the second lines of the couplets were not echoes of the first, but independent confirmations; a whole portrait gallery was etched in steel, every feature clear-cut from needle and acid. There are times in history when national sanity can be restored only by sarcasm. It was so in France, after the excesses of the League and the Religious Wars, when the ridicule of the *Satire Menipée* induced a measure of balance and moderation; it was so also in England

---

[1] *The proceedings . . . against Shaftesbury*, 33.   [2] Ibid. 36–42.
[3] Ibid. 48.

when, after three years of madness, men read *Absalom and Achitophel* and laughed themselves out of their own follies. It was the triumph of native common sense.

In Scotland there was little relief from the trials through which the nation was passing. In July 1681 James, as royal commissioner, presided over a meeting of the Scottish Parliament, at which two Acts were passed, both intended to consolidate Stuart rule in the north. By the first,[1] it was enacted that the right of succession to the crown was unaffected by the religion of the heir; by the second,[2] there was imposed on all office-holders a test of such prodigious length, and such wealth of historical citation, that sworn adherence thereto might well occasion qualms in the scrupulous. This test was used as a means of removing the marquis of Argyle, son of that Argyle who had been offered as a sacrifice in 1661, an object of dislike to the executive because of his whig sympathies, and the occasion of both envy and enmity on the part of his many neighbours, anxious to share in the forfeiture of his great estates. As he was whiggish enough to offer subscription to the test 'in so far as it was consistent with itself and with the Protestant faith', there was now at hand a pretext as base as that which had cost his father his life. He had not lent his men for service in the iniquitous Highland Host; he had opposed the measures of Sharp and Rothes; as the uncrowned king of the Highlands he was an anomaly; and, worst of all, he represented the Protestant interest. His opposition to the exemption of the royal family from the test stirred the easily aroused resentment of James; accordingly, on November 9, 1681, he was committed on charges of treason, perjury, and assuming the legislative power, and convicted on evidence which, as Halifax said, would not have hanged a dog in England. Sentence of death and forfeiture was pronounced on December 23; but, a few days before, the prisoner had succeeded in making his escape. After hiding for a time in London he fled to Holland, where he

---

[1] *Acts of the Parliaments of Scotland*, viii. 239.

[2] Ibid. viii. 244–5. Here the 'true Protestant religion' was defined as that enunciated by the first parliament of James VI. The oath renounced all covenants, leagues and foreign jurisdictions and had to be taken 'without equivocation'.

corresponded with the Rye House conspirators, and fell a victim
at last after the failure of Monmouth's rebellion. The policy
adopted towards Argyle was enforced on all suspected of disaffection. Dragoons harried the western shires in quest of
covenanters, who were either shot out of hand or reserved for
the mercies of the 'bluidy' Advocate, sir George Mackenzie, who
boasted that he had never lost a case for the crown. He gleaned
assiduously in fields from which Graham of Claverhouse had
already extracted a rich harvest, and much of Scottish history
was inscribed on tombstones.

During this, his second,[1] stay in Scotland (Oct. 1680–March,
1682) James had begun by a policy of conciliation, to which there
was a ready response; but, as his exile became more prolonged,
his vindictiveness increased, and his stay in Edinburgh seems to
have accentuated a harsh element in his character. In close
touch with the course of events in England, he fretted visibly at
his enforced abstention from a scene where his presence would
have led to civil war. His misfortunes might have elicited for
him the sympathy of posterity, were it not that his conduct came
to be more and more clouded by an unusual degree of obtuseness
and meanness, qualities so strongly marked as to be attributable
in part to the ravages of a constitutional disease on his mind and
character. His obtuseness was shown by his continued faith in
Sunderland; by the ingenuous confidences of his innumerable
letters to the prince of Orange (all carefully preserved by their
recipient);[2] by his belief in force, preferably French, against
English patriots. Meanness was shown in his sustained resentment against enemies unworthy of a prince's wrath, and by his
readiness to seize on some petty device for avenging himself. He
swore that he would be revenged on the duchess of Portsmouth,
who had played him a 'dog's trick'; he thought that the support
of one of her maids, Mrs. Wall, would serve him in good stead,
and he maintained negotiations with her through colonel Legge.[3]

---

[1] His first stay was from Nov. 1679 to Feb. 1680.

[2] Many of these will be found in *Prinsterer*, v. In the Record Office
(*S.P. Dom.* 8/3) there is a collection of about 200, the last of which were
written in June 1686.

[3] York to colonel Legge, in *Add. MS.* 18477, f. 50, Nov. 22, 1680, quoted
in Campana de Cavelli, *Les derniers Stuarts*, i. 336.

Echoes from this world 'below stairs' had been heard at the trial of Fitzharris. Louis XIV was another friend with whom James was anxious to maintain stricter correspondence, and by whose help he hoped to maintain the prerogative on the basis of a standing army. He was continually urging Charles to act on bolder counsels; 'and who dare advise him to them unless I be with him to help to support him?'[1] It was indeed well for Charles that, throughout the critical period of the exclusion agitation, he was not embarrassed by his brother's presence; indeed there may be some truth in Barrillon's statement that, if the Oxford parliament had been willing to give him money and leave the prerogative intact, he would have agreed to exclusion.[2] Nor was James even consistent in his advocacy of strong measures; for at times he professed only to have reminded his brother of what he should do: 'I merely put him in mind, and pressed him to go on with what was resolved.'[3] It had been a considerable part of Charles's statesmanship *not* to go on with what had been resolved.

By the spring of 1682 England was a safer place for James, and so negotiations began for his return. He resumed communication with the duchess of Portsmouth, the price of her support being a share of the duke's Post Office revenues. This negotiation did not mature; but meanwhile James went to his brother at Newmarket, where he was well received. On returning to Leith in May 1682, in order to bring back his duchess, his ship, the *Gloucester*, was wrecked off the Yorkshire coast, with great loss of life; and contemporaries attributed to him an undue solicitude for his priests, his dogs, and his treasure while the ship was sinking. His return to England was speedily marked by changes which accentuated the reactionary character of Charles's rule. Halifax was again eclipsed; Sunderland, with the help of the duchess of Portsmouth, emerged from obscurity, and was readmitted to the privy council in August 1682, becoming again a secretary of state in January 1683. In September of that year Jeffreys was promoted lord chief justice and shortly afterwards admitted to the privy council. These men, together with Barrillon and the duchess of Portsmouth, constituted the ministry of Charles's last

---

[1] Ibid. i. 349.
[2] Barrillon to Louis XIV, 14/24 July 1681, ibid. i. 362.   [3] Ibid. i. 360.

years; on it was conferred at least the gilt of Anglicanism by the
retention of Hyde (lord Rochester) in office.

The *Ignoramus* returned by the Middlesex grand jury precipitated the long-premeditated attack on the charters, and soon
almost every franchise in the country was subjected to the
scrutiny of lawyers prepared to find pretexts for their forfeiture.
Most of the lords lieutenant and country gentry lent their aid to
this campaign, and in the years 1682–3 compulsion and influence
were freely used to procure the surrender or forfeiture of civic
rights. From the correspondence which passed through the
office of the secretaries of state can be deduced both the local
influence of the landed gentry, and how that influence was
enhanced by their active participation in measures calculated
to redress the balance of power between town and country in
favour of the latter. Thus, in June 1682, lord Ferrers wrote that
he had prevailed with Derby to surrender its charter; he was
willing, if required, to induce several Staffordshire corporations
to do likewise.[1] The city of Norwich asked lord Yarmouth not
to use compulsion in regard to its charter, as 900 citizens had
petitioned against its surrender.[2] Reports from Cornwall and
Devon showed that the gentry there were specially zealous in the
king's service, and even served on petty juries;[3] Nottingham,
where the duke of Newcastle was supreme, surrendered its
charter, but as there was an omission to include the town lands,
the process had to be repeated.[4] Poole was the subject of anathema by the gentlemen of Dorset; because, as the borough was
a county, it was a nuisance to the county of Dorset, and moreover
its corporation was disaffected to the government.[5] At their
suggestion a *quo warranto* was issued. The privileges of the city
of Oxford were examined by Dr. Fell, dean of Christ Church
and vice-chancellor, who insisted that the rights of the university,
especially in regard to the pernoctations of the proctors, should
be safeguarded in the new charter;[6] another potentate who had
to be consulted before the fresh charter was granted was lord
Abingdon. The reasons why proceedings were taken against
the Oxford charter were these: by its Elizabethan charter, the

[1] *Cal. S.P. Dom., 1682*, 229.   [2] Ibid. 274.   [3] Ibid. 347.
[4] Ibid. 423.   [5] *S.P. Dom., 1683/4*, bundle 436, Jan. 23, 1684.
[6] Ibid., Jan. 10, 1684.

market was to be held in Broken Heys and Gloucester Green; but in practice the market was usually kept in the city; there were five aldermen instead of four; three fairs were to be held yearly, but none was kept, and the bailiffs were said to pack juries.[1] Against Plymouth, the count was frauds on the Excise;[2] after a visit from Jeffreys on circuit, Plymouth surrendered its charter.

Most active on behalf of the government was the duke of Beaufort, whose influence was strongest in Wiltshire, Herefordshire, and Somerset. One of his agents gave an account of how he dealt with the recalcitrant corporation of Leominster. The corporation consisted of 25 council men, of whom 14 were 'fanatics' and the others loyal. One of the corporation's duties was the annual election of a bailiff (by a majority of the 25); and when the 14 'fanatics' were reduced to 12 by the death of one and the imprisonment of another, the agent advised the loyal party to absent themselves from the election, in order that a majority could not be secured for the nominee of the 12, and so no bailiff could be appointed. This was good enough for the issue of a *quo warranto*, and Beaufort suggested himself as high steward of the remodelled borough.[3] So too, lord Lindsey asked the king's assent to his acceptance of the office of recorder of the reformed city of Lincoln, and gave an assurance that he would act in the interests of the Court.[4] The duke of Newcastle secured the appointment of one of his nominees to the town-clerkship of Nottingham, and had his dependants installed in the corporation of Newcastle-under-Lyme.[5] As one town after another succumbed to a *quo warranto*, the voluntary surrenders became more frequent, most of them accompanied with that degree of submission expected from defaulting burghers acknowledging the king's mercy conveyed to them by his territorial representatives. A typical example was that of the surrender of its charter by Northampton and its receipt of a new one on September 25, 1681. On that day, the mayor, aldermen, bailiffs, and burgesses walked in their robes to the limits of the town, where they met the earl of Peterborough, lord lieutenant of the

[1] *Cal. S.P. Dom., 1682*, 276.   [2] *P.C. Reg.* 70, June 29, 1683.
[3] *S.P. Dom.*, bundle 438, Oct. 8, 1684, R. Hopton to duke of Beaufort.
[4] Ibid. Oct. 28, 1684, lord Lindsey to secretary of state.
[5] Ibid. Nov. 9, 1684, duke of Newcastle to secretary of state.

county, with a great confluence of nobility and gentry, all on horseback. His lordship, having dismounted, presented the new charter, with a discourse on His Majesty's favour to the borough; while the mayor, in the name of the new corporation, received the document on his knees, 'with due reverence, joy and gratitude of mind'. Then followed a speech by the deputy-recorder, in which he stigmatized the conduct of the evil men recently in authority, and commended the wisdom of the corporation in surrendering its charter in time. 'Is there any among you have been tainted with ill principles? . . . Now there is an eye upon you which will have respect to justice as well as to mercy.'[1]

Of the whig strongholds London was by far the most important; for its overthrow, both time and persistence were necessary. Early in 1678 the city lent a sum of £150,000 for the projected war with France; in the late summer of the same year Charles asked for £200,000; and, though it was feared that this money might be used for suppressing the liberties of the subject or the privileges of the corporation, the request was, nevertheless, granted.[2] The year 1681 was a critical one for London. The two sheriffs, Pilkington and Shute, were noted whigs, and the city indicated its politics in January by petitioning the king for the summoning of a parliament, with a reference to the interruption of public justice entailed by prorogation; this petition was afterwards to figure in the indictment against the city. In June, the freemen in their common hall voted thanks to the lord mayor and common council for presenting this petition, and also accorded thanks to the outgoing sheriffs 'for their provision of faithful and able juries'.[3] These traditions were maintained by the new sheriffs, Bethell and Cornish, and the result was seen in November, when the Middlesex grand jury rejected the Bill against Shaftesbury.

The turn of the tide came in June 1682 when, at the nomination of sheriffs, the lord mayor, sir John Moore, raised his glass to Dudley North, a younger brother of lord chief justice North; who, having acquired wealth as a Turkey merchant, was now embarking on a second career as a tory politician. Since 1674 no one had challenged this method of nominating a sheriff; but

[1] *Bodley, Ashmole*, 1674, no. 79.
[2] R. R. Sharpe, *London and the kingdom*, ii. 455–7.   [3] Ibid. ii. 474.

the city companies and the livery objected to North as their sheriff, and refused to confirm his nomination. In his stead they proposed these three—Papillon the mercer, Dubois the weaver, and Box the grocer, from whom they desired their two sheriffs to be chosen. A poll was conducted by the outgoing sheriffs, Pilkington and Shute, who continued it a few days longer than was warranted by the lord mayor's order; for this offence, Moore reported them to the privy council, which promptly committed the offending sheriffs to the Tower. The king then ordered a new election, the details of which are obscure; but North and Box appear to have obtained some kind of majority through the disqualification of the votes of those whig liverymen who had not taken the oath. Box there- upon resigned in favour of Peter Rich, and shortly afterwards sir W. Pritchard was elected lord mayor; as he, with the new sheriffs, North and Rich, was a tory, this was a victory for the Court.[1] Nor did this end the discomfiture of the large whig element in the city. In the heat of the elections of 1679–81 strong words had been used, and for these full retribution was to be exacted. Pilkington was fined £100,000 in November 1682 on an action of *scandalum magnatum* for having said in public that the duke of York had burnt the city in 1666, and had come from Scotland to cut their throats. A few months after this savage sentence, he was tried, with Shute, Cornish, and Bethell, for riot at the election of sheriffs on Midsummer Day 1682, and again heavily fined. The ex-lord mayor, sir Patience Ward, had had the misfortune to give evidence on behalf of Pilkington at the first trial; for this he was indicted for perjury (May 1683), at the instigation of the duke; but, before sentence, he managed to effect his escape to Holland. Thus was England habituated to methods of justice savouring more of Edinburgh than of Westminster. Even thus, however, the city refused to sur- render its charter, and accordingly a *quo warranto* was issued in January 1682.

After some preliminary arguments,[2] proceedings commenced

---

[1] Ibid. ii. 479.

[2] The arguments and pleadings will be found in *The Case of the Charter of London Stated* (1683) and *The pleadings and arguments . . . upon the Quo Warranto* (1690). See also R. R. Sharpe, *London and the Kingdom*, ii. 494–7.

in the King's Bench on February 7, 1683, when the information recited that the lord mayor, commonalty and citizens claimed, without any lawful warrant or legal grant, to exercise these privileges:

1. To be of themselves a body corporate and politic.
2. To name, elect and constitute sheriffs of London and Middlesex.
3. To hold sessions of the peace.

In the first capacity (so the indictment alleged) the common council had in 1674 passed a by-law imposing a fee of twopence per day on every horse-load of provisions brought into the public markets of the city; and from this and similar charges they had derived about £5,000 per annum to the oppression of the king's subjects. Secondly, they had presented a petition, which was 'in the nature of an appeal to the people'. To the first charge it was answered that the mayor, commonalty, and citizens were seised of the markets in fee, and had the right to levy tolls; they had imposed charges in order to rebuild the markets after the Great Fire. As regards the second charge, Treby, on behalf of the city, contended that the information had been brought against the wrong persons; it ought to have been brought against named persons who had usurped the functions of a corporation. 'The nature of a corporation', he said, 'is a capacity . . . an invisible person and capacity only, which cannot be forfeited.' At the second hearing (April 27, 1683) Pollexfen compared the importance of the case to Magna Carta itself; for not only London, but all the corporations of England were concerned. 'Consider', he said, 'what a vast part is concerned in the corporations of England.' He then cited those which are ecclesiastical or mixed, such as archbishops, deans, chapters, universities, and hospitals; secular, such as cities, towns, and boroughs, and even the very frame of government, since the Commons consist of knights, citizens, and burgesses. The members of a corporation, said Pollexfen, could be dealt with, but not the *persona ficta*, which is 'invisible, immortal, incapable of forfeiture, of treason or felony; having no soul, nor subject to imbecility or death'.

Judgement was pronounced on June 12, 1683, when the Bench declared that a corporation-aggregate might be seized;

that exacting money by pretended by-laws was an extortion, and that the acts of the common council were the acts of the corporation of London. A few days later (June 18) the lord mayor, with representative aldermen and commons, was received by the king at Windsor, where they presented an apology, which was answered by a speech from the lord keeper (North), who told them that their petition should have been presented earlier.[1] In the following September the common council refused by a narrow majority to surrender the old charter, whereupon judgement was entered against the city (Oct. 4, 1683). The corporation was remodelled, and a new charter was granted which effected a revolution in civic constitution.[2] In future, no lord mayor, sheriff, recorder, or town clerk was to be appointed without the royal approval; wherever the king disapproved of a second choice, he should himself nominate. There would therefore be no more whig sheriffs or grand juries; Shaftesbury's stronghold was now a royal demesne, and the proudest corporation in the world was at the feet of a Stuart.

The attack on the charters coincided with the stricter enforcement by the justices of the laws against Papists, Dissenters, and conventicles. Orders to this effect, issued by the privy council, were rigidly enforced in many parts of England; the prisons were again filled, notably with Quakers, and in this campaign many of the country gentry distinguished themselves by their zeal. Thus, from head-quarters at Badminton, the duke of Beaufort co-operated so successfully with his son lord Herbert as to induce the latter to express the hope that soon not a single Dissenter would be heard of in the county of Somerset.[3] An increase of emigration to the colonies at this time caused Jenkins to consider whether this might not be prohibited; another proposal for consideration was that of excommunicating the Dissenters, so that they might be unable either to vote for or be elected to parliament.[4] It was even suggested that the separate community of Walloons and Flemings in Canterbury should be expelled, the grand jury of Kent having presented them as a nuisance to the county.[5]

[1] The proceedings are described in *Bodley, Ashmole* 1674, no. 71.
[2] R. R. Sharpe, op. cit. ii. 503–5.　　[3] *Cal. S.P. Dom.*, *1682*, 24–5.
[4] Ibid. 571, Dec. 9, 1682.
[5] Ibid., *1683*, 103.

In this campaign the government made unsparing use of informers and spies. Hitherto these had been paid by private patrons to ferret out Papists; in 1681 there was money to be had from the Treasury for swearing against prominent whigs, and now (1682-3) a good living could be made by informing against the Dissenters and the smaller fry. A judge, sir Edmund Saunders, thought that the justices might be enlisted in this system of espionage by imposing on them an obligation to reveal to the privy council all matters concerning the state that had arisen in the informations laid before them,[1] a proposal of special interest to justice Edmund Warcup, who had done much subterranean work during the Popish Plot,[2] and was now an active agent on behalf of the government. Throughout England, the informers quickly adapted themselves to the new requirements of the trade; spies prospered on a share of forfeitures and fines, and the success of the tale-bearers was estimated in financial terms; one of them, for example, when petitioning for funds, reminded the king that in the preceding six months he had convicted in London before the lord mayor 'halls, houses and preachers to the value of more than £10,000, and in Westminster to the value of £7,000'.[3] Old-established houses offered tenders for the new business on foot; for instance, the relatives of Oates; one of whom, Clement Oates, gave information to the government of what he had heard from the conversations between Tonge and Titus Oates, and claimed to have discovered the inventor of the cry: 'no popery, no slavery'.[4] More prominent was Samuel Oates, who specialized in sworn informations against his brother's patrons, including Shaftesbury. In the winter of 1682-3 he was finding evidence of a whig plot in the fact that large numbers of short blunderbusses were being made by the London gunsmiths; he was also 'smoking out' the designs of those whigs who had gone to Holland; and, as he wished to keep the business in the family, he announced that he had converted Titus from whiggery; so, if the Doctor were sent for, 'he would offer proposals which I am sure would please Your Majesty'.

---

[1] *Cal. S.P. Dom., 1682*, 105.

[2] His *Journal, 1676-84*, ed. K. Feiling and F. R. Needham, will be found in *E.H.R.* xl.

[3] *Cal. S.P. Dom., 1682*, 520, Oct. 1682. [4] *Ibid.* 245, June 1682.

A share in the confiscated estates of Jesuits was to be the price of this information.[1]

These facts serve to illustrate the collapse of the whig cause. When Shaftesbury was discharged from bail in February 1682 he was a broken man, suffering in health, his spirit almost daunted by the sudden reversal of his party's fortunes. That party was now reduced to a mere handful of men; some eminent and principled, others furtive and dangerous. In the former category were Essex, Russell, and Algernon Sidney. Arthur Capel, earl of Essex, had proved by his tenure of the viceroyalty of Ireland[2] that he was a prudent and sympathetic administrator; his services at the Treasury had won the appreciation of Charles, and he was known to contemporaries as a man of character, industry, and taste. He had joined in the opposition to Danby, and had allied himself, first with Halifax, and then with Shaftesbury. In his political evolution he progressed from limitations to exclusion, and from Orange to Monmouth. Disappointment may have determined this part of his career; for he had hoped to become lord high treasurer. In actual conspiracy he appears to have taken no part.

William, lord Russell, was one of a house destined to play a great part in English liberalism. Opposition to Buckingham had first drawn him out of his reserve; soon he was attacking Danby and the French connexion. In 1678 he was among the parliamentary leaders courted by the French ambassador; that he was one of the dupes of Charles's foreign policy may account in part for his resentment against the Court. Like Essex, he was one of the reformed privy council of 1679; later he was known as a consistent advocate of exclusion, and, though enemies hinted that his anti-popish principles were proof of fear lest his church lands might be confiscated by a popish successor, yet this inadequately accounts for the persistent and reasoned opposition he maintained to the interest of the duke of York. He disapproved the rasher counsels of Shaftesbury; but, on the other hand, by his meetings with Ralph Montagu at Southampton House, he incurred suspicion. Equally eminent was Algernon Sidney, son of the second earl of Leicester, a republican of the type of sir Henry Vane. Though he had refused to participate

[1] Ibid. 236, 538, and ibid., *1683*, 18.　　　　[2] See *supra*, 397–8.

in the trial of Charles I, he was known as a resolute opponent of monarchy; and for the greater part of Charles's reign he was engaged in study and foreign travel. Returning to England in 1677, he unsuccessfully tried to obtain election to parliament: nor did he secure the friendship of Shaftesbury, who at first regarded him as a French spy and a pensioner of Sunderland, an accusation to which some point was given by his acceptance of money from Barrillon. Of the abstract republicans he was considered the most dangerous because prepared to go to extremities with the help of France. Towards the prince of Orange his attitude was one of diffidence, because he knew that absolutism can be based as well on Protestantism as on crypto-Catholicism. Concentration on exclusion was therefore his policy, for which everything was to be sacrificed; but though, after the Oxford parliament, he discussed projects of insurrection with Russell and Essex, he does not appear to have had direct dealings with Shaftesbury or Monmouth.

The younger generation of whig peers was represented by Thomas Grey (1654–1720), styled lord Grey of Groby and later earl of Stamford. He was one of the close associates of Shaftesbury; he received a pardon for his part in the Rye House plot, and at the Revolution took up arms on behalf of Orange. He was a somewhat ineffective whig. Not dissimilar was Forde, lord Grey of Werk, first prominent as an exclusionist; then suspected of concurrence in the Rye House plot. He saved himself after the battle of Sedgemoor by turning king's evidence, and was one of those who came over with William. Older than these was William Howard, third baron Howard of Escrick, who had learned his preaching from the Anabaptists and his plotting from Cromwell's Guards. To the Restoration government he was useful because of the information he could give against his former associates among the Sectaries; during the Third Dutch War he was imprisoned for treasonable correspondence with the enemy; at the trial of lord Stafford he gave evidence against his own kinsman, and he afterwards turned informer against his associates Russell and Sidney. Another associate against whom he swore was John Hampden ('the younger'), grandson of the great Hampden, who had imbibed advanced religious and political principles during his stay in France. Hampden returned to England in 1682, and was afterwards accused of plotting an insurrection with Monmouth, Russell, Sidney, Essex, and Howard. These were afterwards known as the Council of Six.

Whatever may have been the nature of the deliberations of the so-called Council of Six, it is clear that they were all, except Howard, amateurs in the business of plotting. Unfortunately, however, some of them were suspected of association or at least communication with men of a more determined and experienced type, such as the old Cromwellian soldiers Walcot, Rumsey, and Rumbold; the last a maltster, whose house at Hoddesdon (the Rye House), on the way from London to Newmarket, was afterwards to acquire such notoriety. Equally dangerous were Aaron Smith, major Wildman, and Robert Ferguson. Smith, a shady London solicitor, had come into prominence at College's trial; he was already known as an ally of Oates, and he may have been in the pay of William of Orange. It was for his share in the defence of College that he was forced to go into hiding, and soon he was deeply engaged in plots. His skill in covering up his tracks saved him for preferment after the Revolution. John Wildman was another secretive worker who lived to secure a post from William. His seditious activities dated from the days of the New Model Army, and he still perpetuated the visionary politics of Lilburne and the Nag's Head Tavern, combining these activities with astute land speculations which had enriched him during the Commonwealth. It was because he had plotted against Cromwell that he was given control of the Post Office at the Restoration; but his propensity for opening letters caused dismissal, and thereafter he appears to have alternated periods of imprisonment with enjoyment of the favour of Buckingham and the suspicion of the government. Of ripe experience and expert knowledge, he had a simple policy—to assassinate the king and the duke of York, and give the crown to Monmouth; in consequence, like Algernon Sidney, with whom he was associated, he was considered by many whigs as too dangerous, but useful nevertheless as a consultant.

The third member of this group, Robert Ferguson, was the most extraordinary of the three, and perhaps the only one of them having any legitimate grievance against the government. Born in Aberdeenshire, he had obtained a living in Kent, from which he was ejected at the Restoration. He was imprisoned for raising money on behalf of deprived ministers, and on his release became a popular preacher of a somewhat florid type. A supporter of Monmouth, he had sense enough to perceive that the affair of the black box[1] was bad showmanship, since stronger evidence of the marriage of Monmouth's mother would be necessary; by 1681 he had become involved in deeper courses, as intermediary between Monmouth and the whigs; but, unlike Wildman, he stopped short of insurrection. He appears to have been inspired by a measure of genuine religious zeal. He lived, not to enjoy office under William, but to plot with the Jacobites. As pamphleteer, rigorist, and headlong enthusiast he is comparable with William Prynne, and he exercised a somewhat baleful influence on the more loosely-knit men with whom he was associated.[2]

The personage on whose behalf these men were acting was James Scott or Crofts, duke of Monmouth and (after his marriage into that house) duke of Buccleuch. As a youth he was prominent in the more violent escapades of Restoration London; but a certain gracefulness of manner, coupled with a dashing exterior, made him popular with the London mob. He had first incurred the jealousy of the duke of York by his appointment in 1670 to succeed Albemarle as captain-general of the forces; he had distinguished himself under Turenne in 1672, at the siege of Meastricht in 1673, and in 1678, with a small detachment, he had held Ostend. In July 1679, when he returned to London as the clement victor of Bothwell Brig, his popularity was at its height; and, by his conjunction with Shaftesbury, Essex, and the duchess of Portsmouth, he fast became a serious problem to the executive; for as he had helped to overthrow Danby, so he made no secret that he desired the exclusion of his uncle. His Protestantism was patent to all beholders, as his legitimacy was to be revealed in the apocalyptic contents of the black box. His

---

[1] The black box was said to contain the marriage contract between Charles and Monmouth's mother, Lucy Walters. Cosin, bishop of Durham, was said to have entrusted the box to the custody of his son-in-law, sir Gilbert Gerard. For this see under Scott, James, duke of Monmouth, in *D.N.B.*

[2] For a good biography see R. Ferguson, *Robert Ferguson the Plotter*.

decline had begun with the return of James to England in September 1679, when he was deprived of his commission and obliged to leave the country; then his unauthorized return in November caused Charles to deprive him of all his civil and military offices and order him out of the kingdom, which order he disobeyed. He maintained his popularity by public worship in St. Martin's-in-the-Fields, and paid assiduous court to Nell Gwyn, the staunchest supporter of Protestantism in the inner circles of Charles's Court.

It was probably at Shaftesbury's suggestion that he began to show himself to the people in a series of progresses, beginning with Oxford and the western counties in the autumn of 1680. On his coach was painted an emblem presumed to be heraldic— a heart pierced by two arrows, surmounted by a plume of feathers, with two angels bearing up a scarf on both sides.[1] At many points on his route he was well received by the populace, amid shouts of 'No Popery, No Popery'. Thus, his entry into Chard on August 27 was preceded by 500 horsemen, and 'there was not a mute among the crowd that met him'.[2] At Exeter he was received by sir William Courtenay and a crowd shouting 'God bless the Protestant duke'. On the return journey he stayed for a few days in Oxford, where the university ignored his presence, but the city was whig in sympathy, accordingly he was entertained to dinner by the mayor and aldermen, one of the toasts being confusion to the vice-chancellor of the university[3] (Dr. Fell). He also took part at the horse-racing on Port Meadow. In March 1681 he was again in Oxford, with the parliament, and this time maintained a semi-royal state; thereafter he was the public friend and advocate of Shaftesbury and College, thereby imposing a severe strain on the patience of his indulgent father. Further indiscretions led to his deposition from the chancellorship of Cambridge early in 1682. He now talked openly of insurrection, and in the autumn of 1682 he again went on progress.

No pretender to the throne ever worked harder for a following

[1] *H.M.C. Rep.* xii, app., pt. vii. 174, *Le Fleming MSS.*
[2] *Narrative of the duke of Monmouth's late journey into the west* (1680), in *Bodley Pamph.* 149.
[3] Duke of York to princess of Orange in *Prinsterer*, v. 421, Sept. 23, 1680.

than did he. In August he was being entertained by the whig landlords in Staffordshire, including the earl of Macclesfield;[1] in the following month he had a great reception at the Wallasey horse-races, where 'it wanted only a *vive le roy* to complete the rebellion'.[2] Having won the 12-stone plate and a prize of £60 he presented the plate to the mayor's daughter, whom he christened Henrietta. Jeffreys, who was then at Wrexham, noted that lords Derby and Brandon were present. Nor were these his only exploits at this northern race meeting; for he won two foot races 'against the same gent, first stripped, and then in his boots', whereupon the applause was so hearty that he had to ask the spectators to give over.[3] At Liverpool he touched for the king's evil and was made a freeman of the town; throughout Staffordshire and Cheshire—counties said to be 'rotten with whigs'—he was received with enthusiasm. But his movements were being followed by a sergeant-at-arms, and at Stafford he was taken into custody, while at the same time a warrant was issued for Shaftesbury's arrest. Shaftesbury concealed himself in Wapping; Monmouth was bailed out, and again the athletic duke strove to win the populace by the fascination of his appearance and the prowess of his limbs. But his third progress (Feb. 1683) was not a success. He chose the southern counties, and his reception was poor. At Chichester the arrangements for his entry were ruined by the appearance of the high sheriff and justices with a troop of horse, at the sight of which Monmouth 'swore bloodily', but 'no other compliments passed'.[4] Some consolation was offered by the sight of about a thousand people at the Cross, and Monmouth insisted on attending divine service in the cathedral, where the bishop's chaplain drew such a close parallel between rebellion and witchcraft that the duke left hurriedly, leaving some of his suite to curse the preacher.

The northern progress of September 1682 may have been a feeler; at times it had the appearance of an abortive rebellion. Throughout the autumn of 1682 there seems to have been a number of meetings at the house of a wealthy wine merchant named Shepherd, where schemes of insurrection or even assassination may have been discussed, but with what seriousness of

[1] *Cal. S.P. Dom., 1682*, 342.   [2] Ibid. 390, Sept. 11, 1682.

[3] Ibid. 409.   [4] Ibid., *1683*, 70, Feb. 21.

purpose it is impossible to determine. Shaftesbury and the
'Council of Six' had probably become careless, and their talk
reached the ears not only of such men as Wildman and Ferguson,
but of even more obscure desperadoes, such as the Irish adventurer Walcot, a free-thinking lawyer named West, and a London
oil-man named Keeling, one or all of whom may have attended
the deliberations. As the time for the annual pope-burning
approached, the talks assumed a more serious turn; for there
were negotiations by Shaftesbury with the followers of Argyle,
and with Scots refugees from the battle of Bothwell Brig. What
is certain is that there was no leadership, because Shaftesbury
was now nearly distraught with vexation and ill health; and
when, in November 1682, he heard that fresh warrants were out
for his arrest, he fled to Holland, where he died on January 21,
1683. His removal and death destroyed what hope remained
of a successful reaction, leaving his associates compromised by
the wild inconsequences of their leader's decline, and by their
rash confidences to men likely to prove traitors or informers.

Such were the preliminaries to one more mystery of the reign
—the so-called Rye House Plot. On June 12, 1683, there
emerged from an obscurity as murky as that which had preceded
the debut of Oates the salter and oil-man Josiah Keeling, a man
of anabaptist sympathies and a decaying business. Like Oates
before him he had a wonderful story of an attempt to murder
the king, and for some unexplained reason he took his story to
George Legge, lord Dartmouth, who then held a household
office at Court, and was associated in naval affairs with the duke
of York. Legge sent him to the proper quarter, namely to
Jenkins. Meanwhile, news of the 'plot' had leaked out; and
two of the men whose names had been mentioned (Rumsey
and West) appear, if Burnet is to be credited,[1] to have decided
on a novel plan. This was to come in voluntarily with a 'concocted confession' which would not only save their lives, but
might qualify them for employment in detective work against
the numerous emissaries of Satan then flourishing in England.
An alternative explanation (of which there is no proof) is
that the Court prompted the 'confession' in order to implicate
the whigs. The document drawn up by West[2] is comparable

[1] *Burnet*, ii. 360-1.   [2] *Add. MS.* 38847, f. 83 sqq.

in its wildness and inconsistencies with the stories of Oates. In brief, it implicated many persons in one or other of two schemes —the murder of the king and a general insurrection. The object of the latter was to destroy not only the king and the duke of York, but also Halifax and Rochester; the princess Anne was then to be placed on the throne, and married to some 'honest country gentleman' in order to raise 'a Protestant brood of princes'. The former project, that of simple assassination, was to be effected either by 'lopping' the king in the playhouse, or running down his barge on the Thames, or killing him when on his way from or to Newmarket as his coach passed the moat of the Rye House, Rumbold's farm at Hoddesdon in Hertfordshire.

Charles was in the habit of visiting Newmarket regularly in April and October. It so happened that, in April 1683, he had returned from Newmarket a week earlier than usual owing to a fire. Here was the miraculous event which confirmed West as the murder of Godfrey had confirmed Oates. The king returned to Whitehall, and all the members of the Council of Six were arrested, with the exception of Monmouth. At first Essex did not seem to apprehend danger; but later he showed signs of confusion, and he must have realized that, with so many informers around him, his most innocent acts could easily be construed as treasonable. He committed suicide in the Tower on July 13, the day on which the trial of lord Russell began.

Lord Howard, once more an informer, gave evidence against Russell.[1] He said there had been talk of a rising before Shaftesbury's departure; afterwards they feared they might have gone too far. As a member of the Council of Six, Howard described the negotiations with Argyle and the Scots, evidence objected to by Russell, since it gave proof of no overt act; whereupon the court ruled that the assembling of council to raise a rebellion constituted an overt act, and that this had been proved by Rumsey, who swore that, with other persons, he went to Russell's house to find out what resolutions had been come to; by Shepherd, who swore that in October 1682 Monmouth, Ferguson, and Russell discoursed of a way to seize the Guards; and thirdly, by Howard, whose evidence, though admittedly hearsay, was

[1] *The tryals of Thomas Walcot, William Hone, William lord Russell, John Rous, and William Flagg* (1683), 42–6.

confirmed by these two preceding. Russell's defence was that he had been at Shepherd's wineshop accidentally, where he had overheard talk, but had not himself engaged in a plot. ''Tis hard', he said, 'that a man must lose his life on hear-say,' words which adequately describe the evidence on which he was convicted.[1] On July 14 he was sentenced to death with Walcot; and, though powerful family influence was exerted to procure a remission of the sentence, he was executed on July 21 in Lincoln's Inn Fields, after receiving the ministrations of both Burnet and Tillotson, in the presence of a great and silent crowd, some of whom dipped handkerchiefs in his blood.

The next victim was Algernon Sidney, whose trial began on November 21. The indictment[2] alleged that, as one of the Council of Six, he had meditated rebellion; that he had sent Aaron Smith into Scotland in order to promote sedition, and that he was the author of treasonable opinions found in papers left in his study. For the first two counts the only serious witness was again Howard, whose evidence Sidney objected to because he was his creditor, and had admitted to him that he could not procure his pardon until he had done some more jobs.[3] Extracts from Sidney's unpublished papers were read in court.[4] These contained quotations from Bracton, and statements implying that, as the king held his power from the people, he might be deposed if he violated his trust. To this evidence the accused objected that the authorship was not proved, that the papers were merely an answer to Filmer, and that in any event he was not answerable for what he wrote in his study unless he published it.[5] Thereupon Jeffreys, ever apt at quotation, recited these words: 'Curse not the king; not in thy thoughts, nor in thy bed-chamber; the birds of the air will carry it';[6] but how far this helped to substantiate the charge of high treason he did not explain. Burnet, in his evidence for the defence, said that Howard had come to him, and had sworn that there was no plot; as regards the papers, Sidney said that they had no connexion with any political design, and were written many years before. But these pleas were brushed aside by Jeffreys with the malicious innuendo: 'A man convinced of these principles

[1] Ibid. 50.
[2] *The arraignment, tryal and condemnation of Algernon Sidney Esq.* (1684), 1–8.
[3] Ibid. 30.   [4] Ibid. 23–6.   [5] Ibid. 31–3.   [6] Ibid. 35.

and that walks accordingly, what won't he do to accomplish his designs?'[1] The case against him, therefore, was that the principles found in papers attributed to his authorship might lead to treasonable acts if logically carried out; on this hypothesis he was found guilty, and executed on Tower Hill on December 7, 1683, the king having remitted all the sentence except the beheading. It was freely admitted at Court that though there was proof of talk about insurrection, there was no evidence of any plot to kill the king.[2]

John Hampden's trial[3] took place on February 6, 1684. The chief witness was again Howard, but his evidence was now become farcical; for his own remorse removed all conviction from his words; indeed he was alleged to have declared that Russell died an innocent man, and he was said to have confessed to a friend that he could not have a pardon until his drudgery of swearing was over. Lord chief justice Jeffreys, anxious on behalf of this witness, asked whether he had his pardon, and on being assured in the affirmative by the solicitor-general he remarked, 'Then your lordship may be covered'.[4] Evidence was then given of Hampden's 'high misdemeanour' in having agreed that a certain person should be sent to Scotland 'to incite divers persons there to come into England to consult with you, Hampden, concerning aid and assistance to be supplied from Scotland'. This hypothesis was nearly as cloudy as that which had procured the conviction of Sidney. Jeffreys, after a speech in defence of Howard and in accusation of the prisoner, directed the jury to find a verdict of guilty,[5] which was promptly done. His sentence was comparatively light—a fine of £40,000 and imprisonment until he paid it.

One more notable trial remains to be recorded of a period when history was being accelerated by judge and executioner. The duke of York brought an action against Titus Oates on the statute *De scandalis magnatum*, and the case was heard on June 18, 1684.[6] The indictment alleged that Oates had circulated false

[1] *The arraignment, tryal and condemnation of Algernon Sidney Esq.* (1684), 54.
[2] *Baschet*, 155, July 5/15, 1683.
[3] *The tryal and conviction of John Hambden Esq.* (1684).
[4] Ibid. 17.   [5] Ibid. 38–54.
[6] *The account of the manner of executing a writ of enquiry of damages between H.R.H. James duke of York and Titus Oates* (1684).

news and lies about the duke of York, the specific instance being that in December 1682, in a coffee-house, 'amid divers venerable persons' he had held up a letter and proclaimed in a loud voice: 'This letter cost me nine pence and might have been brought for a penny; nobody is the better for it but that traitor the duke of York.'[1] Justice Warcup gave evidence in support of the charge; and Jeffreys (who addressed the accused with scathing emphasis as *Mr.* Oates) demanded that he should be made an example of.[2] The jury took the hint, and assessed the damages at £100,000 with the somewhat superfluous addition of 20s. costs; and so Titus disappeared for a short time from public view, convicted (so strange was the age) not as a perjurer, but as a premature advocate of the penny post. It was indeed a melancholy fate that had overtaken the whigs. Monmouth was in hiding; Shaftesbury had died in exile; Essex had destroyed himself; Russell and Sidney had lost their lives, and Oates had lost his doctorate. The Popish Plot had destroyed about a score of persons, mainly priests or Jesuits; the Stuart revenge, on the other hand, had removed some of the most distinguished representatives of the English aristocracy, and was therefore the more notable as an object-lesson. Supreme above it all was the cynical monarch, comfortable at last; now almost domesticated by the duchess of Portsmouth; his royal person specially protected by a Swiss bodyguard sent over by his solicitous ally Louis XIV.[3] He was still, it is true, being plagued by the prince of Orange, but he had given his nephew 'a slap in the face'[4] by marrying his niece the princess Anne to the Lutheran George of Denmark; so William could no longer claim to be the sole exponent in the family of virtue and Protestantism.

This marriage was acceptable to Louis, since Denmark was among the subsidized allies of France, and it may be numbered with the consequences of the French subsidy on English policy. Abroad, these consequences were also demonstrated. The French king continued his aggressions in the Spanish Netherlands, confident that he could do so without involving himself in war; while

[1] Ibid. 5. [2] Ibid. 19, 21-2.
[3] *Baschet*, 155, July 14/24, 1683. It was commanded by the marquis de Tilladet.
[4] Ibid., May 3/13. The marriage was solemnized on July 28, 1683.

on his side Charles expressed a willingness to help his Spanish ally
by arbitration; but Ronquillo, the Spanish ambassador, knew
that, as arbiter, Charles would decide in favour of Louis; so he
demanded mediation, which in his turn Louis refused to accept.
There was, therefore, an element of futility in the prolonged
negotiations whereby the Spanish and Dutch envoys strove to
induce Charles to honour his treaty with Spain and his promises
of 1681. Moreover, as the Dutch were divided, and as Amsterdam was lacking in sympathy for the policy of William, Louis
was able to proceed on his way unchecked, capturing Luxemburg
in May 1684, and foisting on the humiliated Spanish government a 'truce' of twenty years. For French ascendancy in these
years Charles must accept some of the blame; and Louis was able
to congratulate himself on the advantages secured to him by the
verbal treaty; but not for long, since he had to restore Luxemburg
with other conquests at the peace of Ryswick. He had purchased
the admittedly valueless neutrality of England, but he could not
have foreseen that the England of Charles Stuart would one day
be replaced by the England of king William, and still worse for
him by the England of queen Anne.

A period of more intense reaction followed on the discovery of
the Rye House Plot. In March 1683 Luttrell noted that the
tempers of men were now much altered from what they had been
only a year ago, 'most now seeming Tories',[1] a change nowhere
more clearly illustrated than in the fugitive literature of the
period, in which there were two main motives—hatred of whigs
and dissenters, and unbounded, indeed extravagant devotion to
the crown. In this chorus the voice of the subsidized L'Estrange
was the loudest. He had already exhausted all the similitudes
of vituperation in comparisons of 1681 with 1641; he then
exposed the Popish Plot, contending that Godfrey's death was
due to suicide; he followed up Marvell's *History of Popery* with
a *History of Knavery*, and after 1681 he produced a weekly
news-sheet, called *Heraclitus Ridens*, afterwards named *The
Observator*.[2] L'Estrange knew the importance of exaggeration in
journalism; he distorted the lines of party cleavage, but for

[1] Luttrell, *Brief narration* ... (1857 ed.), i. 252.
[2] For a good account of L'Estrange's literary activities see G. Kitchin,
Sir Roger L'Estrange.

that reason brought them within the vision of a greater number of men.

The principles of L'Estrange were not more extreme than those advocated in the addresses which poured in from loyal grand juries. That from Kent in March 1683 condemned not only popery and fanaticism, but 'all such as pretend to moderation in execution of the laws, where the government is apparently assaulted'; from Bristol, formerly a stronghold of nonconformity, came a petition for the enforcement of the law against conventicles; Northampton sent a long list of disaffected persons, with the suggestion that they should be required to give security for keeping the peace; the jurymen of Devonshire were convinced that the Rye House Plot was attributable to nonconformist preachers; others, such as the grand jury of Southwark, blamed coffee-houses, seditious books, taverns. Other juries thought that greater control might be exercised over the talk at public places of refreshment if the keepers of these places were required to take the sacrament according to the practice of the Church of England.[1]

Charles made no secret of his intention to exact retribution for the Popish Plot.[2] So the campaign against the Dissenters was intensified, and the winter of 1683-4, one of the coldest on record, was a period of exceptional suffering for the recusants, of whom 1,300 Quakers are known to have been imprisoned throughout the greater part of the winter.[3] The year 1684 was that in which the French dragoons commenced their operations against the Huguenots; the same year saw a tentative beginning in England of the same process. But for the earnest solicitations of the justices, dragoons would have been sent into Shropshire in December 1684 in order to apply the methods of persuasion then being applied in Scotland and France;[4] and it was a striking tribute to the strength of English local government that, distorted as it had been by the remodellings, it was yet powerful enough to resist this sinister proposal. In Scotland, where there was no

[1] A large collection of these addresses will be found in *Bodley, Ashmole* 1674.
[2] *Baschet*, 149, Aug. 11/21, 1681.
[3] *S.P. Dom.* 29, bundle 436, State of the Quakers, Jan. 1684.
[4] Ibid., bundle 438, letters from Charles Holt and other Justices to Sunderland, Dec. 8 and Dec. 15, 1684.

such protection for the subject, the reign of terror was unchecked. In December 1684 general Drummond was given a commission to exercise military law and to hang, draw, and quarter all who refused the king's authority. The efficacy of this measure was seen in the fact that men condemned at two were hanged at five.[1] These things provided a warning to any English whig who dared to raise his head; and if he insisted on losing his head, he could read, in the *Apology* attributed to Jack Ketch,[2] a description of the posture most suitable at executions for ensuring 'a quicker despatch out of this world'.

By April 1684 the royal triumph appeared to be complete. Parliament was not again summoned, in spite of the provisions of the Triennial Act, and the king intimated to Barrillon that he had no thoughts of summoning parliament.[3] In the preceding February, by the connivance of the judges, Danby was released from the Tower, and the three surviving Catholic peers, lords Arundel, Powis and Belasyse, were also liberated. The duke of York resumed his effective control over the Navy,[4] and there was talk of reconstituting him lord high admiral; moreover, when Jenkins resigned his secretaryship, Godolphin was installed in his place, and the likelihood of Rochester exchanging his office of first commissioner of the Treasury for that of lord high treasurer served to strengthen the possibility that Charles would still more securely establish himself on the bases of reaction and subserviency, with York and Barrillon as his counsellors and Rochester and Godolphin as his tools. The completion by Louis of his *réunion* annexations, and the return of Dartmouth in April 1684 from the evacuation of Tangier formed a fitting climax to this policy of terrorism at home and surrender abroad.

But the reign, so full of unsolved problems, ended on a note of interrogation. What was the purport of the ministerial changes which caused such surprise in the summer of 1684?[5] A relative

---

[1] Fountainhall, *Chronological notes of Scottish affairs*, 48.

[2] *The apology of John Ketch Esq.* (occasioned by his bungling at the execution of lord Russell) in *Bodley Ashmole*, F. 6.

[3] *Baschet*, 157, March 9/19, 1684.

[4] On May 8/18, 1684, Louis wrote to Barrillon: 'Le roi d'Angleterre ne pourrait prendre une résolution plus convenable au bien de ses affaires et à sa réputation qu'est celle de rétablir le duc d'York dans toutes ses fonctions.' *Aff. Étr.* (*Angleterre*), 152, f. 292.   [5] For this see *Halifax*, i. 420–8.

of Halifax, Henry Thynne, was appointed to the Treasury commission; in August, Rochester, to his disgust, was 'kicked upstairs' into the office of lord president of the council; in November there was talk of sending the duke of York back to Scotland as royal commissioner; there were also rumours of a secret visit of Monmouth to England and a reconciliation with his father; there were even hints of more friendly overtures to the prince of Orange. There seemed a possibility that the moderate and humane counsels of Halifax would at last prevail, and in the *Character of a Trimmer* Halifax delineated for the benefit of Charles a philosophy of kingship wherein were incorporated all the lessons to be deduced from the shame and tragedy of these years. It seemed that an age of marvels was about to be capped by the supreme marvel of all—the repentance of a Stuart.

It is possible, however, that these things are proof not of radical change, but of vacillation or experiment. In April 1684 the verbal treaty of 1681 was at an end, and no fresh commitments were made; but that did not mean the termination of the French connexion. There had been delay and dispute in the payments of the subsidy; the money was in arrears, and some of it was still owing at Charles's death;[1] this may account in part for the omission to renew the engagement in April 1684. Of two facts the correspondence provides proof; that Charles and his brother were determined to rule as the pensionaries of France, and that Louis was willing to pay them, not only to secure acquiescence in French policy, but for a more constructive and disinterested object—to maintain a strong Stuart monarchy in England. But Charles, unlike James, had a genius for obtaining a good bargain; and it is likely that the changes of 1684 were only one more illustration of this instinct. There was a reconciliation with Monmouth, but it was short-lived, for the unfortunate duke refused to write a confession incriminating his associates; and as he would not turn informer, he was ordered to leave the Court.[2] The more friendly attitude to the prince of Orange may have sprung from the fact that in August 1684 the prince's supremacy was seriously

[1] The amount was 470,000 livres. See the letter of Louis to Barrillon, May 15/25, 1685, in Fox, *A history of the early part of the reign of James II*, Appendix lxxxvii.

[2] *Baschet*, 156, Nov. 26/Dec. 6 and Dec. 6/16, 1683.

threatened by the Amsterdam oligarchy, and there was a possibility of reconciliation between the States General and Louis, whereby it became the interest of Charles to support the anti-French element among the Dutch.[1] Otherwise the policy of Charles was perfectly consistent. He confessed that he had taken the side of France for the rest of his life;[2] he was secretly annoyed at William's patronage of Monmouth in Holland;[3] he declared himself resolved to dismiss Halifax from the Council;[4] he recalled Ormonde from Ireland and appointed Rochester in his place; many Catholics were released from prison, and it was freely rumoured that there was a design to create a papist army in Ireland.[5] In neither England nor Scotland was a parliament summoned, and James remained by his brother's side, relentless and vindictive, eager to clutch the sceptre which had so nearly eluded his grasp.

In October 1684 Charles and his brother inspected the troops mustered on Putney Heath, and the tory pamphleteers acclaimed this public demonstration that the crown now possessed a standing army for its preservation against whiggery and dissent.[6] Whither these things tended was a question as difficult as that occasioned in the early months of 1660, when the Rump was confronted by the veterans of Monck. But the question was not to be answered by Charles. On February 1, 1685, he had a seizure, and, after rallying, died[7] before noon on the 6th, after receiving absolution, communion, and extreme unction at the hands of a priest. Before he died he asked for the curtains to be drawn so that he might see the light of day; he besought the reconciliation of his brother and the forgiveness of his queen, and it was in this spirit of solicitude for others that Charles quitted a crowded stage whereon he had seemed as often spectator as actor.

---

[1] *Baschet*, 159, Aug. 11/21, 1684.   [2] Ibid. 159, Aug. 11/21, 1684.
[3] Ibid. 159, Oct. 16/26.   [4] Ibid. 159, Dec. 4/14.
[5] Ibid. 160, Dec. 29, 1684/Jan. 8, 1685.
[6] Some of the pamphlets are in *Bodley, Ashmole*, G. 15. See also *The exercise of musquet and pike as performed before H.M. and H.R.H. at Putney Heath, Oct. 1, 1684*, in *Bodley, Ashmole*, H. 23, no. 4.
[7] For the cause of the king's death see E. R. Crawfurd, *The last days of Charles II*.

XVIII

THE PLANTATIONS AND DEPENDENCIES

THREE main types of settlement have to be considered—(1) the garrison of Tangier and the dependencies in India, the latter administered by the East India Company: (2) the crown and proprietary colonies in the west, represented by Barbados, the Leeward Islands, Jamaica, New York, and New Jersey, together with Maryland, the Carolinas and Pennsylvania; and (3) the New England group, consisting of Massachusetts (with New Hampshire), New Plymouth, Connecticut, and Rhode Island.

Of English possessions in Asia and Africa the most important were those acquired by the Portuguese marriage—Tangier[1] and Bombay. Tangier, which had come into Portuguese possession in 1471, was deemed to be Spanish when Portugal lost her independence in 1580; consequently, after its acquisition by England, there was always the possibility of the revival of Spanish claims. Arrangements were speedily made for the fortification and settlement of this new possession; and in September 1661 Henry Mordaunt, earl of Peterborough, received his commission as governor. Control was vested in a committee of the Privy Council, and to the governor was delegated the power of making laws for the civil government. The port was declared free for five years to all traffic except that from the English plantations and from beyond the Cape of Good Hope.[2] As a further encouragement to commerce it was enacted that foreign merchants might freely trade in the port until six months after the outbreak of hostilities involving their native countries.[3] Tangier was valued in England because it was hoped that from this base an entry might be obtained into the rich Barbary trade of corn, hides, oils, feathers, copper, and gold. This, however, was eventually left to private enterprise.

The first problem was to provide a civil population for the new

---

[1] For a good account of Tangier under English rule see E. M. G. Routh, *Tangier*.

[2] Steele, i. 3369, Nov. 16, 1662.   [3] Steele, i. 3606, Jan. 13, 1675.

African outpost. Some proposed that first offenders should be sent out; others suggested a third part of the population of Scotland; the government eventually dispatched a mixed contingent containing some criminals and political offenders.[1] In order to supplement the recruits for the garrison, deceit had sometimes to be practised; men were enlisted on the understanding that they were intended for Portsmouth, when their real destination was Tangier. The total establishment was estimated to cost £70,000 per annum;[2] and when in 1663 lord Rutherford succeeded Peterborough as governor, the garrison consisted of 2,000 men. By 1678 the civilian population amounted to only 600 persons.[3] From the start, danger came from the Arabs, notably the hordes led by the crafty Ghailan, who, in pursuing his design of creating an independent kingdom in Northern Fez, was destined to prove the bane of the English garrison. Rutherford was killed in a skirmish in May 1664, and was succeeded by lord Belasyse, under whom the port developed a trade with Spain; at the same time, a great defensive mole was constructed. In the Second Dutch War the strategic value of the port was proved; for, using it as his base, sir Jeremy Smith was able to hold the Straits while the French fleet was cooped up in Toulon; it served also to support the fleet of English privateers preying on French and Dutch merchantmen in the Mediterranean. By the end of the war Tangier had received the charter of an incorporated city, having a civil court presided over by the mayor and recorder; while its commercial causes were adjudicated in a court-merchant which met daily.

But Tangier never prospered. It was isolated in a hostile territory: its garrison, barely adequate for defence, could scarcely hold its own against Arab aggressors; moreover, there was little capital circulating in the port. Because of the economies forced upon them, governors had to sacrifice the defences; the garrison was dependent on provisions sent from home, which, owing to the lack of imagination sometimes found in official victuallers, were generally more suited for a Northern winter than an African summer, consisting as they did of salt beef, pork, cheese, and

---

[1] For examples see *Cal. S.P. Dom., 1663–4,* 536, 539.
[2] E. M. G. Routh, *Tangier,* 29.
[3] *H.M.C. Rep.* xi, pt. v. 27. Dartmouth MSS.

oatmeal. Casks of meat which had outstayed their welcome else-where were sometimes thought good enough for dispatch to this Cinderella of the empire. Few 'men of credit' settled in the port, so there was little capital for trade with the Moors; and even that with Spain was carried on mainly by French merchants. It was a place of call rather than a settlement: itinerant Turks and Armenians spread out their glittering wares on the sands before the eyes of a needy populace; but even these, the most insistent of all traffickers, could do little business. There was a chance that a fruit and wine trade with England might have been established, but the difficulty was to find ships, as the port was more fre-quented by men-of-war than by merchantmen; and so merchants had often to entrust their goods to the former, at the cost of naval efficiency. Men such as Palmes Fairborne (deputy governor, 1676–8) devoted themselves to the interests of the settlement; but this self-sacrifice was outweighed by the cynical fatalism of Sun-derland, and the indifference of lord Inchiquin (governor, 1674–80). In 1680, after a siege, the fortifications were almost in ruins.

Events at home precipitated the end. Rumours that Charles intended to sell Tangier caused parliament in 1679 to draft a Bill for annexing it to the imperial crown of England,[1] so that it might not be sold to the French; but the fate of Tangier was sealed when it was made the price of Charles's consent to exclusion.[2] In the winter of 1682–3 Charles tried to sell it to France, but Louis would not have it;[3] an attempt was then made to sell it to Portu-gal, but this also failed.[4] Charles therefore decided to quit possession of a place which he could not afford to keep, and so it was evacuated in August 1683, after elaborate precautions had been taken to destroy the mole. So ended England's most un-fortunate overseas enterprise.

Bombay, 'with all rights, profits, and territories thereto belong-ing' was acquired by the crown in accordance with the eleventh clause of the marriage treaty. The wording of this clause was easily capable of dispute; for it was not clear whether the de-pendencies were included, a doubt which led to prolonged dis-pute. The Portuguese intended by the grant to facilitate English co-operation against the Dutch in the East Indies, and were

[1] C.J. ix. 625, May 20, 1679.   [2] See *supra*, 603.
[3] *Baschet*, 154, Jan. 4/14, 1683.   [4] Ibid. 155, April 23/May 3, 1683.

specially anxious that the religion of the Portuguese merchants should be safeguarded; while the English wished mainly to develop the commercial possibilities of the new acquisition, two points of view never quite reconciled.[1] Difficulties commenced with the arrival, in March 1662, of a fleet with 500 troops to take possession. By the English it was insisted that the dependencies were included in the grant; while the Portuguese were equally certain that only the island was referred to. More pressing was the question: where to land the troops? Oxenden, the agent at Surat, was asked for permission to land them there, but the consent of the Moghul emperor could not be obtained, and eventually the garrison was landed on the unhealthy island of Anjediva, where half of them died from disease. While these men were perishing, an acrimonious correspondence was being conducted by the two governments on the correct interpretation of the treaty, and a stage was even reached when the Portuguese offered to buy back Bombay; but they could not find the money to pay Clarendon's price of £120,000, with £109,000 for the expenses of the expedition.

Not till January 1665 did Humfrey Cooke (the 'Inofre Coque' of Portuguese orthography) take over Bombay as governor, and then only the port and island, a concession deeply resented at home. In terms of a convention not ratified by either government the Portuguese were to have free trade in the port, and the English undertook to respect the religion of Catholics, but all religious refugees and runaways were to be excluded.[2] As the dependencies were not included in this agreement, English ships were subjected to heavy duties at Thana and Karanja. But though Cooke began his governorship by concession, he soon augmented it by acquisition; for before the end of his governorship (1666) he had taken over Mahim, Sion, Dharavu, and Vadala, so that Bombay now included all the islands except Colaba and Old Woman's Island.[3] This policy was followed by his successor sir Gervase Lucas.

So far, Bombay had brought to the Stuart bridegroom not riches, but irritation and expense. In 1666 the cost of ammuni-

[1] See P. B. M. Malabari, *Bombay in the making*, ch. iii; also S. A. Khan, *Anglo-Portuguese negotiations relating to Bombay*.

[2] Malabari, op. cit. 98–9.   [3] Ibid. 103.

tion and victuals amounted to £11,498, while the rents, including the revenue from taverns, Customs, tobacco, and coco-nuts, was only £6,490.[1] Charles's finances were too straitened to permit the retention of a possession which promised nothing but an annual deficit: accordingly, in December 1667 he granted it to the East India Company to be held in free and common socage at a rent of £10 per annum. The royal charter surrendering Bombay to the Company is dated March 27, 1668. By this, the Company acquired full dominion and jurisdiction in the port and island, thereby adding to their trading privileges the prerogative of civil and military government. The right of reversion was preserved to the crown by the terms of the grant, which specified that the laws enacted should be 'consonant to reason, and not repugnant or contrary, but as near as may be agreeable to the laws of England'. There was also a proviso for the exercise of the Roman Catholic religion by Portuguese merchants. On these terms Bombay was taken over by sir George Oxenden, the Company's representative at Surat.

The most notable of the earlier governors appointed by the Company was Gerald Aungier,[2] who first established a civil administration. He divided the inhabitants into orders and tribes, each having a representative; and by this 'Panchayat' system, as it was called, he inaugurated a measure of self-government, with the governor and council as a court of appeal. The most responsible among the English merchants were appointed justices: suits involving more than $3\frac{1}{2}$ rupees were reserved for the governor and council; the nucleus of a civil service was provided by a contingent of Parbhu clerks. Disputed land titles were settled by the summoning of conventions, and, after the confirmation of land titles, the quit-rents were increased. Tolerant and enterprising, Aungier conciliated English, Italian, and Portuguese by respect for their distinctive characteristics; he encouraged traders and weavers to settle; he extended still farther the area under his governorship, until by the end of his administration the population had reached 60,000 and the revenue £9,000. The Company considered, however, that he had taken

---

[1] S. A. Khan, *East India trade in the seventeenth century*, 137.

[2] Malabari, op. cit., ch. iv, and *English Factories in India*, ed. sir W. Foster, 1665-7, 180 sqq.

upon himself more than was proper; so when he died (1677), the salary of his successor was fixed at £300 instead of £500, and the relative importance of Bombay declined. The victim of the Company's economies and maladministration, Bombay came most notably into public prominence in 1683, when captain Richard Keigwin, heading a revolt of the discontented garrison, overthrew the Company's civil representative and had himself elected governor. In his correspondence with Charles II he so ingratiated himself with that monarch as to obtain a full pardon.[1]

In 1687 the fortified Bombay superseded Surat as the head-quarters of the western presidency.[2] By that time sir Josiah Child had become a leading spirit in the East India Company. His policy was to strengthen the coast-line in order to make trade more secure; to accord fair treatment to the natives, without binding himself by legal scruple; to follow the Dutch example of raising a revenue from natives to defray the charge of their protection; to increase the number of trading stations, and to avoid as much as possible the responsibilities and inconveniences of political domination. In the pursuit of this policy he amassed great wealth for himself and his relatives; and the political influence which he was thereby able to purchase accounts in part for the increasing jealousy and hostility with which the Company came to be regarded. After 1680 the Company had to increase its exports of broadcloth in order to conciliate public opinion; but interloping steadily increased, and by the reign of William III, when the interests of the Company became entangled with party politics, its reorganization was inevitable.

Elsewhere in India the foundations of British power were being established. The fort at Madras was strengthened in 1677 against the Marathas by sir Streynsham Masters. Defence was speedily followed by the institution of civil administration; a court of judicature and a bank were instituted, and by 1688 there existed a municipal government in Madras.[3] But with the decay of the Moghul empire the Company had to depend more and more on the guns of its ships and the enterprise of its servants. Of these servants one of the most notable was Job Charnock, appointed

---

[1] For this incident and the career of a remarkable man see R. and O. Strachey, *Keigwin's Rebellion*.   [2] *Cambridge History of India*, v. 101–2.
[3] Sir W. Hunter, *A History of British India*, ii. 233 sqq.

chief of the Bengal council in 1685. In December 1686, when the Company was at war with the Moghul, he proceeded down the Hughli with a small force to the site of the modern Calcutta, where he made a resolute stand against the land forces threatening him on every side;[1] and in the following autumn he erected a factory on the pool of Calcutta, after adventures and privations of almost epic magnitude. He was an empire-builder in the strict sense of that term. When, in 1690, the Company had to accept a contemptuous peace from Aurungzeb, Charnock returned to his ruined settlement on the Hughli and laid the foundations of one more capital in India.[2]

The East India Company had a station at Bantam in Java, from which it was hoped to develop the spice trade; but, early in 1683, the Dutch expelled the English from the fort. This was one of the events which obliged the Company to concentrate on India, and to build up political supremacy on the basis of sea power. Another event occurred which helped the Company to maintain the maritime connexions on which depended sovereignty in the east; this was the capture of St. Helena from the Dutch. The island had been taken over by the Company's ships in 1652; it was lost to the enemy during each of the later Anglo-Dutch wars; but in 1673 it was again seized (by captain Munden), and granted to the East India Company. Thereafter it was the 'sea inn' of the eastern trade. St. Helena was of special importance to English communications because the Dutch were then supreme at the Cape of Good Hope.

On the mainland of South America several attempts had been made to colonize parts of Guiana;[3] and in 1663 Charles granted to Francis, lord Willoughby all the area called Surinam. This settlement was called Willoughby Land, and contained about 4,000 persons who suffered severely from sickness. It was captured by the Dutch in the Second Dutch War, and though recaptured by admiral sir John Harman it was ceded to the Dutch by the treaty of Breda. The insalubrious Cayenne was occupied by the English for ten years (1654–64); it changed hands in the Second Anglo-Dutch War, and was eventually given up to the French. In the West Indies, the Bermudas or Somers Islands had been

---

[1] Ibid. ii. 257.   [2] P. E. Roberts, *History of British India*, 46.

[3] For this see J. A. Williamson, *English colonies in Guiana and on the Amazon*.

granted in 1615 to the earl of Southampton and others, who were incorporated into a company; in 1684 the company's rights were transferred to the crown. From Bermuda were exported provisions to other colonies; among its exports to England were tobacco and cedar wood. The Bahamas were not occupied until 1670.

In the Caribbean are two groups of islands known as the Windward Islands, that is, Barbados, St. Lucia, St. Vincent, and Tobago; and the Leeward Islands, comprising Antigua, Montserrat, Nevis, and St. Christopher. Officially, the ownership of the Caribbean islands was taken over by the king after the Restoration; but actually something of the old proprietary right survived in the terms of the patent of Francis, lord Willoughby, who was appointed governor-in-chief of all the Caribees. He ruled with the assistance of a council and island representatives, and the planters' right to their estate was confirmed by their agreement to pay the four-and-a-half per cent. export duty. Of strategic importance, the Leeward Islands had had to bear the brunt of French attacks during the Second Anglo-Dutch War, the English being driven from Antigua and Montserrat, as well as from their portion of St. Christopher (St. Kitts), while Nevis was preserved for England only at great cost. But in May 1667 the French fleet was decisively defeated in Nevis roads. Antigua and Montserrat had been recaptured a few months earlier, and the English parts of St. Kitts were restored by the treaty of Breda. The administration of these islands had therefore to face the question of obtaining locally a contribution to the cost of defence. It was proposed to start a fund for this purpose, but this was refused in 1682 by a general assembly representing each of the island legislatures; this body also refused to grant a perpetual revenue to the crown, and the planters declined to pay for the maintenance of an agent in England.[1] These refusals implied a challenge not successfully contested by the governments of either Charles II or James II.

Of the Windward group, by far the most important was Barbados,[2] an island having a population reckoned in 1668 at about 20,000 planters and whites, and 40,000 negroes, its trade

[1] C. S. S. Higham, *The Development of the Leeward Islands*, 230 sqq.
[2] For a good account see V. T. Harlow, *Barbados*.

carried on by 10,000 tons of shipping.[1] With its militia of 6,000 men it was the best fortified of the islands, and its 100,000 acres were worth from £10 to £20 an acre. At first tobacco was the staple crop; but this was superseded by sugar, the production of which necessitated a large supply of black labour; this was provided by the Royal African Company, which, after its reconstitution in 1672, was able to dispose of negroes at £16 per head.[2] This increase in the proportion of the African element helped to accentuate the problems of population in Barbados, where unusual conditions prevailed; for land was concentrated in the hands of the large proprietors,[3] and few servants who had served their indentures could hope to acquire a holding; moreover, it had been the practice of Cromwell to ship felons and desperate characters to the island.[4] Another problem was that of overproduction. Sugar, assessed in the Book of Rates (1660) at 30s. per hundred pounds, steadily fell in price owing to gluts and competition from French and Portuguese sugar colonies; by 1685 the price[5] had sunk to 20s. By that time England had lost the European market in refined sugar, but continued to maintain her re-export trade in raw sugar, which, as it needed more shipping than refined, was given preferential treatment when additional duties were imposed in 1685. This policy was at the expense of the refiners in the West Indies, notably Barbados; and caused such discontent that there was at times a danger of the island going over to the French.[6]

The largest and most important of the English West Indian possessions was Jamaica, having an area of over 4,000 square miles. Captured from Spain in 1655 by Penn and Venables, it was the 'pet' colony of the Restoration, for its climate favoured the production of those sub-tropical products most in demand, namely, sugar, coffee, ginger, pepper, and cinchona bark; moreover, it abounded in cattle and horses. Jamaica conformed most closely to the current conception of the ideal plantation; because

[1] *Cal. S.P. Amer.*, *1661–8*, 586–7. Report of lord Willoughby, July 9, 1668. See also ibid. 207, Report of sir T. Modyford, May 10, 1664.

[2] Higham, op. cit. 150–4.

[3] In 1667 they were said to be only 760 in number. *Cal. S.P. Amer.*, *1661–8*, 529.　　[4] Harlow, op. cit. 117.　　[5] Higham, op. cit. 192.

[6] *Cal. S.P. Dom.*, *1676–7*, 464. Notes by Williamson of information about Barbados.

its size favoured both commercial development and effective control; it offered a good market for English manufactured goods; it absorbed many of the negroes sent out by the African Company, and it exported those commodities in demand for home consumption and for re-export to the Continent. Special encouragement was given by the home government. In 1663 its exports were freed from Customs dues for five years,[1] and settlers there were given thirty acres, on condition that they served in arms and reserved one-twentieth of mineral rights to the crown.[2] This special favour was justified by results, for the history of the island under the later Stuarts was one of almost uninterrupted progress. In 1670 the population consisted of about 15,000 persons occupying 209,000 acres; there were about 57 sugar refineries, 49 indigo works, and 47 cocoa walks.[3] The revenue from quit-rents and duties on wine was then £1,870, and the expenses of government, including salaries of governor, deputy governor, major-general, and chief justice, together with upkeep of fortresses, amounted to £3,500. The spiritual needs of the island were seen to by five ministers, each having a salary of £100, paid by the crown.

Privateering[4] was the chief outlet for planters who wished to secure quicker returns on their capital. Near at hand lay some of the richest outposts of the exclusive Spanish empire; and though, in 1660, England was at peace with Spain, it was held by the council in Jamaica that the peace concerned only European waters. That the home government shared this view was seen in the instructions given to lord Windsor, who was sent to Jamaica as governor in 1661; for he was authorized to concert measures with the governor of Barbados against the Spaniards. A start was soon made, and in the following year captain Myngs took St. Iago in Cuba,[5] and early in 1663 there was a landing at Campeche[6] at the southern extremity of the gulf of Mexico. Charles was obliged to disavow these enterprises and leave this irregular warfare to the discretion of the governor; while at Madrid a succes-

---

[1] *Cal. Tr. Bks.*, 1660–7, 725.   [2] *Steele*, i. 3346, Dec. 14, 1661.
[3] *Cal. S.P. Amer.*, 1669–74, 104.
[4] For this subject see C. H. Haring, *The Buccaneers in the West Indies*.
[5] Sir C. H. Firth, *The capture of St. Iago* in *E.H.R.* xiv.
[6] Haring, op. cit. 107–8.

sion of English envoys, including Fanshawe, Sandwich, and Godolphin, were instructed to press for admission into the Spanish
empire, and in particular to secure the entry of negroes. But in
Godolphin's Anglo-Spanish treaty[1] of 1670 there was a clause
enacting that these depredations should cease. Piracy was thus
disavowed by both nations; nevertheless numerous conflicts were
occasioned by the cutting of logwood in the bay of Campeche by
Jamaican adventurers, and cargoes of this wood, though not
contraband, were generally confiscated by Spanish ships. The
English government connived at the cutting of Campeche wood;
but it was suggested that the privateers should cut it only in
unfrequented parts near the sea, and should confine themselves
to that alone.[2] Thus there existed in the years after 1670 a situation not unlike that which preceded the war of 1739 between
England and Spain.

This might be illustrated from the careers of notable pirates.
One of these was the Welshman sir Henry Morgan,[3] who, having
served his indentures in Barbados, went to Jamaica, where he
bought a ship and formed a small stock. In 1666 he was commissioned by governor Modyford to serve under captain Edward
Mansfield in an expedition against Curaçao; and on the latter's
death he became commander-in-chief of the West Indian buccaneers. In June 1668, with 10 ships and 500 men, he sacked
Porto Bello (on the isthmus of Darien), the head-quarters of
Spanish trade in central America, and destroyed the armada
sent against him, capturing 250,000 pieces of eight. In 1670 he
threatened Spanish dominion in Cuba, and was accorded a vote
of thanks by the Jamaican council;[4] this was followed by another
landing in Panama and the destruction of Spanish forts.[5] But
his actions were now disavowed, and his career at sea came to
an end. A second period of usefulness was inaugurated when,
through his favour with king Charles, he was appointed (1674)
lieutenant-governor of Jamaica and second-in-command to lord

[1] *Dumont*, vii, pt. i. 137–9, see *supra*, i. 350.

[2] Godolphin's memorandum for Arlington, May 1672, in Sloane MS. 180,
f. 71.

[3] For his career see the *Transactions of the Society of Cymmrodorion*, 1903–4;
also Haring, op. cit., ch. v.

[4] *Cal. S.P. Amer.*, *1669–74*, 220, May 31, 1671.

[5] Ibid., *1669–74*, 190.

Vaughan,[1] in which shore occupation he distinguished himself by his piety, his interest in churches, and his zeal against pirates; but in old age he appears to have reverted to his dissolute ways,[2] and he became a serious menace to the peace of the island. He shared with colonel Blood and captain Keigwin the honour of Charles's personal esteem.

Like Jamaica, Newfoundland had a special prestige in the hierarchy of English settlements, for it had been discovered by Cabot, and its cod-fishing was of special importance to England because of the seamen who were trained in the fleets. It was thought that, if properly managed, the fisheries might have produced £50,000 per annum in Customs, and could give employment to about 10,000 sailors.[3] But these results were not achieved, because Newfoundland was not under a settled government; the French possessed the best harbours, and were trying to acquire more; there was continual hostility between the fishermen and the denizens of the island, which was regarded by Charles's government as no more than a fishery station. This was illustrated by the rules[4] for its administration which the privy council drew up in March 1671. According to these rules, Englishmen were to have freedom of fishing in any of the rivers or harbours of Newfoundland, to the complete exclusion of aliens; fishing masters were to take out men at the rate of not more than 60 for every 100 tons, and of these every fifth man must be a 'green' man, that is, an untrained seaman. Victuals for the whole season were to be taken out in each ship, the season beginning on March 1 and ending on October 1; sailors were not allowed to remain on the island during the winter. In spite of these rules a small colony of Englishmen succeeded in making a settlement, in the hope of providing for themselves by fish-curing; but their plight was a hard one, because they were frequently despoiled by the fishermen in the summer, while in the winter they had to endure the rigours of the climate. Most of their houses were really taverns. Moreover, both planter and fisherman destroyed much of the timber, for they rooted up young trees to make their stages,

---

[1] *Cal. S.P. Amer.*, *1669–74*, 571.
[2] Ibid., *1681–5*, 515 and 532–5.
[3] Ibid., *1661–8*, 558–9. Reasons for the settlement of Newfoundland.
[4] *P.C. Reg.* 62, March 10, 1671.

and at the end of the season the fishermen threw all their stone ballast overboard into the shallow harbours.[1] In consequence, the home government was insistent in its efforts to induce the planters to go elsewhere, preferably to Barbados,[2] for the reason that the adventurers could catch fish more cheaply than the planters, and because the latter derived most of their products from New England.

On the mainland Virginia was the most important crown colony, and was occupied by Englishmen of substance, almost all of them Anglicans, grouped not in villages as in New England, but in plantations, most of them from 500 to 600 acres. In 1681 it was said that in the whole colony there was only one Papist and 150 Dissenters, the latter being all Sweet Singers of Israel.[3] The executive was vested in the Governor, assisted by a council and an assembly of 41 burgesses. The councillors, who monopolized many of the best-paid offices, were nominated by the governor; and the burgesses, who formed a close oligarchy, were elected by the freeholders.[4] Labour was supplied by indentured servants and by an increasing population of negroes. In temperament the Virginian planter was aristocratic, as befitted one who directed the labour of others; his occupation afforded periods of leisure, and his civilization reflected that of the landed classes in England, which in some respects it surpassed. Education was valued; the numerous Old Free Schools made illiteracy exceptional, and good teachers were recruited from the clergy.[5] The machinery of English local government was preserved intact; justice was administered 'according to the laws of England so far as we are able to understand them'; matters of fact were tried by juries, and included among the fundamental ordinances of the state were Magna Carta, the Petition of Right, and the writ of Habeas Corpus. In at least one respect there was an improvement on English custom, for penalties were more carefully graduated to the offence, and corporal punishment was more

---

[1] *Cal. S.P. Amer.*, *1669–74*, 148–9.

[2] Ibid., *1675–6*, 226–7. Order in Council of May 5, 1676.

[3] Ibid., *1681–5*, 145.

[4] For this see P. A. Bruce, *Institutional History of Virginia in the seventeenth century*, one of the most valuable contributions to the history of America.

[5] Bruce, op. cit., i. 331 sqq.

frequent than hanging; moreover, deeds of conveyance were enrolled in a public record office.

The charge of administration was raised by private levies in each parish for the minister, courts of justice, and payment of burgesses' wages; the sums so raised were not accounted for publicly. There was also the public levy, raised from time to time by the Assembly sitting in Jamestown; this was generally paid in tobacco, and was responsible for the production of much 'trash' tobacco.[1] Another serious difficulty in the management of the colony's revenues was that the general levies might be engrossed by particular persons, and applied to one fort at the expense of another; indeed it was the weakness of the colony's defences against the Indians that constituted the planters' greatest grievance. Another source of difficulty was the over-production of tobacco, which, coupled with the shortage of shipping, frequently caused acute economic distress. But in the midst of these things the House of Burgesses showed a zeal for constitutionalism as great as that of the English House of Commons. Thus in November 1683 they spent a day in wrangling with the Council over the swearing in of the Clerk of Assembly, and the appointment of joint committees. The Council gave way in the matter of the Clerk; the Burgesses then sent up their list of committees, which the Governor (lord Howard of Effingham) rejected, with a rebuke; whereupon the Council sent up an address to the effect that, as the Council had yielded over the Clerk, 'it might as well yield over the joint committees'. The governor then suggested the Stuart expedient of adjournment; but the Burgesses quoted precedents in support of their claim to nominate committees, and the matter was eventually settled by a conference between the two Houses.[2] The spirit of Westminster was abroad in the empire.

Hints of an even more ardent spirit had already been revealed in the rebellion known as Bacon's Rebellion. This arose mainly from the failure of the governor, sir William Berkeley, to listen to urgent requests[3] for protection against the repeated Indian raids. A crisis came with the invasion of the Susquehanna Indians in

---

[1] *Cal. S.P. Amer.*, *1681–5*, 154–5.
[2] Ibid., *1681–5*, 548–9, Nov. 20, 1683. Journal of the Assembly.
[3] Ibid., *1675–6*, 437–8.

May 1676. Meeting with no response from the governor, the men of Charles City County organized themselves into a volunteer force under the command of a remarkable and hot-headed man Nathaniel Bacon, member of a younger branch of the great chancellor's family. Bacon and his men were ordered by Berkeley to disband; when they refused, they became technically rebels, and during the summer months of 1676 the governor, then approaching a vindictive and calculating dotage, was pitted against the supporters of the popular leader. He won time by acquiescing in the demand for a new assembly on an enlarged franchise. Meanwhile Bacon formed an expeditionary force of 500 men, and, when Berkeley summoned the Militia against him, civil war followed. It was in the midst of this (August 3) that Bacon issued a manifesto, called a Declaration of the People of Virginia, signed by him as 'general by consent of the people', and containing an indictment of the government under these heads: taxes on pretext of public works were diverted to favourites; fortifications and trade were neglected; the governor's friends were appointed to judgeships; the governor had made the beaver trade a monopoly, and was protecting the Indians against His Majesty's subjects.[1] One of Bacon's avowed objects was the extirpation of the Indians.[2] The death of the leader in October practically ended a movement which, had it been successful, might have led to a more popular constitution in Virginia, and even to a readjustment of relations with the mother country; it was finally stamped out by ruthless executions. Commissioners were sent out from England for its investigation, and as they reported unfavourably on the conduct of Berkeley, he was sent home in disgrace.

The justification for Bacon's rebellion lay in the bad government of the Virginian oligarchy, a government which left many isolated planters defenceless against raids. In succeeding years the colony fared ill at the hands of some of its governors, notably lord Culpeper, whose object in coming to America was to retrieve his fortunes, an object in which he succeeded at the expense of

[1] Ibid., *1675–6*, 448.
[2] A good account of Virginia and the American plantations in this period will be found in C. M. Andrews, *Colonial Self-Government*, and in E. Channing, *A History of the United States*, vol. ii.

the colony. Otherwise he proved himself a good administrator, and was one of the first to suggest that the King in Council should formulate some uniform scheme of home defence or mutual assistance for the western plantations.[1] Poverty and thriftlessness appear to have caused a general irritability, which Culpeper's successor, lord Howard of Effingham (who succeeded in 1684), did something to intensify by his tactless handling of the Assembly; and not till after the Revolution, which was eagerly welcomed in Virginia, was the prosperity of the colony restored.

The association of Maryland with the Baltimore proprietors dated from their first charter of 1632. Protestants of all sects were encouraged to settle in order to counteract the original Roman Catholic element, a policy which made the position of the Roman Catholic proprietor lord Baltimore one of some difficulty. His almost feudal supremacy was restored at the Restoration; thereafter Maryland was a typical proprietary colony, its prosperity hampered to some extent by discord between the proprietor and his Puritan subjects, who contrived to extract a somewhat precarious subsistence from small, isolated farms and scattered tobacco plantations. As the colony had little shipping, its inhabitants suffered even more than did Virginia from gluts. In 1676 the population was about 20,000, and St. Mary's, then a small port of not more than about 30 houses,[2] was the seat of the Assembly of Burgesses, which held its session of six weeks once a year. These men were 'good ordinary householders, doing more by conscience than by syllogisms'.[3] Conflict between the officials of the Customs and of the proprietary increased with the more strict application of the Navigation laws, and a crisis was very nearly precipitated in 1684 when an English official was murdered by the deputy governor. This act almost caused the forfeiture of the proprietor's charter.[4]

Many of the Puritan settlers of Maryland lived in conditions of almost patriarchal simplicity and detachment. The Susquehanna divided the colony by a broad belt of deep water, thus

---

[1] *Cal. S.P. Amer., 1681–5*, 156. Culpeper to the Lords of Trade and Plantations, Dec. 12, 1681.

[2] Ibid., *1675–6*, 226.

[3] G. Alsop, *Character of the province of Maryland*, in *Narratives of Maryland*, ed. C. C. Hill, 351.   [4] *Cal. S.P. Amer., 1681–5*, vi.

helping to intensify the isolation of the homesteads, where there existed men and women who were perpetuating the traditions of an older and simpler England. They were thus described by an observer:

The Christian natives, especially those of the masculine sex, are generally conveniently confident, reservedly subtle, quick and apprehending, but slow in resolving; and when they spy profit sailing towards them with the wings of a prosperous gale, there they become much familiar. The women are extreme bashful at the first view, but after a continuance of time hath brought them acquainted, they become discreetly familiar and are much more talkative than men. One great part of the inhabitants are zealous, great pretenders to holiness; and where anything appears that carries on the frontispiece of its effigies the stamp of religion, tho' fundamentally never so imperfect, they are suddenly taken with it . . . and are very apt to be catch't. Quakerism is the only opinion that bears the bell away. The Anabaptists have little to say here; the Adamite, Ranter and Fifth Monarchy Man Maryland cannot digest within her liberal stomach.[1]

Maryland was therefore exceptional among the Puritan colonies in these respects: there was no clash of creeds; the fanatical sects were in a minority, and the Protestantism of the colony was tempered by the catholicism of its ruler and proprietor. In regard also to labour the colony was fortunate, for after four years' service the servant might become a freeman with 50 acres of land, a kit of tools, and three suits of clothes.[2]

Very different were the conditions in the Carolinas. The earliest grant of land in Carolina was that of 1629 to sir R. Heath; the first charter to lords proprietors was that dated March 24, 1663. Notable among the proprietors were two men, closely associated with the Usurpation—col. John Colleton, a man of great influence in Barbados, and Anthony Ashley Cooper. For some time both men had had in view the unoccupied lands in Carolina; and when the discontented elements in Barbados talked of another settlement, Colleton suggested an application for these lands. With Clarendon, Craven, Albemarle, Carteret, lord John Berkeley, and sir William Berkeley (governor of

[1] G. Alsop in *Maryland Narratives*, 352 sqq.
[2] Ibid. 358.

Virginia), Colleton, and Shaftesbury constituted the original eight proprietors, each of them contributing £25 capital. By their first charter they were granted the land on the continent between the 36th and the 31st parallel, the patentees to hold the land in free and common socage at a nominal rent, with power to make laws in conjunction with the freemen; they were also given the unusual right of conceding liberty of conscience to the settlers. The intention of this clause may have been to encourage settlers from Barbados, who, by their charter of 1652, were already endowed with this privilege.

There was no immediate response, for by 1672 only about 450 persons had settled in the province;[1] by which time it was thought that indigo, oil, silk, and tobacco might be produced, and, while sugar and cotton could be grown, the winter frosts were considered likely to prove fatal. The meagre population was hampered by shortage of provisions; only in constitutional experiment was there super-abundance. The first set of constitutions, dated 1669, was intended to encourage the settlement of 'ingenious and industrious persons' by the advantages of liberty of conscience, popular choice of governor and assembly, one hundred acres of land for each male, fifty for a female, and one thousand acres for a rent of ten shillings. This scheme owes much to the inspiration of Shaftesbury, and of Locke, who was secretary to the proprietors. It provided for a territorial aristocracy, the eldest called a palatine; the territory was divided into counties, each having eight seigniories, eight baronies, and twenty-four colonies of 12,000 acres; the seigniories pertaining to the proprietors, the baronies to the subordinate nobility, and the colonies to the commonalty. The subordinate nobility was divided into landgraves and caciques according to the number of their baronies. Executive and judicial power was vested in the eight proprietors sitting in their palatine court; they had the prerogative of summoning parliaments, pardoning offences, and vetoing the acts of parliament. The Church of England was to be established by law when occasion permitted, and meanwhile any body of at least seven members was accorded the rights of a church. Persons not members of a church were ostracized but not persecuted. There was no attempt to mitigate slavery. A lack

[1] *Cal. S.P. Amer., 1669–74*, 319.

of elasticity in the original scheme of 1669 led to changes in 1670 and 1682.[1]

As the experiment proceeded, the proprietors showed a zeal and forethought rare in such enterprises. The new-comers were enjoined to raise an adequate supply of provisions; they secured the remission for seven years of Customs duties on wine and silk exported to England; reservations were made for Quakers and Huguenots, and the town of Charlestown was built on a definite plan. With each fresh contingent of settlers the aristocratic owners showed an almost Gilbertian willingness to alter the 'fundamentals' in their favour; but they found some difficulty in soothing the susceptibilities of a party of Scots who 'doubted whether we have sufficiently provided against the oppression of the people by their administrators'.[2] 'We have no other aim', wrote Ashley in 1671, 'in the framing of our laws but to make every one as safe and happy as the state of human affairs is capable of.'[3] The laws were to be the 'equalest' that a state could have; terms which attracted many Protestants from England in the years 1679–1688, so that the population of the colony increased to about 3,000.

But the settlement did not at first answer the hopes of its founders. The proprietors were speedily in debt, and as their holdings depreciated in value, an inferior type of both proprietor and settler succeeded.[4] North Carolina became the refuge of Virginian renegades and the sink of America; a form of slave-trade was developed by capturing Indians and selling them back again; Acts were passed in the legislature prohibiting suits for debt at the instance of foreigners; and, by procuring an Act prohibiting the sale of arms to the Indians, illicit dealers were able to secure a monopoly of this trade. In the most idealist of all constitutions men boasted how for a bowl of punch they could secure the election of whomsoever they would for parliament,[5] and even the most salutary of legislation was often merely a cover for the activities of the organized law-breaker. Unfortunately,

---

[1] For a good account of this subject see J. A. Doyle, *The English in America. Virginia, Maryland, and the Carolinas*, 447–51.

[2] *Cal. S.P. Amer., 1681–5*, 338, Nov. 1682.

[3] Quoted in C. M. Andrews, *Colonial Self-Government*, 141–2.

[4] Ibid. 148.   [5] *Cal. S.P. Amer., 1685–9*, xxii.

the political realists in England and the enemies of Shaftesbury could point to the Carolinas as a sinister comment on idealist experiment.

Next in date after the first settlement of Carolina was the occupation of New York. The Dutch colony, wedged among English possessions, was always in a precarious position; these were added to by the energetic but high-handed conduct of the governor Peter Stuyvesant. Meanwhile, complaints against the Dutch were more eagerly listened to at home, and in July 1663 a committee of the English Council for Plantations was ordered to report on the practicability of an attack on the New Netherlands. After inquiries of the English inhabitants on Long Island the committee in January 1664 reported favourably on the project of driving the Dutch from North America.[1] Action was speedily taken. Having obtained a royal grant (February 1664) and a charter (March 12), James, duke of York, commissioned captain Richard Nicholls to be governor of the new province, and allotted that portion of it between Hudson and Delaware to sir George Carteret, treasurer of the Navy, and John, first baron Berkeley of Stratton, brother of sir William Berkeley of Virginia. In the original patent granted to the duke were included lands not actually occupied by the Dutch, such as Long Island and Nantucket. The town of New Amsterdam fell an easy conquest to a small English fleet on August 26, 1664, and was renamed New York.

Except for the provisions that the laws enacted in the colony must be conformable to the laws of England, and that appeals were allowed to the King in Council, the patent conferred absolute power on the ducal proprietor. The administration of his first governor, Nicholls, was marked by moderation and prudence. He encouraged the Dutch population to remain, on the assurance of liberty of conscience and of all the rights of English subjects; while at the same time he reorganized the settlement on English lines and set himself to increase population and trade. As Ashley showed his distinctive political views in the constitution of Carolina, so the duke of York showed his in framing the polity of his American acquisition; for he prohibited the summoning of a representative assembly, and insisted that the

[1] C. M. Andrews, op. cit. 77–8.

city of New York should be governed as a municipal corporation. Accordingly, mayor and aldermen were appointed by the governor; they were empowered to make only by-laws, and to try only cases involving forty shillings or less. In effect, therefore, Nicholls had to do much of his own legislation.[1] This curtailment of initiative was resented by both English and Dutch, and caused increasing difficulty under Nicholls' successor Francis Lovelace, in whose absence the city surrendered to a Dutch fleet in 1673; but after little more than a year New York was restored to the duke's authority. Under its third governor, major Edmund Andros, an attempt was made to introduce some unity into this cosmopolitan community of English and French, Dutch and German, Protestant and Catholic, and to wrest from Connecticut that part assigned to the duke in the original grant. Though he did not succeed in this last design, Andros nevertheless ruled with as much benevolence as could be included in the narrow limits assigned him by his master.

Their exclusion from legislative functions was keenly resented by many of the towns, notably by those on Long Island, and as the demand for some share in law-making became more insistent, it was coupled with a threat of refusal to pay Customs dues, or to provide money for the upkeep of forts. It was this threat to the revenue that eventually obliged the duke to yield to the demand for a representative assembly; and when in 1682 Thomas Dongan was sent out as governor, the duke empowered him to summon a general assembly of freeholders to co-operate with the governor and council in the raising of revenue and the making of laws.[2] This assembly met in October 1683 and formulated the achievements of English constitutionalism in a Charter of Franchises and Liberties, wherein were rehearsed select fundamentals from Magna Carta, the Confirmatio Cartarum and the Petition of Right.[3] As duke, James confirmed the charter; but afterwards,

---

[1] The code which he drew up contained rules copied from the codes of Newhaven and Massachusetts; it also made allowance for Dutch custom. It allowed toleration. For an account of this see A. E. McKinley, *Transition from Dutch to English rule in New York* in *Amer. H. R.* vi. 693–724. The code was promulgated in Nov. 1667, *Cal. S.P. Amer., 1661–8*, 515.

[2] C. M. Andrews, op. cit. 94–5.

[3] It will be found in *Colonial Laws of New York*, i. 111–16. Cf. also E. Channing, *History of the United States*, ii. 297–8.

as king, he countermanded it, and so Dongan had to rule and tax with the concurrence only of his council. By his gifts of diplomacy and conciliation Dongan continued the work of Andros, and proved himself one of the ablest colonial administrators of the time. Peace with the Indians, defence against the French, development of communications, and increase of population and trade were the concrete results of government by the nominees of the duke of York.

The territory between Hudson and Delaware, granted by the duke to Berkeley and Carteret, was named New Jersey, because it was regarded as compensation to Carteret for loss of his office of governor of Jersey. The form of government adopted by the proprietors was defined in the Concessions of February 1665, whereby liberty of conscience and rights of property were guaranteed. A governor and council were to legislate with 12 representatives of the freemen.[1] There were already in existence a number of Swedish and Dutch settlements in the province, and in 1665 a contingent of men from Jersey arrived, with Philip Carteret (the first governor), a kinsman of sir George. These new arrivals were joined by a number of Puritan immigrants from New England; and, as the proportion of the latter increased, there was imposed on the colony a spirit of theocracy and civic independence inconsistent with the temper of the proprietors and the executive. A Quaker element was added in 1674 when Berkeley sold out his share of the lease to Edward Byllynge, a friend and co-religionary of George Fox; but the duke of York's unwillingness to recognize this transfer delayed the establishment of a Quaker colony in West New Jersey. Difficulty was also caused by the duke's attempt to resume possession of New Jersey (in spite of the lease) and to vest its control in the governor of New York; but eventually East New Jersey (after the resignation of Philip Carteret in 1682) and West New Jersey (after Byllynge obtained his grant from the duke in 1680) became predominantly Quaker colonies. These changes hindered the pursuit of a con-

[1] The original documents for the history of New Jersey will be found in *Archives of the state of New Jersey* (1631–1776), ed. W. A. Whitehead, 1880–1903. A general history of the colony is that by S. Smith. There are good accounts in E. Channing, *History of the United States*, and C. M. Andrews, *Colonial Self-Government*.

sistent policy; and accordingly the Jerseys may be cited as examples of proprietary colonies wherein economic progress was impeded to some extent by the successive bargaining of their owners.

One of these Quaker proprietaries has given his name to the colony of Pennsylvania, which was founded in 1680–2 in order to provide a refuge not only for English Quakers, but for the scattered communities of Friends to be found throughout English North America. Like Ashley, William Penn wished to implant in the virgin soil of the west the seeds ripened from the fruit of political and religious experience in the east. He had acquired his first experience of colonization in the Jerseys; but there he did not have the full personal scope requisite for the realization of his schemes. His influence with the duke of York, and the fact of his being a substantial creditor of the king's, enabled him to secure by charter (dated March 4, 1681) a grant of territory west of the Delaware river, to which was given the name of Pennsylvania. This was supplemented by the addition of New Castle and territory on the right bank of the Delaware in 1682. To Penn, as proprietor, was accorded the right to make laws with the consent of the freemen, and to appoint magistrates. The veto of the crown and the right of appeal to it were safeguarded; and it is notable that by his charter Penn was obliged to observe the Navigation Laws.

The founder's appeal for settlers was answered by Quakers from England, Ireland, Wales, Germany, and Holland. Under the first deputy-governor, William Markham, lands were allotted on a definite scale. These for the most part proved to be very fertile. Philadelphia also was founded, and several industries, including shipping, were established. Penn's ideal was liberty with obedience; but his constitution as formulated in 1682 did not differ materially from that of the other American colonies, consisting of the recognized hierarchy of governor, council, and assembly, except that both council and assembly were elective, and the governor was dependent on his council. More note-worthy were the laws, especially the code known as the Great Law, wherein, on the basis of English jurisprudence, Penn super-imposed his distinctive doctrines. This code provided for liberty of conscience, and limited capital punishment to murder and treason. So far as legislation could do so, the Great Law was intended to foster a very high standard of morals; the same exalted ideals were to be found in the character of the relations which Penn strove to maintain with the Indians. With this auspicious start, the development of the colony was rapid, due in part to the fact that Penn himself supervised its early growth. Progress was, however, impeded by racial and religious disputes, by controversies between council and assembly such as were bound to arise in a constitution where the governor had no independent power, and, lastly, by the personal misfortunes of William Penn.[1]

The common concerns of the New England confederation (Massachusetts, Plymouth, Connecticut, and New Haven) were managed by an assembly of two commissioners from each colony; each of the four states preserving its jurisdiction intact. For long, this confederation had acted as an independent power; for example, in their relations with the Dutch in the New Netherlands; but after the Dutch province came under English rule as New York, the cohesion of the New England federation weakened, and eventually came to an end, leaving Massachusetts pre-eminent, as she had formerly been domineering. Massachusetts was a cause of special disquiet to the statesmen of the Restoration. The colony had passed severe laws against the Quakers—these were tacitly approved at home—but, on the other hand, Anglicans were practically ostracized, and two regicides, Whalley and Goffe, were harboured. So it was resolved to deal with the four New England states; and in April 1664 commissioners were sent out in order to devise measures for settling the peace and security of the confederation. They were well received, except in Massachusetts; where only with difficulty could the General Court be induced to use His Majesty's name in their forms of justice. Indeed the coming of the commission was regarded as a breach of the colony's privileges.[2]

[1] For early accounts of Pennsylvania see *Narratives of early Pennsylvania, Delaware and New Jersey, 1630–1708*, ed. A. C. Myers. (*Original Narrative series*.) The Pennsylvania documents were published in the series *Pennsylvania archives* . . . (Philadelphia, 1852–1907). There are good accounts in E. Channing, op. cit., and C. M. Andrews, op. cit. See also F. R. Jones, *Colonization of the Middle States and Maryland*.

[2] For a good account see P. L. Kaye, *Colonial administration under Clarendon,*

Nevertheless, the charter of Massachusets was confirmed, and its comparative independence left practically unchallenged, mainly because the home government was anxious most of all to knit the plantations in the scheme of the Navigation Acts, and was not at first prepared to press questions of principle in an area so remote. In effect, therefore, by acquiescence in the separatism of the New England federation, the colonial policy of Charles II confirmed principles of government reminiscent more of 1649 than of 1660, and so gave unwitting sanction to a breach between the static fundamentals of New England on the one hand, and the evolutionary politics of England on the other, a breach widened to impassable breadth when, in the eighteenth century, this rigid constitutionalism of the colonists was pitted against a doctrine of parliamentary sovereignty. Meanwhile, however, judicious presents of masts deflected the attention of Whitehall from too close inspection of the implications underlying the potential separatism of the New England colonies.

The history of these colonies throughout the reign of Charles II was predominantly one of prosperity. Trade was good, notably that in provisions and manufactured goods with the other plantations;[1] in the towns, there were ironworks and in the ports shipbuilding; there was abundant supply of timber, from which were made window frames and ready-made houses, for export to a good market in the West Indies. In all, Massachusetts, Plymouth, and Connecticut had 200 sail of ships; they could muster about 50,000 able-bodied men;[2] their merchants were mostly rich, usually thrifty, and always intent on fresh ventures for their capital. In spite of the Navigation Acts the New England shippers built up a considerable connexion with other colonies and a direct trade with Europe;[3] indeed they were the Dutchmen of the empire, deriving no great advantage from their

76–124. The report of one of the commissioners, col. Cartwright, is in Clar. MS. 83, f. 335; it is printed in *New York Historical Society Collections*, xxxiii, 1869.

[1] For an account of their industries see Randolph's report, Oct. 12, 1676, in *Cal. S.P. Amer., 1675–6*, 463–8.

[2] *Cal. S.P. Amer., 1669–74*, 232.

[3] J. A. Williamson in *Cambridge History of the British Empire*, i. 258. For evasions of the Navigation Acts by New England ships see professor C. M. Andrews, ibid. i. 277–9.

soil or climate, but ever ready with equipment and transport for handling the produce of others. With this development of wealth and population there followed extension into the interior, and consequent war with the Indians; while at times Indian reprisals caused a threat of famine, and both the beaver and fishing trades were imperilled. There soon followed assaults from another quarter. The 'peevish' humour of Massachusetts was well known at home, where an opportunity was awaited for an attack on its charter. This came in 1676, after the conclusion of prolonged hostilities with the Indians, who had pillaged Rhode Island; and in June of that year Edward Randolph, as government commissioner, commenced in Boston his inquiry into the laws of the colony, with a view to bringing it more directly under the control of the crown.

After a year of investigation he formulated his accusations. Massachusetts, he contended, was violating the Navigation Acts; the colonists had harboured regicides; they coined their own money; they put Quakers and others to death because of their religion; they imposed an oath of fidelity to their government; they oppressed their neighbours in boundary disputes. They had no right to the land which they called their own, and were usurpers; worst of all, they really constituted an independent commonwealth, for appeals to England were denied, and the oath of allegiance was not taken. Moreover, their laws were arbitrary and objectionable; for example, galloping in Boston streets was punished by a fine of 3s. 4d.; and such diversions as bowling, dancing in ordinaries, playing cards for money, and celebrating Christmas, were all penalized.[1] So the colony was ordered to send commissioners to England to answer these charges; but there was so much delay in sending them, and they were given such restricted powers, that the Lords of Trade had to threaten Massachusetts with a *quo warranto*. Randolph meanwhile remained in the colony as crown collector and surveyor, thereby increasing the resentment of the colonists.[2]

[1] The charges will be found in *Cal. S.P. Amer.*, *1677–80*, 129–31, and 133–4, July 1677.
[2] One of the best modern accounts is that in J. T. Adams, *The Founding of New England* (1930), chapters xiii–xv. Professor Adams shows the influence of the Puritan clergy on the public opinion of New England.

In June 1683 articles of high misdemeanour against the governor and company of Massachusetts were formulated, and a writ of *quo warranto* was issued. But expiry of this writ caused the government to proceed by a *scire facias*, and in October 1684 Chancery adjudged the charter of Massachusetts to be forfeited. At the same time it was decided to annul the charters of Connecticut and Rhode Island, so that these colonies could be merged with Massachusetts, New York, and the Jerseys in a new plantation of New England, directly under the control of the crown. Of this new dominion col. Percy Kirke was selected the first governor; but the death of Charles necessitated another appointment, as Kirke was needed at home; accordingly in May 1686 sir Edmund Andros was appointed governor of this transformed New England. Not till late in 1687 did Andros succeed in adding Connecticut to his dominions, a province which evaded the surrender of its charter by hiding it in an oak tree.[1] The task imposed on the new governor was impossible of fulfilment; for even with the utmost powers of conciliation he could not have done anything to compensate the colonies for their loss of representative assemblies; nor could he have dispelled the rumours of anti-Protestant activities which floated across the Atlantic from the land of James II and father Petre. Accordingly, the Revolution of 1688–9 was repeated almost concurrently in Massachusetts. In April 1689 the Bostoners seized the castle, and imprisoned both Andros and Randolph. A declaration, followed by a Convention, established the Revolution settlement in New England; and Boston, as much as London, might claim the honour of having vindicated against the Stuarts the principles of constitutionalism.

A comparison of the accusations against Andros with those against James II shows how susceptible were the New Englanders to the weight of any man's yoke. Most of the counts against the governor were untrue: of those that were substantiated, the chief were (1) that his carriage to the New Englanders was insolent, and (2) that, to the annoyance of the members of the Old South Church, Boston, he used the building for episcopal services when it was not otherwise being used.[2] 'England', wrote Cotton

---

[1] Andrews, op. cit. 271.
[2] *The Andros Tracts* (Prince Society, 1868), i. xxv.

Mather, 'made and saw a happy revolution. And New England upon (and almost before) the advice of it, made as just and fair an one in conformity to it.'[1] The words in parenthesis are significant. An English traveller in Massachusetts at this time recorded some impressions which provide interesting comment on these events. Of the inhabitants he[2] wrote: 'They are generally very backward in their payments, great censors of other men's manners, but extremely careless of their own. As to their religion, I cannot perfectly distinguish it, but it is such that nothing keeps 'em friends but the fear of exposing one another's knavery. As for the rabble, their religion lies in cheating all they deal with. . . . You must read 'em like Hebrew backwards; for they seldom speak and mean the same thing, but like watermen look one way and row another. Amongst all this dross there runs here and there a vein of pure gold.'

Some New England characteristics may be deduced from the titles of the books most in demand, and from the sermons preached at the executions of malefactors. An inventory[3] of a Boston bookseller's estate included the following assortment, typical of that union of the spiritual with the practical so eloquent of seventeenth-century Puritanism:

> Love's Art of Surveying.
> Christ's Tears for Jerusalem's Unbelief.
> Norwood's System of Navigation.
> Shour of Earthquakes.
> Mr. Doolittle's Funeral Sermon.
> Mr. Doolittle's Call.
> History of the Plot.
> Vernon's Compting House.
> Violations of Property.
> Sion in Distress.
> Stub's Conscience Best Friend.
> Bride's Longing for her Bridegroom's Second Coming.

Men brought up on such literature were not likely to be distinguished for the quality of compromise. Then there were the executions. Felons had sometimes to face three sermons before

---

[1] *The Andros Tracts*, ii. 25.
[2] *John Dunton's Letters from New England* (Prince Society, 1867), 67, March 25, 1686.
[3] Ibid., Appendix B.

they were dispatched; and in one preached by Cotton Mather on March 25, 1686, the victim was addressed in these words: 'The sharp axe of civil justice will speedily cut you down. Oh for a little good fruit before the blow'—an invitation responded to by 'the dying bloody sinner' in a speech against Sabbath-breaking. There is abundant evidence that the New Englanders were re-incarnating a rule of the Saints such as Englishmen, by the end of Charles's reign, had long outlived.

Of this, one instance may suffice. In 1666 appeared the famous poem *The Day of Doom* by William Wigglesworth, in which was graphically described a contest of wits between the supreme judge on one side and accused persons urging divers pleas in arrest of judgement on the other. Calvinist predestinarianism and the forensic possibilities of common law were the inspirations of this effusion; as witness the reply to the fore-doomed who contended that, knowing their hopeless plight, they had adopted the line of least resistance:

> Christ readily made this reply:
> I damn you not because
> You are rejected, or not elected,
> But you have broke my laws.
> It is but vain, your wits to strain
> The end and means to sever,
> Men fondly seek to dash or break
> What God hath linked together.

Equally ineffective was the defence put forward by children who had died in sin. Hence, the heaven depicted by Wigglesworth was not a new Jerusalem, but a new Westminster Hall set up in Geneva; and so, while England was discarding these pre-conceptions of an earlier age, there survived in the west, in their pristine vigour, those scruples and convictions which were destined to trouble the more effete world of George III and lord North.

In conclusion, it may be noted that the colonial administrators of this period knew little of the pride of empire, for they thought of colonies mainly from a utilitarian point of view. This attitude is seen in the methods employed for peopling the plantations. The East India Company, as a highly organized trading and administrative body, was able to recruit a select personnel;[1] but these were not permanent settlers. The population of Tangier was far from selective, as it consisted mainly of the garrison.[2] Of those who went voluntarily to the western plantations many were disbanded soldiers, fugitive rebels, religious recusants, and persons ruined in the Civil Wars. Felons were frequently exported, and might mingle freely with men who had left home not because of crime, but because of high principle; there were also children and orphans, some stolen away, others sent out on indentures. In a sense all the American colonies, other than New England, were penal settlements; though colonies such as Virginia protested vigorously against the policy of sending out 'Newgateers'.[3] There were also Scottish, Irish, and Continental elements. The Irish preponderated in Montserrat; in Barbados they were sometimes considered troublesome, and a preference was expressed for Scottish settlers;[4] elsewhere, notably in New York and New Jersey, there were Dutch and Swedes, and in Newfoundland there were French. Older colonies, such as Massachusetts, Bermuda, and Barbados had surplus men who became frontiers-men elsewhere in the empire;[5] moreover, a steady increase of negro population, notably in the sub-tropical colonies, served to increase the amount of superabundant white labour, and to make urgent the problem of military defence.[6]

This absence of a 'sentiment' of empire is perhaps sufficient to explain why no attempt was made to apply any general administrative policy to the haphazard collection of possessions which were being quietly accumulated. Scarcely any two colonies had the same title-deeds, so there was great diversity in their constitutional rights. Fundamental questions of principle were raised, and the committees of privy council applied themselves with zeal to the study of local circumstances influencing each settlement, but they could not enforce any general principles of

---

[1] *Supra*, i. 224.   [2] *Supra*, 504.

[3] The governor and council succeeded in prohibiting this. *Cal. S.P. Amer.*, *1669–74*, July 17, 1671.

[4] e.g. in Virginia, ibid., *1661–8*, 429–30; in Barbados, ibid. 486; in Jamaica, ibid., *1669–74*, 96.

[5] J. A. Williamson in *Cambridge History of the British Empire*: the Colonies after the Restoration, 249.

[6] *Cambridge History of the British Empire*, i. 266–7.

colonial administration on the heterogeneous possessions which then constituted the Empire.

In two spheres—the legislative and the fiscal relationship between crown and possession—imperial problems were raised and left unsettled. In regard to the first (the legislative connexion) the history of Jamaica is of particular interest. The island differed from other crown colonies because (it was held) the inhabitants had no privileges granted them by letters patent, and the king had found Jamaica 'an acquisition to England' at his accession.[1] On their side, the Jamaicans demanded that the revenue raised by them should be applied in accordance with the directions of the native legislature, and not at the crown's discretion; they therefore objected to a change introduced in 1677 whereby their laws were to be enacted not, as hitherto, 'by the Governor, Council, and representative of the Commons', but 'by the King's Most Excellent Majesty, by and with the consent of the General Assembly'.[2] Throughout this dispute, the Lords of Trade attempted to reduce Jamaica to the status of Ireland as administered by Poyning's Law, supporting their contention with the curious reason that the legislature of Jamaica could not be subject to more accidents than Ireland; to which it was properly replied that the distance of Jamaica from England destroyed the force of the analogy.[3] This was no mere dispute over words; because the colonial legislators feared that the new style of enactment deprived them of deliberative power. So they refused to pass a revenue act; and the crown had eventually to yield, leaving in suspense the question whether the crown had deprived itself of the right to modify the constitution of the island.[4]

This was not unconnected with the question whether the laws of England applied to the colonies. In practice, many of the colonial legislatures embodied fundamental principles of English common law in their legislation; nowhere else indeed were these principles held in deeper veneration. For the proprietary

[1] *Cal. S.P. Amer.*, *1677–80*, 461.

[2] Charles Howard, earl of Carlisle, was instructed to use the new style when he went out as Governor in 1677. *Cal. S.P. Amer.*, *1677–80*, 367–9.

[3] Ibid., *1677–80*, 445.

[4] Ibid., *1677–80*, 622, Oct. 22, 1680. For a full account of this struggle see A. M. Whitson, *Constitutional Development of Jamaica*, 1660–1729, ch. iv.

possessions it was generally a condition of the grant that the laws sanctioned by the proprietor should be in accordance with English jurisprudence. This matter had some constitutional importance; since if English laws were valid in the overseas possessions, then colonists might feel secure in the safeguards which these laws implied; otherwise, if the crown could determine what was law and what was not, then these safeguards might have to be sacrificed. At home, there was not always a clear determination on this subject; for example, the law courts did not know whether the laws of England applied to Barbados or not.[1] But, so far as the later Stuarts had any definite colonial policy, it was to bring the colonies into closer dependence on the crown; inevitably, therefore, in the years when the English borough franchises were being destroyed, a similar process was applied to those plantations which hitherto had maintained some independence. This was the fate of the New England states. After these had lost their charters in 1684, Halifax eloquently pleaded in Council that English laws should be applied to Englishmen in the colonies;[2] but he was overruled, and the remodelled New England confederacy was entrusted to a governor and council, responsible solely to the king, and required to administer a code of laws drawn up by the crown. One characteristic reason was adduced in defence of this policy, namely, that by their subjection the New Englanders would be able to supply 'well-seasoned men' for the reduction of any rebellious colony.[3] Fortunately, the Stuarts did not have to try this experiment.

There was similar dubiety in the fiscal relationship. The colonist had to pay a Customs duty of five per cent. on his exports to England, according to their valuation in the Book of Rates; half of this amount was refunded on enumerated goods re-exported to the Continent.[4] Then followed the Act of 1673 imposing special plantation duties;[5] this was primarily a preventive, not a fiscal measure, but it had some legal importance,

---

[1] Daws v. sir P. Pindar, in *Modern Reports*, ii. 45.

[2] *Halifax*, i. 428.

[3] Randolph to Jenkins April 30, 1681, ibid. 1681–5, 34–6. For a good account of the working of the new constitution under Andros see J. T. Adams, *The Founding of New England*, 398–430.

[4] For this subject generally see G. L. Beer, *The Old Colonial System*, i, ch. iii.   [5] 25 Car. II, cap. vii. See *supra*, i. 239.

because it was the earliest direct tax (other than Customs dues) on colonial produce not initiated by colonial legislatures. In addition to these levies, the colonies were mostly bound by their charters to make payments, some nominal, such as Indian arrows, or sheaves of corn; some more substantial, such as a fifth part of the precious metals found in the soil; but neither of these sources could be considered to provide a substantial or regular revenue. With these exceptions, the proprietary and New England colonies enjoyed a large measure of fiscal autonomy.

It was otherwise in the crown colonies, where there were governors and judges appointed by the crown; there were also forts, and in some cases regiments of English soldiers to be maintained. The general policy of the home government was to raise locally such a revenue, preferably on a permanent basis, as would defray these charges, and make these possessions self-supporting; while the colonial legislatures on their side objected in principle to a permanent revenue, and insisted on such strict clauses of appropriation as to imply complete suspicion of the crown. In this respect, there was a wide repercussion of the financial mismanagement at home; and the suspicion engendered by Charles's extravagance was reflected in the unwillingness of Jamaica, Virginia, and Barbados to surrender control of the revenues which they voted; in consequence, the salaries of officials and the requirements of military defence were often seriously jeopardized. There was an additional complication in Barbados and the Leeward Islands (St. Kitts, Montserrat, Nevis, and Antigua), all of which voted in 1663–4 an export duty of four-and-a-half per cent. From the start there was confusion about this payment. The crown, which had just succeeded to the proprietary rights under the old Carlisle patent, regarded this grant as a return for the confirmation of defective land-titles, and assigned a portion of it to the new Governor, Francis lord Willoughby, in composition for his inherited proprietary rights; while another portion was allocated for payments to creditors of the deceased James Hay, first earl of Carlisle, a Stuart favourite, to whom the West Indian islands not occupied by Spain had been granted by charter in 1627.[1] In effect, therefore, the revenue granted by these possessions was to be used for the liquidation of proprietary claims; but

[1] G. L. Beer, op. cit. i. 171.

the yield did not prove sufficient for this purpose, and the men who paid the tax contended that it should be devoted to the expenses of civil and military administration. This led to much strife and misunderstanding; even more, the defences suffered, and so French and Dutch were able to play havoc in the Leeward Islands during the Second Dutch War. Eventually, the crown had to repudiate the claims of the Carlisle creditors, and apply this revenue to the needs of these islands.[1]

In Jamaica and Virginia the crown, as original owner of the soil, was entitled to quit-rents, which provided a permanent source of revenue. But this was insufficient to meet the costs of administration and defence; so attempts were made to secure additional and equally permanent grants, the proceeds to be applied to the needs of these possessions. The Jamaicans insisted on limiting this extra revenue to periods of two years, in order to ensure the summoning of their legislature; and on one occasion they used the expedient of 'tacking'[2] in order to ensure the passage of Bills. It was only by threat and wheedling that governor Lynch succeeded in 1683 in persuading the island Assembly to vote a revenue for twenty-one years from spirits and licences of taverns, a vote free from the objectionable 'tacking', and in return the crown surrendered the quit-rents.[3] Until 1679, the salary of the governor of Virginia was paid by a local export duty of two shillings on every hogshead of tobacco; but in 1680 the Virginian assembly consolidated this with a poll tax (on immigrants) into a permanent revenue. In return for this, the home government had to acquiesce in the statutes of Virginia which discriminated against English shipping.[4] But elsewhere it was not possible to enforce the maxim that the crown colonies should pay their way. No independent revenue could be obtained from the Bermudas; and for long the quit-rents of New York were insufficient for the salaries of officials. The net result was that, before 1689, the crown derived no financial advantage from the colonies; and was called upon to give satisfactory assurance that what money the colonists raised locally was applied

[1] G. L. Beer, 172–95.

[2] *Cal. S.P. Amer., 1681–5*, 137, Nov. 6, 1681. The Lords of Trade objected to the 'tacking', ibid. 315.

[3] G. L. Beer, op. cit. i. 219.

[4] Ibid. i. 205–6.

solely to colonial needs. When it is added that there was another source of irritation, namely the friction caused by the enforcement of the Navigation Acts, it will be seen that imperial progress in this period did not settle administrative problems, but helped to accumulate them.

XIX

A RECORD OF ACHIEVEMENT

I. SOME ASPECTS OF TRADITIONAL ENGLISH CULTURE

So far as it is possible to describe in one phrase the intellectual character of a generation, the phrase 'sustained curiosity' might be used of the England lying behind the religion and politics of the reign of Charles II. It is true that the spirit of inquiry is the inspiration of every age that can boast any real intellectual achievement; but this is specially true of the later seventeenth century, because, though Bacon and Descartes had already acclimatized scientific scepticism in European thought, it was not till after 1660 that Englishmen definitely applied the new principles, and sought for truth in experiment and research rather than in theological debate. This curiosity was balanced and tempered by a vindication of the native common sense. It is the purpose of this concluding chapter to illustrate some aspects of traditional culture as known to the universities, the schools, and the press; and against this background to set the achievements of those who helped to make this an age of more than usual intellectual progress.

The old grammar schools, one of the glories of Medieval and Tudor England, had trained such men as Cromwell (Huntingdon Grammar School), John Hampden (Lord Williams's School, Thame), John Milton (St. Paul's), and John Selden (Chichester Grammar School); later in the century Newton received some of his early education at Grantham Grammar School, Somers at Worcester Cathedral School, while Locke, like Dryden, was a product of Westminster. But nevertheless these schools show evidence of the decline which overtook many educational foundations in the course of the seventeenth century. Various reasons for this may be suggested. The temper of Restoration England was not favourable to the ideals of frugality and industry embodied in these establishments; there were few great benefactors, and there were many critics, ranging from the statesmen who thought that too many boys were taken from the plough to pore over books, to recluses like Hobbes, who argued that the devotion of these schools to ancient history and classical studies tended to promote republicanism. Other reasons were that, as Dissenters were now debarred by Statute from teaching, the grammar schools lost the services of men pre-eminently fitted for this vocation: still more, there were numerous rival establishments.

But perhaps the main reason why the performance of the older schools compared unfavourably with that of their rivals was that in many cases the first were strictly bound by their original charters, and so did not have the opportunity for initiative or experiment enjoyed by the second. Thus, the curricula of the grammar school showed little deviation from Greek and Latin grammar, a somewhat narrow range of classical authors, with sometimes Hebrew and declamations or themes on abstract or religious topics. Such an education would now be considered narrow, but it was narrow not so much in its choice of material as in its methods and objects; for the classics were studied not as the foundation of the humanities, but mainly as illustrations of rules of syntax, or for the attainment of proficiency in prose and verse composition. This tradition is not extinct, but at least there is a tendency in modern times to value the Latin and Greek languages not altogether as ends in themselves, but as keys to great store-houses of wisdom and inspiration. To-day many men in retirement read or profess to read the classics for intellectual enjoyment; this was rare in the seventeenth century for any but the professed scholars, though sir William Temple was an exception. Intellectual curiosity was as likely to be repressed as encouraged by the education of the endowed school, and in this respect the university was sometimes a continuation of the same routine.

What it meant to be bound by medieval statutes may be illustrated from Winchester College. Our oldest public school was founded by Wykeham as a boarding grammar school for seventy poor scholars and clerks who, after a thorough training in accidence, were to be sent to New College, there to be trained for all the professional posts that might be filled by an educated clergy. The founder's experience of how easily the intentions of a pious donor might be evaded caused him to draw up most elaborate and carefully planned statutes for both foundations;

but even his ingenuity proved no match for that of the generations who had to apply these rules, with the result that the letter of the laws was scrupulously regarded, while their spirit was often ignored. Thus, it was the duty of the senior foundation, New College, to see to it that the sister college carried out the regulations, for which purpose there was an annual scrutiny or examination conducted by the warden of New College and two fellows. For convenience, this was sometimes held half-way between Winchester and Oxford, at the Bear Inn in Newbury; more often it was held at Winchester. At these scrutinies, elections were made to the Oxford College; the scrutineers also required answers to questions concerning the discipline and studies of Winchester; and it was open to all foundationers of the school to bring complaints against any of their fellows or even against the warden himself. On these occasions, therefore, two great dignitaries faced each other, the one prepared to hear accusations by schoolboys against the other, with resort to the Visitor, the bishop of Winchester, as the umpire. It was medieval and democratic; but it may also have encouraged the practice of tale-bearing, which was not then viewed with disfavour.

Among the interrogatories levelled at heads of the Winchester authorities in the scrutiny of 1680 were these:[1] (1) Are there always two bursars at the receipt of money? (the innuendo was patent), (2) do the schoolmaster and the usher teach diligently? (3) do the fellows reside regularly in the College? (4) is Chapel regularly attended by all? (5) are commons served regularly in Hall, and subtracted from those who do not attend? (6) are 'estraneous' persons entertained at College expense? (7) does any fellow, scholar, or servant keep sporting dogs or hawks? (the statutes had limited the founder's charity to the poor), (8) is every one present at the anniversary *obit* for the founder's soul and at the four annual commemorations? (9) is the spare cash locked up in the chest appointed for that purpose by the Founder? (10) are the statutes read three times a year before the whole society in chapel and is a copy kept in the ante-chapel for reference? (11) does every fellow read the statutes privately once a year 'with due attention'? and lastly (12) do

[1] MS. in New College muniments.

the warden and fellows convert to their own use any more of the College estates than that which the statutes allow them?

These questions often evoked accusations of the most personal character; after investigation penalties might be imposed on the delinquents. Scholars who acquired the key of the beer-cellar were punished; a boy who stole money from a school-mate's strong box was expelled; another who made no progress in his studies, and of whom it was said that by no possibility could he make progress, was warned of impending expulsion. This annual inspection descended to the minutest details. Defaulters from chapel were reprimanded; the scholars had to be dressed in that quality of cloth prescribed by the Founder; the bursars had to see to it that the dormitories were supplied with suitable locks; the beer had to be brewed in a proper manner and with good utensils; the choristers had to sing, and the organist was ordered to teach them, in spite of his statement that they were incapable of singing; Latin was to be spoken; the servants were to be respectful, and townsmen were to be kept out of the cellar. No one was spared in this chapter of faults. On one of these occasions the warden of Winchester had to answer certain serious allegations. It was alleged that, at the brewing of beer, he drew off for his own use a large quantity of 'the first brewing, whereby the rest was weaker'; he had neglected to enforce the statute requiring the wearing of furred gowns in chapel, and he rarely dined in Hall. To the first accusation he replied that it was the custom; to the second he made no reply, and to the third he answered that he had married, and had a family. By the time this last confession was elicited there was a display of temper on both sides, moderated somewhat by the use of the sober Latin tongue. He in turn then accused the chaplains of carrying victuals outside the College, contrary to the statutes; to which the chaplains replied that they had a licence for living in the country.

As the observance of these statutes was enforced by a solemn oath, their violation, even in minute respects, was technically perjury; in consequence the very strictness of the rules, however necessary they may have been for a medieval community, was often a pretext for their evasion wherever some defence or exception, however subtle, could be adduced. Such regulations were therefore little better than millstones round the neck of educational progress, and in the seventeenth century they could have provided little more than a training in casuistry. An exceptional example has, it is true, been quoted; exceptional in the sense that then as now Wykeham's foundation was held in special esteem, and moreover it was the model on which the statutes of other schools, including Eton, were based. What was true of Winchester was true of those older institutions which were still attempting to carry out strictly the intentions of their founders; and it is a great tribute to the original spirit of these foundations that, at a later date, they were able quickly to adapt themselves to new conditions, and to rival or surpass establishments which had never known the dead hand of completely obsolete restrictions. But our greatest schools had to wait many years for this change; and the fact remains that in the reign of Charles they were on the whole educationally unproductive.

Nevertheless, there were not lacking schemes of educational reform. The writings of the Bohemian educational reformer Comenius were made known in England by Samuel Hartlib, a prolific writer on pedagogy, husbandry, land surveying, and silk culture; an encyclopaedist, whose enthusiasm for knowledge and its wide diffusion was not without influence on educated society of the Restoration. Later in the reign, a scheme of reform was propounded by Aubrey.[1] He deplored the enormous time and labour spent on grammar and accidence; rather than such slavery, he would prefer that only English and Mathematics should be taught. The home education of the rich he condemned; because young men of position were flattered by servants and dependants, and so, when they entered into the world, they were likely to give offence; nor did he approve of the fashionable academies, which turned out the 'chevalier', or, in plain English, the trooper. Instead of these expedients he proposed that the rich should be educated on more national lines. He would accommodate his ideal school in 'a fair house, with a little park', presided over by a provost, who would be a layman, well travelled, of good birth, and unmarried. He and his staff would have to remain celibate, as their daughters might prove a distraction to the select pupils of this model academy. In

[1] In *Bodley, Aubrey MS.* A. 10.

Grammar he would have three 'informators', none of them English, but all of them Swiss or Scottish; 'men of presence, bonne mine and address', 'not little contemptible rattons'. There were to be teachers of Mathematics, Rhetoric, and Logic; in Rhetoric he included oratory and translations; in Logic, the rudiments of civil law and ethics. Of somewhat less importance were the Penman and the French Dancing Master, who might be non-residents; the cooks were to be French or Swiss, and the porter was not to be an old man, but a 'lusty young fellow', able to speak Latin, and also, if possible, French or German. Mingled with the pupils there were to be ten or twelve Swiss, Dutch, or Scottish boys, fluent Latin speakers, and therefore likely to encourage the young gentlemen to use that language. Even the scullions were to use Latin.

Aubrey's scheme reflects the dissatisfaction with which many enlightened Englishmen regarded the educational methods of their day, and errs on the side of attributing too much importance to foreign models. Moreover, he reveals one pronounced characteristic of the educational practice of that time—the use of Latin as a language in which colloquial proficiency was an end in itself. At the universities, conditions were somewhat better; but even there the incubus of formal routine weighed heavily on grown men. During the Commonwealth their reform had played an important part in Puritan propaganda, and there was a proposal for the establishment of a new university at Durham; but the Restoration effectively quashed these schemes, and for two centuries thereafter the two universities were little more than annexes to the state church. In the later seventeenth century there were, it is true, a number of university and college benefactors, such as Clarendon, Ashmole, Williamson, and Jenkins; there were great vice-chancellors such as Dr. Fell; at Cambridge there were men of international reputation, such as Newton; but nevertheless the fact remains that neither Oxford nor Cambridge was contributing to the intellectual life of the nation in a measure proportionate to the endowments and opportunities enjoyed by them; and both were outstripped by the Royal Society, to which Oxford was at first somewhat antagonistic.[1]

[1] Evelyn (*Diary*, July 9, 1669) records that at the Oxford Encaenia the

Both universities could boast a distinguished list of alumni, including Newton, Barrow, Wren, Halley, Evelyn, Locke, and Pepys; nevertheless, an educational institution must be judged not from the brilliant or exceptional, but from the more numerous and average of its products. Such men were trained in methods still semi-scholastic, and were encouraged by public disputation to draw readily from a narrow range of classical texts for arguments on one side or another of a set theme. Exhibition of this dialectic subtlety had already been condemned by Eachard.[1] The lectures of professors played little part in the life of the undergraduate, who, until the twentieth century, was dependent for tuition almost solely on the resident tutors and fellows assigned him by the college. Thus, at Queen's College, Oxford, one of the Fleming family read with his tutor in Sanderson's *Logic* once or twice a week; on Saturday, he made Latin verses, and in his spare hours he read Florus and Sallust. His tutor, when writing to the pupil's father, said that the boy lacked courage, 'but I hope that disputing in Hall will put some briskness into him'.[2] At Queen's, if one may judge from the Fleming correspondence, the level of tuition was comparatively high, and the tutors were solicitous of their charges' interests; moreover the college profited by the benefactions of sir Joseph Williamson, who provided scholarships for travel in France and Germany,[3] an unusually early recognition of the value of training in modern studies. To Williamson also Queen's owed the establishment of a lectureship in Anglo-Saxon.[4] Another college associated with modern subjects was University College, which numbered a high proportion of scientists among its alumni.[5] At Cambridge, Newton and Barrow were building up the great scientific reputation of the University, and Caius College was ably maintaining its fame in medicine.

But these were exceptional; for elsewhere studies tended to be of the traditional character. Witness the evolution of an

---

Public Orator indulged in 'some malicious and indecent reflections on the Royal Society as underminers of the University'.

[1] See *supra*, i. 99.
[2] *H.M.C. Rep.* xii, app., pt. vii. 148, Sept. 28, 1678; *Fleming Correspondence.*
[3] Ibid. 146.   [4] Ibid. 163, Nov. 1679.
[5] For this see E. J. Bowen, *The study of science in University College, Oxford.*

Oxford professor of Greek. William Taswell graduated bachelor of arts from Christ Church in 1674, and thereupon obtained £4 per annum as a moderator at disputations, then the equivalent of an examination fee. This, with the same sum for tuition and a studentship (i.e. fellowship) of Christ Church, enabled him to remain at Oxford, where he was first employed by Dr. Fell, the Dean of his college, in the somewhat superfluous task of turning Lidyat's Chronological Canons into Latin verse. From this he proceeded to the more useful work of collating the Greek Testament, Livy, and Quintilian with manuscripts in order to prepare new editions. The Dean then offered him advancement—either the post of schoolmaster at £50 per annum, or a tutorship to two noblemen's sons near Oxford, but Taswell preferred his poverty and his studies, so he declined the offer and pawned some of his books. In 1677 he was able to muster £10 for his mastership of arts; but he lost the support of his patron because he voted against Fell's nominee for the public oratorship; three years later, however, he was restored to the favour of the great man, and received six young pupils from him. He was now so well established as a tutor that he bought books and clothes, a gold watch, a silver-hilted sword, a collection of cups, and a supply of bows and arrows; in which state of affluence he was appointed professor of Greek at Christ Church, and he then took holy orders. He recorded one complaint against the Church of England, namely, that on the many days of abstinence prescribed by the Church, his college provided no supper, so he was obliged to dine out on these occasions.[1]

Like Winchester College, the sister foundation in Oxford was labouring under its ancient statutes, and had to suffer also the incubus of Founder's Kin fellows. One of the families from which generations of such fellows was drawn was the great Oxfordshire family of Fiennes, and the measure of their right to places on the foundation may be gauged from a casual reference by Celia Fiennes, who, when she visited New College in the summer of 1695, referred to it as the college 'which belongs to the Fiennes's'.[2] These family rights led to innumerable disputes about precedence; and the social distinctions thus introduced helped to

---

[1] *The autobiography of William Taswell, D.D.* in Camden Miscellany, ii (1853).　　　[2] Celia Fiennes, *Through England on a side-saddle*, 28.

prevent New College from playing that part for which it was fitted by its traditions and endowments. To govern such a close but divided corporation was no easy task; it called forth all the ingenuity and firmness of which warden Woodward was capable. As he had to keep strict watch in his progresses lest manorial rights might fall into desuetude, so in College he had to see that the statutes were observed, that due precedence and ceremony were regulated, and that his own privileges were vindicated against the menace from junior fellows infected with the 'distemperature' of the times. So he began his tenure of office in a characteristic way. From old members he obtained answers to long lists of questions relating to the practice of the College before the anarchy of the Commonwealth; and, with the authority of recorded precedent on his side, he was able to hold his own against the truculent and the disobedient. The place of the Founder's Kin in chapel; the standard of hospitality expected from him; the regulation of 'sleeping days'[1] in the long vacation; his power to appoint and to eject the chaplains, and his right to the 'fee buck' from Whaddon Chase (without the participation of his colleagues)—all these vexed questions were settled once and for all. Even the 'lopp and topp' of the trees in the College garden came within the scope of this inquisition; it must henceforth go to the kitchen, and was not to be used for the fires of fellows in their chambers. None of the ancient rights of his office was allowed to slip away.[2]

As he asserted himself against his colleagues, so he strove to maintain discipline among the junior members of the society; and it may be recalled that many of the fellows were included in this category, as some were little more than schoolboys. Thus, in 1663, there was the case of the fellow who broke two of the statutes. His first offence was that of staying out of college when he was 'gated', that is, confined to its bounds; the second was more complicated: he had taken out bread and beer in his own name and had supplied them to other persons. This was the medieval sin of 'manutention'. Family influence and the inter-

---

[1] Sleeping days may have been those days when attendance at morning chapel was not required.

[2] Miscellaneous memoranda of warden Woodward in New College muniments.

vention of the Visitor were both invoked by the delinquent, who was one of the law fellows; but Woodward, with the consent of the thirteen seniors, sent him down for a period. Against this sentence the offender appealed in the following letter:

Gentlemen. To resist your authoritie or to stand on terms of defiance is not my present purpose; onely to lett you understand what my sense is of my present condition; and if a favourable audience can be granted to mee, which I cannot question from such, who in a special manner live on mercy [a home thrust]. My plea is that for the first breach of the statute, wherein I was ignorantly apprehended, being the Statute of Manutention; my thoughts are with all submission to your judgement, that upon the strictest enquiry I may find some mercy; my threepenny charity being bestowed in no contemptuous manner, or to encourage offenders against your power. Consider, I beseech you the score on which they requested it, and for which I gave it, to entertaine a stranger, the main end which our Founder commends to us, hospitalitie. . . . Then the frequencie, though I accuse none, of such examples made me presume on doing what I did. . . . But such is the extravagancie of youth that I did transgresse my bounds limited, and cannot excuse the times yee object against mee of going abroad, for which I am heartily sorry, and offer myself to be punisht in any sort, unless by my utter ruine, which expulsion will bee.

But withall not to derogate from your power, pray lay it to your hearts whether I am guiltie of perjury in not perfectly submitting to an injunction which the Statutes never dreamt of: it being in one rubrick absolutely decided totidem verbis: Sint manûtentores pro prima vice privati a dimensis per quindenam: pro secunda, per mensem: pro tertia per duos menses: pro quarto, penitus removeantur a Collegio, and if any other rubrick proceeds more vigorously against mee, yet according to Justinian: in dubiis quod minus est prejudiciale eligendum est. . . . Now, Gentlemen, I humblie cast myself at your feet, beseeching you, as able interpreters of the Statutes as ever I believe yett were, to consider whether some milder course may not be taken to preserve you blameless and mee in my place; if not, I am your undone servant.

Thus Woodward had to contend with the lawyers of the College as well as with the lawyers of the Village.

The ingenuity fostered by school and college discipline was not wasted in the larger and more public life of the university;

and spare moments snatched from *studia severiora* might well be spent in the collection of votes or the management of elections; or the chancellor might visit the university, bringing with him a train of persons of quality, on whom degrees by creation were conferred; accordingly, by a well-timed dedication or influence exerted in the right quarter, one might be presented with such persons of quality, and so not only receive a degree free of charge and without examination, but also an introduction into that larger life which surged round the two universities.[1] Many things therefore helped to train some of the qualities requisite for success in the service of church or state. At its lowest, the university system encouraged the informer with money, and the assurance of secrecy;[2] more often it turned out products guaranteed to be invariably fluent and dexterous. This intellectual agility was to be found not only in those studies now designated Arts subjects, but also in the scientific pursuits; and so, while at the Royal Society men were discussing the conclusions to be drawn from ascertained and recorded facts, at the Sheldonian Theatre in Oxford bachelors were debating whether medical practice should be altered because of recent anatomical discoveries; whether contraries might be cured by contraries, and even whether love could be induced by philtres.[3] These may have been vital questions in the fifteenth century, but not in the seventeenth, when real scientific progress was rapid. More useful, perhaps, or at least more elegant were the university prize compositions on such themes as these: Did Duns Scotus write better Latin than Cicero? Is expectation better than fulfilment? Should young men travel abroad? There was a breath from the outside world when in 1680 it was debated: *an tabernae cofficenses sunt permittendae?*[4]

The intellectual agility thus engendered at the universities

---

[1] On the occasion of Ormonde's visit to Oxford in 1677 Dr. Fell warned the duke against this practice. *Carte MS.* 36, f. 374.

[2] For example, the printed announcement issued by the vice-chancellor of Oxford in April 1681 offering a reward of 40s. and a promise of secrecy to informers revealing the names of undergraduates who had recently broken windows. *Bodley, Wood* 276 A, no. 374.

[3] For these Quaestiones debated at Oxford in this reign see *Bodley, Fol.* θ 659.

[4] *Bodley, Wood* 276 A, no. 394.

may be traced also in a new conception of education which came to displace the more pedantic equipment of earlier times. As the capital became more populous, as foreign affairs engaged the attention of intelligent Englishmen, and as the influence of French civilization asserted itself, much of the old insularity disappeared in exchange for a measure of cosmopolitanism, a keen sense of proportion, and a conception of education as a means to a social end, an ideal enunciated by Henry Peacham,[1] who prescribed a method whereby one's 'style' might pass for current, namely: 'Imitate the best authors as well in Oratory as in History . . . with much conference with those that can speak well'. This object was made more easy of attainment by the fact that the education of the middle and upper classes was then more uniform; it was based on the Classics and on the same range of classical texts; consequently, with an apt quotation one could win the plaudits of one's associates, as later one might use it with effect in the House of Commons. But this was only the basis for the polish to be acquired by continual contact with the right kind of society. 'The proprieties and delicacies of English are known to few,' wrote Dryden:[2] ''tis impossible even for a good wit to understand and practice them without the help of a liberal education, long reading and digesting of those few good authors we have among us; the knowledge of men and manners; the freedom and habitude of conversation with the best company of both sexes; and, in short, without wearing off the rust he has acquired while laying in a stock of learning.'

A similar change can be traced, though more insensibly, in the evolution of English prose style. Compare any pamphlet of Prynne or Milton with an essay by Dryden or Addison, and at once there will be noted a complete change in the use of the paragraph; for the earlier writers compress so many facts and opinions into the paragraph that it rarely has any unity of its own, and its dividing lines might often be altered without either improving or spoiling the sequence; whereas the later writers use this division for an essential purpose—for the exposition or completion of one idea, or the comparison of two ideas. This latter method of subdivision promotes easier and quicker

[1] *The Compleat Gentleman*, ch. vi (1661 ed.; first published in 1613).
[2] Preface to *Sylvae* (1685) in *Essays of J. Dryden*, ed. W. P. Ker, i. 253.

reading; because the eye becomes trained to deduce from a few lines something of the essential argument of a whole section; by this method also an exposition may be spun out longer, or greater degrees of differentiation may be introduced. This change may be due to the fact that, with a steady increase in the size of the reading public, authors were beginning to think more of their readers' convenience; they may have been saying less than their predecessors, but they were saying it more clearly, and in such a way that their meaning could be discerned more quickly. At the same time, increasing resort was made to that large class of secondary words derived from Latin either directly or through the French—a change the causes of which were probably as much historical as literary, since Englishmen were now coming into contact with each other in ways necessitating more highly-developed means of expression; for many were entering parliament, aware of the increased consequence attached to expression of opinion in the legislature; others were serving on committees, where their views might be modified or adjusted in confidential discussion; or resort to a coffee-house might bring with it the revelation that there are generally two sides to a question; and so, with the increased volume of the written and spoken word, there dawned on publicists and politicians a clearer realization of the value of circumlocution or reservation in all statements likely to incur public scrutiny.

This process had not gone very far in the reign of Charles, though its beginnings can be detected in the diplomatic and political correspondence, and in the parliamentary oratory. It was fortunate perhaps that, as the language became more pellucid, it became more innocuous; for no democracy can work until it has for its service a sufficiently large stock of non-committal terms, and the England of Charles's reign was at least formulating some of the principles on which democratic government was afterwards based. One consequence of this linguistic development was a deepening of the contrast between the language of the humble and that of the polite; the one remaining a sterling, uninflated currency, surviving mostly in local dialects; while the other was minted in such high denominations that its users were all rich, and gradations of poverty and wealth tended to disappear. Dryden found that in this respect we had been anticipated by the Japanese, who, according to his information, made use of certain words in familiar discourse, while reserving others for studied compositions:

The men of quality have a language quite different from the vulgar. When they write of a sublime subject (for example, religion or affairs of state) they serve themselves of particular terms.[1]

A similar instinct for the non-committal may be traced in the expressed views of men regarding the conduct of life; and in this respect it is noteworthy that we have no native equivalent for the French *savoir faire*, the only phrase to describe those social aptitudes which were now being more closely studied by the heirs of Saxon bluntness and simplicity. In its most ingenuous form this can be seen in the twenty maxims[2] drawn up for his son by 'an eminent lawyer' in 1682. Among his precepts were these: acquire some knowledge of physic, divinity, and law at the university, so that your conversation may be more agreeable, though your knowledge need only be superficial; do not study anything unless there is profit to be had by it; never lend money on the public faith, because common debts like common lands are the most neglected; do not marry a celebrated beauty, because your house will become as frequented as a confectioner's shop; when travelling, see to it that the irreligion of foreign parts does not cause you to neglect divine duties, and remember that God heard Daniel in Babylon; show honour to new families, whatever your opinion of them; avoid writing about the faults of great persons, as your correspondence may be intercepted; and, lastly, always avoid disputes about religion. Lord Chesterfield himself could not have been more sagacious.

The above illustrations from English education and language have been cited to support the contention that, though English civilization was becoming more sophisticated, more self-conscious, and more assimilative of foreign influence, a national distinctiveness was nevertheless preserved. Among the foreign influences was that of the Court. In exile, Charles had acquired a taste for French music and French drama; as king, he exercised some influence in both these spheres. Thus he helped to

[1] Dryden, *Life of St. Francis Xavier*, in *Works*, ed. Scott, xvi, bk. v.
[2] They will be found in *Bodley, Ashmole* G. 12.

create the demand for a new, secularized type of church music, consisting mainly of solo and dialogue, with instrumental accompaniment—a type sometimes florid and theatrical, and not altogether in accord with English taste. Our church music of the Restoration was therefore a somewhat isolated or at least self-contained product, deriving little from older English tradition, and leaving no successor in its wake; but on the other hand its venturesomeness may have helped to stimulate the genius of Purcell, who composed many of his best pieces for church or theatre. But in spite of the very definite French influence to which he was subjected, Purcell preserved characteristics of a distinctively English kind; amid his mannerisms and crudities he maintained a vigorous individuality, which has come to be more generally appreciated by his countrymen in recent years, through the publicity given to his compositions by the Purcell Society. In music as in everything else the king loved experiment; and it was by experiment with new forms that Purcell helped to transmute the old devotional music of the church into the more organized secular music of modern times.[1]

The value of the king's influence on the English drama is more debatable.[2] He was fond of the theatre; his players were part of his retinue, and at least he helped to make the actor a person of more public consequence. The technique of the stage was developed in his reign: scenery was used; important parts were played by actresses; great nobles such as Buckingham, Newcastle, and Rochester emulated the king by their patronage, and the stage became the most fashionable diversion of the Court and of all pretending to social distinction. Nearly all the literary men of the day wrote plays, which were seldom acted for more than a week, with the result that quality was generally sacrificed to quantity. The French influence was seen in the use of rhyme and in the popularity of the heroic play, in which was depicted a world infinitely remote from the actualities of the present; where the characters were mostly stereotyped exponents of the

[1] For a good general account of music in the reign of Charles II see *The Oxford History of Music*, vol. iii, *The Seventeenth Century*, ch. vii, by sir C. H. Parry.

[2] For good accounts of Restoration Drama see the standard books by Allardyce Nicoll and B. Dobrée, *Restoration Tragedy* and *Restoration Comedy*.

grand virtues and the grand manner, always liable to burst
forth into wearisome tirade, and sometimes defying everybody,
including, on at least one occasion, God himself.[1] In such a
world there could be little differentiation of character, so the
author constantly interposed his own sentiments, and contented
himself with putting these into the mouths of his puppets. The
drama of the Elizabethans was often tawdry and obscene, but
it was spontaneous; that of the Restoration contained hardly
an echo of the great events which were being enacted beyond
Whitehall. Against its turgidity and bathos Buckingham's
Rehearsal was a witty and effective protest, a protest which
showed incidentally that Englishmen had now acquired a
keener appreciation of sarcasm as a literary weapon.

Almost as popular as the heroic play was the comedy of
manners. Here there was more scope, but nothing was achieved
comparable to the masterpieces of Molière, for this literary form
was not completely adapted to the English genius. Saint-
Évremond once defined the ideals as the Englishman who can
talk and the Frenchman who can think; the Restoration drama-
tists seldom succeeded in providing either thought or wit. The
accusation of obscenity cannot be levelled by the present age
against any of its predecessors; but, with more justice, much
of the dramatic output of the Restoration may be indicted of
tediousness, for even the courtiers became tired of it; and, in
1682, so diminished was the popularity of the stage, that the
duke of York's company had to combine with that of the king.[2]
Thereafter, the theatre was displaced in importance by the
pamphlet and the newspaper. Thus in drama as in music the
taste of Charles was partly responsible for a diversion from
the main stream of English tradition, a diversion which was not
pure loss, as witnessed by the names of Dryden, Otway, and
Purcell.

In one respect, however, the French influence proved a real
blessing. This was in the development of literary criticism; and,
more especially, in the expression of that criticism by means of
the 'causerie' or short essay, in which literary analysis is effected

[1] Dryden's *Maximin*.
[2] For a very interesting account of this decline see A. Beljame, *Le public
et les hommes de lettres en Angleterre, 1660–1744*.

with moderation and grace. In this the French excelled; but Dryden, who had French models to help him, showed how it could be done almost equally well in English. The essays which he prefixed to many of his compositions are models of clarity and condensation.[1] They are of more than literary interest; for they reflect a subtle change, due perhaps to the greater influence of women in Restoration England, or possibly even to the personal example of Charles himself. It was an entirely different method of expressing disagreement. Hitherto, literary polemic had been handled mainly by scholars, shut up in their studies; it was therefore generally vituperative, and often vindictive; now, in the hands of Dryden, it reflected not the vitiated atmosphere of the study, but a more polite world where there was always a suggestion of femininity, enlivened by the *bons mots* of a king whose humour never failed him. It was not that Dryden had any close personal connexion with the Court, but rather that he interpreted a new attitude of mind popularized by the king and by French influence. In this more rare atmosphere criticism might be both courteous and effective, for the devotee of literature was no longer a pedant but a man of the world; and the 'mob of gentlemen that write with ease' had at least commenced life as gentlemen. Many took their cue from the king, who preferred unhorsing an opponent with a lance to annihilating him with a culverin; hence, at a time when the nation was passing through one of the most sensitive and receptive periods of its history, his personal influence may have counted for much:

Whence is it that our conversation is so much more refined? I must freely and without flattery ascribe it to the Court; and in it particularly to the King, whose example gives a law to it. His own misfortunes and the nation's afforded him an opportunity which is rarely allowed to sovereign princes, I mean of travelling and being conversant with the most polished courts of Europe; and thereby of cultivating a spirit which was formed by nature to receive the impressions of a gallant and generous education. At his return he found a nation lost as much in barbarism as in rebellion; and as the excellency of his nature forgave the one, so the excellence of his manners reformed the other. The desire of imitating so great a pattern first awakened

---

[1] See the edition of these essays by W. P. Ker, with a valuable introduction showing the French influence.

the dull and heavy spirits of the English from their natural reservedness; loosened them from the stiff forms of conversation, and made them easy and pliant to each other in discourse. Thus, insensibly our way of living became more free; and the fire of the English wit, which was before stifled under a constrained, melancholy way of breeding, began first to display its force, by mixing the solidity of our nation with the air and gaiety of our neighbours.[1]

Dryden possibly exaggerated the value of royal[2] and French influence; but of the fact of that influence there can be no doubt. It eventually gave us the age of Pope and Chesterfield for that of Bunyan and Milton. Who is to decide between them?

Wider than the influence of university, school, or court was that of the popular press.[3] There was first the newspaper. At the close of the Commonwealth two publications of a government news-book were in circulation—the *Mercurius Politicus*, published on Thursdays, and the *Public Intelligencer*, on Mondays, both compiled by Marchamont Needham; but in December 1659 a rival journal the *Parliamentary Intelligencer* was brought out by Henry Muddiman, one of the professional journalists of his age. This newspaper had a definite object—to popularize the demand for a free parliament; and when this object was achieved, Muddiman succeeded in acquiring a more official status for his papers. For some years he had a monopoly of supplying printed and written news to the public, in return for which monopoly he conveyed intelligence to the government. As the press came to be more effectively controlled by the Licensing Act and by the supervision of the secretaries of state, Muddiman was displaced in importance by Roger L'Estrange, who combined the two roles of government agent or spy and editor of a semi-official weekly paper named *The Intelligencer*; but Muddiman was left as the most important of the news-letter-writers, who sent their weekly summaries at regular intervals to

[1] Dryden, *Defence of the Epilogue*, in *Essays*, ed. W. P. Ker, i. 176.

[2] A useful corrective to Dryden's estimate is provided by Halifax's *Character of Charles II*, in *Halifax*, ii. 343–60. Halifax thought that Charles told his good stories too often, and that the frank manner of expression acquired abroad was not always in accord with English taste.

[3] For the history of the press in England see H. R. Fox Bourne, *English Newspapers*; J. B. Williams, *A history of English journalism to the foundation of the Gazette*; S. Morison, *The English Newspaper* (1932).

clients on payment of a fee, generally £5 per annum. In November 1665, when court and parliament were at Oxford, Arlington secured the publication of the bi-weekly *Oxford Gazette*, an infringement of L'Estrange's monopoly which was made possible by the special privileges of the University Press. This journal was afterwards printed in London, and was known as the *London Gazette*; but at first it was not fully official because (owing to disagreements between the two principal secretaries of state) rival papers were licensed. The Great Fire destroyed these competitors; so in this fortuitous way the *London Gazette* came to be a semi-official organ. The meeting of the Oxford Parliament in 1681 provided another occasion for journalistic activity; but this was short-lived. In the last four years of the reign L'Estrange pilloried Whigs and Dissenters in *Heraclitus Ridens* and *The Observator*: newspapers which, though frequently parodied, did not have to face the sustained competition of rival journals.

The newspapers were small, closely-printed sheets, containing a few items of foreign and domestic intelligence, together with announcements of horses stolen and strayed, and advertisements of quack medicines. There was a certain amount of specialization; for in 1675 appeared *The City Mercury or Advertisements Concerning Trade*, a journal intended for the needs of merchants and the commercial world. In this were trade announcements: such as ships offered for sale, houses and shops to be let, offers from purchasers of life annuities, and the time-tables of stage-coaches. It does not appear to have been long-lived.[1]

While the newspaper provided for those who wished to be abreast of the times, there was a great increase in that literature whose object was merely to provide diversion. As this was not written for a critical public, and was intended to attract purchasers from those who do not usually spend money on books, its productions were not likely to be found in the studies of the learned, nor among the well-bound folios of the rich; they were circulated 'below stairs', and found a resting-place behind the pots and pans in the kitchen. In this way a reading public grew up. Accounts of murders, fires, and disasters, in rhyme or prose, with or without the help of the woodcut, satisfied in some

---

[1] Copies will be found in *Bodley, Nicholl's Newspapers*, i.

measure the human demand for accounts of the marvellous. These are evidences not that crime and misfortune were more than usually common, but that thousands of humdrum existences were varied by resort to that half-real world in which the literary artist worked. Thus there were ghost stories, such as that of the haunted house in Cherry-Tree Alley, near Bunhill Fields, where the apparition took the form sometimes of a man, sometimes of a dog, and manifested itself by pulling the clothes from people in bed. The owner of the house intimated that he proposed to ask a divine to 'lay' the ghost.[1] Another early example of this kind of literature was the story of the hackney coachman who picked up a curious passenger in Fleet Street. Some uncanny influence at once permeated the vehicle; the horses became restive; and when the fare dismounted, he turned first into a bear, and then 'of a sudden vanished away in a terrible flash of fire with great sparks, as if a flambeau had been dashed against the wall'.[2] This was in 1684. But if there were few ghost stories, there were many that bordered on the miraculous, a favourite theme being that of the man or woman who slept for unusually long periods. Thus there was the Dutchman, a patient in St. Bartholomew's Hospital, who slept regularly for five days and nights every August. Nor was this all, for on these occasions he had dreams which came true; and at the same time his mother had identical dreams. On one occasion, the dream was about two fellow patients in the hospital; the one he saw 'hurried to a dismal, dark carstle' (sic), while the other was taken away 'to a place of bliss'. Sure enough, these two men died while the sleeper was dreaming about them. A woodcut showing the Dutchman in bed added to the novelty of this story.[3]

A new and more vivid world was coming more prominently into existence, peopled by men who were heightened above the ordinary human dimensions; for whom glory, disaster, and death were as things of ordinary routine. It was as unreal as that of the heroic drama, but it made a much stronger and wider appeal. This world of imagination was not so densely peopled as its counterpart of to-day, when there are so many devices for bridging the gulf between fact and fancy, but in Charles's

<hr/>

[1] In *Bodley, Ashmole* G. 12, no. 214.   [2] Ibid., no. 213.
[3] *The sleepy man awak'd* . . . in *Bodley*, 2702 e. 1.

England its existence was being noted as a new phenomenon. 'It is nothing', said an observer, 'to kill a man this week, and with ink instead of *aqua vitae* to bring him alive the next; to drown two admirals in a week, and to buoy them up again the next, so that many of these pamphlets may be better termed The Weekly Bills of Truth's Mortality.'[1] The student of this literature cannot but notice the great increase in its popularity after 1679, an increase sometimes attributed to the lapsing of the Licensing Act in that year; but this cannot be the sole cause, because the executive still retained some power of censorship, and exercised it by proclamation;[2] moreover the pamphlets here in question were not of a character likely to offend the licensing rules. It is equally probable that the Popish Plot stimulated the vogue for the miraculous; and so, at a time when there was real difficulty in distinguishing the natural from the supernatural, when the extraordinary was not the exception but the rule, it is not surprising that the purveyor of the wonderful came into his own; indeed, for perhaps the first time in English literature, the lie became a legitimate motive, and to tell it well became one of the recognized objectives of art. Not for some time was this accomplished with real skill, but meanwhile there were some creditable attempts.

Some of these attempts are not without interest in the history of that literary form which came to displace the epic, the lyric, the elegy, and the funeral oration, namely the novel. Many critics find the seventeenth-century prototypes of the novel in long, rimed romances, such as Davenant's *Gondibert* (1651), or in the comparatively short stories of Aphra Behn, or even in the wearisome narratives of madame de Scudéry; but it is possible that humbler ancestors had a share in the development of this literary type. It is at least likely that some of the more obscure romancers of the Restoration period were seeking for expedients intended to create the illusion of verisimilitude. The poorest device was to say that, if the reader doubted the truth of the events narrated, he could obtain confirmation by interviewing the inhabitants of a particular place; or, if even that were not enough, by inspecting the remains of the villains of the piece on

[1] *The Tears of the Press* (1681), in *Bodley, Ashmole* 730.
[2] *Steele*, i. 3699. See *supra*, 515.

a specified place of hanging.[1] A slight improvement on this was to say that the qualities of the hero or heroine would sufficiently appear in the sequel about to follow, a subterfuge adopted in a historical novel entitled: *The English Princess or the Duchess Queen: a relation of English and French Adventures, a Novel*[2] (1678). This title was certainly an attractive one; but after being lured into a record of cosmopolitan adventures, the reader was asked to accept this unconvincing description of the heroine, queen Margaret of Scotland: 'as to her body, nothing was wanting that might render it perfect; her complexion was fair, and the round of her face inclined near to a perfect oval'. These descriptions of female beauty or virtue are still notorious stumbling-blocks for the male novelist.

It was in the romances of roguery that the lie was told well; indeed, the tramp is a progenitor of the novel, as the burglar of the detective story. These rogue stories had begun as translations of Spanish picaresque novels; but in the later part of the seventeenth century original narratives were being produced, and there was at least one extensive cycle relating to the exploits of a single great rogue. This was the German Princess, alias Mary Carleton, alias Jenny Voss, whose real name was Mary Moders. She was born in humble circumstances at Canterbury in 1634 and had a local reputation as a cheat. Her marriage to John Carleton, who pretended to be a lord, brought her a wider circle of acquaintance and opportunity, which she utilized to the fullest advantage, as may be seen in the numerous accounts of her exploits.[3] After being tried for bigamy, she went on the stage in a play depicting her own career;[4] she then returned to thieving, and is said to have emulated the exploits of colonel Blood by stealing the more picturesque valuables, such as the lord

---

[1] These were the tests suggested in a story about a witch and her two sons who murdered a Mr. Harrison, who came to life again and was transported to Turkey. The inhabitants of Camden and the remains on the gibbets on Broadway Hill would provide confirmation. (*Bodley, Wood* 401, no. cxci.)

[2] In *Bodley*, 8 R. 72 Art.

[3] For instance, F. Kirkman, *The Counterfeit Lady Unveiled* (1673), in *Bodley, Wood* 267. See also E. Bernbaum, *The Mary Carleton Narratives* (1914). See also the account in the *D.N.B., s.v.* Mary Carleton.

[4] *The German Princess.* It was seen by Pepys on April 15, 1664.

chancellor's mace.[1] She was executed at Tyburn in 1673. It was said by one of her biographers that when young she was addicted to pleasure, loved fine clothes, delighted in reading books, especially love stories, and sometimes imagined herself a princess.[2]

In at least one of the rogue stories can be detected that attention to minute detail afterwards so brilliantly exemplified in the work of Defoe; in this way an apparent irrelevancy is only one of many units making a concerted work of art. Examples abound in *The English Rogue*, by R. Head (1680). Thus, in his boyhood, the hero of this romance killed a turkey and was extremely proud of his exploit. This youthful pride might have been emphasized by a free use of adjectives; but Head makes it convincing by recording a trivial incident—the boy stuck some of the turkey's feathers in his cap, and, through constantly looking at these proofs of his prowess dangling before his eyes, he became squint-eyed. So, too, his mother was always admiring his beauty. More conventional writers would have tried to describe the boy's charms; but Head merely records the fact that, at table, the mother so doted on her son 'that she forgot to eat'. These are small things, but they show the beginnings of a new aim in English literary art—the presentation of falsehood in such a manner that it seems as natural as the truth.

The Popish Plot may also be held responsible for an increased interest in national history, an interest accentuated by hatred of France as personified in Louis XIV. Hitherto men had read history in sombre folios or long chronicles; for the learned, there were the researches of Selden, Coke, and Spelman; but now, for perhaps the first time, it was possible to read at least some of it in the short biography, such as that of Mary, Queen of Scots,[3] a book specially written for those who doubted the truth of the Plot. There were also published historical comparisons of parliaments, such as those of 1680–1 with those of 1640–1;[4] and there were reprints of old books, such as Doleman's *Conferences about the next succession to the throne of England*,[5] or Birkenhead's

---

[1] *The German Princess Revived, or the London Jilt*, 1684, in *Bodley, Ashmole* F. 5.
[2] F. Kirkman, *The Counterfeit Lady Unveiled*, 9.
[3] *History of the life of Mary, Queen of Scots*, 1681, in *Bodley, Ashmole* F. 6.
[4] *Multum in Parvo*, by Theophilus Rationalis, in *Bodley, Pamph.* 146.
[5] Printed by the Whigs in 1679 in support of the exclusionist cause.

sarcastic *Assembly Man*. More important than these was a new venture—a short, general history of England, from the 'beginnings'. This was H. Cressey's *The Plain Englishman's Historian* (1679), a compendium of only 140 pages: 'a brief epitome of English History', which traced national origins to heroic sources; for it began with the landing (2855 B.C.) of Brutus on our shores. Most famous of all was Gilbert Burnet's *History of the Reformation in England* (commenced in 1679), a work which received such a welcome as to earn for its author the congratulations of both Houses of Parliament. Condemned though he is by modern experts, Burnet was nevertheless our first popular historian.

Almost as wide in their appeal were those books which popularized scientific theories about the origin of the universe, the constitution of matter, and the nature of the human body. Then as now there was some distinction between those researchers who were patiently contributing to the sum of knowledge, and those who, possessed of the gift of exposition, were familiarizing the layman with what was already known. A good example of this latter class was Thomas Burnet, master of the Charterhouse, whose *Sacred Theory of the Earth* (1684) was dedicated to Charles, and was much appreciated by that monarch. In this book the early history of the globe was described. The world was nearly 6,000 years old, and had been produced from a liquid chaos; its surface was at first perfectly smooth— no rocks, no mountains, no seasons; the air was calm and serene, and natural conditions produced a golden age amid 'the first innocency of Nature'. This perfect state was ended when the world fell into an abyss, where it suffered the Deluge, or forty days' rain, which created mountains and valleys through erosion; this fact alone, noted the author, was sufficient to disprove Aristotle's doctrine of the permanence of the earth's form. An entirely new world emerged from the Deluge; for the crust of the old earth had fallen into the abyss of waters, everywhere there were changes and irregularities, such as storms, rains, and seasons; into this new world only about eight people survived. Everything pointed to the view that the world would eventually be destroyed by fire. This would prove to be a mixed fatality: that is, a divine judgement supported by natural causes. Among the natural causes were the sulphureous quality of the soil, and the hollow construction of the ground; moreover, Scripture tells us that the Fire will start at the seat of anti-Christ, obviously in Rome, and the country round about, where the earth contains much sulphur and there are fiery mountains and caves. Rome will therefore be swallowed in a lake of fire. But there are men who incur an even greater measure of divine wrath than the papists: these are the infidels and atheists, who will be the first to perish. However antiquated Burnet's views may appear, it should be recalled that scientific geology did not begin until the nineteenth century, and moreover, Burnet handled his great theme with a dignity of expression which at least stimulated respect for the mighty forces at work in the universe.

Both popularizer and researcher recognized the need of harmonizing the new discoveries with truth as already revealed in the Scriptures; in this sense, there was no antithesis between the two, and the greatest scientists of the period, such as Newton and Boyle, were men of profoundly religious character. But at least this spread of scientific knowledge, even where crude or inaccurate, may have helped to break down a barrier which had been immeasurably strengthened by the Reformation and its consequences—the barrier of dogmatism. Before the human mind could be set in order, much heavy lumber had therefore to be removed. This was the theme of a notable book published in 1661: *The Vanity of Dogmatizing*, by Joseph Glanvill, a book which showed what a tiny fraction of our experience can be explained or accounted for in a completely satisfactory way. The human body was itself, he contended, a mass of unexplained problems;[1] the motion of a wheel round its centre was inexplicable on currently accepted hypotheses;[2] sensation and memory were not completely accounted for; we live in a world of mysteries of which we perceive only an infinitesimal part. Aristotle's teaching, he thought, was completely inadequate for the new world of nature being unravelled before men's eyes; moreover the Stagyrite's philosophy had been responsible for no new invention, and was impious.[3] Because of the mutual 'dependence and concatenation' of causes we cannot know one thing without

[1] *Vanity of Dogmatizing*, ch. v.　　　　　[2] Ibid., ch. vi.
[3] Ibid., ch. xix.

knowing all.[1] Dogmatizing is therefore the effect of ignorance, the disturber of the world, and the consequence of a narrowness of spirit. This plea for philosophic doubt was perhaps premature; it was enunciated in an age when most men were still thinking in definite, theological terms; but it aptly embodied that constructive scepticism which Bacon and Descartes had already applied to the preconceptions of their times.

This mingling of tradition with free inquiry is to be found in much of the philosophy and science of the later seventeenth century. It may be illustrated from chemistry. Here the ancient Greek and Arab traditions had been modified in the sixteenth century by Paracelsus, and later by van Helmont of Brussels; their views were further developed by Sylvius (Francis Dubois), who was born at Amsterdam in 1614. Briefly, Sylvius correlated all diseases with chemical properties, everything being referred to acids and alkalis; diseases were therefore divided into two main classes, according as they were due to the acridity of one of these substances. The bile is one of the main factors producing such acridities, according as it is influenced by food, air, and emotion; thus fevers are caused by acid acridity of the pancreatic juice. In England these doctrines were developed by the physician Thomas Willis (1621–75), who is also known in the history of medicine for his important researches into diabetes. Willis adopted the three primary chemical qualities of Paracelsus, namely salt, sulphur, and mercury. Salt is the cause of fixity in bodies, and is the residue left after burning; mercury is the spirit which volatilizes their constituent parts, and is isolated by distillation; sulphur causes colour and combustibility, and thus unites the spirit to the salt. On this basis he expounded a whole theory of medicine. He held that, in the process of digestion, an acid ferment is produced in the stomach; together with the sulphur of the food, this forms the chyle. The chyle enters into fermentation in the heart; in other words, the salt and sulphur are set on fire. This combustion produces the vital flame, which permeates all life; it creates also the vital spirits in the brain by a process of distillation. Fevers are attributable to an effervescence of the blood; spasms and convulsions are caused by explosions of salt and sulphur; gout

[1] Ibid., ch. xxii.

is due to the coagulation of the blood; scurvy is caused by the blood becoming 'vapid'.[1]

Such were the main principles of the Iatrochemists, so called because they referred all medical phenomena to chemical processes. For the student of science, these doctrines show an attempt to utilize, in the healing art, the chemical researches into the properties of metals which Paracelsus had inaugurated in the preceding century; and they directed attention to one of the most fruitful fields of modern research—the chemical composition of the blood. For the student of history they have this interest, that they illustrate the vast importance of chemistry in the speculative inquiries of the seventeenth century, and the influence of that science in spheres where it no longer has a monopoly; indeed, it can be demonstrated that much of the thought of the later seventeenth century was coloured by chemical similes and doctrines. Thus, human character like the human body was determined mainly by chemical composition. The 'humours' illustrated the balance of components in this composite entity, the preponderance of any one of the four elements producing certain distinctive idiosyncrasies, so clearly defined that they might be deduced from the complexion, the hair, or the eyes.[2] A humour was defined[3] as 'a moist and running body into which the food in the liver is converted'. It might be of different kinds—sanguine, phlegmatic, choleric, or melancholic, and an excess of one might produce disturbance amounting to a disease, such as Melancholy, the fashionable complaint of the century; while the ideal character was based on a perfect balance of all four elements. Chemistry was an essential element in the inquiry of the time, not, as is sometimes supposed, because Charles dabbled in laboratory experiments, but because its principles and nomenclature underlay so much of seventeenth-century thought.

[1] T. Thomson, *History of Chemistry* (2nd ed.), 184–201; W. C. Dampier-Whetham, *A History of Science*, 124–8. See also C. Singer, *A short history of Medicine* and *Studies in the history and method of Science*, and E. J. Holmyard, *Makers of Chemistry*.

[2] A good account of the humours and their importance in literature will be found in Dr. Percy Simpson's introduction to his edition of Jonson's *Every Man in his Humour* (1919).

[3] W. Vaughan, *Directions for Health* (1633), 127.

Increasing resort to mineral wells helped to spread this popular interest in chemistry; indeed, one of our earliest text-books of chemistry is a guide-book to the spa at Bath,[1] and for long men were induced to think of health and sickness in metallurgical terms. Metals were classified in a hierarchy which put gold at the top, because the most solid, the most heavy, and completely devoid of impurities, as was proved by the fact that it lost nothing in heating; silver came next; most impure of all was iron; intermediate were the 'half metals', such as bismuth, or tin glass, and antimony; there were also the minerals some-times classified as 'spirits', such as mercury, sulphur, arsenic, and cadmium. All these had their medicinal qualities. Sulphur provided a valuable fumigant, and could be taken internally in rhubarb as a purge by the choleric man; but for the same pur-pose the melancholic man would resort to senna or polypody. Nitre appears to have been grouped with elements like sulphur; it was of great value for its supposed qualities, and was used in juleps. Public health was thought to be influenced and even determined by the purity of the nitre available; and Boyle believed that the supplies of saltpetre could be classified in this way, that from the East Indies being the purest.[2] Scurvy was attributed to impure nitre,[3] plague to its exhalations in the air.[4] Some writers resolved the whole question of health into sulphur and nitre: 'Nitro-sulphurous spirits or salts are, as it were, the soul of the world, and the authors and carriers of all produc-tions and generations'.[5] With these explanations at hand, few diseases were attributed to occupation or nutrition, with the possible exception of rickets, then coming to attract the atten-tion of the physician because of its wide prevalence. This disease was said to be due to 'a soft and debauched way of living',[6] probably the reverse of the truth. Another substance to which great importance was attached was tartar. This might be adventitious or innate; the former being one of the by-

[1] E. Jorden, *Discourse of natural bathes* (1631).

[2] Boyle, *Works* (ed. 1772), i. 327. Boyle concluded that the differences in nitre were due to differences in the soil from which it was dug.

[3] G. Castle, *The Chemical Galenist* (1667), 41.

[4] N. Hodges, *Loimologia*, 32. See also *supra*, i. 292–3.

[5] G. Castle, op. cit. 61.

[6] Ibid. 44.

products of digestion, which usually found a lodging in the joints, where it produced gout.[1]

So long as Chemistry and Medicine were thus interlocked, the progress of each was impeded; phenomena had to be interpreted to comport with the doctrine of the four 'elements' and the three 'primaries'; nor, until Boyle defined it, was the conception of a chemical element understood. There were other instances of this interlocking. Many of the seventeenth-century thinkers were mathematicians, or had had a mathematical training; the importance of Harvey's discovery, coupled with the influence of Descartes, helped to create a school which linked medicine with mathematics or even hydraulics. From this point of view, physiology was a branch of mechanics. Contemporary, therefore, with the Iatrochemists, there were the Iatrophysicists; the first thinking in terms mainly of minerals and acids, the second in terms of pressure and suction. To these may be added a third school, the Galenists, who claimed to follow the older traditions of the Greek and Arabic doctors.[2] While it is true that modern research favours this use by one science of the discoveries of another, yet this stage cannot be reached until each of the great branches of science is thought worthy of independent investigation. It was perhaps the most important intellectual achievement of Charles's reign that medicine, surgery, chemistry, physics, and astronomy all came to be regarded as great sciences, each having its distinctive aims and methods; and even more, that in all these subjects the authority of tradition was finally set aside in favour of independent investigation and experiment. If for this only, the period of the Restoration was one of the most important in the history of human thought.

2. THE ROYAL SOCIETY: SCIENTIFIC RESEARCH

Towards this achievement the universities at first contributed little; it is to the Royal Society that we owe the differentiation of the sciences and the encouragement of research. The Royal Society had its origin in the meetings of certain philosophers and inquirers which can be traced as far back as 1645; these

[1] H. Nollius, *Hermetical Physick* (1655 trans.), 294 sqq.
[2] A. H. Buck, *The Growth of Medicine*, 419–20.

men, detached from the troubles around them, were an informal group, called the Invisible College, a name which may have emphasized their dissociation from the religious and political parties of the time. After 1648 they held gatherings at Oxford, where their members included Dr. Wilkins, warden of Wadham College; Dr. Ralph Bathurst, afterwards president of Trinity College, Oxford; Seth Ward, afterwards bishop of Salisbury, and Dr. Petty. For a time Oxford was the centre of the new experimental philosophy, because in the university city were held the meetings of the Invisible College; Dr. Willis presided over an experimental club, which met at an apothecary's shop (Tillyard's in the High Street); and next door but one in the same street Boyle had a laboratory, into which he introduced the first teacher of practical chemistry in England—Peter Sthael, a native of Prussia.[1] These activities were outside the super-vision of the University; but in 1683 Oxford acquired a labora-tory of its own—the Ashmolean (now the 'old' Ashmolean), a benefaction of the antiquary Elias Ashmole, and Chemistry was there taught by the indefatigable Dr. Plot.[2]

With the Restoration, the Invisible College resumed its meet-ings at Gresham's College, when it numbered fifty-five; and, after a lecture given on November 28, 1660 by Christopher Wren, it was proposed to found a college for 'physico-mathematical learning', the members to pay a subscription of 1s. per week.[3] For nearly two years the society existed on this basis; but, by charter of July 15, 1662, it was incorporated as the Royal Society, and received a mace from Charles II. Its first president was lord Brouncker, who was succeeded fourteen years later by sir Joseph Williamson, and in 1680 by Boyle. In 1682 the members had so increased in number that it was necessary to discriminate carefully among the candidates for admission; this was possibly owing to the prestige bestowed on the Society by the king, who was himself interested in experiments, and enjoyed the conversa-tion of ingenious men. Many eminent workers contributed to the success and prestige of the Society. Thus Dr. Jonathan

[1] R. T. Gunther, *Early Science in Oxford*, i. 9–22. For a good, short history of the Royal Society in this period see H. B. Wheatley, *Early history of the Royal Society*. See also E. J. Bowen, *The study of science in University College, Oxford*.
[2] For this see Gunther, op. cit. i. 43 sqq.   [3] Wheatley, op. cit. 7.

Goddard made telescopes, which were more useful and less expensive than his 'drops'[1]; and in Robert Hooke the Society had not only a curator of experiments and (afterwards) an enterprising secretary, but a noted mathematician, architect, optician, and physicist; one of the most ingenious and prolific researchers of his day, who, while he anticipated many discoveries, did not have the sustained power requisite for bringing them to maturity. Among its fellows were to be found practically all the men of note in the reign of Charles II; for these included Newton, Boyle, Dryden, Petty, Evelyn, Sandwich, Barrow, Buckingham, and Pepys.

The scope of the Society's inquiries may be gathered from the names of the committees and their purposes. Among these were the mathematical, the astronomical and optical, the chemical, the agricultural, and those for correspondence and the history of trade. The communications were classified into the following, among other categories: mechanics and trade; journals of the weather; statics and hydraulics; architecture, ship-building, geography, navigation, voyages, and travels; pharmacy and chemistry; monsters and longevity; grammar, chronology, history, and antiquities. These attest the diversity of the Society's interests,[2] and serve to show that the Royal Society was not a scientific institution in the narrow sense of the term, but a body for the encouragement, collection, and classification of knowledge on almost every conceivable subject. By its agency also were conducted extensive inquiries which would now be the subject of royal commissions. Such an inquiry was that into English agriculture.[3] In this way the whole character of philosophic speculation (in the wider sense of the term) was completely changed. Hitherto the investigator had worked as a solitary student; he had been taught to despise the methods of the 'sooty empiric', and to place his faith in books; he published his results in Latin, and would have resented most strenuously the criticism that he had strayed from accepted authority. Now he was encouraged to go into his workshop or laboratory or the outside world in order to use his powers of observation; his

[1] See *supra*, i. 331.
[2] See A. H. Church, *Royal Society Archives: Classified Papers* (1907).
[3] See *supra*, i. 60-1.

results were communicated in English to a body of men with whom he could discuss their relevance or import; and he was induced to think, not that men were at the end of their knowledge of nature, but at the beginning. Similar forces were at work in the scientific Academies of France and Italy.

Nor were these things confined to a small and select circle; for in 1665 began to appear the *Philosophical Transactions*, printed for the Royal Society and edited by its first secretary, Henry Oldenburg. This was intended to give publicity to the 'undertakings, studies and labours of the Ingenious in many considerable parts of the world'. Its first number was prefaced by a statement of the importance of communicating scientific knowledge through the press. There then followed an account of improved optic glasses made in Rome; there was a communication by Hooke intimating that, with a 12-foot telescope, he had seen a spot in one of the belts of Jupiter; to this was added an account of a book in the press—Boyle's *Experimental History of Cold*; there was also a description of a 'very odd, monstrous calf' born at Lymington in Hampshire; and finally there was a short article on the new 'American whale fishing about the Bermudas'. Subsequent numbers maintained this variety of topic, and so provided reading of interest to every man of intelligence. The mercury mines of Friuli; a method of producing wind by falling water; revelations by the microscope of minute bodies on the edges of razors, on blighted leaves, on the beard of the wild oat, on sponges, hair, the scales of a sole, the sting of a bee, the feathers of a peacock, the feet of flies, and the teeth of sharks; a baroscope for measuring minute variations in the pressure of the air; a hygroscope for discerning the watery steam in the air (these were Hooke's inventions); Mr. Wing's Almanac giving the times of high water at London Bridge; a new way of curing diseases by transfusion of blood; the process of tin-mining in Cornwall; and the making of mulberry wine in Devonshire— these are only a minute number of the subjects on which writers conveyed information derived from their experience and investigation. Such things may well appear commonplace or jejune to a surfeited or over-educated world; but in their original freshness they must have opened up new worlds to men circumscribed by the older traditions.

Of actual intellectual achievement, many examples might be cited from the careers of scientific men in the reign of Charles. It may suffice to record a few of the results obtained in medicine, surgery, chemistry, and physics; for which purpose the names of Sydenham, Wiseman, Boyle, and Newton may be selected. The last two were members of the Royal Society; the first two were not.

Thomas Sydenham (1624–89) came of an old Dorsetshire family, and varied his studies at Oxford with service in the Civil Wars (on the parliamentary side). Having obtained a medical degree and a fellowship of All Souls he began to study medicine with such facilities as the university then afforded, these consisting mainly of the specimens which the enterprising Petty provided for the dissecting-room. Further military service and studies at Montpelier delayed his establishment in practice; nor, until 1663, did he obtain the licentiate of the College of Physicians. Thereafter he built up a good practice in London. He suffered much from ill health, and his personal experience of gout enabled him to write an important account of that ailment. By contemporaries he was held in high esteem, because of his zeal and ability as a physician, and from a certain nobility and modesty of character, but otherwise he was not numbered among the notable men of his time. Two treatises, *Methodus curandi febres* and *Observationes Medicae*, brought him into European notice.

Sydenham's importance in the history of the healing art lies in the fact that he was the first to illustrate accurate clinical observation of disease. That observation could be trained, and that it must be trained in order to achieve scientific results, was the principle which he taught and acted upon; that it is a truism to-day does not detract from the importance of its earlier enunciations in medical history. He defined this principle in four axioms: (1) all diseases must be reduced to certain definite species, as the botanists have done for plants; (2) 'every philosophical hypothesis that has inveigled the writer's mind should be set aside', and the clear and natural phenomena of the disease, no matter how small they may appear, should be recorded; (3) in describing a disease it is necessary to distinguish between the 'peculiar and perpetual phenomena' and those that are accidental and adventitious; (4) the seasons of the year are to be observed, because some diseases follow the seasons as do birds and plants. In these axioms[1] was Sydenham's challenge to the traditional practice as derived from Galen; even more, he showed how these new methods might be applied. Accordingly he recorded his observations of plague, ague, cholera, and fevers as he had witnessed them in different years; and from these observations he made his recommendations for treatment. He did not believe in bleeding as a universal panacea, and considered that idiosyncrasy and habit should be considered before this was resorted to. He succeeded in a fairly accurate diagnosis of measles—accurate enough to distinguish it from small-pox; and he noted also the liability of measles to result in bronchial complications—peripneumonia was the name which he gave to the broncho-pneumonia which frequently supervenes. His treatment of this ailment did not differ greatly from that of modern physicians—namely warmth, light diet, and a linctus for the cough.[2]

Sydenham was by no means the first English physician to use his powers of observation; for Francis Glisson (1597–1677), who was professor of Physic at Cambridge, adopted the same method for the study of morbid conditions, and embodied his investigations in a standard treatise on rickets (1650). But it was Sydenham who first advocated and applied these new principles of clinical medicine to the whole range of the healing art, thus systematizing and illustrating what others were applying to particular diseases or special branches of the subject. In Surgery there was also an important advance, exemplified in the work of Richard Wiseman (?1622–76). Like Sydenham he had seen much military service (on the royalist side), which proved of great value to him, since it enabled him to study his subject at first hand. When he was about fifteen he was apprenticed to a surgeon; in 1652 he was made free of the Barber-Surgeons, and in 1672 he was sworn sergeant-surgeon to the king. He had a considerable practice, in the course of which he did much to differentiate his profession from that of barber and bone-setter on the one hand and physician on the other; indeed he helped

[1] These will be found in the author's preface to *The whole works of . . . Dr. Sydenham* (8th ed. 1722).   [2] Ibid. 131–4.

to make surgery a scientific subject. Before it could be differentiated, there were required a nomenclature and a set of definitions; in this respect the work of Wiseman was to prove of permanent importance. Here is his definition of a wound; it is a model of concision and clarity:

A wound is a solution of continuity in any part of the body suddenly made, by anything that cuts or tears, with a division of the skin.[1]

Wiseman coupled this scientific spirit with devotion to a sentiment; for as a royalist he believed in the efficacy of the royal touch for Scrofula, or the King's Evil, and he described those cases which he thought specially amenable to treatment from this source.[2] Moreover, he had considerable power of literary expression, and his volume of *Chirurgical Treatises* is one of the most remarkable 'case books' in the history of medicine; so clearly written as to win the commendation of Dr. Johnson, and so easily understandable as to provide the lay reader with much information about the practice of both medicine and surgery in the later seventeenth century. He used the knife only when absolutely necessary; he was quick to detect every circumstance that might help better diagnosis or promote speedier cure. Thus he noted the effect of air on his patients; that of Hampstead he thought particularly good; he recorded also the case of a patient who improved in Knightsbridge and relapsed in Holborn.[3] He believed moreover in the value of exercise, and the benefits to be derived from adapting diet to bodily habit. Many of the cases which he attended were not surgical at all, and he frequently prescribed the powerful drugs then in vogue; but, in the midst of his work as a general practitioner specializing in fractures and wounds, he helped to lay the foundations of the great traditions of British surgery, to be built upon in the next century by Hunter, and entirely remodelled in the nineteenth by Lister.

Like Wiseman, Robert Boyle knew the need for scientific definition and nomenclature. Chemists, still labouring under the four Aristotelian categories of matter, could not distinguish

[1] R. Wiseman, *Eight Chirurgical Treatises* (4th ed. 1705), 322.
[2] He recommended for royal treatment those cases where the tumours were about the neck, and also where the lips or eyes were affected. Ibid. 241.
[3] Ibid. 370.

between element and compound; until there was such a distinction, little progress could be looked for in chemistry. It was Boyle who supplied the definition of an element:

I mean by elements . . . certain primitive and simple, or perfectly unmingled bodies; which, not being made of any other bodies, or of one another, are the ingredients of which all those called perfectly mixed bodies are immediately compounded, and into which they are ultimately resolved.[1]

The author of this definition was one of the most distinguished and creative men of his age. The Hon. Robert Boyle (1627–91) was a son of the first earl of Cork. After a short stay at Eton (in the provostship of sir Henry Wotton) he travelled in Italy; and like many of his contemporaries he devoted himself to study and research while the great Civil Wars were being fought out. One of the Invisible College, he was induced by Petty to interest himself in dissection; but from his earliest days chemistry was his favourite subject. By means of an air-pump, invented by Hooke, he demonstrated the compressibility and weight of the air; while by his experiments in hydrostatics he succeeded in elucidating the laws of fluid equilibrium. He was in touch with most of the learned men of his time, including Newton, Locke, Evelyn, and Sydenham; and his busy life, passed in indifferent health, was marked by intense piety, and even fervour. He had the modesty of genius.

The achievements of Boyle in the many fields which he investigated have not yet been adequately valued;[2] but from his published writings the non-scientific reader may gauge something of the general importance of these achievements. His best-known work *The Sceptical Chymist* was published in 1661 and is in dialogue form; one of the speakers, Themistius, being an exponent of the older traditions, while Carneades, that is Boyle, shows how unsound are many of his assumptions. The hypotheses of the four 'elements' fire, air, earth, and water are shown to break down as a universal description of matter; nor is there even any evidence that any one of these is simpler than the substances of which they form a component; so, too, with the three

[1] Boyle, *The Sceptical Chymist.*
[2] A step in this direction has been made by Dr. Fulton's *Bibliography of the Writings of Robert Boyle* (1932).

'primaries' salt,[1] sulphur, and mercury. In this way it was possible for Carneades to define the real nature of an element, a conception of such vast importance for scientific investigation that its import could not at first be realized. It was too early for any isolation or enumeration of the elements; but once the significance of Boyle's distinction was realized, the process could not be long delayed.

His miscellaneous writings touch on many questions of moment. He impugned Hobbes's disparagement[2] of experiments; the philosopher of Malmesbury may be noted as perhaps the last exponent of the view that truth is evolved in the mind, and must never be sought for in the crucible. Failures in chemical experiments were thought by Boyle to be due to the practice of adulterating drugs;[3] generally, therefore, the materials available were 'sophisticated'. Throughout his writings he pleaded for a recognition of the need for practical as distinct from theoretical chemistry; characteristically, he was obliged to support this with the argument that, by such experiments, 'some meliorations' of mineral and metallic bodies might be effected.[4] His plea would have had little weight had it not been continually reinforced by illustration; invariably his conclusions were supported by very full and clear records of practical demonstration, and in the course of these he came upon many lines of investigation which have not been fully worked out until comparatively recent times. This is true of his inquiries into the nature of phosphorus and phosphorescent substances (then known as the 'noctiluca'); the illumination from these might, he thought, be used in places, such as the gun-rooms of ships, where candle-light might cause an explosion;[5] it is true also of his suggestion that a freezing mixture might be made with saltpetre as one of its ingredients.[6] He knew the importance of saltpetre (i.e. potash) in vegetable life; and, after researching into soils and seeds, he threw out a hint that fertility might be vastly increased by the use of chemical fertilizers.[7] He was fully aware of the importance

[1] In the sense defined *supra*, 717.
[2] *An examen of Mr. T. Hobbes his Dialogue* in *Works of the Hon. Robert Boyle* (6 vols. 1772), i. 186.
[3] *Two essays concerning the unsuccessfulness of experiments* in *Works*, i. 218 sqq.
[4] *Works*, i. 359.   [5] Ibid. iv. 384.   [6] Ibid. ii. 632.   [7] Ibid. iii. 404.

of crystalline form as a guide to chemical structure. These are only a few instances to show how Boyle had entered very far into the domain of modern chemistry.

His writings have a range of speculation paralleled only by those of Descartes, Pascal, and Newton. As he cleared chemistry of dangerous preconceptions, so he removed from metaphysics the hypothesis of substantial forms. The substantial forms were supposed to be entities or inseparable qualities of matter, quite distinct from its physical or chemical qualities; thus both steam and ice tended to return to their substantial form—that is, water; and so, on this assumption, there was generated in matter some force which preserved and restored its identity. The doctrine had been of great service to the theologians. Boyle had little difficulty in showing that extraneous causes such as heat or solution were in themselves sufficient to account for those predeterminable qualities of matter. This does not mean that he adopted a materialist interpretation where his predecessors had invoked a spiritual cause; for, while the Epicureans held that the universe of atoms was not made by a deity, and the Cartesians that matter, having had its original impetus from God, needed no further influence from that source, Boyle rejected both theories; holding that neither explanation was sufficient to show how matter was brought 'into so orderly and well-continued a fabric as this world'. There was divine creation and divine energizing of the orderly creation in which men lived.[1] Hence the possibility of miracles.[2]

It was in this mingling of the experimental with the speculative that Boyle was greatest. Side by side with accounts of practical investigations there are in his writings disquisitions of a general and often lofty nature, in which he shows how the religious spirit is quickened and deepened by exploration of the forces of nature. Thus in his *Discourse about the final causes of natural things*[3] he instances the membrane covering the eye of the frog as evidence of design; for, as the frog is amphibious, living among sedges and prickly things, it must have a strong protection over the eye. 'God declares his intentions particularly in the making of his creatures'; if these declare the divine purpose, still more is that purpose revealed by sun, moon, and stars.

[1] Ibid. iii. 38–48.   [2] Ibid. iv. 201.   [3] Ibid. v. 392.

But this consideration of final causes must not be an excuse for neglect to study any of the infinite intermediaries interposed before that end. Observation of natural phenomena, he claimed, was in itself an incitement to devotion: 'they who would deter men from the scrutiny of nature tend to deprive God of much of the glory due to him'.[1] Thus Boyle placed the justification for scientific study on very high ground. He taught and exemplified a conception of religion very much higher than any expounded in the formularies of his time; and he allied it to speculative inquiries which opened up new fields in scientific research. Added to this, his character and birth gave to his words a weight and influence which would have been less had his origin been obscure, or his personal reputation dubious. Boyle made the man of science eligible in good society;[2] no longer could he be dismissed as a quack or dabbler in alembics; no longer were culture and intelligence deemed incompatible with test-tubes and crucibles.

While Boyle did much to explode obsolete hypotheses, his work cannot be estimated except in reference to the revival of the atomist theory which Gassendi initiated. This revival helped to discredit the Aristotelian system; indeed it was the Latin poet Lucretius, not the Stagyrite, who was to prove the inspiration of real scientific achievement. Boyle as an atomist was a direct continuator of Gassendi and Galileo; and as an exponent of this *philosophia corpuscularis* he held that everything was reducible to 'one catholick or universal matter'. The corpuscle constituting this matter had magnitude, shape, motion or rest, and was indivisible and indestructible. What Boyle interpreted in chemical terms Newton interpreted in mathematical and physical; in this way was perfected one of the most remarkable achievements of human thought.

Sir Isaac Newton (1642–1727) was the greatest product of the new scientific movement; but while his achievements can be linked with those of contemporaries and predecessors, his genius and the range of his investigations had a universality which elevate him above the eras and periods recognized by the

[1] *The usefulness of natural philosophy*, ibid. ii. 15.

[2] According to an (alleged) Irish epitaph, Boyle was the 'father of Chemistry and the son of the earl of Cork'.

historical student. Moreover he was not a popularizer, and it needed all the persuasions of his friend Halley to induce him to consent to the publication of his *Principia* (1687); hence an accurate statement of his theories and discoveries can be expressed only in mathematical or physical terms. But, on the other hand, no student of English civilization under the later Stuarts can afford to ignore Newton on the ground that he is of exclusively scientific interest; for it was through his influence that whole branches of scientific investigation were transformed, and the outlook of educated man entirely altered.

Early in his career Newton approached the problem of gravitation, and in 1666 the fall of an apple in his orchard is said to have suggested to him the idea of a force which varied in proportion to the square of the distance. Earlier thinkers such as Descartes had supposed the existence in space of a primary substance or ether which accounted for those qualities of matter not directly attributable to extension; but to Newton it seemed that the fall of the apple illustrated a force which could be determined empirically. For the time, however, the problem had to be set aside, because of one serious difficulty, namely, that while the sun and planets could be treated as masses, each concentrated at mathematical points (owing to the disproportion between their size and their distance apart), this (seemingly) approximate method was inapplicable to the earth and the apple, because of their small distance apart in proportion to the size of the earth. Meanwhile several important advances were made which ultimately made it possible for Newton to solve the problem. The French physicist Picart obtained a more accurate measurement of the radius of the earth; and the Dutch scientist Huygens established the relation between the length of a pendulum and its time of vibration; and, most important of all, in investigating the movement of a mass describing a circular path, he determined the acceleration of the force impelling such a moving mass to the centre in terms of the velocity of the mass and the radius of its path. In 1685 Newton, prompted by Halley, returned to the problem of 1666, and he now made the vital discovery that, where there is gravitational pull, the mass of the gravitating sphere may be assumed to be concentrated at its centre. The result was a general law of gravitation, namely that its force varied directly in proportion to the product of masses and inversely to the square of their distance apart; a discovery which enabled him to link the phenomena of astronomy with the fall of bodies to the surface of the earth. Observation of the motion of the moon in its orbit enabled him to confirm this empirical law; and in this way he made it possible to determine the movements of the whole solar system. There were many immediate results of great consequence. Thus the tides could now be explained in terms of the inertia of water and the gravitational attractions of sun and moon;[1] hitherto many inquirers had attributed them to chemical causes.[2]

Accurate statement of Newton's discoveries in mathematics, optics, astronomy, and physics is for the scientist; here it may be permissible to note one general result of his influence. He definitely severed science from metaphysics in the sense that he made clear the scope and purpose of each. Scientific knowledge in its incomplete and empiric form could never, he held, be metaphysics, which is concerned only with real and final causes. These he did not try to determine, and he stated his law of gravitation not as the cause of gravitation, but as a formula by which its phenomena might be measured. Nevertheless, he believed that a complete knowledge of the universe would show it to be not a mechanism, as Descartes had supposed, but a providential arrangement;[3] not something originally set going and left to its own devices, but a coherent unit continually directed by some unseen and intelligent force. To him, therefore, the world was both geometrical and theological; religion and science were thus not antagonists, but were ultimately explicable each in terms of the other. This conception was bound to prove a potent influence in intellectual development. By thinking of gravity in universal, not terrestrial, terms Newton extended infinitely the horizons of men's minds, and linked the fall of a

---

[1] For a good account of the stages by which Newton evolved his law of gravitation see W. C. Dampier-Whetham, *A History of Science*, ch. iv.

[2] e.g. J. Philpot, *Brief discourse of that grand mystery of nature, the flux and reflux of the sea* (1673), where tides are attributed to a 'vitriolated, volatile or ammoniack salt'.

[3] A. J. Snow, *Matter and gravity in Newton's physical philosophy*, 81.

stone with the movements of the planets in a system more awe-inspiring than anything ever conceived by prophet or philosopher. Both the infinite and the infinitesimal were thus acclimatized in thought, the twin conceptions best fitted to inspire a more reverent approach to the problems of knowledge.

3. SOME ILLUSTRATIONS OF RESTORATION THOUGHT AND ACHIEVEMENT

Restoration England abounded in great and interesting men; few ages of history were so prolific of genius and ability. This can be evidenced by even the scantiest of selections. There was sir Christopher Wren, not only a scientist of real eminence but the architect of a restored capital; Halley, the continuator of Galileo, one of the first of astronomers among the last of astrologers; Purcell, whose music is at last coming into its own; prince Rupert, who, having achieved fame in the field, proved himself one of the most dashing of Charles's admirals, as well as an inventor, a patron of exploration, and an artist—a medley of activities eminently characteristic of his age. Or tribute might be paid to Clarendon as a historian; or to Burnet, who started a new school of autobiography by making the indiscretion a literary motive; or to Prynne, who by his researches in the Tower inaugurated the professions of archivist and scientific historian. Modern specialization makes such kaleidoscopic brilliance impossible or difficult of achievement; but in Charles's England the world was nearly three centuries younger, and the nation had the vigour and confidence of adolescence. At least a fraction of the total intellectual achievement of the Restoration may be deduced from its evidence of three things: curiosity, revolt, and good sense. The first may be illustrated from Petty, Evelyn, and Pepys; the second from Bunyan and Hobbes; and the third from Locke and Halifax.

Few careers[1] can have been more diversified than that of sir William Petty (1623–87). Born at Romsey in Hampshire, he showed a keen, boyish interest in everything mechanical; he

---

[1] See the account by *Aubrey*, ii. 139 sqq. For a good modern biography see that by lord Edmond Fitzmaurice. See also *The Petty Papers*, ed. marquis of Lansdowne, 2 vols., 1927, and *The Petty-Southwell Correspondence*, ed. marquis of Lansdowne, 1927.

loved to watch artificers at work, and he learnt many of the secrets of their trade. He served in boyhood at sea; but defective eyesight ended his career as a sailor, and for a time he studied abroad, notably at Caen, Amsterdam, and Paris. In 1649 he took a degree at Oxford and was one of the Invisible College. For a time he taught anatomy at the university, supplying his own specimens, which were brought by water from Reading and preserved by a special process of his own; and as the professor of Physic disliked dissecting, Petty's teaching found ready appreciation, so that he was 'beloved by all the ingeniose'. He soon found more lucrative employment; for in 1652 he was appointed physician-general to the Army in Ireland, and later he was commissioned to carry out the land-surveying requisite for the Cromwellian scheme of Irish resettlement, a task for which he was well qualified by his mathematical knowledge; and his 'Down' survey is one of the first attempts at surveying on a scientific scale. From this he derived advantage as well as reputation; indeed he was said to have acquired an estate in every province of Ireland. After the Restoration he devoted himself to the study of navigation, and was one of the men in whose conversation the king delighted. His double-bottomed ship performed at least one successful trip across St. George's Channel, but it does not seem to have done all that was expected of it, and was afterwards wrecked. One of the original fellows of the Royal Society, he abounded in novel ideas, the most notable being his belief in the value of statistics as the sound basis of efficient government. He wanted to be Registrar General of England, but as that office was not yet in existence he had to content himself with the posts of judge of admiralty in Ireland and a commissionership of the Treasury. As economist, he exposed the fallacies of those who limited wealth to the precious metals; he showed the vital importance of population in economic speculation; and he constantly reiterated the advantages of profiting by the Dutch example of free, unfettered commerce, encouraged by a state which did not throw all its energies into the crushing of religious dissent, or the enforcement of prerogative rights.

Judged by the reports of contemporaries Petty must have been a singularly attractive man; unusually well-informed, and yet anxious to learn; possessed of a dynamic force which communicated some of its energy to those with whom he came into contact. Nor was his demeanour always of that seriousness which one would expect in the patriarch of political economy, for he was known as a good mimic; he could preach in various styles; and once, when challenged to a duel by sir Alan Brodrick, he proposed weapons suitable to his short-sightedness, namely a dark cellar and hatchets. At the Royal Society he aptly suggested that the general annual meeting should be held not on St. Andrew's Day but on St. Thomas's Day, because the saint who insisted on personal verification was indeed the right patron for that society. Humour, enterprise, sociability, and an extremely broad and enlightened view of the good that might come from the collection and co-ordination of information and its proper use by the state—these were the qualities which made Petty distinctive in an age of remarkable men. 'There is no darkness but ignorance' might have been his motto. It is characteristic that, like Hobbes, he did not read much, because he knew the dangers that may come from too ardent pursuit of learning for its own sake; and he typified many of the best qualities of the 'practical' Englishman, with a touch of genius to set off his more matter-of-fact qualities.

John Evelyn (1620–1706) was the son of a landowner and was born at Wotton in Surrey. As a young man he travelled in France and Italy, as well as in England, in the course of which travels he developed a keen appreciation of art and architecture; his *Diary* also shows some appreciation of landscape, and he may have been susceptible to the environment of his Surrey home. Travel, with reading and gardening, was his main occupation in the time of troubles; but he was not a solitary, for he was in frequent communication with Wilkins and Boyle, and he was one of the first fellows of the Royal Society. During the Second Dutch War he did good work as a commissioner for the sick and wounded; he remained at his post in the Plague; in 1671 he was appointed a member of the Council of Plantations; and for a time, in the reign of James, he was one of the commissioners of the privy seal. He twice declined the honour of presidency of the Royal Society. His numerous writings cover a great range of subject, including 'sculpture' (i.e. engraving), gardening, silviculture, navigation and trade, numismatics, and the problem of London smoke. His *Diary* is a classic, of great value not only as a record of incidents, but for its revelation of a singularly graceful and thoughtful character, free from the pettiness and self-seeking so common among his contemporaries.

The dissoluteness of Restoration England helps to place the qualities of Evelyn in sharper relief. He had many of the attributes characteristic of the best type of Englishman—loyalty to the throne, devotion to his family, a high sense of duty, moderation in speech, and regularity of conduct. These were not the virtues which brought men success or fame in the reign of Charles; nor would they have been remarked by posterity had they not been coupled with a rich humanity, which enabled him to participate fully in all the best movements of his time. He is remembered for no single achievement, but his personality was a refining influence in a society where there was a temptation to relax every restraint; and in a minor key he voiced that intelligent curiosity which inspired the highest intellectual achievements of his time. He set a high standard, for he was an embodiment of the qualities which constitute the gentleman, and he proved that landed wealth was not incompatible with public spirit, refined taste, and a fair measure of learning.

His thirst for information was shared by Samuel Pepys, whose *Diary* is a serious rival to the plays of Shakespeare, and about whose activities there is a considerable literature which shows no sign of diminishing. His personal habits, his butterfly amours, his early risings and late to-beds, his childlike glee at the signs of his steady rise in life—all these have entered into our literary currency, though Pepys probably never intended that they should. Perhaps the secret of his charm is that he could take such genuine pleasure in small things. 'All the morning in my cellar ordering some alterations therein, being much pleased with my new door into the back yard'[1]—had he been a man of introspection he would not have had this interest in the door into his back yard. So too his delight when he was first addressed as Esquire; hence also the energy which he put into the cause of his further advancement; indeed, he rose several times at four in the morning to learn the multiplication table.[2]

[1] *Pepys*, Jan. 31, 1662. [2] Ibid., March 25, 1660.

Indirectly, he once gave the explanation of his own charm; for, after spending some time in the company of a major Waters, 'a most amorous, melancholy gentleman, under a despair in love', he noted that for this reason he found the major poor company.[1] Pepys is always good company, because though he was continually falling in love he never allowed these episodes to destroy his buoyancy; and like a cork he quivered with every ripple from the sea of life.

The involuntary revelation in his Diary that he was human has helped to obscure the fact that Pepys was a great administrator, possibly the greatest in the history of the British Navy. Where previously there had been indifference and ignorance, he stimulated zeal and the spirit of inquiry; and he was a pioneer in naval research, collecting vast materials now distributed in great libraries.[2] Curiosity was the mainspring of his herculean labours, as this enabled him to master the most profound technicalities, and was accompanied by an unfailing optimism; a curiosity for which nothing was too small—it might be the nautical history lurking behind the street-names of London, or the arrangement of his books, or the nature of the timber used by Noah in the building of the Ark—all these things provided welcome material for his omnivorous mind. A landsman by nature, he yet learnt more of things nautical than any sailor of his day, and he devoted that learning to the service of the Navy. In few men were the habitudes and passions of life so completely co-ordinated as in him; for he was able to return from the distractions of the park or the bargaining of the yards to the work of preparing a parliamentary report, or the devising of new official forms; with equal facility he could lose his heart to a woman and find his soul in a ledger. Living in an England ignorant of maritime affairs and often indifferent to them, having a landsman for a patron saint, and a proverb 'the sea and the gallows refuse nobody', he helped to inspire in his countrymen both a greater interest in ships and the sea, and some measure of pride in English sailors.

The greatest of diarists, Pepys was also the greatest of civil

[1] Ibid., July 9 and 11, 1662.
[2] In the British Museum, the Bodleian, and the Pepysian Library in Magdalene College, Cambridge.

servants. Eminence in this latter profession requires a sense of responsibility and a capacity for enforcing that sense on subordinates in a manner which shall be effective without being offensive. It is in the wording of the official rebuke that this quality calls for exercise, and here Pepys was breaking fresh ground, as may be seen in this letter[1] written on behalf of the Navy Board to negligent dockyard officials:

Gentlemen,

In answer to yours wherein we find you making complaint that the displeasure of this Board in the particular therein mentioned had been occasioned by our not being acquainted with what you had lately wrote on the same to Mr. Hayter, we cannot but take notice thereof as too obvious an instance of the perfunctoriness with which we find the service of His Majesty generally attended to by the officers of the yards; and assure you that we are in no little measure troubled to find such a proof thereof in reference to yourselves; who, had you considered our letter of the 14th. of December last with a regard anyway suitable to what you ought to pay to all that comes to you from this Board, you could not have overlooked the first three lines of our said letter, but found reason then, as we doubt not you will do now to be ashamed of your own negligence rather than judge us backward to do you the right due to you in that particular. . . . Therefore let not your want of considering your instructions longer occasion any prejudice to His Majesty by your not performing them.

We are,
Navy Office,   Your Very Loveing Friends,
22nd Jan. 1669.   Brouncker, Mennes, Pepys.

The structure of the first sentence could be improved, and the valedictory subscription might have been written by scribes of an earlier school; but in its restrained phrasing and pontifical detachment this letter has all the dignity and authority of Whitehall.

Had they known each other, Pepys would have found Bunyan 'very odd', and Bunyan would have assigned Pepys high office in the administration of the city of Carnal Policy. *The Pilgrim's Progress* was published in 1678, and its success proved both immediate and continuous. Its author has been the subject of praise and patronage because he, a tinker and former repro-

[1] *Add. MS.* 9307, f. 86.

bate, wrote the greatest allegory in the English language. But he was not of the gipsy race, for he was descended from a long line of English small-holders; he had a settled habitation; and the sins which he had to live down do not appear to have been more serious than profanity and sabbath-breaking. Itineracy he did not regard as a sin, nor imprisonment a shame. He cannot be definitely grouped with any one sect; indeed he rose above the distinctions of creeds, and directed his appeal not to one church but to all men. He spent many years in prison when he might have obtained liberty by undertaking to give over his mission; and he announced his message to an England wherein every fibre seemed to be relaxed.

The language of compromise is smooth and facile; that of rebellion is hard-grained and piercing. Unencumbered with book-learning, and burning with the fires of a conviction more enduring than that of Luther or St. Augustine, Bunyan permeated every sentence with a vigour such as no amount of training could have achieved. Compared with that of his contemporaries, his style is like some strange survival from a more primitive and elemental life. Everywhere men were learning to write agreeably, to see both sides of a question, to think in terms of their readers' likes and dislikes, and to keep going, in the cadence of the paragraph, the stately procession of the innocuous or the evasive; whereas, for Bunyan, each word had a sterling individuality. Hence with a few deft touches he can bring a man to life. Witness how the jury in Vanity Fair springs into animation:

And first among them Mr. Blind Man, the foreman said: I see clearly that this man is a heretic. Then said Mr. No Good: Away with such a fellow from the earth. Ay, said Mr. Malice, for I hate the looks of him. Then said Mr. Love Lust: I could never endure him. Nor I, said Mr. Live Loose, for he would always be condemning my way. Hang him, hang him, said Mr. Heady. A sorry scrub, said Mr. High Mind. My heart riseth against him, said Mr. Enmity. He is a rogue, said Mr. Liar. Hanging is too good for him, said Mr. Cruelty. Let us despatch him out of the way, said Mr. Hate Light. Then said Mr. Implacable: Might I have all the world given me, I could not be reconciled to him; therefore let us forthwith bring him in guilty of death. And so they did.

Bunyan devoted himself to a campaign not against sin, but against complacency. Any moralist can discredit the first; it was the tinker of Elstow who routed the second. By prayer and patience, the pilgrim might escape Giant Despair; but Mr. By Ends, whose principles were both harmless and profitable, was a far more elusive enemy. In the course of Christian's pilgrimage a climax was reached when Mr. By Ends, having failed in his onslaught on the hero's convictions, was joined by a powerful band of auxiliaries; these being Mr. Hold-the-World, Mr. Money-Love, and Mr. Save-All, old schoolfellows of Mr. By Ends, all having been educated at the academy kept by Mr. Gripe-Man, a schoolmaster in Love-Gain, a market-town in the county of Coveting. The pupils had been so well taught the art of getting 'either by violence, cozenage, flattery, lying or by putting on a guise of religion' that each of them could have kept school himself; and so, when they joined forces, they could make out an impregnable case for associating religion with profit. Did not Abraham and Solomon grow rich in religion? Did not Job say that a good man shall lay up gold as dust? Surely piety was justified by its material results; nor could anything be more reasonable than to be both virtuous and successful. With this proposition the attack on Christian was renewed, and old Mr. Hold-the-World (as the most moderate in demeanour) was put up to propound the question. The reply of Christian was devastating: 'Even a babe could answer ten thousand such questions.' The man who takes up religion for the world will throw it away for the world; the Scriptures ring with judgements meted out to the formalists and the hypocrites; the Pharisees, Judas Iscariot, and Simon the Sorcerer are the eternal prototypes of Mr. By Ends' principles and Mr. Gripe-Man's pedagogy. There could be no resisting the torrent which flowed from Christian's lips; for it caused Mr. By Ends and his company to stagger and fall behind.

Thus did Bunyan weave a halo round the uncompromising and the uncomfortable; and he raised a tribunal more solemn than any by which he was himself judged—that of human conscience. He set spiritual values against the petty objects for which humanity strives, and he practised as well as preached a doctrine in which these values had supreme and solitary force. That his book should still be read wherever the English language is used is a tribute not only to his supreme literary gift, but to the finer things in that rule of the Saints which was terminated by the coming of Charles Stuart.

Another great rebel was Thomas Hobbes of Malmesbury (1588–1679), who, after desultory study at Oxford, was for twenty years tutor and secretary to the Cavendish family. During the Commonwealth he spent some years in France, and gave mathematical lectures to Charles II, with whom he shared a lively intelligence and from whom he received a small pension. He knew most of the learned men of his day and had acute controversies with many of them, notably in matters mathematical. He preserved his faculties to a ripe old age, and was fortunate in that he was allowed to die a natural death; for on at least one occasion the Commons proposed to burn the *Leviathan* and the bishops proposed to burn its author. In appearance he was tall, erect, and bright-eyed; at times he dallied with hirsute adornments, but he deprecated a full beard, as implying philosophic professionalism.[1] The amateur status was thus preserved, and his life in the country afforded long periods of meditation without books; indeed he believed that if he had read as much as his contemporaries, he would have been as stupid as they.

His books, notably the *Leviathan* (1651), puzzled and deceived many readers, who found in his readiness of scriptural quotation and apotheosis of absolute power what appeared to be no more than the divine right theory in another guise; on the other hand, most of those who fathomed his meaning regarded his books as works of darkness, and at least one sinner was obliged publicly to recant his blasphemy, debauchery, and Hobbism.[2] Clarendon wrote a book[3] specially intended to undeceive those who regarded the *Leviathan* as a legitimate defence of monarchy. Hobbes often wrote in a somewhat oblique way, partly because it was safer, and partly because his peculiar literary style was well adapted to the veiling of original and daring thought in words

---

[1] *Aubrey*, i. 339–40.

[2] *Recantation of Daniel Scargil in Great St. Mary's, Cambridge, 1669*, in *Bodley, Wood*, 608.

[3] *A brief view and survey of the dangerous and pernicious errors to church and state in Mr. Hobbes's Leviathan* (1676).

apparently innocuous. His 'starcht, mathematical method' does not always lend itself to easy interpretation; but his English is always terse and virile.

Hobbes did many things by contraries, and a clue to the meaning of his *Leviathan* may be obtained by starting at the end. His last chapter: 'Of the benefit proceeding from darkness and to whom it accrueth' is apparently an exposure of the practices of the Roman Catholic Church; but closer inspection reveals the fact that he is attacking the whole of religious professionalism, under whatever name it may be practised. His argument is that, on the basis of revelation, the clergy have established a cult, having its distinctive language, its supernatural invocations, its terrifying threats, its demonology, and 'frivolous distinctions, barbarous terms and obscure language' (these taught in the Universities)—in fine, a complete paraphernalia of weapons for cheating the laity and dividing their allegiance. The benefit accruing to the clergy from this darkness consists of money, power, and reputation. Almost the last sentence makes it clear that he was not thinking only of popery; 'for it is not the Roman clergy only that pretends the kingdom of God to be of this world'. Here is Hobbes's starting-point. It was not merely that he was agnostic or anti-clerical; for he himself had no grievance against any particular religion, and he frequently attended the services of the Anglican church, because he liked its order and ritual. His position was fundamental. He believed that, by means of clerical obscurantism, the whole of contemporary thought had been tinged with conceptions which destroyed the possibility of clear and exact analysis; nor, until the state assumed all the secular powers and privileges of the church, would such exact thought be possible of exercise.

His purpose was therefore primarily an intellectual one—to destroy not a doctrine but a whole attitude of mind. Reading backwards in his book, the implications of this are illustrated. In his forty-sixth chapter he treats of 'darkness from vain philosophy and fabulous tradition'. Prominent in these categories is the hoary doctrine of substantial forms; with these 'separated essences', argues Hobbes, the theologians have been able to play many tricks; for, as they juggle with the bread and wine, so they give out that 'faith, wisdom and other virtues are sometimes poured into a man, sometimes blown into him'. Some would think that no great harm results; but Hobbes believed that thereby was set up a rival power to the state. 'Who will endeavour to obey the laws, if he expect obedience to be poured or blown into him? Or who will not obey a priest that can make God, rather than his sovereign, nay than God himself? Or who that is in fear of ghosts will not bear great respect to those that can make the holy water that drives them from him?' Probably few of Hobbes's readers read so far as this chapter. Some may have stopped at chapter xxxviii, where Hell is stated to be determined not 'by any note of situation, but only by the company'; those who persevered as far as chapter xxvii would have read some disturbing things about miracles, and this statement: 'a private man has always the liberty, because thought is free, to believe or not believe in his heart those acts that have been given out for miracles'; or this: 'the first rainbow that was seen in the world was a miracle, because the first, and consequently strange'. These passages might have been written by Voltaire; but Voltaire had an easier and less dangerous task. There was a hint of his real meaning in chapter xxxii, where he speaks of the 'captivity of our understanding'; by this, he understands not a submission of the intellectual faculty, but a submission of the will to a power which has no right to demand such obedience. This obedience, he thought, was stimulated by a whole host of accessories—by an anthropomorphic conception of the deity, by revelations in dreams, and by prophets. He would accept a prophet only if he preached the established religion and performed a real miracle.

These daring heresies were skilfully concealed in a heavy undergrowth of scriptural quotation, and the wolf which entered among the lambs was thickly covered with wool. He devoured many of the choicest specimens in the flock. Man in the state of nature had already been badly mauled by the Jesuits; but by the time Hobbes had finished with him his bones seemed those of a non-gregarious animal. The social contract had been fattened up by the Huguenots, and was regarded as an exhibition specimen, having a record of awards and prizes which completely discredited his one-time rival of the absolutist breed; there remained only an empty fleece when the wolf had finished;

for the contract was shown to bind only the subject, not the sovereign. There was the celebrated *Jus Naturale*, or natural inborn right, a pedigree creature, for which international triumphs were prophesied, though some thought it too good for this world; but after a little skirmishing (with words) this also was dispatched; for the *Jus Naturale* was proved to be Natural Right, that is Natural Liberty, that is Natural Licence, that is Anarchy, and so fit only for the state of savagery. Then followed a whole batch of *Leges Naturales*, each the embodiment of some virtue, such as justice, complaisance, and pardon; these were destroyed one after another; for it was demonstrated that they had their force not from any innate or supernatural power, but simply from the fact that they had the backing of the state. There remained only Liberty and Law. But even they succumbed. For Liberty had no separate existence, being merely what was left over after the decrees of the sovereign had been subtracted from the total of human activity; while Law, so far from being the emanation of reason, or discussion, or morality, was merely what the sovereign commanded. Not a single ideal was left.

Probably few who read those chapters of the *Leviathan* realized what a holocaust was taking place. If there was a cherished social or political aspiration, that was enough to invite attention from Hobbes; his aim was to undermine a whole fabric of thought, but he burrowed so deeply that few realized what he was doing. In place of the old structure torn by rival allegiances he substituted one which was completely enveloped by the secular power. The sovereign had taken upon himself the person of the state; all acts and opinions had their sanction in him; he was the incarnation of the secular spirit, enforcing opinions deemed necessary not for the salvation of the soul but for the safety of the state; himself the clearly defined source of authority, and the unlimited extent of his power the guarantee of peace. So expressed, Hobbes's opinions might seem to have merely academic import; but the date (1651) of his book should be recalled. It was a time when it might well have seemed that the whole principle of secular government was at stake. The king of England had recently been executed, and a 'purged' House of Commons was assuming executive functions; France was plunged in the wars of the Fronde; elsewhere there was revolt and disaffection; and in the background was the Roman Catholic Church, the one united political force, towering above innumerable and quarrelling Protestant sects. An acute observer might well have quailed at the prospect; and at least the remedies of Hobbes were not half-measures.

These remedies appeared to surrender every human sentiment in politics, to disparage everything hitherto accepted as good, and to exclude the possibility of progress. In place of the natural instincts which make men social and therefore political, Hobbes appeared to erect a mechanical and crushing despotism, a Moloch on whose altars were sacrificed all that men had hitherto held true or sacred. In this work of destruction Hobbes was doing in the seventeenth century what Calvin had done in the sixteenth century, and what Lenin was to do in the twentieth; the work of all three was primarily intellectual, and had the limitations inherent in all systems which ignore human nature. It is therefore not surprising that English political theory has derived more from Locke than from Hobbes; more from the traditionalism of Burke and the optimism of Bentham than from the cast-iron theorems of those who reduce politics to an exact science; for representative English thinkers have started from Aristotle's assumption that man is a social and political animal, and have rejected theories which force men into some preconceived conception of the state.

In mentality therefore the philosopher of Malmesbury was un-English; but his theories were to find their most complete vindication in Restoration England; and if he was not the inspiration of later Stuart absolutism, he was its prophet. Charles was restored without conditions; he was protected against seditious talk by a special treason act; he was given absolute control over all the armed forces; his judges often considered themselves merely the mouthpieces of the royal will; he was empowered by statute to remodel corporations, and so was enabled to destroy those 'worms' which, according to Hobbes, consumed the entrails of the body politic. Each of these things had been advocated as a principle in the *Leviathan*. Still more, the Test Act of 1673 and the Act of 1678 imposed a state religion, for a political purpose and by secular penalties; with this cement

Charles established an impregnable power, whereas James transferred his foundations to the shifting sands of compromise and toleration. Hobbes's ideal was peace for the subject and liberty of thought for the philosopher; these things have been secured not by weak but by strong government; not by a division of power but by its concentration and monopoly in one clearly defined source. In all governments there must be an element of coercion; the question is not of its amount but of its justification. In the Hobbesian state its justification was the necessity for enforcement of internal peace and security, a tolerable coercion because its purpose is clear, simple and constant, in contrast with those states where coercion is complex and capricious, because used on behalf of ever-changing dogmas or ideologies. Men agree more readily about what is treason than about what is heresy. Moreover, Hobbes's sovereign was indivisible and endowed with all the force at its command, a doctrine compatible with delegation of power and with toleration of all opinions not inimical to public safety. On the other hand, a divided sovereignty brings civil war, and a sovereign unable to enforce its decrees ends in anarchy or annihilation.

In contrast with these two extremists, Bunyan and Hobbes, were those who, like Locke and Halifax, vindicated the characteristic English quality of good sense. As a thinker, John Locke (1632-1704) is almost the complete counterpart of Hobbes; for he did not specially pride himself on freedom from inconsistency; nor did he penetrate deeply into those *arcana* which might disturb his readers; and, above all, he wrote plain English, seldom disguising his meaning in metaphor, sarcasm, or innuendo. He therefore had none of that recondite charm which makes Hobbes beloved of connoisseurs; in its place he had that clarity and high seriousness which seldom fail to carry conviction. It is true that his published works belong to a period after Charles's reign, as Hobbes's *Leviathan* to a period before it; but both philosophers have this interesting link with the reign, that, while the Restoration period witnessed the application of some of Hobbes's most characteristic doctrines, the same period created that public opinion which made possible of realization many of the ideals professed by Locke. The one pushed to extremes the results obtainable from the older mechanical method of reasoning; the other restored human nature to its place in the state, and propounded a system which, though liable to logical objection, was nevertheless eminently practicable and reasonable.

The events of his earlier years helped to accentuate the balance which was so distinctive of Locke's maturity. His schooling at Westminster was under strict Puritan auspices; but later he made friends among the Royalists, and became one of the Oxford pioneers who afterwards formed the Royal Society; so too, though he welcomed the Restoration for its return to political normality, he deplored the religious and political excesses by which it was followed; and, as early as 1667, in a manuscript essay on toleration, he expounded his view that while there should be an established church, outside its frontiers there should be a toleration of independent opinion, with the exception of Catholicism and Atheism, which he thought dangerous to the state. At Oxford he had obtained an introduction to mathematical and oriental studies; but his mind was bent on less academical pursuits, and this may account for his choice of medicine as a career. His medical services brought him into contact with Shaftesbury in 1668, and the two were closely associated, first in the constitution-making for Carolina (the first draft, dated June 1669, is in Locke's handwriting), and, later, in the administration of the reconstructed council of trade, of which Shaftesbury was president, and Locke secretary (1673). To the end Locke remained faithful to his patron; but he was the friend of Shaftesbury the idealist, not Shaftesbury the plotter, a fact which did not prevent his expulsion from Christ Church in 1684, in consequence of an order from Sunderland. Meanwhile he had completed his education by travel in France and Holland, and the fruits of his meditation were to be reaped after the Revolution, notably in his *Essay on Toleration* (1689), the *Two Treatises of Government* (1690), and his *Essay concerning humane understanding* (1690).

The *Essay on Toleration* raised the subject from the level of theological polemic, and placed it on almost universal grounds. In general, he contended that toleration was due to all who are themselves tolerant; conversely, the state should expel only those whose principles incite either to persecution or to subversion.

In this way he gave an abstract setting to the latitudinarian doctrines of the whigs. To the same party he did a signal service by his *Treatises of Government*. Primarily written as a confutation of Filmer, the *Treatises* disposed of two things: first, the sovereignty which divine right genealogists traced back to Adam; and, secondly, the social contract as distorted by Hobbes, whereby men were supposed to have surrendered their powers to an irresponsible abstraction. He started from the assumption that man had once been in a state of nature, but he wisely avoided any attempt to describe that state; for he claimed that it was merely a non-politic condition, similar to that which prevails between two independent states not bound by treaties or agreements. The beginnings of the body politic were, he held, to be found in common consent, every one putting himself under an obligation to submit to the determination of the majority; and, in order to promote that preservation of property, which he claimed to be the main object of the state, there were required an established and known law, an impartial judge, and a power to give execution to the sentences of the judge.

On this stock Locke grafted those tender scions of whig doctrine which even in Charles's reign had given promise of a rich maturity. Still using the old categories, he declared that, once men have established themselves in a body politic, the first and fundamental natural law impels them to establish a legislative power. This is not only the supreme power, but 'sacred and unalterable in the hands where the community have once placed it'; nor does it rule by extemporary decrees, but by 'promulgated standing laws, and known, authorised judges'. Hence a clear distinction between the legislative and the executive; the latter responsible to the former, and the former responsible to the people. But as the world is in a constant state of flux, that part of the legislative which consists of elected representatives must, in course of time, be reformed or altered so as to correspond with changes in the distribution of population. Prerogative he defined not as something outside or above the laws, but as a power in the hands of the Prince to provide for those exceptional cases which cannot be left to the determination of the laws.

Other writers have constructed the ideal state and fitted man into it; Locke, on the other hand, built his edifice on the foundation of experience, and adjusted the categories and preconceptions of an earlier philosophy to accord with the results of that experience. Metaphysically his conclusions may have been untenable; but humanly and historically they were sound. Another factor may have helped to give his views wider currency, namely that he was neither a lawyer nor a stylist. Earlier in the century the cause of constitutionalism had been fought by men such as Coke, Selden, and Spelman, all of them learned or erudite rather than intellectual; but Locke expounded the same cause not from statutes or law books, but from general considerations of expediency and reasonableness. Moreover, his exposition gained wide acceptance not by brilliant but by moderate expression; not once is the reader perturbed by a deviation from the course of lucid and consecutive reasoning; there are neither lapses nor epigrams in the writings of Locke. He could therefore be understood by a very wide class of reader; and it was characteristic that, after their visits to England, both Montesquieu and Voltaire returned to France enthusiastic disciples of that cause for which Shaftesbury fought and his secretary wrote.

Another empirical thinker was George Savile, marquess of Halifax (1633–95), whose counsels are filled with a mellow wisdom and personal detachment reminiscent more of the repose of eighteenth-century classicism than of the acerbities and strivings of his age. At times his statesmanship was somewhat ineffective; for generally he preferred retreat to failure, nor would he have died for a lost cause. His natural gifts, his wealth, and his social status all help to account for his pre-eminence; but he had none of the austere consistency of Clarendon, nor the creative force of Shaftesbury. Yet in his career and writings will be found a measure and balance by which the excesses of his contemporaries may be revealed as excesses. To Clarendon he might have applied these words: 'to know when to leave things alone is a high pitch of good sense'; to Shaftesbury and the political idealists: 'the best definition of the best government is that it hath no inconveniencies but such as are supportable; but inconveniencies there must be'; to the religious zealots: 'singularity may be good sense at home, but it must not go much abroad'; to the divine-right clergy: 'experience maketh more prophets than revelation'; to the learned professions: 'the clergy and the lawyers, like the free-masons, may be supposed to take an oath not to tell the secret'.[1] Halifax sounded no clarion-call to action, but his tuning-fork served to discredit the slightest violation of harmony.

This quality pervades his writings, and gives them a unity of spirit and direction. It can be seen in his *Character of a Trimmer*, where he showed that mistakes, like everything else, have their periods, 'and many times the nearest way to cure is not to oppose them, but stay till they are trussed with their own weight';[2] in his *Letter to a Dissenter*, where he counselled patience until 'the next probable revolution';[3] in his *Advice to a Daughter*, where, after hinting tactfully at the inequality of the sexes, he gave this counsel: 'let your method be a steady course of good life that may run like a smooth stream'.[4] It was a simile which had already been used by Denham:

> O could I flow like thee, and make thy stream
> My great example as it is my theme,
> Though deep yet clear, though gentle yet not dull,
> Strong without rage, without o'erflowing full.[5]

There was the same shrewd discrimination in his character-sketches; his picture of Charles II is by far the most faithful of contemporary portraits. 'His wit was better suited to his condition before he was restored than afterwards. The wit of a gentleman and that of a crowned head ought to be two different things'.[6] 'That some of his ministers seemed to have a superiority did not spring from his resignation to them, but to his ease. He chose rather to be eclipsed than to be troubled.'[7] There was the same discernment in his appreciation of a very different character—that of Gilbert Burnet. He saw that Burnet's faults as a historian rose mainly from the warmth of his heart and the

---

[1] These are taken from the miscellaneous thoughts and reflections of Halifax in *Halifax*, ii. 505–27.   [2] Ibid. ii. 337.

[3] Ibid. ii. 377. This should not be taken as a prophecy of the Revolution of 1688.

[4] Ibid. ii. 392.   [5] Denham, *Cooper's Hill*.

[6] *Halifax*, ii. 355.   [7] Ibid. ii. 351.

depth of his humanity. 'Dull men do not miss one blot he makes; and being beholden to their barrenness for their discretion, they fall on the errors which arise out of his abundance.'[1] What Halifax said of the critics of Burnet may be applied to many of the critics of Macaulay.

By rights Halifax ought to have been a cynic. 'God hath made mankind so weak that it must be deceived. The several sorts of religion in the world are so many spiritual monopolies';[2] 'Anybody that is fool enough will be safe in the world, and anybody that can be knave enough will be rich in it.'[3] These remarks might have been made by Hobbes or La Rochefoucauld. But it was seldom that he indulged this humour. He had a strong sense of patriotism. For him good sense meant a penetrative quality, a power to see ourselves and others in perspective, an instinct for perceiving the sham and the false, where others find truth and virtue. But in a world where there are as many opinions as human beings, he thought that private conviction might often have to yield to peace and decorum; that good sense should give way to common sense. He expounded this ideal in these words:

Little words and motions of respect and civility do often recommend men more to the company than the knowledge of all the liberal sciences; but the truth is, all good sense hath something of the clown. in it, and therefore though it is not to be suppressed, it must be softened so as to comply with that great beast the world, which is too strong for any man, though never so much in the right, to go to cuffs with.[4]

Here was defined that high social accomplishment whereby a man can so express his personal opinions that he retains both his individuality and his friends. It is an ideal not easy of achievement, but it was at least made possible by that good nature which Clarendon had already noted as a national characteristic, a virtue which, surviving Plague, Fire, and Plot, provided a basis for the training of those qualities which enable

[1] Ibid. ii. 531. Here Halifax was thinking mainly of Burnet's *History of the Reformation.*
[2] Ibid. ii. 502.   [3] Ibid. ii. 523.
[4] Halifax to Henry Savile, March 29, 1680, in *Savile Correspondence* (Camd. Soc.), 150.

men to co-operate harmoniously in the life of the well-ordered state.

Thus the reign of Charles II, which ended the experiments of Puritan idealists and led insensibly to the rule of expediency and practical politics, was a period of discovery and achievement, neither so spectacular as the Elizabethan age nor so incontestably pre-eminent as the era of Chatham and Pitt, but a period nevertheless wherein were tested and brought to maturity many of the greatest qualities of the English race.

BIBLIOGRAPHICAL NOTE

The contractions here used are those set forth at the beginning of Vol. I of this book with these additions:

Bulletin of the Institute of Historical Research.	*Bull. Inst. H. R.*
Cambridge Historical Journal.	*Camb. Hist. J.*
Economic History Review.	*Econ. Hist. Rev.*

THE standard bibliography is Professor G. Davies's *Bibliography of British History 1603–1714* (1928), which must now be supplemented by the bibliographies in *English Historical Documents*, viii, 1660–1714, edited by Professor A. Browning. For Scottish history, H. M. Paton's *The Scottish Records* (1933) should be used, and reference may be made to a select bibliography in *Econ. Hist. Rev.* iii (1931). For Ireland, there are lists in *Irish Historical Studies*, a journal which began to appear in 1938, and includes both Eire and Ulster within its scope; for Wales, there is the *Bibliography* by R. T. Jenkins and W. Rees (1931). The annual *Writings on American History* began to be published in 1906; and the *Writings on British History*, which A. T. Milne has been editing for the Royal Historical Society, begins at 1934.

In practice, every researcher has to build up his own bibliography. He will be greatly helped by the monumental *Catalogue of Printed Books* in the British Museum, of which the first volume appeared in 1931, and the fiftieth (to *Denz*) in 1954. For miscellaneous and manuscript sources he should consult, as a general guide, the *Bulletin of the Institute of Historical Research*, with its supplements, because these contain not only important articles by scholars, but summaries of theses, *corrigenda* to the *D.N.B.*, and notes regarding the migration of manuscripts, a topic which is also dealt with in *Archives*, the journal published twice yearly since 1949 by the British Records Association. This journal also gives information about facilities for access to manuscripts and guidance for the preservation of documents. In this connexion it may be noted that, in the last generation, there has been great development in the organization and efficiency of county archives, so that today there can be few counties in England where provision has not been made for the custody and classification of muniments, as well as arrangements for accessibility thereto by students. This development may well have great influence on the direction of historical studies in the near future, since the amount of local material easily available is so vast. As well as this, there are now more journals devoted in whole or in part to historical studies. The *Huntington Library Bulletin* has been issued since 1938 as a *Quarterly;* the *Journal of the National Library of Wales* first appeared in 1939; the *Historical Journal of the University of Birmingham* dates from 1947–8. A welcome revival is that of the *Scottish Historical Review*, which made its reappearance in 1947.

Of the sources which have been made available in print since 1933 the most important are the *Calendars of Domestic State Papers* from 1 July 1683 to 5 February 1685 (3 vols., 1934, 1938, and 1938 respectively: Her Majesty's Stationery Office); the third volume has an introduction by F. Bickley. These documents have special interest as authentic evidence of the characteristics of non-parliamentary Stuart rule, and help to prepare the way for the sequel in James's reign. Generally, their contents convey the impression that the ruthless suppression of the Rye House Plot and the relentless search for more victims created an atmosphere of tension not unlike that which has been experienced by some continental countries in this century. The prisons were filled with Dissenters and Quakers; many conspirators were in hiding, or had fled abroad, hoping to make plans for their return; innumerable informers, some for money, some as the price of their lives, were retailing stories in which it is almost impossible to disentangle the true from the false; and the reappearance of old Oliverians gave some point to talk of revolution. The loud hysteria of the Popish Plot was followed by the silence and furtive whispering which greeted the Stuart revenge. Most significant of all was the concerted and wholesale attack on the corporations, which was intended not only to give the crown complete control over the local administration but to ensure the return to parliament of burgesses who would be completely subservient, whenever it was deemed necessary to summon parliament. It was natural that the full implications of all this should be revealed in Scotland, where, because of the comparative backwardness of political institutions, a totalitarian régime could more easily be established. On 14 June 1684 the Secret Committee of the Scottish Privy Council was ordered to raise the Highland clans 'for preventing and suppressing commotions' in Fife and in the south-west; those suspected of complicity in the late 'commotions' were to be examined 'by torture and other effectual means' (*Calendar*, May 1684–Feb. 1685, p. 55).

Of the volumes more recently published by the Historical Manuscripts Commission, two are of special interest for this period: the supplementary *Report of MSS. of Montagu Bertie, twelfth earl of Lindsey,* at Uffington House, Stamford, 1660–1702, edited by C. G. O. Bridgeman and J. C. Walker, 1942; and *MSS. of R. R. Hastings* at Ashby de la Zouch, 1947. Of these the first is miscellaneous, including private, semi-official, and official documents. Some relate to Treasury business; some to the contracts of the Navy Board; some to Danby's imprisonment in the Tower and the efforts to obtain his release. There is an account of Charles Bertie's mission to Denmark in 1671, when he was instructed to adjust differences about saluting the flag. On p. 155 there is a memorandum on the coal trade; on p. 162 an account of the operations in the Mint. The second of the above sources is of some interest for its notes on speeches and proceedings in the House of Lords, 1670–95, some in the handwriting of the seventh earl of Huntingdon. These new publications add to the great mass of original material already available for this period. A selection from original material will be found, in convenient form, in Professor Browning's *English Historical Documents*, viii, 1660–1714 (1953), with valuable introductions, bibliographies, and appendixes. This book is of great service for the study and teaching of the period.

Of general books covering the reign of Charles the most comprehensive is *The Later Stuarts*, by Sir George Clark, which first appeared in 1934, in the Oxford History of England. This may be supplemented by books dealing generally with certain aspects of the subject, such as Professor Mark Thomson's *A Constitutional History of England 1642–1801* (1938) and Sir D. L. Keir's *The Constitutional History of Modern Britain 1485–1937* (4th ed. 1950). Among the more specialized books and contributions to learned journals the following may be enumerated:

(a) Crown and Parliament. Two important diaries of members of the Commons are now available in good editions, namely, that of John Milward, 1666–8, edited by Caroline Robbins (1938), and that of Sir Edward Dering, 1670–3, edited by B. D. Henning (New Haven, 1940). Miss Robbins has contributed an account of the Oxford session of the Long Parliament in October 1665 to *Bull. Inst. H. R.* xxi (1948). Mr. E. S. de Beer has analysed the membership of the Court party in the Commons 1670–8 in *Bull. Inst. H. R.* xi (1934); and a general account of parties and party organization in Charles's reign is that by A. Browning, in *Trans. R. H. Soc.*, 4th series, xxx (1948). Division lists are rarely come by for this period, but one for the Exclusion Bill has been communicated to *Bull. Inst. H. R.* xxiii (1950) by Professor Browning and Miss Doreen Milne. All these contributions have done much to elucidate the complicated history of Charles's Long Parliament. Reference should also be made to G. Davies, *The Elections of Richard Cromwell's Parliament, 1658–9*, in *E.H.R.* lxiii (1948), as evidence of the strength of Royalists and Presbyterians on the eve of the Restoration. In *Camb. Hist. J.*, vii (1941), will be found a general account of the Whig theory of the constitution by Mr. B. Behrens.

Of books relating to the crown there are few serious studies. In the *Huntington Library Bulletin*, x (1946–7), Professor Davies has subjected the concluding lines of Dryden's *Absalom and Achitophel* to careful examination in order to link the poem with the king. An episode in Charles's diplomacy is handled by Mr. K. H. D. Haley in his *William of Orange and the English Opposition 1672–4*, a study based mainly on the Dutch archives. Less directly, the king has come into his own again in Mr. Peter Laslett's scholarly and sympathetic edition of the *Patriarcha* and other works of sir Robert Filmer (1949). M. A. Thomson's *The Secretaries of State 1681–1782* (1932) is a worthy successor to the brilliant study by Miss F. M. G. Evans (Mrs. Higham) on the same subject for the period 1558 to 1680 (1923). Miss Doris M. Gill has contributed an informative account of the Treasury in the years 1660 to 1714 to *E.H.R.* xlvi (1931); and in her study of the relations of the Treasury with the Excise and Customs commissioners in *Camb. Hist. J.* iv (1932) she shows the increased control exercised by this body over subordinates.

(*b*) Finance, Commerce, and Trade. Although Professor E. Hughes's *Studies in Administration and Finance 1558–1825* (1934) is concerned mainly with the Salt Tax, it may be regarded as possibly the first serious attempt to study the Stuart fiscal system. It may be supplemented by the same writer's *The English Stamp Duties 1664–1764*, in *E.H.R.* lvi (1941). In vol. li (1936) of the same journal there is an analysis of the Hearth Tax by Miss L. M. Marshall which shows how this levy combined most of the evils of the Stuart system. The banker-goldsmith Edward Backwell is studied by Miss D. K. Clark in *Econ. Hist. Rev.* ix (1938); and the same writer has contributed 'A Restoration Banking House' to *Essays . . . in honour of Wilbur Cortez Abbott* (Cambridge, Mass., 1941). Although concerned mainly with a later century, W. R. Ward's *English Land Tax in the Eighteenth Century* (1953) contains much of interest for the earlier period. For commerce and shipping generally reference should be made to L. A. Harper, *The English Navigation Laws* (New York, 1939); and to Miss V. Barbour's *Capitalism in Amsterdam in the Seventeenth Century* (Johns Hopkins Press, 1950). Trading relations with Spain are the subject of Miss J. O. MacLachlan's *Trade and Peace with Old Spain 1667–1750* (1940); those with France are examined by Miss M. Priestley in her *Anglo-French Trade and the Unfavourable Balance Controversy*, in *Econ. Hist. Rev.*, 2nd series, iv, no. 1 (1952), where she shows that the unfavourable balance was much less than was commonly supposed. The part played by merchants in Mediterranean ports is illustrated by H. Koenigsberger (for Naples and Sicily) in *E.H.R.* lxii (1947) and A. G. Ambrose (for Aleppo) in *Econ. Hist. Rev.* iii (1931–2). Of general importance for our overseas trade are Miss L. S. Sutherland's *The Law Merchant in England in the XVIIth and XVIIIth Centuries*, in *Trans. R. H. Soc.*, 4th series, xvii (1934), and Sir George Clark's *The Barbary Corsairs in the Seventeenth Century*, in *Camb. Hist. J.* viii (1944).

For English industry in this period reference should be made to the very full and informative *The Rise of the British Coal Industry 1550–1700* (2 vols. 1932), by Professor J. U. Nef. But objection may be taken by some readers to the phrase 'Industrial Revolution', when applied to this period; moreover, it is by no means certain that increasing resort to coal implied increasing industrialization, because much of the coal was used for domestic purposes; while, in the metal industries, coal had by no means displaced wood.

(*c*) Local Government and Social Life. Two valuable bibliographies for this subject are *Local History Handlist . . .*, published in 1947 by the Historical Association; and F. G. Emmison and Irvine Gray, *County Records* (1948). Studies of borough corporations are well represented by Philip Styles, *The Corporation of Bewdley under the later Stuarts*, in *University of Birmingham Historical Journal*, i, 1947–8. In vol. iii of the same journal Mr. Styles, in his *Census of a Warwickshire Village* (Fenny Compton), has made an interesting contribution to the subject of rural population. Newark in the period 1549–1688 is the subject treated by Mr. C. G. Parsloe in *Trans. R. H. Soc.*, 4th series, xxii (1940); a county, *Dorset* (1952), is the subject of Mr. R. Douch, a book which contains much guidance for the local historian. Wage assessments in Herefordshire after 1666 provide the subject of Mr. R. K. Kelsall in *E.H.R.* lvii (1942). Some important work has been done on the history of London. Its population in the later seventeenth century is studied by P. E. Jones and A. V. Judges in *Econ. Hist. Rev.* vi (1935–6); and two pieces of research are of great interest for this period: T. F. Reddaway, *The Rebuilding of London after the Great Fire* (1940), and N. G. Brett James, *The Growth of Stuart London* (1935). In his *Studies in Stuart Wales* (1952) Mr. A. H. Dodd has described the revival of the Welsh gentry after 1660.

Much information about local turbulence and the means for its suppression will be found in Max Beloff's *Public Order and Popular Disturbances 1660–1714* (1938); R. B. Schlatter's *The Social Ideas of Religious Leaders 1660–1688* (1940) connects social conditions with contemporary religious opinion. Additional evidence about social and economic conditions will be found in *The Journeys of Celia Fiennes*, ed. C. Morris (1947). *Life in a Noble Household 1641–1700* (1937) by Miss Gladys Scott Thomson is based on the papers of the duke of Bedford. Miss Joan Parkes's *Travel in England in the Seventeenth Century* (1925) may now be supplemented by the volumes of T. S. Willan, *River Navigation* (1936) and *The Coasting Trade* (1938), which both cover the period 1600–1750. H. C. Darby, *The Draining of the Fens* (1940), is of capital importance for the study of land and agriculture in the period.

(*d*) *Scotland, Ireland, and the Plantations.* In his *Religious Life in Seventeenth-century Scotland* (1937) Professor G. D. Henderson has greatly added to our knowledge of social and intellectual conditions in Scotland. *Scottish Population Statistics*, edited by J. G. Kyd for the Scottish History Society (3rd series, xliv, 1952), relates mainly to the eighteenth century, but contains some information about the later seventeenth; the same is true of K. H. Connell, *Population in Ireland 1750–1845*, and J. C. Beckett's *Protestant Dissent in Ireland 1687–1780*. More directly concerned with our period is E. Maclysaght's *Irish Life in the Seventeenth Century* (1950). The older books by W. E. H. Lecky and J. A. Froude are by no means so obsolete as is commonly supposed.

For the Plantations generally, two of the most important sources are *Proceedings and Debates of the British Parliaments respecting North America*, ed. L. F. Stock, 3 vols. (Washington, 1924–30), which incidentally serves as a partial index to the voluminous *Journals* of the Lords and Commons; and E. Donnan, *Documents illustrative of the History of the Slave Trade to America* (3 vols., Washington, 1930–2). For the slave trade, A. B. Keith's *West Africa* (1933) should also be used. For Newfoundland, there is R. G. Lounsbury, *The British Fishery at Newfoundland 1634–1763* (New Haven, 1934); for the Hudson's Bay Company, the *Minutes* for 1679–1684, edited by E. E. Rich, appeared in 1946. A selection from a wide range of sources will be found in K. E. Knorr, *British Colonial Theories 1570–1850* (1944). In 1933 appeared A. P. Newton's *The European Nations in the West Indies, 1493–1688*.

(*e*) *Biographies and Miscellaneous.* For biographies, the *D.N.B.* should be consulted, supplemented by the *corrigenda* in the *Bull. Inst.*

H.R.; also *The Complete Peerage*, edited by G. E. Cokayne, an invaluable source, now in process of completion. The standard life of Shaftesbury is that by Miss L. F. Brown (New York, 1933); of Pepys, that of Sir Arthur Bryant, 3 vols. (1947–9). Mr. C. H. Hartmann has contributed two biographies: *Charles II and Madame* (1934) and *Clifford of the Cabal 1630–73* (1937). A scholarly account of a great ecclesiastic is C. E. Whiting's *Nathaniel Lord Crewe, Bishop of Durham 1674–1721* (1940). M. Ashley's *John Wildman, Plotter and Postmaster* (1947), is of value for its account of early republicanism in England. Colonel B. Fergusson's *Rupert of the Rhine* (1952) provides a short, well-balanced biography. Although concerned mainly with events before 1660, Mr. B. H. G. Wormald's *Clarendon: Politics, History and Religion, 1640–1660* is of interest for the understanding of Clarendon.

Of miscellaneous sources, there may be cited J. Walker, *Censorship of the Press during the Reign of Charles II*, in *History*, xxxv (1950); and in the same journal Miss D. Ross, *Class Privilege in XVIIth-century England* (xxviii, 1943). D. C. Coleman's *Naval Dockyards under the later Stuarts*, in *Econ. Hist. Rev.*, 2nd series, no. 2 (1953), is a good account of a neglected subject, and provides a useful list of the tonnage of H.M. ships completed each year 1660–88. Another important contribution to this subject is *The Tangier Papers of Samuel Pepys*, edited by E. Chappell for the Navy Records Society (1935). *The Diary of Robert Hooke 1672–80* has been edited by H. W. Robinson and W. Adams (1935); another, more extensive Diary, that of John Evelyn, was edited in six volumes by E. S. de Beer (1955).

Among the more important contributions to this subject within the last few years may be mentioned: G. Davies, *The Restoration of Charles II 1658–1660* (1955), a faithful record of events from the death of Cromwell to the accession of Charles; J. L. Cope, *Joseph Glanvill, Anglican Apologist* (Washington University Studies, St. Louis, U.S.A. 1956), of great interest for the conflict of religious and scientific thought; Miss Jane Lang, *Rebuilding of St. Paul's after the Great Fire of London* (1956), shows the part played by Wren and his associates; P. Fraser, *The Intelligence of the Secretaries of State and their Monopoly of Licensed News 1660–1688* (1956), describes the secretaries' use of spies, particularly in the wars with the Dutch; A. P. Thornton, *West India Policy under the Restoration* (1956) shows the difficulties in the way of framing a colonial policy in Restoration England. K. G. Davies, *The Royal African Company* (1957) is an important contribution to the study of company organization and of the slave trade; Sir Godfrey Fisher's *Barbary Legend: War, Trade and Piracy in North Africa, 1415–1830* (1957) dispels many misconceptions on the subject; S. B. Baxter's *The Development of the Treasury 1660–1702*

(1957) explains how the Treasury attained 'maturity' in this period; G. R. Cragg, *Puritanism in the Period of the Great Persecution 1660–1688* (1957) shows the increasing severity with which the Puritans were treated after 1681; R. Schlatter (ed.), *Richard Baxter and Puritan Politics* (1957) illustrates the political opinions of Baxter by extracts from his writings; E. E. Rich, *History of the Hudson's Bay Company 1670–1870* (1958), vol. 1 carries the narrative down to 1763; P. Laslett, *John Locke. Two Treatises on Government* (1960). Mr. Laslett shows that the Treatises were written in 1679–1680, during the Exclusion controversy; J. R. Jones, *The First Whigs: the Politics of the Exclusion Crisis 1678–1683* (1961). Mr. Jones's researches into the composition of the Exclusion parliaments helps to confirm the older view that it is legitimate to speak of Whig and Tory in this period.

Notable biographies for this period include: J. Summerson, *Sir Christopher Wren* (1954), a well-balanced study; M. Cranston, *John Locke* (1957), the standard biography; and J. P. Kenyon, *Robert Spencer, Earl of Sunderland, 1641–1701* (1958), an important study of an enigmatic statesman who influenced the policy of three reigns.

INDEX

Acadia, i. 313, 314.

Administration, local, ii. 486–99.

Admiral, lord high, i. 258.

Admiralty, board of, i. 259.

Africa, English possessions in, i. 251, 314. See also *Tangier*.

Africa, Royal Company of Adventurers trading into, i. 230, ii. 665.

Agriculture, English, and geology, i. 36–7; and draining, 55–7; and enclosing, 57–9; fertilizing and improving, 59–60; new crops, 60–1; corn and grain, 65–6; the labourer, 84–5; the copyholder, 85–90. See also *Land* and *Royal Society*.

Aids, royal, ii. 434. See also *Wards, court of*.

Aire, river, i. 40.

Aix-la-Chapelle, treaty of (1668), i. 335.

Albemarle, duke of, see *Monck, George*.

Alexander VII, pope, i. 347.

Alliance, Triple, i. 332–4.

Allin, captain Thomas, i. 287, 302.

Andros, major Edmund, ii. 677–8, 683.

Angling, i. 105.

Anglo-Dutch wars, see *War, Anglo-Dutch*.

Anne, princess, afterwards queen, and a Swedish marriage, ii. 557; and an English marriage, 648; and her Danish marriage, 651–2.

Annesley, Arthur, first earl of Anglesey, i. 27, 152, 155.

Annuities, life, i. 113.

Antigua, i. 307, 313, ii. 664.

Apple, culture of the, i. 62.

Appropriation of supplies, ii. 427, 443–4, 535.

Archdeacon, the, ii. 496–7.

Argyle, marquis of, see *Campbell, Archibald*.

Arlington, earl of, see *Bennet, Henry*.

Army, the, and politics, i. 2 seqq.; and constitutional reform, 8, 15; the standing, 253–4; voted a grievance (1673), 379–80; debates on (1674), 385; parliamentary grant for, ii. 444; obscurity in legislation about, 456; status of the soldier, 504–8; Commons' fear of (1678), 553–4, 574. See also *Courts martial, Militia, Prerogative*.

Articles, lords of the, ii. 409.

Arton, William, i. 364.

Arundel, i. 43.

Arundell, Henry, third baron Arundell of Wardour, i. 338, 344, ii. 564, 573, 574, 654.

Ashdown, forest of, i. 71.

Ashley, lord, see *Cooper, Anthony Ashley*.

Atherstone, i. 78.

Attorneys, see *Lawyers*.

Aubrey, John, and educational reform, ii. 696–7.

Aungier, Gerald, governor of Bombay, ii. 661–2.

Aylesbury, vale of, i. 36.

Ayscue, sir George, admiral, i. 285, 300, 301.

Backwell, Edward, banker, ii. 426.

Bacon's rebellion (Virginia), ii. 539, 670–1.

Badminton, i. 63.

Banckers, admiral, i. 359.

Bankers and goldsmiths, i. 127, ii. 445, 448–9.

Banking, early history of, ii. 441–4.

Baptists, the, i. 217.

Barbados, ii. 664–5, 688.

Barnardiston, sir Samuel, ii. 469, 531, 629.

Barnardiston v. *Soame*, ii. 462.

Barratry, ii. 502.

Barrillon, Paul, French ambassador, ii. 546, 547, 548, 549, 551, 577, 585, 594, 599, 622–3, 654.

Bath, i. 46, 107, ii. 474.

Batten, sir William, admiral and administrator, i. 257, 258.

Baxter, Richard, i. 199, 214.

Beaufort, duc de, French admiral, i. 297.

Beaufort, duke of, see *Somerset, Henry, first duke*.

Bedfordshire, i. 37, 42.

Bedingfield, father, ii. 565.

Bedloe, William, ii. 568–9, 574–5, 587.

Beer, i. 76–7. See also *Excise*.

Behn, Aphra, ii. 712.

Belasyse, John, baron Belasyse, ii. 568, 573, 654, 658.

Bellings, sir Richard, i. 203, 339, 342.

Benevolence, or free gift, a (1661), ii. 432.